D0856966

OXFORD MEDIEVAL TEXTS

General Editors

J. W. BINNS   W. J. BLAIR

M. LAPIDGE   T. REUTER

WILLIAM OF MALMESBURY
SAINTS' LIVES

William of Malmesbury
SAINTS' LIVES

LIVES OF SS. WULFSTAN, DUNSTAN, PATRICK, BENIGNUS AND INDRACT

BY

M. WINTERBOTTOM

and

R. M. THOMSON

CLARENDON PRESS · OXFORD

BX4659
.G7
W54
2002x

0 90017729

OXFORD
UNIVERSITY PRESS

Great Clarendon Street, Oxford OX2 6DP

Oxford University Press is a department of the University of Oxford
and furthers the University's aim of excellence in research, scholarship,
and education by publishing worldwide in

Oxford New York

Auckland Bangkok Buenos Aires Cape Town Chennai
Dar es Salaam Delhi Hong Kong Istanbul Karachi Kolkata
Kuala Lumpur Madrid Melbourne Mexico City Mumbai Nairobi
São Paulo Shanghai Singapore Taipei Tokyo Toronto

and an associated company in Berlin

Oxford is a registered trade mark of Oxford University Press
in the UK and in certain other countries

Published in the United States
by Oxford University Press Inc., New York

© M. Winterbottom and R. M. Thomson 2002

The moral rights of the authors have been asserted

Database right Oxford University Press (maker)

First published 2002

All rights reserved. No part of this publication may be reproduced,
stored in a retrieval system, or transmitted, in any form or by any means,
without the prior permission in writing of Oxford University Press,
or as expressly permitted by law, or under terms agreed with the appropriate
reprographics rights organizations. Enquiries concerning reproduction
outside the scope of the above should be sent to the Rights Department,
Oxford University Press, at the address above

You must not circulate this book in any other binding or cover
and you must impose the same condition on any acquirer

British Library Cataloguing in Publication Data

Data available

Library of Congress Cataloging in Publication Data

Data available

ISBN 0-19-820709-3

1 3 5 7 9 10 8 6 4 2

Typeset in Ehrhardt
by Joshua Associates Ltd., Oxford
Printed in Great Britain
on acid-free paper by
Biddles Ltd,
Guildford and King's Lynn

PREFACE

THE present volume is the third in a projected series of five which will offer editions and translations of all of William of Malmesbury's historical works. The bulk of the work—collation of the manuscripts, construction and translation of the Latin texts—was carried out by MW. The organization and indexing of the volume, and the writing of the Introduction, were done by RMT. The editors have collaborated in footnoting the texts, and every part of the book has been subject to discussion between us both. We would like to thank those who have aided our labours by answering questions or reading portions of the work: Professors Richard Sharpe, Margareta Steinby, and James Carley, Drs Martin Brett, Paul Hayward, David Howlett, and Christine Rauer, Nicolette Winterbottom, and, as ever, the general editors of OMT. We owe a debt of gratitude to many libraries, but we should like to mention in particular the Librarian of the Gloucester Cathedral Library. The preparation of this book for the press roughly paralleled that of the important set of conference papers, *St Wulfstan and his World*, edited by Julia Barrow and Nicholas Brooks. We are most grateful to the editors for allowing us access to 'pre-prints' of relevant contributions. Finally, we are very conscious of how much we owe to the co-operation of the Press, to our incomparable copy editor, John Cordy, and to the skills of Joshua Associates Ltd.

M.W.
R.M.T.

AUG 3 0 2002

CONTENTS

ABBREVIATED REFERENCES   ix

INTRODUCTION   xiii

VITA WULFSTANI   1
    Text and Translation   7

VITA DUNSTANI   157
    Text and Translation   165

THE FRAGMENTARY LIVES
    Introduction   305
    Vita Patricii   315
    Vita Benigni   344
    Vita Indracti   368

INDEX OF SOURCES   383

GENERAL INDEX   387

ABBREVIATED REFERENCES

AA SS	*Acta sanctorum* (first edn. Antwerp/Brussels 1643–1894)
Adelard	Adelard, *Vita S. Dunstani*, in *Memorials*, pp. 53–68
AG	William of Malmesbury, *De antiquitate Glastonie ecclesie*, ed. and trans. J. Scott, *The Early History of Glastonbury* (Woodbridge, 1981)
Anglo-Latin Literature 900–1066	M. Lapidge, *Anglo-Latin Literature 900–1066* (London and Rio Grande, OH, 1993)
ANS	*Anglo-Norman Studies*
ASC	*The Anglo-Saxon Chronicle*, ed. and trans. D. Whitelock, D. C. Douglas, and S. Tucker (London, 1961)
ASE	*Anglo-Saxon England*
Atkins I, II	I. Atkins, 'The Church of Worcester from the eighth to the twelfth century', part I, *Antiquaries Journal*, xvii (1937), 371–91, part II, ibid., xx (1940), 203–28
B.	B., *Vita S. Dunstani*, in *Memorials*, pp. 3–52
Barker, *A Short Architectural History*	P. Barker, *A Short Architectural History of Worcester Cathedral* (Worcester Cathedral Publs., ii: Worcester, 1994)
BHL	*Bibliotheca Hagiographica Latina*, ed. Bollandists (2 vols.: Brussels, 1898–1901; *Novum Supplementum*, ed. H. Fros, 1986)
Bieler	*Four Latin Lives of St. Patrick*, ed. L. Bieler (Scriptores Latini Hiberniae, viii: Dublin, 1971)
Blackwell Encyclopaedia	M. Lapidge *et al.* (eds.), *The Blackwell Encyclopaedia of Anglo-Saxon England* (Oxford, 1999)
Bodl. Libr.	Oxford, Bodleian Library
BRECP	J. Greatrex, *Biographical Register of the English Cathedral Priories of the Province of Canterbury c.1066–1540* (Oxford, 1997)
Byrhtferth, *Vita S. Oswaldi*	(Byrhtferth of Ramsey), *Vita S. Oswaldi*, in *HCY* i. 399–475
Comm. Lam.	William of Malmesbury, *Commentary on Lamentations*, in Bodl. Libr., MS Bodl. 868
Councils	*Councils and Synods*, i (AD 871–1204), ed.

	D. Whitelock, M. Brett, and C. N. L. Brooke (2 vols.: Oxford, 1981)
CCSL	Corpus Christianorum Series Latina
Darlington	*The Vita Wulfstani of William of Malmesbury*, ed. R. R. Darlington (RHS Camden 3rd ser., xl, 1928)
DB	*Domesday Book*, ed. J. Morris *et al.* (Chichester, 1975–)
Eadmer	Eadmer, *Vita S. Dunstani*, in *Memorials*, pp. 162–249
EETS	Early English Text Society
EHR	*English Historical Review*
Ekwall	E. Ekwall, *The Concise Oxford Dictionary of English Place-Names* (4th edn.: Oxford, 1960)
English Benedictine Libraries	*Benedictine Libraries; the Shorter Catalogues*, ed. R. Sharpe *et al.* (Corpus of British Medieval Library Catalogues, iv: London: The British Library, 1996)
Farmer, 'Two biographies'	D. H. Farmer, 'Two biographies by William of Malmesbury', in *Latin Biography*, ed. T. A. Dorey (London, 1967), pp. 157–76
Fasti	J. Le Neve, *Fasti Ecclesiae Anglicanae 1066–1300*, ii. *Monastic Cathedrals*, ed. D. E. Greenway (London, 1971)
GP	William of Malmesbury, *Gesta pontificum Anglorum*, ed. N. E. S. A. Hamilton (RS, 1870)
GR	William of Malmesbury, *Gesta regum Anglorum*, I text and transl. by R. A. B. Mynors, R. M. Thomson, and M. Winterbottom, II commentary by R. M. Thomson (2 vols.: OMT, 1998–9)
HBC	*Handbook of British Chronology*, ed. E. B. Fryde *et al.* (3rd edn., RHS Guides & Handbooks, ii: London, 1986)
HCY	*Historians of the Church of York and its Archbishops*, ed. J. Raine (3 vols.: RS, 1879–94)
Heads	D. Knowles, C. N. L. Brooke, and V. C. M. London, *The Heads of Religious Houses, England and Wales, 940–1216* (Cambridge, 1972)
Hemingi Chartularium	*Hemingi Chartularium Ecclesiae Wigorniensis*, ed. T. Hearne (2 vols.: London, 1723)
HN	William of Malmesbury, *Historia novella*, ed. E. King, trans. K. R. Potter (OMT, 1998)

JG | *The Chronicle of Glastonbury Abbey: An Edition, Translation and Study of John of Glastonbury's Cronica siue Antiquitates Glastoniensis Ecclesiae*, ed. J. P. Carley, trans. D. Townsend (Woodbridge, 1985)

JW | *The Chronicle of John of Worcester*, ed. and trans. R. R. Darlington, P. McGurk, and J. Bray (OMT, 1995–)

Leland, *Coll.* | *Joannis Lelandi Antiquarii De Rebus Britannicis Collectanea* . . . (2nd edn., 6 vols.: London, 1774)

Leland, *Comm.* | *Commentarii de Scriptoribus Britannicis, autore Ioanne Lelando*, ed. A. Hall (Oxford, 1709)

Mason | E. Mason, *St Wulfstan of Worcester c.1008-1095* (Oxford, 1990)

Memorials | *Memorials of Saint Dunstan*, ed. W. Stubbs (RS, 1874)

Mir. | *El Libro De Laudibus et Miraculis Sanctae Mariae de Guillermo de Malmesbury*, ed. J. M. Canal (2nd edn., Edizioni 'Ephemerides Mariologiae': Rome, 1968)

NLA | *Nova Legenda Anglie*, ed. C. Horstman (2 vols.: Oxford, 1901)

NMT | Nelson's Medieval Texts

ODML | *Dictionary of Medieval Latin from British Sources* (Oxford, 1975–)

OMT | Oxford Medieval Texts

Osbern | Osbern of Canterbury, *Vita S. Dunstani*, in *Memorials*, pp. 69–161

Otto, *Sprichwörter* | A. Otto, *Die Sprichwörter und sprichwörtlichen Redensarten der Römer* (Leipzig, 1890)

Peile | *William of Malmesbury's Life of St Wulstan Bishop of Worcester*, trans. J. H. F. Peile (Oxford, 1934)

PL | Patrologia Latina

Polyhistor | William of Malmesbury, *Polyhistor*, ed. H. Testroet Ouellette (Binghamton, NY, 1982)

RHS | Royal Historical Society

Robinson, *Times* | J. Armitage Robinson, *The Times of Saint Dunstan* (Oxford, 1923)

RS | Rolls Series

S | P. H. Sawyer, *Anglo-Saxon Charters* (RHS Guides and Handbooks, viii: 1968), cited by document number

St Dunstan | *St Dunstan: his Life, Times and Cult*, ed.

N. Ramsay, M. Sparks, and T. Tatton-Brown (Woodbridge, 1992)

St Oswald of Worcester   *St Oswald of Worcester*, ed. N. Brooks and C. Cubitt (Leicester, 1996)

St Wulfstan and his World   *St Wulfstan and his World*, ed. J. Barrow and N. Brooks (Aldershot, forthcoming)

Taylor and Taylor, *Anglo-Saxon Architecture*   H. M. and J. Taylor, *Anglo-Saxon Architecture* (3 vols., Cambridge, 1965–78)

Thomson, *William of Malmesbury*   R. M. Thomson, *William of Malmesbury* (Woodbridge, 1987)

Two Saxon Chronicles   C. Plummer and J. Earle, *Two of the Saxon Chronicles Parallel* (2 vols.: Oxford, 1892–9, repr. with a bibliographical note by D. Whitelock, 1952)

VCH   *Victoria History of the Counties of England*

VD   William of Malmesbury, *Vita S. Dunstani*

Vita Aedwardi   *The Life of King Edward who rests at Westminster*, ed. and trans. F. Barlow (2nd edn., OMT, 1992)

VW   William of Malmesbury, *Vita S. Wulfstani*

Wulfstan of Winchester, *Vita Æthelwoldi*   Wulfstan of Winchester, *The Life of St Æthelwold*, ed. and trans. M. Lapidge and M. Winterbottom (OMT, 1991)

INTRODUCTION

The present volume contains the hagiographical writings of the monk, historian, and scholar, William of Malmesbury (*c*.1090–*c*.1143):[1] his Lives of Wulfstan and Dunstan, which survive complete, and those of Patrick, Benignus, and Indract, which exist now only as fragments.[2] The complete Lives (especially the first) are reasonably well known and have both been edited before;[3] the fragments are edited here for the first time, and for the first time also we attempt to offer an assessment of William as hagiographer, and of the relationship between his historical and hagiographical output.

Medieval historians sometimes made reference to different conventions for the writing of history and hagiography, but in practice often blurred them.[4] William of Malmesbury included considerable quantities of hagiographical material in his two major histories of England, and the Saints' Lives which constitute the bulk of his *opera minora* are noticeably historical.[5] Each genre contains material of a kind one would expect in the other, and two of the Lives offer more detailed treatment of personalities who were already prominent in the *Gesta regum* and *Gesta pontificum*.[6] Moreover, there is reason to think

[1] For William's biography, see *GR* II, pp. xxxv–xlvii and the literature cited there. *GR* includes, for instance, accounts of the lives and miracles of SS. Æthelthryth, Æthelwold, Aldhelm, Augustine of Canterbury, Cuthbert, Eadgyth, Edmund k. and m., Edward k. and m., Edward the Confessor, Gregory, Kenelm, Mildburh, Mildred, Oswald k., Oswald bp., Wigstan, and Wihtburh. *GP* includes Ælfgifu, Ælfheah, Æthelburh, Æthelthryth, Æthelwold, Aldhelm, Anselm, Audoenus (Ouen), Augustine of Canterbury, Birinus, Byrnstan, Cuthbert, Cyneswith, Cynethryth, Eadburh, Eadgyth, Ecgwine, Edmund, Edward k. and m., Edward the Confessor, Eorcenwald, Frederick, Frideswide, Hadrian, Ivo, Kenelm, Letard, Mildburh, Mildred, Oda, Oswald k., Oswald bp., Paternus, Patrick, Swithhun, Wærburh, Wigstan, Wihtburh, Wilfrid, and Wulfstan.

[2] Strictly speaking, we should also count as hagiographical William's *De miraculis beatae uirginis Mariae* (*Mir.*), although it is in no sense a *Vita*. And *GP* book v is a *Vita et miracula* of St Aldhelm, combined with a history of Malmesbury abbey. It will receive appropriate consideration in our forthcoming OMT edition and translation of *GP*.

[3] See below, pp. 5, 160.

[4] e.g. Gregory of Tours, *Historiae*, as discussed by W. Goffart, *The Narrators of Barbarian History* (Princeton, 1988), pp. 127–53. On hagiographical literature and its conventions, see R. Aigrain, *L'hagiographie* (Paris, 1953); H. Delehaye, *The Legends of the Saints* (London, 1962).

[5] See below, pp. xxvii–xxxviii.

[6] With *VW* cf. *GR*, cc. 269. 2, 303, 306. 4, *GP*, cc. 137–49; with *VD* cf. *GR*, cc. 144. 2–3, 146. 2, 147. 2–4, 148. 1, 149. 1–4, 161, 164, 165. 1, *GP*, cc. 18–19, 75–6, 87, 255. References to Patrick, Benignus and Indract are in *GR*, cc. 22–4, 35C. 3, and in *GP*, c. 91.

that William was approached to write the hagiographies by two of the communities which had supported him, with hospitality and resources, while he conducted research towards his major historical works. The Life of Wulfstan was commissioned by the prior and convent of Worcester, the Lives of Dunstan, Patrick, Benignus, and Indract by the monks of Glastonbury. William was a *confrater* of Glastonbury, and clearly spent much time there.[7] He may have enjoyed a similar connection with Worcester, since he demonstrably exchanged material with its house-chronicler, John, and knew Priors Nicholas and Warin, as well as other monks.[8] At both places he drew on the rich stores of ancient books and documents.

William's personal commitment to these hagiographical projects is hard to gauge; he was, one feels, impressed and attracted by Wulfstan; he understood the historical importance of Dunstan but, as we shall see, the task set him by the Glastonbury monks presented certain dilemmas which he would probably rather have been spared. Certainly, the Lives of Wulfstan and Dunstan can be seen as related to William's passionate commitment and contribution to a larger enterprise: of demonstrating to contemporaries and rescuing for posterity the achievements of pre-Conquest England. This enterprise had been begun by the previous generation, and culminated in William's own major works. This incentive, however, hardly applies to the Celtic saints; William did not think much of Celts in general,[9] and probably only 'did' these saints because Glastonbury pressed him to.

DATES

William's Saints' Lives are not easy to date, either absolutely, or relatively to each other and to his other writings. All were written later than redaction A of the *Gesta regum Anglorum* (*GR*), finished in or soon after February 1126 (though most of it was written about a year earlier).[10] It is probable that *VW* was already planned by this time, for in *GR* there seems to be a reference to it as a future

---

[7] *GR* II, p. xxxii n. 25.

[8] *GR* II, p. 13, and the literature cited there; Thomson, *William of Malmesbury*, pp. 73, 75, 122, 127–30; for William's acquaintance with Nicholas, Warin, and the monk Eadric, see *VW* Ep., iii. 3. 3, 9–10, 13, 16–17.

[9] *GR*, c. 409. 1 n.; J. Gillingham, 'The context and purposes of Geoffrey of Monmouth's *History of the Kings of Britain*', in his *The English in the Twelfth Century* (Woodbridge, 2000), pp. 19–39, at 29.

[10] See *GR* II, pp. xvii–xviii and n. 2; xxxv.

undertaking.[11] The account of Wulfstan in the *Gesta pontificum* (*GP*), the earliest state of which was completed in mid-1125, used Coleman's Old English Life, of which *VW* is a translation.[12] Other than that, the fact that *VW*'s prologue is addressed to Prior Warin of Worcester is unhelpful, since he was in office for about two decades (*c*.1124–*c*.1142). A passage in *GP* shows that *VD* was not yet in prospect.[13] This and the Lives of Patrick, Benignus, and Indract seem to have been written more or less en bloc, as part of a project which also included the writing of William's *On the Antiquity of Glastonbury* (*AG*). *AG* was written after 1126, when Henry of Blois became abbot of Glastonbury, and before 1 December 1135, the *terminus ante quem* of redaction **BC** of *GR*, in which extracts from *AG* were included.[14] *AG* was already envisaged while William was writing *VD* i, which refers forward to it; *VD* ii, however, was written later than the main body of *AG*, to which it refers back.[15] Both books of *VD* were complete by the time William wrote the prologue to *AG*. It is addressed to Henry as bishop of Winchester, so it must have been written later than 17 November 1129, the date of Henry's consecration. In it William says that, at the request of the Glastonbury community, he has already written a Life of Dunstan in two books. He adds that 'some years ago', that is presumably at an earlier date still, he had written the Lives of Patrick, Benignus, and Indract, which the monks had checked for correctness—so presumably they too were commissioned works.[16] Finally, in *VD* ii William refers to *GR* 'quae ante aliquot annos edidi'.[17] We might summarize this by saying that *VD* and *AG* were written more or less simultaneously, *c*.1129–30, the other Lives of Glastonbury saints a very few years earlier. One can only marvel at the quantity of scholarly writing produced by this Benedictine monk during the decade *c*.1120–30.

SOURCES

VW purports to be a Latin version of a now-lost Old English Life by the Worcester monk Coleman (d. 1113), who had been Wulfstan's

---

[11] *GR*, c. 268. 2 and n.
[12] *GP*, cc. 137–48. *GR*, c. 303, retold in *VW* ii. 1. 4–6, may also reflect knowledge of Coleman.
[13] *GP*, c. 19 (p. 32).
[14] *GR* II, pp. xxvii–xxxii. The *terminus ante quem* is the death of King Henry I.
[15] See below, p. 234. There is also a reference in *AG back* to *VD* i (below, p. 202 n. 4).
[16] *AG* prol. (pp. 40–1).   [17] *VD* ii. 14. 2.

chaplain.[18] William's description of what he was doing as (effectively) 'translation'[19] must be taken with a grain of salt, given the freedom with which he customarily treated what he pronounced to be verbatim citations of earlier texts.[20] He himself admits that he is going to omit passages of alleged direct speech ('declamatiunculae', which he thought likely to be inaccurate) and of general moralistic reflection (which he thought irrelevant).[21] He explicitly added a few stories told him by Prior Nicholas,[22] and another about a priest at Bruton (Somerset) of whom he had heard.[23] In ii. 16 he tells a story about Coleman himself, in terms which make it difficult to believe that Coleman was its source. Although he has retained Coleman's division into three books,[24] he announces and explains his resiting of the break between books i and ii.[25] It has recently been suggested that Coleman wrote in a style, employing alliteration and chains of rhythmical doublets, which William felt bound to abbreviate.[26] On the other

---

[18] *VW* Ep. 3–4. On Coleman, see *BRECP*, pp. 790–1.

[19] *VW* Ep. 4: 'Huius ego ut uoluistis insistens scriptis nichil turbaui de rerum ordine, nichil corrupi de gestorum ueritate.'

[20] Farmer, 'Two biographies', p. 166. Compare, for example, William's treatment of the letters of Alcuin in *GR* and *GP*, studied in Thomson, *William of Malmesbury*, ch. 8.

[21] *VW* Ep. 4, i. 16. 5, iii. 18. 3. A. Orchard, 'Parallel Lives: Wulfstan, William, Coleman and Christ', in *St Wulfstan and his World*, suggests that Coleman included a good deal of hagiographical comparison, most of which William omitted.

[22] *VW* iii. 9. 2–3, 10. 3, part of 13, all of 17. At iii. 3. 3 he cites a story, presumably from Coleman, concerning a monk called Eadric, 'with whom I also am personally acquainted'.

[23] *VW* iii. 29. See below, p. 153 n. 7, for discussion of the possibility that William was born not far from Bruton.

[24] Farmer, 'Two biographies', pp. 166–7, errs in supposing that William was responsible for the addition of book iii. The matter is settled by William's reference (i. 16. 5) to Coleman's break between books i and ii as 'decisionem *primam*'. We are not primarily concerned here with the character of Coleman's original Life except insofar as it can be distinguished from William's reworking of it, but valuable remarks on Coleman's structure, language, and intention will be found in A. Gransden, *Historical Writing in England c.550–c.1307* (London, 1974), pp. 87–9, and Orchard, 'Parallel Lives'. Orchard suggests that Coleman's Life was modelled on Wulfstan of Winchester's *Vita Æthelwoldi*.

[25] *VW* i. 16. 5.

[26] Orchard, 'Parallel Lives', studies Coleman's vernacular style as revealed in the longer marginal notes by him in various Worcester manuscripts. He observes that 'by comparison with what is found in the *Gesta regum* and *Gesta pontificum*, William's *Vita Wulfstani* appears somewhat overwrought, and that, particularly when one compares parallel accounts of the same episode in Wulfstan's career from the *Gesta pontificum* (where William is paraphrasing Coleman's work) and from the Latin *Vita Wulfstani* (where the relationship is presumably closer) the preciousness of the prose, not to mention what might be termed the "doublet-quotient", rises dramatically. At such times, perhaps, one can sense something of the ornate quality of Coleman's evidently rather complicated cadences.' But the difference may simply be due to William's ideas of what was fitting for hagiographical as distinct from historical prose.

hand, in *GP* he included three stories about Wulfstan not apparently from Coleman, and not retold in *VW*.[27] This is reassuring; it suggests that William took his brief to 'translate' Coleman's Life seriously enough to accept some limitations on his freedom to supplement it from elsewhere. Further reassurance is provided by the speed at which the work was carried out: inside six weeks, according to William himself.[28] Finally, there is the evidence of the entry in John of Worcester's long annal for 1062, which sums up Wulfstan's career to that point and shows substantial verbal agreement with *VW*. Since, as Darlington showed, John was drawing on Coleman's Life, not on *VW*,[29] the divergences are also significant. Most of these are extra details in the annal: that the writer had heard from Wulfstan himself of his passing up to four days and nights without sleep; that he succeeded Prior Æthelwine, in the time of Bishop Ealdred; that at the time of Wulfstan's own election as bishop there were two apostolic legates in England, one of them Ermenfrid bishop of Sion; that the reluctant Wulfstan was persuaded to accept the episcopal office by a recluse named Wulfsige. The question is, of course, whether these details were taken by John from the text of Coleman, or whether they are additions. The first of them—information imparted by Wulfstan in person—must at least derive from a source earlier than John himself (who died after 1140). The source could have been his elusive predecessor as chronicler, the monk Florence (d. 1118), but it might equally have been Coleman. The possibility must he entertained, therefore, that William's pruning of Coleman's account included the omission of some personal names.[30] What does seem certain is that Coleman's Life was William's *only* written source, apart from a few classical and biblical tags, and one or two references drawn from his own *GR*.

VD and the Life of Patrick, on the other hand, are both cunningly-constructed pastiches of several pre-existing Lives, either ready to hand at Glastonbury, or seen by William on his wider travels while gathering material for *GR* and *GP*. For Dunstan he had access to the early Lives by B. and Adelard, plus the later ones by Osbern and Eadmer of Canterbury. He knew two versions of the B. Life: one with the original prologue, which he was shown at Glastonbury,[31] and

[27] *GP*, cc. 144, 146, 149 (pp. 285, 286–7, 288–9).
[28] *VW* iii. 29. 3.
[29] Darlington, pp. xi–xvi. The overlap with *VW* occurs within i. 1–12.
[30] William does in fact admit to having done this at *VW* i. 16. 5 and ii. 19. 4.
[31] *VD* i. pr. 7.

another revised before the mid eleventh century at St Augustine's Canterbury.[32] He seems to have found copies of this latter version both there and at Bury St Edmunds,[33] again probably while chasing material for *GR* and *GP*. Both Adelard's Life (in the form of lections for the saint's Office) and Osbern's were widely available, and William might have had them at Malmesbury itself.[34] It is virtually certain that he knew the even more recent one by his admired friend Eadmer, but he makes almost no demonstrable use of it, for reasons that we will attempt to divine below.[35] He also mentions writings in Old English, and quotes from one of them, Æthelwold's prologue to his Old English translation of the Benedictine Rule.[36] But he seems also to have known of a Life in Old English which has not survived. Because this observation has not been made before, and has important consequences, it requires demonstration in detail.

Both Osbern and William seem to have thought in terms of two 'old' Lives of Dunstan, one in English, one in Latin.[37] William provides three crucial pieces of information about the English Life (we shall call it Eng.): firstly, one of the two 'old' Lives said that Dunstan was offered the see of Crediton but refused it, while the other made the see Winchester.[38] As B. gives the Crediton version, it follows that Eng. named Winchester.[39] William remarks that it is easy to suppose that Dunstan was offered both, and this is the line he takes at *VD* i. 23. Now the other three Latin Lives, by Adelard, Osbern, and Eadmer, all give Winchester.[40] It is therefore worth pursuing the hypothesis that all three made particular use of Eng. Secondly, William says that the two old Lives 'often' give different information: 'dicunt quidem plerumque unus plus altero, sicut se habebat

---

[32] See *Memorials*, pp. xxvi–xxx; M. Lapidge, 'B. and the *Vita S. Dunstani*', in *Anglo-Latin Literature 900–1066*, pp. 279–92, but, for the relationship between the MSS, M. Winterbottom, 'The earliest Life of St Dunstan', *Scripta Classica Israelica*, xix (2000), 163–79. He argues that the original version is found in St Gall, Kantonsbibl. (Vadiana) 337 (C); a revised text is found in Arras, Bibl. municipale 812 (A); the text in BL Cotton Cleopatra B. xiii (Stubbs's B, renamed D by Winterbottom) was copied from A's ancestor, with abbreviation and further revision.

[33] *AG*, cc. 1 (pp. 44–7) and n. 13 (p. 186), 2 (pp. 48–9) and n. 19 (p. 187); *GR* II, p. 400.

[34] *Memorials*, pp. xxx–xxxii, xli–xlvii.

[35] See below, pp. xx–xxiii.

[36] Below, p. 238 and n. 2.

[37] *VD* i. prol. 7; ii. prol. 3–4; Osbern, c. 1 (p. 70); cf. also Eadmer, prol. (p. 164), referring to 'scripta ueter*um*'. But he could in principle have meant B. and Adelard.

[38] *VD* ii. prol. 4.

[39] B., c. 19 (p. 29).

[40] Adelard, lect. iv (pp. 56–7); Osbern, c. 22 (p. 95); Eadmer, c. 12 (p. 185).

scribentium memoria uel intentio.'[41] This is true of B. as compared
with Adelard, Osbern, and Eadmer. Thirdly, he says, or at least
appears to say, that *both* Lives were 'published' (*edita*) with dedications to Ælfric, archbishop of Canterbury from 995 to 1005.[42] This is
certainly true of B.[43] Both Lives, then, were written before, but not
very long before, 1005 (before late 1004 for B.).[44] In view of their
common dedicatee, it is difficult to believe that there was no
relationship between them; nonetheless their contents appear to
have been strikingly different. Osbern says that he was told, presumably by members of the Canterbury community, that some
material, translated from Latin into English, had survived the fire
there in 1067. This material we take to have been Eng. Osbern,
therefore, saw his task as to translate it back, with God's help.[45] As he
has just told us that he has read B., this is evidence for a substantial
difference between B. and Eng.: a difference that would make
(re-)translating Eng. worthwhile.

Of Adelard's Life, Stubbs commented: ' . . . it is not to be understood
as solely or even mainly drawn from' B.[46] Instead, 'the legend had, in
the seven or eight years that intervened between the two, had time to
grow, and had grown luxuriantly'.[47] In fact, it is probable that Eng.
already contained this luxuriant growth.[48] Whoever 'translated' it, if
their source was B., took the opportunity to add, subtract, and alter at
will. William, like Osbern, had access to both B. and Eng., but whereas
Osbern may be supposed to have relied heavily on Eng., William's
policy was to produce a compromise version.

Comparison of the accounts of the death of Eadred can be used as a
test case.[49] In B., the king becomes ill and sends Dunstan to get the
treasure he was storing.[50] In Adelard, Osbern, and Eadmer, the king
sends *for* Dunstan to confess him.[51] There is no mention of the

[41] *VD* ii. prol. 3.
[42] *VD* i. prol. 7. Adelard's Life, on the other hand, was dedicated to Archbishop
Ælfheah (1006–12).
[43] B., c. 1 (p. 3).
[44] Because a copy was sent to Abbo of Fleury, who died on 13 Nov. of that year
(*Memorials*, pp. xxvii–xxviii).
[45] Osbern, c. 1 (p. 70).
[46] *Memorials*, p. xxxi.   [47] p. lx.
[48] This line of reasoning involves the assumption that Adelard, though a monk of St
Peter's Ghent, either could read OE or had oral information equivalent to the content of Eng.
[49] For another comparison which one might expect to have produced a similar picture,
but which turns out to be complicated and confusing, see below, p. 235 n. 10.
[50] B., c. 20 (p. 31).
[51] Adelard, lect. v (p. 58); Osbern, c. 24 (p. 98); Eadmer, c. 14 (p. 187).

treasure: so this can be seen as the 'pious' (that is, more purely hagiographical) alternative. William's compromise version makes the king send for Dunstan, who brings the treasure without being asked.[52]

William lambasts Osbern heavily, and refers to the 'old biographer' in terms which would suggest heavy reliance on him. For example, William says that the story of King Eadwig's amours is only to be believed on the basis of the 'auctores antiquos',[53] presumably B. and Eng. (for Adelard does *not* tell the story): that is, he would not believe it if Osbern alone had told him. It is in this light that one must read the data on William's sources supplied in Table I below.[54] *Prima facie* it presents a picture of William making choices between the accounts of B. and Osbern in either direction and in about equal measure, or conflating them. In view of William's criticisms of Osbern, this makes him appear hypocritical. We suggest, however, that even in those cases where he is borrowing Osbern's very language, the choice he was making was really between the accounts of B. and Eng., Osbern's main source. And what determined that choice was often simply which of the two accounts was the longer and more detailed. This explains why Adelard, whose stories are almost always briefer than the comparable versions in either B. or Osbern (= his main source, Eng.), hardly makes a showing.

We still need, however, to make sense of William's criticism of Osbern, which is odd on three counts: in the first place, in *GR* William had praised him for his work as a hagiographer and liturgist, not only in general but specifically for his Life of Dunstan:

I would gladly add more facts . . . about this great man [Dunstan], but I am restrained by Osbern, precentor of Canterbury, who has written his life with Roman elegance, being second to none in our time as a stylist as well as leading the field without dispute in music.[55]

In the second place, William's summary account of Dunstan's miracles in *GP*, c. 19, is almost entirely dependent upon Osbern.[56]

---

[52] *VD* i. 25.
[53] *VD* i. 27. 2.
[54] See below, pp. 161–3.
[55] *GR*, c. 149. 3.
[56] In the order of William's telling, the miracles are from Osbern, cc. 4, 6–7, 10, 17, 18, 26, 34, 14, 19 (fox and wolf; William has fox only), 26–7, 21, 30, 16, 33, 19 again, 24, 20, 37, 38, 19 again, 40. Those from cc. 14, 30, 34, and 37 are unique to Osbern. But Dunstan's prophecy of the death of Eadgyth is from the *vita* by Goscelin, and 'Ode se gode' and the vision of the Kyrie are not in Osbern, but in Eadmer, *Vita S. Odonis (Anglia Sacra* ii. 86), and *Vita Dunstani*, cc. 27 (p. 203), 30 (p. 207). William says that the posthumous miracle of the thief rescued from death by precipitation was not in writing.

Finally, at least for the modern reader there seems a disproportion
between the relative triviality of most of Osbern's alleged errors on
the one hand, and William's stringent and repeated condemnation of
them on the other. These sins fall into three categories. In descending
order of their gravity as seen by William, they are: (*a*) historical
errors, above all the assertion that Dunstan was Glastonbury's first
abbot; (*b*) exaggeration, and the inclusion of allegedly verbatim
speeches; (*c*) theological errors.[57] Why was William so concerned to
discredit Osbern in *VD*, after he had praised him so highly in *GR*?
Any attempted answer can only be conjectural, but it seems likely that
this puzzle is bound up with another: the relationship between *VD*
and the Life of Dunstan by Eadmer. Stubbs thought that William
made no use of Eadmer's *Vita*.[58] This would be *prima facie* odd, given
that William admired Eadmer and clearly knew him well,[59] made use
of most of his writings,[60] and could hardly *not* have known his *Vita
Dunstani*, written it seems while Archbishop Anselm was still alive
(that is, before 1109).[61] There are indeed signs of such acquaintance,
both in *VD* and elsewhere. In the first place, their approaches are
strikingly similar: Eadmer, like William, criticized Osbern for historical errors, though he used him as the basis of his narrative (especially
for the period covered by William's book i); and both (claim to) use
earlier sources with which to supplement or correct Osbern.[62] In *GP*,
William's account of the state of Canterbury when Lanfranc arrived
appears to derive from a passage in Eadmer's Life.[63] In *GP* and *VD*
his account of Oswald's ploy to rid Worcester of secular clerks must
come from Eadmer.[64] Finally, a handful of smaller details are

---

[57] *VD* i. prol. 2–6, 15. 5, 32, ii. prol. 1, 4. 2–3, 33. 2, 35. At i. prol. 9 William offers a
partial excuse for Osbern's errors, 'because he had to do without old documents as a result
of the fire which, as he said in his prologue, ravaged the church of Canterbury'.

[58] *Memorials*, pp. xxxv–xxxvi.

[59] Thomson, *William of Malmesbury*, pp. 71, 73.

[60] Eadmer's *Historia novorum* and *Vita Anselmi* are extensively used in *GR* and *GP*; *Vita
Wilfridi* and *Vita Odonis* in *GP*, probably his *Vita S. Oswaldi* in *GR*, *GP*, and *VD*, *De
excellentia B. Mariae* in *Mir*.

[61] R. W. Southern, *St Anselm and his Biographer* (Cambridge, 1963), p. 281 n. 2.

[62] Eadmer, prol. (pp. 162–4); *VD* i. prol. 7. And the source of Eadmer's corrections, like
William's, seems to have been Worcester: A. Gransden, 'Cultural transition at Worcester
in the Anglo-Norman period', in *Medieval Art and Architecture at Worcester Cathedral* (The
British Archaeological Association, Conference Transactions, i: 1978 for 1975), pp. 1–14,
at 9–10.

[63] *GP*, c. 44 (pp. 70–1), Eadmer, c. 16 (pp. 237–8); the observation was made by
Southern, *St Anselm and his Biographer*, p. 247 n. 1.

[64] *GP*, c. 115 (p. 248); *VD* ii. 13; Eadmer, c. 22 (p. 197). But it could also have come
from Eadmer's *Vita S. Oswaldi*, c. 20 (*HCY* ii. 24–5).

common to the accounts of William and Eadmer alone.[65] In other words, the puzzle is why, when William evidently knew Eadmer's work perfectly well, and despite his admiration for its writer, he chose to make so little use of it.

William's evidently deliberate avoidance of Eadmer, and his criticism of Osbern, may both have to do with the claim, apparently first made by the Glastonbury monks in the early 1120s, to possession of Dunstan's body. At this time, it seems, they began to maintain that it had been 'translated' from Canterbury about a century earlier, to protect it from the ravages of the Danes. On the preposterousness of this claim Eadmer addressed a strongly-worded letter to the Glastonbury community.[66] William must have known of Eadmer's view, and probably shared it; indeed this is implicit in the very opening sentences of *VD*:

Most holy fathers, in the celebration of the love and honour of your most blessed father Dunstan our pious zeal strives to compete with the whole of England. And it may be that ours is the greater glory in this contest, seeing that we love as a former pupil one whom they look up to as a saint and an archbishop. So it is that we can join love to our reverence, yielding in neither to those of Canterbury, who boast that they once had him as their primate.[67]

Surely, if William thought that Glastonbury had Dunstan's body, here was the place to say so, loud and clear; his failure to do so is therefore significant. The fact is that his commission to write *VD* put him in a most embarrassing position: he had to satisfy Glastonbury, and yet he surely had no desire to attack Eadmer or his community. Eadmer was his friend, and Canterbury, like Glastonbury, had supported his historical and bibliographical researches. We suggest that his solution was, on the one hand, to distance his work from Eadmer's by making almost no use of it, and no explicit reference to

---

[65] (1) *VD* ii. 8. 2 'Ode the goode' (so Q), *GP*, c. 19 (p. 30) 'Ode se gode'; similarly Eadmer, c. 27 (p. 203) and *Vita S. Odonis* (*Anglia Sacra* ii. 86) 'Odo se gode'; (2) *VD* ii. 19. 3 'hoc miraculum . . . clericis', cf. Eadmer, c. 34 (p. 213); (3) in *Mir.*, pp. 161–2, occurs the story of the miraculous supply of mead (cf. *VD* i. 12), basically as Osbern, c. 15 (pp. 85–7), but saying that Ælfgifu (there 'Ethelfleda' as in B. c. 9 (p. 16): see below, p. 192) was nurse of the royal children, a detail otherwise found only in Eadmer, c. 8 (p. 175). (4) The brief mention of Dunstan's vision of the Kyrie in *VD* ii. 26. 5, and the more elaborate account in *GP*, c. 19 (p. 31), may depend upon Eadmer, c. 30 (p. 207). But see below, p. 285 n. 3.

[66] ed. *Memorials*, pp. 412–22; trans. and discussion by R. Sharpe, 'Eadmer's letter to the monks of Glastonbury concerning St Dunstan's disputed remains', in *The Archaeology and History of Glastonbury Abbey: Essays in Honour of the Ninetieth Birthday of C. A. Ralegh Radford*, ed. L. Abrams and J. P. Carley (Woodbridge, 1991), pp. 205–15.

[67] *VD* i. prol. 1.

it, and on the other to make a show of defending Glastonbury against Canterbury by using the deceased Osbern as his target. Eadmer had already criticized Osbern, so Canterbury could hardly object if William did so too. Osbern's (and thus by implication Canterbury's) main slight to Glastonbury was identified by William as his failure to register its venerable antiquity. The other criticisms of Osbern unrelated to Glastonbury were doubtless designed to diminish his credibility in general; the carping nature of some of them suggests that William's intention might even have been satirical.[68] Still, William had to deal with the question of the translation of Dunstan's body from Canterbury to Glastonbury, of which the Glastonbury monks must surely have expected an account. This, we conjecture, he could reasonably postpone until he produced book iii, on Dunstan's posthumous miracles; and perhaps for this reason he never wrote that book, of which no trace has been found. There is indeed an account of the translation in *AG*, but it seems to be a later interpolation, doubtless necessary precisely because William failed to provide such an account in the first place.[69]

Of all William's hagiographical works, *VD* is the one in which his experience and interests as a historian are most to the fore. So far as his sources are concerned, this means that he provided extra detail and context from a variety of writings other than the earliest Lives of Dunstan. We find him referring to his own *GR*, to the *Anglo-Saxon Chronicle*, to Wulfstan of Winchester's *Vita S. Æthelwoldi*, and to Goscelin's *Vita S. Edithae*. He probably made use, also, of important

---

[68] Unfairness and the absence of a sense of proportion are part and parcel of the satirical technique: see the remarks on this score in R. M. Thomson, 'The satirical works of Berengar of Poitiers: an edition with introduction', in his *England and the 12th-Century Renaissance* (Variorum Collected Studies Ser. dcxx: Aldershot, 1998), XIII, at pp. 97, 101–3.

[69] *AG*, c. 23 (pp. 72–5). There is no doubt that William could not have written the chapter as it stands: note e.g. the insistent cursus and use of the word *exemplariter* (unattested in his other writings), the historical error in dating the Danish landing in eastern England to 1012 (see *AG*, p. 195 n. 60), and the nonsensical dating of the 'translation' to 1012, 'the second year after the murder of the archbishop St Ælfheah', itself implicitly dated 1012! All the same, there are some possible William fingerprints: (1) *silere preter religionem existimantes*. Cf. *GR*, c. 29. 3 [= *GP*, c. 75 p. 159] 'dissimulare preter religionem uidebatur'; also [from JG] in the *Passio S. Indracti* (below, p. 370): 'preter religionem estimantes . . . preterire.' (2) *anima in quietas sedes translata*. Cf. *VD* ii. 5. 1 'episcopum in quietas sedes transduxit'; *GR*, c. 124. 2 'quieta sede composuisse' (of a translation). (3) *caritatis qua nutriculam amplectebantur* (of the monks' love for Glastonbury). Cf. *VD* ii. 17. 1, where Dunstan is said to have often visited Glastonbury, 'felicitatis et religionis suae nutriculam'. None of these parallels is decisive, but it is just conceivable that something of William's may lie below this chapter. It is also interesting for its remarks on the way in which Dunstan favoured Glastonbury monks at Canterbury.

and relevant letters in the collection made at Canterbury *c.*1000, BL, MS Cotton Tiberius A. xv.[70]

Due to its fragmentary state, there is less to say about William's manipulation of the sources used in his *Vita Patricii*. He used four in particular: firstly, the *Vita tertia*, written in Ireland some time between *c.*800 and William's day. This he found in version Π, the English family, sub-version *g*, whose most distinctive feature, significantly, is its identification of Patrick's burial place, Dun Lethglaisse (Downpatrick), with Glastonbury.[71] Doubtless that was where this sub-version originated, and one imagines that that was where William found it. He also used the lost source (*W*) of the *Vita secunda* and *Vita quarta*, which survive only in continental copies.[72] Finally, he had access to Patrick's own *Confessio* and *Letter to Coroticus*. These are found together today in five manuscripts, including the Passionals BL Cotton Nero E. i (s. xi med., Worcester), and Salisbury, Cathedral Libr. 221 and 223 (formerly Bodl. Libr. Fell 4 and 3) (*c.*1100, Salisbury).[73] William could have known any of these, and presumably Glastonbury also had a copy.[74] But most of the material in William's Life connecting Patrick with Glastonbury is not derived from any of this, or from any other surviving writings. Whether it already existed in written form, or whether it came to William orally, there can be no doubt that it originated specifically at Glastonbury itself.

Still less can be said about the sources for the fragmentary Lives of Benignus and Indract. For most of their content there are no surviving earlier written materials at all. At the beginning of his account of Benignus, William took some scraps of information from the *Vita tertia* of Patrick;[75] the rest of his text (as far as we have it) represents Glastonbury tradition, otherwise unrecorded. For Indract,

[70] See below, p. 283 n. 7.

[71] Bieler, pp. 22–4, 183 n. Bieler, however, errs on p. 24 in saying that William also knew the (very rare) Life by Muirchu; of the four passages he cites as proof, three are found in Patrick's *Confessio*, c. 1. The fourth ('haud procul' instead of 'non longe') is far too unsubstantial to make a case.

[72] Bieler, pp. 1–13. A. Correa, 'William of Malmesbury's *Vita S. Patricii* and his source', in *Saint Patrick*, ed. D. Dumville (Woodbridge, 1993), pp. 265–71, at 267, suggests tentatively that William might have known a single lost source rather than the two Lives mentioned above.

[73] L. Bieler, *Codices Patriciani Latini* (Dublin, 1942), p. 2.

[74] The Glastonbury library-catalogue of 1247 contains an exceptionally large number of hagiographical collections, including a dozen Passionals (*English Benedictine Libraries*, pp. 194–7).

[75] See below, p. 344 and n. 1.

likewise, no earlier written material exists. The relationship of William's Life to the anonymous Life that survives in the twelfth-century manuscript Bodl. Libr. Digby 112, and the possibility that William used its Old English exemplar, now lost, are discussed below, pp. 310–11.

POPULARITY AND INFLUENCE

William's hagiography was far less well-known than his *GR* and *GP*, for understandable reasons. So far as the *VW* is concerned, Wulfstan's cult was never very popular away from Worcester.[76] It is surprising, therefore, that the sole surviving copy of *VW* should have been made in a Cistercian scriptorium, probably that of Holm Cultram far to the north, where it was kept by the fourteenth century.[77] At Worcester itself William's Life was laid under contribution for other hagiographical compositions. An abridgement was made in the late twelfth century, probably by Prior Senatus, an accomplished writer who died in 1207.[78] This survives in two copies: one, probably made at Worcester, was at Durham Cathedral Priory by the late fourteenth century; the other is from the Cluniac abbey at Reading or its cell at Leominster. Even more abridged versions survive in another three manuscripts, two without provenance, one from the Hampshire nunnery of Romsey.[79] In the thirteenth century a metrical Life was composed, perhaps by the well-known poet Henry of Avranches, using *VW* or Senatus' abridgement as its basis.[80]

[76] Darlington, pp. xix, xlvi–lii; Mason, pp. 265–84; R. C. Finucane, *Miracles and Pilgrims: Popular Beliefs in Medieval England* (London, 1977), pp. 130, 159, 169. Nonetheless, a wall-painting at Norwich Cathedral, probably s. xiii med., illustrated the miracle referred to below, pp. xxxiii–xxxiv and nn. 116–17: D. Park, 'Simony and sanctity: Herbert Losinga, St Wulfstan of Worcester and wall-paintings in Norwich Cathedral', in *Studies in Medieval Art and Architecture presented to Peter Lasko*, ed. D. Buckton and T. A. Heslop (Stroud, 1994), pp. 157–70; D. Park and H. Howard, 'The medieval polychromy', in *Norwich Cathedral: Church, City and Diocese, 1096–1996*, ed. I. Atherton, E. Fernie, C. Harper-Bill, and H. Smith (London, 1996), pp. 379–409, at 380–3.

[77] See below, p. 3 and n. 1.

[78] Darlington, pp. xx–xxii, 68–108. On Senatus, see M. G. Cheney, *Roger, Bishop of Worcester, 1164–1179* (Oxford, 1980), pp. 58–66. To Darlington's single MS (the Durham copy) should be added Gloucester Cath., MS 1, fos. 153–62 (see below, p. 3).

[79] Darlington, pp. xxi–xxii; see below, p. 4.

[80] R. Flower, 'A metrical Life of St Wulfstan of Worcester', *The National Library of Wales Journal*, i (1940), 119–30; P. Grosjean, review in *Analecta Bollandiana* lxxiii (1955), 259–60. The work is preserved in Aberystwyth, National Library of Wales, Peniarth 386, a Worcester MS s. xiii².

Dunstan's cult was much more widespread, but centred on Canterbury, where *VD* was unlikely to be read.[81] Canterbury's interests aside, the work was too polemical, too overtly historical, and too pro-Glastonbury to be widely influential. Adelard already provided the text of the Office, and the *Vita* by Osbern, a hagiographer's hagiographer, remained far more popular than William's critique of it.[82] Yet he did not go far enough to please the Glastonbury monks, any more than with *AG*.[83] Thus the work survives complete (at any rate the first two books) only in a single copy, written, in an obscure context, in the late fifteenth and early sixteenth centuries.[84] Much earlier, by the second half of the twelfth century, it was known at Worcester, where it was used to interpolate a surviving copy of Eadmer's Life.[85]

Not surprisingly, the fragmentary Lives also had a restricted circulation. One would not expect the Life of Patrick to have had an audience outside Glastonbury, let alone those of such obscure local saints as Benignus and Indract.[86] Patrick was already well served by Lives to which William added only Glastonbury material of no interest elsewhere. Benignus and Indract, too, unimportant in themselves, were only venerated locally. In the case of the latter, mystery surrounds the relationship of William's to the Digby Life. This Life survives in a copy no later than William's time, and was almost certainly written at and for Glastonbury; yet William seems not to have used it.[87] Perhaps, as with Osbern's Life of Dunstan, William preferred to use Digby's Old English source rather than Digby itself; if his own Life had survived intact we might know more.

What is clear, however, is that William's works survived and were

---

[81] On the cult, see N. G. Ramsay and M. Sparks, 'The cult of St Dunstan at Christ Church, Canterbury', in *St Dunstan*, pp. 311–23.

[82] Eighteen copies of his work are listed in *Memorials*, pp. xlii–xlvii, seven of them continental, most of them twelfth-century. One of the earliest even accords Osbern the dignity of an author-portrait: M. Budny and T. Graham, 'Dunstan as hagiographical subject or Osbern as author? The scribal portrait in an early copy of Osbern's *Vita Sancti Dunstani*', *Gesta*, xxxii (1993), 83–96.

[83] This is the reason why, notoriously, *AG* only survives in a version heavily revised by the local monks: see Scott in *AG*, pp. 27–33.

[84] See below, p. 159 and nn. 1–3.

[85] See below, pp. 159–60.

[86] The 1247 catalogue includes two copies each of *GR* and *AG* (*English Benedictine Libraries*, p. 191), and a collection containing Lives of Dunstan and Benignus (pp. 196–7), which might or might not have been William's.

[87] M. Lapidge, 'The cult of St Indract at Glastonbury', in *Anglo-Latin Literature 900–1066*, pp. 419–52, at 434–6.

used in the communities for which they were written. The monk John of Glastonbury (perhaps John Seen) used William for the accounts of the local saints which he inserted in his own chronicle, written in the 1340s.[88] But about the very same time John of Tynemouth brought some of these works back into the main stream of English hagiographical writing. In the great collection of saints' Lives known as *Sanctilogium Angliae, Walliae, Scotiae et Hiberniae*,[89] he included a Life of Wulfstan based on Senatus' abridgement of William (and on *GP*), while at Glastonbury he found copies of the Lives of Benignus and Indract and used them as sources for his own.[90] It was there, too, that John Leland, visiting between 1536 and 1540, found copies of *VD* and the Lives of Patrick, Benignus and Indract, quoting extracts from the first and a snippet of information from the last. Leland, ironically, probably appreciated William's hagiography more than anyone else before or for a long time after.

VALUE

We should first consider the value of the Lives as sources of information about their subjects. In this respect they differ widely from each other. For Wulfstan, William is effectively the main primary source, given the loss of Coleman's Old English Life.[91] All his sources of information were persons—Coleman and his own informants, the monk Eadric, and Prior Nicholas—who knew Wulfstan intimately. This, allied to William's instincts as a historian, means that Wulfstan emerges as a distinct and distinctive personality, not just a hagiographical exemplar. He is shrewd though not highly educated; he is simple but not naive; he is an active, widely-travelling pastor, who sometimes drives himself and his *familia* hard; he is very severe on sexually active clergy; he is tolerant, though, of his hard-drinking

---

[88] See below, pp. 307–10.

[89] *Nova Legenda Anglie* (*NLA*) is a later, revised version of it.

[90] Darlington, p. xxii; and see below, pp. 308–12. On the other hand, the *NLA* Life of Dunstan was based upon Osbern. This is brought out clearly by Stubbs's annotation to his edition of the *NLA* Life in *Memorials*, pp. 325–53. This is the more striking as the author was at Glastonbury, where he used *AG*: *Memorials*, pp. 352–3.

[91] See Mason, pp. 286–96, Farmer, 'Two biographies', pp. 165–6. It continued to exist and be thought useful long enough to be shown to Innocent III in 1203, when Wulfstan was canonized: Darlington, pp. xlvii, 149–50. Even later than this date there was still at least one Worcester monk capable of reading Old English: N. R. Ker, 'The date of the "tremulous" Worcester hand', in his *Books, Collectors and Libraries*, pp. 67–9; C. Franzen, *The Tremulous Hand of Worcester: A Study of Old English in the Thirteenth Century* (Oxford, 1991).

knights, though he himself is unostentatiously abstemious.[92] A few examples of his direct speech—normally eschewed by William—and characteristic utterances ('Crede mihi') reveal his cast of mind; and there is a brief physical description.[93] Although his interaction with and reaction to England's new rulers are recorded, Wulfstan was not a major political figure, or important in the English Church outside his own diocese; he is presented instead as an example of the best of the old, Bedan world (which William thought had generally been in decline prior to the Conquest),[94] with little in one sense to offer the new—apart from timeless Christian virtues which William thought were much needed. Some of this might reasonably be thought to reflect the 'real' Wulfstan, but of course some of it has to be put down to the genre.[95] Some of it might also be quite mistaken. For example, the fact and the character of Wulfstan's reforming zeal could indeed be interpreted as a resuscitation of ancient values held within the English Church, as William would have it; but they were also suspiciously in tune with the latest continental legislation.[96] It is possible, therefore, to see Wulfstan as remarkably up to date and uninsular, well able to make common cause with someone like Archbishop Lanfranc in framing conciliar decrees and seeing to their implementation. This is arguable; what is certain is that the portrait in *VW* is far from complete or balanced. The picture of Wulfstan that emerges from Hemming's Cartulary still includes the ingredients of piety and moral uprightness, but the main emphasis is upon his energy and effectiveness as a recoverer, defender, and manager of the Cathedral Priory's estates.[97]

---

[92] *VW* ii. 1, iii. 2–4, 10, 12, 16.　　　　　　[93] *VW* ii. 3, iii. 1. 1, 17. 2.

[94] e. g. *GR*, c. 245. 3–6.

[95] For the genre in its English context, see M. Lapidge, 'The saintly life in Anglo-Saxon England', in *The Cambridge Companion to Old English Literature*, ed. M. Godden and M. Lapidge (Cambridge, 1991), pp. 243–63. An impressive attempt to penetrate beyond the hagiographical view of Wulfstan is A. Williams, 'The cunning of the dove: Wulfstan and the politics of accommodation', in *St Wulfstan and his World*. Also S. Baxter, 'The representation of lordship and land tenure in Domesday Book', in *Domesday Book: New Perspectives*, ed. D. Bates and E. Hallam, forthcoming.

[96] See below, pp. 124 and n. 5, 128 and n. 1.

[97] Esp. *Hemingi Chartularium* i. 282–6; and see below, p. xxxii and n. 108. Even so, Hemming (i. 271) says of Wulfstan that 'totum se Dei seruitio mancipabat, nec ullo modo, cum plurimum quidem posset, secularibus negotiis implicare se uellet: immo, ne occasione aliqua honoris aut potentie eis implicaretur, quasi mortem deuitabat, apostolici memor precepti, "nemo militans Deo implicet se negotiis secularibus"', and at i. 284 he is described as 'secularium rerum minime cupidus'. See also the Life of Abbot Æthelwig of Evesham, as preserved in *Chronicon abbatiae de Evesham*, ed. W. D. Macray (RS, 1863), pp. 89–90, where Wulfstan is described as 'uir religiosus, simplex et rectus', even though bribery is alleged to have played a part in his litigation against Archbishop Thomas.

There is little of this in *VW*, which stresses the bishop's unworldliness, or at least his involvement in royal and ecclesiastical administration on sufferance only.

Stubbs's assessment of *VD* was that William had no fresh information to add to the extant early Lives apart from some otherwise unrecorded Glastonbury and Malmesbury tradition; however, we have argued above that it is William who offers the clearest testimony to the existence of a now-lost Old English Life used by himself and apparently by the Canterbury writers. If this is true, then the texts of William, Osbern, and Eadmer can be used in combination to recover at least the blurred outlines of this lost early witness where it differs from the account in B. William's technique of combining the evidence of Eng. and B. when appropriate, or of choosing the longest version of a story told by more than one early source, resulted in the longest of the Lives: 75 pages in Stubbs's edition, compared with 50 pages for B., 16 for Adelard, 60 for Osbern (without the *Miracula*), and 61 for Eadmer (again excluding the *Miracula*). William mainly followed B.'s order, but sometimes altered it drastically in the interests of chronology. As with Wulfstan, he omitted passages of Dunstan's allegedly direct speech (mainly provided by Osbern), and Osbern's sometimes lengthy passages of panegyric and moral reflection.[98] He added very few stories not found in one or other of his two main sources. As with Wulfstan, but perhaps more obviously, the result should be regarded with caution: we have to deal with an attempt to create historical verisimilitude rather than with history-writing in the fullest sense. *VD* is certainly beguiling in its presentation of the most clearly-delineated picture of Dunstan, and the best integrated into a broad historical context. The first of these characteristics involves a clear focus and emphasis on Dunstan's unique characteristics: his skill at craft-work, gift of prophecy, relations with kings, and pro-monastic policy. Especially in relation to these last two areas, William can be seen (particularly as compared with B.) adding historical context and reference (some of this occupying whole chapters), and providing 'normal' human motivation to explain Dunstan's movements and career-pattern. He has a larger view of Dunstan as reformer, connecting him with Edgar, Æthelwold and Oswald, and others. This is often the contribution of the source-material not directly concerned with Dunstan's hagiography.[99] But in

---

[98] Osbern, cc. 4–5, 7–9, 11–12, 14, 16, 18 (pp. 73–4, 76–9, 81–3, 85, 87–8, 91–2), etc.
[99] See below, pp. 161–3.

the last analysis, this compelling picture is the result of William's historian's instinct, and of his clever manipulation and interpretation of his sources. With the possible exception of the Old English Life, it is unlikely to have resulted from his having had access to early information now lost to us.

For the three Lives of Celtic saints, William's work is most usefully approached as a source for religious practices at Glastonbury abbey, and for its attempts to assert its antiquity and the value of its pre-Conquest traditions. About Patrick he has nothing underivative except a quantity of otherwise unrecorded Glastonbury tradition. For the exiguous cult of Benignus he is the unique source; for Indract he is parallel to the twelfth-century Digby Life. But William's literary support for the assertions by Glastonbury and Worcester of their glorious traditions was in turn part of a wider movement, involving many of the larger and older Benedictine foundations in England.

This phenomenon has attracted a good deal of scholarly attention in recent years, though much remains to be done.[100] Among its earliest practitioners were foreigners: Folcard of Saint-Bertin, monk of Christ Church Canterbury and (?acting-)abbot of Thorney *c.*1068–1084/5, and Goscelin of Saint-Bertin, precentor of St Augustine's abbey Canterbury (d. after 1114).[101] Canterbury remained the focus of this activity for some time, due to two successive precentors at Christ Church: Osbern, who died perhaps in 1094, and Eadmer, who died after 1124.[102] Most of what these men wrote, naturally,

---

[100] e.g. Southern, *St Anselm and his Biographer*, pp. 248–51; Gransden, *Historical Writing in England c.550–c.1307*, chs. 5 and 7; S. J. Ridyard, '*Condigna Veneratio*: post-Conquest attitudes to the saints of the Anglo-Saxons', *ANS* ix (1987 for 1986), 179–206; D. Townsend, 'Anglo-Latin hagiography and the Norman transition', *Exemplaria*, iii (1991), 385–433; *Three Eleventh-Century Anglo-Latin Saints' Lives*, ed. and trans. R. C. Love (OMT, 1996), pp. xi–xlviii; P. A. Hayward, 'Translation-narratives in post-Conquest hagiography and English resistance to the Norman Conquest', *ANS* xxi (1999), 67–93; idem, 'The *Miracula inventionis Beate Mylburge virginis* attributed to "the Lord Ato, Cardinal Bishop of Ostia"', *EHR* cxiv (1999), 543–73. Also, with particular reference to Worcester, Gransden, 'Cultural transition at Worcester in the Anglo-Norman period'.

[101] On Folcard, see Barlow in *Vita Ædwardi*, pp. lii–lix; on Goscelin, ibid., pp. xlvi–lii, and appendix C (pp. 133–49), and R. Sharpe, 'Goscelin's St Augustine and St Mildreth: hagiography and liturgy in context', *Journal of Theological Studies*, new ser. xli (1990), 502–16. Their writings are listed in R. Sharpe, *A Handlist of the Latin Writers of Great Britain and Ireland before 1540* (Turnhout, 1997), pp. 116–17, 151–4.

[102] On Osbern, see J. Rubenstein, 'The life and writings of Osbern of Canterbury', in *Canterbury and the Norman Conquest: Churches, Saints and Scholars, 1066–1109*, ed. R. Eales and R. Sharpe (London, 1995), pp. 27–40; on Eadmer, see Southern, *St Anselm and his Biographer*, esp. pp. 274–313. Their writings are listed in Sharpe, *Handlist*, pp. 407, 104–5.

concerned saints linked with Canterbury's past, but Goscelin was a quasi-professional hagiographer, who was engaged, for example, by the nunneries of Barking and Wilton, and the monasteries of Winchcombe, Chester, Ramsey, and Ely. By the early twelfth century other houses were either imitating, or reacting against, Canterbury's initiative, often using hagiography to support their own history and alleged privileges: at Bury with Hermann's *De miraculis sancti Edmundi* (*c*.1100), at Durham with the *Libellus de exordio atque procursu Dunelmensis ecclesiae* by the precentor Simeon (d. *c*.1130), at Evesham with the *Vita S. Ecgwini* by Prior Dominic (d. 1125).[103] William's Lives can be seen as part of this larger enterprise, of which he was certainly conscious. He was well acquainted with the work of Goscelin, Osbern, Eadmer, and Dominic;[104] like the first three he was precentor of his house. This is highly significant, for one of the responsibilities of the precentor was to ensure that saints' feasts were celebrated in the appropriate manner. This might involve the compilation, copying, or renewal of a multi-volume Passional covering the whole Christian year.[105] This exercise in turn might easily lead to the discovery that the cult of a particular saint was not well supported with written material. In such a circumstance a conscientious and energetic precentor might either commission a new Life, or write it himself. To put it another way, a good choice for precentor might well be a man with appropriate literary gifts as well as liturgical expertise.

This enterprise should not, of course, be seen as a single, coordinated campaign with an overall design or strategy; rather, it was focused within particular religious communities, who were as much in competition with each other as they were concerned to assert their ancient traditions in the face of the rapacity of Norman magnates or the scepticism of Norman prelates. Nonetheless, the intention of each community, and thus the effect of the whole, was to

---

[103] Sharpe, *Handlist*, pp. 178 (not naming the editions in *Memorials of St Edmund's Abbey*, ed. T. Arnold (3 vols.: RS, 1890–6), i. 26–92, and F. Liebermann, *Ungedruckte Anglo-Normannische Geschichtsquellen* (Strassburg, 1879)), 203–81, 607–8, 99–100. Simeon of Durham's work is now ed. and trans. D. Rollason (OMT, 2000).

[104] Goscelin is referred to by name in *GR*, c. 342; Osbern likewise in *GR*, cc. 149. 3, 342. 1; Eadmer likewise in *GR* i. prol. 3, with reference to *Hist. nov.*; in *GP*, cc. 45–66, his *Vita S. Anselmi* is laid heavily under contribution. Dominic is nowhere mentioned by name, but his *Miracula BVM* are used in *Mir.*, his *Vita S. Wistani* in *GR*, c. 212, and *GP*, c. 161 (pp. 297–8), and his *Vita S. Ecgwini* in *GP*, c. 230 (p. 384).

[105] See M. E. Fassler, 'The office of the cantor in early western monastic rules and customaries: a preliminary investigation', *Early Music History*, v (1985), 29–51, esp. pp. 50–1.

strengthen and rehabilitate the cults of Insular (mainly English) saints in the face of Norman ignorance or downright disbelief.[106] The very existence of William's hagiographical work, and its choice of subjects, owes something to this aim. He was the 'professional', called in by Worcester and Glastonbury to ratchet up their local cults in the face of Canterbury's noticeable and increasing potential for hagiographical hegemony. This aim also shaped the way in which he *presented* his saints.

VW shows this most clearly, presenting Wulfstan much as Eadmer saw him: 'the one sole survivor of the old Fathers of the English people'.[107] However, it is impossible to say how much of its assertion of 'English' against 'Norman' values is owed to Coleman rather than to William himself. That English values (and property) were already felt to be under threat at Worcester in the time of Wulfstan and Coleman is shown by the passages of commentary in Hemming's Cartulary, where the Normans are explicitly ranked with the Vikings as major depredators of Worcester's estates.[108] The fact that Coleman wrote his Life in the vernacular, at least as late as *c*.1100, may also be relevant. Certainly the Norman Samson, bishop of Worcester 1096–1112, a secular cleric appointed by William Rufus, is unlikely to have been sympathetic to his predecessor's ethos or its celebration.[109] Perhaps Coleman even wrote in the vernacular because Samson would be unable to understand it. However that may be, *VW* presents its hero as the confident and unapologetic representative of the pre-Conquest Church and its values in the face of Norman superiority. Thus, Wulfstan's simplicity is contrasted with Norman grandeur

---

[106] Norman disbelief should not be exaggerated, however: R. W. Pfaff, 'Lanfranc's supposed purge of the Anglo-Saxon Calendar', in *Warriors and Churchmen in the High Middle Ages: Essays Presented to Karl Leyser*, ed. T. Reuter (London and Rio Grande, OH, 1992), pp. 95–108.

[107] Eadmer, *Hist. nov.*, p. 46.

[108] *Hemingi Chartularium* i. 248–71, 282, and especially ii. 391: 'Hunc libellum . . . Wlstanus . . . scribi fecit . . . ut sciant, quid eorum cure commendatur, queue terrarum possessiones huic sancte ecclesie iuste competunt aut iure competere debent, quantumue etiam a malignis hominibus iniuste subtractum sit, primitus a Danis hanc patriam inuadentibus, postea uero ab iniustis prepositis et regiis exactoribus, ad ultimum quoque istis temporibus a uiolentis Normannis, qui, si quid ab aliis, ne deriperetur, retentum fuit, ui, dolis, et rapinis studentes iniuste diripuerunt, hancque sanctam ecclesiam suis possessionibus et rebus, uiculis et terris spoliauerunt.'

[109] *GP*, c. 150 (pp. 289–90 and n. 3). 'Coleman's decision to compose a *Life* in Old English seems self-consciously anachronistic': Orchard, 'Parallel Lives' (above, p. xvi n. 21). He notes that Coleman's Life was 'almost the last work known to have been composed in Old English prose', and that William describes Samson in terms which were an ironic reversal of his view of Norman self-restraint.

(Geoffrey bishop of Coutances and the cat-skins) and education
(Wulfstan as his own lawyer).[110] He is conscious of the holy bishops
who were his predecessors (weeping at the demolition of their old
church to make way for his new one).[111] His first recorded act after his
consecration was to dedicate a church to Bede: 'an excellent choice for
his first dedication, for Bede had been the prince of English letters'.[112]
He does the king's business conscientiously but not by choice; he does
not charge for his services like modern (that is, Norman) prelates.[113]
Mason suggests that the stories of his defence of the royal power in
the rebellions of 1075 and 1088, which must have been known to
Coleman, were omitted by him because they did not fit in with this
interpretation.[114] On the other hand William, perhaps following
Coleman, drew attention to Wulfstan's good relations with Harold
Godwinesson.[115] This interpretation of Wulfstan's character and
episcopate, admittedly, was not confined to Worcester and William;
it was to enjoy long and wide currency. In 1211, King John told
legates of Innocent III:

When William the Bastard, conqueror of England, wanted to deprive him of
the bishopric because he did not know French, St Wulfstan answered, 'You
did not grant me my pastoral staff, and I will not surrender it to you.'
Instead, he went to the tomb of St Edward, and said in his native language,
'Edward, you gave me my staff, and now I cannot hold it, because of the
king, so I commit it to you. And if you can defend it, then defend it.' He
rammed the staff into the tombstone and the staff was miraculously
transfixed to St Edward's tomb, so that nobody present could dislodge it
except St Wulfstan.[116]

King John told this story to illustrate and justify the English tradition
of the royal right to appoint to bishoprics; but it is likely that the story
originated as anti-Norman polemic, probably at Westminster. The
earliest known version of it, in which the initiative is taken by

[110] *VW* iii. 1. 2, ii. 1. 3–6.
[111] *VW* iii. 10. 3.
[112] *VW* i. 14. 1. But Bede was perhaps a hero of Coleman's also. Coleman annotated
CUL Kk. 3. 18, a copy of the OE Bede, *HE*, the main text of which was written by
Hemming.
[113] *VW* i. 7. 1, iii. 2. 1, 9. 1, 16. 2.
[114] Mason, p. 293. Wulfstan's role in both is mentioned by JW s.aa. 1074, 1088.
[115] *VW* i. 7. 3.
[116] Mason, p. 282, from the Burton Annals in *Annales Monastici*, ed. H. R. Luard (5
vols.: RS, 1864–9), i. 211. See also her 'St Wulfstan's staff: a legend and its uses', *Medium
Aevum*, liii (1984), 157–79. King John's interest in Wulfstan is discussed by P. Draper,
'King John and St Wulfstan', *Journal of Medieval History*, x (1984), 41–50.

Lanfranc at a (non-existent) Council of Westminster, is found in Osbert of Clare's *Vita S. Edwardi Confessoris*, written *c*.1138–9.[117] Dunstan, of course, could not be used in this way. Instead, the centrally important point in *VD* is the nature of the reform programme itself, supported by members of the royal house and involving not one, but a group of outstandingly active and holy individuals. It is a picture of a Golden Age of English Christianity, achieved by a harmonious partnership of the archbishop and king. In presenting Dunstan in this setting, William might have had an eye towards the difficult relationship between Archbishop Anselm and Kings William II and Henry I.[118] Towards the end of *VD*, though, there appears one remarkable and very overt assertion of 'Englishness': this is William's comment on Æthelred II's marriage to Emma—more extreme than anything in the far longer and highly critical treatment of this reign in *GR* :

> To prolong the harm he did so that it affected posterity, he contrived that his successors should lose all England, by marrying Emma, daughter of Richard duke of Normandy, the result being that in after years the Normans were able to claim England as of right and bring it under their control, something better seen today than put down in writing.[119]

This is William at his most English, identifying himself as such much more strongly than in his balanced remarks in *GR* on the merits of the English versus Norman claims to succeed Harold.[120] The difference has, of course, something to do with the different audiences for whom he was writing. It suggests that the culture of at least two major west-country Benedictine houses was still strongly influenced by pre-Conquest values.

Finally, the Lives reveal William's own qualities as writer and scholar. Although the genre is hagiography, *VW* and *VD* in particular testify to his ability as a historian, even if we did not have *GR* and *GP*, in which his real greatness was given full scope. Part of William's

---

[117] ed. M. Bloch, 'La Vie d'Edouard le Confesseur par Osbert de Clare', *Analecta Bollandiana*, xli (1922), 5–131, at pp. 17–44. The story finds a place in all the abbreviated versions of *VW* (Darlington, pp. xxxi–xxxiii, 77–8), but there is no reason to suppose that it was current at Worcester in William's time.

[118] As he recorded it in *GR*, cc. 315, 332, 333. 9, 413–17, and *GP*, cc. 45–66. In *GP*, c. 44 (p. 72), William makes an explicit comparison and contrast between the difficulties faced by Archbishop Lanfranc and the favourable environment in which Dunstan and his colleagues operated.

[119] *VD* ii. 34. 3–4.

[120] *GR*, cc. 228. 7, 238. 2–4.

conception of the historian's task was rhetorical; thus the point of writing *VW* was to replace a Life in the 'barbarous' vernacular with one dressed in elegant, classicizing Latin. It is characterized by the employment of a wide but not abstruse vocabulary, absence of cursus, and the unusually—perhaps uniquely—large number of quotations or echoes from classical authors, above all from his beloved Virgil: below we have identified thirty-five classical quotations or echoes in *VW*, and thirty-seven in *VD*. Rhetorical concerns manifest themselves in other ways in *VD*, for instance in the criticism which it includes of the style and organization of the 'rustic' early Lives.[121] In *GR* he had characterized a similar Latin style ('hermeneutic') by the technical word 'suffultum' (inflated), lifting the word from Osbern, but upstaging him by naming its source, the pseudo-Ciceronian *Rhetorica ad Herennium*.[122]

But the use of rhetoric could be carried too far, and William was equally concerned that the information available to and purveyed by him should be authoritative. He therefore draws attention to the antiquity of his sources, and is prepared, other things being equal, to value the ancient above the more recent.[123] This is the basis for part of his criticism of Osbern: that he was *too* rhetorical, sacrificing accuracy in his attempt to achieve elegance, that he had not conducted sufficient research into the ancient sources on the one hand, and that in order to compensate he invented or exaggerated on the other.[124] For William, information *not* obviously based upon the early sources was suspect, no matter how well-expressed. And with a high value on antiquity goes a similarly high rating for the use of the vernacular. Now William, notoriously, valued Latin as the language of civilized discourse par excellence. As we have observed above, and as William stated elsewhere, he saw his task as a historian to render in elegant Latin what had been hitherto conveyed imperfectly, either in inferior (usually meaning verbose) Latin, or in 'barbarous' language, usually meaning English.[125] Nonetheless, English had a peculiar attraction and value for him.[126] This was partly because it was, quite simply, the native language of one of his own parents,[127] and because it was fostered by two of his culture-heroes: Bede and Alfred.

---

[121] VD i. prol. 2, where 'antiquis' could refer both to B. and Eng.

[122] *GR*, c. 132 n. Osbern refers to B.; William, however, applies 'suffultum' to the lost 'ancient volume' on the exploits of King Æthelstan.

[123] *VD* i. prol. 7, 9; i. 32; ii. prol. 2.

[124] *VD* i. 32, ii. prol. 1–2.   [125] *GR* i. prol. 2–4.

[126] *GR*, cc. 49. 4, 68. 3, 122. 4, 123. 1–3.   [127] *GR* iii. prol. 1.

In *GR* he noted that Bede had died in the act of translating the Gospel of St John into Old English, and he gave a very full description of the translations made or commissioned by King Alfred.[128] Moreover, documents in that language were venerable and could be credited with at least a kind of naïve, rustic truthfulness. And so he has nothing positive to say of the literary qualities of Coleman's Life of Wulfstan,[129] nor perhaps of the Old English Life of Dunstan; as far as William was concerned the notion of 'literary' qualities in a vernacular text was probably an oxymoron. But these documents conveyed precious information, and the 'rustic' English Life of Dunstan was certainly to be preferred as a source over and against the elegant latinity of Osbern. Of course the early sources did not always agree. William is one of the rare medieval historians who explicitly acknowledged this. He sought for ways to cope with it, usually by simply alerting his readers to the disagreement, or by some kind of conflation, rather than a choice between right and wrong.[130]

One of the most interesting features of these works is the attention given to physical objects. William was interested in them both in their own right, and as evidence with which to support his narrative. This is a frequently-noted characteristic of his historical work as well, most to the fore in *AG*.[131] In *VW* he mentions Wulfstan's involvement in the construction of a bellcote, and of the splendid new cathedral church.[132] In *VD* he shows that he knows some of the technical vocabulary associated with Anglo-Saxon church architecture: the best example is *porticus*, which he once equates with *alae*.[133] He explains the origins and reason for the dedications of the two pre-Conquest churches at Worcester, Dunstan's modifications to Ine's church at Glastonbury (tower and *porticus*), and his walling and raising the ground level of the cemetery there.[134] He also mentions items of church furniture: Dunstan's organs at Glastonbury and Malmesbury, to which he also gave a set of bells and a liturgical ewer.[135] These were the sort of objects likely to interest a precentor, and it is evident that William had seen them, although the Malmesbury gifts were already

---

[128] *GR*, cc. 60. 2, 122. 4, 123. 1–3.

[129] On the contrary, see *VW* Ep. 3: 'uitam eiusdem patris, si attendas ad sensum lepore graui, si ad litteram simplicitate rudi'.

[130] *VD* ii. prol. 3–4. Cf. *GR*, c. 9. 1.

[131] R. W. Southern, 'Aspects of the European tradition of historical writing IV: the sense of the past', *TRHS*, 5th ser., xxiii (1973), 243–63, at p. 255.

[132] *VW* i. 8. 6, 14. 4, iii. 10. 4.   [133] *VD* i. 3. 4, 16. 1.

[134] *VD* ii. 4. 2, i. 16.   [135] *VD* i. 4. 4, ii. 10. 3–4; *AG*, c. 67 (pp. 136–7).

recorded in Faricius' *Vita S. Aldhelmi*. The organs are only hinted at
by Osbern (another precentor), who says that Dunstan learned to play
musical instruments 'sicut Dauid psalterium sumens, citharam
percutiens, modificans organa, cimbala tangens',[136] later specifying
that he actually played the drum, harp and 'other instruments'.[137]
The inscription on the Malmesbury organ, and perhaps the presence
of a similarly inscribed one at Glastonbury, may have led William to
amplify Osbern's words so as to make Dunstan a player as well as a
promoter of the instrument in the England of his day. On the other
hand, as Farmer observed, William did not find everything he might
have. It is perhaps surprising that, while at Glastonbury, he did not
come across the famous manuscript dubbed in modern times 'St
Dunstan's Classbook', partly in Dunstan's hand, with the frontispiece
of the saint, clearly identified by accompanying verses, at the feet of
Christ. At least, it is hard to believe that William would not have
mentioned it had he seen it.[138]

All of these preoccupations can be found in William's historical
works; the difference between his historical and hagiographical works
is more clearly visible in his treatment of the miraculous. In the *Gesta
regum*, for instance, *miracula* occur in abundance; but they take the
form of marvels, magic, and freaks of nature more often than miracles
in the strict sense, that is, supernatural occurrences related to the
outstanding holiness of a particular individual. They scarcely affect
the main action, and William's attitude to their veracity sometimes
appears ambivalent. Either he explains them as quasi-'natural'
occurrences, or they are rationalized or toned down from the version
in William's sources, in favour of more 'normal' and credible human
motivation and activity.[139] In the hagiographical works, on the
contrary, miracles are very much related to the special powers
acquired by the saint: not only those generalized powers vouchsafed
to any saint by virtue of his or her relationship with God, but powers
inherent in each saint's individual character. Thus, in *VW* a number
of miracles relate to Wulfstan's tireless pursuit of his pastoral duties,
and occur in the context of baptisms or dedications of churches.[140] In

---

[136] Osbern, c. 8 (p. 78).   [137] Osbern, cc. 9–10 (p. 80).
[138] Farmer, 'Two biographies', p. 162. The book is now Bodl. Libr., MS Auct. F. 4. 32;
facsimile edn. *Saint Dunstan's Classbook from Glastonbury*, ed. R. W. Hunt (Umbrae
Codicum Occidentalium, iv: Amsterdam, 1961); M. Budny, '"St Dunstan's classbook"
and its frontispiece: Dunstan's portrait and autograph', in *St Dunstan*, pp. 103–42.
[139] *GR* II, p. xliv and n. 78, c. 363 n.
[140] *VW* i. 15, ii. 5–7, 9, 14–15 etc.

VD Dunstan is shown to have had the gift of foreknowledge, especially of the fate of his kings.[141] The explanation for this difference is simply the shift to the hagiographical genre; it is even more pronounced in William's *Miracles of the Virgin*.

On the other hand, William was still a historian's hagiographer, with an eye to what was unique, personal, and particular, and to the specifics of period and context, rather than to that which was held to be timeless and generally exemplary. Here he parts company sharply with Osbern, whose generalized moral reflections and comparisons he neither admitted nor imitated.[142] In the same way, in at least one instance, he explicitly excised this sort of material from Coleman's account.[143] In William's view, the general contributed nothing to a better understanding of the particular, and it was elucidation of the particular that was his main concern. This is the concern of a historian, not a hagiographer. And over and above that, William was keen to fit his characters into a convincing historical framework, and to get the non-miraculous facts right.

---

[141] *VD* i. 10, 17, 21, 25, 31; ii. 4, 23–4, etc.

[142] e.g. Osbern, cc. 4 (pp. 73–4), 8 (p. 78), 31 (p. 106), 40 (p. 119); and see also above, p. xxi n. 57. The same is true of William's treatment of the life of Aldhelm in *GP*, cc. 188–227, as compared with the earlier Life by Faricius of Abingdon (*BHL* 256), ed. *AA SS*, Maii vi. 84–93, J. A. Giles, *Vita quorundam Anglo-Saxonum* (Caxton Soc., 1854), pp. 119–56, repr. PL lxxxix. 63–84. Faricius had very little hard information about Aldhelm, and padded his account by comparing his hero with biblical characters and other saints.

[143] *VW* iii. 18. 3.

VITA WULFSTANI
LIFE OF WULFSTAN

INTRODUCTION

The Life of Wulfstan, in what appears to be a complete and authentic form, is transmitted in only one manuscript, BL Cotton Claudius A. v, fos. 160v–99v. The manuscript as a whole is a composite of three original books, put together by Sir Robert Cotton: (*a*) fos. 2–45, a fourteenth-century Peterborough Chronicle; (*b*) fos. 46–135, a twelfth-century copy of the so-called first recension of William's *Gesta pontificum* (known as B); and (*c*) fos. 135–200, a collection of four saints' Lives, s. xii ex. By s. xiv (*c*) was at the Cistercian abbey of Holm Cultram (Cumberland), where it may have been made.[1] The prefatory letter and the prologue are written at the end of the Life. We call this witness C.

This sole witness is, however, fortunately backed up by the evidence of several abridgements. Darlington exploited in particular what he called D, Durham, Cathedral Library B. IV. 39b, where a shortened Life of Wulfstan follows Senatus' Life of St Oswald of Worcester and precedes the Miracles of Wulfstan (printed in full by Darlington, pp. 68–108; see also pp. xx–xxi).[2] The book was written soon after 1235, probably at Worcester, though it was at Durham by 1391.[3] To this we may now add Gloucester, Cathedral Library 1 (G), a Cluniac manuscript from Reading or Leominster, dated *c*.1200, which contains both the Life and (some of) the Miracles.[4] Of the Life,

---

[1] There is a detailed description in A. W. Wade-Evans, *Vitae Sanctorum Britanniae et Genealogiae* (Cardiff, 1944), pp. xvi–xvii, where it is suggested that the relevant part of the MS was made at Worcester. This is untrue; not only are the script and decoration untypical of Worcester or of the west midlands generally, but the flex punctuation is characteristic of a Cistercian scriptorium.

[2] The abbreviated Life has been ascribed to Senatus because (*a*) Senatus stated that he had written Lives of Oswald and Wulfstan (Cheney, *Roger, Bishop of Worcester*, p. 66), and (*b*) the abbreviated Life in D follows a Life of Oswald attributed to Senatus by its *titulus*. On the other hand, one might wonder why the D Life of Wulfstan, if it were also by Senatus, did not have a similar *titulus* ascribing it to him. As the Life is a mere abridgement of William's, stylistic comparison with Senatus' other writings is not relevant.

[3] Described in T. Rud, *Codicum Manuscriptorum Ecclesiae Cathedralis Dunelmensis Catalogus Classicus* (Durham, 1825), pp. 244–5. On fos. 50, 52, 62v, and 88 occur painted initials in a style which persisted at Worcester from the late eleventh until the early thirteenth century. The manuscript appears in the 1391 list of books kept in the Spendement at Durham Cathedral Priory: *Catalogi Veteres Librorum Ecclesiae Cathedralis Dunelmensis*, ed. B. Botfield (Surtees Soc. i, 1834, publ. 1838), p. 29.

[4] Described in N. R. Ker, *Medieval Manuscripts in British Libraries ii. Abbotsford–Keele* (Oxford, 1977), pp. 934–9.

G contains all but i. 1 (ii. 17 is out of order, after ii. 19). It is often wrong against DC (especially in the later sections), but often enough right with C against D[1] to make it certain that it is an independent witness. Both G and D, whose common ancestor we call δ, are prefaced by a new and inauthentic opening ('Gesta . . . patrono'), replacing William's letter to the monks of Worcester and his prologue (see Darlington, pp. xx and 68). And this feature links to GD a very much more abridged version found in BL, MS Cotton Vespasian E. ix (Darlington, pp. xxi and 111–14).[2]

The abbreviation that lies behind δ gave rise to two further versions. The more important is H, BL, MS Harley 322, a collection of saints' Lives written in the second half of the thirteenth century. Related to H,[3] but even more abbreviated,[4] is the version found in BL, MS Lansdowne 436 (R), a fourteenth-century Passional from Romsey. Both these versions have no prologue, but start instead with an introductory passage printed by Darlington, p. 68 n. ('Temporibus Ædwardi . . . sanctorum'), then proceeding direct to 'celibem' in D's i. 2. H and R are independent of each other,[5] and independent too of GD.[6]

The particular service of GD (= δ) is to make up in some measure for the loss of a folio in C, which caused the mutilation of iii. 2–3. But as they are descended from a complete copy that is independent of C,[7]

---

[1] G wrong against CD, e.g. (we cite by D's chapters) i. 8 dependerent] pependerent (penderent *p. c.*); 11 inde] hinc; 15 mordicus] morsibus; 18 serere] habere; ii. 9 labuntur] uitantur. CG agree against D's variants at e.g. i. 7 exposuit] exponit D; 13 decedens] discedens D; 26 abscidi iuberet] iuberet abscidi D; ii. 8 sermo se intulit] se intulit sermo D.

[2] The whole MS is a Cotton makeup, of which the *Vita* occupies fos. 10–14v. *Pace* Darlington (p. xxii), there is no connection between this section and the preceding cartulary of the Worcestershire priory of Westwood. Two leaves follow, in a similar but not identical hand and format, containing the beginning of a Life of St Hugh of Lincoln. This may have been part of the same book as fos. 10–14, but as all the leaves are now mounted as singletons, this must remain uncertain. It may be relevant that in BL Lansdowne 436 (see below) the abbreviated *VW* is followed by Osbern's Life of Dunstan, then the same Life of St Hugh.

[3] Thus (against GD) HR also agree on e.g. (D's chapters) i. 2 celibem ⟨enim⟩; ergo (after 'precipitatis', as C) *om.*; aperit (as C)] aperuit; i. 7 uir] ubi; ei] illi.

[4] In particular R omits the whole of D's Book ii.

[5] H of course cannot be descended from the later and much shorter R. Nor can R be descended from H, which shows unique errors at e.g. (D's chapters) i. 2 qualiter] taliter; i. 7 pauimentum (as C)] pauimento.

[6] Errors of GD against CH(R) include (D's chapters): i. 9 tunc temporis *om.*; i. 30 turgidos] tragidos.

[7] The *apparatus criticus* gives many examples of readings of δ that we prefer to those of C; those most clearly showing independence include i. 8. 6 gressus; ii. 5. 1 intorqueret; ii. 16. 3 opifex; ii. 21. 3 maiusculos. In some other cases conjecture on δ's part cannot be ruled out.

their readings are of importance throughout the text, and we have used them to confirm, correct, or challenge the readings of C at disputable points. HR, though less useful, can, where present, act as a check on GD.

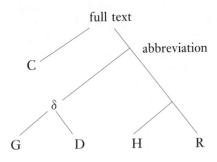

EDITORIAL PRINCIPLES

VW was first printed, in an excerpted form, by Henry Wharton in *Anglia Sacra* (2 vols.: London, 1691), ii. 239–70, using C.[1] The complete text was printed by Darlington in 1928, and on this were based the excellent complete translation by J. H. F. Peile, and the selective one by M. J. Swanton.[2] Darlington printed a text which (his errors apart) is very close to a transcript of the Cotton manuscript. Our aim is to give a critical edition. We have therefore felt free to print our own conjectures and those of others at many points. Wharton's readings are attributed in the apparatus to 'Whar.', Darlington's to 'Darl.' (but conjectures made only in his notes are signalled '[Darl.]'). Conjectures implied by the translation of Peile are signalled '[Peile]'. Two emendations attributed to Dr B. J. Gibson were made during an Oxford seminar.

C has been corrected by a second hand. Where such changes are clearly correct we almost never note the original reading (though see iii. 10. 3; elsewhere readers may get (most of) the information from Darlington). Where they appear to be wrong, we do note them ($C^{p.c.}$). It should be observed that in a number of places the corrector has

---

[1] See Darlington, p. vii, for a fuller critique. Wharton's version was reprinted in *Acta Sanctorum Ordinis Sancti Benedicti* (9 vols.: Paris, 1668–1701), ix (Saec. VI pars 2), 840–65, and in PL clxxix. 1735–72.

[2] *Three Lives of the Last Englishmen*, trans. M. J. Swanton (New York and London, 1984), pp. 91–148. Swanton omitted those portions of *VW* which he thought definitely not based upon Coleman.

changed the order of words; like Darlington, we follow the corrector without comment. Again like Darlington, we do not signal various places where the second hand has added a long mark, apparently for the convenience of readers (so over the 'a' of 'Merlaue' at iii. 4. 1).

It should be noted that, to simplify the apparatus, δ is used to signify the agreement of G and D, and H* to signify a reading of H where R is not available. Mention of C in the apparatus where no other MS readings are given does *not* imply anything about the readings of any other manuscripts that may (or may not) be present at that place (though other manuscripts are naturally cited where their readings might throw light on what William wrote). This is because D and its relations so frequently rewrite as well as abbreviate the complete text that it would be unrewarding to provide a full apparatus; Darlington gives a complete transcript of D, collated with H(R), and this can be consulted by those interested; page references to his edition are given wherever D and its relations are cited.

At iii. 2–3 a folio has been lost in C; in the lacuna we print the text of D. Variants of G in this passage are nugatory and have been ignored. Nor did H and R prove any more useful here, and their readings have been suppressed; though we do record one place (iii. 3. 2) where GH share an error against D, perhaps by accident.

The spelling has been normalized to the system reconstructed for William from the *Gesta pontificum* autograph and employed in our edition of the *Gesta regum* (see *GR* I, pp. xxvi–xxviii; readers may turn to Darlington for usually reliable information on C's orthography). In the process we have silently corrected various minor slips of the scribe (e.g. i. 1. 4 sacrametarium; ii. 5. 2 inuolunt; iii. 16. 3 stratro); again Darlington gives most of the details for those who would like to know them.

We have introduced a system of sub-sections to ease reference to the often long chapters.

TEXT AND TRANSLATION

Incipit epistola Willelmi ad fratres Wigornenses in Vita[a]
uenerabilis Wlstani eiusdem loci episcopi

Domino uenerabili Guarino priori[1] et omni reuerentissimo Wigornensi[b] conuentui, Willelmus amorem filii, clientelam famuli.

1. Dudum a uobis iussus in sancti patris nostri Wlstani uita[c] manum ponere, aliquandiu subterfugi offitium. Subterfugii causae plurimae, sed ea uel prima uel maxima, quod, cum sim imparis meriti conscius, ulteriora uiribus arrogo si sanctum laudo. Non est enim spetiosa laus in ore peccatoris.[2] Huc accessit et preceptum uestrum non mediocriter labefactauit metus ne obedientiam meam quorundam pulsaret liuor, si opus inuaderem ut hactenus intemptatum ita meliori relinquendum. His causis exterritus linguam obstinato frenassem silentio, nisi spes de pietate beati antistitis concepta mederetur formidini, accurreret solatio. 2. Consueuit enim beatus Wlstanus nudis etiam se uerbis amantes cum[d] offensarum remissa donare, tum protectionis suae umbone defendere. Multo magis igitur perpetuam de se meditanti scripturam et uenia fauebit et emolumento sermonis non deerit. Dignabitur etiam Dominus Christus de hoc opere amoliri omnem inuidiam, quod susceptum est non scientiae supercilio sed sincerae deuotionis obsequio. Quapropter eius ope fretus, fatiam quod imperastis. Non ulterius munus meum obnubet meticulosa cunctatio, sed moram preteriti temporis exsecutionis celeritate compensabo.

Et uos quidem, domini, uitalis adhuc aurae[3] compotes probe cognoscetis me nichil dicere quod non sit solida ueritate subnixum, quod non sit probabilium uirorum testimonio compertum, adeo antiquorum mentibus insederunt uisa, adeo iuniores amplectuntur audita. 3. Posteris uero quando gestorum memoria frigebit, poterit subesse dubitatio nisi testem idoneum produxero. Quocirca quia non nisi exacta fide deberent recitari gesta sanctorum, dabo uadem non improbabilem dictorum meorum. Is erit Colemannus monachus

---

Both Letter and Prologue are given by C after the text of the Life (see above, p. 3)
  [a] uitam *Whar.*   [b] Wigorn (*with a stroke over the last two letters*) C   [c] *Perhaps read* uitam   [d] *ed.* (see GR I, p. 14); tum C

[1] Occ. as prior 1133 × 1140; his exact term was probably 1124–42: *BRECP*, p. 888.
[2] Ecclus. 15: 9.
[3] Cf. Virgil, *Aen.* i. 387–8 ('auras/uitalis'); also echoed in *GP*, c. 271 (p. 433): 'uitalibus auris'.

Here begins the letter of William to the monks of Worcester,
on the Life of the revered Wulfstan, bishop of that place

To his revered lord Prior Warin[1] and to the whole very respected monastery of Worcester, William sends a son's love and a servant's duty.

1. Though I long since received your order to set my hand to a Life of our father St Wulfstan, for some time I shirked the duty. Many were the reasons for my hesitation, but first and foremost was the fact that I am conscious of the limits of my merit, and know that I am taking upon myself more than my strength can bear, if I set out to eulogize a saint. For 'praise is not seemly in the mouth of a sinner'.[2] In addition, my willingness to obey your command was greatly affected by the fear that I should, if I obeyed, be assaulted by the envy of certain persons, for taking on a task hitherto untried and preferably left to a better man. So I was frightened off, and I should have curbed my tongue into obstinate silence, if a hope I formed of the kindness of the blessed bishop had not cured my fear and provided solace. 2. For St Wulfstan is accustomed to be at hand to help even those who love him superficially, granting them remission of their offences, and defending them with the shield of his protection. Much more, then, will he forgive one who contemplates a continuous narrative about him, and assist his expression. Further, Christ the Lord will surely deign to remove all envy from a work that is undertaken not out of pride in erudition, but in a spirit of sincere devotion. Relying therefore on His aid, I shall do what you ordered. No longer will fearful hesitation lour over my task. Instead, I shall make up for my past delay by completing it quickly.

Now you, my lords, while you go on breathing the air of life,[3] will be well aware that I say nothing that does not rest on a firm foundation of truth and is not known on the witness of reliable persons, for the older among you will remember what they saw, and the younger what they have heard. 3. But what of posterity? When the recollection of events grows cold, doubts may arise, if I do not bring forward a credible witness. So, since the deeds of saints should not be retailed except in all scrupulousness, I shall provide a guarantor for my words who will command no little respect: your

uester,[1] uir nec scientia imperitus nec sermone patrio infacetus. Scripsit enim Anglice, ne gestorum auolaret memoria, uitam eiusdem patris, si attendas ad sensum lepore graui, si ad litteram simplicitate rudi: dignus cui fides non derogetur in aliquo, quippe qui nouerit intime mores magistri ut discipulus, et religionem ut quindecim annis capellanus. 4. Huius ego ut uoluistis insistens scriptis nichil turbaui de rerum ordine, nichil corrupi de gestorum ueritate. Sane uerbis quae uel dicta sunt uel in tempore dici potuerunt enarrandis supersedi, consulens in omnibus ueritati, ne uideretur periclitari.[2] Otiosi enim est hominis et suae indulgentis facundiae cum gesta suffitiant uerba nundinari, nisi forte sint aliqua quae propter eximium sui splendorem breuem exigant mentionem. Quae cum ita sint, hanc queso michi redhibete gratiam, ut ab hoc opusculo et emulos dignemini summouere, et obsequium meum piissimi Wlstani sensibus quo presentiores estis insinuare, domini uenerabiles et merito amabiles patres.[3]

Explicit epistola

Incipit prologus

Multa et ut nostra fert opinio innumera sunt in scripturis sanctis quibus diuina dignatio mentes mortalium ad bonae uitae cultum informat, cum*a* precepta tum exempla.[4] Illis qualiter uiuendum sit instruimur, istis innuitur quam sint Deo iuuante factu facilia quae iubentur. Natura porro hunc quibusdam ingenerauit animum, ut quanuis utraque sciant necessaria, magis tamen exemplorum quam exhortationum eos prolectet auditus, et ueterum quidem gestis pro antiquitatis assurgunt reuerentia, sed alacriori capiuntur dulcedine si alicuius sancti qui nuperrime fuerit uita producatur in medium, in qua sicut e speculo conspicentur, ut ita dictum sit, uiuum religionis simulacrum. Accedit*b* enim iocundae relationi nouitas, ne aliquis desperet a se per Dei gratiam fieri posse quod audit ab alio de proximo factum fuisse. 2. Vnde non contempnenda, sicut opinor, cura successit animo beati Wlstani episcopi Wigornensis uitam nequaquam posteris inuidere, sed eam stilo qualicumque aeternae

---

a ed.; tum C, AG p. 40   *b* C, AG p. 40; -dat C*p.c.*, Darl.

[1] Occ. 1089, d. 1113; *BRECP*, pp. 790–1. No writings of his have been identified, but his hand has been tentatively recognized in a number of Worcester MSS: N. R. Ker, 'Old English notes signed "Coleman"', in *Books, Collectors and Libraries*, pp. 28–30; W. P. Stoneman, 'Another Old English note signed "Coleman"', *Medium Aevum*,

monk Coleman,[1] a learned man and a master of his native tongue. Unwilling that the memory of Wulfstan's deeds should flit away and be lost, he wrote in English a Life that in content was agreeable and serious, and in style simple and unaffected. No one should doubt his word on any detail, for he knew Wulfstan's character intimately, having been his pupil, and his religious practice too, as one who was his chaplain for fifteen years. 4. As you wished, I have kept to his narrative, in no way disturbing the order of events or falsifying the facts. It is true that I have omitted to recount the words that were spoken, or could have been spoken under those circumstances, for my design everywhere has been to avoid the shipwreck of the truth.[2] It is for an idle man, too much in love with his own eloquence, to traffic in words when actions are sufficient—though perhaps some of particular magnificence may demand brief notice. This being so, please do me a favour in return: deign to divert envious critics from this little work, and to make my service known to the pious Wulfstan, for you are in closer touch with him than I, my revered lords and deservedly loved fathers.[3]

Prologue

There are many—in my view countless—things in Holy Scripture by which God sees fit to train the minds of mortals to cultivate a virtuous life, both precepts and examples.[4] The former equip us how to live, the latter give us a hint how easy it is, with God's aid, to carry out His orders. Now nature has so formed some people that, though they know both to be vital, they are more inclined to listen to instances than to exhortation. They respect the doings of the ancients out of a reverence for antiquity; but they are captivated by a livelier sweetness if the life of a very recent saint is published. Here they can see, as if reflected in a mirror, the (so to speak) living image of a religious life. For to the pleasantness of the story is added the nearness of the events, so that the reader does not despair of doing, by the grace of God, what he hears another has done very recently. 2. So I think I have done well to conceive the idea of favouring posterity with a Life of St Wulfstan, bishop of Worcester, and of handing it down for

---

lvi (1987), 78–82. There are more remarks on translation from English in *AG*, c. 49 (p. 106).

[2] Similarly *VD* ii. prol. 1–2.

[3] So end William's *Deflorationes Gregorii*, printed by H. Farmer, 'William of Malmesbury's commentary on Lamentations', *Studia Monastica*, iv (1962), 283–311, at p. 310.

[4] Cf. *AG* prol. (p. 40, first paragraph).

mandare memoriae.[1] Fuit enim uir ut nostris temporibus affinis, ita priorum patrum uirtuti non absimilis. Quapropter benigno lectori grande paciscor commodum, ut quamquam eum non minus quam priscos pro miraculorum gloria suspitiat,[a] familiariter tamen pro recenti aetate mores eius emulo exercitii pede sequi contendat. Nec uero haec dico quod multis hanc beatitudinem arrogem, ut sicut ipse fuit imitator Christi, sic possint eum imitari. 3. Pauci quin potius, pauci quos aequus amabit Iesus poterunt,[2] quasi longo ad eum respitientes interuallo,[3] uirtutum ipsius uestigiis insistere, potius quam ipsas sibi perfecte insculpere: adeo (quod salua maiorum reuerentia dixerim) nullo in continentia uitiorum inferior fuit, adeo uirtutum studium, ceptum a tenero, felici ad senectam continuauit proposito. Quocirca par fuerat ut scriptor gestorum eius esset limatus lingua et probatus scientia,[b] quatinus sullimia facta non humili proferrentur eloquio[4] et laudata laudator sequeretur exemplo. Michi uero nec[c] oratoria facultas suppetit nec de integritate uitae animus applaudit. Sola me palpat et urget obedientia, ne munus quod fraterna necessitudo[5] imponit, sponsum presertim et animae fructuosum, obstinate recusem. Assit michi Spiritus sancti clementia, ut eodem inspirante noster dirigatur stilus quo auctore bene operatus est Wlstanus.

4. Et quidem qui rethoricis nituntur institutis ita sermonem suum instituunt ut primo[d] auditorem suum beniuolum, mox attentum, postremo docilem reddant.[6] Quem dicendi morem ego quoque cum res expostulat non omitto. Hic porro eo modo rethoricari extra propositum est. Est enim ex habundanti argumenta querere, ubi et ad credendum fides excitat et ad legendum materia inuitat. Qua de causa pio patri lectores non defuturos arbitror dum polus rotabit sidera,[7] dum ulla in mundo erit littera. Hanc ipse[e] sibi apud homines

---

[a] *[Peile] (cf. ii. 7. 3)*; suspiciat C   [b] conscientia *would fit the continuing parallel between style and morals (cf. esp.* nec . . . animus applaudit). *But cf. GP p. 195* ('probatissimus . . . scientia').   [c] uero nec *Whar.*; nec *(mg. m. 2)* uero C   [d] *[Darl.]*; post C   [e] *ed.*; ipso C

[1] Cf. *AG* prol. (p. 40, second paragraph).

[2] Cf. *GR*, c. 62; a remarkable adaptation of Virgil, *Aen.* vi. 129–30: 'pauci, quos aequus amauit/Iuppiter'.

[3] Cf. Virgil, *Aen.* v. 320: 'proximus huic, longo sed proximus interuallo'; also below, ii. 1. 8, and *GR*, c. 15. 4.

[4] The ancient doctrine of 'the fitting', that is, that the style should suit the subject matter. See, for instance, Cicero, *Orator* 101: 'is erit igitur eloquens . . . qui poterit parua summisse, modica temperate, magna grauiter dicere', cited by Augustine, *De doctrina christiana* iv. 96.

[5] This suggests that William enjoyed confraternity rights with Worcester, as he did with Glastonbury: *GR* II, pp. xxxii–xxxiii n. 25.

eternal remembrance, however poor my style.[1] For though he lived so close to our own time, he resembled the fathers of old in virtue. And so I am guaranteeing my kind reader a great advantage: while he looks up to Wulfstan no less than to the ancients because of the splendid miracles he performs, he can feel closer to him because of his recent date, and strive to follow his example with an emulous foot.

I do not say this because I claim for many the happiness of being able to imitate Wulfstan in the way that *he* imitated Christ. 3. Few, few indeed, of those whom the just Jesus shall love,[2] will be able to contemplate Wulfstan as it were from a long way back,[3] and tread in the footprints of his virtues, let alone stamp them upon themselves in all perfection. Indeed (I say this with all due respect for our forefathers) he was in no way inferior to them in his avoidance of vice, and with a fortunate persistence in his principles he carried through to old age an enthusiasm for virtue formed in his tender years. Therefore it would only be right that the narrator of his story should be both polished in style and accomplished in learning, so that lofty deeds could be expressed in no mean language,[4] and so that the praiser could follow in practice the things he praises. But *I* have no ability in oratory, and no consciousness of an unsullied life to cheer me. I am coaxed and urged along merely by my duty of obedience, not to be so obstinate as to turn down a task imposed on me by ties of brotherhood,[5] particularly as it is something that I have promised to do and that will bear fruit for my own soul. May the Holy Spirit attend me in His mercy, and may His inspiration direct my pen, just as He forwarded Wulfstan's own good works.

4. Now those who have a rhetorical training to fall back on start what they have to say by making their hearers first well disposed, secondly attentive, and thirdly ready to learn.[6] And this procedure I too follow when the topic demands. But *here* it is out of place to use rhetoric in that way. It is superfluous to look for proofs when faith excites one to belief and the content attracts the reader. Hence I think the holy father will not lack readers, so long as the sky turns and the stars go around,[7] and while any trace of letters remains in the world.

---

[6] Similarly *GR* iii. pr. 3. William refers to the description of the purpose of the proemium, as found in e.g. *Auctor ad Herenn.* i. 4. 6: 'Id ita sumitur ut attentos, ut dociles, ut beniuolos auditores habere possimus.' Similarly, 'argumenta querere' alludes to the rhetorical doctrine of *inuentio*, and 'ad legendum materia inuitat' may allude to *elocutio* (expression).

[7] Cf. Claudian, *In Rufin.* ii. 527: 'dum rotat astra polus, feriunt dum litora uenti'; a closer echo is in *GR*, c. 237. 6.

per Dei misericordiam uiuens locauit et post fata tenet gratiam. Sed hactenus prohemium[1] traxisse suffecerit; nunc caelesti freti auxilio opus destinatum tali ordiemur initio.

Explicit prologus

Incipit Vita sancti Wlstani episcopi et confessoris

1. Pagus est in regione Mertiorum non incelebris, Warwicensis dictus. Is habet uillam[2] Icentune[3] uocatam, cuius iam inde a proauis incolae parentes uenerabilis*a* Wlstani fuere. Pater Athelstanus, mater Wlfgiua*b* nominati,[4] nec tenues censu nec natalibus abiecti, ita utentes seculo ut redderent quae sunt Cesaris Cesari et quae sunt*c* Dei Deo,[5] illud perfunctorie, istud studiose. Industria in illis cum generositate certabat, ut alterum facultatum copiam, alterum uirtutum studium subpeditaret. Coniugali affectu magis quam pruritu coniuncti,*d* meruere filium in preclarum Anglie decus euasurum. 2. Puero Wlstanus uocabulum datum, ex anteriore*e* materni et ex posteriore paterni nominis compositum.[6] Spei felicis infans felici auspitio utrorumque parentum nomen mutuatus,*f* qui utrorumque sanctitatem in se transfunderet, nescio an etiam incomparabiliter supergressurus. Eorum siquidem penitus euanuisset memoria si non eos filius conspicua sanctitate animi extulisset in speculam.

Primis elementis litterarum apud Euesham[7] initiatus, perfectiori mox*g* apud Burch[8] scientia teneras informauit medullas. Gratum dictu quantum iam tunc futurarum uirtutum indolem crebris partur- iebat inditiis, uix dum primum pueritiae limen egressus, ita quod maturum, quod sanctum predicabilis pueri spirabat et loquebatur modestia. 3. Ieiuniis quantum id aetatis homo pateretur operam non negare, humiles in excelsum orationes porrigere. Pueriles garritus,

---

a D (*p. 69*); uenerabis C   *b* ed.; Wlfgeua C, D (*p. 69*); Wlfgeoua *John of Worcester s.a. 1062*   *c* Cesaris Cesari et quae sunt D (*p. 69*); *om.* C   *d* D (*p. 69*); -uicti C
e parte *may have dropped out; Whar. inserted it after* nominis   *f* D (*p. 69*); mutuatur C
g morum D (*p. 69*), *rightly?*

[1] The word is also used in *GP*, c. 187 (p. 331).
[2] We have invariably translated 'uilla', frequently used by William, as 'vill'. This covers the full range of William's meanings: village, small town, estate, or manor. It is not always easy to determine which particular meaning he had in mind.
[3] Until the mid-eleventh century a single estate which had earlier belonged to Worcester; it was then split in two and both parts alienated. The name is now preserved in two villages, Long Itchington about eight miles east of Warwick, and Bishop's Itchington, about nine miles south-east: Mason, pp. 28–9.
[4] With the whole of 'Pagus . . . Wlfgiua', cf. JW s.a. 1062 'Hic Deo amabilis . . .

By God's mercy Wulfstan won this grace for himself among men while he lived, and he maintains it after his death. But my proem[1] has gone on long enough: now, relying on the aid of Heaven, I shall begin the work I have in mind as follows.

BOOK ONE

1. In the district of the Mercians there is a county of some note called Warwickshire, and in it a vill[2] named Itchington,[3] where the revered Wulfstan's forebears lived for many generations. His father was Æthelstan, his mother Wulfgifu,[4] and they were neither poor nor of low birth. Their attitude in this world was to render unto Caesar the things which are Caesar's and unto God the things that are God's,[5] the former with minimal care, the latter with all zeal. In them hard work competed with nobility of spirit, the former bringing a fair income, the latter enthusiasm for virtue. They were united by marital affection rather than sexual lust, and well deserved to have a son who would prove to be an ornament to England. 2. He was given the name Wulfstan, made up of the first part of his mother's and the second of his father's.[6] The child had fair hopes, and fair too the omen which gave him a name taken from both parents, considering that he was destined to pour into himself the sanctity of both, and perhaps to surpass it beyond all comparison. For their memory would altogether have passed away if the conspicuous holiness of their son had not raised them to prominence.

He took his first steps in letters at Evesham,[7] and then shaped his tender mind with deeper knowledge at Peterborough.[8] It is pleasant to record the extent to which even then, scarcely over the threshold of boyhood, he gave constant signs of the nature of the virtues to come, for this modest and praiseworthy boy breathed and spoke all that was grown up and holy. 3. He observed fasts so far as was possible at such an age, and lifted up humble prayers on high. He rejected childish

---

Wlfgeoua nomine'. On the circumstances of Wulfstan's parents, and the possible identification of his father as a priest in the *familia* of St Oswald, see Mason, pp. 29–32.

[5] Matt. 22: 21; Mark 12: 17; Luke 20: 25. Also in *VD* i. 14. 1, *GP*, c. 49 (p. 87).

[6] R. I. Page, 'Personal names, Old English', in *Blackwell Encyclopaedia*.

[7] Doubtless he did not stay long: Mason, p. 34. See iii. 17. 1 below, where Wulfstan sends the monk Nicholas to Lanfranc's Canterbury to complete his monastic education.

[8] So also JW s.a. 1062. Peterborough was perhaps a surprising choice, given its distance from Worcester. Mason, p. 35, suggests that it may have been due to Archbishop Wulfstan's close links with the house. Wulfstan was presumably there *c*.1020, certainly before 1035, the year of Cnut's death (see below).

illecebrarum fomitem, primum in se, tum in aliis aspernari. Maturae uitae uestigiis instare, adeo ut coeuos et etiam maiores natu suplicibus conueniret precibus quatinus sibi bene uiuendi simulacrum ipsi bene uiuendo effigiarent: si quid perperam faceret arguerent, ipse libens correctioni manus daret. Deuotio prouexit usum, ut nichil uideret imitandum quod non formaret in exemplum. Monstrabat nimirum his factis se sapientem et esse et fore, iuxta quod diuina sapientia Salomonis innexuit litteris: 'Corripe' inquit 'sapientem, et amabit te.'[1]

4. Nec minus illud in se naturaliter rapiebat, quod olim philosophia ex aditis effudit suis, semper aliquem bonum uirum ante oculos mentis proponendum, cuius respectu mores componantur.[2] Non enim a iustitia facile deuiat qui semper uel Deum uel hominem cogitat, cuius timore peccata compescat.

Habebat tunc magistrum, Ernuuium[a] nomine, in scribendo et quidlibet coloribus effingendo peritum.[3] Is libros scriptos, sacramentarium et psalterium, quorum principales litteras auro effigiauerat, puero Wlstano delegandos curauit. Ille pretiosorum apicum captus miraculo, dum pulchritudinem intentis oculis rimatur et scientiam litterarum internis haurit medullis. Verum doctor, ad seculi spectans commodum, spe maioris premii sacramentarium regi tunc temporis Cnutoni, psalterium Emmae reginae contribuit.[4] 5. Perculit puerilem animum †facti†[b] dispendium, et ex imo pectore alta traxit suspiria. Meror inuitauit somnum, et ecce consopito assistens uir uultus angelici tristitiam propulsat, librorum reformationem promittit. Nec minus pollicito, sed multo post, euenit, sicut progrediens sermo dicere perget.[5]

Itaque uernans aetas pueritia exclusa adolescentiam induxerat, et erat Wlstanus quanto aetate auctior tanto sanctitate prouectior. Denique numquam, ut ea fert aetas, aliqua labe castimoniam prodidit, sed integri pudoris palmam in caelum tulit.[6] Aderat ei in cunctis diuinae gratiae liberalitas, ne uacillaret arbitrii libertas.[7] Senserat ipse olim infusum sibi caelitus castitatis munus, nec quin diceret ingrato silentio indulsit, sed caeleste nectar quod hauserat sine liuore aliis

---

^a *ed.*; Erueuium *C*   ^b *Corrupt; one expects* depositi *or the like*

[1] Cf. Prov. 19: 25.
[2] Seneca, *Epist.* xi. 8–10; also echoed in *Mir.*, p. 116 lines 136–9.
[3] Perhaps Earnwig, abbot of Peterborough 1041–52 (*Heads*, p. 60).
[4] The story is discussed by T. A. Heslop, 'The production of *de luxe* manuscripts and the patronage of King Cnut and Queen Emma', *ASE* xix (1990), 151–95, at pp. 159–62.
[5] i. 9.
[6] Cf. generally *Comm. Lam.* (Farmer, 'Lamentations', p. 303 n. 49); for *in caelum tulit*, cf. *GP*, c. 137 (p. 278), also in relation to Wulfstan's virginity.

chattering, first in himself and then in others, regarding it as an incentive to temptation, and trod in the footprints of maturity to such a degree that he begged his contemporaries and even his elders to live good lives themselves and so provide him with a model for a good life: if he did anything wrong, they should reprove him, and he would willingly put out his hands for correction. His piety forwarded his practice, so that he saw nothing worth imitating that he did not make into an example. Surely by such behaviour he showed that he was and would continue to be wise, in accordance with what was put into words by the Wisdom of Solomon: 'Reprove the wise man, and he will love you.'[1] 4. And it was equally in his nature to embrace what philosophy once proclaimed from its innermost shrines, that one should always put before oneself some good man to act as a model for the formation of character.[2] For he cannot easily diverge from the path of justice who always takes thought of either God or man, and uses fear of them to curb his sins.

He had at that time a teacher called Earnwig, an expert in writing and colouring.[3] He had picked out in gold the capital letters in two manuscripts, a sacramentary and a psalter, and these books he entrusted to the boy Wulfstan. He was captivated by the wonder of the precious letters, and he pored attentively over their beauty while drinking deep the content of the words. But his teacher looked to worldly advantage, and in hope of a greater reward presented the sacramentary to Cnut, who was king at that time, and the psalter to Queen Emma.[4] 5. The boy's mind was shattered by the loss, and he sighed many a deep sigh. Grief brought on sleep; and lo, while he slept, a man of angelic countenance stood over him and drove away his sadness, promising restitution of the books. That was fulfilled, though much later, as we shall see.[5]

So Wulfstan left boyhood behind and came into the spring time of adolescence. The older he grew, the more advanced he became in holiness. For instance, he never, as tends to happen at that age, allowed any stain to betray his chastity, and he took to heaven the prize of unblemished virginity.[6] In all things God's grace lavished on him unshaken self-control.[7] He had long since felt that Heaven had poured into him the gift of chasteness, and he did not keep this ungratefully silent: the heavenly nectar he had drained down himself he was ready to pour out for others without stint. 6. I shall tell how

---

[7] Cf. *Comm. Lam.* (Farmer, 'Lamentations', p. 303 n. 50 on freewill).

propinauit. 6. Quod quatinus actum sit dicam, ut posteris liqueat quanta Dei gratia iuuenem et preuenerit et subsecuta sit.

Reuerso de Burch ad parentes puella e uicino nata ad naufragium pudoris[1] et illecebram uoluptatis molesta erat. Denique manum prensitare, oculo annuere, et cetera quae sunt moriturae uirginitatis inditia †lasciuis etiam gestibus*[a]* impudicitiaef*[b]* facere solebat. Sed cum is castitatis instinctu impudicae desideria frustraretur, hoc modo pene illum uenata est. Conuenerat in campum frequens cetus adolescentum, cuinam †letius†*[c]* ludo uacans non diffinio. Cursitaba-tur ut fieri solet in talibus uirentis graminis aequore, plausui et fauori adhortantium respondebat stridulus aer. 7. Emicat inter*[d]* alios[2] Wlstanus, communique cunctorum iuditio illius ludi triumphum reportat. Agrestium multitudo in laudes acclamat, easdemque ut eius famularetur auribus repetit et geminat.[3] Delectaretur alius his neniis, et flatu adulantium concitatus bullatas[4] in corde formaret ampullas. At ille nec uel corporis nutu uel animi motu laudantibus adquieuit. Quocirca, ut de hoc diabolus uictus alio modo triumpharet, puellae predictae quae*[e]* propter*[f]* astaret infudit animo ut accurreret. Illa non segnis gestibus impudicis, motibus inuerecundis, plausibilem psaltriam agit,*[g]* id*[h]* ut amasii[5] sui seruiret oculis.[6] Nec minus*[i]* ille, qui uerbis et tactui non cesserat,*[j]* infractiori gestu totus resolutus in amorem anhelabat. Veruntamen reducto continuo ad bonum animo, et lacrimas fudit et fugam in dumosa et uepribus hirsuta loca intendit. 8. Iacebat ergo longiuscule, aliis nichilominus secus iocum conti-nuantibus. Ibi multa uoluenti et plurimis se ipsum accusanti sopor irrepsit. Fuitque tunc prodigium conspicari. Nubes enim serena et blando fulgore oculis intuentium alludens superne descendit, et aliquandiu iacentem obnubens stupori*[k]* spectantibus fuit. Discussit protinus splendor nubis nebulam uanitatis, et ludibundos animos adolescentium grauitatis afflauit aura. Precipitatis ergo cursibus illuc

---

[a] lasciuis etiam gestibus *del. B. J. Gibson*   *[b]* impudicitie *C; del. ed.*   *[c] C, partly in erasure*; certius *Gibson*   *[d] Perhaps read* ante. *Cf. Virg. Aen. v. 318–19* longeque ante omnia corpora Nisus/emicat (*also 337*)   *[e] Ambiguous in C*   *[f]* prope *Whar. (cf. GP p. 189); see VD p. 311 (propter), GR 218. 3 (both attested)*   *[g]* egit *δHR (p. 70); but cf. above* ut . . . famularetur . . . repetit et geminat   *[h] om. δHR (p. 70); perhaps read* id ideo ut (*cf. iii. 5. 2* hoc ideo ut, *VD ii. 9. 3* id ideo ut)   *[i] Perhaps read* mora *[j] Whar.*; cessaret (*corr. to* -arat) *C*   *[k] Whar. (cf. iii. 22. 1)*; -ris *C*

[1] Cf. *Comm. Lam.* (Farmer, 'Lamentations', p. 296 n. 38).

[2] Virgil, *Aen.* v. 318–19.

[3] A parallel scene of children at play is found in Bede, *Vita Cuthberti*, c. 1 (ed. Colgrave pp. 156–7).

this came about, so that posterity may know for sure what grace of God went before and after him.

On his return from Peterborough to his parents, he was troubled by a girl of the district who was designed by nature for shipwrecking chastity[1] and luring men into pleasure. She would grab his hand, wink at him, and do everything that signifies virginity on the point of departure. Spurred on by the impulse to chastity, he outwitted the shameless girl's desires. But she almost caught him in the end. There had assembled in a field a large troop of youngsters (I am not prepared to specify the game they were playing). As usual on such an occasion, they raced about on the verdant sward, and the applause and favouring shouts of those egging them on met a response from the shrill air. 7. Wulfstan shot out among the others,[2] and by common consent took first prize in the contest. The crowd of rustics shouted their praises, and repeated and redoubled them to flatter his ears.[3] Anyone else might have taken delight in such trifles, and been encouraged by the windy flattery to let the bubbles[4] of vainglory form in his heart. But Wulfstan gave no encouragement by any movement of body or mind to those who praised him. The Devil, defeated here, tried to triumph in another way, and prompted the girl I have mentioned, who stood nearby, to run up. Nothing loath, she employed indecent gestures and movements to act the role of a dancing-girl in search of applause, all to play the slave to the eyes[6] of her sweetheart.[5] Though he had not yielded to her words and touch, he was so affected by her alluring gestures that he gave himself over wholly to love. But he immediately came to his right mind, shed tears, and bolted to a spot bristling with thorns and brambles. 8. He lay there some way off while the others went on with their sport unheeding, and sleep crept over him as he pondered deeply and belaboured himself with reproaches. Then a portent was to be seen. Down from above came a bright cloud that played on the eyes of those watching with a pleasing glow; for a while it veiled the prostrate Wulfstan, and bemused the spectators. Instantaneously the brightness of the cloud dispelled the fog of vanity, and breathed an air of seriousness over the sportive minds of the young people. They ran up at full tilt, and anxiously pressed Wulfstan to tell them what the sign

---

[4] The word is used in a literal sense at *VD* ii. 16. 1.

[5] Cf. the use of *amasia* in *Comm. Lam.* (Farmer, 'Lamentations', p. 296 n. 38).

[6] Just before, Wulfstan's ears have been tempted (*famularetur*, lit. 'to be the servant of') by the plaudits of the crowd. Now his eyes are tempted by this flirtatious girl.

contendunt, sollicitisque sermonibus Wlstanum adorsi quid illud
fuerit signi requirunt. Nichil ille negandum ratus, ut flamma caelestis
amoris quae in illum reluxerat scintillaret in sotios, rem omnem
ordine aperit.[a] Nuper se stimulis carnis aculeatum[1] ⟨in⟩[b] immensum
excanduisse; nunc superno rore irrigatum et uentre et totis uitalibus
algere. 9. Sperare se ulterius incentiuo carnis cariturum, et iuuante
Dei clementia nulla inquietandum molestia. Dictum propheticum
comitata est ueritas rerum. Numquam enim deinceps animum uel
oculum eius sollicitauit ullius formae miraculum, numquam turbu-
lenta eluuies dormientis interpellauit quietem.

Hoc se Colemannus ab Hemmingo[c] suppriore[2] didicisse asseuerat,
qui ab ipso Sancto postmodum episcopo ea se audisse memoraret.
Solebat enim reuerentissimus pater pro aetate et capacitate audien-
tium moderari sermonem, et nonnumquam sua inferre facta, ut non
diffiderent se illa posse facere quae illum audissent per Dei gratiam
implere ualuisse. Ita illud quod ante dixi[3] pueris, istud iocunda
hilaritate narrabat ephebis.[4]

2. Interea uterque adolescentis parens secularis uitae pertesus alios
pannos, alios mores et deuoto ardebat animo et frequenti uoluebat
susurro.[d] Quippe iam eis aetas progressior et fortuna despectior
imminebat. Nec multa morari quin desideriis facerent satis: pater
apud Wigorniam monachi habitum, mater in eadem urbe sanctimonialis suscepit uelum. Pannorum mutatio inuitauit bonorum exercitium,
ut non esset otiosum alterasse uestes nec auxisse uirtutes. Ita deuotione
simplici et studio efficaci propositum exsecuti, diebus suis expletis
naturae cessere.[5] Remansit interim Wlstanus in seculo spetie non
mente, non animo sed corpore. Veruntamen ut altioris gradus exemplo
in se uirtutum spetiem deliniaret, paulatimque mundana dedisceret,
Brihtegi Wigornensis episcopi[7] sese curiae[6] dedit. 2. Suscepit eum

---

[a] *C δ (p. 70); aperuit HR, perhaps rightly*   [b] *suppl. ed.*   [c] *ed.*; Hemmingo *C*;
Hemingo *δ (p. 70)*   [d] *Whar.*; susurrio *C*

[1] Used of Eadgyth's *uenter* in *GR*, c. 218. 4, paralleled by *VD* ii. 23. 3.
[2] Occ. in Wulfstan's time and *c.*1104, compiler of Hemming's Cartulary; *BRECP*,
p. 819.
[3] Meaning the story about the books (above, 4–5).
[4] For Wulfstan's overriding concern with sexual abstinence, especially among the
clergy, see below, i. 6, iii. 8. 1, 12. It has been thought that this concern was based on
a desire to imitate the Desert Fathers. Worcester Cath., MS F. 48, is a collection of the
Vitas patrum and related texts made in his time (perhaps at his request, and annotated by
Coleman): P. Jackson, 'The *Vitas patrum* in eleventh-century Worcester', in *England in the*

had meant. He thought he need hold nothing back, and told them the whole story, so that the flame of heavenly love that had shone on him should be reflected on to his companions. He had recently (he said) been pricked[1] by lusts of the flesh, and had blazed up to an enormous heat; but now he had been watered by the dew of heaven, and was cold in his groin and in his whole innards. 9. He hoped that from now on he would be free of fleshly impulse, and would by God's mercy have no further trouble on that score. His prophetic words came true. Never after that was his heart or eye distracted by anyone's striking beauty, never was his quiet sleep interrupted by a wet dream.

Coleman says he had this story from the sub-prior Hemming,[2] who mentioned that he had had it from the saint himself, when he was bishop later on. For the revered father would vary his conversation according to the age and understanding of his audience, and would sometimes introduce events involving himself, so that his hearers would not despair of doing things which they heard that thanks to the grace of God *he* had been able to do. So he used to tell the previous story[3] to boys, but this one (with a pleasant twinkle) to youths.[4]

2. Meanwhile both the young man's parents grew tired of life in this world, and longed devotedly for a different dress and a different way of life. They frequently discussed the matter, for old age and a reduction in their fortunes loomed over them. They did not wait long before putting their desires into practice; his father took a monk's habit at Worcester, and his mother a nun's veil in the same city. The change of garb encouraged practice in good things, so that it should not be a waste of time to alter clothes without an increase of virtue. They held to their resolve with simple piety and practical zeal, lived out their days and yielded to nature.[5] During this period Wulfstan remained in this world in appearance, not in mind, in body but not in soul. But so as to sketch out in himself the shape of virtue by the example of someone of higher rank, and gradually unlearn the ways of this world, he handed himself over to the 'court'[6] of Brihtheah bishop of Worcester.[7] 2. The bishop was glad to have him, and embraced

---

Eleventh Century, ed. C. Hicks (Woodbridge, 1990), pp. 119–34. However, this concern was also a modern one, taken up by the papacy from the time of Leo IX (1049–54).

[5] With this information cf. JW s.a. 1062 'Qui ambo . . . gauderent.'

[6] An odd use of the word (also below, i. 8. 4, ii. 13. 3, iii. 3. 1 (*curiales*), 8. 1, 16. 1, 19. 1, *VD* ii. 30. 1 (*curialis*)). At this date it was normally reserved for the king, otherwise the papacy: *ODML* ii. 537. In *VW* it seems to mean any one of (*a*) the bishop's *familia* proper, (*b*) the bishop's lay household (including his knights), or (*c*) the room or building in which

[See page 22 for n. 6 cont. and n. 7]

libens antistes et affinium suffragio et sua benignitate in iuuene Dei
gratiam fauorabiliter exosculatus. Nec ille fauori suo deerat, sed eum
probitate morum etiam ab improbissimi et asperi propositi hominibus
extorquebat, quippe a quo mens insolentior, uox preruptior, gestus
solutior, incessus fractior exulabat, fugitans proteruiae, immunis
petulantiae, quodque illi aetati maximo est ornamento, seruantissimus
custos uerecundiae. Cumulabat pectoris gratiam spetiositas corporis,
quam*a* licet inter uirtutes non numerem, non tamen omnino excludo,
quia sicut ars opificis in commodiore materia elucet, ita uirtus in
pulchritudine formae splendidius eminet.[1] 3. His artibus ita sibi
amorem pontificis conciliauerat ut ultro eum ad presbiteratum promoueret,[2] quanuis ille uix egreque ad consensum adduci potuerit.
Memorabile in iuuene quod eo gradu se indignum putauit, nec minus
quod acceptum dignis moribus illustrauit. Nec ergo ad accipiendum
aspirauit per arrogantiam, nec semel susceptum decolorauit per
inertiam: adeo inedia et omni parsimonia corpus attenuare et animae
uires dilatare curabat, adeo mente sobrius, sermone serius, reuerendus
aspectu, iocundus affectu, laicum uestibus, monachum moribus
agebat.[3] Si uero in quopiam*b* uidisset reatum, ita sermonem temperabat
ut rigor acerbae correptionis transiret in materiam laudis.[4] Non enim
asperum uideri poterat quod, licet durum sonaret, intus caritatem
redoleret.

3. Obtulit ei plusquam semel antistes aecclesiam suburbanam,[5] cuius
opulenti reditus ad cotidianam stipem satis superque[6] sufficerent. Ille
offerentem suspenso in posterum consilio sepe frustratus, tandem
uehementius instanti quid animi gestaret aperuit: fluctuantem seculi
statum menti suae uilescere; monachum se fieri uelle, totam uitam
suam non per partes Deo libare cupere. Hoc accepto responso

---

a *Whar.*; quem C   *b* *Whar.*; quempiam C

the bishop resided. In *GP*, c. 7 (p. 15), *curia* is used of an archbishop (meaning either
building or household), and at c. 54 (p. 102) we find the separate *curiae* of archbishop and
pope almost becoming one. Eadmer (*Hist. nov.*, p. 13) has Lanfranc build a *curia* for
himself at Canterbury, unambiguously a physical structure.   [7] Bp. 1033–8.

[1] Physical, in particular aristocratic, good looks had, however, for a long time been
included as a standard, though not essential, item in a saint's dossier: C. S. Jaeger, *The
Envy of Angels: Cathedral Schools and Social Ideals in Medieval Europe, 950–1200*
(Philadelphia, 1985), pp. 106–16, this instance p. 108. Cf. also *VD* ii. 9. 1–2.
[2] Wulfstan's career from this point until 3. 1 is recalled again at iii. 2. 1, with additional
details.
[3] Cf. *GP*, c. 137 (p. 278).

with all favour the grace of God in the youth, with the backing of
Wulfstan's relatives and his own kindness. Wulfstan helped to win
such favour, which he could extract, thanks to his uprightness, even
from men of wicked and harsh character; for insolence of mind,
hastiness of speech, effeminacy of gesture or gait were all foreign to
him, he avoided impudence and was untouched by impropriety,
and—a particular mark of distinction at such an age—guarded his
modesty with the greatest care. The grace of his heart was capped by
the beauty of his body; though I do not count that among the virtues,
I do not altogether rule it out, for, just as a craftsman's art shines
forth in superior material, so virtue stands out more splendidly in a
beautiful form.[1] 3. By such means Wulfstan had so won over the
bishop's love that Brihtheah, unasked, advanced him to the priesthood,[2] though Wulfstan could scarcely be induced to consent. It is
remarkable in a young man that he thought himself unworthy of the
rank, and that when he had taken it he brought lustre to it by worthy
behaviour. So he did not, through arrogance, long to receive it, but
neither, when he had taken it on, did he disgrace it by sloth: to such
an extent did he endeavour to slim down his body by fasting and
every kind of restraint, and thus to widen the scope of his soul, and so
true is it that, sober as he was in mind, grave in speech, reverend in
appearance, pleasant in temper, he resembled a layman in his dress
and a monk in his manners.[3] But if he saw a fault in anyone, he so
guarded his tongue that any austerity of bitter correction passed over
into material for praise;[4] for that which, while sounding harsh, yet
breathed the charity within could not be thought excessive.

3. More than once the bishop offered Wulfstan a church on the
outskirts of the city,[5] whose rich revenues would be more than
enough[6] to support him. He put off a decision several times, and
finally, when Brihtheah insisted, told him his real view. The world, in
its uncertain state, was growing cheap in his eyes; he wished to
become a monk, for he desired to offer up the whole of his life, not
just parts, to God. At this reply, the venerable bishop leapt for joy,

[4] Cf. *VD* i. 1. 3: 'in suae laudis materiam transduxit'.
[5] In 969 Oswald leased to one of his clergy the church of St Peter, at the south-west
corner of Worcester, with adjacent land (S1327). This could have been the same church,
and certainly the passage describes a similar arrangement. A lease of 1003 × 1006 (S1385)
mentions another extramural church, St Martin's. For both, see D. Hooke, *Worcestershire
Anglo-Saxon Charter-Bounds* (Woodbridge, 1990), pp. 284, 356.
[6] A cliché also used in *GR*, c. 303. 1, *GP*, c. 23 (p. 36), and below, iii. 23. 4.

uenerabilis episcopus magno exiliuit gaudio, iuuenilemque calorem monitionum suarum in maius animauit classico: felicem esse qui mundanas nausiaret illecebras, quarum momento temporis euanescit uoluptas, sed totam uitam mordet conscientiae asperitas; (2) felicem esse qui monachus fieri uelit, quod id sit genus hominum quanto despectius mundo crucifixum, tanto pretiosius Deo proximum, si non mores ab habitu degenerent. Ita uotis amborum concordibus, dum quod unus cuperet alter urgeret, Wlstanus apud Wigorniam induit monachum,[1] Brihtego indulgente fauorem et habitum.[2]

Hic si quispiam rethorum more spatiari cupiens auditoribus proponat quanta bona faustus dies ille Wigorniae attulerit, qui primo Wlstanum monachum uidit, profecto uoto excidet,[a] propositum implere non ualens. Quocirca quod lingua nequit exprimere, conetur uel animus ruminare. 3. Illud non tacendum, quod numquam nostro aeuo fuit monachus aut a uitiis remotior aut in uirtutibus perfectior. Quocirca, sinceritate uitae ipsius explorata, fratres illius aecclesiae non multo post puerorum fatiunt custodem, mox cantorem, postremo secretarium,[3] quatinus haberet liberiorem copiam orandi et uberiorem de uirtute in uirtutem crescendi materiam. Quam ille occasionem dignanter amplexus dies ieiuniis et uigiliis totas continuabat noctes. Numerabat in delitiis quod nos inertes homines magno ducimus supplitio, diebus omnibus ad unumquemque uersum septem psalmorum genua flectere, idem noctibus in psalmo centesimo octauo decimo[4] facere. 4. In occidentali porticu aecclesiae,[5] ubi erat altare omnium sanctorum cum tropheo uexilli Dominici, obserato aditu Christum uocare, lacrimis pulsare caelum, aethera onerare planctibus.[6] Plumam et ullum omnino lectum non

---

[a] excidet *Whar.* (*cf. iii. 20. 3*); incidet C

---

[1] Similarly *GP*, c. 138 (p. 279). For the expression 'induit monachum', see Col. 3: 9–10: 'expoliantes uos ueterem hominem cum actibus eius et induentes nouum', and *ODML*, s.v. 'induere' 2. e–g.

[2] Cf. JW s. a. 1062 'monachicum habitum . . . suscepit'. John of Worcester says that Wulfstan was encouraged to take this step by his mother.

[3] The term is used in *Mir.*, p. 96 lines 897–8 ('et dicitur secretarius quod sit secretarum gazarum conscius'), apparently as a synonym for 'thesaurarius', which is the word used in relation to Wulfstan by JW s.a. 1062 (ii. 588). Comment in Mason, p. 53, translating as 'sacrist'. So also C. D. Ducange, *Glossarium mediae et infimae Latinitatis* (rev. edn., 8 vols.: Paris, 1840–57), s.v.   [4] Ps. 118 (119).

[5] On the meanings of *porticus*, see below, p. 176 n. 1. Here probably a western annexe is meant, like the one for which evidence can be seen at Breamore (W. Rodwell and C. Rouse, 'The Anglo-Saxon rood and other features in the south porch of St. Mary's church, Breamore, Hampshire', *Antiquaries Journal*, lxiv (1984), 298–325, at pp. 299–300, 315, 319). There were two pre-Conquest churches at Worcester: St Peter's, built by Bishop

and used the clarion call of his exhortations to make the younger man's ardour even more lively. Happy (he said) the man who was sickened by worldly temptations, the pleasure of which vanishes in a moment, leaving the rest of one's life to the torments of a bitter conscience. 2. And happy the man who wanted to be a monk, and so join a class of men crucified to the world and despised by it, but so much the more valuable in their closeness to God—so long as their behaviour does not fall below the standards of their habit. So there was no difference in their prayers: what one desired the other was urging. Wulfstan became a monk at Worcester,[1] Brihtheah support-ing him and granting him the habit.[2]

If anyone at this point wished to spread himself like an orator and tell his hearers how great were the good things brought to Worcester by the auspicious day which first saw Wulfstan a monk, he would surely fail of his desire and find himself unable to complete his plan. So what tongue cannot express the mind must try to reflect upon. 3. What cannot be kept silent is that never in our age was there a monk further removed from vice or more perfect in virtue. The monks of the church, accordingly, having tested the uprightness of his life, soon made him novice-master, then cantor, and finally sacrist,[3] so that he could have more time for prayer and richer scope for growing from virtue to virtue. He made good use of this opportunity, and spent all day in fasting and all night in vigils. He counted as luxury what we lazy mortals think of as a penance, to genuflect every day at each verse of seven psalms, and to do the same at night in the 118th psalm.[4] 4. In the west *porticus*[5] of the church, where there was an altar of All Saints with a crucifix, he would bar up the entrance, and calling on Christ beat at the door of heaven with his tears and burden the sky with his laments.[6] He had no feather-bed—

Boisil 680 × 691, and still standing in Wulfstan's time, when it is last mentioned; and St Mary's, built by Oswald after 961. This was the main cathedral church until replaced by Wulfstan himself: Barker, *A Short Architectural History*, pp. 10–11. Work on the new cathedral started in 1084, according to the early fourteenth-century *Chronicon prioratus de Wigornia* (*Annales Monastici*, iv. 373). Nothing is known of the architecture of either church, and it is not clear which one is referred to here.

[6] Cf. Virgil, *Aen.* ix. 24; for other echoes by William, see *GR*, c. 49. 6 n. To the references there add *GR*, c. 405. 2, and *GP*, c. 49 (p. 84). With 'Quocirca, sinceritate uitae . . . planctibus' cf. JW s.a. 1062 'statimque in ipso initio . . . corpus macerans'. John of Worcester adds that Wulfstan was 'so devoted to pious vigils—passing as he did not only a night but even, very often, a day and a night, and sometimes (something we should scarcely believe if we had not heard it from his own lips) four days and nights without sleep—that he would have run into danger by parching of the brain if he had not hastened to satisfy nature by a taste of sleep'.

habere,[1] sopori non indulgere sed surripere. Super gradus ante altare capite posito se humo exponere, uel etiam codice aliquo uertici summisso super lignum tenuem inuitare soporem.[2] Ante unumquodque decem et octo altarium quae in ueteri aecclesia[3] erant septies in die prosterni. Haec dura non putare, sed quod alii putarent imitari.*[a][4] Cumque prae omnibus esset in uirtutibus sullimis, erat tamen singulis humilitate acclinis, ut aliqua uilia quae alius facere fastidiuit ille incunctanter expleret.

4.[5] Mos beato uiro increuerat noctibus aecclesias in uicino positas psalmorum excubiis frequentare, et in singulis orationum uota apud Deum deponere. Ibat ergo per medium cimiterium nec titubanti gressu nec ulla mentem hebetatus formidine. Regebat iusti animum ipse Christus, ut nullae illum turbarent tenebrae, nulla quateretur solitudine. Deuotione usus incaluit, uel consuetudinem pene in naturam conuertit.[6] Hoc effectum ut ad aecclesiam apostolorum principis quadam nocte ueniret. Haec quondam sedes episcopalis fuerat, sed eam sanctus Oswaldus clericis irreligiosis uacuauerat, certo*[b] et rationabili commertio[7] potestatem apostoli ad matrem Domini mutuatus.[8] Stabat ergo ante altare iam in preces effusus, iam totus in Deum gestiens. 2. Tum uero antiquus hostis, qui numquam deest quin uel bona nobis inuideat uel mala suggerat, cuiusdam rusticani simulacrum indutus orantem talibus interpellat. Quae illum dementia in tam opacae horrore noctis[9] eo adduxisset? Importunum eius aduentum esse, nec sibi placere. Quocirca luctamen inter se competere, quod experiri uellet cuius esset roboris qui esset animi tam audacis. Haec et immani rictu et uoce fremebunda. At Wlstanus parum motus, qui nichil minus opinaretur quam hostem tali

---

[a] mirari *tempt. Darl.*   *[b]* Perhaps read recto (*cf. GP p. 39* iuste et rationabiliter)

[1] For other references by William to feather beds, see *GR*, c. 199. 7 n.

[2] With 'Plumam . . . soporem' cf. JW s.a. 1062 'Denique . . . reclinabat.'

[3] Meaning St Mary's church (see below, iii. 10. 3).

[4] Cf. JW s.a. 1062: 'quod officium [i.e. prioris] ualde laudabiliter adimplens, prioris conuersationis austeritatem minime reliquit, immo, ut ceteris exemplum bene uiuendi daret, multipliciter adauxit.'

[5] The story is also in *GP*, c. 138 (pp. 279–80), with variations. No mention is made there of Wulfstan's wound, and the account adds, as further evidence of Wulfstan's fearlessness, that he crossed broken bridges without getting off his horse. For another instance of saintly courage before visible demons, see *VD* i. 31. 1; for fear of churchyards, *GP*, c. 75 (p. 163).

[6] Similar expressions are in *VD* i. 31. 1 and *Comm. Lam.* (Farmer, 'Lamentations', p. 303 n. 49); cf. *Mir.*, p. 116 line 129. Otto, *Sprichwörter*, pp. 90–1.

or bed of any sort;[1] he did not indulge in sleep, but snatched it. He would lie on the ground with his head on the steps before the altar; or he would even put a book beneath his head and woo a light slumber resting on some wooden board.[2] Seven times a day would he prostrate himself before all the eighteen altars in the Old Church.[3] He did not think such things hard, but instead took as a model what others thought hard.[4] And though he was high above all others in virtue, he was nonetheless humbly submissive towards individuals, ready to do without hesitation servile tasks that another was too fastidious to put his hand to.

4.[5] The habit had grown on the blessed man of going by night to churches in the vicinity to keep vigils with the singing of psalms and to pray to God in each. So he would go through the middle of a graveyard with firm step and no dulling fear. Christ in person guided the mind of the just man, so that no darkness confounded him, no solitary place shook his purpose. Practice grew warm through piety, and virtually turned custom into nature.[6] Hence it was that one night he went to the church of the foremost of the apostles. This had formerly been the episcopal seat, but St Oswald had rid it of irreligious clerks and, by a lasting(?) and reasonable exchange,[7] borrowed for the mother of our Lord the power of the apostle.[8] So there stood Wulfstan before the altar, already pouring out his prayers and yearning wholly after God. 2. But then the Old Enemy, who never fails to grudge us good things or put bad ideas in our minds, took on the guise of a yokel and interrupted Wulfstan's prayers with a harangue. What madness had brought him there on such a terrible black night?[9] His coming was untimely, and he did not like it. What was needed was a fight: he wanted to find out the physical strength of someone whose heart was so bold. This he poured out with appalling grimaces and a roaring voice. But Wulfstan, not suspecting for a moment that the Devil was concealing himself beneath such a

---

[7] Cf. *GP*, c. 79 (p. 175): 'Nunc de presulatu in abbatiam mutatus, commertio nostra aetate non insueto'.

[8] Oswald's replacement of clerks by monks, and his building of St Mary's church (in St Peter's cemetery), are referred to in *Hemingi Chartularium* ii. 342–3; *GP*, c. 115 (p. 248), and *VD* ii. 4. 2 and 13. 1. Commentary on the relative positions of the two churches is provided by C. C. Dyer, 'The Saxon cathedrals of Worcester', *Transactions of the Worcestershire Archaeological Society*, 3rd ser. ii (1968–9), 34; N. Baker and R. Holt, 'The city of Worcester in the tenth century', in *St Oswald of Worcester*, pp. 129–46, at 143–4.

[9] The same expression, applied to similar events, in *Mir.*, pp. 65 lines 59–60, 130 line 560; *GR*, c. 178. 2.

se celare inuolucro, psalmorum seriem non interrupto exsequebatur
ordine. Et casu uel potius diuino nutu uersum illum ruminabat,
'Dominus michi adiutor; non timebo quid fatiat michi homo':[1]
dicentem hostis inuadit, duris ulnarum internodiis corpus ieiuniis
attenuatum astringens. 3. Ille primo monstrum brachiorum obiectu
repellit, mox etiam uicario certamine aggreditur. Quippe comperto
quod diabolus sub illo simulationis lateret pallio, fidei arma concutiens, in certamen animatur. Durauit haec lucta non paruo noctis
tempore, nescias maiore impudentia diaboli an confidentia Sancti.
Facinus hostile et improbum, spiritum homini corporaliter congredi
non tam probandarum uirium causa quam probatarum inuidia!
Confidentia uiri prompta et laudabilis immani furiae non cedere,
quae plerumque Deo permittente noscitur terras et maria turbare.
Quapropter tandem larualis umbra, succumbens animosae fidei
acrique fetore uicinum turbans aerem, in auras confusa euanuit.
4. Ne tamen nichil uideretur fecisse,[2] pedem iusti quanta poterat
iniquitatis mole conculcans, non secus quam ignito perfodit cauterio.
Penetrauit labes illa in ossa, teste Godrico eiusdem conuentus
monacho,[3] qui, ut auctor est Colemannus, sepe se illud uidisse
diceret; uulnus an ulcus dicam ignoro. Idem etiam Colemannus
asseuerat notum sibi fuisse agrestem illum cuius spetiem inimicus
assumpserat, idoneum nimirum hominem, et atrocitate roboris ⟨et⟩[a]
scelerum immanitate et torua deformitate uultus, in quem se
improbissimus latro transformaret, a quo procedit quicquid horri-
dum, quicquid fedum mundus uel uidit uel uidebit.

5. Adolescebat temporis processu in Wlstano germen omne uirtutum, precipueque obedientia et ad prelatos subiectio. Quamlibet enim
durum, quamlibet iuberetur asperum, statim producebat[b] uelle,
quanuis non suppeteret posse. Vnde et ex diuinae gratiae fonte
scaturiuit in eum amor hominum, ut omni deliniendum putarent
obsequio quem acceptum habebat caelestis dignatio, antistes maxime,
qui sic in Wlstanum affitiebatur animo ut quouis honore dignum
putaret. Nam et[c] strenue peracti offitii industria spem altioris
dignitatis salubriter exsequendae,[d] si conferretur, infuderat. Hac

---

[a] *suppl. ed.*   [b] *Perhaps read* procudebat   [c] *Perhaps read* ei   [d] *ed.;* -di C

[1] Ps. 117 (118): 6.
[2] Similar expressions are in *AG*, c. 15 (p. 64); *GP*, c. 74 (p. 150).
[3] Occ. 1092, *c.*1104, on the first occasion as chamberlain: *BRECP*, p. 811.

disguise, was quite unconcerned, and continued his psalm-sequence without a break. By chance, or rather by God's will, he was savouring the verse 'The Lord is on my side; I will not fear what a man might do unto me',[1] when the Enemy attacked, pinioning in his sinewy arms a body wasted away by fasting. 3. Wulfstan first pushed the monster away, then went over to the offensive. For he had by now realized that the Devil lurked beneath that disguise, and brandishing the arms of the faith he found courage for the battle. No small stretch of the night this wrestling bout lasted, and it is hard to know which was the greater, the impudence of the Devil or the self-confidence of the saint. It was the deed of a wicked enemy for a spirit to fight in the body with a man, not so much to test his strength as out of envy of strength already tested. The man's confidence, ready for anything and beyond praise, would not give in to the foul fiend, that is known often to plague land and sea when God allows it. And so at last the ghostly figure, yielding to spirited faith, and polluting the neighbour-hood with an acrid smell, vanished in confusion into thin air. 4. But so that he should not seem to have failed altogether,[2] he trod on the good man's foot with all the force wickedness could muster, and pierced it as though with a red-hot iron. The damage penetrated to the bone, so Godric, monk of that house,[3] bore witness; according to Coleman, he said he had often seen—I do not know whether to call it wound or ulcer. The same Coleman avows that he knew the rustic whose shape the Devil took on, a man well suited from his superhuman strength, wicked character and grim ugliness, to be the one into whom that most wicked bandit transformed himself—he from whom proceeds all that the world has seen or will see in the way of horrible and foul things.

5. As time went by, a shoot of all virtues flowered in Wulfstan, particularly obedience and submission to those over him. Whatever he was ordered to do, however hard or unpleasant, he immediately provided the will even if the ability was not available. As a result, from the fountain of God's grace, there showered over him the love of men, so that they thought one whom Heaven deigned to find acceptable should be flattered by every kind of obedient attention: particularly the bishop, who felt so warmly towards Wulfstan that he thought he deserved any and every honour. For the hard work he put into his duties encouraged him to hope that he would carry out a higher office with sound judgement, if it were to be conferred on him.

occasione[1] prepositus ut tunc, prior ut nunc dicitur,[2] monachorum constitutus, statim materiam qua uirtus emineret arripuit, multis incommodis intus forisque propulsatis. 2. Nam res exteriores antecessorum incuria pessumdatas ingenii uiuacitate in solidum restituit, et interiores freno regulari cohercuit. Quod ut efficatius faceret uitae suae subiectis religiosa porrigebat exempla, erubescens scilicet predicare quod fastidiret facere.[3] Ipsam porro doctrinam non suo confingebat ingenio, nec coturnato et plausibili proferebat eloquio. Quin potius maiorum nostrorum scriptis inuigilans hauriebat sitibundo pectore fluenta doctrinae, quae postea mellito eructaret gurgite (licet enim michi de beati Gregorii uita[4] dictum mutuari, quod a Colemanno in patriam linguam ut pleraque alia uersum ego transfudi denuo in Latinum). Itaque cum in omnibus diuinae scripturae libris, tum in his diligentes pretendebat excubias qui sibi castimoniam commendarent. Eius integritatem in se alacriter exsequi, corruptionem in aliis acriter insequi, ut uno liquebit exemplo.

6. Erat in eadem urbe matrona et domesticis opibus locuples plusquam sufficeret uictui et quae formae liniamentis curioso intuentium lenocinaretur aspectui, frequentius in aecclesiam ueniens, sed magis ut uisentibus esset spectaculo quam diuinae lectionis intenta oraculo. Quod eo claruit quia uerbis adulatoriis tanti uiri animum sollicitare presumpsit: incassum, quia pulchritudo eius et promissa infra pudicitiam Wlstani fuere. Et diu quidem multumque cecum uulnus[5] secreto aluerat, sed timore repulsae dissimularat. Tandem cum cupidine superante depuduisset eam castimoniae, prioris iuxta se in aecclesia forte stantis pannos tactu impudenti temerauit. Quam cum ille oculi uigore perstrinxisset, ipsa omnipotentis Dei nomen contestata ne suum aspernaretur eloquium rogauit. 2. Tum Wlstanus, arbitratus eam peccata uelle confiteri, substitit et in

---

[1] According to JW s.a. 1062 (ii. 590–1), this was in the time of Bishop Ealdred (after 1046), and after the death of Prior Æthelwine (after 1051: *Heads*, p. 83).

[2] But in *Hemingi Chartularium*, i. 279, Wulfstan is styled 'prior' and Wilstan 'praepositus' (and at i. 261 Ælfstan is 'prior', Witheric 'praepositus'): Mason, p. 62 n. 84. The two monks seem to have acted on behalf of the ageing Prior Æthelwine. Wilstan became abbot of Gloucester in 1058 (*Heads*, p. 52). For a different use of 'praepositus', see below, iii. 2. 2. K. Hallinger, *Gorze-Kluny: Studien zu den monastischen Lebensformen und Gegensätzen im Hochmittelalter* (Studia Anselmiana, fasc. 22–5: 2 vols., Rome, 1950–1), ii. 781–868, esp. 854 seq., discusses the change from 'praepositus' to 'prior', promoted particularly by Cluny during the eleventh century. In relation to the English, and monastic cathedral contexts, see E. John, 'The church of Worcester and Oswald', in *Belief and Culture in the Middle Ages: studies presented to Henry Mayr-Harting* (Oxford, 2001), pp. 142–57, esp. 148–50.

As a result, he was made[1] what was then called provost but is now called prior of the monks;[2] and thus at a stroke he won scope for his virtue to stand out. He did away with many faults both inside and outside the monastery. 2. For the neglect of his predecessors had ruined the external affairs of the house, and it needed Wulfstan's lively intelligence to put them on a firm footing again; and matters within he controlled with the curb of the Rule. To do this more effectively, he offered his subjects the pious example of his own life, for he would have blushed to preach things he shrank from doing himself.[3] Moreover, what he taught was neither the product of his own free invention nor expressed in a style that asked applause for its melodrama. Rather, he spent wakeful hours studying the writings of our forebears, and greedily drank in the rivers of their teaching, so that later he could emit them with honeyed flow. (For I may surely borrow a phrase from the Life of St Gregory,[4] which, like much else, Coleman turned into his native language and I have translated back again into Latin.) So Wulfstan spent much time in careful study of all writings from Holy Scripture, but especially those that pressed upon him the virtue of chastity, whose preservation he eagerly pursued in himself, and whose sullying he roundly attacked in others—as will appear from a single instance.

6. There lived in Worcester a married lady who had greater private means than mere livelihood required, and whose beauty pandered to the gaze of the curious onlooker. She was a frequent attender in church, but she came rather to show herself than because of any desire to concentrate on the word of God. This became clear, for she tried with winning words to attract the great man. To no avail, for Wulfstan's chastity was on a different plane from her beauty and her promises. Long did she foster in secret a hidden wound,[5] but hitherto she had concealed it for fear of rebuff. Finally, her desire got the better of her, and she grew ashamed of being so bashful. When the prior chanced to stand next to her in church, she polluted his habit with a shameless touch. He glared at her, but she appealed to him in the name of Almighty God not to ignore her words. 2. Wulfstan thought she wanted to confess her sins, and he stopped and drew

---

[3] With 'antistes maxime . . . facere' cf. JW s.a. 1062 'Post aliquod tempus . . . multipliciter adauxit.'

[4] Paul the Deacon, *Vita Greg.* i. 2 (PL lxxv. 42).

[5] Virgil, *Aen.* x. 733 (cf. iv. 2); another echo in *Mir.*, p. 119 line 232.

partem concessit. At femina oportunitatem nacta sermones malesua-dos*^a* femineisque blanditiis sed uipereis dolis infectos[1] sancto uiro assibilat.*^b* Ex longo tempore eius se colloquium meditatam, ut si non refugiat*^c* suggereret quod amborum utilitati conduceret.*^d* Habere se domum, ut sumptibus affluentem ita procuratore carentem, quod uterque parens obierit et maritus non assit. Debere sapientiam ipsius tantae curae accedere, ut eius arbitratu et regatur familia et dis-pensetur pecunia. Quibus dictis cum inferret ille ut pecuniis in pauperes erogatis se ipsam uelari faceret, ea subiecit: Quin immo se hoc optare et orare, ut paululum propositi*^e* rigore inflexo suum dignaretur cubile.[2] 3. Leue uel nullum peccatum esse si femineo potiatur amplexu. Si etiam esset grandiusculum, elemosinis ex suo redimeret quicquid ueniabilis culpa obfuscaret. Ad hoc opes sibi affluere, nec uoluntatem deesse. Non tulit prior ulterius, sed loquentis uoce interrupta pretentoque fronti crucis signaculo 'Fuge' inquit 'cum eo quo digna es odio, fomes lasciuiae,*^f* mortis filia, uas Sathanae'.[3] Verba increpatoria subsecuta est alapa, quam ille zelo castitatis fatiei mulierculae gannientis[4] tanto nisu infregit*^g* ut illisae crepitus palmae ualuas etiam exiret aecclesiae. Migrauit per urbem huiusce facti fabula, totisque compitis per multos dies cantabatur qualiter alter Ioseph[5] muliebrem lasciuiam et animo respuit et manu compescuit.

7. Nec solum in monachos sed et in uulgus misericordiae suae respergebat semina. Crebro enim summo mane diurnis expeditus offitiis conspicuum se prebebat ante fores aecclesiae, ut facilior esset aditus uolentibus se conuenire. Ibi igitur sedulus et pius explorator diem plerumque ad sextam, plerumque ducebat ad uesperam, dummodo uel uim passis quanta posset ope concurreret uel pauper-iorum filios baptizaret. Iam enim uenalitas ex infernalibus umbris

---

^a *ed.*; male suasos *C*   ^b *Perhaps read* assibilabat (sibilabat δ, *p. 73*)   ^c refugiat (*with blot on last letter*) *C. For the tense cf.* assit *below.*   ^d condeceret *C*^{*p.c.*} (*but cf. i. 11. 2*)   ^e δ*H**(*p. 73*); pre- *C*   ^f lasciuie δ*H**(*p. 73*); laciuie *C*   ^g *C* (*cf. ii. 18. 3*; *GR 178. 2*; *Ter. Adelph. 200*); impegit δ*H** (*p. 73*) (*cf. ii. 18. 2*)

¹ A similar expression in *VD* ii. 20. 1.   ² Virgil, *Ecl.* iv. 63.
³ Cf. *Passio S. Agnetis* (*BHL* 156), in *AA SS* Ian. ii. 351–4, at 351: 'Discedite a me, fomes peccati, nutrimentum facinoris, pabulum mortis', quoted by Aldhelm, *De uirginitate prosa*, in *Aldhelmi Opera*, ed. R. Ehwald (*Monumenta Germaniae Historica, Auctores Antiquissimi*, xv: Berlin, 1919), c. 45 (p. 298 lines 17–18); spoken by St Agnes. The *Passio* was translated by Ælfric: *Ælfric's Lives of the Saints*, ed. W. W. Skeat (EETS, orig. ser. lxxvi, lxxxii, xciv, and cxiv, 1881–1900), this passage at i. 170.

aside with her. The woman took her chance, and whispered in the holy man's ear seductive words imbued with a woman's coaxing but a viper's wiles.[1] She said that she had for a long time planned a conversation with him; if he did not turn tail, she could make a suggestion that would be to the advantage of both of them. She had a house flowing over with money but with no one to look after it, for both her parents had died and she had no husband on the spot. So wise a man as Wulfstan should take over this important role, so that his judgement could see to the administering of the household and the allocation of the cash. At this, Wulfstan rejoined that she should give away her money to the poor and have herself made a nun. She replied that what she really wanted was this, to have Wulfstan make some concessions in the rigour of his principles and to join her in bed.[2] 3. It was (she said) a slight sin, if sin at all, to embrace a woman, and even if it were quite a big one, she could use her resources to pay for it in alms, if so venial a fault made any blot on his soul. She was wealthy, and she was willing. The prior could stand it no longer. He interrupted her in full flight, and crossing himself said, 'Away with you, and take with you the hatred you deserve, you tinder of wantonness, daughter of death and vessel of Satan.'[3] These admonitory words were followed by a slap, which he, in his zeal for chastity, administered to the face of the gabbling[4] woman with such force that the smack of his palm could be heard right through the door of the church. The story went the rounds of the city, and every street corner for many days heard talk of how this second Joseph[5] had rejected a woman's lewdness, and quelled it with his hand.

7. Nor was it only on the monks, but on the ordinary people too that he scattered the seeds of his mercy. For very often, early in the morning, when the daily office was over, he showed himself before the church doors, so that he could be more easily available to those who wanted an interview with him. Here, therefore, assiduous in his piety, he would often pass the day till Sext or Vespers, if it meant he could give all possible help to victims of violence, or baptize the children of the poorer class. For by that time bribery had made its appearance from the shades of Hell, with the result that priests would

---

[4] Used of women in *GR*, c. 229, *VD* i. 6. 2.

[5] Gen. 39: 6–12, the episode of Joseph and Potiphar's wife. Like the woman here, she made a shameless grab at his clothing.

emerserat, ut nec illud gratis presbiteri preberent infantibus sacramentum, si non infarcirent parentes marsupium.[1] Horum igitur Wlstanus miseratus inopiam, illorum animo*[a]* et facto pertundens auaritiam, in baptizandis pauperibus ultroneae[2] dignationis impendebat offitium. 2. Currebatur ad eum ex urbibus et agris, ab illis precipue quorum non intererat dare nummum ut soboli suae mercarentur lauacrum. Transfusa est a tenuiori fortuna in diuites consuetudo, ut nemo fere illius regionis iure baptizatum aliquem ex suis putaret quem Wlstanus non baptizasset. Conciliabat hanc suspitionem[3] non falsa de sanctitate uiri opinio et de religione non temeraria presumptio. Ferebatur ergo per Angliam ipsius famae preconium, adeo ut potentissimi tunc optimates Anglorum eius amicitiam et auidissime optarent et constantissime tenerent. Hanc sibi securitatem in secundis, euasionem in sinistris, tutelam in cunctis pollicebantur. 3. Quorum Haroldus, et maiorem potentiam conscientia opum spirans et iam tunc regnum magnanimitate morum affectans,[4] unice diligebat uirum, ita ut in itinere positus triginta miliaria de recto calle non dubitaret diuertere ut eius colloquio curarum suarum moles posset auocare, ita uoluntati eius et clientelae deditus ut Wlstanum tantum puderet iubere quantum Haroldum non pigeret facere. Nec minorem comiti Sanctus refundebat gratiam, eius confessiones benigne accipiens et orationum apud Deum fidus interpres. Eiusdem dilectionis terebat orbitam Aldredus, post Brihtegum Wigornensis episcopus, uir multum in secularibus astutus nec parum religiosus.[5] Is domino priori pro reuerentia sanctitatis granditer obsequi, humiliter parere,[6] prorsus in omnibus ut parenti gratissimo deferre.

8. Nec illud subtraho lecturis, quod non minori quam cetera quae dicta sunt dignum est illustrari titulo. Animaduertens enim penuria predicationis populum a bonis moribus diffluere, omni dominica et maioribus sollemnitatibus in aecclesia infundebat ei monita salutis. Putares ex euangelicis et propheticis aditis uerba intonare quae ille ex alto stationis plebi pronuntiabat, adeo ut tonitrua fulminabant in

---

[a] C *adds* miseratus; *del. ed.*

[1] Ælfric, in the 990s, prohibited the taking of money for baptizing: *Councils*, i(1), p. 211. In the eleventh century the prohibition was repeated by councils on the Continent; it was made again in England at the Legatine Council of Westminster, Sept. 1125, canon 2: *Councils*, i(2), no. 130 (p. 738).

[2] i.e. without asking for payment.

[3] i.e. the doubt about whether baptism by any other person might be ineffective.

[4] Note William's attitude to him, less positive than in *GR*, e.g. cc. 228. 7–8, 238. 1–2.

not give even this sacrament to infants unless parents greased their palms.[1] Wulfstan took pity on the poverty of the parents, and in thought and deed chastised the greed of the priests; and he gave the poor baptism of his free will.[2] 2. People flocked to him from town and country alike, particularly those who were not prepared(?) to use cash to buy their children's baptism. The custom passed from the poor to the rich, so that few in the district thought one of their offspring properly baptized if Wulfstan had not officiated. This doubt[3] was the reward of his justified reputation for holiness and the well-founded presumption of his piety. Hence Wulfstan's fame was the talk of all England, so much so that the most powerful English noblemen of the day were avid to gain and keep his friendship, promising themselves thereby safety in good times, escape in ill, and a helping hand in every matter. 3. One of them was Harold, who thirsted for greater power on account of his wealth and was already showing by his lordly behaviour his designs on the throne;[4] yet he had a particular liking for Wulfstan, to such a degree that in the course of a journey he was ready to go thirty miles out of his way to remove, by a talk with Wulfstan, the load of anxieties oppressing him. He was so devoted to serving Wulfstan and doing what he wanted that the holy man was as ashamed to ask something as Harold was willing to comply. The saint repaid these favours to the earl, hearing his confession sympathetically and faithfully mediating his prayers to God. Ealdred, bishop of Worcester after Brihtheah, trod the same affectionate path: a man wily in secular affairs, but not without piety.[5] Out of respect for his holiness, he was the devoted servant of the lord prior and obeyed him humbly,[6] deferring to him in everything as to a beloved father.

8. I do not propose to deprive my readers of another matter that deserves to be recorded no less emphatically than the rest. Wulfstan noticed that the people were drifting away from good behaviour because they were short of sermons; and so every Sunday and on the major feast days he would pour out salutary advice for them in church. You might have thought that the words he proclaimed to the common people from his high pulpit were thunder from the innermost shrines of apostles and prophets: thunderclaps they were to wicked men, but refreshing showers of rain to the elect. He did this in

---

[5] bp. 1044/6–1061 (1062); he was not Brihtheah's immediate successor, as William was aware (*GP*, c. 136 (p. 278)).   [6] Cf. *GP*, c. 209 (p. 354).

improbos, adeo ut imbres irrigabant electos. Fatiebat hoc summa modestia, et quantum ad se sub humilitatis latebra. Veruntamen ita latere uolentem inuenit et carpsit inuidia,[1] quanuis carpentem caelestis uindicta non preterierit, sicut ex consequenti clarebit.

2. Erat in eadem aecclesia transmarinae nationis monachus, Winrichus nomine,[2] si ad litteram[a] spectes eruditissimus, si ad copiam facundiae dicendi ualidus, si ad calliditatem seculi prudentissimus, si ad morum elegantiam pulchre compositus perindeque[b] hominibus acceptus et carus. Idem alias et ira preferuidus[c] ad succensendum quod displiceret torquente liuore accommodus. Is[d] de predicatione Sancti multa cauillari solitus quaedam ad hanc sententiam exsequebatur. Contra regulas esse quod offitium antistitis preriperet, solius pontificis esse populo predicare, qui solus tradita sibi et indulta potestate peccata posset absoluere. Monacho silentium et claustrum competere, non pompatico gestu et sermone populi auribus insultare. Videri ergo magis alicuius ambitum dignitatis quam exsecutionem pietatis.[3] 3. Haec ille non iam tantum a tergo, sed etiam quadam die amariore bile succensus in os obiectauit Wlstano. Contra ille scuto patientiae armatus paucis occurrit. Nichil esse magis Deo gratum quam populum pessumeuntem in uiam ueritatis reuocare, ideoque non se omissurum. Sin aliud quod gratius esset Christo addiscere posset, incunctanter facturum. Ita tunc discessum et dormitum est.

At uero ut Deus ostenderet quanti beati uiri factum penderet, horrifica calumniatorem uisione concussit. Cum enim ad quietem composuisset membra in lecto, ad tribunal iudicis ignoti raptus est animo. 4. Ab eo itaque graui seueritate increpatus cur seruum suum pridie de bono predicationis obiurgasset, dum se parum expurgat, iussus est in pauimentum sterni et cedi. Ita succedentibus sibi lictoribus acriter fustigatus nichil aliud inter tormenta nisi 'Miserere, Domine, Domine miserere!' clamitabat. Tandem laxatus interrogatur num preconem suum ulterius prohiberet, quo minus homines ad

---

[a] $C^{p.c.}$ *adds* iam, *wrongly* (*cf. esp. VD* i. *21. 5*); per- *C*   [b] [*Darl.*]; pereundeque *C*; proindeque *Whar.*   [c] *ed.* [d] *ed.*; his *C*; hic *Whar.*

---

[1] Cf. ps.-Quintilian, *Decl. maiores* xiii. 2: 'sic quoque me latentem inuenit inuidia' (twice cited by Jerome).   [2] The name is German.
[3] A similar story in Gregory, *Dial.* i. 4 (PL lxxvii. 169); cf. below, ii. 16. 3. The basis of Winrich's position was entirely orthodox: only ordained priests should preach, not monks or laity: classic texts are e.g. Leo I, *Epist.* cxviii and cxix (PL lv. 1040, 1045–6). Although the 'normative' Anglo-Saxon texts generally assign the duty of preaching to bishops and mass-priests alike, the Constitutions of Oda (*Councils* i(1), no. 20, pp. 71–2) and I Cnut 26 (F. Liebermann, *Die Gesetze der Angelsachsen* (3 vols.: Halle, 1903–16), i. 305–6) only treat

all modesty, and, so far as he was concerned, shrouded in a cloak of humility. But though he was eager to stay hidden, he was found out and carped at by Envy[1]—though, as will appear, the carper was not passed over by punishment from on high.

2. In the same church was a monk called Winrich, a monk from overseas:[2] very learned, if you considered his mastery of letters; a powerful speaker, if you considered his flow of eloquence; a very sensible person, if you considered his astuteness in worldly matters; smooth and therefore acceptable and agreeable to people, if you considered the polish of his manners. But for all that he was on other occasions quick to anger, and was liable to grow heated in a torment of envy when something displeased him. This man made a habit of constantly cavilling at the holy man's preaching, on the following lines. It was against the rules: Wulfstan was usurping the duties of the bishop. It was the bishop's task, and his only, to preach to the people, for only he, by the power handed down and granted to him, could give absolution of sins. A monk's role was silence in the cloister, not assaulting the ears of the people with sermons as melodramatic as the gestures that accompanied them. Such behaviour looked more like canvassing for office than the performance of a religious duty.[3] 3. In the end he did not just say things like this behind Wulfstan's back: one day, heated by a more bitter attack of bile than usual, he flung them in Wulfstan's face. Wulfstan armed himself with the shield of patience, and made a brief reply. Nothing was more acceptable to God than the summoning of an errant people back to the way of truth; and he would not give up. If he came to hear of anything *more* acceptable to Christ, he would do it at once. They parted on that note, and went off to their beds.

But, to show his appreciation of the blessed man's behaviour, God struck the slanderer with a terrible vision. For when he had settled down to sleep, he found himself rapt in his mind before the tribunal of an unknown judge. 4. The judge rebuked him sternly for upbraiding His servant the day before for the good he did by his sermons. He could find little or no excuse, and was ordered to lie on the floor for a beating. So a succession of attendants gave him a severe cudgelling. Nothing else did he cry in his agony but 'Pity me, Lord! Lord, pity me!' In the end he was released, and the judge asked him

bishops; so Winrich, though a foreigner, may have been invoking a strict interpretation current in pre-Conquest England. Martin Brett informs us that he knows of no relevant texts which actually encouraged monks to preach. The issue was, however, to become a lively one in the twelfth century: G. Constable, *Monastic Tithes* (Cambridge, 1964), pp. 145–85.

curiam suam euocaret. Ille, cui nichil illius temporis necessitas non extorqueret, per quicquid sanctum est deierauit se non modo ultra non prohibiturum sed etiam ultro ad predicationem et eum et alios impulsurum: tantum*ᵃ* sibi miseratio iudicis uitam prorogaret in posterum, ut illius euaderet angoris articulum. 5. Ita fide data ne temeraret promissa, dimissus est. Mox ergo ut potuit, potuit autem statim ut illuxit, prioris pedibus aduoluitur, genua exosculatur, commissum fatetur, offensam deprecatur. Interrogatus repentinae mutationis causam, ordinem uisionis iuratus exposuit. Vadabantur ueritatem narrationis lacrimae sinceris precibus expromptae. Liuores in scapulis protuberantes testabantur nichil eum uanum uidisse, nichil molle sensisse. Nec difficulter ueniam a Sancto impetrauit, ad cuius benedictionem sanitas rediit, dolor omnis euanuit.

Fidem ergo de presentibus exemplis mereatur et omni ambiguo liberetur antiquitas, quae nobis simile factum in beato Ieronimo representat. 6. Parum enim discrepat illum fuisse cesum propter libros gentilium, et istum propter prohibitae*ᵇ* predicationis offitium. Idem est pene propter gentilium nugas diuinam scripturam negligere et eandem predicari nolle.[1]

Illud fuit tempus quo super aecclesiae[2] tectum machinabatur fabricam, in qua dependerent campanae.[3] Eam uero fabricam quo proprio nomine quam proxime appellem in promptu non habeo. Ad illam ergo erigendam moliebatur gradus scalarum, quibus operantes insisterent, et pendulos in aere gressus*ᶜ* firmarent. Iamque funibus subuectae stabant scalae plures proceritate in caelum minantes,[4] quibus manus artificum quaeque munus exsequeretur iniunctum.

ᵃ *Whar.*; tandem C   *ᵇ* *Perhaps read* prohibitum   *ᶜ* δHR (*p. 74*); gradus C

[1] It is perhaps odd that Winrich is equated with St Jerome. 'Fidem . . . representat' is the reverse of William's usual argument, that past miracles told on good authority make reports of recent ones more credible. Cf. Jerome, *Epist.* xxii. 30 (on which the whole episode is modelled), alluded to also in *Mir.*, p. 132 lines 609–14, and quoted in *Polyhistor*, p. 87. See *GR* II, p. 218 (another example below, ii. 19. 4), on the way in which William uses past miracles to make modern ones credible. On the other hand, in *GR*, c. 445. 1, he argues as he does here: 'There were at that time [i.e. the early twelfth century] in England many persons distinguished for their learning and famous for their religious life . . . . By their admirable lives they made the stories of the past time seem credible; we cannot accuse old tales of being untrue, when recent facts prove that they might easily have happened.'

[2] Presumably the work was done on St Mary's church (see above, c. 3. 4 n.). A similar miracle is told in Wulfstan of Winchester, *Vita Æthelwoldi*, c. 34 (pp. 52–3).

[3] William's careful wording shows that he does not mean a belfry (i.e. a substantial tower with bell-chamber), for which at least one word was available to him: OE 'belhus',

whether he would go on trying to prevent His preacher summoning men to His court. The urgency of his predicament would have made him say anything, and he swore by all that is holy that he would make no more objections, but would go out of his way to encourage Wulfstan and others to preach: only let the judge in His mercy prolong his life and save him from this extreme of anguish. 5. So he guaranteed not to go back on his promises, and was sent away. As soon as he could—and he could as soon as it grew light—he prostrated himself at the prior's feet, kissed his knees, confessed his offence, and begged forgiveness. Asked why he had so suddenly changed his tune, he related the vision in detail, on oath. His tears, the result of the sincerity of his prayers, guaranteed the truth of the story, and the weals raised across his shoulders attested that he had seen something real and felt something hard. He easily won the forgiveness of the holy man, and at his blessing health returned and all pain vanished.

Let antiquity then win credence from modern instances, and be freed of all doubts. For in the case of St Jerome it exhibits for us a similar event. 6. There is little difference between Jerome being scourged for reading heathen books and Winrich for taking it upon himself to get preaching stopped. It is much the same to neglect holy scripture in favour of heathen nonsense and to wish it not to be proclaimed.[1]

That was the time when Wulfstan was working at a structure on the church[2] roof for bells to hang in—I do not have the exact word available for such a thing.[3] Anyway, to further the work he made ladders for the men to stand on and steady their steps as they hung in mid-air. And now the ladders, which had been sent up by rope, stood there in some number, menacing the heavens with their height,[4] so that each group of workmen could carry out its allotted

---

glossed by Ælfric as 'cloccarium'; *ODML* s. v. 'clocarium' ('campanarium', 'campanile' are only attested later than William's day). What he is describing here is a bellcote, a small structure on a church roof in which bells were hung. Early churches with this feature are Anglo-Saxon Escomb (Co. Durham: Taylor and Taylor, *Anglo-Saxon Architecture*, i. 234–8, ii. pl. 463) and romanesque Adel (outside Leeds: N. Pevsner, *Yorkshire: The West Riding* (The Buildings of England: 2nd edn., Harmondsworth, 1967), pp. 338–9 and pl. 4(a)). In each case the structure is situated above the gable at the west end. We are grateful to Christine Rauer for help with this note.

[4] Cf. *GR*, c. 249. 3: 'turres proceritate sua in caelum minantes'. Probably a reminiscence of Gildas, c. 3. 2: 'nonnullis castellis, murorum turrium serratarum portarum domorum, quarum culmina minaci proceritate porrecta in edito forti compage pangebantur', or Aldhelm, *De virg.* (*prosa*), c. 47 (ed. Ehwald, p. 301 lines 4–5), itself based on Gildas.

7. Quorum unus audatior, dum ceteris preruptius*ª* arduos meditaretur ascensus, preceps ruit. Astabat eminus Sanctus, et dum ille longum per inane uolueretur crucem calamitati opposuit. Tu affuisti, Christe, miraculo, tu affuisti ruentis miseriae ut manum subiceres,*ᵇ* Rex*ᶜ* misericordiae. Casus enim ab altitudine pedum ad minus quadraginta non solum corpus non attriuit sed nec etiam animum frigente sanguine ut solet hebetauit. Surrexit ergo incolumis, suae quidem reputans temeritati quod cecidit, sed Wlstani sanctitati quod euasit. Cuius presentiam si fortuna subtraxisset, non solum unam, sed, ut uulgo dicitur, si centum haberet animas efflasset.[1] Poteram per amplificationem miraculum istud exponere, sed insulsum*ᵈ* est exaggerare uerba ubi ammirationem sui res exigit ipsa.

9. Interea rex Eduardus Aldredum episcopum Coloniam ad seniorem imperatorem Henricum direxit,[2] quaedam negotia quorum cognitionem causa non flagitat compositurum. Qui cum in imperatoriae augustae dignationis oculis inuenisset gratiam, aliquot ibi dierum continuatione laborum suorum accepit pausam. Ei seu pro sui reuerentia seu quia tanti regis legatus esset, multi multa, quidam sacramentarium et psalterium de quibus supra dixi[3] dedit in xenium. Ambos enim codices, ut suae memoriae apud illas gentes locaret gratiam, Cnuto quondam miserat Coloniam.[4] Aldredus ergo prophetiae quondam Wlstano dictae ignarus, patriam cum renauigasset, libros pro merito uitae illi soli competere arbitratus restituit. Suscepit ille caeleste depositum, magnifice gratulatus et gratias agens Deo quod religioso non fraudaretur desiderio.

10.[5] Eadem tempestate,[6] cum Kinesius Eboracensis archiepiscopus diem clausisset, Aldredus Wigornensis episcopus successioni accla-

---

ª δ *HR* (*p. 74*); proruptuis C   *ᵇ* [*Darl.*]; subieceras C (*the last seven letters in* ras.*)   *ᶜ* [*Peile*]; res C   *ᵈ* insulsum C, *app. corrected from* insultum

---

[1] We have been unable to find a parallel for this expression.

[2] Henry III (1039–56). The journey is recorded by John of Worcester and *ASC* (D) s.a. 1054. Ealdred was sent to negotiate the return of Edward son of Edmund Ironside to England from Hungary. On his embassy, which lasted for about a year from July 1054, see J. Nelson, 'The rites of the Conqueror', in her *Politics and Ritual in Early Medieval Europe* (London, 1986), pp. 375–401, at 391–3, and M. Lapidge, 'Ealdred of York and MS. Cotton Vitellius E. XII', in *Anglo-Latin Literature 900–1066*, pp. 453–67, at 460–5. It was perhaps on this visit that Ealdred obtained a copy of the influential 'Romano-German Pontifical', now BL Cotton Vitellius E. xii, fos. 116–60. Cambridge, Corpus Christi Coll. MS 163, is a copy of its exemplar, made at Worcester in Wulfstan's time for a nunnery: M. Budny, *Insular, Anglo-Saxon, and Early Anglo-Norman Manuscript Art at Corpus Christi*

task. 7. One of the men in his foolhardiness was essaying the difficult ascent more hastily than the rest when he fell headlong. The holy man was there to help, though at some distance, and while the man spun all that way through space he pitted the Cross against the calamity. You, Christ, were present to work a miracle, you were there as the poor wretch came down, ready to place your hand beneath him, King of Mercy. For the fall, from a height of at least forty feet, not only did not shatter the man's body; it did not even knock him out by the chilling of his blood, as normally happens. So he got up unharmed, blaming his own heedlessness for the fall and giving Wulfstan's holiness the credit for his escape. If Wulfstan had chanced not to be there, the man would have lost not a single life; he would, as the saying goes, have lost a hundred if he had had them to lose.[1] I could have exaggerated this miracle in the telling; but it is uncouth to pile on the words when the bare fact makes one astonished.

9. Meanwhile King Edward sent Bishop Ealdred to Cologne to the elder emperor Henry,[2] to settle certain matters which it is not to my present purpose to explain. Finding grace in the eyes of the august emperor, he stayed a few days there to rest from his labours. He received many presents from many people, out of respect for himself, or because he represented so great a king, and in particular the sacramentary and psalter which I mentioned before.[3] For both books had previously been sent to Cologne by Cnut, to keep his name in favour with those peoples.[4] Ealdred, who did not know of the prophecy uttered to Wulfstan of old, returned home, and, thinking that in view of the merits of his life the books were suitable for him and him only, he gave them back to Wulfstan. He received them as something that Heaven had held in trust for him, showing extreme joy and thanking God that his pious wish had been granted.

10.[5] At the same time,[6] Cynesige archbishop of York ended his days, and Ealdred bishop of Worcester was acclaimed his successor; this

---

College, Cambridge: An Illustrated Catalogue (2 vols.: Kalamazoo, 1998), i. 593–8; M. Gullick, 'The origin and date of Cambridge, Corpus Christi College MS 163', *Transactions of the Cambridge Bibliographical Society*, xi (1998), 89–91.

[3] i. 1. 4.

[4] They must, then, have been splendid books if it was thought that they would make such an impression.

[5] The story of Ealdred's journey to Rome is told in more detail in *GP*, c. 115 (pp. 251–2); for example, it is there said that he was accompanied by the bps. of Wells and Hereford.

[See page 42 for n. 5 cont. and n. 6]

matur. Id Eduardo regi simplicis quippe animae bene uisum. Ille Romam pro more profectus, Nicholaum tunc temporis papam[1] uotis suis primo abhorrentem inuenit. Nam nec ille Wigornensi presulatui renuntiare nec papa nisi cederet Eboracensi eum pallio insignire uolebat; adeo illum amor Wigorniae[2] deuinxerat ut maioris honoris nomen eius pretio supponeret. Diu igitur multumque conflictu habito, Aldredus reflexo pede Sutrium[3] uenit, Tostino comite[4] qui cum eo uenerat magnas efflante minas quod nummi quos Anglia quotannis Romano papae pensitat hac occasione ulterius non inferrentur.[5] 2. Veruntamen predonibus irruentibus,[6] usque ad dolorem et miserationem uidentium nudati, Romam redire contendunt. Quae res rigorem apostolicae sedis hactenus inflexit ut Aldredus pallium mereretur Eboracense Wigornensis aecclesiae discessionem pactus, meliori dumtaxat persona quae in eius diocesi posset inueniri ab eo in illam subroganda. Huius igitur conditionis arbitros et quaedam alia aecclesiastica negotia in Anglia expedituros cardinales[7] adductos archiepiscopus regi exhibuit. Excepit eos Deo deuotissimus princeps more illo suo paucis imitabili,[8] quo soleret in omnibus aecclesiae Romanae conuenire moribus. 3. Ita summa reuerentia honore summo apud se aliquandiu habitos iterum ductoris tutelae delegauit. Familiarius enim ei conuiuerent cuius mores longo comitatu addidicissent[a] et commertia linguae[9] non ignorarent, denuo ad curiam in Pascha reducendi. Aldredus, apostolici precepti tenorem secutus omnemque pene Angliam cum eis peruagatus, imminente Quadragesima in Wigorniam pedem reflexit. Inde in predia sui iuris

---

[a] Whar.; addidiscissent C

Wulfstan's promotion to the bishopric of Worcester is recounted, more briefly, in GP, c. 139 (p. 280). There more initiative is credited to Ealdred, who is said to have been motivated by his belief that he would easily be able to control the guileless and inexperienced Wulfstan. The main initiative is also given him in Hemingi Chartularium ii. 405–6, and there too he is said to have noted Wulfstan's guilelessness, but in a positive sense.

[6] 'Eadem tempestate' is wrongly used. William presumably intended to link only the death of Cynesige and appointment of Ealdred, not to link both of these events to Ealdred's embassy to Cologne six years earlier. Cynesige d. 22 Dec. 1060; Ealdred was appointed soon after (Mason, p. 72), dying in 1069.

[1] Pope Nicholas II (1058/9–1061). See JW s.aa. 1060–1.
[2] This apparent justification of flagrant pluralism may have been intended ironically.
[3] See Vita Ædwardi, pp. 52–3 and nn. 128–9, 131. In fact the embassy transacted a great variety of business. The most pressing issue was doubtless the state of the English Church in general, especially the position of Archbishop Stigand.
[4] Brother of Harold Godwinesson: F. E. Harmer, Anglo-Saxon Writs (2nd edn., Stamford, 1989), p. 575.

seemed the proper course to King Edward, that straightforward soul. In accordance with custom, Ealdred went off to Rome, to find Nicholas, the current pope,[1] at first reluctant to accede to his wishes. Ealdred was unwilling to renounce the bishopric of Worcester, and if he did not the pope was unwilling to distinguish him with the pallium of York. Love of Worcester[2] had so captivated him that he prized it higher than the grander name of York. After a long struggle, Ealdred turned back to Sutri,[3] accompanied by Earl Tostig,[4] who had come with him and on this pretext was now huffing and puffing with threats that the money paid yearly by England to the pope of Rome would not be forthcoming any longer.[5] 2. But the party was attacked by robbers[6] and stripped naked, to the sorrow and outrage of those who saw them, and had to come back in haste to Rome. This circumstance so far softened the hard line of the pope that Ealdred got his pallium for York after agreeing to leave Worcester, so long as he replaced himself at Worcester with the best person to be found in the diocese. To bear witness to the fulfilment of this condition, and to transact other church business in England, Ealdred took with him certain cardinals,[7] and presented them to Edward. The king, devoted as ever to God, received them in his characteristic and more or less inimitable way,[8] striving as usual to adapt himself in all respects to the customs of the church of Rome. 3. He kept them with him for some while, showing them the greatest respect and honour, and then gave them back to the care of their escort: they would feel more comfortable with someone whom they had come to know well on their long journey together, and who knew their language;[9] and they could be brought back to court at Easter. Ealdred kept to the letter of the apostolic precept, and travelled over almost all England with them, returning to Worcester when Lent was approaching. Then he went off to certain estates in his jurisdiction,

---

[5] i.e. Peter's Pence. See H. R. Loyn, 'Peter's Pence', in his *Society and Peoples: Studies in the History of England and Wales, c.600–1200* (London, 1992), pp. 241–58.

[6] Their leader was identified by Plummer in *Two Saxon Chronicles* ii. 250, as Count Gerard of Galeria. His attack on the Englishmen is also mentioned by Peter Damian in his *Disceptatio synodalis* (*Monumenta Germaniae Historica, Libelli de Lite* i. 91). The pope excommunicated him for it.

[7] According to JW s.a. 1062 (iii. 590–1) there were two of them, one being Ermenfrid, bp. of Sion. In 1070, as legate of Pope Alexander II, he was present at the Council at Winchester at which Archbishop Stigand was deposed (JW s.a.).

[8] Perhaps pointed, more recent monarchs not having been very good at this, according to William's ideas: *GP*, cc. 49 (pp. 85–91), 52–5 (pp. 97–104 and n. 1), 56–60 (pp. 106–15).

[9] Cf. *Mir.*, p. 93 line 838 and below, ii. 12. 2.

profectus stabilem eis mansionem apud Wlstanum priorem indixit.[1]
Illi consilium non aspernati libenter in otium concesserunt, post uiae
labores pausae adquiescentes. Aderat eis humanitas hospitis nichil
pretermittentis quo minus Anglorum dapsilem liberalitatem et
liberalem dapsilitatem experirentur. 4. Ipse interea, et solitae orationis instantiam et ciborum inediam non oblitus, propositum pertinaciter urgebat: totis noctibus psalmicinas[2] protelans excubias, genua
crebro flectens, somno penitus illudens. Tribus in ebdomada diebus
omnis cibi abstemius, noctem perinde ac lucem continuabat ieiunio;
ipsis etiam diebus, ne ullo saltem laberetur uerbo, perpetuo linguam
cohibebat silentio. Tribus reliquis porros caulesue coctos uel elixos
†panis cibaria† aditiens[a] uictum transigebat. Dominicis porro propter
festi reuerentiam pisce uinoque frugalitatis parsimoniam soluebat,
magis ut contineret naturam quam deliniret gulam: singulis preterea
diebus tres pauperes affectuose colens, quibus Dominici sequax
mandati et uictum cotidianum et pedum exhibebat lauacrum.[3]

11. Haec cardinalibus fuerunt incitamento ut eius mirarentur uitam,
laudarent doctrinam: quam reuerentiorem fatiebat dum anticiparet
exemplo quod predicaret uerbo. Denique ad curiam reuersi, dum
Wigornensis episcopi uentilaretur electio, nomen eius tulerunt in
medium: eum antistitio dignum qui sacerdotio plus uenerationis
adiceret quam ipse per illud dignitatis acciperet, cuius responderet
natura industriae, in quo conquadraret uita sapientiae. Eam enim esse
demum sapientiam, si bene uiuas, si dicta factis preuenias. 2. His
laudibus suscitauerunt †maiorem uiri†[b] animum Eduardi regis, in
cuius pectore nichil umquam nundinator aecclesiarum, nichil
umquam deprehendit auarus quod suis conduceret artibus.[4] Astipu-
labantur uotis cardinalium archiepiscopi Cantuariensis[5] et Eboracensis, ille fauore, iste testimonio, ambo iuditio. Accedebant laudibus
etiam comites Haroldus et Elgarus,[6] par insigne fortitudinis, non ita
religionis: ingens momentum causae facti,[7] adeo ut certatim concitatis equitibus pro Wlstano mitteretur. Nuntii breui multa miliaria

---

[a] *Read something like* elixos ⟨comedendo⟩, panem cibarium aditiens   [b] maiorem
uiri] *Reuter conjectures* maiore ui

---

[1] With 'Huius igitur conditionis . . . indixit' cf. JW s.a. 1062 'Contigit nanque . . .
proximi pasce.'
[2] The adjective 'psalmicinus' appears to be a hapax legomenon; see *GR*, c. 204. 4 n.
[3] John 13: 14 (and, for 'panem cotidianum', Luke 11: 3).
[4] *Mir.*, p. 73 line 303 (where Canal is wrong to read 'condiceret').

and appointed them a fixed abode with Prior Wulfstan.[1] They took this advice, and were glad to enjoy some relaxation after their hard travelling. Their host treated them kindly, omitting nothing that would give them an idea of the lavish liberality and liberal lavishness of the English. 4. Wulfstan meanwhile did not forget to press on with his customary prayers and fasting, and stuck rigidly to his principles, staying awake for whole nights to sing psalms,[2] frequently genuflecting, and making utter mock of the claims of sleep. Three days a week he abstained from all food, continuing his fast for twenty-four hours, while during the day he curbed his tongue to complete silence, for fear he should make a slip even in a single word. On the other three weekdays he supported life on leek or cabbage, cooked or boiled, together with coarse bread. On Sundays, to mark the festival, he would relax his frugal diet so far as to take fish and wine, rather to keep body and soul together than to pander to his appetites. Further, he every day lavished affectionate attention on three poor persons, following our Lord's command by giving them their daily bread and washing their feet.[3]

11. All this caused the cardinals to admire his way of life and to praise his teaching, which he made the more worthy of respect by practising what he preached. In the end, when they were back at court and the election of the bishop of Worcester was under discussion, they brought up Wulfstan's name. Well worthy of a bishopric, they said, was one who brought the priesthood more cause for veneration than he received from it in the way of prestige; whose qualities were matched by his application, his life by his wisdom: for true wisdom is to live an upright life and act before you speak. 2. These praises made a deep impression (?) on King Edward, in whose heart no trafficker in churches, no profiteer ever found anything that suited their ways.[4] The cardinals' prayers were backed by the archbishops of Canterbury[5] and York, the one with support, the other with evidence, both with considered judgement. Two earls joined in the chorus of praise, Harold and Ælfgar,[6] a pair remarkable for bravery, if not for piety; and their support carried such weight[7] that horseman were sent off hot-foot to summon Wulfstan. The messengers travelled many miles in a short time, and their conscientiousness spurred on their

---

[5] Stigand, archbp. 1052–70.
[6] Earl of Mercia 1057–d. ?1062. See Harmer, *Anglo-Saxon Writs*, pp. 546–7; Mason, p. 81; Barlow in *Vita Aedwardi*, p. 77 n. 190.
[7] Cf. *GR*, c. 376. 1: 'ingens momentum desolatis futurus'.

progressi stimulis industriae celeritatem maturauere negotii. Sanctus ergo ad curiam exhibitus iubetur suscipere donum episcopatus. Contra ille niti, et se honori tanto imparem cunctis reclamantibus clamitare. 3. Adeo concors populus in unam uenerat sententiam ut non peccaret qui diceret in tot corporibus unam in hoc dumtaxat negotio conflatam esse animam. Sed ut multos uerborum circuitus in summam conferam, frustra cardinales cum archiepiscopis triuissent operam nisi refugienti pretendissent papae obedientiam. Qua ille obiecta confusus cessit, et assensus est electioni, merens, inuitus, impulsus. Preclare meritoque obstinatio unius uiri cessit hic uoluntati Dei et populi. Prouectum autem eius non temere uoluntatem Dei dixerim, qui numquam contrarium intenderit et fortuitu commissa fructuosa penitentia[1] diluerit. 4. Illud sane non omiserim, fuisse tunc apud Euesham abbatem Ailwium nomine,[2] maximae quantum ad seculum prudentiae, quantum ad religionem non minimae. Quocirca sepedictus Aldredus, pro pacto quod fecerat Apostolico, nonnullo tempore fluctuauerat animo utrum ad episcopatum eligeret Ailwii perspicacem industriam in seculo an Wlstani simplicem religionem in Deo. Erant enim illi uiri Wigornensis diocesis diuerso respectu prestantissimi. Veruntamen multum hinc indeque libratis causis, quanuis Ailwius sollicite anniteretur partibus, succubuerunt diuinae prouidentiae humanarum prestigiarum cautelae.[3]

12. Rex ergo Eduardus Wlstanum Wigornensi episcopatu ex solido inuestiuit, licet illum Aldredus potentia qua uigebat multis et pene omnibus, ut post clarebit, prediis uellicauerit.[4] Id Sanctus licet egre, ut postea ostendit, ferret, tamen dolorem silentio suppressit, cedendum tempori arbitratus. Non multo autem post consecratus est Eboraci ab eodem archiepiscopo, quod Cantuariensi Stigando Romanus papa interdixisset offitio.[5] Causam interdictionis non est huius

---

[1] Cf. Luke 3: 8.

[2] Æthelwig (1058–77). On him see *Chronicon abbatiae de Evesham*, ed. W. D. Macray (RS, 1863), pp. 87–96; R. R. Darlington, 'Aethelwig, abbot of Evesham', *EHR* xlviii (1933), 1–22, 177–98. His skill and experience in worldly matters are also noted in *Hemingi Chartularium* i. 270–3 (in contrast to Wulfstan); but Hemming also tells of an extraordinary miracle associated with Wulfstan, illustrative of the bitter memory Æthelwig left at Worcester because of his successful abstraction of some of its estates.

[3] Wulfstan's Lenten austerities, described in 10. 4, and the account of Wulfstan's election in 11, are summarized by JW s.a. 1062.

[4] Also c. 13 and ii. 1 below. Archbishop Wulfstan of York (1002–23), previously and for some time simultaneously bishop of Worcester, was remembered by the monks as a despoiler of their property because he appropriated some of their estates to his new see; Archbishop Ealdred retained the same lands on his translation from Worcester to York: JW s.a. 1070 (iii.

business to a swift conclusion. So the holy man made his appearance at court, and was told to take up the offer of the see. He objected, and cried out—while all the rest shouted back their disagreement—that he was not up to so great an honour. 3. The people were so united in a single view that it would not be wrong to say that in this one matter all those bodies had but a single soul. But to cut a complicated story short, the cardinals and archbishops would have wasted their time if they had not thought to point out to the reluctant Wulfstan his duty of obedience to the pope. He was confounded by this objection, yielded, and agreed to his election, sorrowful, unwilling, and under compulsion. It was right and good that one man's obstinacy should give way on this occasion to the will of God and people. And I should not be rash to call his advancement the will of God, for Wulfstan never meant to resist it, and made up by a fruitful penitence[1] for something he had done unwittingly. 4. I should not fail to record that at Evesham the abbot at this time was Æthelwig,[2] a man of great good sense in worldly affairs and not a little in religious. This was why Ealdred, bearing in mind the deal he had done with the pope, had for a while been undecided whether to choose as bishop Æthelwig, the clear-sighted and hard-working man of business, or Wulfstan, the straightforward man of God. These, in any case, were in their different ways the two outstanding men of the diocese of Worcester. But after much balancing of the candidates' claims, and despite Æthelwig's pressure in his own interest, the prudent stratagems of man gave way to the providence of God.[3]

12. King Edward therefore invested Wulfstan with the bishopric without reservation, though Ealdred used his considerable influence, as will appear, to rob him of many, indeed almost all, of his estates.[4] As he showed later, the holy man bitterly resented this, but he kept his peace, suppressing his feelings on the principle that he must yield to circumstances. Not much later he was consecrated at York by this same archbishop, for the pope of Rome had banned Stigand archbishop of Canterbury from officiating.[5] The reason for the ban

---

12–13); *GP*, c. 139 (p. 280); Mason, pp. 24 n. 111, 86–7. For more of William's thoughts about bishops of Worcester who became archbishops of York, see *GP*, c. 115 (pp. 248–52).

[5] Similarly JW s.a. 1062: 'Consecratus est igitur episcopus a uenerando Aldredo, Eboracensium archiepiscopo, eo quod Stigando Dorubernie archiepiscopo officium episcopale tunc a domno apostolico interdictum erat'. Nonetheless, JW goes on to claim that Wulfstan made his canonical profession to Stigand. On the reason for this implausible statement (to deny Abp. Thomas of York support for his claim to jurisdiction over Worcester) see Williams, 'The cunning of the dove' (above, p. xxviii n. 95).

temporis allegare; scire uolentem alias[1] nostrae docebunt litterae. Nec uero sine diuino nutu credi fas est prognosticon hoc ei fuisse: 'Ecce uere Israelita, in quo dolus non est!'[2] 2. Nichil enim uerius experietur qui eius conuersationem uiderit, audierit, legerit. Ipse porro impositionem episcopatus adeo ingrate tulit ut diceret, sicut qui presentes fuere testantur, maluisse se decapitari quam illud onus pati.[3] Adeo ad quaeque deuia terrarum profecto preparasset fugam, nisi quidam amici suspectam adhibuissent diligentiam. Enimuero animabant deiectum merore animum hi blanditiis, illi monitis: blanditiis, genibus eius et pedibus reuerenter affusi, nonnumquam etiam osculabundi; monitis, ne caeleste munus gratuito infusum impatientia decoloraret, sed tolerantia insigniret. Obedientiam uirtutum omnium esse signaculum, cui qui refragandum putaret nec digne haberetur claustralis monachus nec popularis episcopus. 3. Quocirca non solum modeste ferret, uerum et Deo gratias ageret, qui eum sullimasset in gradum per quem inferioribus uellet esse consultum. Haec illi. Nec uero dubitandum est ingenti sanctum pectus sudasse conflictu, dum in eo aequas partes facerent et huc illucque raptarent hinc amor inde timor,[4] iste ne sub insueto labaret onere, ille ne tot probabilium uirorum imperiosae auctoritati et populorum religosae deuotioni uideretur resultare. Enimuero quanto sibi uidebatur indignior, tanto erat acclamatio pertinatior, dum fidem prouide amministrandi muneris faceret idem*a* quod ad amministrandum meticulosus accederet. Stulti enim est ad illud se inconsiderate ingerere quod ignoret quanti sit laboris expedire.

13. Ordinatus ergo, ut dicere ceperam, et sub pretextu honoris Eboraci ab Aldredo relictus, non pauco tempore Wigorniam absentia sua contristauit. Eius interim aecclesiae redditus usibus suis applicabat archiepiscopus.[5] Postmodum reuerso uix septem uillas contulit,

---

a One expects id ipsum

[1] 'alias' means 'in other works', 'elsewhere' (so also *VD* ii. prol. 1), referring to *GR*, c. 199. 10–11, *GP*, c. 23 (pp. 35–7).

[2] John 1: 47. The story is also in *GP*, c. 139 (p. 280). JW s.a. 1062 (ii. 590–3) does not mention the *prognosticon*. It was recorded, apparently independently of *VW*, in the list of prognostics in Cambridge, Trinity Coll. R. 7. 5, fos. 250v–1, compiled after 1123: G. Henderson, '*Sortes biblicae* in twelfth-century England: the list of episcopal prognostics in Cambridge, Trinity College MS R. 7. 5', in *England in the Twelfth Century: Proceedings of the 1988 Harlaxton Symposium*, ed. D. Williams (Woodbridge, 1990), pp. 113–35, esp. 116, 131.

[3] With 'Ipse porro . . . pati' cf. JW s.a. 1062 'Illo uero obstinatissime renuente . . .

is irrelevant at this point; anyone who wishes to know it may consult other writings of mine.[1] But it is entirely right to believe that it was not without God's will that Wulfstan's prognostic was: 'Behold an Israelite indeed, in whom is no guile!'[2] 2. For anyone who has heard, seen, or read of his way of life will agree that no words could be more true. Wulfstan, however, was so bitter about the way in which the bishopric had been thrust upon him that he said (so eyewitnesses testified) that he would have preferred to be beheaded than have to put up with this burden.[3] Indeed he would for sure have made off to some remote spot if friends had not taken pains with him which he thought excessive. They cheered him up in his depression by coaxing and by advice. The coaxing took the form of respectful prayers at his knees and feet, and sometimes even kisses. The advice was that he should not let his impatience spoil a gift given him freely by Heaven, but add lustre to it by his willingness to bear it. Obedience was the seal of all the virtues, and anyone who thought to kick against it did not deserve to be either a cloister monk or a bishop of the people. 3. So he should not merely take it cheerfully: he should give thanks to God for raising him to a position by means of which He wished benefit to accrue to those inferior to him. That was their advice. But there is no doubt at all that the holy man's breast sweated in a titanic conflict, love and fear equally balanced, and pulling him now one way, now the other:[4] fear that he might fail under an unaccustomed load, love prompting him not to appear to be opposing the orders and the authority of so many prestigious persons and the devoted piety of the people. The unworthier he seemed in his own eyes, the more persistent the cries of the rest; and the fact that he felt trepidation in approaching the job seemed proof of his being likely to do it with prudence: only a fool would rush headlong into something without knowing the trouble it would involve.

13. As I began to say, Wulfstan was ordained by Ealdred, and left at York on the pretext of doing him an honour. For no short period he saddened Worcester by his absence, while the archbishop diverted the revenues of the church to his own purposes.[5] When Wulfstan

---

succumbere uelle.' John of Worcester adds that his obstinacy was reproved, and his mind changed, by the admonition of a recluse named Wulfsige.

[4] Cf. Ovid, *Heroides* xii. 61: 'hinc amor, hinc timor est.'

[5] See above, 12. 1. The unfavourable view of him expressed here and in JW s.a. 1070 (iii. 12–13 and n. 2) must be balanced by other evidence: *Vita Aedwardi*, p. 52 n. 130; the anon. twelfth-century 'Chronicle of the Archbishops of York', in *HCY* ii. 344–54. For

ceteras omnes pertinaciter usurpans. At Wlstanus, qui nichil apud eum uiribus agendum nosset, ita paulatim precibus arrogantis animi cupiditatem contudit ut cuncta preter duodecim uillas iuri aecclesiae reformaret.[1] Eas quo tempore et quali labore pater noster retraxerit, sequens stilus edocebit.[2]

14. Sed ut ad id quod exorsus fueram regrediar, Wlstanus in episcopum sullimatus statim ad offitia pietatis animum intendit. Nec mora in medio: altera enim ordinationis die beato Bedae dedicauit aecclesiam,[3] pulchre illi primae dedicationis prebens principium, qui fuisset litteraturae princeps de gente Anglorum.[4] Eo enim die tam proflua predicatione populum irrorauit ut non dubitaretur Wlstanum per Spiritum sanctum eadem niti facundia quae quondam linguam mouisset in Beda. Nec solum tunc sed et omni uita ita fama predicationis plebem mulcebat ut cateruatim eo uideres agmina confluere quo auditum esset eum aecclesiam ded- icare. 2. Ipse quoque ultro rapiebat materiam ut semper Christum sonaret, semper Christum auditoribus proponeret, postremo Chris- tum etiam, ut ita dicam, repugnantem parti suae attraheret. Ita enim obstinate insistebat ieiuniis et uigiliis, ita uiolentas orationes initiebat caelo, ut non immerito de ipso eiusque sequacibus Dominus dixerit 'Regnum caelorum uim patitur, et uiolenti rapiunt illud'.[5] Tanto aequilibrio uitam informans ut utramque professio- nem teneret et neutram amitteret: sic episcopus ut religione non abiuraret monachum, sic monachus ut auctoritate representaret episcopum.[6] Remotissimus ab hominum moribus quos nostra

---

modern comment, see Lapidge, 'Ealdred of York and MS. Cotton Vitellius E. XII', pp. 453–67; J. M. Cooper, *The Last Four Anglo-Saxon Archbishops of York* (Borthwick Papers, xxxviii: York, 1970), pp. 23–9; V. J. King, 'Ealdred, archbishop of York: the Worcester years', *ANS* xviii (1996), 123–37. The views reflected in JW and *VW* are not found in the documents or commentary in Hemming's Cartulary: see N. R. Ker, 'Hemming's Cartulary', in his *Books, Collectors and Libraries*, pp. 31–66; S. Keynes, 'Hemming', in *Blackwell Encyclopaedia*, pp. 231–2. On the contrary, Hemming honoured Ealdred as the main backer of Wulfstan's promotion, and as a donor of property to the monks of Worcester: *Hemingi Chartularium* ii. 395–6, 405–6. However, the same record represents Abbot Æthelwig of Evesham as having abstracted no fewer than seven Worcester manors: *Hemingi Chartularium* i. 272–3, 279 (and see below, p. 60 n. 8). One wonders whether later Worcester tradition, reflected by Coleman, William, and John of Worcester, saw fit to transfer the sin of a fellow-monk (Æthelwig) to a secular cleric (Ealdred). This might constitute an argument for dating the writing of Coleman's Life as late as possible (i. e. not long before his death in 1113).

[1] Similarly *GP*, c. 139 (p. 280). The twelve manors are also mentioned by Hugh the Chanter, *The History of the Church of York*, ed. and trans. C. Johnson, rev. M. Brett,

eventually returned he gave him scarce seven vills, obstinately
keeping hold of the rest for himself. Wulfstan knew that there was
nothing to be done with him by force, but gradually his prayers wore
down the arrogant greed of Ealdred, who restored all but twelve vills
to the jurisdiction of the church.[1] When our father won them back,
and the trouble he had to take, will be told later.[2]

14. But to return to the story I embarked on: Wulfstan immediately
on his elevation as bishop put his mind to works of piety. There was
no delay: the day after his ordination he dedicated a church to the
blessed Bede,[3] an excellent choice for his first dedication, for Bede
had been the prince of English letters.[4] That day Wulfstan's flow of
preaching so watered the people that it was not in doubt that he owed
to the Holy Spirit his command of an eloquence that had once moved
the tongue of Bede. And indeed all his life long, not just on this
occasion, the people were so seduced by the report of his preaching
that you might have seen them flocking in droves wherever it was
reported he was to dedicate a church. 2. For his part, he went out of
his way to collect material that would enable him always to speak of
Christ, always to put Christ before his hearers, and finally to bring
Christ over to his side even (if I may so put it) when Christ was
reluctant. For he persevered with such determination in fasts and
vigils, and flung such violent prayers at Heaven, that it was not
without reason that the Lord said of him and his followers: 'The
kingdom of heaven suffereth violence, and the violent take it by
force.'[5] His life kept so fine a balance that he held to both professions
without losing either: he was the bishop without abjuring the monk in
his religious practice, and the monk while preserving a bishop's
authority.[6] He was far removed indeed from the ways of the men

C. N. L. Brooke, and M. Winterbottom (OMT, 1990), pp. 2–3. Williams, 'The cunning of
the dove', suggests that they were the episcopal manors, of which there were precisely that
number.   [2] ii. 1.
    [3] This dedication to Bede is the only early one known: D. H. Farmer, *The Oxford
Dictionary of Saints* (Oxford, 3rd edn., 1992), p. 44. Only three other dedications to Bede,
all much later than this, are listed in F. Arnold-Forster, *Studies in Church Dedications* (3
vols.: London, 1899), ii. 60–6, iii. 343 (none of them in Worcestershire).
    [4] See *GR* I index s. v. 'Bede' for references to similar eulogies by William.
    [5] Matt. 11: 12.
    [6] For earlier examples of this hagiographical topos, see N. Wright, 'Alfred burns the
cakes: the *Vita prima Sancti Neoti*, *telesinus*, and Juvenal', in his *History and Literature in
Late Antiquity and the Early Medieval West* (Variorum Collected Studies Ser., diii:
Aldershot, 1995), XV, p. 3. Also i. 2. 3 above.

producunt secula:[1] si consuleretur consiliosissimus, si rogaretur
facillimus; (3) cum aliquid esset impetrandum absolute deliberans,
celeriter pronuntians, cum iudicandum, ad iustitiam propensior, nec
diuitem palpans pro pecunia nec pauperem pulsans pro penuria;
nulli adulationi deditus nec sibi adulantibus gratus; timore principum numquam a iustitia decedens, numquam amori eorum honore
aliquo nisi debito assurgens. Laudatus de bono indulgebat Dei
gratiae, non suae arrogantiae. Vituperatus ignoscebat uituperantium
errori, conscientiae suae gratulatus: quamquam id raro admodum
fuerit, quia, cum ipse omnem hominem amore caritatis foueret ut
sobolem, uicissim omnes eum diligebant ut parentem. 4. Cordis
alacritate et hilaritate fatiei superna prelibans gaudia, iam caelestis
laetitiae fontem spe presumebat, quem nunc re indefitienter haurit
et potat. Qui quanuis semper animo intimis hereret, non tamen eum
segnem aut hebetem in extimis homines experti sunt. Plures in
omni diocesi basilicae per eum inchoatae animose et egregie
perfectae,[2] presertimque episcopalis sedis aecclesia, cui a fundamentis ceptae supremam imposuit manum,[3] ubi et numerus monachorum ampliatus et ad normam institutionis regularis compositus.[4]
Sed haec et postmodum facta et cotidie oculis apposita compendio-
sam relationem desiderant. Quocirca, ut in campo liberioris materiae nostra decurrat oratio, reliquarum[a] rerum ordinem expedito
prosequamur otio.[5]

15. Preter alia quibus presulatum ornabat, etiam hoc habebat,
diocesim sedulo peragrare, infantibus quod reliquum esset sacramen-
torum[6] supplere, fidem populorum in bonum acuere. Oratorium
quodcumque se uianti obtulisset nulla uel precipiti necessitate
urgente preteribat insalutatum,[7] quin immo ingressus Deo et sancto

---

[a] *Whar.*; reliquiarum C

[1] For other disapproving comments by William on the clerical morals of his day, see
GR, cc. 314, 338–9, *GP*, cc. 68, 73, 90, 122 (pp. 127, 145 and n. 5, 195 and nn., 263 n. 2).
[2] *VW* alone records seven such instances: here, ii. 9. 1, 15. 1, 17. 1, 22. 1, iii. 10. 1–2, 15. 1.
[3] See Wright, '"Industriae Testimonium"; William of Malmesbury and Latin poetry
revisited', *Revue Bénédictine* ciii (1993), 482–531, at p. 496 n. 56, for William's use of the
expression 'summam/supremam manum imponere', probably derived from Lucan v. 483–4.
[4] Wulfstan's famous Alveston Charter of 20 May 1089 mentions an increase in the number
of monks from just over a dozen to fifty: *The Cartulary of Worcester Cathedral Priory
(Register I)*, ed. R. R. Darlington (Pipe Roll Soc., n.s. xxxviii: London, 1968 for 1962–3),
p. 8 no. 3. The early twelfth-century chapter-house provided seating for ninety-five monks,
but only sixty-two appear as benefactors in the Durham *Liber uitae* of *c*.1104: Atkins II,
pp. 212–13, 218–20. For Wulfstan's new church, see below, p. 122 and n. 3.

produced in our century.[1] If he was asked his advice, he was excellent at giving it; if he was begged for something, he was ready to listen. 3. When a request had to be considered, he was thorough in his deliberation but swift to come to a view. When judgement had to be given, he leaned towards justice, neither flattering the rich for the sake of money, nor oppressing the poor because of their poverty. He was not given to flattery, and showed no favour to those who flattered him. He never turned aside from what was just for fear of princes, and never responded to their love for him by giving them more honour than was due to them. If he was praised for the good he did, he rejoiced in receiving the grace of God, with no thought for his own pride. If he was criticized, he forgave his critics' error and rejoiced in the knowledge of his own rectitude. But that happened but rarely, for, just as he cherished every man as his own child out of love of charity, so they all in return loved him as a parent. 4. In his lightness of heart and cheerfulness of countenance he had a foretaste of the joys above, and his hope allowed him to draw in advance on the fountain of heavenly pleasure which he now in very fact drains without stint. Though he was constantly concerned with inner things, men did not find him dilatory or sluggish when it came to outer things. Many were the churches throughout the diocese that he began with vigour and completed to an excellent standard,[2] not least his own cathedral, which he started from the foundations and put the finishing touches to,[3] increasing the number of the monks and making them behave in accordance with the Rule.[4] All this, which occurred later and is daily before our eyes, needs only a brief account here. In order then that my story can run free in a field of wider scope, let me at my leisure go through the rest of the tale in order.[5]

15. Besides other ways in which he brought distinction to his office, he was assiduous in travelling through his diocese, giving infants any sacraments[6] they lacked, and spurring the faithful on to good works. No crisis, however urgent, would cause him to leave without a greeting[7] any oratory that he chanced upon in his visitations; but

---

[5] William seems to be saying that, as Wulfstan's building of churches was not restricted to the pre-Conquest period covered by book i (or indeed perhaps all came after the Conquest), and is any case obvious to any reader who looks about him, he does not need to go into detail. In fact, he returns to the topic in iii. 10.

[6] The word seems to imply confirmation rather than baptism: Mason, p. 95 n. 41.

[7] Cf. *Mir.*, p. 98 line 958, *Vita Indracti*, below, p. 370.

cuius esset templum preces cum lacrimis semper, ut quidam ait,[1] in statione paratis thurificabat. Hoc more quadam die, dum ad comitatum euocatus per Euesham iter haberet et sotii obstreperent quo minus ad aecclesiam diuerteret, audire supersedit. Itaque ingressus ante sancti Egwini se prostrauit exuuias,[2] plurimus ibi pro sua suorumque salute precator. 2. Facta oratione, monachos omnes salutatione sua et osculo dignatus salubri etiam predicatione demulsit. Erat ex eodem conuentu monachus cui iam dudum diuturna febris internas depasta medullas[3] morti*[a]* ut putabatur affinem lecto apposuerat. Is*[b]* ut adesse cognouit episcopum misit nuntium qui suas ad eum lacrimas deportaret, quatinus eius mereretur conspectum, priusquam efflaret supremum. Audito nuntio antistes aduentum non excusauit, sed etiam in sotios itineris moram et diei processum pretendentes hoc dictum retorsit: 'Meum est Creatoris mei de uisitando infirmo preceptum implere.[4] Quod si uobis obnitentibus non impleuero, et hic decesserit, preuaricati mandati reus ero.' 3. Simulque cum dicto ad decumbentem ingressus, salutaribus promissis dolorem attenuauit, superstiti penitentiam, abeunti uiaticum pollicitus. Ille, qui nichil*[c]* minus optaret quam penitentia non peracta uita excedere, Sancti applorauit misericordiae, ut ei a Deo*[d]* impetraret commeatum uitae. Mouit Wlstanum egrotantis miseria et desperatio iam conclamata. Totis ergo in misericordiam uisceribus profluus leuansque iuxta prophetam[5] ad Deum cor cum manibus, orauit: 'Deus omnipotens ineffabilis clementiae, per cuius indultum confessio peccata diluit, ante cuius conspectum accusator sui iustus*[e]* efficitur,[6] te supliciter deprecor ut huius infirmi longius protelare digneris uitam, quatinus per penitentiam eius quandoque mundiorem recipias animam.' 4. Dixit, et orationem benedictione condiuit. Vtraque intrarunt in caeli penetralia, ut non moraretur pius Dominus quod fidelis precabatur famulus. Statim enim ut egressus est episcopus egressum est pariter quicquid dolebat languidus. Omnis infirmitas effugit, uigor salutis refusus*[f]* incommodum depulit. Nam

---

[a] morti *Whar. mg.* (*cf. δH*, p. 75*); mori C   *[b]* *ed.*; his C   *[c]* *ed.*; nichilo C
[d] a Deo *ed.*; adeo *Darl.*   *[e]* *ed.* (*cf. Prov. 18: 17*); custus C; custos *Darl.* (*suggesting* insons*)   *[f]* *ed.* (*cf. GP p. 243*); effusus C

[1] Juvenal vi. 273–4.

[2] Ecgwine, bp. of Worcester from after 693 until 717, founder of Evesham abbey: Farmer, *The Oxford Dictionary of Saints*, pp. 153–4, and M. Lapidge, 'The medieval hagiography of St. Ecgwine', *Vale of Evesham Historical Society Research Papers*, vi (1977), 77–93.

[3] Cf. Paulinus of Périgord, *De uita S. Martini* i. 320–1 (CSEL xvi (1), p. 32): 'huic

he would go inside and offer up prayers to God and the patron saint
of the place, accompanying them with tears that were always (as
someone puts it)[1] 'ready at their posts'. It was in accordance with this
principle that one day, when he had been summoned to the shire
court and was passing through Evesham, he refused to listen when his
companions objected to him turning aside to the church. So in he
went, and prostrated himself before the remains of St Ecgwine,[2] with
many a prayer for himself and his people. 2. After praying, he saluted
and kissed all the monks, and gave them the comfort of his beneficial
preaching. Now to this house belonged a monk whose innards had
long been wasted by a fever,[3] which had put him to bed, near, as was
thought, to death. When he heard of the bishop's presence, he sent a
message conveying the tearful request that he be allowed to see him
before he breathed his last. At this news the bishop did not try to find
an excuse not to go to see him, but retorted to his companions when
they pointed out the delay to their journey and the lateness of the
hour: 'It is my duty to obey the commandment of my Creator on the
visiting of the sick.[4] If I do not obey because of your obstruction, and
this man dies, I shall be guilty of the sin of disobedience.' 3. And
with these words he went in to the man, bed-ridden as he was, and to
lessen his distress made promises of salvation: penitence if he lived,
the last sacrament if he was departing. *He* wanted nothing less than to
die without being shriven, and he threw himself on the holy man's
mercy, begging him to obtain the viaticum from God. Wulfstan was
affected by the sick man's wretchedness and his desperate state,
which all now accepted as irremediable. He became all pity, and,
raising (as the prophet says)[5] hand and heart to God, he prayed:
'Almighty God of ineffable clemency, by whose indulgence confession washes away sins, before whose sight the self-accuser is made
just,[6] I humbly beg you, deign to prolong the life of this sick man, so
that by his penitence you may in the end receive his soul in a purer
state.' 4. These were his words, and he flavoured his prayer with a
blessing. Both prayer and blessing found their way within the portals
of heaven, and the merciful Lord did not delay to do what His faithful
servant asked. The moment the bishop departed, there departed too
all the invalid's pain. His sickness quite fled away, health flowed back
into him, driving out all discomfort. Indeed he immediately struggled

febris totas penitus depasta medullas/extorsit . . . uitam.' Also echoed in *VD* i. 3. 1, and
more remotely in *GP*, c. 256 (p. 409): 'medulam [*sic*] mediterranei soli depascebatur'.
  [4] Matt. 25: 36.   [5] Lam. 3: 41.   [6] Prov. 18: 17.

continuo in pedes conatus[1] poposcit pannos, clamauit calceos, lectum quem diu fouerat aspernatus. Putabant eum presentes alienata mente loqui, ut fit plerumque cum occupato cerebro et turbata rationis sede cogitur infirmus non*[a]* sua uerba iactare. Veruntamen perstitit Egelricus[2] (id enim monacho nomen) Deum et episcopum pro sospitate reddita benedicere, idque aliis lecto relicto et sensu integro pretendere.

16. Quinto[3] anno collati Wlstano episcopatus rex Eduardus fato functus*[b]*[4] ingens seminarium discordiae reliquit Angliae, hinc Haroldo, inde Willelmo comite Normanniae legitimo eam iure clamantibus. Et tunc quidem Haroldus, uel fauore impetrata uel ui extorta corona, regnum paulo minus totum obtinuit.[5] Soli Northanimbri magnum et gentile tumentes[6] interim parere distulere, aquilonalem ceruicositatem australi (ut dictitabant) mollitiei subiugare non dignati. Animabat eos ad tirannidem et insolentia sua ingentes eorum alebat spiritus Tostinus, eiusdem regis frater nec fortitudine degener, si ardens ingenium tranquillis studiis applicare maluisset. 2. Qui postmodum in eadem prouintia, cum Haroldo rege Norreganorum,[7] quem in suffragium asciuerat, cesus,[8] penas inconsultae animositatis pependit. Sed haec posterius; tunc uero Haroldus eo profecturus ut contumatiam eorum lenioribus curaret remediis, quandoquidem ferro frangere consilium non erat, sanctum uirum secum adduxit.[9] Sic enim fama sanctitatis eius etiam abditissimas penetrauerat gentes ut nullam non arrogantiam molliturus crederetur. Nec uero citra opinionem rei fuit euentus. Namque illi populi ferro indomabiles, semper quiddam magnum a proauis spirantes, pro reuerentia episcopi in iura Haroldi facile concesserunt, et profecto perseuerassent nisi eos Tostinus, ut dixi, auerteret. 3. Sane licet esset pontifex bonus mansuetus et lenis, non tamen ad improbos indulgebat blanditiis, sed uitia eorum arguens minacibus infrendebat uerbis; sin id parum procederet, aperto eis preconabatur

---

[a] ed. (cf. *VD* i. 3. *1* aliena); nunc C   *[b]* *Whar.*; fluctus C

[1] Cf. Statius, *Theb.* vi. 807: 'ab humo conantem'.
[2] Occ. as a monk of Evesham 1077 and *c.*1104: Mason, p. 94 n. 33.
[3] This should really be 'quarto': 1062–6.   [4] 5 Jan. 1066.
[5] For discussion of William's ambivalent attitude to Harold's succession, see *GR*, c. 228. 7–8 n.
[6] Statius, *Theb.* viii. 429, also echoed in *VD* i. 15. 6, with the same application to the Northumbrians.
[7] Harold III Hardrada, king of Norway 1045–66.

to get to his feet,[1] demanded his clothes, cried for his shoes, and spurned the bed he had so long cherished. Those present thought his words mere madness, for it often happens that a sick man is reduced to hurling about words not his own when his brain has been taken over and the seat of his reason has become disturbed. But Æthelric[2] (for this was the monk's name) stood it out, and blessed God and the bishop for restoring his health, which he demonstrated to others by abandoning his bed and regaining all his faculties.

16. In the fifth[3] year of Wulfstan's bishopric, King Edward died,[4] leaving England a hot-bed of discord, for on one side Harold, on the other William duke of Normandy were claiming the throne as of legal right. For the moment, Harold won the crown by favour, or extorted it by force, and took over almost the whole realm.[5] The only people to put off taking allegiance were the Northumbrians, 'with all the pride of their race';[6] as they frequently put it, they did not care to see their northern granite subject to those softies in the south. Tostig inspired them to rebellion, and by his own arrogance fostered their high spirit. He was the king's brother, and true to his high birth. If only he had chosen to use his ardent nature in the cause of peaceful ambitions! 2. Later he paid the penalty for his imprudent spirit when, again in Northumbria, he was killed[8] alongside Harold king of the Norwegians,[7] whom he had called in to help him. But this came later. For the moment, when Harold was about to go north to curb their contumacy by gentler methods (for he had no thought of trying to break them by war), he took the holy man along with him.[9] The report of Wulfstan's holiness had reached even the most remote peoples, and he was thought capable of softening any and every arrogance. Things turned out in such a way as to confirm this view; the Northumbrians, unconquerable in war, and as spirited as their ancestors had always been, made no difficulty about giving way to Harold's rule out of respect for the bishop. And no doubt they would have stayed that way had not Tostig, as I say, led them astray.

3. Though Wulfstan was a good, mild, and gentle bishop, he did not deal with the wicked by blandishments. He would castigate their vices and utter menacing words. If that did not work, he would give

---

[8] Stamford Bridge, 25 Sept. 1066.
[9] Cf. *GR*, c. 200. 2–3, with rather different emphasis. For Harold's expedition against the rebellious Northumbrians in 1065, see I. W. Walker, *Harold, the Last Anglo-Saxon King* (Stroud, 1997), pp. 111–13.

uaticinio quanto multandi essent suplitio. Nec facile umquam uel prudentem hominem coniectura uel uatem prophetia fefellit. Multa et illo itinere et alias crebro prescita et prenuntiata sunt. Denique Haroldo palam testificatus est quanto[a] detrimento et sibi et Angliae foret nisi nequitias morum correctum ire cogitaret. Vivebatur enim tunc pene ubique in Anglia perditis[b] moribus, et pro pacis affluentia delitiarum feruebat luxus. Ille uitiosos et presertim eos qui crinem pascerent insectari, quorum si qui sibi uerticem supponeret ipse suis manibus comam lasciuientem secaret. 4. Habebat ad hoc paruum cultellum, quo uel excrementa ungium[1] uel sordes librorum purgare consueuerat. Hoc cesariei libabat primitias, iniungens per obedientiam ut capillorum ceterorum series ad eandem complanaretur concordiam. Si qui repugnandum putarent, eis palam exprobrare mollitiem, palam mala minari. Futurum ut qui erubescerent esse quod nati fuerant, qui emularentur capillorum fluxu feminas,[2] non plusquam feminae ualerent ad defensandam patriam contra gentes transmarinas. Quod in aduentu Normannorum eodem anno claruisse quis eat in infitias?

5. Quorum quoniam attigimus tempora, hic primo libello statuatur meta. Ita enim concinnius fieri posse puto, si quid sanctissimus uir Anglorum tempore, quid Normannorum fecerit enucleate digessero. Colemannus enim in episcopatus eius electione decisionem primam fecit.[3] Illud autem conscientiae uestrae[c], domini fratres,[d] non celauerim, me nomina[e] testium[4] pene omnium suppressisse, ne uocabulorum barbaries[5] delicati lectoris sautiaret aures, nec minus alta uerba ⟨et⟩[f] declamatiunculas[6] quasdam quas ille ab aliorum sanctorum gestis assumptas prona deuotione inseruit. Sicut enim superius dixi,[7] quisquis rem per se satis eminentem uerbis exaltare molitur, ludit operam. Quin immo dum uult laudare infamat potius et

---

[a] δHR (*p. 76*); quanto et C   [b] C (*cf. GR 80. 4*); peruersis δHR (*p. 76*)
[c] *Whar.*; contientie nostre C   [d] *Perhaps read* domini et fratres (*cf. Ep. 4 above, VD p. 250*)   [e] nec C[a.c.]; *there may be a lacuna before* nomina (*see the translation*). [f] *suppl.* [*Peile*]

[1] Cf. Lucan vi. 543: 'excrementa manus'.

[2] For long hair as a sign of effeminacy, and the disquiet it caused among clerics in the late eleventh century, see *GR*, c. 314. 4 and n., *HN*, c. 4. The same passages have equivalents for 'ut qui erubescerent esse quod nati fuerant'; cf. also John of Salisbury, *Policrat.* i. 5: 'obliuiscantur quod nati sunt'.

[3] William's comments on Coleman's organization suggest that he was following it for the most part (see above, p. xvi, and below, p. 100 n. 3). In *GP*, cc. 137–49, he varies it significantly, by dealing with Wulfstan's character *before* giving examples of his miracles (note the opening words of c. 142).

them plain prophecies of the punishment that would afflict them. As a man of sense, he rarely failed in a guess; as a prophet he rarely failed in a prophecy. Many were the things that on that journey and often elsewhere he foresaw and foretold. For instance, he told Harold straight out what damage he would do both to himself and to England unless he had a mind to put right the wickedness of current behaviour. For at that time, almost everywhere in England, morals were deplorable, and in the opulence of peace luxury flourished. Wulfstan employed invective against the wicked, not least those who grew their hair long. Indeed if any of these offenders put his head within range, the bishop would personally snip a flowing lock. 4. For this purpose he kept a small knife, which he used to tidy up his finger-nails[1] or clean blots off books. With this he would take the first fruits of their tresses, enjoining them by their vow of obedience to return the rest of their hair to the same level plane. Anyone who thought it worth objecting he would openly charge with effeminacy, and openly threaten with ill: men who blushed to be what they had been born, and let their hair flow like women,[2] would be no more use than women in the defence of their country against the foreigner. No one would deny that this was shown to be very true that same year when the Normans came.

5. Since I have reached the Norman period, let this be the halting place for my first book. For it seems neater if I separate out what the holy man did in the time of the English and what in the time of the Normans. It is true that Coleman made his first break at the point where Wulfstan was elected bishop.[3] But I will not, lord brothers, conceal from you that I have ⟨not always followed Coleman's lead. For example,⟩ I have withheld the names of almost all the witnesses,[4] so that barbarous names[5] should not wound the sensibilities of the fastidious reader, and also removed the grand language and little declamations[6] that he borrowed from the Lives of other saints and put in with all too eager piety. For, as I said before,[7] whoever tries to use language to heighten something that is grand enough in itself is just

---

[4] For Coleman's witnesses, see e.g. ii. 1. 8, 19. 1.

[5] William comments on barbaric names in *GR*, c. 115.

[6] A rare word, perhaps derived by William from Jerome, *Comm. in Hos.* i. 2. 16–17 (CCSL lxxvi, p. 29): 'neque . . . oratoriis debeo declamatiunculis ludere', or *Dial. contra Pelag.* iii. 5 (PL xxiii. 574A): 'nunc mihi puerilibus declamatiunculis ludendum est'. Both works were excerpted by William in his *Polyhistor*. A similar sentiment is in *VD* ii. prol. 2; see below, p. 234 n. 6.

[7] Ep. 4.

attenuat, quia uideatur non posse niti argumento proprio, si fulciatur patrocinio alieno.

Explicit liber primus

Incipit liber secundus

1. Interea Willelmus Normanniae comes, Angliam ueniens congressusque prelio cum Haroldo,[1] cede ipsius et Anglorum strage regnum ditioni suae asseruit. Vbi, sicut prefatus sum,[2] claruit prophetiae ueritas, quod tanta fuit miserorum prouintialium imbecillitas ut post primam pugnam numquam communi umbone ad libertatem temptarint assurgere, quasi cum Haroldo robur omne deciderit patriae.[3] Rex porro Willelmus nullo umquam sanctum uirum affecit incommodo, quin immo multo eum honore ueritus patrem et uenerabatur amore et dignabatur nomine.

Wlstanus ergo, benignitatem temporum nactus, multas Wigornensis aecclesiae possessiones, quas uel olim Danorum impudentia uel nuper Aldredi archiepiscopi potentia eliminauerat,[4] usibus debitis reformauit. 2. Sic ei regis fauebat dignatio, sic sanctitas rerum dominos[5] ad se diligendum inuitat, sic religio aliis timendos ad sui reuerentiam inclinat. Aldredo sane successit in Eboraco Thomas Baiocensis canonicus,[6] litterarum scientia insignis, seculari prudentia non ignobilis, morum compositione multis preferendus, musica certe tunc temporis facile omnium primus.[7] Contra hunc uir Domini Wlstanus questionem instituit de uillis aecclesiae suae, quas, ut predictum est, ab Aldredo peruasas nec umquam redditas ille quasi legitimo sibi defensitabat iure.[8] Thomas e diuerso non solum predia non reddenda putabat, uerum etiam, seu quod nouus Anglus esset seu aliquorum susurro[a] persuasus,[9] Wigornensem aecclesiam sui iuris

---

[a] susurro *Whar.*; -rrio *C*

[1] Hastings, 14 Oct. 1066. [2] i. 16. 4.

[3] Cf. *GR*, c. 228. 11: 'quasi cum Haroldo . . .', and n. ad loc.

[4] See above, i. 12. 1, for Ealdred's alleged abstractions. The Danes are mentioned more than once in Hemming's Cartulary as despoilers of Worcester's property (see above, p. xxxii and n. 108).

[5] Virgil, *Aen.* i. 282.

[6] Ealdred d. 11 Sept. 1069. Thomas was archbp. 1070–1100.

[7] So also *GP*, c. 116 (p. 258).

[8] i.e. referring to the twelve manors which Wulfstan had not succeeded in wresting from Ealdred: see above, i. 13. Commentary in Mason, pp. 110–13; A. Williams, 'The spoliation of Worcester', *ANS* xix (1997), 383–408. For the relationship between York's claim over

wasting time. Indeed in his desire to praise he is in fact degrading and belittling his topic, because he looks unable to rely on his own material if he has to prop himself up with the aid of another.

BOOK TWO

1. Meanwhile William duke of Normandy came to England, fought with Harold,[1] killed him, wrought slaughter among the English, and brought the kingdom under his sway. Here, as I said,[2] the truth of Wulfstan's prophecy shone clear: such was the weakness of the wretched people that after the first battle they never again tried to rise with a common purpose to assert their liberty, as though with Harold the whole strength of the land had fallen away.[3] But King William never caused the holy man any problems. Rather, he honoured and respected him, venerating him as a father and dignifying him by that name.

So Wulfstan took advantage of the good times, and brought back to their proper status many possessions of the church of Worcester which had been taken away by the shameless Danes of old or more recently by Ealdred's overweening power.[4] 2. For such was the favour that the king deigned to afford him; indeed holiness causes even the lords of the world[5] to love it, and piety wins respect from those whom others dread. Ealdred, anyway, was succeeded at York by Thomas canon of Bayeux,[6] famous for his literary knowledge, a man of good sense in worldly affairs and superior to many in character; in music he was by far the greatest expert of his day.[7] It was against this dignitary that Wulfstan, that man of the Lord, brought a case concerning the vills of his church, which Ealdred, as I have said, had overrun and never returned, and which Thomas was now keeping as his lawful property.[8] Thomas, for his part, not merely thought the estates should not be given back, but—whether because he was new to England, or because he was persuaded by the whispers of certain persons[9]—claimed that the church of Worcester was his. Rule over it,

---

Worcester and the issue of the primacy of Canterbury, see M. T. Gibson, *Lanfranc of Bec* (Oxford, 1978), pp. 116–21. Worcester was adjudged to Canterbury at the council of 1072 (see below, p. 64 n. 3).

[9] Cf. Lanfranc, *Scriptum de primatu* (*The Letters of Lanfranc Archbishop of Canterbury*, ed. and trans. H. Clover and M. Gibson (OMT, 1979), pp. 40–1), in which Thomas is similarly described: 'nouus . . . homo et Anglicae consuetudinis penitus expers uerbis adulatorum plus aequo et bono exhibebat.' Either Coleman or William presumably had this document in mind; William quotes almost the whole of it in *GP*, cc. 25–7 (pp. 39–43).

esse clamabat: dominatum illius legitima successione sibi competere, antecessorum suorum fuisse. 3. Eam causam magno egit impetu primo Angliae, mox etiam, Lanfranco Cantuariensi archiepiscopo presente, apud Alexandrum papam[1] Romae. Non tulit id Lanfrancus, qui priuilegium aecclesiae suae periclitari sciret si taceret, sed ea respondit quae magis iustitia quam dolor imperauit. Tum papa qui Lanfrancum utpote magistrum suum quondam grauaretur offendere, sed nec Thomam uellet premere, arbitrii a se remouens inuidiam causae cognitionem in concilium Angliae traiecit.[2]

Magno ergo conflictu et procerum Angliae conuentu res acta. Assistebat Thomae Odo, immane quantum[3] opulentus, et qui diuitiis certaret cum rege, quem contingebat sanguine. Frater enim eius erat uterinus, comes Cantiae, Baiocarum episcopus.[4] 4. Hunc comitabatur uniuersitas magnatum, pars pretio redempta, pars adulationibus deprauata. Solus Lanfrancus partes tutabatur iustitiae. Nam et rex in fauorem fratris uergebat pronus, quamquam nonnichil in eius animo ponderaret Lanfrancus. Quid plura? consistunt partes, uentilatur causa. Egreditur Thomas cum suis, quid opponeret, quid oppositis responderet compositurus. Wlstanus interim indulgebat sopori, dulci quiete membra confotus.[5] Alter reuersus multo sensuum acumine, multo uerborum flumine dixit. Ille a sotiis expergefactus psalmos ore, preces corde ingeminat. 5. Tandem iussus exire ut strictiori consilio responsum poliret, cum paucis secum egressis horam nonam incepit et percantauit; illis porro referentibus ut alia magis quam psalmos curaret et id propter quod uenerat expediret, respondit: 'Stulti, nescitis quod Dominus dixit: "Dum steteritis ante reges et presides nolite cogitare quomodo aut quid loquamini. Dabitur enim uobis in illa hora quid loquamini."[6] Ipse idem Creator Dominus Iesus Christus qui hoc dixit potest michi hodie sermonem conferre quo causae meae rectitudinem defendam et illorum tortitudinem destruam.' Preclarum plane dictum hominis! 6. Habebat tunc in manibus Vitas beatorum pontificum Dunstani et Oswaldi, qui ambo quondam diuersis temporibus Wigorniae presederant, quorum ut imitabatur uitam sic tuebatur sententiam; et mira prorsus oculorum

---

[1] Alexander II (1061–73).

[2] The story is told in more detail in *GR*, c. 302 (and see note ad loc.). The Council itself was held *c.* 8 April 1072: *Councils*, i(2), no. 91 (pp. 591–607).

[3] See *GR*, c. 1. 2 n.

[4] Earl 1066/7–82, 1087–8, d. 1097. For the story which follows, see *GR*, c. 303, and *GP*, c. 143 (pp. 284–5), both quoting more of Wulfstan's direct speech.

he said, belonged to him by lawful succession, as it had belonged to his predecessors. 3. He pursued this case with great energy first in England, and then before Pope Alexander[1] in Rome, in the presence of Lanfranc archbishop of Canterbury. Lanfranc felt strongly about the matter, for he knew that the privileges of his own church were at risk if he held his tongue; but he made replies dictated by justice rather than by resentment. The pope was reluctant to offend Lanfranc, his own one-time teacher, but he was also unwilling to find against Thomas; so to avoid the invidiousness of making a decision he transferred the hearing to a council in England.[2]

The matter was taken up with great passion and a fine turn-out of English magnates. On Thomas' side was the excessively[3] rich Odo, a rival in wealth to the king as well as his relation by blood: for he was his uterine brother, earl of Kent, and bishop of Bayeux.[4] 4. With him went along the mass of magnates, some bought for cash, others corrupted by flattery. Only Lanfranc was on the side of justice. As for the king, he was inclined to support his brother, though Lanfranc had some weight in his considerations. So the parties took their place and the case was discussed. Thomas went out with his people, to settle what he should plead and what he should reply to the pleas of others. Wulfstan meanwhile took a nap, relaxing his limbs in agreeable repose.[5] Odo came back, and made a speech of great acuity of content and flow of language. Wulfstan was woken up by his companions, and sang psalms aloud while praying in his heart. 5. In the end he was told to withdraw to work out a more polished and organized reply. With the few who accompanied him he began Nones and sang it right through. They represented to him that he had other things to worry about besides psalms, and that he should get down to what he had come for. He replied: 'You are fools. You don't know that the Lord said: "When you stand before kings and rulers, take no thought how or what you shall speak. For ye shall be given in that hour what you should say."[6] Our Maker, Lord Jesus Christ, He who said this, can today give me the words to defend the rightness of my cause and bring these men's crookedness to naught.' An excellent saying indeed! 6. Wulfstan at that moment held in his hand the Lives of the blessed bishops Dunstan and Oswald, who had both at different times in the past ruled over Worcester; and just as he imitated their lives, so did

---

[5] With such studied nonchalance cf. Anselm in *GP*, c. 49 (p. 88), and in Eadmer, *VA* i. 27.

[6] Cf. Mark 13: 9 and 11, Matt. 10: 18–19.

fidei perspicatia illos se coram profitebatur cernere quos[a] causae non
dubitabat assistere. Ita ingressus causam non difficulter obtinuit.
Siquidem interroganti regi quid in suo inuenisset consilio, cum
respondisset: 'consilium meum in uobis est', continuo ille (cor
quippe regis in manu Dei)[1] edictum annitente Lanfranco proposuit
episcopum Wigornensem Cantuariensi archiepiscopo subiectum esse
debere, nichil in illum iuris Eboracensi competere. 7. Quin etiam
duodecim uillas, quas Aldredus usque ad diem mortis suis assigna-
uerat commodis, indulsit Wigornensi aecclesiae, regia sane liberalitate
archiepiscopo data prediorum compensatione.[2] Cumulauit miraculum
quod in eodem concilio apud Pedridan[3] habito episcopatus ei
Cestrensis[4] a Lanfranco archiepiscopo uisitatio commissa est. Ea
enim prouintia quae habet tres pagos, Cestrensem Scrobbesberiensem
Statfordensem,[b] erat adhuc propter longinquitatem Normannis inaccessa et propter barbariem impacata. 8. Ea res diu fuit sermonis
materia hominibus, affluentiam in eo Dei gratiae mirantibus. Duos
enim episcopatus discedens[c] concilio reportabat qui unum quasi
amissurus uenerat. Huius narrationis Colemannus testem citat Walk-
elinum Wintoniensem episcopum,[5] in uirtutibus tunc temporis
Lanfranco sed longo interuallo proximum.[6] Eum siquidem plusquam
semel narrantem audiuit[d] quomodo uir sanctus pene solus tot
optimatibus et ipsis magno elimatis acumine obnitentibus uictor
abierit.[7]

2. Sed haec hactenus. Nunc ad enarranda quaedam quae per
Wlstanum Christus ostendit miracula, uelificante Spiritu sancto, in
altum laxemus carbasa. Propheticae sanctitatis eius multa fuere
inditia, quorum[e] uel duo perstrinxisse suffecerit. Aldwinus[8]

---

[a] δH* (*p. 79*); quo C   [b] Scrobbesberiensem Statfordensem *ed.*; Crobernensem
Tefordensem C   [c] DH* (*p. 79*); dec- CG   [d] [*Darl.*]; -iui C   [e] *Whar.*;
quarum C

---

[1] Prov. 21: 1.
[2] The loss to York of the twelve manors is recorded by Hugh the Chanter, pp. 18–19.
[3] So also JW s.a. 1070 (iii. 16–17 and n. 10). Held probably after Easter (24 April) 1071,
this council presumably met at North or South Petherton (Somerset), royal manors on the
Parret: Darlington, pp. xxix–xxxi; Lapidge, 'The cult of St Indract at Glastonbury' (above,
p. xxvi n. 87), p. 446. Williams, 'The cunning of the dove' (above, p. xxviii n. 95), suggests
that 'The Petherton meeting may have been a preliminary hearing, intended to settle the
points at issue between Wulfstan and Thomas, before the more important matter of the
primacy was resolved'. This resolution took place at the Council held at Winchester and
Windsor, Easter 1072.
[4] The see of Lichfield was moved to Chester in 1075, so that either Coleman or William

he follow their principles. And—so wonderful is the acuteness of the eyes of faith—he professed to see them face to face, for he had no doubt of their support for his case. So in he went, and won the case with no difficulty. When the king asked what counsel he had found, he replied: 'My counsel is in you.' Forthwith the king (for 'the king's heart is in the hand of God')[1] issued an edict, with Lanfranc's backing, that the bishop of Worcester should be subject to the archbishop of Canterbury, while the archbishop of York should have no competence over him. 7. Further, the twelve vills that Ealdred had usurped to the day of his death, William granted to the church of Worcester, though with regal largesse he compensated the archbishop with other estates.[2] To add to the miracle, in the same council on the Parret,[3] Wulfstan was given by Archbishop Lanfranc the visitation of the see of Chester.[4] For that province, which has three shires, Cheshire, Shropshire and Staffordshire, was still inaccessible to the Normans because of its remoteness and not yet pacified because of its uncouthness. 8. This circumstance was long a talking-point, for people were astonished at the boundlessness of God's grace in him; he had left the council carrying off two sees, though he had entered it reconciled to losing the one he had. As witness to this story, Coleman cites Walkelin bishop of Winchester,[5] who was at that time next in virtue to Lanfranc, though a long way behind him.[6] For he heard him more than once telling how the holy man almost single-handed confronted so many nobles of great acuteness and polish, and departed victorious.[7]

2. But enough of this. Now, with the Holy Spirit blowing in our favour, let us haul up our sails and head for the deep, to narrate some of the miracles that Christ showed through Wulfstan. Many were the signs of his holiness as a prophet, but it will suffice to touch on two. A certain Ealdwine,[8] a monk of no education, had essayed the

---

has committed a slight anachronism. For the changes in the name of this diocese, see *HBC*, p. 253 n. 1. A similar account is given, but without specifying the see, in *GP*, c. 143 (p. 285). Wulfstan governed the diocese from late 1070 until 29 Aug. 1072, when Peter was consecrated bishop. Obviously Lanfranc must have asked him to undertake this task soon after he was made archbishop, and not following the Council of 1072.

[5] bp. 1070–98.   [6] Above, i. prol. 3 n.

[7] Cf. Virgil, *Aen.* x. 859–60: 'hoc solamen erat, bellis hoc uictor abibat/omnibus'. Similarly echoed in *GR*, c. 135. 4.

[8] The story is also told, more clearly, in *GP*, c. 145 (pp. 285–6). For instance, it is said there that Wulfstan himself made Ealdwine a monk, and that he was joined at Malvern by some thirty persons.

quidam, habitu monachus, litterarum expers, cum congregationem religionis apud Maluernum adoriri conatus esset, post aliquot annos immensitate laboris deterritus cepto desistere cogitabat. Sed quia preter conscientiam patris diocesis*a* eius decedere temerarium esset, eo adito difficultatem rei et tenuitatem pecuniae sanctitati eius applorauit: uelle se Ierosolimam iter moliri, ut si alios nequiret, saltem se ipsum Dei seruitio manciparet. 'Non,' ait pontifex, 'crede michi' (hoc enim sollemni iuramento utebatur)[1] 'quia, si scires quantam religionem Deus in illo loco futuram preuidit, multum gauderes.' Perstitit ille hoc nisus oraculo, et ueritatem uaticinii, sicut hodieque uidetur, exsecutus est sudore proprio.[2]

3. Non est dissimile quod sequitur. Occasionem, ut dixi,[3] uisitandi Cestrensem episcopatum nactus, crebroque per Scrobbesberiam transiens, in oratorio sancti Petri[4] tunc illius urbis minimo frequentes orationum protelabat excubias. Mirantibus urbicis et causam sedulo percunctantibus cur posthabita quam sanctam Mariam nominabant aecclesia[5] illud oratorium suis nobilitaret precibus, respondisse constat episcopum: 'Credite*b* michi, hoc oratorium quod modo uilipenditis erit in posterum locus gloriosissimus totius Scrobbesberiae et gaudium omnis prouintiae, eumque et diligetis*c* uiui et ibi iacebitis mortui.' Haec ille tunc dixit, sed rem non infra promissum impletam esse nunc est celebratius quam ut necesse sit ad hoc inculcandum nostrum spatiari stilum.

---

a [*Darl.*]; diocesi *C*   *b* *DG^(p.c.) H**(p. 92); crede *CG^(a.c.)*   *c* *C^(p.c.)*, δ*H**(p. 92); diligitis *C^(a.c.)*, *Darl.*

[1] This form of words (used by Christ in John 4: 21) was intended to fulfil Christ's injunction against swearing oaths (Matt. 5: 34–7). It was enjoined on monks in the late eighth-century Carolingian supplement to the Benedictine Rule, 'Memoriale qualiter', c. 7: ed. J. Semmler in *Initia Consuetudinis Benedictinae: Consuetudines Saeculi Octavi et Noni* (Corpus Consuetudinum Monasticarum, i, ed. B. Albers *et al.*: Siegburg, 1969), pp. 177–282, at p. 277: 'Iuramentum aliud nemo proferat nisi "Crede mihi", sicut in Euangelio legimus Dominum Samaritanae affirmasse, aut "Certe", aut "Sane".' The work was widely known in England by the tenth century, and translated and glossed in OE: ed. A. S. Napier (EETS, orig. ser. cl: London, 1916). A copy of s. xi ex. is in Cambridge University Library, MS Ll. 1. 14, fos. 70–108, of unknown English provenance. For further detail, see M. Lapidge in Wulfstan of Winchester, *Vita S. Æthelwoldi*, pp. lvi–lvii and nn. Christ's injunction was commented upon by Ælfric, in his homily on the decollation of John the Baptist: *Ælfric's Catholic Homilies: the First Series*, ed. P. Clemoes (EETS, 2nd. ser. xvii: Oxford, 1997), p. 454. This homily is included in Bodl. Libr. MS Hatton 116, written at Worcester s. xii¹. Wulfstan was not the first to take Christ's injunction seriously and to interpret it in this way; the expression was also frequently used by the hero of the *Vita S. Ioannis Eleemosynarii* by Leontius, trans. Anastasius Bibliothecarius: *BHL* 4388; PL

foundation of a religious community at Malvern; but after some years he was frightened off by the immensity of the task and contemplated giving up. But because it was rash to quit without informing the father of the diocese, he went to Wulfstan and complained to him of the difficulty of the task and the shortage of money. He wanted, he said, to make the pilgrimage to Jerusalem, so that if he could not bring others to the service of God he could at least serve Him himself. 'No,' the bishop said, 'believe me' (for this was his customary oath)[1] 'that if you knew how great the religious life God has foreseen will flourish there, you would rejoice greatly.' Relying on these inspired words, Ealdwine stuck to his resolution, and by his own sweat brought about the fulfilment of the prophecy, as we see today.[2]

3. What follows is very similar. Wulfstan had occasion to visit the diocese of Chester, as I have said,[3] and on his frequent journeys through Shrewsbury he would often undertake prayerful vigils in the oratory of St Peter,[4] at that time the church of least importance in the city. The townspeople were surprised, and kept asking why he downgraded the church called after St Mary[5] and dignified this chapel with his prayers. It is beyond doubt that the bishop's reply was: 'Believe me, this oratory that you now belittle will in the future be the most glorious place in all Shrewsbury, and bring joy to the whole province; you will love it while you live, and lie in it when you are dead.' Those were his words then, but that they were fulfilled to the letter is now too well known for me to have to spread myself in pressing the point.

---

lxxiii. 337–84. This work was evidently common in late eleventh-century England: R. Gameson, *The Manuscripts of Early Norman England* (*c.1066–1130*) (London, 2000), nos. 315, 371, 608, 776.

[2] Great Malvern, founded in 1085, soon after a dependency of Westminster (*Heads*, p. 90). Ealdwine apparently became first prior.

[3] ii. 1. 7.

[4] A small wooden church in the suburb outside the east gate of Shrewsbury, founded by Siward son of Æthelgar, a kinsman of Edward the Confessor. It was later granted by Roger de Montgomery, earl of Shrewsbury, to Odelirius, father of Orderic Vitalis. In 1083, on Odelirius' advice, Earl Roger vowed to found and endow an abbey in that place. See *DB 25 Shropshire*, 3b. 1: 'in Sciropesbirie ciuitate fecit Rogerius comes abbatiam, et ei dedit monasterium Sancti Petri ubi erat parochia ciuitatis'. Roger's charter, though of dubious authenticity, may be correct in dating the actual foundation to 1087. It was populated by Benedictine monks from Séez. See *VCH Shropshire* ii. 30–7; Darlington, p. 26 n. 15; *Heads*, p. 71 and n. 1; Mason, pp. 109–10.

[5] Perhaps the church of St Mary mentioned in Domesday (*DB 25 Shropshire*, 3d. 3; *VCH Shropshire* i. 310) as holding 1 virgate in the city.

4. Contulerat diuina dignatio uirtutum gratiam Sancto, ut more priscorum patrum in depellendis ualitudinibus esset egregius: merito, ut qui uitae illorum emularetur exempla signorum mereretur insignia. Quorum aliqua quae nostram non effugere memoriam compendio transcurram. Et quoniam superius de monacho apud Euesham sanato dixi,[1] nunc de regionis eiusdem muliere castigata breuitate miraculum subnectam. Erat enim eius prouintiae incola femina cui non inops substantia familiares lares impleuerat, sed nequam spiritus mentem prudentia uacuarat. Et paulatim quidem †desipientem pertemptans aditum procedente tempore dementiam extremam[2] intrauerat†.[a] 2. Iamque ad hoc miseriae processerat ut relictis parentum affectibus, affinium necessitudinibus, per deuia camporum uel quo eam tulisset impetus uagaretur. Hoc parentes, qui cetera moleste uidissent, non ferendum rati, comprehensam uinculis innexuerunt. Nimium id dure, dixerit aliquis. Sed enim seueritatem secuta est misericordia, et quo maior erat miseria maiora uenabantur remedia. Conducti medici qui noto artifitio morbum fugarent. Adducti presbiteri qui salubri exorcismo animum reuocarent. Inter quos prior Eueshammensis, qui Colemanno huiusce rei fuit testis et index,[b] sicut ceteri, spe sua frustratus[c] abscessit. Nam utrique, et medici et clerici, omnibus conatibus consumptis, illi antidota, isti exorcismos uentis exposuerunt. 3. Veruntamen cognatis non paruo res constitit, quin fortunas suas magno impensarum emungerent dispendio.[3] Inopes ergo spei, exules consilii, ad priorem de quo predixi reuertuntur, eum, quia bonae uitae hominem nossent, quid opus sit facto consulunt: si quid spei reliquum sciret ediceret, facturis[d] procul dubio nisi uires suas excederet. Ille librato consilio[4] exhibendam censet Wlstano episcopo: fidere se itemque illos debere quod nulla ualitudo ante illum auderet subsistere, qui se gauderet Creatoris sui iussis subicere. Dicto probato ad episcopum perrectum, nec difficulter quod optabatur impetratum. Mox enim ut mulierem uidit, miseriae patientis medullitus indoluit. 4. Calamitatis immanitas euocauit planctum, planctus inuenit remedium. Protenta ergo

---

[a] *Read something like* quidem ⟨ad⟩ [*cf. GP p. 229; or better* in] desipientem . . . irritauerat [*cf. GP p. 185*]   [b] δH* (*p. 80*); iudex *C*   [c] *ed.* (*cf. GR 52. 2, 309. 2*); spem suam frustratus *C*; spe frustrata δH* (*p. 80*)   [d] facturus *C*[a.c.]

[1] i. 15. 2–4.
[2] Cf. Sallust, *Jug.* iii. 3, also echoed by William in *GR*, c. 121. 1 (and see n.), *HN*, c. 40.
[3] Cf. the woman cured by touching the hem of Christ's garment (Mark 5: 26), who had also previously undergone expensive and ineffective medical treatment.

4. God had deigned to confer on the holy man the grace of miracles, so that like the fathers of old he was remarkable for driving away illness. Indeed it was only right for one who vied with the examples of the lives of saints to receive the distinction of working miracles. I shall briefly recount some that have not been forgotten. And, since I spoke previously of the curing of a monk of Evesham,[1] I shall now give a short account of a miracle affecting a woman from the same area. She had a good deal of money; but though it had filled her household coffers, an evil spirit had emptied her mind of sense. Gradually it tested the defences of the silly woman, then it took her over until as time went on she had fallen into an extreme of madness.[2] **2.** By now she had reached such a point of wretchedness that she had left her loving parents and the support of her relatives, and was wandering the byways of the countryside or wherever her whim took her. Her parents had seen what had gone before with great distress, but this they thought beyond endurance; they caught her, and shackled her. That was too harsh, some may say. But on this harshness followed mercy, and the more she suffered the greater the remedies they tried to hunt down. Doctors were hired to drive away the disease by their well-known arts. Priests were summoned to bring back her senses by health-giving exorcism. Among these was the prior of Evesham, who was Coleman's witness and informant in this matter. But like the rest he had to go away, his hopes dashed. For both doctors and clerics wasted all their effort, antidotes and exorcisms cast uselessly on the winds. **3.** But all this cost the relatives dear, and the vast expense threatened to drain all their resources.[3] So with no hope or plan they went back to the prior, and, knowing him to be a man of exemplary life, asked him what was to be done. If he was aware of any remaining possibility, he must tell them: they would of course do it if it was not beyond their powers. He weighed things up,[4] and suggested that she should be shown to Bishop Wulfstan. He was sure, and so should they be, that no illness would dare to look him in the face, for it was his joy to subject himself to the commands of his Maker. They thought this a good idea, and went to the bishop. Their wish was easily granted. As soon as he saw the woman, he felt for her suffering to the bottom of his heart. **4.** Her terrible affliction evoked his laments, and lament found a cure. He stretched out his hand and

---

[4] Cf. e.g. *Mir.*, p. 54 line 194.

manu benedictione feminam[a] impertiuit, nescio quid archanae orationis immurmurans. Nulla in medio mora: statim resumpsit egrota sensum, statim sapuit sanum, affines cognouit, episcopum benedixit. Ipse diuinum munus uerbis salutaribus prosecutus est: iret cum pace domum, benediceret non Wlstanum sed Deum; uirtutes amaret, uitiis modum poneret, pudicitiam non perderet, ne deterius aliquid ei contingeret. Nec potuerunt esse ieiuna predicationis semina quae tam peritus seuit agricola. Mulier enim post modicum sanctimonialis accepit uelum, tota uita Dei preceptis posthabuit seculum.

5. Similem uirtutem in simili morbo alias exhibuit. Cliue uocant uillam accolae in pago Gloecestrensi.[1] Mansitabat ibi agrestis uitae et conditionis homo, qui cotidiano manuum exercitio[b] egre uitam toleraret.[2] Hunc tam infestus afflauerat spiritus ut proxima quaeque uel manibus discerperet uel uastis molaribus corroderet, in remotiora dentes moleret, intorqueret[c] conuitia, iacularetur sputa. Vltima necessitas indigenas conciuit[d] ut non putarent negligendum quod uidebant pernitiosum, illos presertim quorum pro cognatione seu uicinitate intererat ut miserum miserarentur. Crudis ergo loris renitentem innexuerunt, sed ea ille uel mordicus apprehensa conscidit uel leui negotio ut stuppea fila dirupit.[3] 2. Tum illi, maiori uiolentiae dignos nexus commenti, ferreis catenis reclamantem inuoluunt et posti uel spondae lecti affigunt. Ita pressus inconditos ruditus potius quam clamores emittebat, adeo ut longe positos rabido strepitu exterreret. Crederes ex ore uno loqui exercitum, tanta erat uariarum confusio uocum. Hos dolores affines hominis conquesti sunt antistiti in eadem sui iuris uilla manenti. Rogant ut misero presentiam non negaret suam, qui pre sarcinae importabilitate ad eum nequiret afferri. Nichil Sanctus cunctatus et ab imo pectore affectuosa ducens suspiria illos preeuntes ad domum comitatus est. Patiens uero pontifice uiso, totis intremiscens membris, diros stridores intonare, iniurias euomere, patulo rictu, sputorum diluuio, magno

---

[a] ed. (cf. VD ii. 30. 2); femina C   [b] C adds non; del. ed. (cf. GR 29.3)   [c] δHR (p. 81); ut torqueret C   [d] ed. (cf. Peile); consciuit C

---

[1] Bishop's Cleeve (Glos.), formerly an independent minster, by Wulfstan's time little more than an episcopal estate centre, later a manor of the bishop of Worcester. C. Dyer, *Lords and Peasants in a Changing Society* (Cambridge, 1980), pp. 23, 44–5; P. Sims-Williams, *Religion and Literature in Western England, 600–800* (Cambridge Studies in Anglo-Saxon England, iii: Cambridge, 1990), pp. 157–8, 169–70.

[2] Cf. *GR*, c. 29. 3: 'ut inhabitantes egre cotidianum uictum expedirent'. A similar demoniac appears in *GP*, c. 261 (pp. 416–17).

gave the woman his blessing, murmuring some recondite prayer. There was no delay: the rich woman at once recovered her wits, and became of sound mind; she recognized her relatives and blessed the bishop. He followed up his godly work with salutary words: she should go home in peace, and bless God, not Wulfstan. She should love virtue, and set a limit to sin; and she should preserve her chastity, for fear of worse afflicting her. Seeds of preaching sown by so skilled a farmer could not be fruitless: after a while the woman took the veil as a nun, and all her life put the commands of God above the calls of this world.

5. On another occasion he performed a similar miracle to remedy a similar affliction. At a vill in Gloucestershire called by its inhabitants Cleeve,[1] there dwelt a man of rustic life and rustic class, who scratched a living by daily toil with his hands.[2] On him had lit so hostile a spirit that things nearby he tore apart with his hands or crunched in his great fangs, while at things further off he ground his teeth, hurling abuse and spitting. Finally the people around about were driven to the conclusion that they should not ignore something they saw to be dangerous: and particularly those whose relationship or physical vicinity gave a special interest in pitying the wretch. So despite all his struggles they tied him up in raw-hide thongs. But these he either gripped in his teeth and bit through, or snapped with ease as though they were hempen string.[3] 2. Then they devised bonds that would stand up to greater force, and while he screamed defiance they bound him in iron chains and shackled him to a door post or bed leg. Thus constrained, he uttered what were inarticulate roars rather than shouts, terrifying people some way off with the insensate racket. You might have thought that a whole army was speaking from a single mouth, such was the variety of confused sounds that issued forth. The man's relations complained of these problems to the bishop while he was staying in the vill, which came under his jurisdiction, and begged him not to refuse to come to see the poor man, who could not be brought to him, it being impossible to carry him. The holy man did not hesitate for a moment, and heaving deep sighs of sympathy he went with them as they led the way to the house. But the patient, at the sight of the bishop, trembled all over, thundered out terrible cries, and vomited forth abuse; his mouth wide open, he raged against

---

[3] *Mir.*, p. 140 lines 865–6: 'stupea fila disrumpens'.

in Sanctum bachatus hiatu. 3. Tanto incommodo sacerdos indoluit, et expansis in caelum manibus orauit: 'Domine Iesu Christe, qui per mortem tuam genus humanum a diaboli potestate liberasti, qui legionem demonum ab homine fugatam in porcos abire siuisti,[1] libera hunc hominem a diabolo, et redde ipsi rectum intellectum.' Conuersusque ad demonem 'Discede,' inquit 'immunde spiritus, ab hac imagine Dei, et da honorem Spiritui sancto.' Mirum est dicere, mirum est credere quod sequitur. Confestim qui fuerat mentis inops efferos animos exuit, et felleos desinens intorquere oculos resipuit. Conualuitque in horas sanitas et episcopo ad sua redeunte ille omnino renuntiauit dementiae. Idemque post haec non paucis uiuens annis miraculorum beati uiri etiam post eius obitum testis fuit, tanto fidelius quanto expertus in se felitius.

6. Alio tempore ad eandem post aliquot dies uenturum uillam nuntius a dapifero missus preuenit, necessaria sumptuum expediturus. Erat autem ex eo genere hominum quos armigeros uocant,[2] malo auspitio iter ingressus. Iam enim aliquantum progressum spiritus inquietus arripiens dire inquietabat, Dei iuditio nonnumquam occulto, numquam iniusto.[3] Itaque mentis impos fugiensque hominum consortia in siluam quae proxima erat euasit, ibi noctes diesque moratus. Sed enim indignitas rei accendit agrestium animos ut eum comprehensum arctissimis funibus alligarent. 2. Veruntamen non multo post, incautiorem nactus custodiam frustratusque uincula, saltum repetiuit. Tanto fuit incolis terrori ut nichil magis cauerent quam illuc accedere ubi scirent illum esse, siue quod aliquem eorum confecerat dampno, siue quod sit a natura comparatum ut eos homines horreant qui humanitatem abiurant. Interea uenit episcopus, sane in noctem uergente uespera, quia tardiuscule quam hora poscebat progressus fuerat. Iam ergo discumbenti hominis miseria est nuntiata, magna seruientium querimonia. 3. Sacerdos nichil moratus pro more suo cunctis pietatis indixit offitium pro patiente preces fundere et 'Pater noster' dicere. Hoc enim consuetudinis sibi

---

[1] Mark 5: 9–13, Luke 8: 26–39: 'The demon Legion'.

[2] It is not clear what OE word lies behind William's 'armiger', or what kind of person he had in mind.

[3] Cf. Cassiodorus, *Expositio S. Pauli: Epist. ad Rom.*, c. 9 (PL lxviii. 469): 'Dei iudicia . . . plerumque sunt occulta, nunquam tamen sunt iniusta'; Caesarius, *Serm.* xl. 1 (CCSL ciii,

Wulfstan, spitting profusely. 3. The holy man felt for him in his trouble, and raising his hands to the heavens prayed: 'Lord Jesus Christ, who by your death freed the human race from the power of the Devil, and allowed a legion of demons to be driven from a man and enter into pigs,[1] free *this* man from the Devil, and give him back his right mind.' And turning to the demon, he said: 'Unclean spirit, go out from this image of God, and honour the Holy Spirit.' What followed is wonderful to relate and to believe. He who had been out of his mind at once cast off all his madness, stopped rolling his bloodshot eyes, and regained his senses. Hour by hour his sanity returned, and when the bishop went home he altogether gave up his madness. After that he lived for not a few years, witnessing to the miracles of the blessed man even after Wulfstan's death, and gaining the more credence because he had had the good fortune to be their object.

6. On another occasion, when Wulfstan was due to go to the same vill in a few days' time, he was preceded by a messenger sent by his steward to deal with some necessary expenditure. He was of the class of men called esquires,[2] and unlucky was the omen with which he had started on his journey. For after he had gone some way, an unquiet spirit took hold of him and sorely disturbed him; such was the judgement of God, which may sometimes be hidden but is never unjust.[3] So, out of his mind and avoiding human company, he went off into a nearby wood, and spent night and day there. But the country folk were stirred by the shame of the thing to seize him and bind him tight. 2. But soon, taking the opportunity of a moment when his guard was inattentive, and escaping from his fetters, he went back to the wild. He was so terrifying to the people round about that their last idea was to approach anywhere he was known to be, either because he had harmed one of them, or because it is only natural to shun contact with those who have renounced their status as men. Meanwhile the bishop arrived on the scene, as evening was passing over into night, for he had made slower progress than the hour demanded. As Wulfstan was going to bed, the plight of the man was reported by loud complaints from his staff. 3. The priest did not waste a second, but as ever told everyone to do what piety suggested: pray for the patient and say the Lord's Prayer. For it was his habit,

p. 177): 'Iudicia Dei . . . plerumque sunt occulta, nunquam tamen iniusta' (the opening words of the sermon). Cf. also *Mir.*, p. 114 lines 85–6 'Dei occultum iudicium'.

asciuerat ut, quocumque loco, quacumque hora excessum alicuius audierit uel incommodum, statim presentes moneret orare uel ut defunctus in pace quiesceret uel egrotus infirmitatem euaderet. Miranda clementia Christi, predicanda gratia uiri! Eadem nocte profugus adolescens exuto mentis stupore uillam rediit nullo reuo- cante, eadem nocte contubernio se curialium immiscuit; nullumque deinceps quoad uixit dementiae inditium dedit.

7. Villa est episcopatus Kemeseya dicta,[1] in qua pro necessariorum oportunitate manebat. Venerat eo ex Cantia pauper, et inter alios cotidianam stipem capientes assederat: miser, cui preter egestatis incommodum morbus irrepserat quem regium uocant,[2] et ita lenta tabe omnes artus infecerat ut non diceres eum uero uti corpore sed uiuo circumferri cadauere.[3] Horrori erat omnibus eum cernere, qui totus uirulenta stillabat sanie; fastidio sermones eius audire, qui non putaretur loqui sed raucum ululare. Denique dispensator episcopi Artur,[4] cuius testimonio et hoc et quaedam alia nituntur, sepe ab eo rogatus ne colloquium suum despiceret, non semel refugit. 2. Tandem adiurationem nominis Dei reueritus substitit, et copiam loquendi fecit. Ille summurmurat et uix intellectus anhelat oriundum se Cantiae, plenum infanda ualitudine, ut uideret, esse. Ter manifesto conuentum somnio ut spe sanitatis uenerabili se presentaret episcopo; hac gratia uenisse. Vt haec domino insinuaret, per Deum orare. Suggessit minister postulata, sed non grate ab eo auditus est qui humanae gloriae nollet obnoxius esse. Quin immo non suum esse respondit ullum, presertim tantum, attemptare miraculum. 3. Abiret ergo et infirmo uictum uestemque preberet, ut saltim huius compen- satione humanitatis consolaretur fatigationem itineris. Ita cassa fuisset suggestio, nisi Eilmeri presbiteri[5] successisset sollicitudo. Huic pro uitae reuerentia sanctitatis post Wlstanum profecto palma cessisset,

---

[1] Kempsey (Worcs.), formerly an independent minster, by Wulfstan's time an episcopal estate centre, later an episcopal manor: S154; JW s.a. 868; Dyer, *Lords and Peasants*, pp. 11, 28–30, 36–7, 45; Sims-Williams, *Religion and Literature*, pp. 170–1, 375–6.

[2] *GP*, c. 73 (p. 145), and below, iii. 18. 1. See *GR*, c. 222 n., for the various diseases which went under the name of the 'King's Evil'. To the literature cited there, add K. Manchester and C. Roberts, 'The palaeopathology of leprosy in Britain: a review', *World Archaeology*, xxi (1989), 265–72.   [3] Cf. *GP*, c. 276 (p. 440).

[4] As Mason comments (p. 178 n. 66), the name is not common in this period. This man may therefore be Arthur the Frenchman, in 1086 a tenant of Westminster Abbey in Powick (Worcs.): *DB 16: Worcestershire*, 8: 10e.

[5] In *GP*, c. 141 (p. 282), William mistakenly calls him Egelricus. He was probably Æthelmær the priest, whose death is entered in the Calendar in Bodl. Libr., MS Hatton

the moment he heard of a death or an illness, wherever he was and whatever the hour, to instruct those present to pray, either that the dead man should rest in peace, or that the sick man should recover from his infirmity. Wonderful the mercy of Christ, remarkable the grace of the man! That very night the young wanderer put off his mental block, and came back to the vill of his own volition. And that night too he rejoined the household, giving no hint of madness from that day until he died.

7. There is a vill in the see called Kempsey[1] where Wulfstan was staying because it could supply the necessities of life. There was a pauper there, come from Kent, who had taken his seat among others begging for their daily alms. Poor fellow, quite apart from his neediness, what they call the King's Evil[2] had crept up on him, so infecting all his limbs with its slow wasting that you would have said he did not have a real body at all, but was carried around in a living corpse.[3] Everyone shuddered at the sight of him, for he dripped all over with a festering pus. And everyone shrank from listening to him, for they thought he did not so much talk as wail tunelessly. For example, the bishop's steward Arthur,[4] on whose testimony this and other stories rest, though the pauper frequently begged him not to think it demeaning to talk with him, more than once turned away. 2. Finally, out of respect for an oath in God's name, he paused and gave him a chance to talk. In a low murmur scarcely to be understood, the man gasped out that he came from Kent, and (as he could see) was wracked by an appalling disease. He had three times been told in a vivid dream to look to the revered bishop for a hope of a cure, and that was why he had come; he begged Arthur in God's name to let his master know this. The servant handed on the message, but had an unfriendly reception, for Wulfstan had no thought of exposing himself to the perils of glory among men. Indeed he said it was not for him to attempt any miracle, let alone one so great as this. 3. Arthur should go and give the sick man food and clothing, to compensate him by this kindness at least for the fatigue of the journey. And so the pauper's message would have been in vain if the thoughtful priest Æthelmær[5] had not intervened. So respected was this man's life that he would have won second place for holiness

113 (s. xi, Worcester), on 29 Mar.: pr. E. S. Dewick and W. H. Frere, *The Leofric Collectar compared with the Collectar of St Wulfstan, together with Kindred Documents of Exeter and Worcester* (2 vols.: Henry Bradshaw Soc., xlv, 1914 for 1913, lvi, 1921 for 1918), ii. 601.

nisi eam seueritate grauasset. Constat enim beatum episcopum hilariores sepe abrupisse sermones,[1] si presbiter uel*ª* coniueret uultu uel argueret nutu. Ceterum ad morum congruentiam ita caste sobrius ut nichil uere in eo lacerare inuidia, nichil falso laudare amicitia posset. Harum rerum contuitu presul eum granditer suspitiebat, missam eius cotidie inhianter audiens. Ambo enim emulo religionis contendebant offitio, ut nullum diem preterirent sine missae sacrifitio. 4. Is igitur egrotum suscipiens hospitio pio blanditiarum delinibat obsequio. Commentus est etiam quomodo episcopo miraculum quod palam extorquere non posset furtim surriperet. Eius fuit occasio aqua qua post missam sanctas diluerat*ᵇ* manus. Hanc presbiter ministro supradicto datam iussit infundi balneo egroti. Lauit leprosus uisu horridus, carne maculosus.[2] Sed mirum in modum continuo pustularum tumor desedit,*ᶜ* letiferum uirus effluxit, et (ne plura) omnis caro in puerilem puritatem refloruit. Quin etiam impetigo et scabies capitis abolita, cesaries capillis succrescentibus reformata.

8. Lundoniam ad curiam proficiscens apud uillam Wicumbe dictam[3] ueteris tecti*ᵈ* ruinam minantis hospitio successit. Mane, cum iam abscessum meditaretur, domus tota crepitare, tignaque cum trabibus deorsum uergere ceperunt. Turbati seruientes ad unum omnes foras exilierunt, solum dominum intus obliti, adeo inconsiderata formido mentes eorum perculerat. Iam uero foris positi, memores domini sui,*ᵉ* magnis eum inclamabant uocibus, ut exeundo sibi consuleret antequam edes tota corrueret. 2. Nemo enim, periculo suo salutem illius mercari uolens, ut eum educeret intrare presumebat. Sed ille tanti discriminis immanitate constantior ultro etiam clamoribus arguebat: 'Modicae fidei,[4] putatis quod me ruina opprimat?' dixit, nec priusquam animalia sarcinis impositis promoueri uidisset pedem domo extulit. Cum uero egressus esset, statim horrifico fragore domus tota

---

ª C adds non; *del. ed.*   *ᵇ* D*ᵖ·ᶜ·*G*ᵖ·ᶜ·*HR (*p. 82*); -eret CD*ᵃ·ᶜ·*G*ᵃ·ᶜ·*   *ᶜ* resedit δHR (*p. 82*); *but cf. ii. 15. 6; Celsus vii. 18. 4* tumor . . . desidit   *ᵈ* C; tecti et δH* (*p. 82*), rightly?   *ᵉ* memores domini sui δH*(*p. 82*); *om.* C

[1] A striking reminiscence of Suet., *Tib.* xxi. 2: 'ut nonnumquam remissiores hilarioresque sermones superueniente eo abrumperet' (not employed in *GP* loc. cit.).
[2] In *GP*, c. 73 (p. 145) is another description of a leper, said to have the 'King's Disease'.
[3] High Wycombe (Bucks.). This and the next story imply that Wulfstan stayed there regularly, showing that Wulfstan already used the route from Worcester to London still

after Wulfstan himself had he not made his sanctity burdensome by
the sternness of his character. It is a fact that the bishop often cut
himself off short in the middle of some pleasant conversation[1] if the
priest winked or nodded his disapproval. But to balance this (?),
Æthelmær was so chaste and sober that envy could find no handle for
justified criticism, and friendship no scope for false praise. Taking all
this into account, the bishop had a high regard for him, and heard his
mass avidly every day, for they had a competition in religious
observance: no day was to go by without a mass being offered.
4. So Æthelmær gave the sick man a lodging, comforting and
coddling him. What is more, he contrived a way of obtaining
surreptitiously from the bishop a miracle he could not extort
openly. He made use of the water with which Wulfstan had
washed those holy hands after mass. The priest gave this to the
servant I have mentioned and told him to pour it into the patient's
bath. In went the leper, a horrid sight with his spotty skin.[2] But
miraculously the swollen boils went down, the deadly poison drained
away, and, in a word, his whole skin was rejuvenated and became as
clear as a child's. The itchy scabs on his head disappeared, and his
hair was renewed as his locks grew again.

8. On a journey to London to attend the court, Wulfstan stopped at a
vill called Wycombe,[3] where he lodged in an old building whose roof
threatened to fall in. When he was thinking of leaving in the morning,
the whole place began to creak, and the rafters and beams started to
give way. The servants in their fright rushed outside to a man,
forgetting all about their master, who was left inside by himself, such
was the heedless panic that had struck them. Once outdoors, they
remembered about their lord, and shouted loudly to him to look to
himself and get out before the whole building collapsed. 2. For no
one was willing to purchase Wulfstan's safety at the price of risk to
himself, or thought of going inside to bring him out. But he was
unperturbed by the horror of the situation, and went so far as to shout
at *them* : 'O ye of little faith,[4] do you think I am going to be crushed?'
And he refused to take a step out of the house until he saw the animals
loaded and moving on. But as soon as he had came out, the whole
place shook with a dreadful crashing sound, and then came down,

normal in the seventeenth century, i.e. via Pershore, Moreton-in-Marsh, Islip, High
Wycombe, Beaconsfield, and Uxbridge: J. Ogilby, *Britannia* (London, 1675), Pls. I and II.
    [4] Matt. 16: 8 etc.

concussa parietes et tectum in unum ruderum chaos confudit. Miro
prorsus et pulchro signo, ut Sancto intus posito domus casum suum
suspenderet, eo uero egresso continuo debilitati cederet!

9. Hic ponit miraculum Colemannus in eadem exhibitum uilla, annis
quidem posterius sed ueneratione grandius.¹ Contexendas ergo res
putauit communione paginae quae licet dissiderent tempore con-
gruerent dignitate.² Id miraculum eiusmodi fuit. Erat ibi uir Swertlin
nomine,ᵃ ³ opibus ex facili confluentibus fortunatus et in Sancti
reuerentiam pronus. Denique sumptibus suis edificatam aecclesiam
a nullo nisi ab eo consecrari uolebat; tunc enim demum dedicatam
putaret si Wlstanus dedicasset. Fluctuabat autem sententiae incerto,
quod fieri non posset inconsulto diocesis illius episcopo. Sed sustulit
fluctus animi licentia facilitate Remigii Lincoliensis episcopi⁴ cum
gratia impetrata. 2. Die igitur dicta uenit episcopus et dedicationi
aecclesiae, sermoni ad populum, confirmationi puerorum sollicitam
impendit operam. Quibus explicitis domum uiri pransurus ingredi-
tur. Tum mater familias, quoniam sexus sui uerecundia et episcopi
reuerentia inhiberet cum eo colloquium serere, Colemanni auribus
dolorem suum exponit. Pedissequam suam iniquo morbo tabescere,
utpote cuius caput infando tumore lasciuiat, lingua extra palati
concauum promineat. Linguam ipsam ita protuberare ut magis
uideatur esse bouis quam hominis.⁵ Victum ei omnem negatum, et
si quid sumatur non esse cibum dentibus commasticatum sed potum
cocleari infusum. 3. His acceptis monachus quod sua intererat fecit,
mittens decumbenti aquam quam eo die pater ad consecrationem
aecclesiae benedixerat. Nec eo contentus rem episcopo insinuauit.
Habebat ille unum ex aureis quos ab urbe quondam Bizantio, modo
Constantinopoli, bizantios uocant.⁶ Is aureus erat de lanceae cuspide

---

ᵃ *δH** (*p. 83*); surnomine (*sic*) C

¹ The logic is unclear, and the text uncertain, considering that William proceeds to say
that the two miracles were 'equal in importance'.
² Evidence that William is following Coleman's order.
³ Probably Suarting (Swerting), who with his ?brother Harding held Bradenham near
West Wycombe of the king in 1086, as well as other lands: *DB 13: Buckinghamshire*, 57: 15,
57: 14–17, 17: 13; *VCH Bucks.* i. 276.
⁴ Bp. of Lincoln ?1067–92. Buckinghamshire was within the huge diocese of Lincoln.
On the jurisdictional problem of bishops dedicating churches in other dioceses, see
M. Brett, 'The English abbeys, their tenants and the king (950–1150)', in *Chiesa e
Mondo Feudale nei Secoli X–XII* (Miscellanea del Centro di Studi Medioevali, xiv: 1995),
pp. 277–302, at 288, citing Eadmer's report of a judgement on the subject by Wulfstan.
⁵ Cf. *Mir.*, p. 84 lines 584–90, showing William's medical knowledge: 'permisit eum

walls and roof and all, in a chaotic heap of rubble. It was a wonderful
and fine miracle that while the holy man was inside the house delayed
its collapse, but that it succumbed to its weakness the moment he
came out.

9. It is at this point that Coleman places a miracle that took place in
the same vill, years later, but more impressive;[1] he thought it
appropriate to bring together on the same page events that though
separated in time were equal in importance.[2] The miracle was as
follows. There lived there in Wycombe a man called Swertlin.[3] He
was well off, for wealth flowed in with no difficulty, and much
inclined to reverence for the holy man. For instance, it was his wish
that the church built at his expense should be consecrated by no one
but him; he would regard it as dedicated only if Wulfstan had
officiated. But he was in some uncertainty, because the dedication
could not go forward without the approval of the bishop of the
diocese. But his anxiety was removed by a licence, freely granted by
the kindness of Remigius bishop of Lincoln.[4] 2. On the agreed day
the bishop arrived, and flung himself into the dedication of the
church, a sermon to the people, and the confirmation of children.
When this was over, he went into the rich man's house to take lunch.
Then the mother of the house, being inhibited from striking up a
conversation with the bishop because of her sex and her respect for
him, told her tale of woe to Coleman. She had a maid who was
wasting away grievously, for her head was subject to a rampant
swelling; her tongue was far too big for her mouth, protruding so far
that it looked more like a cow's than a woman's.[5] She could take no
sustenance, or if she did it was not food chewed in the mouth but
drink given by spoon. 3. Hearing this the monk did his part, sending
the patient water that the bishop had blessed that day for the
consecration of the church. Not content with that, he reported the
matter to Wulfstan. The bishop possessed one of those gold pieces
known as bezants[6] after the city once called Byzantium but now

aliquandiu pati colli tumorem incommodum, qui ingrauescens per dies, perrepsit ad
fauces, adeo ut intercluderet et ciborum et faucium meatum . . . Siquinanciam uocant
medici genus illud pessimi morbi, quod si foras collum cum rubore protuberet, curabile
opinantur, sin minus et intra fauces tumor maneat, indubitabilem mortem pronuntiant.'

[6] The usual Western name for the standard Byzantine gold coin called solidus or
nomisma (after 1092 hyperpyron). Other instances of their presence in late eleventh-
century England are in *Mir.*, p. 134 line 700, *GR*, c. 354. 1. Surviving examples are
described by V. Laurent, 'Byzance et l'Angleterre au lendemain de la conquête normande',
The Numismatic Circular, lxxi (1963), 93–6, and 'Un sceau inédit du patriarche de

percussus quae perfidi persecutoris manu impacta Domini Saluatoris perforauit latus.[1] Huius intinctione aquam sanctificatam mulierculae direxit, salubrem antea fuisse multis expertus. Medicabilem potum sanitas matura subsequitur, sicut matrona eidem Colemanno post aliquot dies, et ipsa iurata et testibus nixa, innotuit.

10. A[a] Wigornia in uillam[b] quadam uice uiam carpebat, extremus ut semper agminis sui, ne psalmos ullius colloquium interpolaret. Casu adequitabat ei Colemannus. Interea conspicatus cecum eminus inclamantem innuit monacho ut elemosinam porrigeret, id ipsum a se postulari arbitratus. At cecus, qui altioris laetitiae spem animo conceperat, equitanti se adiungens Colemanno calamitates ingerit suas. Oraret pro Deo episcopum ut paulisper contineret gradum. Manifesta sibi somnii uisione ostensum quod oculis lumen refundere posset si uellet. Suggestioni ceci serenus predicabilis uiri assensus accurrit, et rem episcopo precibus mixtis allegauit. 2. Refugit ille diu multumque causatus non esse meriti sui miracula facere. Sed quantulum erat quod a sancto pectore non posset Colemannus extorquere! Nec enim prius abstitit, pie uiolentus et laudabiliter importunus, donec ex equite peditem faceret. Ita super oculos ceci psalmo 'Ad te leuaui'[2] cantato et adiecto crucis signaculo reliquum uiae contendit explere. Post haec octo dierum fluxit intercapedo, cum Colemannus Wigorniam regressus illum quem liquerat cecum repperit perspicua oculos luce inuestitum.[3] Quae res in laudem Dei cum[c] illi tum aliis qui nouerunt et mentes accendit et ora resoluit.[4]

11. Huic miraculo illud proxima similitudine accedit, quod Wiltoniae fecit. Venerat eo, an quod eum animus ferret uel quod uia conduceret incertum michi. Frequenti sanctimonialium exceptus laetitia inter eas

---

[a] δH* (*p. 83*); e C   [b] *If the vill is not to be identified, one expects* aliquam uillam   [c] *ed.*; tamen C (tum *Darl.*)

Jérusalem Sophrone II trouvé à Winchester', ibid., lxxii (1964), 49–50; M. Biddle, 'Excavations at Winchester 1962–1963: Second interim report', *The Antiquaries Journal*, xliv (1964), 188–219, at p. 195; K. Ciggaar, 'England and Byzantium on the eve of the Norman Conquest (The reign of Edward the Confessor)', *Anglo-Norman Studies*, v (1982), 78–96, at p. 88. This one, however, had the status of a relic, and had presumably been obtained from Constantinople on that basis.

[1] John 19: 34. In *GR*, c. 135. 4, William tells of the lance given by Count Hugh of Paris to King Æthelstan in 926, said to have been Charlemagne's, and to have been identical with the Holy Lance which pierced Christ's side. Æthelstan bequeathed it to his successors, but William does not say where it was in his day. It is hard to imagine that

Constantinople. This coin was struck from the point of the spear, driven home by the hand of a treacherous tormentor, that pierced the side of our Lord and Saviour.[1] He gave the poor woman water that had been made holy by having the coin steeped in it, for he had found this had cured many in the past. Healing followed soon on the medicinal draught, as the lady told Coleman some days later, on oath and with witnesses to support her story.

10. On one occasion Wulfstan was on his way from Worcester to a vill. He was, as ever, at the end of his troop, to make sure that his psalms were not interrupted by any conversation, and as it happened Coleman was riding at his side, when he caught sight of a blind man shouting from some way off. He signed to the monk to offer the man alms, thinking that this was what was wanted. But the blind man had conceived the hope of a deeper joy than that. He attached himself to Coleman as he rode along, and poured out his woes to him. In God's name would he beg the bishop to halt awhile. He had been shown in a vivid dream that Wulfstan could if he wished restore the sight of his eyes. This met with a ready assent from the estimable Coleman, who told the bishop the tale, adding his own prayers. 2. Wulfstan was long reluctant, with many an objection that he was not worthy to do miracles. But it had to be a grand thing that Coleman could not wring from that holy heart, and he did not desist from his pious violence and praiseworthy importunity until he had made him dismount. So Wulfstan sang the psalm 'Unto thee have I raised'[2] over the blind man's eyes, added the sign of the Cross, and hurried on with his journey. After this there was an interval of eight days. When Coleman got back to Worcester he found the man he had left blind endowed with clear vision.[3] The circumstance fired the hearts and loosed the tongues[4] of Coleman, and others who learned of it, to praise of God.

11. He performed a very similar miracle at Wilton, where he had gone perhaps as the fancy took him, or because it was on his way somewhere else. The nuns greeted him with much pleasure, and he took his seat in a large group of them. In the congregation was a

---

a gold bezant could have been made from this or any other lance; the intended sense may have been 'struck by'.

[2] Ps. 24(25): 1.

[3] This suggests that the 'vill' referred to in 1 is not Wycombe (cc. 8–9), but somewhere not far from Worcester.

[4] Cf. e.g. Virgil, *Aen.* iii. 457.

assedit. Erat eiusdem congregationis femina Gunhildis[1] dicta, regis Haroldi de quo superius sermo se intulit filia.[2] Huius oculos adeo infestus tumor inuaserat ut et moles palpebrarum uisum obduceret et massa carnea oppleret. Hinc querimonia delata pontifici iussa est adduci. Nam et memoriae paternae nonnichil deferendum arbitratus dignam uirtutibus suis misericordiam exhibuit, totis pro miseria mulieris uisceribus turbatus. Oculis igitur signum crucis pretendit, et, ne multo uerborum circuitu citum retardem miraculum, continuo detectis et erectis palpebris lucem serenam infudit.

12. Rex Willelmus consuetudinem induxerat quam successores aliquandiu tritam postmodum consenescere permisere. Ea erat ut ter in anno cuncti optimates ad curiam conuenirent de necessariis regni tractaturi, simulque uisuri regis insigne, quomodo iret gemmato fastigiatus diademate.[3] Loca et tempora curiae dicere non est presentis materiae. Huius igitur moris necessitate uir sanctus astrictus Wintoniam ante Pascha ire maturabat. Iacebat in semita homo natalibus Francus, quem interna uiscerum exagitabant tormenta. Volutabant eum[a] in diuersum immensi dolores, sicut anguis uarios se torquet in orbes.[4] 2. Iactabat eiulatus flebiles et plangoribus ipsum contristabat et uerberabat aerem. Quibus plerique uiantum adducti piam quidem querelam impendebant, sed medelam non poterant. Venit tandem in tempore, uenit oportune Wlstanus qui deturbaret incommodum, afferret remedium. Is[b] ubi uocem dolentis et paulo minus ut uidebatur animam agentis accepit, mox equo descendit. Secuti sotii exemplum concitatis saltibus ad humum uenere. Iam uero infirmus, quadrupedantium audito fremitu, quid esset percunctatus ab his qui linguae commertia nossent, Wlstani episcopi comitatum esse addidicit. 3. Accepto Wlstani uocabulo, quod obscurum nec apud Francos erat, continuo uires resumpsit, et quantis poterat animae conatibus benedictionem efflagitauit. Nec fuit impetratu difficile quod fuerat fidei postulasse. Aquam igitur benedictam in uase corneo decumbenti porrexit, acclinis ad eum quidem corpore sed erectus mente. Caritas enim refocillabat eum poculo, sed pulsabat

---

a *Darl.*; cum (*or* eum) C   *b* *ed.*; his C

[1] For Gunnhild and her presence at Wilton, see Darlington, p. 34 n. 3; Barlow in *Vita Aedwardi*, p. 137 n. 31; Walker, *Harold*, pp. 195–6.   [2] e.g. i. 16. 1.
[3] *ASC* (E) s.a. 1085 (*recte* 1086) (p. 162). M. Biddle, 'Seasonal festivals and residence: Winchester, Westminster and Gloucester in the tenth to twelfth centuries', *ANS* viii (1985–6), 51–72.

woman called Gunnhild,[1] a daughter of the King Harold I mentioned earlier.[2] So serious a tumour had taken hold of her eyes that the swollen lids blocked her vision and the fleshy growth covered it over. Her complaint was notified to the bishop, and he ordered her to be brought in. He thought he owed a debt to her father's memory, and he showed her the mercy appropriate to his virtues, moved as he was to the depth of his being by the woman's wretched plight. So he made the sign of the cross over her eyes; and—not to let any verbiage slow down so swift a miracle—the eyelids at once uncovered and lifted up, and he poured bright light into her eyes.

12. King William had introduced a custom that his successors for some time complied with but afterwards allowed to lapse. Three times a year the great men would all come to court, to deal with vital business affecting the realm, and at the same time to see the king in his pomp, how he went crowned with a bejewelled diadem.[3] It is not relevant here to describe the places and times when the court was held. But it was bound by this custom that Wulfstan once came hurrying to Winchester before Easter. In the road lay a Frenchman, who was being wracked by severe internal pains, that made him roll from side to side, just like a snake twisting itself in varying coils.[4] 2. He was uttering piteous wails, and he saddened the very air with his lamentations. This attracted the attention of many of the wayfarers, who contributed pious words of sympathy but had no cure to offer. At last, and most opportunely, came Wulfstan to drive away the complaint and supply a remedy. Hearing the voice of a man in such pain and apparently on the point of death, he hastily dismounted, and following his lead his companions leapt briskly to the ground. The sick man heard the whinnying of the horses, and asked those who could converse in his language what was going on. They told him that this was the retinue of Bishop Wulfstan. 3. The name was by no means unknown even among the French, and hearing it he at once summoned up the strength to demand a blessing with all the emphasis at his command. What it had taken faith to ask was not difficult to obtain. Wulfstan handed the recumbent man holy water from a cup of horn, bending over him in the body though upright in the mind; his charity revived the man with a drink, but his prayers were beating at the doors of heaven. The man got up, healed, and one

---

[4] 'anguis . . . orbes' is almost a complete hexameter.

caelum oratio. Surrexit homo incolumis, eodemque momento et uni fuit terminus orationis et alteri repulsa ualitudinis. Denique statim iter ad Wintoniam cum ceteris, sicut incepit alacriter, ita consummauit feliciter.

13. Vicus Wigornensi diocesi attinet Wic ab antiquo dictus, ubi, quod mirum sit dicere, de dulcibus stagnis confitiuntur salinae publicae.[1] Huius erat mulier indigena, cuius natales ita natura formauerat ut nec multum diues altum tumeret nec multum humilis humi reperet.[2] Eiusdemque mediocritatis sortita maritum pro fortuna mediocriter uictitabat. Sed enim nulla umquam inconcussa felicitas, nulla umquam sine turbine laetitia egris arridet mortalibus.[3] Huius quoque domesticos successus interpolauit repentinus morbus, morbus qui non solum unum membrum sed etiam omnes artus premeret, qui omnes articulos nodositate quadam constringeret. 2. Accreuit in dies auctior labes, et mulierem grabato inuexit. Ipsa interim, nec minus maritus, medicorum opem immodicis sumptibus sollicitabant. Illi sedulo instare, arti suae non deesse; quod minus possent facto, promissis supplere, commeatum deliberandi sepius frustrati.[a][4] Euacuabat enim omnem industriam, attenuabat omnem efficatiam fortuna, uel quod magis crediderim caelestis prouidentia, huiusmodi opus antistitis sui fore speculata. Iamque multo tempore in penum congesta defecerant, cum illa humana ope desperata ad Christi fugit suffragia. 3. Consulte et prouide; affuit enim Deus ipsius[b] inspirator consilii, ostenditque per uisum quod liberaretur incommodo si litteras suscipere mereretur a Wlstano episcopo. Habebat ipsa in curia filium, Colemanni discipulatui traditum. Qua familiaritate nixa legatio episcopales mature infudit auditus. Per Frewinum[5] igitur, tunc diaconum postea monachum, uirum magnae fidutiae constantisque laetitiae, directum scriptum huiusmodi: 'Sanet te Iesus Christus, Segild' (hoc enim uocabulum matronae). Quae alacri fide suscepit munus antistitis, non multo post causam salutis experta. Primo enim

---

[a] commeatum . . . frustrati] *Obscure*   [b] *Perhaps read* ipsi

[1] On the economic importance of the salt industry at Droitwich, see D. Hooke, 'The Droitwich salt industry: an examination of the West Midland charter evidence', *Anglo-Saxon Studies in Archaeology and History*, ii (1981), 123–69; J. D. Hurst, *A Multi-Period Salt Production Site at Droitwich* (Council for British Archeology Research Report, cvii, 1997).
[2] A similar expression is in *GR*, c. 262. 2, and cf. Hor. *Ep.* ii. 1. 251.
[3] Cf. e.g. Virgil, *Aen.* ii. 268.

and the same moment saw the end of Wulfstan's prayer and the routing of the sick man's illness. So the bishop immediately took the road to Winchester with the rest, and completed his journey with success as he had started it with eagerness.

13. There is a town belonging to the diocese of Worcester long known as Droitwich, where, remarkably enough, sweet water lakes produce salt for public consumption.[1] One of its natives was a woman born to a position in which she neither swelled with pride in great wealth nor crept along the ground[2] in undue humility. She married a husband of the same modest standing, and lived the middling life her fortune required. But no felicity ever goes unshaken, no happiness smiles on wretched mortals[3] without a storm. This woman too found her domestic serenity interrupted, by a sudden illness, the sort that attacks not just a single limb but the whole body, leaving all the joints as though in knots. 2. Every day the affliction grew worse, and the woman became confined to her bed. All this time, she, like her husband, had been spending excessive sums in trying to get help from doctors. They practised their art and were sedulous in their treatment; what they could not *do* they made up for with promises, often . . . (?).[4] For all their efforts were nullified, all their results whittled away by fortune, or, as I should rather suppose, by heavenly providence, which foresaw that this was a task for its favourite, the bishop. For a long time their savings had been getting low; and in the end the woman, despairing of human aid, had recourse to the help of Christ. 3. That proved a good idea. For God inspired a plan, showing her in a vision that she would be granted relief if she was found worthy to receive a letter from Bishop Wulfstan. She had in Wulfstan's 'court' a son, handed over to Coleman for instruction. This intermediary took advantage of the connection, and told the story to the bishop. By the hand of Freowine,[5] then deacon but later monk, a very reliable man of constant good humour, a letter of the following purport was sent: 'May Jesus Christ cure you, Segild!' (that was the woman's name). She received the bishop's gift with lively faith, and not long afterwards found that it brought a cure. Applied first to the most

---

[4] There is more on doctors being useless in ii. 4. 2.
[5] Occ. 1093 (described as a 'clericus' of the bishop), *c*.1104; Mason, p. 182 n. 75, *BRECP*, p. 809. Also mentioned below, ii. 21, iii. 4.

maxime ^adolentibus locis applicita dolorem sedabat scedula; mox omnem morbum depulit,^a uigorem refudit.

14. Exuberabat ei uariis de causis miraculorum gratia, sedulam operam dante Domino quatinus mundo innotesceret quam grato fidelis famulus eum demereretur obsequio. Semper enim tota uita curam corporis illis posthabuit rebus quibus conciperet terrenorum fastidium, quibus hauriret appetitum caelestium. Quandocumque dioceses circumiret numquam sine missa, sine sermone populum dimitteret, id crebro et diligenter faceret. Numquam uictui die indulsit quoadusque quanticumque numeri pueros undecumque aduectos consignasset.[1] Hoc a primo solis ortu ad lucem occiduam actitabat, non solum diebus hibernis sed et solibus aestiuis. 2. Sepe illum duo milia ut parum, sepe tria et quod excurrit, uno die confirmasse non perfunctoriis testibus approbatur.[b][2] Hoc non modo in iuuentute, cum et uiridis aetas[3] et ipsa bene fatiendi uoluptas ad laborem uocaret, uerum etiam cum iam gemmea canities niue caput aspergeret et ipse tenui ualitudine uix corporis uiribus animum sequeretur. Stupori erat omnibus quod, octo plerumque clericis qui crismatorium ferrent uicissim fatigationi succumbentibus, ipse indefessus persisteret. Fallebat nimirum tantos labores amor Dei, ut mens senectuti non cederet sed labente corpore uictrix euaderet.

Hunc porro cum,^c ut dixi, semper inops cibi morem transigeret semel apud Gloecestram, uenerabilis abbatis Serlonis[4] precibus deuictus, omisit. 3. Dictis enim ex more missis iam ad pueros egressurum idem abbas conuenit, ut eo die refectorium fratrum presentia nobilitaret sua. Plurima esse quare roganti durus esse non deberet: primo ut pausae adquiescens sanitati consuleret, secundo ne uideretur aspernari quod seruorum Dei uellet deuotio, quorum uoluntati nonnumquam ipse Dominus Iesus placido se indulgeret assensu. Huc accedere quod interim puerorum turba digereretur in seriem, quo haberet ipse itum et reditum expeditiorem. Paruit his antistes, certatim omnibus annitentibus inflexus. Interea uulgus in

---

^{a–a} scedula sedauit dolorem, mutata de loco ad locum membrana, membra reparauit, morbum depulit δH* (*p. 85*)   ^b *Whar.*; approbat *C*   ^c *Darl.*; eum *C*

---

[1] For 'consignare' meaning 'to sign with the Cross', see *ODML* ii. 451. Cf. the use of 'signare' in *VD* i. 21. 2.

[2] Confirmation of such numbers would have been impossible, unless Wulfstan omitted to lay his hand on each child's head and pronounce the name of each: R. W. Pfaff, 'The

painful spots, the parchment eased the pain; later it drove the trouble away altogether, allowing her old vigour to flood in again.

14. The grace of miracles, which took different forms, came freely to him, for the Lord was concerned that the world should know how welcome to Him was the service of His loyal servant. For all his life Wulfstan put care for his body second to the things that helped him to reject earthly matters and indulge his appetite for what is heavenly. Whenever he visited his dioceses, he would never let the people go without a mass and a sermon, officiating frequently and with all care. He never indulged in food by day, until he had signed[1] the children, whatever their number, who were brought to him from all around. This was what he always did, from dawn to dusk, and not only in the winter but in the heat of summer too. 2. Often in a single day, as careful witnesses prove, he confirmed at least two, often three or more, thousand:[2] and that not only in his youth, when green age[3] and the very delight of good works led him to work hard, but even when the shining white sprinkled his head with snow, and his frail health scarcely allowed his body the strength to keep up with the impulses of his mind. It was a matter for general wonder that, when eight priests carrying the chrism in turn gave in to fatigue, he kept going without tiring. Such exertions he did not notice, in his love for God; his mind did not yield to old age, but came away victorious as his body failed.

As I have said, he always went without food when he was celebrating confirmation in this manner; but once, at Gloucester, he did make an exception, at the urgent request of the venerable Abbot Serlo.[4] 3. For after the saying of the usual masses, when Wulfstan was going outside to the children, the abbot asked him to honour the monks' refectory by his presence that day. There were (Serlo said) many reasons why he should not be hard and turn down this request. First, he could have a rest and take some thought for his health. Secondly, he would avoid giving the impression that he was spurning something dear to the hearts of devoted servants of God, to whose wishes even the Lord Jesus would sometimes grant a gracious assent. What was more, the mob of children could be lined up in the interval, so that he would find it easier to come and go among them. The bishop agreed with all this, swayed by the pressure of them all.

Anglo-Saxon bishop and his book', *Bulletin of the John Rylands Library*, lxxxi (1999), 3–24, at p. 19.

[3] Cf. e.g. Isidore, *Etymol.* xii. 1. 32.   [4] 1072–1104: *Heads*, p. 52.

cimiterio multa inter se serere, nunc hoc nunc illud quod in buccam uenisset[1] dicere. 4. Quorum unus adolescens, cui aetatis lubricum petulantiae uerba suggereret, subinde talia iactitabat: 'Quid expectatis episcopum, qui cum monachis uentrem implet suum? Immo agite, si quis infantem suum consignari desiderat, ad me ueniat', simulque luto arrepto frontem proximi infantis illiniens obscena murmurauit uerba. Processit in ulteriora uesania, tali clamore fatuum factum prosecuta: 'Frontem isti ligate, consignatus est!' Hactenus cachinni, hactenus lasciuia. Sed non impune: quanuis enim et factum et dictum adolescentuli excepisset risus populi, caelestis tamen ultio non defuit, quae et donum suum et famuli obsequium derisum indigne tulit. 5. Mox enim auctor arrogantiae palam omnibus furere cepit, illo proculdubio mouente sensus exterius ad cuius nutum interiores iuuenis exagitarat affectus. Ita miser crinem rotare,[2] rictus torquere, ad maceriam caput impingere. Plaudit plebs miraculo, et sullata in altum laude seuientem eliminat loco. Ille, incerto gressu effreni cursu nunc huc nunc illuc uagatus, in puteum uel potius cenum cimiterio proximum saltu delatus est, ubi profecto euomuisset animam nisi cognatorum diligentia funibus cohercitum*[a]* portasset ad diuersorium. His ad aures episcopi delatis, doluit ille tam pro iuuenis culpa quam pro pena. Et benedictione quidem missa statim patiens resipuit; sed credo pro his quae furens egerat uel tolerauerat aliquantis post diebus fati munus expleuit.

15. Ad eandem iterum urbem a reuerentissimo accitus abbate dedicauit aecclesiam.[3] Densa populorum constipatio aderat, quod, ut fere fit, penitentiarum remissae inhiaret et ipsius presertim antistitis benedictionem magnipenderet. Hinc ipsius mentem tacitam pertemptabant gaudia,[4] quia uideret tam effuso fauore, uelut lenis aquae inundantem impetum, populum ad Dei seruitium confluere. Non ergo torrentem eloquii sui sitientibus subtraxit, sed eum larga caritate infudit. Multum enim diei occupauit predicatio, dum eis habundanter inculcaret quod maxime tenendum cognosceret: (2) pacem dico, qua nichil dultius audiri, nichil desiderabilius appeti, nichil postremo melius inueniri a mortalibus potest; pacem quae sit

---

[a] extractum *δH** (*p. 86*), *more appropriately*

[1] Otto, *Sprichwörter* s.v. bucca 1.　　　　[2] Lucan i. 566. Cf. *GP*, c. 142 (p. 284).
[3] The story is told, more briefly, in *GP*, c. 142 (pp. 283–4).
[4] Virgil, *Aen.* i. 502.

Meanwhile the crowd in the cemetery gossiped mightily, saying whatever came into their heads.[1] 4. One youth, whose dangerous age prompted wanton language, kept taunting them: 'Why wait for the bishop? He's filling his belly along with the monks. Come on, if anyone wants his child signed, try me.' And he snatched up some mud, and smeared the forehead of the nearest baby, murmuring an obscene incantation over it. The madness went further, and the stupid action was taken up with a shout of 'Bind this one's forehead, he's been signed!'. Thus far mirth and high jinks. But not without punishment. Although the youth's words and action had won the laughter of the crowd, vengeance from heaven was at hand, for God resented the mock made of His gift and of the obedience shown by His servant. 5. Soon the boy responsible for the presumptuous behaviour began to rave in front of them all. No doubt he [i.e. the Devil] who had stirred up the youth's emotions within him now dictated his external movements. So the wretch began to toss his hair about,[2] grimace, and batter his head against a wall. The mob applauded the miracle, praised God in the highest, and drove the lunatic from the scene. Wandering hither and thither, with unsteady steps and quite out of control, he fell head first into a well or rather a sewage pit near the cemetery, and would have spewed up his life there had not his attentive relations tied him up and carried him to an inn. This was brought to the bishop's attention, and he grieved as much for the boy's punishment as for his sin. After he had sent a blessing the patient immediately regained his wits; but a few days later, I suppose because of what he had done or undergone, he completed his allotted span.

15. The reverend abbot invited Wulfstan on another occasion to Gloucester, to dedicate a church.[3] There was a big crowd present, eager, as often happens, for release from penances, and in particular appreciative of the bishop's blessing. This caused his own heart to be 'touched in silence by joys',[4] to see people flocking to pay their respects to God with such enthusiasm, like the surging flood of some gentle stream. So he did not refuse the torrent of his eloquence to those who thirsted for it, but poured it into them with the generosity of charity. Preaching took up most of the day, as he drove into them in good measure what he knew they most needed to grasp. 2. Peace is what I mean: for mortals can hear nothing sweeter, long for nothing more desirable, find nothing better. Peace is the beginning and end of man's salvation, and as it were the bottom line of the orders of God. It

salutis humanae principium et terminus, quae mandatorum Dei quasi limes extremus. Denique illam in ipso redemptionis auspitio angelicum melos intonuit, eam Dominus iam iamque crucem meditatus discipulis dedit, eam resurgens sicut triumphale xenium eisdem reportauit.[1] Loquebatur haec uulgo episcopus et ideo necessario inserebat exempla;[2] sed ego quia litteratis loquor, notiora sunt quae dico quam ut exemplificari*a* desiderent.

Multi sane antea inpacabiles*b* eo die ad pacificos reuocati assensus.[3] Alterutrum se incitabat populus, et si quis resultandum putaret consulebatur episcopus. 3. Hinc cuidam Willelmo cognomento Caluo oborta*c* fidutia ut querelas suas ferret in medium. Is casu non industria occiderat hominem, nec a cognatis occisi ullo poterat pacto mercari amicitiam, ullo pretio impetrare ueniam.[4] Sepe temptauerat uenerandus abbas reducere illos in concordiam, sed omnes conatus in uentum effuderat. Fratres erant quinque, qui pro nece germani tantas fremebant furias, tantas fulminabant minas ut quemlibet exterrere possent. Quis enim non corde labaret cum tot homines aeui maturos ⁻ eosdemque robore audacissimos in caput unum assurgere uideret? Tunc quoque producti et ab episcopo rogati ut illius delicti gratiam facerent turbulente prorsus abnuerunt. 4. Addiderunt facto non mitiora uerba, malle se omnino excommunicari quam necem fratris non ulcisci. Tum sacerdos ad plenam satisfactionem aduoluitur eorum pedibus, sicut erat pontificatus*d* insignibus amictus, iterabat preces iacens in terra, commeatum etiam missarum et benefitiorum tam Wigorniae quam Gloecestrae defuncto pollicitus. Nichil illi pro tanta flexi humilitate omnem abiurabant concordiam. Tantus eos dolor interitus fraterni succenderat ut totam sibi humanitatem adimerent. Quantus enim erat furor beatam illam canitiem in puluere uolutatam despicere, quam etiam ipsos angelos puto reueritos fuisse! 5. Addebatur contemptui eius diuina iniuria, et pontificalem uestem humana calcabat arrogantia. Quocirca presul, qui parum blanditiis promouerat, seueriori remedio inueteratis occurrens morbis, facile discrimen esse aiebat inter filios Dei et filios diaboli. Si enim ueritati

---

a *ed.*; -are *C*   *b* in pacabiles [*sic*] *C*; implacabiles δ (*p. 87*); in placabiles *H**
c δ*H** (*p. 87*); aborta *C*   *d* pontificatis *C^{p.c.}*

---

[1] Luke 2: 14, John 14: 27, Luke 24: 36.
[2] On preaching in the vernacular at Wulfstan's Worcester, see M. McC. Gatch, *Preaching and Theology in Anglo-Saxon England* (Toronto, 1977), pp. 44, 56–7.
[3] Cf. *GP*, c. 142 (p. 283): 'offensas utrimque donauere'.

was peace that the song of the angels thundered out at the very beginning of the Redemption, peace that the Lord gave to His disciples while He was contemplating His Passion, peace that He brought back in triumph as a present for them when He rose from the dead.[1] The bishop was talking to ordinary people, and so had to include instances.[2] But as I am writing for the literate, what I say is too well-known to need exemplification.

Many who had hitherto been unappeasable were that day brought back to peaceful accord.[3] The people egged each other on, and if anyone thought fit to object the bishop was brought in. 3. This is how one William the Bald plucked up courage to publicize his complaint. He had killed a man not intentionally but by accident, and could not buy the friendship of the slain man's relatives on any terms, or win their forgiveness at any price.[4] The revered abbot had often tried to reconcile them, but all his efforts had been vain. There were five brothers concerned about the death of the man, and such were their furious threats that anyone might have been frightened out of his wits. Who would not have flinched to see so many grown men, with all the daring of physical strength, turning upon a single victim? So they were brought forth on this occasion, and begged by the bishop to forgive the offence; but they shook their heads violently. 4. What is more they added equally resentful words: they said they would rather be excommunicated than fail to avenge their brother's killing. Then the priest, to make them full amends, grovelled at their feet just as he was, dressed in his episcopal vestments. He lay there on the ground, repeating his prayers, and promised masses and spiritual benefits for the dead man at Worcester and at Gloucester. But they were not moved, for all his humility, and swore they would never be reconciled. Their sorrow at their brother's death had so enflamed them that they had lost all human sentiments. What madness to look without a pang on those blessed white hairs rolling in the dust, when even angels would, I think, have respected them! 5. Not merely was Wulfstan treated with contempt, but injury was inflicted on God: the arrogance of men trampled on the robes of a bishop. So Wulfstan, having got nowhere by entreaty, applied a harsher remedy to a disease

---

[4] An apparently unique anecdote, cited as a late example of intention to pursue a feud without accepting compensation, by A. Kennedy, 'Feud', in *Blackwell Encyclopaedia*, pp. 182–3, at 183, and discussed by P. Hyams, 'Feud in medieval England', *The Haskins Society Journal*, iii (1991), 1–21, at pp. 2–4, making an interesting comparison of Wulfstan's strategies with those used by the Peace of God movement on the Continent.

creditur, immo quia creditur, dicenti 'Beati pacifici, quoniam filii Dei uocabuntur',[1] liquet profecto filios esse diaboli qui paci aduersantur;[2] cuius enim quis opera facit, eius et filius dicitur.[3] Acclamauit populus ita esse, ita se uelle; simul et contemptores conuitiis incessebat. Secuta est e uestigio maledicta populi diuina ultio, uno ex fratribus eodemque acerrimo statim insano facto. 6. Volutabatur ad humum miser, mordicus terram apprehendens, digitis effodiens, spumas uirulentas iaciens, fumigabundis etiam (quod uix alias audierim) membris, ut teterrimus odor uicinum infestaret aerem. Quid animi tunc fuisse putas reliquis haec uidentibus? Desedit tumor mentium, insolentia euanuit, arrogantia emarcuit. Cerneres illos ultro quod contempserant affectare, pacem offerre, misericordiam implorare. Metus sui reuerentiam extorserat, pietas fratris humilitatem induxerat. Quippe non secus in se quam in illo ultum iri timebant facinus, quod aeque omnes inuoluerat. Mouit haec rerum faties clementiam antistitis, statimque post missam patienti salutem, ceteris securitatem, omnibus reformauit pacem.[4] 16. Haec fuit occasio ut Wlstano de pace loquenti nemo presumeret refragari.[5]

Gaudebat pater de filiorum prouectibus, quia sciret quod illorum salus ad suum redundaret premium.[6] Propterea quantum sua intererat multum eorum bona urgebat, 'instans' secundum apostolum 'oportune, importune, in omni patientia et doctrina'.[7] Sin uero minus commode posset, quod quidem in extremo aetatis prae dolore tibiarum fuit, Colemanno predicationis delegabat offitium, magnipendens in eo munditiam uitae, prestantiam personae, profusam facundiam, litterarum peritiam. 2. Quae cum uir ille non perfunctorie haberet, non tamen ad Wlstani poterat gratiam aspirare, ut tam grate audiretur a plebe. Quandocumque enim episcopus de pace loquebatur inhianter audiebatur, alter non ita, sed auditores aut

---

[1] Matt. 5: 9.

[2] Cf. John 8: 44.

[3] Cf. Isidore, *Sententiae* i. 16. 16 (CCSL cxi, p. 59): 'cuius doctrinam quisque sequitur, huius et filius nuncupatur; . . . filii Dei nuncupantur qui praecepta Dei custodiunt.'

[4] This part of the story goes on longer in *GP*, c. 142 (p. 284).

[5] This emphasis on Wulfstan as a peace-maker is commented upon by Orchard, 'Parallel lives'. He draws attention to the apparently unique prayer on fo. i of Bodl. Libr., MS Hatton 113, a book closely connected to Wulfstan (see above, p. 74 n. 5, below, pp. 93 n. 7, 112 n. 1): 'Oremus omnes Deum Patrem omnipotentem ut sanctam ecclesiam suam pacifice gubernet et protegat, subiciens ei principatus et potestates, detque nobis quietam et tranquillam uitam, et adiuuet ut stabili fide in confessione sui nominis perseuerare mereamur, per Christum.'

[6] Similarly of Dunstan in *VD* i. 17. 4.

that had become ingrained. He said that it was easy to distinguish between sons of God and sons of the Devil. 'If—indeed because— belief is accorded to the Truth when He said: "Blessed are the peacemakers: for they shall be called the children of God",[1] it is quite clear that the sons of the Devil are those who stand out against peace.[2] For if you do the works of anyone, you are called his son.'[3] The crowd shouted that this was true, this was what they wanted, and they hurled abuse at Wulfstan's despisers. All at once, upon the curses of the people followed vengeance from God: one of the brothers, and that the fiercest, suddenly went mad. 6. The wretch rolled on the ground, biting at the soil and digging it up with his fingers. He foamed poisonously, and— something I have scarcely heard tell of— his limbs smoked, so that a foul smell polluted the air around. What do you think the rest felt when they saw this? Their swelling pride collapsed, their insolence vanished, their arrogance withered. You might have seen them going out of their way to embrace what they had despised, offering peace and begging for mercy. Fear for themselves had enforced this reverence, pity for their brother had brought on this humility; for they were afraid that an offence in which they were all implicated would be avenged on themselves as well as on him. The scene aroused the mercy of the bishop, and straight after mass he restored health to the sufferer, reassurance to the other brothers, and peace to all.[4] 16. The result of this was that no one henceforth presumed to answer back when Wulfstan was talking of peace.[5]

Like a father he rejoiced in the advancement of his sons, because he knew that their salvation redounded to his own credit.[6] So he did all he could to urge them on to good works, being, as the apostle says, 'instant in season, out of season, with all long-suffering and doctrine'.[7] But if he could not easily do it himself, as happened at the end of his life because of pain in his shins, he would delegate the task of preaching to Coleman, whose pure life, personal stature, eloquence, and learning he highly valued. 2. It is true that Coleman had all these characteristics to a high degree, but he could not aspire to Wulfstan's heights, and was not heard by the people with such pleasure. For whenever the bishop spoke of peace they listened avidly. But it was different with Coleman: his listeners either barracked or walked out.

---

[7] 2 Tim. 4: 2. The importance that Wulfstan placed on preaching is exemplified in the great collections of English homilies produced at Worcester in his time, and probably by his authority: Bodl. Libr., MSS Hatton 113 and 114, and Junius 121.

succlamabant aut abibant. Veruntamen et in hoc uindicta caelestis sacerdoti seruiuit, ut discerent omnes et in offitialium eius ueneratione ipsius honori assurgere. Erat in Wigornia[a] minister Ernmerus nomine, ex illo cementariorum genere quos litores[b] uocant. Hic cuidam homini ex eodem uico digladiabili odio[1] infensus, si quando Colemannum de pace loquentem audisset, statim discessu suo predicationi simul et monacho ualefatiebat. 3. Adulabatur interim sibi et cordi suggerebat blanditias: episcopum non loqui, et propterea quod a monacho diceretur impune posse contempni. Deo aliter uisum.[2] Non enim multo post idem opifex[c] confractis machinis super quas ad liniendam maceriam[d] stabat miserabilem semperque sibi duraturam erumnam incurrit, ambo crura debilitatus. Et eo quidem anno cubili accumbit, sed numquam tota uita pedes non doluit. Multisque pro exemplo, pene correctioni fuit,[e] ut nullus fere per nomen Wlstani rogatus pacem auderet infitiari.

17. Nec erat quicquam quod magis caueretur a suis quam ut culpis eorum irritatus uel moueretur animo uel excederet uerbo. Quamquam ille in neutrum facile laberetur, aut si umquam certa hoc et necessaria causa, ut exemplo palam erit. Eielsius[f] quidam, qui minister regis Eduardi fuerat,[3] ad uillam suam Langene supra Sabrinam positam euocauit antistitem ad consecrandam aecclesiam. Venit ille, ut numquam in talibus moras nectens, sed locus capacitati populi defuit, qui undatim ad eum solito more confluxerat. 2. Preter haec erat in cimiterio arbor nucea patulis frondibus umbrosa, quae lasciua[g] ramorum amplitudine diem inuidebat aecclesiae. Eam inuitatore ascito iussit abscidi episcopus. Congrueret enim ut si spatium negasset natura ipse suppleret industria, nedum quod illa dederat ille suis occuparet ludibriis. Solebat enim uir ille sub eadem arbore presertim aestiuis diebus aleis uel epulis uacare uel aliis ludis hilaritatem allicere. Quapropter non solum non humiliter paruit,

---

[a] δH^* (*p. 88*); -iam *C*   [b] *C* (-es *in ras.*); lictores δ (*p. 88*); littores *H**   [c] δH^* (*p. 88*); pontifex *CH*   [d] δH^* (*p. 88*); materiam *C*   [e] multisque . . . fuit] *The text is uncertain; perhaps delete* pro, *so that both nouns can be predicative datives, adding* et *after* exemplo. pene = paene *seems feeble, and it may represent* poenae *and be a gloss on* correctioni. [f] *Domesday Book spells the name* Elsi. *William will probably have written* Elfsius *or* Elsius. [g] *ed.* (*cf.* luxuriante δHR, *p. 89*); lasciuia *C*

---

[1] Similarly *GR*, cc. 14. 1, *GP*, cc. 107 (p. 240), 142 (p. 283). The rare word 'digladiabilis' may derive from Prudentius, *Cath.* iii. 148: 'hoc erat aspidis atque hominis digladiabile discidium.' For the story cf. i. 8. 2–6.

[2] Cf. Virgil, *Aen.* ii. 428: 'dis aliter uisum'. See *GR*, c. 419. 2 n.

But here too punishment from heaven came to Wulfstan's aid, so that everyone learned to honour him by showing respect to his subordinates. There was at Worcester a man on the staff called Earnmær, one of the kind of masons called plasterers. He nurtured a deadly hatred[1] against someone in the same town, and if he ever heard Coleman on the topic of peace he would make a prompt exit and bid farewell to sermon and monk alike. 3. He flattered himself with the cheering reflection that it was not the bishop speaking, and that what a monk said could safely be ignored. God thought otherwise.[2] Not much later, this same workman was standing on a contraption he used when plastering a wall; it broke, and he sustained an injury that aroused the pity of others and brought him lasting distress, for he damaged both legs. That year he spent in bed, and never afterwards did he lose the pain in his feet. He served as an example to many, and almost as a means of reforming them, so that virtually nobody dared to refuse reconciliation when begged in the name of Wulfstan.

17. Wulfstan's people were especially concerned to avoid his being provoked by any fault of theirs into irritation or harsh language. Not that he fell readily into either, or if he ever did it was for some good and clear reason, as the following case shows. One Ælfsige, who had been a thegn of King Edward,[3] invited Wulfstan to his vill of Longney on the Severn to dedicate a church. He never made difficulties about something like that, but when he arrived he found that there was not enough room for the people who had, as usual, come in droves to hear him. 2. What is more, there was in the churchyard a nut tree which provided shade with its spreading leaves, but whose luxuriant branches denied light to the church. The bishop summoned his host and gave orders for the felling of the tree: it was only proper that, if nature had not provided enough room, he should supplement it by his own efforts, and certainly not take over for his own low pursuits space that nature *had* given—for the man had the habit of spending leisure time under the tree, especially on a summer's day, dicing or feasting, or indulging in some other kind of jollification. That was why the man, far from obeying humbly,

---

[3] He held Longney in chief as a king's thegn, and probably lands elsewhere: *DB 15: Gloucestershire*, 1: 66, 11: 14, 78: 1, 12. The manor farm at Longney still adjoins the churchyard immediately to the south, and is presumably the site of Ælfsige's house. For the cursing of the tree Mason, p. 166, compares Christ's cursing of the barren fig-tree in Matt. 21: 18–22. See also R. Morris, *Churches in the Landscape* (London, 1989), pp. 79–80; J. Blair, *The Church in Anglo-Saxon Society* (Oxford, forthcoming), ch. 8.

sed etiam pertinaciter contradixit, tamque, ut postea confessus est, erat impudentis amentiae ut mallet aecclesiam non dedicari quam arborem abscidi. 3. Tum uero Sanctus, nonnichil hac proteruia motus, maledictionis iaculum in arborem intorsit, quo illa uulnerata paulatim sterilescens et fructu caruit et radicitus exaruit. Qua infecunditate ita possessorem exacerbauit ut quam possederat cum inuidia, desiderauerat cum gratia, sterilitate pertesus abscidi iuberet. Hoc idem paterfamilias Colemanno reuerso*[a]* postea retulit, et in signum miraculi locum ostendit; fixumque apud se semper habuit et dixit, nichil Wlstani maledictione amarius, nichil benedictione dultius inueniri.[1]

18. Multotiens enim qui tranquillum animum uiri peruicatia sua turbauerunt caelestem ultionem experti sunt. Verbi causa exemplum subtexam. Venerat statim post Pascha in uillam cui Bloccelea nomen,[2] aderatque dies octauarum qua Dominus noster geminato post resurrectionem suam miraculo ueram carnem obseratis foribus intulit cenaculo.[3] Missam dicturus omnia ornamenta altaris infra sollemnitatis decorem esse offendit, informes cereos, candelabra cotidiana, mantilia diuturnum squalorem preferentia. 2. Quapropter astanti clericello innuit ut ueloci cursu cubiculario rei correctionem iniungeret. At minister, qui sepe clementia mansueti pontificis abusus esset, commoto felle pergrandem colaphum puero impegit. Cesus ille ad dominum rediit, indices sui doloris lacrimas reportans. Tanta seruientis arrogantia infremuit antistitis ira, turbato etiam uultu prodita. Veruntamen intra pectus eam cohibens rem omnem pro tempore quieto dissoluit silentio. Sed mirabilem in modum, eadem hora qua ira mentem pontificis in aecclesia concussit, morbus ministri corpus in cubiculo turbauit. 3. Quo ictus ad terram decidit, flatu pene intercepto, sensu certe amisso. Similis ergo iam iamque morituro iacebat, ita color a fatie, calor a corpore, sermo ex ore fugerat. Accursum undique ad iacentem, causa subiti casus sollicite quesita, diligenter inuenta. Quia innocenti

---

[a]   *The sense seems to demand* reuersus

[1] Here William might have inserted the story of Wulfstan cursing the army of Roger of Montgomery, which he tells in *GP*, c. 144 (p. 285). See above, p. xxxiii.

[2] Blockley (Glos.), once an independent minster; by 855 the church was in the bishop's hands (S207), and by Wulfstan's time it was an episcopal estate centre; later an episcopal manor: *Gloucestershire Studies*, ed. H. P. R. Finberg (Leicester, 1957), pp. 5–11; Sims-Williams, *Religion and Literature* (above, p. 70 n. 1), p. 172; J. K. West, 'Architectural sculpture in parish churches of the 11th- and 12th-century west midlands: some problems

obstinately refused, and fell, as he later admitted, into such impudent madness that he was prepared to see the church undedicated rather than have the tree cut down 3. The saint, in no small degree provoked by this impertinence, hurled the spear of his curse at the tree. From the wound it gradually grew barren, failed in its fruit, and shrivelled up from the root. This sterility so irked the owner that in his annoyance he ordered the felling of a tree he had jealously owned and dearly longed to keep(?). The bishop told the story later to Coleman, when he returned to the vill, and showed him the spot in proof of the miracle. And Coleman always maintained and expressed the firm view that nothing could be more bitter than the curse of Wulfstan, or more agreeable than his blessing.[1]

18. Indeed it very often happened that those whose perversity ruffled his tranquillity were given a taste of punishment from on high. I will provide an instance. He had come straight after Easter to a vill called Blockley.[2] It was the first Sunday after Easter, the day on which our Lord, in a second miracle following his resurrection, though the doors were closed, brought his very flesh into the dining room.[3] Wulfstan was about to say mass when he found all the ornaments on the altar in no fit state for the rite: shoddy candles, ordinary candlesticks, and cloths with the dust of every day on them. 2. So he signed to the minor clerk who stood by him to hurry and tell the chamberlain to put things right. But the attendant, who had often abused the clemency of the easy-going bishop, flew into a rage, and gave the boy a great smack. He returned to his master, his tears witnessing to his pain. The bishop was enraged by the attendant's high-handed behaviour, and showed it in his face. But he restrained his feelings and for the moment let the whole thing go. But remarkably enough, at precisely the moment when anger disturbed the composure of the bishop's mind in the church, the servant's body was disturbed by illness in the bedroom. 3. He fell to the floor under its impact, almost without breath, and certainly unconscious. There he lay, like one about to die: the colour had drained from his face, the heat from his body, and he could not say a word. Everyone ran up to him as he lay on the ground, and the reason for his sudden collapse was carefully

in assessing the evidence', in *Minsters and Parish Churches: the Local Church in Transition 950–1200*, ed. J. Blair (Oxford, 1988), pp. 159–67, at 164 and n. 44.

[3] The first Sunday after Easter, when Christ appeared to the disciples in the upper room: John 20: 19. The first of the 'twin miracles' was presumably the Resurrection itself.

puero alapam infregerat, iratum episcopum fuisse; illum nunc sacrilegi ausus penam pendere. Deposcendam ergo ab illo ueniam, pro quo culpa inuenerat uindictam. Huius rei legatione familiari monacho quem persepe nominaui[1] data, cunctorum uoces pertulit ille. Nec mora, benedictione concessa, tam facile sanitas astitit confitenti quam perniciter morbus ingruerat peccanti.

19. Veniam ad illud miraculum quod, quia nostris temporibus est factum, pene sibi fidem abrogat. Quod Colemannus fore non ignorans, multis illud suffulsit testibus, ne auditorum credulitate uacillante triumpharet perfidia. Et primo quidem cum recens auditum Wigornensibus intulisset, quidam arguerunt eum mendatii, non ueritatem facti sed fauorem Sancti esse cauillati. Hoc ille acrius instare, et testes legitimos producere, uiros numero et dignitate prestantes. Nec prius abstitit quam duras frontes obtunderet, dum predicabiles homines se illud expertos esse dicerent et per quicquid sanctum est iurarent. Id fuit huiusmodi. 2. Vicus est maritimus Bristou dictus,[2] a quo recto cursu in Hiberniam transmittitur, ideoque illius terrae barbariei[3] accommodus. Huius indigenae cum ceteris ex Anglia causa mercimonii ut sepe in Hiberniam annauigabant. Iamque in altum processerant cum mutata caeli clementia diem abstulit, noctem induxit. Seuiebat fragor uentorum, diluuium imbrium, ut solui mundus estimaretur. Militare putares procellas in excidium miserorum nautarum: rudentibus diruptis, malo effracto, remis excussis; procedebat nauigium casu non uiribus, fortuna non arte.[4] Pallebant[a] omnes morte uentura, tribusque diebus cum noctibus inopes somni expertes cibi uitam traxerunt. 3. Deus pie, quanta miseria hominum pendulo metu mortem operientium! cum leuius, ut puto, sit uitam uiriliter abrumpere quam ignauum interitum expectare. Quarto die, cum iam terga daret quicquid superfuerat animi,

---

[a] C(*corr. from* psallebant)*HR*; pallescebant (*corr. in D from* palescebant) δ (*p. 90*)

[1] i.e. Coleman.

[2] On Bristol and its trade with Ireland see D. Walker, *Bristol in the early Middle Ages* (Bristol Branch of the Historical Association, xxviii: 1971); M. Horton, 'Bristol and its international position', in *'Almost the Richest City': Bristol in the Middle Ages*, ed. L. Keen (British Archaeological Assoc., Conference Transactions xix, 1997), pp. 9–17, at 10–12; A. Gwynn, 'Medieval Bristol and Dublin', *Irish Historical Studies*, v (1947), 275–86, esp. p. 278.

[3] For more scornful remarks on Irish mores, see *GR*, cc. 51. 1, 409. 1 and n., and J. Gillingham, 'The beginnings of English imperialism', in his *The English in the Twelfth Century*, pp. 3–18, at 9–18.

sought—and found: they realized that, because he had slapped an innocent boy and the bishop had grown angry, he was now paying the penalty for his sacrilegious action. He must therefore beg pardon from him on whose behalf his fault was being punished. The conveying of this message was entrusted to the monk in Wulfstan's confidence whom I have often named,[1] and he brought to the bishop the views of them all. He did not delay in granting his blessing, and health returned to the chamberlain when he confessed as quickly as the illness had come upon him when he sinned.

19. I now come to a miracle that almost beggars belief, because it happened in our own day. Coleman foresaw this problem, and gave the story the support of an array of witnesses, in case the credence of hearers should waver and disbelief triumph. At first when he told the monks of Worcester the news, some accused him of lying, objecting that the story stemmed not from fact but from bias in the saint's favour. Coleman pressed his point the more emphatically, and produced legitimate witnesses, men numerous and high in rank. And he did not give up until he had got it into their thick heads, for there were respectable persons ready to swear by everything that is holy that they had witnessed the miracle. The story went like this. 2. There is a town on the sea called Bristol,[2] from which there is a direct passage to Ireland; hence it is very convenient for intercourse with that barbarous part of the world.[3] Some Bristolians, accompanied by other Englishmen, were, as often, on a voyage to Ireland for purposes of trade. They had already got well out to sea when the weather turned foul, the light failed, and darkness fell. The winds raged and howled, the rain came down in floods. It looked as though the end of the world was nigh. You might have supposed that the squalls were at war to the death with the hapless sailors. Ropes snapped, the mast broke, oars went overboard, and the ship drove ahead more by luck than judgement.[4] Everyone was pale at the prospect of death, and three days and nights, without sleep and without food, they hung on to life. 3. Good God, think of the misery of men waiting for death on a tenterhook of fear!—for it is surely easier to cut short life like a man than to await an ignoble end. On the fourth day, when what spirit remained was in retreat, God, who would not wish the death of the wretched but rather their

---

[4] Another storm like this is described in *GP*, c. 224 (p. 377).

Deus, qui nollet mortem miserorum sed uitam,[1] inspirauit cuidam ut diceret: 'Vos qui estis ex episcopatu reuerentissimi Wlstani, cur non precamini Dei misericordiam,[a] ut per eius intercessionem fatiat nos euadere hanc miseriam?' Rapuerunt ex ore[2] illius uerbum ceteri, una uoce imis medullis in orationem effusi. Nec multo post Omnipotentis clementia in illo mortis horrore positos erexit, exhibens non quidem crediderim Wlstanum, sed effigiem eius presentissimam. Mirum id sit dicere; sed enim ueritati non resultat tot et tantorum uirorum assertio. 4. Ibat ergo per nauem, armamenta consolidans, rudentes coaptans, modo singulos modo uniuersos appellans. Reuocarent animos, antempnas erigerent, funes uel cingulis innecterent; futurum Deo propitio ut suo auxilio breui appellerent. Promissionem secutus est effectus. Statim enim Hiberniae portui allapsi, nec multo post felicibus auris Angliam reuecti disseminauerunt ubique miraculum. Nec diffitendum est nostro tempore potuisse fieri quod aliquotiens per antiquos sanctos Deus fecerit. Siquidem legimus aliquos, plerumque rei conscios, plerumque nescios, opem tulisse absentibus, et adhuc corporis inuolucris impeditos prout sibi libuit spiritu exhibitos. Quorum nomina supersedeo dicere, ne uidear alienae indulgere materiae.[3]

20. Hoc sane miraculum tanti apud uicanos ualuit ut nichil eis magis animo staret quam quod ille iubendum putaret. Denique ab eis morem uetustissimum sustulit, qui sic animis eorum occalluerat ut nec Dei amor nec regis Willelmi timor hactenus eum abolere potuisset.[b 4] Homines enim ex omni Anglia coemptos maioris spe questus in Hiberniam distrahebant, ancillasque prius ludibrio lecti habitas iamque pregnantes uenum proponebant. Videres et gemeres concatenatos funibus miserorum ordines et utriusque sexus

---

[a] [*Peile*]; miam (*with a mark of abbreviation*) C (miseriam *Darl.*)   [b] H* (*p. 91*); potuissent C; potuerunt δ

[1] Cf. Ezech. 33: 11 (cf. 18: 32).
[2] Cf. Virgil, *Aen.* vii. 118–19, also echoed in *GR*, c. 239. 3, *GP*, cc. 6, 130 (pp. 13, 270), *VD* i. 21. 4.
[3] William has obviously chosen to omit material present in Coleman's Life. The abbreviation of *VW* (Darlington, p. 90) mentions St Nicholas. Mason, p. 184 n. 76, compares Columba: *Adomnan's Life of Columba* ii. 42, ed. and trans. A. O. and M. O. Anderson (OMT, 1991), pp. 166–71.
[4] On Wulfstan and the slave-trade, see also *GR*, c. 269. 2 and D. A. E. Pelteret, *Slavery in Early Medieval England: from the Reign of Alfred until the Twelfth Century* (Woodbridge, 1995), pp. 59, 76–8, 224–5. Wulfstan's position was an entirely orthodox one; what he

life,[1] inspired someone to say: 'You who are from the diocese of the revered Wulfstan, why don't you pray for God's mercy, that by Wulfstan's intercession He may have us escape from this distress?' The others snatched at these words,[2] and with a single voice launched out into heartfelt prayers. Not long afterwards the clemency of the Almighty uplifted them in those horrid straits by showing them not (as I believe) Wulfstan himself but an image of him, ready to help them. It may sound extraordinary, but the evidence of so many distinguished persons cannot clash with the truth. 4. The shape went through the ship, strengthening the tackle, splicing ropes, addressing men singly or all together. They should pluck up their courage, haul up the yards, and contrive sheets, even if they had to use their own belts. God willing, they would soon make land with his help. His promise was fulfilled. At once they came into an Irish port, and not much later returned with favouring winds to England, where they spread the miracle abroad. No one can say that what God did several times through saints of old could not have happened in our time too. For we read that holy men, sometimes consciously, sometimes unaware of what they were doing, have brought help while not present, and, though still hampered by the integument of the body, have been free to appear in the spirit wherever they willed. I forbear to give names, so as not to seem to be digressing.[3]

20. This miracle made such an impression on the people of Bristol that they formed no principle more fixed than to do what he thought fit to tell them. For instance, he put a stop to an ancient habit of theirs which had become so ingrained that neither love of God nor fear of King William had hitherto been able to abolish it.[4] For they would buy up men from all over England and sell them off to Ireland in hope of a profit, and put up for sale maidservants after toying with them in bed and making them pregnant. You would have groaned to see the files of the wretches roped together, young persons of both

---

opposed was not the institution of slavery as such, but the sale of persons destined to be sent abroad. Pelteret's evidence shows that slavery was common in Anglo-Saxon England, and he suggests that the Norman kings were prepared to let it continue because it was profitable to them. Nonetheless it was prohibited 'outside the country' in clause 9 of the *Leges Willelmi* (*English Historical Documents 1042–1189*, ed. D. C. Douglas and G. W. Greenaway (2nd edn., London, 1981), p. 400) and outlawed altogether in canon 28 of the council of Westminster 1102 (*Councils*, i(2). 678). See also Mason, pp. 184–6.

adolescentes,[1] qui liberali forma, aetate integra, barbaris miserationi essent, cotidie prostitui, cotidie uenditari. Facinus execrandum, dedecus miserabile, nec beluini affectus memores homines necessitudines suas, ipsum postremo sanguinem suum, seruituti addicere! 2. Hunc tam inueteratum morem et a proauis in nepotes transfusum Wlstanus ut dixi paulatim deleuit. Sciens enim ceruicositatem eorum non facile flecti, sepe circa eos duobus mensibus sepe tribus mansitabat, omni dominica eo ueniens et diuinae predicationis semina spargens. Quae adeo per interualla temporum apud eos conualuere ut non solum renuntiarent uitio sed ad idem fatiendum ceteris per Angliam essent exemplo. Denique unum ex suo numero, qui pertinatius obuiaret preceptis episcopi, uico eiectum mox luminibus orbauere. In qua re deuotionem laudo, sed factum improbo, quanuis semel incitatis agrestium[2] animis nulla queat obsistere uis rationis.

21. Legatu Willelmi regis et Thomae archiepiscopi semel ad Eboracum ante Pascha proficiscens ut ibi crisma benediceret, Snotingaham uenit. Is uicus est famosus, quem Trenta non ignobilis fluuius ibidem transmeabilis alluit. Premittit ministros qui pararent hospitium totius comitatus capax. Et tum forte uicecomes aberat.[3] At uero uxor eius, bonae actionis femina, nuntios dignanter excepit, eoque magis quod essent Wlstano episcopo dediti. Nam sanctitatis eius fama etiam illius aures dulci perflauerat aura. Referentibus illa nec fidem prorsus abnuerat nec penitus accommodauerat. 2. Nutabat ergo sententiae incerto. Quapropter precursores uerbis adorsa sedulo explorat, sollicite per nomen Dei adiurat: liberarent eam hoc ambiguo, an religio episcopi famae conueniret suae. Respondit percunctanti Frewinus quod erat ueritatis, quod moderationis, ut nec rem deprimeret nec ulterius fide attolleret: episcopum Dei seruum esse, libenter et simpliciter eius seruitium facere, illud in se et in aliis diligere. Altius intendit questionem mulier, ut eius solutionem de caelo attraheret: euidenter appariturum quod Dei famulus esset, si eius edulio profuturus piscis reti accurreret. 3. Iam enim plus tribus

---

[1] We have translated on the presumption that the 'adolescentes' made up the 'ordines', rather than being supplementary. This would be clearer if the 'et' were omitted after 'ordines'.

[2] Cf. *VD* ii. 25. 2: 'multa . . . inflixit incommoda, ut est agrestium cum incipiunt saeuire proteruia'. 'Agrestis', here applied to townspeople, must refer metaphorically to their habits.

[3] For his possible identity (there are at least four possibilities), see J. A. Green, *English Sheriffs to 1154* (London, 1990), p. 67.

sexes,[1] whose youth and respectable appearance would have aroused the pity of barbarians, being put up for sale every day. An accursed deed, and a crying shame, that men devoid of emotions that even beasts feel should condemn to slavery their own relations and even their flesh and blood! 2. It was this long-established custom, handed down from generation to generation, that, as I said, Wulfstan gradually got rid of. He knew there was no easy way to influence such stubborn people, and so he would often live in the district for two or three months at a time, going to the town each Sunday and sowing the seed of the word of God. The seed flourished among them over a period, so that they not merely renounced this evil practice, but gave all Englishmen a lead in doing the same. For example, one of their own number, who was recalcitrant in his flouting of the bishop's commands, they drove out of town and then blinded. I applaud the piety lying behind the action, however much I deplore what they did. But once countrymen are aroused, they are not amenable to reason.[2]

21. Once Wulfstan had to set out before Easter for York to bless the chrism there. He had been summoned by King William and Archbishop Thomas. On the way he came to Nottingham, a well-known town washed by the noble river Trent, which can be crossed at that point. He sent servants ahead to arrange lodging sufficient for his entire retinue. The sheriff[3] was away, as it happened, but his wife, a practical lady, gave the messengers a civil welcome, the more so because they were devoted to Bishop Wulfstan. For her ears too had received the sweet breath of the fame of his sanctity. To such reports she had neither altogether denied credence nor completely assented. 2. So she was in a state of doubt. She accordingly interviewed the advance party, and made careful enquiries, adjuring them in the name of God to free her from her conundrum: did Wulfstan's piety correspond with the reports of it? Freowine's reply was in accordance with the truth, steering a middle course between playing down the facts and exaggerating them beyond belief. The bishop, he explained, was the servant of God, and did His service in willingness and simplicity: that was what he liked, in himself and in others. The woman probed deeper, hoping to bring down a solution to her question from on high: it would be quite obvious that he was the servant of God if a fish entered her nets and gave him something to eat. 3. For it was now more than three months since any fish had

mensibus omnis in his locis piscium captura desiuerat. Dubietatis ergo nodum ille pro misericordia sua sibi solueret, qui quondam cicatrice uulnerum Thomae firmasset ambiguum.[1] Haec secum. Ceterum nuntiis egregio confotis hospitio suos piscatum mittit, euentum rei fortunae indulgens arbitrio. Continuo illi, quorum (ut dixi) artem omnes conatus illuserant pridem, quinque isitios immane quam turgidos insuerunt retibus.[2] Veruntamen homines qui commodis consulentes suis in exiguo mendatium ponerent tres maiusculos[a] furati duos herae attulere. 4. Illa immenso gestiens tripudio eos domino exhibuit, et palam omnibus rem totam exposuit. Nichil dubietatis superesse quin Dei gratiam haberet. Orare obnixe ut benefitiorum eius compos, orationum particeps, memoriae assecla fieri mereretur. Hoc primo die, hoc secundo, cum detecta latronum fallatia reliqui pisces recepti auxere miraculum. Nam et hoc ad eius sanctitatem referendum rata quem Deus nollet toto fraudare commodo, uotum oblato cumulauit xenio.

Inter haec pulchrum est animaduerti quam in promptu spiritum prophetiae habuerit, cum[b] in multis tum in hoc quod subtexam. 22. Sewius quidam non mediocrium diuitiarum homo in sua uilla Readecliue fecerat aecclesiam.[3] Eam a Sancto dedicari religiosis uotis inestuans, ab archiepiscopo cuius erat diocesis petierat licentiam[4] et impetrauerat. Sato rumore in uulgus quod munus dedicationis exsecuturus esset Wlstanus, constipatis eo uentum est agminibus. Multus eo die fuit sermo ad populum, cum semper pro more de pace actitaret episcopus. Quo fretus ac plurimum bonae spei concipiens, tenuis homo substantiae processit. 2. Is multis precibus supplicauit antistiti ut inter se et quendam prediuitis fortunae qui astaret uirum pacem reformaret. Amborum nomina siue consulto siue quia exciderant pretermittit Colemannus. Veruntamen diuitem fuisse declarat presbiterum, sed presbiteratum propter opum conscientiam[5] peierasse. Euocatus ergo et bis terque de pace precibus episcopi pulsatus, petitiones arroganti fastu exinaniuit. Tum ille in superbum

---

^a δH* (p. 92); mansiunculos C　　　　^b ed.; tum C

[1] John 20: 24–9.
[2] Evidence of early medieval fish-traps on the Trent near Nottingham is adduced by C. R. Salisbury, 'Primitive British fishweirs', in *Waterfront Archaeology*, ed. G. L. Good, R. H. Jones, and M. W. Ponsford (Council for British Archaeology Research Report, lxxiv, 1991), pp. 76–87.
[3] Sewy or Sæwig occ. among the king's thegns in Domesday Book. He held lands at Ratcliffe-upon-Soar as well as elsewhere: *DB 28 Nottinghamshire*, 30. 20; *VCH Notts.* i. 285, mentioning a priest and church there.

been taken in those parts. Her knotty problem would be solved in His mercy by Him who once had reassured doubting Thomas by showing him the scars of His wounds.[1] This was her secret plan. But she gave the messengers a royal welcome, and sent her people off to fish, leaving the outcome to chance. Straight away the fishermen, whose arts (as I said) had been baffled for all their efforts over a long period, took five enormous salmon in their nets.[2] But they were quite ready to tell a lie where their own interests were involved, and they filched the three biggest fish, taking two back to their mistress. 4. She was overjoyed, and showed the fish to the lord bishop, telling everybody the whole story: there was no room for doubt now that Wulfstan had the grace of God. She prayed fervently that she should be found worthy to be the object of his spiritual benefits, to be mentioned in his prayers, and to foster his memory. This she did on the first and again on the second day, when the miracle was increased by the appearance of the remaining fish, for the trickery of the thieves had been found out. The woman thought this too redounded to the credit of Wulfstan's holiness, for it seemed that God was unwilling to deprive him of the full benefit of the catch, and she backed up her prayer with the offer of a present.

Amid all this, it is a pleasure to observe how ready to hand he kept the spirit of prophecy, as on the following occasion. 22. One Sæwig, a man of some means, had built a church in his vill at Ratcliffe.[3] In his piety he was anxious to have it dedicated by the holy man, and he had made a successful application for a licence to the archbishop of the diocese.[4] The rumour got about that Wulfstan was to officiate, and the roads were packed as they came to hear him. There was a long sermon to the people that day, and the bishop as always made his subject peace. Relying on that, and with good hopes, a man of slender means came forward (2) and begged the bishop to restore concord between himself and a certain very rich man who was present. The names of both are left out by Coleman, either on purpose, or because they had slipped his memory; but he states that the rich man had been a priest, though he had forsworn his priesthood because of his wealth.[5] This personage, therefore, was summoned forth, and two or three times assailed by the bishop's prayers in the interest of peace. But he frustrated the requests in the arrogance of his pride. Then Wulfstan

---

[4] Cf. ii. 9. 1.
[5] i. e. his wealth corrupted his morals; cf. *Mir.*, pp. 114 lines 76–7 'pro diuitiarum conscientia', 148 line 1111–12 'pro conscientia opum'.

presentem prophetiam intentans ait (uerba enim ipsa non pretermit-
tam):[1] 3. 'Non uis' inquit 'pacem? Amen dico tibi, uenit hora et in
proximo est quod uoles et ei et aliis misereri, et non poteris. Petes
misericordiam et negabitur tibi.' Nichil ille motus iter uel potius
fugam ad domum celerabat. Sed enim fortuna, diu homini lenocinata,
tunc autem scorpiacea cauda[2] prosecuta inimicos eius superinduxit.
Quibus uisis sotii qua quisque poterat dilapsi, ipse interfectus ueri
uaticinii periculum fecit, utile sane aliis factus exemplum, si modo[a]
mortales possint utilitatibus suis prospicere, ne presumant sanctorum
uirorum preceptis obuiare.

Explicit liber secundus

Incipit tertius

1. Hactenus et dixi et dixisse iuuat miracula, pauca sane, sed quae
suffitiant ad documentum sanctitatis Wlstani. Nunc interiorem[b] eius
uitam et mores dicere aggrediar.[3] Primoque de corporis qualitate
dicendum. Statura fuit temperata, maximis cedens, minimos super-
grediens, omnium membrorum aequalitate compositus. Congruebat
habitudini corporis serenitas mentis, ut quemuis ad reuerentiam sui
alliceret. Valitudinis prosperrimae, quam ipse et modestia cibi et nulla
indulgentia somni adiuuabat. Indumenta eius, lectisternia, calcia-
menta moderata, nec arrogantis pretii nec abiectae uilitatis. Vitabatur
in utroque fastus, quia et in sordibus luctuosis potest esse iactantia;[4]
pronius tamen ad id quod esset humile uergebat, ut totum deesset
pompae et nichil desideraretur gratiae. 2. Itaque semper omnis
ostentationis refugus, in cunctis diuitiis[c] agninis tantum amitiebatur
pellibus.[5] Vnde quadam uice, a Gaufrido Constantiensi episcopo[6]
benigne reprehensus, facetissimis hominem respersit salibus. Cum
enim interrogasset cur agninas pelles haberet qui sabelinas uel

---

[a] *ed. (cf. GP p. 80* si modo . . . nancisceretur); quomodo *C*   [b] *C (cf. VD ii. 26. 1)*;
exteriorem *δH* (p. 93)*   [c] induuiis (*adding* suis) *δH* (p. 93)*

[1] William emphasizes a case where he *does* give the exact words, contrary to his usual
practice (see above, p. xvi).
[2] Similar expressions are found in *GR*, c. 50. 2, *GP*, c. 246 (p. 398), *HN*, c. 34.
[3] Cf. *VD* ii. 26. 1, *GR*, c. 122. 1; modelled on Suetonius, *Aug.* lxi. 1: 'referam nunc
interiorem ac familiarem eius uitam quibusque moribus . . . egerit . . .'.
[4] Augustine, *De serm. Dom. in monte* ii. 41 (PL xxxiv. 1287), also quoted in *GR*, c. 218.
2, *GP*, c. 87 (p. 189).
[5] But Wulfstan may not always have dressed so modestly. An inventory of items kept in
the Cathedral precentory in 1401 (Worcester Cathedral, Dean & Chapter Muniments
C. 370), includes 'unum preciosum monilem for⟨m⟩atum ad modum litere M. et gemmis

launched a prophecy at the proud man before him. He said (for I shall not pass over the exact words):[1] 3. 'Do you not want peace? Amen, I say to you, the hour comes and is very near when you will wish to pity both him and others, and you will not be able. You will seek pity, and it will be refused you.' The man took no notice, and hurried, or rather fled, to his house. Fortune had long smiled on him, but now it showed the sting in its tail[2] and brought his enemies upon him. His companions, seeing them, slipped away where they could, leaving him to be killed and prove the prophecy true to his cost. That makes a useful example to others, if only mortals could look to their own advantage, and not presume to go against the orders of holy men.

BOOK THREE

1. So far I have told of miracles, and I am glad to have told them: only a few, to be sure, but enough to prove the holiness of Wulfstan. Now I shall turn to his inner life and character.[3] First, his appearance. He was of middle height, shorter than the tallest, taller than the shortest, and well-proportioned throughout. Correspondingly, he had the serenity of mind that could attract anyone to respect him. He enjoyed excellent health, himself looking after it by his restraint in food and sleep. His dress, bedding, and shoes were moderate in quality, neither ostentatiously expensive nor self-deprecatingly cheap. He avoided both kinds of pride: there can be display even in mourning garments.[4] But if he tipped in either direction, it was towards the humble: but in such a way that while all pomp was absent there was no lack of grace. 2. So he shrank from all showing off; despite the wealth at his disposal, he would only wear lamb-skins.[5] When he was on one occasion told off for this in a kindly tone by Geoffrey bishop of Coutances,[6] he retorted with some witty remarks. Geoffrey had asked why he had lamb-skins when he could and should

ornatum quod fuerat Wulstani episcopi.' This may have been the fastening for a vestment; the M presumably stood for 'Maria'.

[6] 1049–93. The story is also told in *GP*, c. 141 (pp. 282–3). According to William in *GP*, c. 165 (p. 302), after Wulfstan's death the Worcester monks presented Bishop Robert of Hereford with his cape lined with lambskin. Cf. Legatine Council at Westminster, 1127, canon 11 (*Councils*, i(2), p. 749): 'Nulla abbatissa, nulla sanctimonialis carioribus utatur indumentis quam agninis uel cattinis nigris'; Council at Westminster, 1138, canon 15 (*Councils*, i(2), p. 778): 'Prohibemus . . . sanctimoniales uariis seu grisiis, sabellinis, marterinis, hereminis, beuerinis pellibus . . . uti.' Cf. B., c. 7 (p. 13): 'maluit sponsare iuuenculam cuius quotidie blanditiis foueretur quam more monachorum bidentinis indui panniculis.'

castorinas uel uulpinas habere posset et deberet, eleganter respondit eum et homines prudentiae secularis gnaros uersutorum animalium pellibus uti debere, se nullius tergiuersationis conscium pelliculis agninis contentum esse. Cumque ille instaret referretque ut uel saltem cattos indueret, 'Crede michi,' respondit Wlstanus, 'sepius cantatur Agnus Dei quam Cattus Dei.' Haec uerba Gaufridi risus excepit, admodum delectati quod ipse posset illudi nec alter posset inflecti.

2. Excepto si quando cum monachis reficeretur, semper in regia[1] considentibus militibus palam conuiuabatur. Indecens enim et illiberale testabatur esse si clam obsonaretur, domesticis interim mussitantibus: quamquam numquam post religionis habitum nec ante aliquot annos unctioribus cibis corpus curauerit, sed semper sagimini,[a] semper carnibus preterquam piscium ualefecerit. Quem morem qua sibi occasione indixerit non ab re fuerit si altius repetam. Brihtegus, ut premissum est,[2] episcopus eum a primis ordinibus in presbiteratum promouerat, promotoque aecclesiam uillae quae Hauekesberia dicitur[3] delegauerat. Erat tum ille primae lanuginis ephebus,[4] nec tamen ut inuestis aeui homo seculi luxibus consumebat operam. 2. Inter haec,[5] nondum ab esculentis dapibus abhorrens, iussit quadam die aucam coqui. Ales uero ueru infixus torrebatur sedulo, delicato pueri familiaris artifitio. Distillabat ignea ui expressus aruinae liquor; fuerat enim de altilibus aucis lectissima. Pars ministrorum prunas suggerere,[6] pars condimentum[b] molere, omnes in nidorem prurire, uoluptatemque uerbis dissimulare non posse. His captus presbiter ipse quoque in delectationem animum resoluerat, spe aucam prelibans. Iamque pene mensa posita importuna sed necessaria causa[7] extitit quae ipsum et prepositum[8] cibi extorres domo extrusit. Ita inanis discedens momentaneae uoluptatis culpam arguebat animo: miseram carnem ad tanta instigari mala; delectationem effluere, peccatum manere. Carnem non[c] . . .

---

[a] *Whar.*; sagimine *C*, δ*R* (*p. 93*); sanguine *H*   [b] *Perhaps read* condimenta (*Thomson*)
[c] *C has lost a folio here, and the abbreviated and adapted text of* δ (*pp. 94–5*) *is used instead.*
See above, pp. 4, 6.

---

[1] 'Regia', unusually employed here, may refer to a particular building or room where Wulfstan conducted his business as a king's baron. The knights reappear at c. 16. 1 below.
[2] i. 2. 3–3. 1.
[3] Hawkesbury (Glos.), an episcopal manor.
[4] Virgil, *Aen.* x. 324.
[5] The content of 2–3 similarly in *GP*, c. 137 (p. 279).

wear sable, beaver, or fox. He replied neatly that Geoffrey and other men well versed in the way of the world should wear the skins of crafty animals, but *he* was conscious of no shiftiness in himself and was happy with lambskin. Geoffrey pressed the point, and suggested he could at least wear cat. But 'Believe me,' answered Wulfstan, 'the Agnus Dei is more often chanted than the Cattus Dei.' That made Geoffrey laugh: he was pleased that he could be made fun of and that Wulfstan could not be moved.

2. Except when he ate with the monks, he would always dine publicly in his 'palace',[1] his knights sitting down with him. For he declared it improper and mean to gorge in private, while the servants grumbled. But never after he took the habit, and not for some years before that, did he ever indulge in rich food, but bade a long farewell to fat and flesh, except for fish. It will not be irrelevant if I tell the full story of what occasioned his imposing this rule on himself. Bishop Brihtheah, as I said earlier,[2] had moved him up the grades to the priesthood, and then given him a church in the vill of Hawkesbury.[3] He was then a very young man,[4] but he did not for all his youth waste time on the luxuries of this world. 2. All the same,[5] he had not yet conceived a distaste for succulent food, and one day he ordered a goose to be cooked. The bird was put on the spit and carefully roasted, a skilled servant-boy giving it his fastidious attention. In the heat of the fire the fat dripped off, for this had been the choicest of the birds being fattened up. Some of the servants piled on the coals,[6] others ground up ingredients for the seasoning, everyone was lusting after the smell, and could not help talking about the pleasure it gave them. The priest was affected too, and was in a transport of delight as he awaited the taste of the goose. The table was nearly ready when an untimely but unavoidable summons[7] meant that the priest and the reeve[8] had to hurry from the house, leaving their meal behind. As he went away empty, he blamed himself for his short-lived pleasure. Wretched (he thought) is the flesh that can be stirred to such evil; the pleasure drains away, but the sin remains. Flesh does not . . .

---

[6] Cf. Virgil, *Aen.* v. 103.

[7] A *placitum*, according to *GP*, c. 137 (p. 279), where further details are given.

[8] Above, at i. 5. 1, William has told us that 'praepositus' is equivalent to 'prior'. Here, however (and in iii. 19. 1), someone humbler than a prior must be meant, and the 'praepositus' was presumably the reeve who administered the manor of Hawkesbury. Cf. B., c. 18 (p. 28), for Dunstan's brother Wulfric as reeve of the monastery's properties.

[δ] 3. A se itaque penam exegit: uoluptatem unius horae totis abstinendo compensauit temporibus. Vouit, et uoti se compotem fecit, numquam ulterius se id genus cibi comesurum. Inferebantur autem ante eum pisces et condimenta, lac et lactea: quorum nonnulla esu degustans sola olera libentius insumebat. Legebantur ad mensam eius libri edificationi accommodi, cunctis interim summum prementibus silentium. Iam uero quiete data epulis,[1] exponebat lectionem patria lingua, ut caelestem impertiret alimoniam quibus corporalem ministrauerat. Post prandium, cum aliis ceruisia uel idromellum pro patrio more porrigeretur in potum, ipse aquam puram bibebat, solo ministro conscio, ceteris pretiosum liquorem esse estimantibus.[*a*] Et primis quidem annis meram aquam hauriebat, procedente uero senio uino uel ceruisia mixtam.

3. Disciplinam domus suae tam in laicis quam in ordinatis seuerissime exercebat; legem enim tulerat ut omnes curiales sui tam missae quam omnibus horis non deessent. Custodes ad hoc constituit, ut nullum impune ridere sinerent; alioquin aut potu eo die carebat, aut palma ictum ferulae excipiebat. Neminem laicum de suis quoquam mitteret cui non preces septies in die dicendas iniungeret, hoc congrue asseuerans, ut sicut clerici septem horas, ita laici septem orationes Deo libarent.[2] Si quis ante eum iuraret, statim ferulae uindicta sequebatur.[3] 2. Hoc etiam in sermone ad populum sepe inculcabat, ne quis iuramento[*b*] assuesceret, ne hac occasione in periculum peierandi duceretur. Sed et indigne ferebat si quis coram eo aliorum uitam roderet uel carperet mores, quoniam hoc summae malitiae deputabat. Noctibus autem cum pauxillulum somni recepisset, confestim surgebat. Sepe legebat psalterium, sepe orationum librum,[4] in quo non minus quam in psalterio erat quemque semper sinu gestabat, et horas de sancta Maria dicebat,[5] solus nonnumquam omnia, ne quietem aliorum impediret, quandoque cum sotio quem [C] [cete]ris uigilantiorem deprehendisset.

[*a*] *William no doubt wrote* existimantibus   [*b*] *D* (*p. 95*); iuramenta *GH**

[1] Virgil, *Aen.* i. 723.
[2] Similar details are also given in *GP*, c. 140 (pp. 281–2).
[3] Cf. ii. 2 for Wulfstan's attitude to oaths.
[4] Almost certainly the so-called *Portiforium of Saint Wulfstan* (Cambridge, Corpus Christi Coll. MS 391): Budny, *Insular, Anglo-Saxon, and Early Anglo-Norman Manuscript*

[δ] 3. He therefore inflicted a penance on himself, compensating by life-long abstinence for one hour's pleasure: he vowed, and kept the vow, that he would never eat that sort of food again. Instead he was brought fish and seasoning, milk and milk products; he would have a taste of some of these, but he only ate vegetables if he could help it. At his table were read improving books, while all kept complete silence. When the meal was over,[1] he commented on the lection in his native tongue, so as to provide heavenly sustenance for those he had given food for their bodies. After lunch, when the others were, by English custom, offered beer or mead to drink, *he* took pure water; only the butler was aware of this; the rest thought it was something stronger. In his early years he drank pure water; as old age came on, he would mix it with wine or beer.

3. He kept discipline in his house rigorously, and extended it to lay as well as ordained; for he had laid it down that all those in his 'court' should attend mass and all the Hours. He posted guards to ensure that no one was allowed to laugh without being punished; if anyone did, he went without drink that day, or received a cut of the cane on his hand. He would never send a layman of his anywhere without enjoining him to say prayers seven times a day, making the logical declaration that the lay should offer seven prayers to God just as clerks offered seven Hours.[2] If anyone swore an oath in his presence, punishment from the cane followed at once.[3] 2. He often made the point to the people in his sermons that no one should get habituated to swearing oaths, for fear it might lead to perjury. But he was also angry if anyone in his presence carped at the lives of others or criticized their behaviour; he put this down to sheer wickedness. At night, after taking a very little sleep, he would get up promptly. He would often recite the psalter, or a book of prayers[4] to which he was as devoted as to the psalter, and which he carried around constantly in his pocket; and he would also say the Hours of St Mary.[5] Sometimes he did all this alone, so as not to prevent others sleeping, but sometimes with some companion [C] he found more wakeful than

---

Art at Corpus Christi College, Cambridge, i. 629–44, with bibliography p. 634. Made at Worcester between 1064 and 1069, with later additions.

[5] Cf. *Mir.*, p. 114 lines 80–1. On the development of the Office of Mary in late Anglo-Saxon England, see M. Clayton, *The Cult of the Virgin Mary in Anglo-Saxon England* (Cambridge, 1990), and idem, 'Virgin, cult of', in *Blackwell Encyclopaedia*, pp. 461–2.

3. Quorum unus Edricus nomine,[1] quem et ego noui, quadam nocte cantanti consedit. Sed cum ille nichil soliti pensi pretermittere uellet, pertesus morarum monachus manu etiam episcopo ut desineret significare presumpsit. Quo somnolentiam eius nutu arguente, resedit inuitus, perstitit oscitabundus. Mox cum se cubitum collocasset, magna ui per uisum concussus, flagris quin etiam cesus, inconsultae temeritatis penas dedit. Postremo data fide[2] quod numquam ulterius bonum hominem a bono deterreret uel impediret opere, tam horrificae uisionis periculo solutus est.

4. Matutinas semper in aecclesia cantitabat quantocumque spatio dispararetur ab hospitio. Illuc ibatur ningueret, plueret, quaecumque porro incommoditas aeris esset. Si luto uia sorderet, nichilo[a] minus. Si crassitudo tenebrarum caelum subtexeret, nichilo segnius. Eluctabatur ille omnem difficultatem itineris, dum modo ueniret ad aecclesiam: ut non falso posset dicere Deo: 'Domine, dilexi decorem domus tuae.'[3] Hac consuetudine cum quadam uice ante Natale Domini curiam proficiscens apud Merlaue uillam[4] accepisset hospitium, dixit suis mane se ad aecclesiam iturum. Ea longe aberat, simul et lutosa uia quemlibet etiam die ambulantem deterreret. Preterea ninguidus imber uel nix pluuialis (utroque enim modo seuiebat aer) impedimento essent. 2. Haec clericis obtendentibus ille perstitit in sententia, nec deici potuit. Velle se ad aecclesiam ire, uno saltem uel etiam nullo comite, tantum monstraretur sibi uia, ne incerto erraret tramite. Ita uotis episcopi contra se fluentibus, cessit clericorum improbitas, iracundiamque silentio frenauit. Quorum ⟨unus, nomine⟩[b] Frewinus, mente preruptior manu domini apprehensa geminauit culpam, ducendo eum qua palus undosior, qua uia infestior esset. Ille luto ad genua immersus, uno etiam calceo priuatus, interim dissimulauit

---

[a] *H*;* nichil *C,* δ (*p. 95*) (*so also* δ*H* in the next occurrence of the word below*) [b] *Supplied by ed.* (*cf. iii. 3. 3* quorum unus Eadricus nomine). *The story is told more clearly in* δ (*p. 96*): Clerici, hoc nichilominus egre ferentes, ex se tamen unum delegerunt qui episcopum duceret. At ille, Frewinus nomine, ceteris mente . . . (*'The clerks took this badly, but nevertheless chose one of their number to escort the bishop. This man, by name Freowine, more headstrong than the rest . . .').*

---

[1] Two monks of this name are listed, tentatively, in *BRECP*, p. 801: the man who was a monk under Wulfstan, also occ. *c.*1104, and the other in a document dateable 1125 × 1139. But William's personal reference (written after 1125) must mean that they were one and the same. Eadric wrote fos. ii–xi[v] (computus and kalendar) of Bodl. Libr., MS Hatton 113 (vol. I of Wulfstan's Homiliary), to which his obit was added at 23 November: 'Obiit Edricus monachus et sacerdos qui scripsit hunc compotum.' One of the other hands may

the rest. 3. One such, called Eadric,[1] with whom I also am personally acquainted, sat with him one night as he chanted. The bishop was unwilling to leave out anything in his usual quota, but the monk grew tired of the long-drawn out process, and presumed even to sign to the bishop to stop. Wulfstan reproved his sleepiness with a nod of his own, and Eadric sat down again unwillingly, and stuck it out drowsily. Later, when he had gone off to bed, he was heartily struck, even lashed, in a vision, and so paid the penalty for his ill-considered presumption. In the end he guaranteed[2] that never again would he try to deter or hamper the good man in doing good work, and was released from the peril of that horrid vision.

4. He always sang Matins in a church, however far away it might be from his lodgings. He went there come snow, come rain, in fact whatever shape the inclemency of the weather was taking. If the road was foul with mud, he went none the less; if thick darkness shrouded the sky, he was just as energetic. He overcame all the difficulties a journey presented, so long as he got to church; and he could with truth say to God: 'Lord, I have loved the beauty of thy house.'[3] On this principle, when he was once on his way to court just before Christmas, and had taken lodgings at the vill called Marlow,[4] he told his people that he would go to church in the morning. It was a long way off, and the mud on the road was such as to put off any walker even by daylight. What was more, a snowy rain or rainy snow (for the bad weather was providing both in abundance) would delay him. 2. These were the representations of the clerks; but he stuck to his resolution and could not be budged. He wanted, he said, to go to church, and he would go with one companion, or even none provided they showed him the way, so that he did not stray off the route. As the wishes of the bishop were going against them, the clerks stopped being tiresome and reined back their anger in silence. One of them, the headstrong Freowine, compounded his fault by taking his master's hand and guiding him to wherever the standing water was deepest and the road most unfriendly. Wulfstan went in up to his knees, and also lost a shoe, but for the moment he kept quiet about his ill-treatment. For the clerk's purpose was to make the bishop regret

be Coleman's: A. G. Watson, *Catalogue of Dated and Datable Manuscripts . . . in Oxford Libraries* (2 vols.: Oxford, 1984), i, no. 520.
    [2] Cf. the Jerome-inspired story in i. 8. 5, 'fide data'.
    [3] Ps. 25(26): 8.
    [4] Marlow (Bucks.).

iniuriam. Eo enim clericalis procedebat[a] intentio, ut et tunc episcopum cepti pigeret et postmodum consiliis suis accederet. Iam uero multo die, artubus gelante rigore premortuis, ad diuersorium regressus, tum demum et suum incommodum et clerici delictum aperuit. 3. Precepit etiam ut quereretur calceus,[b] nullo conuitio in contumacem inuectus sed atrocitatem facti uultus hilaritate attenuans.

Erat enim dominus pontifex magnae tolerantiae, qua ita mentem armauerat ut nulla eum illusio turbaret, nullum incommodum in peccatum concuteret. Nam plerumque quidam eum uel aperte obuncabant uerbis uel occulte uellicabant ludibriis. Sed ipse aduersus haec et ⟨omnia⟩[c] extrinsecus a seculo uenientia sic stabat intrepidus ut sequeretur[d] animo, non tamen caderet uerbo. Nec enim ei hanc laudem arrogare uolo quam affirmare non ualeo, ut nec animo moueretur. Affectiones enim animi nulla umquam religio delere potuit uel poterit, quas et si ualet ad horam compescere non ualet in aeternum auferre.

5. Missas cotidie ad minus duas audire. Ad utramque oblationem suam non negligere, ipse tertiam cantare. Si quo equitandum esset, ascenso animali continuo psalterium incipere, nec pausam nisi ad finem facere. Adiungebantur letaniae cum collectis pluribus, et uigiliae cum uesperis pro animabus. Tum, si uia protelaretur ad suffitientiam horum, repetebatur psalterium.[1] Adequitabant clerici et monachi, uel seriem uersuum excepturi uel amminiculaturi memoriae, si quando uideretur titubare: 2. hoc ideo ut dediscerent inanes fabulas, quae potissimum se uiantibus ingerunt. Quanto enim aspectui lenocinantur plura,[e] tanto copiosior loquendi occurrit materia. Cubicularius presto habebat marsupium, quod esset omnium egentium aerarium. Nemo enim umquam ingemuit repulsam, qui a Wlstano mendicauit elemosinam. Iam uero uia permensa, cum uentum esset ad hospitium, non ante, ut supra dixi,[2] quietis intraret cameram quam cum precibus salutasset aecclesiam. Ipsas porro domus totius diuersorii iubebat lustrari a presbitero cum aqua benedicta et crucis uexillo. Sic fugarentur aduersa, sic introducerentur secunda.

---

[a] *DH** (*p. 96*); precedebat *CG*   [b] *δH** (*p. 96*); calceus et *C*   [c] *suppl.* [*Peile*]
[d] *Perhaps read* quereretur   [e] *ed.*; plurima *C*

his intention on this occasion and take more notice of his views in the future. In the end, his limbs numb with the freezing cold, he got back to the hospice in broad daylight; and only then did he reveal the ordeal he had gone through and the clerk's sin. 3. He ordered a search for the missing shoe, though he did not abuse the obstinate Freowine, and his cheerful face made light of the seriousness of the offence.

Indeed the lord bishop was very tolerant, and he had so armed his mind with long-suffering that he was disturbed by no mockery and not forced to err by any discomfort. For quite often some people *did* openly abuse him or taunt him in secret. But against these and all things with a worldly origin he stood so firm that, though he was well aware of them, he did not let slip a word he might have regretted. For I do not wish to claim for him the credit for something I have no grounds for asserting, that he was not even moved in his mind. No religion has ever been able to get rid of feelings, and never will; even if it can restrain them for an hour, it has no power to remove them for ever.

5. He heard at least two masses a day, not neglecting his own offering at either, and himself singing a third. If he had to go anywhere on horseback, he started the psalter the moment he mounted the beast, not stopping till he reached the end. Litanies and many collects were added on, and vigils and vespers for the souls of the dead. Then if the journey was so long that these were used up, the psalter would be repeated.[1] At his side rode clerks and monks, ready to take up verses where he stopped or to jog his memory if he seemed to be faltering. 2. The idea of this was to get them out of the habit of empty gossip, which particularly affects wayfarers; for the more there is to pander to the sight, the more there is to talk about. A chamberlain kept a purse to hand, to act as a treasury for all poor men. No one who begged alms of Wulfstan ever complained of a rebuff. When the journey was over and they came to a hospice, he would not (as I have said)[2] enter the tranquillity of his room before saluting the church with his prayers; and he would order a priest to purify the very rooms of the whole lodging with holy water and a Cross. In this way what was hostile would be driven away and what was favourable brought in.

---

[1] Cf. *GP*, c. 140 (p. 282).   [2] i. 15. 1.

6. Semper orabat aut predicabat uerbo si uacaret; sin minus, mente affixus caelo, inhiabat Deo. Iaceret, staret, ambularet, sederet, semper in ore psalmus, semper in corde Christus. Quid quod etiam dormiens corpore uigilabat oratione? Si quando nimio precum labore defatigatus quieti membra composuisset, cedebat quidem naturae ut dormiret, sed uel per se uel pulsante alio experrectus psalmum inchoabat 'Conserua me, Domine'[1] uel 'Diligam te, Domine'[2] uel cetera huiusmodi quae orationem sonarent. **2.** Aestiuis diebus post prandium plerumque indulgebat lecto, sed, quod mirum quis dixerit, non poterat in somnum resolui nisi aliquo coram legente inductus. Si lector munus exerceret suum, uidebatur dormitare; altero cessante confestim abrumpebat soporem. Legebantur enim ante ipsum sanctorum Vitae et scripturae edificatoriae. Vere pronunties uitam hominis fuisse quasi quoddam caeleste speculum,[3] ex quo totius sanctimoniae resultaret simulacrum, fuisse quasi diuinae uoluntatis specimen[a] quod conduceret religioni, quod responderet saluti, quod postremo conquadraret decori.

7. Homines ad confessionem peccatorum uenientes iocunde suscipiebat, benigne refouebat, confitentes gratissima humanitate audiens,[b] non arroganti gestu fastidiens, lacrimabiliter condescendens illorum delictis, non resiliens sicut inauditis. Quae res effecerat ⟨ut⟩[c] ex tota uenientes Anglia ea quae nulli alii crederent illi confiteri non erubescerent. Non pudebat ergo illi dumtaxat dicere quod pigebat fecisse. Ipse quoque parem in confitentes refundebat gratiam, sedulo ne desperarent ammonendo, qualiter peccata cauerent, qualiter commissa diluerent instruendo. Nec illud minori, nescio an maiori, predicatione dignius quod eos semper familiariores in posterum haberet quorum peccata et penitentias nosset.

8. Egentium curam maxima componens diligentia, ante se illos sedilibus gregatim disponebat, affluenter quaeque necessaria impertiens. Filii diuitum curiae suae mancipati offitio dapes epulanti pro more inferebant. Eis salutaria sedulo infundebat monita, arrogantiam non habere, humilitatem induere, in primis munditiam carnis non ledere, ne impulsu aetatis lubrico fedarent corpus in uoluptatum

---

[a] uoluntatis specimen *ed. doubtfully*; uoluptatis speculum C　　　　[b] audie[ns] C
[c] *suppl. ed.*

[1] Ps. 15(16): 1.　　　　　　　　　　　　　　　　　　[2] Ps. 17(18): 2.
[3] Cf. *GR*, c. 35. 3 ('puritatis . . . speculum').

6. He always prayed or preached aloud, if he had time. If he did not, he cleaved to heaven in his mind and longed after God. Lying, standing, walking, sitting, he ever had a prayer on his lips, ever had Christ in his heart. Further, even when asleep in the body he was awake in prayer. If ever he was exhausted by excessive prayer, and composed his limbs to rest, he went to sleep as nature demanded, but woke, either spontaneously or at another's nudge, and started a psalm, 'Preserve me, O Lord'[1] or 'I will love thee, O Lord',[2] or others of this prayerful kind. 2. On summer days he generally favoured his bed after lunch, but remarkably enough he could not relax into sleep unless he was read to. If the reader went on with his task, Wulfstan appeared to be asleep; if the other stopped, he immediately awoke with a start. Saints' Lives and edifying writings were read to him. You could say with all truth that the life of the man was like a heavenly mirror[3] from which an image of all that is holy was reflected. It was like a model of God's will(?), conducive to piety, answering to salvation, and in line with what is correct.

7. He welcomed agreeably and affably cheered those who came to confess their sins. When they did so, he listened with the most pleasant humanity, not disdaining them with a show of arrogance. Tearfully he stooped to the level of their sins, not shrinking away from them as though none such had been known before. As a result, people coming from all over England did not blush to confess to him things they would have entrusted to no other. There was no shame in telling *him* what they were sorry to have done. He showed equal goodwill to those who confessed to him, constantly urging them not to despair, and furnishing them with methods by which they could avoid sin in future and wash away their guilt. No less—perhaps more—praiseworthy the fact that afterwards he always treated with greater familiarity those whose sins and penances he knew.

8. He saw to the care of the needy with the greatest attention, seating throngs of them in front of him and giving them the necessities of life in abundance. Sons of the rich who had been appointed to serve at his 'court' customarily brought him his meals when he dined. He was particular in deluging them with salutary advice: not to be arrogant, to put on humility, and in particular to avoid violating the cleanliness of the flesh, so as not at their dangerous age to defile the body in a morass of pleasures. These same young men he forced to serve the

uolutabro. Eosdemque cogebat genibus flexis pauperibus mensam et cibos apponere, et pro disciplina ministrantium aquam manibus infundere. Si quis eorum conscientiam alti sanguinis spirans uel uultu superbiam proderet, contumacem arguebat: ⟨omnia⟩[a] alia esse in quibus mallet offendi quam pauperem uel nutu contristari. 2. Dominicum mandatum obseruandum, ut seruiatur egenis; quicquid enim pauperi accedit emolumenti transire in reuerentiam Domini. 'Quod' inquit '⟨uni⟩[b] ex minimis meis fecistis michi fecistis.'[1] Illis iuuenculis et diuitum liberis sanitatis etiam arridere gratiam. Contra si casu fortuna hilaritatem uultus subtraheret, gauisuros si quis assistere, si quis saltem eos dignaretur aspicere. His et talibus pius doctor quamlibet rudium animorum decoquebat insolentiam, ut assuescerent[c] egenis exhibere reuerentiam. Sane pueros elegantis formae dignanter sacrarum manuum tactu et osculis demulcens, amplectebatur in eis diuinae compositionis gratiam, materiamque boni ex decore liniamentorum elitiebat, dictitans subinde: 'Quam pulcher est Creator qui tam pulchras creaturas facit!'

9. In singulis uillis suis singulas habebat ediculas, in quibus se obiectis repagulis a mane post missam includebat, ibique, solitudinem qua maiorem in heremo non haberet nactus, liberos in contemptum mundi et in speculationem Dei librabat mentis obtutus. Nec erat qui meditantem interpellaret, nisi cum clericus pulsatione hostii tempus prandii uel horarum nuntiaret. Eratque hoc claustrum inter cameram[2] et priuatam domum, domesticis tantum consciis ne uideretur esse ostentator religionis. Hac se cohibebat inter homines solitudine[d] semper quidem, sed maxime tempore Quadragesimae, ut hoc modo furaretur corpusculo quod toto fugitabat animo.

2. Erat enim, ut uenerabilis prior Wigornensis Nicholaus michi dixit, non solum orator multiplex sed etiam diligens. Denique cum ad uersum psalmi ueniret quo affectum in Deum suscitare posset, utpote 'Inclina, Domine, aurem tuam et exaudi me, quoniam inops et pauper sum ego',[3] hunc inquam et alios eiusmodi bis terque repetens, erectis

---

[a] *suppl. ed.*   [b] *suppl.* [*Darl.*]   [c] (sic) assuescerent δH* (*p. 97*); maturescerent C
[d] δH* (*p. 97*); sollicitudine C

[1] Matt. 25: 40.
[2] The 'camera' was the more private and less formal of the two main components in a domestic house of the period: J. Blair, 'Hall and chamber: English domestic planning 1000–1250', in *Manorial Domestic Buildings in England and Northern France*, ed. G. Meirion-Jones and M. Jones (London, 1993), pp. 1–21, at 4.

poor on bended knee, bringing them table and food, and to pour water on their hands like servants. If any of them, in the inflated awareness of his high birth, showed a sense of his worth even by the look on his face, Wulfstan would reprove his disobedience. 'I would prefer' he used to say 'to be offended in any other way than by the saddening of a poor person, even by a nod. 2. The Lord's command must be obeyed, that the needy should be served. For whatever profit accrues to a poor man passes over to become reverence towards the Lord: "Inasmuch as ye have done it unto one of the least of these my brethren, ye have done it unto me."[1] On young men like you, sons of the rich, there smiles also the grace of good health. But if by some chance Fortune were to take away the cheerful look on your faces, you would be glad if anyone was ready to stand by you or even give you a glance.' With words like these, the pious teacher whittled away the insolence of minds however callow, so that they might become used to showing respect to those in need. Boys of elegant appearance he marked out by fondling them with his holy hands and kissing them, for he embraced in them the grace of God's handiwork. He drew a moral from the beauty of their features, often exclaiming: 'How beautiful must be the Creator who makes such beautiful creatures!'

9. In every one of his vills he had a special room where he would put up the shutters and isolate himself from morning mass onwards. Here he enjoyed a solitude as profound as any he could have found in the desert, and here he launched his mind on the contemplation of God, while despising this world. No one would interrupt his meditations, except when a clerk banged at the door to announce lunchtime or the Hours. This reserved spot lay between the chamber[2] and the privy, and only the household staff were aware of it, for he did not wish to look as though he was flaunting his piety. Such was the solitude in the midst of men to which he restricted himself always, but especially in Lent; his intention being to steal from his frail body what he fled from with all his mind.

2. Now, as the reverend prior of Worcester Nicholas told me, he was both versatile and sedulous in his prayers. For instance, when he came to a verse of a psalm which enabled him to arouse his emotion towards God, such as 'Bow down thine ear, O Lord, hear me, for I am poor and needy',[3] he would (I say) repeat this and such like verses two

---

[3] Ps. 85(86): 1.

in caelum oculis, ingeminabat. Diligentiam quin etiam orandi, sicut idem prior auctor est, non solum in se sed et in suis diligenter obseruabat. Transgressiones autem suorum et tolerabat oportune et arguebat pro tempore. 3. Denique si quem monachorum uideret matutinae sinaxi deesse, quanuis tunc dissimularet, ceteris post offitium somno cedentibus neglectorem leniter suscitans debitum implere cogebat, ipse uice ministri cantanti respondens. Quid hoc mirabilius homine, quid isto humilius pontifice? Nec turbulento spiritu in dormientem efferatus pulsabat pede,[1] lacessebat*a* uoce, nec rursus pretereunter peccatum subditi negligendum arbitratus ad ueniam commissi regredi compellebat. In uno ergo monitorem, in altero supparem, in utroque benignum Deoque dignum exhibebat antistitem. De Nicholao sane reuerentissimo plura libet dicere, si prius quae de moribus Wlstani habeo in manibus potuero explicare.

10. Diocesim suam, ut supra tetigi,[2] sollicite peragrabat, nichil quod sui intererat offitii pretermittens. Id ut commodius fieret, semel in anno metam ponebat, ualitudini suae occurrentiumque fatigationi prospitiens. Per totum enim episcopatum, precedente*b* archidiaco-norum[3] ammonitione, tantum uulgus eius se infundebat occursui ut nequiret numerari. Quorum dum infirmitatibus seruire cogeretur, erat quidem res ponderis et grauedinis, sed emicabat animus sulleuator oneris et uictor laboris.

Per totam parrochiam[4] in sui iuris prediis aecclesias struebat, in alienis ut struerentur instabat. 2. Apud Wesbiri[5] ex antiquo aecclesia fuerat, sed tunc semiruta et semitecta remedium desiderabat. Eam ille reparauit in solidum, fastigauit in summum, parietes cemento, tectum plumbo refitiens, delegatisque uillarum et decimarum redditibus librisque offitialibus sollemni dono Wigornensi aecclesiae dedit, ibique monachis positis Colemannum totiens dictum prefecit. Ver-untamen cum esset in diuinis domibus apparandis ita ut dixi sollers et

---

a [*Darl.*]; lacessabat *C*   *b* *Whar.*; procedente *C*

[1] Cf. Horace, *Carm.* i. 4. 13: 'pallida mors aequo pulsat pede'. Also echoed in *GR*, c. 204. 1.

[2] i. 15. 1.

[3] At this date there was apparently only a single archdeacon (see below, 15. 1 n.), but William may be intending to refer to a sequence rather than more than one simultaneously.

[4] Here synonymous with *diocesis*, the word he has just used, and the older term for the province ruled by a bishop: *The Oxford Dictionary of the Christian Church*, ed. F. L. Cross and E. A. Livingstone (3rd edn., Oxford, 1997), p. 482.

[5] Westbury-on-Trym (Glos.): for the earlier history of Worcester's possession, see

or three times, and redouble them with his eyes raised aloft. The same prior is witness to the fact that he was a stickler for careful prayer not only in himself but in others. If his own monks transgressed he would tolerate the offence or rebuke it as the occasion suggested. 3. For instance, if he saw that one of the monks was absent from morning mass, he would seem not to notice at the time, but later, when all the others went to sleep after the office, he would gently rouse the offender and force him to complete what was due, himself playing the role of the priest in reply to his chanting. What more remarkable than a man like this, what more humble than such a bishop? He did not get upset and fly into a rage with the sleepy-head, kicking[1] or abusing him; but neither did he think that the fault of someone subject to him should be passed over and forgotten, and he would force him to return to be forgiven for what he had done wrong. In the one aspect he showed himself an adviser, in the other a virtual equal, and in both a kindly bishop and one worthy of God. Of Nicholas, that most reverend man, I have more to say; but first, if I can, I will complete what I have to tell of the character of Wulfstan.

10. As I mentioned above,[2] he was systematic in visiting his diocese, and he left undone nothing that formed part of his duty. To make this easier, he called a halt once a year, with a thought for his own health and the energies of those who came to meet him. For throughout his bishopric, the preliminary notice given by the archdeacons[3] led to so great a crowd flocking to greet him that it could not be numbered. He had to look to their infirmities, and it was a weighty and tiring business enough; but his mind triumphed, making light of the burden and overcoming the labour.

Through all his diocese[4] he built churches on lands that were in his jurisdiction, and pressed for such building on the lands of others. 2. At Westbury[5] there had been a church from olden times, but now it was half ruined and its roof was half gone: it clamoured for help. Wulfstan repaired it completely right to the roof-tree, re-pointing the walls and renewing the lead on the roof. He provided it with the revenues of vills and tithes and with service-books, and handed it over

---

Heads, p. 97; *Hemingi Chartularium* ii. 407–8, 421–4; Dyer, *Lords and Peasants*, pp. 16, 19, 28–30, 37; Mason, pp. 168–9; Sims-Williams, *Religion and Literature* (above, p. 70 n. 1), pp. 174–6; P. Wormald, *How do we Know so Much about Anglo-Saxon Deerhurst?* (the Deerhurst Lecture, 1991: Deerhurst, 1993), pp. 2–7. Refounded *c*.963–4, again refounded *c*.1093, the cell was disbanded by Wulfstan's successor Samson (1096–1112: *GP*, c. 150 (p. 290)), and Coleman returned to Worcester.

diligens, in secularibus propemodum esse uidebatur hebes et negli-
gens. Nusquam enim in uillis suis aulas, nusquam triclinia fecit,
nimirum qui non solum in istis forensibus sed etiam in aecclesiis
operosa grauaretur architectura. Magis enim deputabat talia humanae
pompae et iactantiae quam diuinae uoluntati et gratiae. 3. Quod
Nicholaus dicebat eo die potuisse uideri quo uetustam aecclesiam
Wigorniae fecit detegi. Stabat ipse in cimiterio tacitus et subinde
congemiscens.ᵃ Scaturiebatᵇ quippe in animo eius cogitatio quae
ingentem imbrem lacrimarum ferens tandem erupit. 'Nos' inquit
'miseri sanctorum destruimus opera, pompatice putantes nos facere
meliora. Quanto prestantior nobis sanctus Oswaldus, qui hanc fecit
aecclesiam, quot sancti uiri religiosi in ea Deo seruierunt!' Et licet
astantes referrent non debere illum tristari sed potius laetari, quem
Deus ad hanc seruasset gratiam, ut sic uideret magnificari aecclesiam,
in lacrimarum proposito tenax fuit.[1] Nec desunt qui dicant predixisse
illum aecclesiae nouae incendium,[2] quo subsequentibus conflagrata
est annis. Sed non placuit pro uero presumere quod discrepat.
Relinquatur ergo in medio. 4. Tunc autem et nouam aecclesiam
perfecit, nec facile inuenias ornamentum quod eam non decorauerit,
ita erat in singulis mirabilis et in omnibus singularis.[3] Quocirca, ut
magnificentiae nichil deesset, septuaginta duas marcas argenti scrinio
innexuit, in quo beatissimi Oswaldi predecessoris sui exuuias simulque multorum sanctorum locauit. Ea res ᶜmultorum populorum et
episcopi Rotberti[4] et abbatum frequentiaᶜ octauo idus Octobris facta,
quo die translatio predicti Sancti eiusdemque octaua reliquiarum
omnium loci memoria fieri annuatim iussa. Hoc ideo excogitatum
quia depositio Sancti quae in Quadragesima est non ita commode fieri
potest. Sciat porro lector idem quondam scrinium a beato Oswaldo[5]
factum, sed a Wlstano ampliatum.

　　ᵃ conquiniscens *C* ᵃ·ᶜ·; *the correction might be wrong*　　ᵇ δ (p. 106); -ibat *CH*, perhaps*
rightly　　ᶜ⁻ᶜ *The text is uncertain*

---

[1] Similarly *GP*, c. 141 (p. 283).
[2] This refers to the fire recorded by JW s.a. 1113, in more detail by William in *GP*, c.
149 (pp. 288–9), involving the miraculous preservation of Wulfstan's tomb. The
abbreviator of *VW* (Darlington, p. 106) uses similar language to describe a fire and the
same miracle, said to have been witnessed by Bernard bp. of St David's (1115–48), who
later described it in a letter to Pope Eugenius III (1145–53). Darlington (pp. xx–xxi) dated
this fire to 1147, and Mason (pp. 272–3, 275–6) assumes that it was different from that
recorded by William. But it is hard to imagine that they were not one and the same.
Perhaps Bernard was not yet bishop when he witnessed it.
[3] On Wulfstan's church, see R. Gem, 'Bishop Wulfstan II and the romanesque

solemnly to the church of Worcester, putting monks in and giving
Coleman charge of it, the same man I have so often mentioned. But
though he was, as I have said, skilled and energetic in the fitting out of
God's churches, Wulfstan could seem almost lethargic and negligent
in secular matters. He never built halls or banqueting rooms in his
vills. No wonder! for he had an aversion to elaboration of architecture
not only in such secular buildings but even in churches. He regarded
such things as having more to do with human pomp and circumstance
than with the will and grace of God. 3. Nicholas said this could be
observed on the day he had the roof taken off the old church at
Worcester. He stood there in the churchyard speechless and with
many a groan, for his heart was full of a thought that brought a great
shower of tears before it burst out at last into words: 'We wretches are
destroying the works of the saints, thinking in our insolent pride that
we are improving them. How superior to us was St Oswald, maker of
this church! How many holy and devout men have served God in this
place!' Those present told him he should be glad rather than sad, for
God had preserved him to see the church so exalted; but he kept to
his course, and wept on.[1] There are those who say that he foretold the
fire in the new church,[2] which gutted it years later. But I have decided
not to affirm as true something on which the evidence is conflicting.
So let it remain in doubt. 4. But on this occasion he went on to
complete the new church, and you will not find it easy to think of an
ornament that was not brought to decorate it, so wonderful was it in
its details, so unique in every respect.[3] To ensure that its splendour
lacked nothing, he put 72 marks of silver into the shrine in which he
placed the remains of his predecessor, the blessed Oswald, and those
of many holy men. This took place on 8 October, in the presence of a
great crowd including Bishop Robert[4] and abbots (?). This day is
appointed for the annual celebration of the translation of the saint,
and its octave for the commemoration of all the relics in the place.
The idea was thought up because the day of the saint's death, being in
Lent, is less suitable. The reader should also know that the shrine was
made earlier by Oswald,[5] though Wulfstan enlarged it.

cathedral church of Worcester', in *Medieval Art and Architecture at Worcester Cathedral*,
pp. 15–37; Barker, *A Short Architectural History*, pp. 17–46; C. Guy, 'Excavations at
Worcester Cathedral 1981–91', *Transactions of the Worcestershire Archaeological Soc.*, 3rd
ser. xiv (1994), 1–74.
    [4] i. e. Robert Losinga ('of Lorraine'), bp. of Hereford 1079–95.
    [5] Darlington (p. 53 n. 1) thought 'Oswaldo' a slip by William for 'Aldulfo', and indeed
Ealdwulf, Oswald's successor, had placed the bones of the saint in a shrine in 1002 (JW

11. In animarum fidelium auxilium maxima tenebatur miseratione, ut etiam temeritatem per cimiteria equitantium perpetuo compesceret edicto. Multa ibi sanctorum iacere corpora, quorum animabus quae apud Deum sunt debeatur reuerentia. Veruntamen parum hac profecit industria, quia nichilominus hodieque sanctorum calcatur reuerentia. Quandocumque et ubicumque, ut superius dixi,[1] alicuius audiret obitum, statim 'Pater noster' presentibus indicto ipse tres psalmos,[2] 'Laudate Dominum, omnes gentes', 'De profundis', 'Laudate Dominum in sanctis', cum precibus dicebat. 2. Ita oratione pro anima deposita fiebat defuncto si tempus sineret sermo breuis et perfunctorius uel longus et necessarius. Missam pro mortuis nullo non die cantari fatiebat, preter dominicas et maiora sollemnia. Remittebat enim festiuitati quod pietati debebat, ut tanto magis augeret ueniam quanto minus urgeret causam. Erat ergo dulcedinis quod ceteris diebus orabat, amplissimae spei quod in dominicis cessabat. Neutro eum autem Dominus fraudaret, quoniam arridebat Domini clementia ubi plaudebat serui confidentia.[3]

12. Labem impudicitiae oderat, integritati fauebat in omnibus et maxime sacrati ordinis hominibus. Quorum si quempiam castitati comperisset deditum, familiarium eum partium facere et ut filium diligere.[4] Vxoratos presbiteros omnes uno conuenit edicto, aut libidini aut aecclesiis renuntiandum pronuntians. Si castimoniam amarent, manerent cum gratia; si uoluptati seruirent, exirent cum iniuria.[5] Fueruntque nonnulli qui aecclesiis quam mulierculis carere mallent.

s.a.). However, the reliquary used on that occasion had been made by Oswald himself to house the remains of Wilfrid and other northern saints which he had brought from Ripon: Eadmer, *Vita S. Oswaldi*, cc. 25–6 (*HCY* ii. 30–2); *Miracula S. Oswaldi*, c. 4 (*HCY* ii. 49). Wulfstan must have re-used this reliquary, after he had had it enlarged and refurbished.

[1] ii. 6. 3.   [2] 116 (117), 129 (130), 150.
[3] In this contorted passage, William comments approvingly on Wulfstan for not having mass sung for the dead on Sundays and feast days, as *pietas* might seem to demand. He mentions three interconnected considerations: (*a*) To over-press the case of the dead before God might be less effective in winning them pardon from Him than a less insistent approach. (*b*) Missing out feast-days was a reflection of the firmness of his hope in God's mercy. (*c*) God would reward Wulfstan for not singing the masses on feast-days as well as for singing them on ordinary days, because in His mercy He took pleasure in Wulfstan's confidence in Him (as shown by his not singing them every day).
[4] His own chastity (for which cf. i. 1. 9) is noted in *Hemingi Chartularium* ii. 405: ' Vidit enim [Ealdredus] in illo castitatem uigere.'
[5] Mason, pp. 162–4, comments that Wulfstan's measures were more severe than those promulgated at the Council of Winchester, 1076: *Councils*, i(2). 616–17, 619. But they would seem to have been a reasonable interpretation of canon 2 of the Council of Lisieux of 1064 ('de uillanis presbiteris atque diaconibus, ut nullus abinde uxorem uel

11. His overwhelming sense of pity compelled him to help the souls of the faithful. He even tried to restrain by an unlimited edict the rash behaviour of those who rode horses through cemeteries. He said that many holy men's bodies lay there, and that reverence was due to their souls, which are with God. But he got little profit of his trouble; notwithstanding him, the respect due to holy men is trodden underfoot even today. Whenever and wherever (as I said earlier)[1] he learned of someone's death, he at once told those present to say the Lord's Prayer and himself said, with accompanying prayers, three psalms,[2] 'O praise the Lord, all ye nations', 'Out of the depths', and 'Praise ye the Lord in his sanctuary'. 2. After these prayers for the soul, there was given for the deceased a sermon, brief and cursory or long and serious (?), according to the time available. He had the mass for the dead sung every day except Sundays and high feasts. For he gave up to the feast what he owed to piety, so as to win the more forgiveness for the dead because he did not press their case. It was a sign of his sweet character that he prayed on the other days, a sign of his high hope that he gave up on Sundays. But the Lord would not deprive him of the fruit of either practice, for the clement Master smiled when His servant gave Him praise by trusting in Him.[3]

12. He hated the blot of unchastity, and approved of chasteness in all men, especially those in holy orders. If he knew a priest devoted to it, he made him part of his intimate circle and loved him like a son.[4] Married priests he dealt with in a general edict, laying down that they should renounce either their lust or their living. If they loved purity, they could stay with his blessing; if they were the servants of pleasure, they could leave with his curse.[5] And there were not a few who preferred doing without their churches to giving up their women.

concubinam seu introductam mulierem duceret: qui uero a tempore Rotomagensis concilii duxerat perderet': L. Delisle, *Journal des Savants*, 1901, pp. 516–21, at 517), elaborated as canon 13 of the Council of Rouen of 1072 (Mansi, *Concilia*, x. 33D-40C), and restated baldly as canon 15 of the Council of Winchester, 1070: 'Quod clerici aut caste uiuant aut ab officiis recedant' (*Councils*, i(2). 576). The canons of this last council were copied into one of Wulfstan's legal reference-books (see below, p. 128 n. 1). Probably another of his books was Cambridge, Corpus Christi Coll., MS 265, written at Worcester s. xi med. On clergy and women it offered examples of earlier legislation such as the following: (p. 127) 'Nulla femina cum presbitero in una domo habitet. Quamuis enim canones matrem et sororem et huiuscemodi personas in quibus nulla sit suspicio cum illo habitare concedant, hoc nos modis omnibus idcirco amputamus, quia in obsequio sub occasione illarum ueniunt aliae feminae quae non sunt ei adfinitate coniunctae et eum ad peccandum inliciunt.' See N. R. Ker, *Catalogue of Manuscripts containing Anglo-Saxon* (Oxford, 1957 and 1990), pp. 92–4.

Quorum aliquos uagabundos fames absumpsit, aliquos res familiaris
aliunde quesita in extremum tutata non destituit. Pauci quos sanior
regebat ratio abdicatis illicitis preclaro in aecclesiis suis consenuere
otio. Quare antistes, cauens in posterum, nullum ulterius promouit ad
presbiterum qui non de castitate seruanda daret sacramentum.

13. Humilitatis[1] eius ubique, maxime inter monachos, multa fuere
inditia. Quando erat Wigorniae, missam maiorem cotidie fere dicebat,
offitio ultroneo sepius quam ab illo cuius septimana esset rogatus.[2]
Fertur enim solitum dicere, quod tamen fide Nicholai dixerim,
monachum se loci esse, septimanam ut ceteros aecclesiae debere,
ideoque quod suo explere nequiret ordine suppleret pro aduentus
tempore. Collationi[3] sepe interesse, deinde in aecclesia confessione
facta et benedictione data redire ad sua. Summo diluculo ceteris
quiescentibus in aecclesiam se matutinus agebat.[4] Vbi si aliquis
fratrum, ut fit plerumque, missam dicere uolens non haberet adiutoris
solatium, ipse incunctanter ministri subibat offitium. Ipse in pueris et
ceteris quos perperam uestitos uidisset dignanter acclinis pendulos
componebat sinus, rugasque dissidentes redigebat in seriem.[5]

14. Asserentibus quibusdam quod tam dilecta humilitas citra episcopalem dignitatem esset respondebat: 'Qui maior est uestrum, erit
minister uester.[6] Ego sum episcopus uester et magister, ideoque
debeo esse uestrum omnium minister, secundum Domini preceptum.' Nec enim umquam ad uoluntatis suae supinabatur arbitrium, in
omnibus Dei preceptis obsecundans: moribus gratissimus, nulla
acerbitate cohabitantes offendens, nulla ingratitudine obsequentes
confundens, sepe suis usibus aptata retrahens, dummodo suorum
commoditatibus consuleret, faceret diceret omnia quae ad offitium
spectarent suum. Haec non solum exhibebat Wigorniae, sed ubicumque in diocesi sua peteretur uenire ad cenobia. 2. Nec enim petentes
dura fronte suspendere uel morarum ambagibus aduentum suum
excusare solebat. Quandocumque ei confirmandi pueri nuntiarentur,
ut ante dixi,[7] statim petitionibus nuntiantium assurgebat, si uigilaret

---

[1] Wulfstan's religious observances are similarly described in *GP*, c. 140 (pp. 281–2),
where his singing of the Psalter is also emphasized.
[2] i. e. to act as celebrant at the masses for the week. In *GP* the monk is called
'septimanarius', i. e. hebdomadary, for which see *ODML* s. v. 'hebdomadarius' 2b–c.
[3] The monks' mealtime reading.   [4] Virgil, *Aen.* viii. 465. Also in *VD* i. 10. 4.
[5] Cf. *Mir.*, p. 78 line 436.   [6] Matt. 23: 11.
[7] Esp. ii. 14. 1–2, but cf. also i. 7. 1, 15. 1, and ii. 9. 2.

Some became vagrants and died of starvation. Some had private means from other sources which kept them going to the end. Some few of sounder principles gave up what was forbidden, and grew old in their churches, at ease and of good repute. The bishop therefore took heed for the future, and gave up promoting to the priesthood any one who would not give his oath to stay celibate.

13. Many were the signs of his humility[1] on all sides, especially among his monks. When he was at Worcester, he generally said High Mass every day, more often spontaneously than because he was asked to do it[2] by the monk whose week it was. He used to say—such is the story; but I tell it on the testimony of Nicholas—that he was a monk of the place and owed the church a week like the others: so that what he could not do in his own turn, he would make up when he chanced to be present. He often attended collation;[3] then after making confession in church and giving the blessing he would return to his quarters. At crack of dawn, when the rest were still asleep, he would betake himself to the church of a morning.[4] There, if as often happens one of the brothers wanted to say mass but had no one to help him, Wulfstan would not hesitate to perform the office of server. When he saw boys or others incorrectly dressed, he would deign to bend down and adjust the hang of their folds and bring rebellious creases back into line.[5]

14. Some said that such earnest humility was beneath a bishop's dignity. But he answered: ' "He that is greatest among you shall be your servant."[6] I am your bishop and master, and so I ought, in accordance with our Lord's command, to be servant of you all.' For he did not bow down to the whims of his own will, but in all things followed the precepts of God. He was most pleasant in his character, and gave offence to none of those with whom he lived by any harshness; nor did he distress those who obeyed him by any ingratitude. He often went without (?) things intended for his own use so long as he could serve the convenience of his people and say and do everything that pertained to his office. And this not only at Worcester, but wherever in his diocese he was requested to visit a monastery. 2. For he did not hold up petitioners with a frowning face, or explain away his unwillingness to come by alleging complicated reasons for delay. Whenever he was told that there were boys to confirm, he would, as I have said,[7] immediately leap up to respond to

reiectis quae habebat in manibus, si dormiret continuo somno excussus. Erant tunc temporis altaria lignea,[1] iam inde a priscis diebus in Anglia. Ea ille per diocesim demolitus ex lapidibus compaginauit alia. Vnde fiebat ut nonnumquam uno die duo in aliqua uilla, secundoque et tertio alias profectus totidem dedicaret altaria. Ita impigre quocumque uocabatur aderat ut non eum migrare sed uolare crederes. *Quo tempore miraculum quod ea fecit occasione* non patiar obduci silentio.

15. In ipso dedicandorum altarium itinere uenit ad locum cui uicinabatur aecclesia nouiter ab Egelrico archidiacono[2] facta. Hanc ad dedicandum paratam episcopus sciens imminente crepusculo archidiaconum conuenit. Iret protinus et iam aecclesiae consecrandae competentia pararet. Eo se uenturum diluculo, et affuturum offitio. Expalluit ille tam repentino precepto, sed nichil aliud excusationis nisi de apparatus inopia referre potuit: multis obsoniis tanto comitatui opus esse; ipsum quidem paruo contentum fore, sed sotiorum se importunitati timere. 2. 'Vade,' ait episcopus, 'fac quod ad te attinet; Deus seruos suos undecumque*b* pascet. Quia tam in proximo sumus, Dei opus fatiemus.' Necessitas extorsit celeritatem clerico, ut continuo profectus necessaria consecrationi maturaret. Adiecit munificentiam ut conuiuantium*c* usui apta cuncta expediret. Sola[3] erat hidromelli penuria, quod in uno uase illoque non grandi ab amicis emendicauerat. Venit ergo episcopus factoque propter quod uenerat alias iter intendebat. Depulit intentionem archidiaconus nisusque amicorum precibus remansionem illius diei deprecatus est. 3. Post prandium inuitatoris precepit dapsilitas ut de uase quod dixi cunctis propinaretur. Contendebat liquor cum haustoribus et quasi de fonte

---

a-a *The text is uncertain*   *b* *Apparently* = alicunde (*cf. iii. 19. 2*)   *c* *ed.;* couiuantium *C* (conuiantium *Darl.*)

---

[1] Their replacement in stone was decreed in canon 5 of the Legatine Council at Winchester, April 1070: *Councils*, i(2). 575. These canons were copied, in a contemporary hand, onto fos. 2v–3 of Bodl. Libr., MS Junius 121, a book of ecclesiastical law made for Wulfstan. Wulfstan was himself summoned to this council: *Councils*, i(2). 568. For fixed altars stone had been decreed as early as the sixth century, but in England wood seems to have been common until much later: J. Braun, *Das christliche Altar in seiner geschichtlichen Entwicklung* (2 vols.: Munich, 1924), i. 104; C. A. Ralegh Radford, 'The portable altar of Saint Cuthbert', in *The Relics of St Cuthbert*, ed. C. F. Battiscombe (Oxford, 1956), pp. 326–35, at 328–9.
[2] *Fasti*, p. 104: first occ. as a tenant of the bp. of Worcester in 1086, latest (as archdeacon) in a document of 1100 × 1108. At some time between 1096 and 1112 the single archdeaconry of Worcester diocese was divided in two, and Æthelric occurs, in an

the request. If he was awake, he threw aside what he was busy with; if he was asleep, he started up instantly. At that time there had from olden days been wooden altars[1] in England. He had them destroyed throughout his diocese, and new ones made of stone. As a consequence he sometimes would dedicate two altars in one day at some vill, then go on elsewhere and dedicate two more the next day and the day after that. He arrived so quickly wherever he was summoned that one might have supposed he flew rather than travelled. I will not leave shrouded in silence a miracle he did on one such occasion.

15. On a journey devoted to the dedication of altars he came to a place near a church newly built by Archdeacon Æthelric.[2] The bishop knew it was ready for consecration, and he contacted the archdeacon as night was coming on: he was to go off at once and make ready what was needed for the consecration of the church. He himself would come at dawn and take part in the rite. The archdeacon blenched at so peremptory an order, but he could find no plea other than that he was short of what was required. So great a company needed much in the way of victuals, and while the bishop himself would be content with but a little, he was afraid of the demands his companions might make. 2. 'Go,' said the bishop, 'and do *your* part. God will feed his servants from some source. Because we are so close, we shall do God's work.' Necessity lent wings to the cleric: he set off at once, and hurried on what the consecration demanded. He added generous gifts, so that everything suitable for the diners' use should be available. Only mead was in short supply:[3] he had begged it from friends, but it was only enough to fill a single and by no means large jug. So the bishop arrived, did what he had come to do, and proposed to go on elsewhere. The archdeacon persuaded him to change his mind, and had his friends' prayers to back him in begging him to stay for the day. 3. After lunch the host's lavishness prompted him to order the serving of all the guests from the jug I have mentioned. The liquor kept pace with those who gulped it down; it bubbled up as though from a spring, and grew with

undated context, with the other archdeacon Hugh. He is presumed to have died before 1114, by which time the archdeacons were Hugh and Richard. Darlington (p. xxxv n. 3) thought that the miracle recorded here might have occurred at the village of Cutsdean (Glos.), where Æthelric had a priest. For other details of this man and his evidently close connections with Wulfstan, see Darlington ut supra, and Mason, p. 166 n. 43.

[3] William tells a similar story, similarly worded, of Dunstan in *VD* i. 12 (after B., c. 10 (pp. 17–18)). Wulfstan of Winchester recounts a similar miracle in *Vita S. Æthelwoldi*, c. 12, and was himself imitated by Goscelin, *Vita S. Wulfhildae*: M. Esposito, 'La vie de sainte Vulfhilde par Goscelin de Cantorbéry', *Anal. Boll.* xxxii (1913), 10–26, at p. 19.

scaturiens dampnis increscebat suis. Crederes farinae hidriam uel lecithum olei quibus Saraptenam uiduam ipse pascebat qui pasci uenerat.[1] Ignoro an excellentiore gratia, quia ibi trium hominum[2] sustentata est natura, hic multorum satietas expleta. Et hoc quidem magnum, sed maius quod sequitur, quia post triduum inuentum est uas semiplenum quod tantae multitudini sufficere uideretur nec totum. Nec uero archidiaconus clam tulit factum, sed communicauit aliis ad episcopalis sanctitudinis inditium.

16. Res ammonere uidetur ut, quia de potu sermo se intulit, dicam quid monstri cuidam accidit qui contra uetitum eius potauit. Habebat ipse in curia sua milites multos,[3] non quo uoluptati esset aut eius blandiretur animo frequens seruientium multitudo (nec enim in corde parturiebat iactantiam si haberet multorum obsequelam), sed rex Willelmus ita fieri preceperat, quod sereretur rumor in uulgus Danos aduentare[4] et iam iamque affore. Nec a uero deuiabat opinio, uenissentque profecto nisi aliae res intercessissent. Causam minarum et obicem impedimentorum in Gestis Regum Anglorum exposui,[5] quae ibi si quis uolet amicus lector inueniet. Quocirca, ut ceperam dicere, rex timore percitus coacto concilio*a* quid opus esset facto in medium consuluit. 2. Omnium fuit sententia Lanfranco auctore curias magnatum militibus muniendas, ut si forte res exigeret communi umbone rempublicam et priuatas fortunas omnes contra barbaros tuerentur. Ideo episcopus plures retentans affluentibus mulcebat stipendiis et delicatis saturabat obsoniis. Id cum sepe, tum solito habundantius quadam die. Et primo quidem crebrioribus poculis adducta hilaritas uarios, ut in conuiuiis solet, sermones inuenit. A sermonibus processum in iurgia et pene in arma; quibus Sanctus offensus pauloque commotior omnem strepitum pincernarum cessare et ne quisquam in domo illa ea die potaret precepit. Ceteris nutui iubentis seruientibus solus Nicholaus, quod eum antistes maiori dignaretur gratia, penum ingressus temerauit preceptum. Inde dormitum se recipiens horrificisque insomniis

---

a δH* (*p. 99*); consilio C

[1] 3 Sam.(1 Kgs.) 17: 16. The biblical story was doubtless the ultimate source for later accounts of miracles of this type.

[2] One person only in the *VD* story.

[3] Wulfstan's knights and the heavy drinking of his household are mentioned again in *GP*, c. 139 (p. 281). There it is said that Wulfstan would keep them company, while drinking from a tiny glass. Cf. above, iii. 2. 1 and 3.

its own loss. You might have supposed it 'the barrel of meal' or 'the cruse of oil' with which he [Elijah] who had come to be fed himself fed the widow of Zarephath.[1] But perhaps here a greater grace was shown: *there* the bodily needs of three persons[2] were met, *here* a multitude was fed to satiety. This indeed was a great miracle, but greater was to follow. After three days the vessel was found half-full although it did not seem large enough to provide drink for so many even when full. The archdeacon did not keep the story quiet: he passed it on to others, to demonstrate the sanctity of the bishop.

16. As a story about drinking has come up, it seems a hint that I should say what a portent afflicted one who drank against the orders of Wulfstan. In his 'court' he had many knights:[3] not because a throng of servants pleased or gratified him, for his heart felt no pride in having many at his beck and call; but King William had given the order for this, because a rumour was going about that the Danes were on their way[4] and would arrive at any moment. This belief was in fact true, and they would indeed have come had not other factors intervened. The reason for the threat and the obstacles that brought it to naught I have explained in the *History of the English Kings*,[5] and a friendly reader will be able to find it there if he so wishes. So, as I was about to say, the king was very scared; he summoned a council and threw open discussion on what should be done. 2. On Lanfranc's motion all agreed that the courts of the magnates should be reinforced by the presence of knights, so that if need be everyone could unite to defend public weal and private fortunes against the barbarian. And so the bishop began to maintain a sizeable force, keeping them happy with high pay and filling them up with choice food. That often happened, and one day more lavishly than usual. At first the cheerfulness brought on by frequent rounds of drink led as usual in feasts to conversation on different topics. From talk it went on to quarrelling, and almost to the use of weapons. The holy man was put out and rather annoyed by this. He told the waiters to stop bustling about, and forbade any more drinking in the house that day. The others obeyed his request; Nicholas alone, relying on the special favour he enjoyed with the bishop, went to the cellar and flouted the order. Then he took himself off to bed, where he was assailed by

---

[4] Cf. *ASC* (E), s.a. 1085. For the institution of 'household' knights, with reference to this passage, see B. Golding, *Conquest and Colonisation: the Normans in Britain, 1066–1100* (London, 1994), pp. 133–4.   [5] c. 258. 3 and n.

impulsus, stridores diros emittebat. 3. Exiluit strato Colemannus, qui prope cubabat, expergefactumque tantorum motuum causam interrogat. Ille, quod procul a Christiano sit, demone se urgeri respondit: pro transgressione precepti nullam sibi requiem dari. Persuasus autem a sotio ut psalmo et cruce fantasiam discuteret, denuo in soporem resoluitur. Denuoque et tertio horrores eosdem aut maiores expertus, intellexit tandem solum esse remedium si ab illo impetraret ueniam cuius iussum uiolando meruerat penam. Is tum more solito in aecclesia solitariis orationibus Deo lucubrabat. Affusus ergo genibus pii patris peccatumque confessus, benedictionem gratanter obtinuit, salutem non difficulter elicuit.

17. Sane,[1] ut occasione magistri etiam uenerabilis discipuli memoria eat in paginas nostras, Nicholaus[2] clarissimae progeniei quantum ad Anglos fuit. Parentes eius sanctum uirum magna coluere reuerentia, multis commodis amicitiam eius pignerati. Puerum baptizauit ipse, litterisque nobiliter instructum continuo ut aetas tulit semper ad latus habuit. Mox ut plena informationis perfectio in eum conflueret, Cantiam misit, sub disciplina Lanfranci aliquandiu militaturum. Idemque postea tempore Thiulfi episcopi[3] factus prior multa in breui experimenta industriae dedit. Idque quod magis conducibile arbitror, sic litteras habitatoribus loci uel doctrina infudit uel exemplo inculcauit ut summis aecclesiis Angliae etsi cedunt numero non uincantur studio. 2. Porro Nicholaus Wlstani dicta et facta referre uoluptati habebat, in hoc fortasse culpandus quod uitam eius stilo non commisit.[4] Nullus enim eam memoriae mandare posset ueratius quam nemo ipso nosset presentius. Denique uerba eius, etiam quae fortuitu effunderet, numquam fere pondere caruisse dicebat, ut istud: Demulcebat paterna benignitate caput ipsius, cui iam refugis a fronte capillis dampnosa cesaries erat.[5] Tum ephebus alludens episcopo 'Pulchre' inquit 'seruas capillos meos, qui omnes effugiunt.' 'Non,' respondit ille 'crede michi, quam diu uixero caluus eris.' Nec minus dicto fuit, sed ipsa pene septimana qua spiritus Wlstani reliquit terras quicquid reliquum erat capillorum in fronte Nicholai effluxit in auras.

---

[1] Much the same story in *GP*, c. 147 (p. 287).

[2] Occ. as a monk by *c*.1080, prior from *c*.1116, d. 1124: *BRECP*, p. 858.

[3] Bp. 1115–23.

[4] Orchard, 'Parallel lives' (above, p. xvi n. 21), suggests that William would have preferred an account of Wulfstan's life from Nicholas, rather than from Coleman, whose 'overblown prose' William had to curtail.

[5] Cf. Lucan x. 132; for other echoes by William, see *GR*, c. 439. 2 n.

fearful dreams and began to let out frightful screams. 3. Coleman, who slept nearby, leapt out of bed, woke Nicholas up, and asked why he was so upset. He replied, in words ill-befitting a Christian, that he was being harassed by a demon: because of his disobedience, he could get no rest. He was prevailed upon by his fellow to drive off the illusion with a psalm and the sign of the Cross, and went to sleep again. But a second and third time he underwent the same or greater terrors, and eventually realised that the only solution was to ask the pardon of the man whose order he had disobeyed and so brought on this well-deserved punishment. Wulfstan at that moment was, as so often, awake in the service of God, praying alone in the church. Nicholas fell at the devout father's feet and confessed his sin. He received Wulfstan's willing benediction, and had no difficulty in obtaining relief.

17. I should like to take the opportunity provided by his master to bring into my pages the memory of his revered pupil.[1] On his English side, Nicholas[2] was of exalted descent. His parents paid the holy man high respect, and won his friendship by the many services they did him. Wulfstan baptized Nicholas as a child, gave him a fine education in letters, and kept him continually at his side when he was old enough. To complete his training, he sent him off to Canterbury to serve awhile under Lanfranc. Later, in the time of Bishop Theulf,[3] Nicholas became prior, and in a short period gave many proofs of his hard work. And, something I think particularly to his credit, he so inculcated letters into the occupants of the place, by both teaching and example, that, though they may be inferior in numbers, they are not surpassed in zeal for study by the highest churches of England. 2. Further, Nicholas loved to tell over the doings and sayings of Wulfstan, and could perhaps be criticized for not writing his biography.[4] For no one could have more truthfully recorded a life that no one knew more intimately at first-hand. For instance, he would say that Wulfstan's words, even chance utterances, almost never lacked substance. Thus, Wulfstan was once stroking Nicholas' head like a kind father; his hair was already beginning to thin, and the locks were receding from his forehead.[5] The young man said lightly to the bishop: 'It is a good thing that you are trying to save my hair, for it's all in retreat.' 'Believe me,' was the reply, 'you will not go bald as long as I live.' This came true. In almost the very week that Wulfstan's spirit left the earth, the hair remaining on Nicholas' forehead disappeared into thin air.

18. Omni die in Quadragesima, ut ante dictum lector recolit,[1] pauperibus post ablutionem pedum et manuum stipem impendebat cibariam, idque libentius noctibus quam diebus, uitans uidelicet iuditia hominum quae in utranuis partem amore labuntur aut odio. Vbi si inter alios assedisset aliquis quem morbus occupasset regius,[2] illius uero pedes pressare tenatius, osculari dultius, oculos porro in ipsis figere ulceribus. Iam uero in cena Domini totam diem perinde ac noctem succedentibus inuicem sibi pietatum offitiis exigebat. Et licet semper esset in Dei cultum suspensus, illo tamen die maxime curabat ne quid seculare suis irreperet actibus. Post matutinas cum monachis in maiori cantatas aecclesia in cubiculum regressus, aquam calidam cum manutergiis inueniebat paratam ab offitialibus quorum id erat munus. 2. Ibi multis pauperibus ut dixi dilutis, omnium etiam uestimentorum indulgebat compendium, manu sua ipse caritatem ministrans.[3] Tum ad momentaneam quietem membris compositis, ministri totam aulam implebant pauperibus, quantum densatis agminibus, quantum confertis ordinibus sedere poterat. His omnibus cum pater calceos et uictum manu prebuisset sua, si ei diceretur 'Domine, modo requiesce, bene fecisti', respondebat 'Parum feci, sed uoluntatem habeo preceptum Domini mei fatiendi.' Inde secedebat in aecclesiam, totaque die usque ad nonam mundanorum refugus caelum anhelabat. Sequebatur penitentium reconciliatio, missae celebritas, crismatis benedictio. 3. Quae omnia quanuis Colemannus magno uerborum circuitu egerit, michi pretermittere consilium fuit, propterea quod non episcopale offitium designare sed uitam eius describere susceperim. Quid enim ad rem ea dicere quae et alii fatiunt nec aliter quam in libris continetur facere possunt?[4] Illud sane pretereundum non opinor, aspectum eius ita fuisse penitentibus gratiosum ut, cum eum conspicarentur oculo, Dei angelum imaginarentur animo. Est enim naturae ingenitum ut per illum te speres assequi peccatorum remissam in quo nullam cognoueris offensam. Eo die cum reconciliatis comedere, post cenam monachis omnibus pedes abluere, pocula cum osculis ministrare solitum accepimus, sic a media nocte usque ad profundum alterius noctis crepusculum mundo se subtrahere consuetum.

---

[1] i. 10. 4.   [2] See above, p. 74 and n. 2.

[3] Similar observances are mentioned of Bishop Byrnstan of Winchester in *GP*, c. 75 (p. 163).

[4] William sees no point in describing things that every bishop, not just Wulfstan, did,

18. Every day of Lent, as the reader will recall me saying,[1] after washing the feet and hands of the poor he would give them alms in the form of food. He preferred to do this at night rather than by day, for he tried to avoid the judgement of men, which slides one way or the other out of love or dislike. If someone afflicted by the King's Evil[2] had taken his seat with the others, Wulfstan would squeeze his feet more tightly and kiss them more tenderly, while keeping his eyes fixed on the actual sores. On Maundy Thursday he would spend all day and all night in one pious duty after another. And though he was always anxiously concerned to serve God, he took particular care on that day that nothing worldly should creep into his activities. After the singing of Matins with the monks in the greater church, he would go back to his room, where he found hot water and towels laid out by the officials whose task it was. 2. There, as I have said, he washed many paupers, and gave them a change of all their clothes, administering charity with his own hand.[3] Then, while he took a short nap, his staff filled the whole hall with paupers, as many as could sit there in packed rows. When the father had personally given them all shoes and food, someone might say to him: 'Master, take some rest now, you have done well', but he would reply: 'I have not done enough; but it is my wish to do the bidding of my Lord.' Then he used to go apart into the church, and all day till Nones flee worldly things and long for heaven. Next came reconciliation of the penitent, celebration of mass, and blessing of the chrism. 3. Coleman has given elaborate details of all this, but I have decided to pass them over, because it is my plan to write the man's life, not lay down the bishop's duties. What is the point of telling of what other people as well do, and indeed cannot do except in the manner laid down in books?[4] But I do not think I should pass over the fact that his face was so appealing to the penitent that when they looked at him they imagined they were looking at an angel of God. Indeed it is natural to hope to receive remission of your sins through one in whom you know no offence. That day, so we learn, he would eat with the newly reconciled, wash the feet of all the monks after supper, and serve drinks along with kisses. Then from midnight to the late dusk of the following night, he would withdraw from the world.

and indeed had to do in view of the written instructions (such as Gregory the Great's *Pastoral Rule*) governing their conduct. This is a good example of the sort of generality that William did not include in his own saints' Lives.

19. Anno ante obitum suum proximo tanta in cena Domini[1] offitium istud curauit efficatia ut superiorum annorum nichil fuisse putaretur diligentia. Presagiebat profecto illud se facturum ultimo, cunctosque ministros sollicitudinis percellebat miraculo. Indixerat singulis prepositis ut ex singulis uillis preberent unius hominis uestimenta omnia, decem hominum calceos, centum hominum uictum.[2] Eadem etiam cubiculariis nundinanda preceperat, ut quod minus haberent predia suppleret curia. Ter ea die impleta est aula egenis, sic constipatis ut uix egreque quisquam progredi posset, adeo cunctos aditus occluserant agmina, longa serie et confusa herentia.[3] 2. Fremebat domus magno tumultu, abluebantque monachi et clerici pedes considentium. Ipse sedebat in medio, episcopali nixus subsellio (labor immensus uires exhauserat), ut uel psaltes esset qui ablutor esse non posset. Erat interea mens misericors, quae uellet satisfieri cunctis ne ullus abiret inanis. Et quidem semel et secundo discesserunt omnes uestibus ornati, nummis et calceis laeti, omnes uentribus suffarcinati. Iam uero cum tertio locaretur pauperum ordo, suggessit in aurem monachus episcopo pecuniam et uestes defecisse, in angusto etiam uictum esse, dapiferum cubiculariosque*ᵃ* conuentos expensas negare. Quid ergo lauari pedes attineret quando quod lotis daretur non esset? 'Immo,' inquit episcopus, 'fiat preceptum Domini; non deerit largitas eius, ut alicunde pascantur serui. Ministri mei pro me facere nolunt; uolent cum me non habebunt.' 3. Vix haec locutus fuerat, et ecce tres ingressi sunt nuntii, alter alterius calcem pene pro festinatione terentes.[4] Primus pecuniam allatam, secundus equum adductum, tertius boues donatos episcopo nuntiauit. Ille leuatis in caelum oculis et manibus exultauit miraculo, non tam sui causa quam pauperum emolumento. Monachi flere pre gaudio, et tali aggratulari domino. Ab omnibus benedici Deus, qui non fraudaret uota in se sperantium, nec pateretur uel ad horam contristari Wlstanum. Ita

---

ᵃ dapiferum cubiculariosque *ed.* (dapiferumque et cubicularios *Whar.*); dapiferumque cubicularios *C*; dapiferum et cubicularium δ (*p. 101*); dapifer puerum et cubicularium *H**

---

[1] John 13: 1 seq.

[2] The idea was not new; cf. the ordinance of King Æthelstan (F. L. Attenborough, *The Laws of the Earliest English Kings* (Cambridge, 1922), pp. 126–7), commanding all his reeves to 'provide a destitute Englishman with food, if you have such an one [in your district], or if you find one [elsewhere]', to each 'an amber of meal, a shank of bacon or a ram worth four pence every month, and clothes for twelve months annually'.

[3] Cf. Lucan i. 492–3, also echoed in *GR*, c. 348. 3. *VD* ii. 30. 2 provides another example of crowded doors.

19. A year before his death, he went so far in carrying out these duties on Maundy Thursday[1] that the care taken in earlier years was reckoned to have been quite eclipsed. He must have had a premonition that he would be doing it for the last time, and he struck all his staff with amazement at this solicitude. He had instructed each of the reeves to provide from every vill a complete suit of clothes for one man, shoes for ten, and provisions for a hundred.[2] He had ordered his chamberlains to buy up these same things, so that his 'court' would supply any deficiencies left by the estates. Thrice that day the hall was filled with the needy, so close packed that one could move through them only with difficulty, the throng having so blocked all the entrances, huddled together in a long and disorderly queue.[3] 2. The house was in uproar. Monks and clerks were washing the feet of those who sat there. Wulfstan was in the midst of them, resting on a bishop's seat (for the enormous labour had drained his strength) so as to be able to sing psalms even if he could not wash feet. His mind meanwhile was full of mercy, wanting to satisfy the needs of all so that none should go away empty-handed. Once and a second time they all went out clothed, happy at receiving coin and shoes, and all with full stomachs. But when the third sitting of paupers was in place, a monk whispered in the bishop's ear that the money and clothes had run out, and that the food stocks were getting low, while the steward and chamberlains had been approached and were refusing money. What was the point of washing feet if there was nothing to give to those who had been washed? 'No,' said the bishop, 'let the Lord's commandment be kept. His generosity will not fail, and He will ensure that His servants are fed from somewhere. My staff are refusing to act for me. They will be willing enough when they have me no longer.' 3. The words were scarcely spoken when lo! three messengers came in, almost treading on each others' heels in their haste.[4] The first announced to the bishop that money had been brought, the second that a horse had been led up, the third that oxen had been donated. Wulfstan raised his eyes and hands heavenwards, and rejoiced at the miracle, not so much for his own sake as because of the gain to the poor. The monks wept for joy, and applauded so remarkable a master. All blessed God for not frustrating the prayers of those who put their hopes in Him, and not allowing Wulfstan to be saddened even for an hour. So the sale of the horse and the realizing

---

[4] There is a similar 'miracle' in *VD* ii. 7. 2–3.

equus in pretium redactus, boues in nummos conflati cum pecunia nuper allata egenorum profecere compendiis.

20. Premonuerat ministros uelle se ad illud Pascha conuiuari accuratis epulis*a* cum bonis hominibus. Id illi falso interpretati opulentorum plerosque conuocauerant.*b* Iamque Paschae dies illuxerat, cum ille in aulam pauperibus quantos capere poterat introductis precepit inter eos sedili locato epulas sibi apponi. Excepit illud dapifer ingenti indignatione animi. Multo enim infrendens murmure lacerabat lenitatem uiri, dicens competentius esse ut episcopus conuiuaretur cum paucis diuitibus quam cum multis pauperibus. Ad hoc ille respondit illos diuites esse qui nossent et possent uoluntatem Dei facere; illis debere seruiri qui non haberent unde redderent.[1] 2. Redditurum Deum compensationis gratia quod non haberent egeni relatione uicaria. Laetius se uidere istum consessum quam si ut sepe consedisset regi Anglorum. Multo enim, ut dixi, eum suspitiebat rex honore, multo proceres, ut qui sepe ipsum ascirent conuiuio et assurgerent eius consilio, ipsi crebro qui persequerentur iustitiam, ingenita quibusdam natura ut in aliis percolant ad quod ipsi aspirare non ualeant. Quid dico de optimatibus Angliae? Reges Hiberniae magnis eum uenerabantur fauoribus. Rex Scottiae Malcolmus[2] cum uenerabili coniuge Margareta ipsius se dedebat orationibus. Penetrauerat regionum intima, regnorum extrema sanctitatis eius fama. Papa Romanus, Barensis archiepiscopus, Ierosolimitanus patriarcha epistolis quae adhuc supersunt eius ambierunt apud Deum suffragia.[3] 3. Nulla postremo pene fuit mundi gloria quae nolentem renitentemque non sequeretur. Eratque certamen inter uirum et gloriam, dum quo eam acrius fugeret ille, eo instantius eum illa urgeret.

Sed de talibus hucusque circumuagari licuerit, dum transitum eius lacrimabilem quidem terris sed exultabilem caelis adoriri formidat oratio. Nunc enim pro mediocritate scientiae dicturus te rogo, Domine Christe, ut sic in eo dixerim uel dicere possim munera tua,

---

a Whar.; eplis (*with a barred l, i.e.* epistolis) C   *b* conuocauerunt δH* (*p. 101*)

[1] Luke 7: 42.
[2] Malcolm III Canmore, 1058–93, and his queen Margaret.
[3] Apparently Urban II (1088–99); Ursus (d. 1089) or Elias (d. 1105); Marcus II or Euthymius (d. 1099). The letters are not known to survive. With the passage 'Reges Hiberniae . . . suffragia' cf. Einhard, *Vita Karoli* c. 16 (ed. Halphen, p. 46): 'Scottorum quoque reges sic habuit ad suam uoluntatem . . . ut eum nunquam aliter nisi dominum . . .

of the value of the oxen, along with the money just brought, saw to the needs of the indigent.

20. He had warned his staff in advance that he wanted that Easter to dine formally with good men. They had taken that the wrong way, and invited a large number of rich personages. Easter Day dawned, and Wulfstan brought as many paupers into the hall as it could hold, and requested to be served with a meal at a chair placed among them. The steward was furious, and grinding his teeth grumbled aloud at the man's softheartedness, saying it was more appropriate for a bishop to dine with a few rich men than with many poor. He replied that those men were rich who knew how to do God's will and were capable of doing it; those needed serving who had nothing from which to repay the service.[1] 2. God would, by way of compensation, return on behalf of the poor what they could not afford to give themselves. He was happier to look on this company than if (as often happened) he had sat down with the king of the English. For, as I have said, the king and noblemen regarded him with great honour, often inviting him to dinner and taking notice of his counsel, including, often, those who were themselves liable to harry justice, it being natural to some people to respect in others what they cannot aspire to themselves. Nor was it just the great men of England. The kings of Ireland revered and favoured him. Malcolm king of Scotland[2] and his respected wife Margaret entrusted themselves to his prayers. The fame of his holiness had penetrated deep into every land, and to the furthest parts of every realm. The pope of Rome, the archbishop of Bari, and the patriarch of Jerusalem canvassed his help before God in letters that still survive.[3] 3. Finally, there was almost no worldly distinction that did not pursue him for all his unwillingness and reluctance. There was a competition between the man and glory: the more anxiously he fled it, the more closely did it press on his heels.

But enough of such rambling reflections, by which I have been trying to put off approaching a story I dread to tell, that of his passing over, which brought tears on earth though joy in heaven. But now I shall tell the story so far as my insufficient knowledge permits; and I ask you, Lord Christ, to ensure that I have spoken and may speak of

pronuntiarent. Extant epistolae ab eis ad illum missae quibus huiusmodi affectus eorum erga illum indicatur', and Asser, *De rebus gestis Alfredi*, c. 91 (ed. Stevenson, p. 77): 'Nam etiam de Hierosolyma ab Elia patriarcha epistolas et dona illi directas uidimus et legimus.'

quatinus et tibi sit placitum et sibi non ingratum. Tua enim sunt, Domine, prorsus quae in Wlstano laudamus, quia tuum est omne quod uiuimus. Quapropter misericordem omnipotentiam tuam quantum possum queso, ut hanc*ᵃ* acceptes lucubratiunculam, ne quantulicumque fructu laboris excidam.

21. Proximo post ista quae nuperrime dixi Pentecoste graui per omnes artus tactus molestia lecto accubuit. Iussit continuo equis concitatis familiaris sui Rotberti episcopi Herefordensis[1] aduentum rogari. Rotbertus, quod nuntiabatur audito, confestim affuit, et Wlstanus humanorum excessuum confessione facta etiam disciplinam accepit (ita uocant monachi uirgarum flagra, quae tergo nudato cedentis infligit acrimonia).[2] Quantus hic uir, qui aeuo inualidus, morbo infractus, conscientia etiam serenus, non abstinuerit flagellis corporis, ut discuteret si quid reliquum erat animae sordis! 2. Ab eo tempore usque in Circumcisionem Domini[3] uidebatur aliquando leuius habere, aliquando recidebat in lectum: ita pigra sed assidua febre agebatur in exitum. Labes corporis augebat uires animae, ut si quid in eo erat immaturum aeternae gloriae feruor infirmitatis posset decoquere. Post Circumcisionem supradictus episcopus et uenerabiles diocesis suae abbates, Serlo Gloecestrae Geraldus Theokesberiae,[4] decumbentem uisitarunt. Hos ipse primum pro more suo se ipso accusato iure absoluit suo, extremum eis ualefatiens. Ebulliebat in dies uis ualitudinis, maturabatque Christus transitum qui uocabat ad caelum. 3. Interea non feriabatur ille a Dei seruitio, sed ueterum non oblitus studiorum orabat plerumque uerbo, semper animo, magisque sedens quam iacens aures psalmis, oculos altari applicabat, sedili sic composito ut libere cerneret quicquid in capella fieret. Ante octo dies decessus sui a Thoma priore[5] loci sacrae inunctionis suscepit offitium, cotidiano post haec eucharistiae uiatico tutatus exitum.

Supremum efflauit tertio decimo kalendas Februarii, paulo post mediam noctem sabbati. Annus erat incarnationis Dominicae millesimus octogesimus septimus,*ᵇ* regni Willelmi iunioris decimus, post

---

ᵃ *ed.*; hac C   *ᵇ* *So C; the date is given variously in the other MSS* (1067 D (*p. 102*), 1061 G, 1097 H*, 1095 *Vesp.*)

---

[1] See above, p. 123 and n. 4. Wulfstan had ordained Robert priest: JW s.a. 1079.

[2] For monastic discipline, see *The Monastic Constitutions of Lanfranc*, ed. and trans. D. Knowles, rev. edn. C. N. L. Brooke (OMT, 2002), pp. 146–52.

[3] 1 Jan.

[4] 1072–1104, 1102–9. At this date Gerald was probably abbot of Cranbourne, founded *c.*980, from 1102 a cell of Tewkesbury: *Heads*, p. 87.

your gifts in him in such a way that you may be pleased and he not displeased. For yours indeed, O Lord, are the things we praise in Wulfstan, because it is your gift that we live at all. Wherefore with all my power I beg, Almighty and Merciful one, that you accept this little work on which I have been labouring, so that I do not lose the fruits of my effort, however small it may have been.

21. At the Pentecost following the events I have just described, Wulfstan was struck down by severe discomfort in all his limbs, and took to bed. He at once sent messengers hot foot to ask his friend Robert bishop of Hereford[1] to come. Robert, hearing the news, came at once. Wulfstan made confession of the shortcomings to which men are heir, and also received 'discipline', for that is what monks call the strokes of the rod inflicted harshly on the bared back.[2] What a man!—who, though feeble with age, broken by illness, and quiet in conscience, yet did not flinch from corporal punishment to shake off any remaining stain on his soul! 2. From that time until the Lord's Circumcision[3] he seemed to be easier at times, while at others he would relapse into bed again, such was the effect of the slow but incessant fever that was driving him towards his end. The failure of his body only increased the powers of his soul, so that the heat of his illness could sweat off anything in him that was unprepared for eternal glory. After Circumcision, Robert and two venerable abbots of his diocese, Serlo of Gloucester and Gerald of Tewkesbury,[4] visited the sick man. He first, as was his wont, accused himself; then by his privilege he absolved them of their sins, and said goodbye to them for the last time. The severity of his illness welled up as the days went by, and Christ hurried on his passing, for He was calling him to heaven. 3. In the meantime Wulfstan took no holiday from serving God; never forgetting his old ways, he prayed often in words, always in the mind, and sitting rather than lying kept his ears attentive to psalms and his eyes fixed on the altar, for he placed his chair where he could see without obstruction what went on in the chapel. Eight days before he died, he received the office of the sacred unction from Thomas, prior of the house,[5] and after this daily safeguarded his departure with the viaticum of the Eucharist.

He died on 20 January, shortly after Saturday midnight. The year was AD 1087, the tenth of King William the younger; it was 34 years,

---

[5] Prior from before 1080 until his death in 1113: *BRECP*, pp. 883–4.

annos suscepti episcopatus triginta quattuor, menses quattuor, dies tredecim,[a] anno aetatis circiter octogesimo septimo.[1] 4. Hic porro mirari quis poterit quod longeuitatis suae futurae non ignarus ipse uiuens fuerit. Quod cum sepe alias tum semel in capitulo dulcissime pronuntiauit. Circumsedentibus enim fratribus et multa ut fit mutuo sermone serentibus, cum repente obstipo capite[2] sopori cessisset, singultantibus omnium lacrimis quasi festino eos obitu destituturus conclamatus est. Nec multo post discusso somno cum causam ploratus addidicisset,[b] respondit his fere uerbis: 'Crede michi, quantum senile corpus durare poterit, non moriar, nec nisi longo senio dissoluetur haec compago. Postquam autem excessero, tunc uobis presentior ero, nec aliquis ex eis quos timetis uobis poterit nocere, si Deo uelitis fideliter seruire.'

22. Lauerunt ergo corpus, quod iam spe resurrectionis perpetuae prefulgidum stupori et uenerationi uisentibus fuit: ita perspicuo nitore gemmeum, ita miranda puritate lacteum erat. Denique nasus, qui uiuenti citra modum protuberabat, ita pulchre defuncto subsedit et incanduit ut mirum uisentibus esset. Illud porro quod dicam non nullo presentibus fuit miraculo. Anulus quem ad consecrationem pontificatus acceperat nonnumquam ante hanc horam[c] exciderat. Multis enim ante obitum annis ita caro digitorum exinanita fuerat ut uix pellicula herere uideretur ossibus,[3] adeo uel longeuitas uel quod magis affirmauerim abstinentia corpus attenuauerat. 2. Inde fiebat ut crebro laberetur anulus, magno dolore monachorum proximam antistitis mortem ominantium.[4] Eos ille benigno miseratus animo clementis suadelae demulcebat oleo. Frontem tristitia[d] soluerent: anulum non defuturum si quererent; eum sibi sine ambitu acquisitum, in humum portandum. Haec sepius dicta et facta;

---

[a] So C; the other MSS (DGH* (p. 102) and Vesp.) agree on quattuor   [b] Whar.; addicisset C   [c] Whar.; ad horam C   [d] tristia C[p.c.]

[1] As Darlington showed (p. xliii n. 1), these reckonings do not produce a single date. (1) The AD year of 1087 given in MS C is wildly wrong, presumably by scribal rather than authorial error. One conjectures that the exemplar of the surviving MSS had indistinct roman numerals at this point (see the app. crit.). (2) But William himself made a mistake, for the tenth year of William II's reign and thirty-fourth of Wulfstan's episcopate, however calculated, cannot be made to coincide (they are approximately a calendar year apart). The correct year was 1095, which was Rufus's eighth year and Wulfstan's thirty-third. (3) For the length of his pontificate cf. Hemingi Chartularium ii. 407: 'Mansit autem in episcopatu xxxii. annis, mensibus iiii. et iii[bus] septimanis.' (4) 13 kal. Feb. (20 Jan.), a Saturday, is correct, and is that assigned his obit in Bodl. Libr., MS Hatton 113, fo. iii. Yet in the explicit to VW William gives the day as 14 kal. (19 Jan.). JW s.a. 1095 (iii. 74–5, and see

four months and thirteen days since he took up his bishopric. He was
about 86 years old.[1] 4. At this point it is remarkable to observe that
while alive he was not unaware of his future longevity. He proclaimed
it in a particularly engaging fashion on one occasion in chapter. The
brothers were sitting around him conversing vigorously as usual,
when Wulfstan's head suddenly drooped[2] and he went off to sleep.
Everyone started to sob, thinking that he was about to rob them of
him by a swift demise, and giving him up for lost. But soon he shook
off his slumber, and learning the reason for their grief replied in more
or less the following words: 'Believe me, I shall not die so long as my
aged body can last out; and my frame will only disintegrate after a
prolonged old age. But after I am gone, I shall be the more present
with you, and no one of those you fear will be able to do you harm, if
you are ready to serve God in all loyalty.'

22. So they washed the corpse. It inspired amazement and reverence
in those who saw it, gleaming as it already was in the hope of eternal
resurrection; for it shone bright like a gem, and was white with a
remarkable purity. His nose, excessively prominent while he lived,
retreated and paled so beautifully in death that those who saw it
marvelled. There was a further circumstance that much surprised
those present. The ring he had received at his consecration as bishop
had several times fallen off before this moment. For many years
before his death the flesh on his fingers had become so wasted that
skin seemed scarcely to cling to bone:[3] so much had his long life, or,
as I should prefer to say, his abstinent life worn down his body.
2. The result was that the ring often slipped off, to the great distress
of the monks, who took it as a presage of the bishop's imminent
death.[4] His kind heart felt pity for them, and he soothed them with
the oil of his merciful persuasion. They must smooth away their
frowns; the ring would be there if they went to look for it. He had
received it without asking for it, and he would take it to his grave.

n. 1) says that it occurred on a Saturday which, however, he wrongly dated 18 Jan. This is
the more surprising, as at Worcester Wulfstan was early on commemorated on 20 Jan.:
Mason, p. 257 n. 5. His death is also recounted in *GP*, c. 148 (pp. 287–8), quite differently
and without a date.

[2] Persius iii. 80.

[3] Cf. Virgil, *Ecl.* iii. 102, also echoed in *GR*, c. 232. 3, and *GP*, c. 76 (p. 170).

[4] JW (iii. 74–5) records that 'God did not allow anyone to pull off from his finger the
ring with which he had received episcopal consecration, so that the holy man should not
mislead his people even in death; for he had very often predicted to them that he would
never lose it whilst alive or even on the day of his burial.'

anulus crebro lapsus numquam omnino amissus, semper inuentus. Tum uero, ut ceperam dicere, quidam temptauerunt subtrahere digito, siue ut memoriae loco haberent siue ut fidem promissi probarent. Verum multis conatibus ultro citroque irritis cepto destiterunt, sic nodositas articulorum, sic pellis et neruorum integritas omne deludebat ingenium.

23. Effertur*a* [1] interea corpus, proceditur ad aecclesiam, quam ipse de uetusta fecerat nouam, locatur ante altare cum feretro, circumsedente clero. Ibi nocte illa cum sequenti die ac nocte orationum inferiae, lacrimarum exequiae Deo turificantur. Erat tunc Rotbertus antefatus Herefordensis episcopus in curia regis,[2] homo seculi quidem fretus prudentia sed nulla solutus illecebra. Huic, eadem hora qua Sanctus rebus excessit, uisus est astare, multum mutatus ab illo[3] Wlstano quem proximis uidisset annis, ita stellanti luce perspicuus, uiridanti uultu roseus erat. Episcopalibusque uestimentis amictus et baculum tenens in manibus his compellare uidebatur iacentem: 2. 'Veni nunc, dilecte frater Rotberte, Wigorniam: uolo ut iusta michi persoluens humo corpus, Deo animam commendes.' Talia contra Rotbertus putabatur referre: 'Domine et dilecte amice, precipis michi ut te sepeliam, cum iam quinque annis non te uiderim huius uigoris?' 'Dimitte,' aiebat Wlstanus, 'sic est uoluntas Dei, quam oportet impleri. Velociter nunc perge, nec uerba mea negligenter accipe.' Tum episcopus, tam manifestae uisionis motus oraculo, statim solutus est somno, regis auribus uisum intimauit. Cuius permissu accepto, concitato equitatu rapiebat arua morantia,[4] Wigorniamque ire pergebat. Leuabat immensum laborem uis sanctae amicitiae, qua iam inde ab episcopatus initio deuinctus fuerat uiro, fauitque benignis uotis diuinitas, ut ante ad locum ueniret quam tempus humandi esset. Nam et monachi consulto moras protraxerant eius operientes aduentum.

3. Hoc modo prima nocte spiritus Wlstani amicum pontificem sed

---

a δH* (*p. 103*); offertur C

[1] The story in 1–2 was also told, with important variations, in *GP*, c. 165 (pp. 301–3). There Wulfstan is still alive when he appears to Robert in a vision, he foretells Robert's own imminent death, and after the burial the Worcester monks present him with Wulfstan's cape. A briefer version of the story in 2 is told by JW s.a. 1095 (iii. 74–5). According to the same source (iii. 76–7), Wulfstan appeared again to Robert, a month after his death, reproving him for his poor conduct as a bishop and urging him to emend his life.

[2] He (and thus presumably the royal court) was at Cricklade (Wilts.), according to JW (iii. 74–5). According to *ASC* (E) s.a. 1095, the king was at Wissant for Christmas (of

The scene was many times repeated; the ring often slipped off, but it was never lost for ever, and always retrieved. But now, as I started to say, some tried to remove it from his finger, either as a keepsake, or to test the promise he had made. But though they kept twisting it one way and the other, they failed, and gave up their attempt; all their arts were foiled by the knotted joints and the firmness of skin and sinew.

23. Meanwhile[1] the body was brought out for burial. The procession came to the church, which he himself had made new from old, and body and bier were placed before the altar, with the clerks seated around. There that night and the following day and night sacrifices of prayer and obsequies of tears were paid to God. At that time, Robert bishop of Hereford was at the king's court;[2] he was a man who relied on his wits to make a way in the world, but he had not been corrupted by the world's temptations. At the very hour the holy man died, he appeared standing before Robert, very different[3] from the Wulfstan he had seen in late years, so brilliantly did he shine with starry light, so rosy-hued and fresh of face was he. He was clad in his bishop's vestments, and held his staff in his hand. These were the words he seemed to address to the sleeping Robert: 2. 'Come now to Worcester, dear brother Robert. I want you to pay me the proper rites, and commend my body to the earth, my soul to God.' Robert was thought to have replied: 'Lord and beloved friend, are you asking me to bury you, when I haven't seen you so vigorous these five years?' 'Be that as it may,' said Wulfstan. 'Such is the will of God, which must be fulfilled. Go now, and swiftly; do not disregard my words.' The bishop was stirred by the prophecy of so clear a vision. He awoke at once, and told the king what he had seen. Receiving his permission to leave he ate up the miles that delayed the progress of his swift horses[4] as he journeyed to Worcester. The exertion was eased by the strength of the holy friendship which had bound him to the man ever since he became bishop. And his kindly prayers were favoured by God, that he might arrive before the funeral. Indeed the monks had purposely held things up in expectation of his coming.

3. So it was that on one night the spirit of Wulfstan roused his

1094), entered England 'after the fourth day of Christmas' (28 December), and was at Winchester for Easter. JW s.a. 1094 (iii. 72–3) says that on his return to England, which he dates to 29 December, 'he led an army into Wales to fight the Welsh'. If this is true, then he could certainly have passed through Cricklade at the right time (around mid-January).

[3] Virgil, *Aen.* ii. 274.   [4] Cf. *VD* i. 12. 2.

longe positum in exequiarum suscitauit offitium. Sequenti uero nocte, quasi de peregrinatione domum reuersus, multa miranda exhibuit presentibus. Quidam monachorum, longi laboris pertesi, quo quisque poterat in angulos concesserant ut liberiori otio sine arbitris soporem adorirentur. Eis omnibus continuo aderat, stertentes pulsans, semisopitos suscitans: confestim surgerent, somnolentiae renuntiarent; inciperent psalterium a capite, finirentque cum commendatione animae. 4. Fecerunt illi quod iusserat, nacti ex necessitate uirtutem,[1] ut dum quod esset libitum facere nequirent, ei quod licitum esset quoquo modo acquiescerent. Eorum erat unus qui facinus immane animo quidem uolutarat sed necdum in opus produxerat. Ei Sanctus fremebundus apparuit, cogitationem sceleris improperans, immanitatem exaggerans, executionem comminatus. Satis superque[2] fuisse quod cogitasset, ideoque ab expletione temperaret. Si sibi uellet esse consultum, cohiberet factum. Breui enim penas daturum eodemque anno moriturum, si non absisteret illo peccato. Exterritus monachus minarum fulmine simul et tormento conscientiae fidem dedit, eo abiurato de quo arguebatur, se ulterius mancipatum iri regulae.

24. Dies dominica quae fuit sepulturae aderat, iamque prefatus episcopus aduenerat, inditium uisionis uera fide uix pre festinatione anhelans. Ipse missis ex more celebratis beatum funus sepultura curauit. Tum uero, quasi nichil ante fletum esset, itum est in planctum, perrectum in gemitum. Exclamabat turba in plangorem, quem repercussum testudinum conuexa multiplicabant.[a] Nec erat simplex fletus aut simulatus, sed exprimebantur ueris singultibus lacrimae,[3] religionis ruinam,[4] patriae miseriam in uno testantes homine. 2. Difficulterque discerneres qui iustiores fletus sui causas allegarent, clerus an populus, dum hic pro tutela pastorem, ille pro disciplina doctorem clamaret; senes an pueri, dum hi maturitatem, hi dulcedinem desiderarent; diuites an pauperes, dum isti opum abstinentiam, illi expensarum munificentiam predicarent. Immiserunt tandem amantissimi patris ossa sepulchro.[5] Sed memoria numquam

---

[a] *Darl.* (*by accident?*); -icant *C*

---

[1] *GR*, c. 5. 2; Otto, *Sprichwörter*, p. 241.   [2] See above, p. 23 n. 6
[3] *VD* i. 15. 4, of King Edmund.
[4] *VD* ii. 33. 3, of the death of Dunstan.
[5] The tomb is described, in language difficult to interpret, in *GP*, c. 148 (p. 288).

friend the bishop, far away as he was, to take his burial service. But on the next night, as though home from a far journey, Wulfstan showed great wonders to those there to see them. Some of the monks, tired out after their long labours, had withdrawn to such corners as they could find, to court sleep more freely without anyone to observe them. Wulfstan was instantly at their side, nudging the snorers and rousing the drowsy. They must get up at once, and bid farewell to sleepiness. They must start on the psalter from the beginning, and at the end add the commendation of his soul. 4. They did what they were told, making a virtue of necessity:[1] not being able to do what they liked, they acquiesced as best they could in what was permitted. There was one who had been turning a dreadful crime over in his mind, though he had not yet put it into effect. The holy man appeared to him in a towering fury, rebuking his wicked design, stressing its horror, and warning of the danger of carrying it out. It was enough and more than enough[2] that he had had the idea; so he must forbear from putting it into practice. If he wanted to serve his own interest, he should not proceed to the act. For if he did not desist from that sin, he would pay the penalty all too soon, and die that same year. The monk was terrified by the thunderous threats, and equally by the torments of his own conscience; and he gave a pledge that he would drop what he was accused of and henceforth bind himself to observance of the Rule.

24. The Sunday appointed for the funeral came. Bishop Robert had already arrived, scarce able, such was his haste, to pant out the truth of his vision. He celebrated in person the customary masses, and saw to the burial of the blessed body. Then indeed, as though there had been no lamentation before, they proceeded to wail and groan. The crowd shouted words of grief that the vaulted roof of the church re-echoed and redoubled. It was no superficial(?) or pretended weeping; genuine were the tears forced out by their sobs,[3] as they proclaimed in one man's death the collapse of religion[4] and the disaster to England. 2. It would have been difficult to decide who could supply the juster reasons for their tears: the clergy or the people, the former bewailing the pastor for the protection, the latter the teacher for the instruction they had lost; the old or the young, the former missing his ripeness, the latter his sweet character; the rich or the poor, the former praising his abstinence from riches, the latter his generous expenditure. At last they placed the bones of their beloved father in his grave;[5] but the

in eorum sepulta est animo. Non enim conuentum uel ciuitatem facile inuenies ubi defuncti episcopi reuerentia non dicam maiori sed nec pari colatur cura. Hoc omni ebdomada si dies uacat,[1] hoc cum se ad eius obitum anni uolubilitas uersat. Monachi psalteria et missas, ciues largissimis expensis elemosinas frequentant. Ipse quoque ultroneus accurrit uotis precantium, nec est ullus cum fide petens qui non mereatur suffragium.

25. Libet enim duobus exemplis palam facere quod nec etiam in minusculis rebus amantes sui patiatur contristari. Non multo post eius transitum liber quem epistolarem uocant[2] ab aecclesia subreptus est. Intentabatur culpa in secretarium,[a] cuius custodiae fuisset illusum. Fremebat in eum prior, grauis disciplinae ultionem, nisi liber redderetur, comminatus. Monachus, multa questione ultro citroque habita sed elusus opera, tandem aliquando ad Sancti recurrit suffragia. Nota beatae animae pietas spem dedit preces suas cassatum non iri. Itaque aduolutus tumulo petitiones immurmurat, uota continuat, ut antiquae pietatis non oblitus libri dampnum resarciret, minas prioris obtunderet. Paciscitur[b] etiam ut ad uicem suffragii toto anno candelam ad sepulchrum accenderet et quindecim psalmos diceret.[3] Eo die processit ad populum sermo et diligens de libro questio. Paululum morae in medio. Nam ante uesperum codex redditus est, mulierculae cuiusdam inditio quae furem arguit, latebram prodidit.

26. Eodem fere tempore seruiens aecclesiae laicus, cuius fideli opera sacrista sepe fuerat usus, librum sibi subreptum ingemuit. Cumulabat merorem quod alienus fuerat, debitoremque creditor uehementer urgebat. Quocirca cotidie acclinis tumulo rogabat Deum ut per merita episcopi librum restitueret et rapacitatem furis digna pena percelleret. Sibi propter hoc meritum curae futurum ut deinceps fidele impenderet aecclesiae obsequium. Elapsi erant aliquot dies, et

---

[a] culpa in secretarium *ed.*; culpam secretarium (*corr. to* culpa secretario) *C*   [b] *ed.*; pasciscitur *C*

---

[1] i.e. if the day is not already occupied by another Feast.

[2] A service-book containing the readings, mainly from the Epistles, for mass thoughout the Christian year: H. Gneuss, 'Liturgical books in Anglo-Saxon England and their Old English terminology', in *Learning and Literature in Anglo-Saxon England*, ed. M. Lapidge and H. Gneuss (Cambridge, 1985), pp. 91–141, at 110. No example survives from this period, and very few from later.

[3] The Psalms were probably the fifteen Gradual Psalms (119–133): J. Harper, *The Forms*

memory of him was never buried in their hearts. You will not easily find a monastery or a city where reverence for a dead bishop is cultivated, I do not say with greater, but even with comparable assiduity. This is shown every week, if there is a free day,[1] and when the turning year brings round the anniversary of his death. The monks sing many a psalm and say many a mass. The citizens give constant alms from generous pockets. Wulfstan too comes unbidden to answer their prayers, nor is there anyone who asks with faith and is not found worthy of help.

25. I should like to make clear by two instances that even in the slightest of matters he is unwilling that those who love him should be made sad. Not long after his passing what they call the Epistle Book[2] was taken from the church. Responsibility was laid on the sacristan, whose guardianship of the book had been at fault. The prior raged at him, threatening the direst penalties if the book were not returned. The monk looked high and low, but to no avail; and in the end he had recourse to the help of the holy man. The well-known pity of the blessed soul gave him hope that his prayers would not be in vain. So he prostrated himself before the tomb, murmuring his petition and praying for a long time that Wulfstan should remember his old pity, make good the loss of the book and draw the sting of the prior's threats. He also made a bargain: in return for help he would burn a candle at the grave for a whole year, and sing fifteen psalms.[3] The story got out that day, and careful search was made for the book. There was little delay. Before evening the codex was returned, thanks to a poor woman, who informed on the thief and revealed where the book was hidden.

26. At much the same time a lay servant of the church, whose loyal services had often been employed by the sacristan, had the theft of a book to bewail. What made it worse was that the book belonged to someone else, who was angrily demanding its return. Every day he lay before the tomb begging God to restore the book for the sake of the merits of the bishop, and to strike down the greedy thief with a suitable penalty. He would make sure in return that he gave the church his best service in the future. Some days went by, and the

and Orders of Western Liturgy from the Tenth to the Eighteenth Century (Oxford, 1991), p. 300. William's Latin is obscure; presumably he means fifteen Psalms per diem throughout the year, with a candle burning continuously, replaced as required.

ipse assiduabat preces. Id ipso Ascensionis die solito enixius solitoque profusius fecit. Et forte tum diluculo latrocinii conscius audatia sua ingressum templi temerauit. Nondum orationem remiserat alter, et ille subito furore arreptus demoniaco*a* horrificos stridores attollere cepit. 2. Quin etiam librum sinu extractum ostendere, et quando quoue modo surripuisset exponere. Ita cum predo alienam mentem induit fidelis orator sua recepit. At uero frater patientis, eiusdem loci monachus, homo non iners nec imprudens, non difficulter a ceteris obtinuit ut implorarent dulcedinem Sancti quatinus sanam mentem repararet furenti. Fecerunt hoc sincerae fraternitatis affectu, nec multo post gauisi sunt impetratae sanitatis effectu. Hinc mos inoleuit illius loci monachis ut omnes corporum inequalitates, omnes animorum turbines non secus ac si uiuenti grato susurro*b* insinuent. Recipit ille largo caritatis sinu cunctorum uota, mancipatque facto a Deo*c* impetrata. Quod si aliquis cassus abit non crediderim sanctae animae impotentiam sed uel precatorem indignum uel rem quam*d* precatur non necessariam.

27. Multos de gloria eius dulci quiete animarunt somnia, multos luce palam confortarunt uisa, quorum paucula tetigisse suffecerit. Erat quidam Dei seruus inclusus, orationibus et solitudini ut id hominum genus deditus. Ei antiquus hostis qui nequiret auferre religionem inuidebat quietem, multas sancto uiro struens molestias, ingenti conflictu nequissimi spiritus ut non dicam una die, certe nec hora uacarent insidiae. Poteratque reclusus fatigari, nec poterat uinci, cum aliud esset fragilitatis humanae, aliud opis diuinae. 2. Hanc luctam compescuit sanctissimi antistitis oratio, missa ei a Wigornia interiori tunica, quam staminiam dicimus, quam ille extremum agens flatum indutus fuerat. Mirabile et uenerabile dictu quod sequitur. Statim ut indumentum accepit, immo ut uidit, fugerunt infestationum nebulae, rediit sereni cordis tranquillitas. Nichil quod stimularet ulterius persensit, nichil quod peniteret suspirauit. Quapropter meritum suum infra sanctitatem Wlstani esse comperiens, tunicam loco reliquiarum uenerabatur. Multo enim studio inuolutam cum soporem meditaretur superponebat capiti, quod esset tutelae contra fantasias inimici.

---

a [*Peile*]; demoniaci *C*   *b* δ*H** (*p. 104*); susurrio *C*   *c* a Deo *ed.* (*cf. i. 15. 3*); adeo *Darl.*   *d* *ed.*; qua *C*

sacristan persisted in his prayers. He prayed more earnestly and at greater length than usual on Ascension Day. It chanced that at dawn on that day the man guilty of the theft dared to enter the church. The other had not yet stopped praying, and the thief, seized by a sudden attack of demonic madness, began to utter hideous shrieks. 2. What is more he took the book from his pocket for the sacristan to see, and told him when and how he had removed it. Thus the thief lost his wits and the man who had believed and prayed received back what he had lost. But the afflicted man's brother, a monk of the place and a man of energy and sense, had no difficulty in persuading the rest to beg the holy man, in the sweetness of his nature, to give back the madman his wits. They did this out of sincere brotherly love, and not much later were able to rejoice in the restoration of his sanity. It was because of this incident that the monks of the place started the habit of telling Wulfstan, in a grateful whisper, as though he still lived, of all their bodily afflictions or mental troubles. He receives the prayers of all in the generous embrace of his charity, and puts them into effect, after obtaining God's assent. But if someone goes away empty-handed I should not suppose that the holy man's soul had been unable to help, but that either the petitioner was undeserving or his petition unnecessary.

27. Many were inspired at dead of night by dreams of his glory, many were strengthened by visions seen in clear daylight. It will be enough to mention a few cases. There was a servant of God living in seclusion, devoted like all of his kind to prayer and solitude. The Old Enemy, unable to rob him of his faith, grudged him his repose, and contrived many troubles to harass the holy man; and great were his efforts, so that no day or even hour was free from the assaults of the wicked spirit. The recluse might be exhausted, but he could not be defeated: the one was a matter of human weakness, the other resulted from the aid of God. 2. The conflict was ended by the prayers of the holy bishop, for the anchorite was sent from Worcester the inner tunic, which we know as linsey-woolsey, that Wulfstan was wearing when he drew his last breath. The sequel is wonderful and awe-inspiring to relate. The moment he received the garment, or rather the moment he saw it, the clouds that had been troubling him fled away, and the calm of a serene heart returned. He never afterwards felt anything to trouble him, never had longings to rue. So, realizing that his own deserts were beneath the level of Wulfstan's holiness, he revered the tunic as a relic. When preparing himself for sleep, he would fold it with great care and place it over his head as a protection against the illusions sent by the Enemy.

28. Idem[1] quadam die iam sole in noctem occiduo, cum grandem strepitum ad fenestram pulsantis[2] attonitis hausisset auribus, percunctatur auctorem. Responsum est a foris*a* Wlstanum esse Wigornensem episcopum, amicum eius; petere ut si aquam in promptu habeat manibus diluendis suggerat. Remunerationi futurum quod aecclesiam ingressus horas amico cantaret. Ad amicitiae preterea pignus daret sibi caracallam quam haberet. Recluso respondente se nullam habere, idque pontificem non latere, ille promissum retulit habiturum e uicino, si figeret mentem in Deo. 2. Tanta uero lux ex pontificalis ut uidebatur corporis resultabat simulacro ut circumpositas regiones hoc perstringeret corusco.[3] Iam uero ingressus aecclesiam et post genuflexionem orationemque cruce frontem signatus horarum offitio[4] dedit auspitium. Respondebant ei tres puellae prope astantes quae pro liniamentorum gratia et spetiei miraculo[5] essent*b* humano generi spectaculo. Cantibus explicitis ea quae in medio stans eminentia staturae uideretur ceteris prestare benedictionem conquiniscenti[6] episcopo indulsit. 3. Interea solitarius lectum pulcherrime stratum et caracallam superpositam imaginatus, cum suggessisset antistiti quatinus quod rogauerat acciperet, hoc responsum accepit: haberet ipse cum gratia, maioris quandoque gloriae pignus. Mandaret preterea Wigornensibus offitiosissimas salutes: magnas eis gratias agere, maximas habere, quod tanto tempore*c* orationibus inuigilarent. Omnia proficere ad eorum compendium, dum totum in eorum refunderetur sinum quicquid pro eo putarent fatiendum. Ita euanuit uisio, quam Dei seruus postero mane fidei declarauit inditio.

29. Instabant fideliter monachi, missitabantur per Angliam epistolae doloris interpretes, amoris indices. Rogabatur ut si Deus cuipiam aliquid de ipsius salute innotesceret ipse bono nuntio anhelantium uota expleret. Fuit hoc tempore apud Briuentonam*d*[7] bonae uitae

---

a a foris *ed.* (*cf. HN 32*); afforis *C*, δ*H** (*p. 105*)   *b* essent *H** (*p. 105*); ess*** *C* (*suffering from a blot*); uidebantur δ   *c* opere *C^{p.c.}*   *d* δ (*p. 105*); Briuentunam (*or* Brau-) *H**; Brumetonam *C*

[1] The story seems to lack point, as the promise of greater glory to come (presumably promotion to a bishopric) is left unfulfilled.

[2] Cf. *GR*, c. 178. 2 'pulsantis strepitum'.

[3] Cf. *GR*, c. 54. 1, of Bede: 'in extremo natus orbis angulo doctrinae corusco terras omnes perstrinxerit.'

[4] See above, p. 111 and n. 5.

[5] Cf. *VD* i. 27. 2 'miraculo pulchritudinis'; *Mir.*, pp. 97 line 914 'faciei miraculo', 123 lines 342–3 'formae miraculo'; *GR*, c. 45.1 'miraculo uultus'.

28. One day[1] at nightfall, this same recluse heard to his astonishment a great racket of knocking[2] at his window, and asked who was there. The reply from outside was that it was his friend Wulfstan bishop of Worcester, asking to let him have water to wash his hands, if there was any available. In return, Wulfstan would go into the church and sing the Hours for his friend. Further, he asked the recluse, as a pledge of his friendship, to give him a cope he had. The recluse said he had no cope, as the bishop well knew. Wulfstan promised he should have one forthwith, if he fixed his mind on God. 2. So great a light gleamed from the semblance of (as it appeared) the bishop that it dazzled the vicinity with its brilliance.[3] So Wulfstan entered the church, genuflected, prayed, signed his forehead with the Cross, and began the Office of the Hours.[4] The responses were given by three girls standing near: wonderfully beautiful they were,[5] and graceful in form, so that a mortal might think them an amazing sight. When the singing was over, the middle girl, who looked taller than the rest, gave the benediction to the bishop as he crouched there.[6] 3. Meanwhile, the recluse saw in a vision a bed beautifully made up and a cope laid on it. He hinted to the bishop that he should take what he had asked for. Wulfstan answered that the recluse was welcome to keep it, as a token of greater glory to come. Further, he should convey Wulfstan's most dutiful greetings to the monks of Worcester: he was most grateful, and sent them his warmest thanks for having prayed for him over so long a time. It was all to their advantage: everything they thought fit to do for him would be poured back into their bosoms. So the vision vanished; and in the morning the servant of God noised it abroad, to show his faith.

29. The monks in their faith pressed ahead, sending letters throughout England to express their grief and show their love. They requested that if someone received from God tidings of Wulfstan's salvation, he should send the good news and answer the prayers of his anxious people. There was at that time in Bruton[7] a priest of good

---

[6] 'conquiniscere' also above, apparatus to iii. 10. 2, *Mir.*, p. 109 line 1248.

[7] Darlington (p. 67) noted that 'It is unwise to suggest any identification in view of the material difference between the forms in which the name occurs and the uncertainty which overhangs the early life of William of Malmesbury.' But the place is surely Bruton, a 'uicus regius' (*GP*, c. 222 (p. 374)) in Somerset, near the border with Wiltshire. It might well have been a minster, and was a mint between the 990s and 1030s: M. Aston, 'Post-Roman central places in Somerset', in *Central Places, Archaeology and History*, ed. E. Grant (Sheffield, 1986), pp. 49–77, at 53, 58, 59 fig. 7. 7, 74. The name is spelt 'Briwetone' or

presbiter, Dunstanus nomine, cuius sanctitatis suauem*ᵃ* fragrantiam iam inde a pueritia audisse me memini. Huic consimili uirtutum studio aduigilabat eiusdem uillae reclusa, nulli uirorum sanctitate inferior femina. Nescires quem preferres, ita emulis certabant bonis, presbiter instruendi doctrina, mulier parendi disciplina: insignis religionis homines quos Deus theoricis speculationibus dignaretur nondum hac uita carentes. 2. Isti Wigornensibus mandauerunt nichil de salute Wlstani dubitari debere. Vidisse se illum inter sanctos choros nichilo minus quam ceteros habentem gloriae, et aliquanto plus quam aliquos inferioris gradus habentem gratiae. Quorum qui non credit dictis in religionem committit, quam ut dixi tanta coluerunt instantia ut nil nostro*ᵇ* presertim seculo supra. Denique quicquid dicebant ita excipiebatur quasi ex caelestibus insonuisset templis, quasi ex diuinis profunderetur aditis.¹

3. Explicuisse michi uideor iussa uestra, patres et domini, ut Vitam sanctissimi uiri qualicumque stilo exculperem. Obedientiam ergo exhibui, etsi uotum uestrum non expleui; uestri erit iuditii an utrumque.² Excusat uoluntas impotentiam, quia, etsi nequiui quod debui, feci quod potui. Paciscar ergo, queso, aeternam uobiscum de paruo labore gratiam, quia studio uestro et uoluntati sex septimanis paulo minus lucubraui. Par ergo erit ut, post huius animae corporisque discidium, totidem diebus pro me Deo immoletis hostias quot noctium ego Wlstano consecraui excubias. Valete.

*Explicit Vita sancti Wlstani episcopi et confessoris, cuius sancta depositio celebratur quarto decimo kalendas Februarii.*³

ᵃ Whar. (but perhaps read suauifragr- *?);* suaue C   *ᵇ* nil nostro *ed.;* nostro nil C

'Briuuetone', in Domesday Book: *DB 8 Somerset*, 1, 9; 21, 91; 24, 1736; Ekwall, p. 71; in *GP* William spells it 'Briwetune', and shows that he knew the place well. Indeed, the combined evidence of both texts suggests that William was born not far away. According to his own account, Aldhelm was the builder of the larger church, while the smaller had his altar, donated by King Ine. These associations might explain why William became a monk at Malmesbury.

repute called Dunstan. I remember that from childhood I used to hear of the sweet fragrance of his holiness. He was looked after by a female recluse of the same vill; she was no less zealous for virtue than he, and was a woman inferior in sanctity to no man. It was difficult to know whom to place first, so well-matched were they in their competition in good: the priest in teaching, the woman in obeying. They were people of remarkable religious faith, whom God thought worthy to receive the gift of spiritual contemplation while still in this life. 2. These persons sent a message to the monks of Worcester to say that there should be no doubt of Wulfstan's salvation. They said they had seen him among the holy choirs, with no less glory than the rest, and with rather more grace than some of lower rank. Anyone who does not believe their words is offending against religion, which they, as I have said, so earnestly cultivated that there is nothing that surpasses it, especially in our age. In fact, whatever they said was received as though it spoke from the temples of heaven, and issued from the sanctuaries of God.[1]

3. I think, fathers and lords, that I have carried out your orders, to write, in however poor a style, the life of a most holy man. I have obeyed, even if I have failed to do all you wished. You will have to judge if I have succeeded in both.[2] Good intentions are an excuse for inability. If I have been unable to do what I ought, I have done what I could. I therefore ask to obtain from you your lasting favour in return for a short labour. I have spent almost six weeks' work by night on what you so earnestly asked. So it will be commensurate if, after the separation of this body from this soul, you should sacrifice to God on my behalf on as many days as I have spent wakeful nights on Wulfstan. Farewell.

Here ends the Life of St Wulfstan, bishop and confessor, whose holy Deposition is celebrated on 19 January.[3]

---

[1] Cf. i. 1. 4 (with n.) and i. 8. 1.   [2] i.e. by both obeying and not failing.
[3] See above, p. 142 n. 1.

VITA DUNSTANI
LIFE OF DUNSTAN

INTRODUCTION

The text is preserved as a whole in only one manuscript, Bodl. Libr., MS Rawlinson D. 263 (Q), given to Thomas Hearne by James West in 1726. The date and origin of this manuscript are both mysterious. Book i was copied by two similar scribes probably from the Low Countries, writing gothic textura characteristic of the second half of the fifteenth century; the opening initial, however, is typical English work of that date. The second scribe ended at the foot of fo. 33v with the rubric 'Explicit liber primus. Incipit prologus Secundi'.[1] Book ii was written in a hand which is either an accomplished Italian humanistic cursive of similar date, or an italic hand of the first half of the sixteenth century, which could just as well be English.[2] However, it is hard to imagine that the second part of the manuscript was written at any great interval of time after the first. The same red and green initials are found in both parts, and in both corrections and marginal notes were made in two humanistic cursive hands, which look to be fifteenth- rather than sixteenth-century. We may conjecture, then, that this book was made for a member of the Glastonbury community, the second part perhaps during a stay in Italy, and that it is to be identified with the copy seen at Glastonbury by John Leland.[3]

In the surviving fragment of a large and handsome Passional, BL, MS Cotton Nero E. 1, fos. 189–222 (s. xii 3/4, probably from Worcester),[4] occurs an abbreviation of Eadmer's Life (fos. 200v–

[1] The scribe added a ninth leaf to the quire in order to finish precisely at the end of book i. He obviously knew, on the one hand that there was a second book, on the other that he would not be the one who would copy it. One can only guess at the underlying circumstances.

[2] RMT examined the MS closely, and showed it to Professors James Carley, Andrew Watson and Albinia de la Mare, and Drs Martin Kauffmann and Peter Kidd. About the hands and decoration of bk. i all were in agreement. As to bk. ii, Professor de la Mare, an acknowledged expert on humanistic script, thought the hand italic and sixteenth century, while acknowledging the difficulties signalled above.

[3] See above, p. xxvii. For a perhaps analogous instance of books associated with William of Malmesbury being copied on the Continent, see Thomson, *William of Malmesbury*, pp. 54–5.

[4] This is *not* part of the famous 'Cotton-Corpus Legendary' (BL Cotton Nero E. i part i + part ii fos. 1–180, 187–8 + Cambridge, Corpus Christi Coll. 9), made at Worcester s. xi 3/4 with later additions: P. Jackson and M. Lapidge, 'The contents of the Corpus-Cotton Legendary', in *Holy Men and Holy Women: Old English Prose Saints' Lives and their Contexts*, ed. P. Szarmach (Albany, NJ, 1996), pp. 131–46. Nero E. i, fos. 189–222, is from

3v), into which some (often adapted) extracts from William's Life have been inserted.[1] These extracts (N) are taken from *VD* i. 26–27. 1; ii. 6. 6; ii. 7. 1–3 and 10; ii. 8, 15, 18–19, 27–9 and 33. 3 and 5. Occasionally they give a reading that seems preferable to what is found in Q. John of Glastonbury also used the Life, but his adaptation does not help at any crucial point.

John Leland saw the Life in two books, and summarized Dunstan's life on the basis of it in *Comm.*, pp. 161–3, citing some passages verbatim (from i. 4. 2–3, i. 17, ii. 10. 5 [where he wrongly thinks William is speaking of 'Ealfridus'], and ii. 11). Leland's excerpts give no superior readings, except '⟨a⟩ litteris' at i. 4. 4 and perhaps 'praecellebat' at ii. 11.

We print the text of Q, with some corrections made by the only previous editor, Stubbs, and by ourselves. We ignore a few slips of the scribe's pen. We do not give a full collation of N, most of whose variants are patently without value, but it is cited where it seems possible or certain that it gives a superior reading. The orthography has again been corrected to conform with William's established practice (see above, p. 6).

We have introduced a system of sub-sections to ease reference to the often long chapters.

In the *Memorials* edition Stubbs provided a running concordance of *VD* with the earlier Lives by means of sidenotes. These notes did not distinguish between parallel accounts, and those which William really used as sources. In the following tables the distinction is made by means of brackets, which denote accounts certainly or probably known to William, but of which there is no proof that he made use. In Table I accounts which, certainly or probably, he did not use, are omitted. In particular, it is usually impossible to say whether William

---

the end of a separate book, wrongly dated by Stubbs s. xiii. Perhaps by mere coincidence, it too appears to be have been made at Worcester: its initials, in 1–3 of red, green, and blue, are diagnostic, with motifs characteristic of the Worcester scriptorium. Later in the book appear red or blue initials added s. xiii in. A rubric occupying the first two-and-a-half lines of fo. 189 has been erased (by Cotton?); this was almost certainly the explicit of the previous item (the next two-and-a-half lines are the incipit of the next). At the foot of fo. 220v (s. xvi) is 'Post tertium diem ?antius quod Iohannes Newynam'. The Feasts run from 15 May to 1 August, so the original volume was probably the *pars aestivalis* of a Passional in more than one volume. See M. Lapidge in Wulfstan of Winchester, *Vita Æthelwoldi*, pp. clxxvi–clxxvii.

[1] For details, see Stubbs, p. l n. 1, where the words said to be abridged from p. 293 in fact come more or less untouched from p. 295 (= ii. 6. 6), and where 'p. 294' should read 'p. 295'.

was using Eadmer rather than his source Osbern (see above, pp. xxi–xxii); Eadmer is therefore omitted.

TABLE I. *VD* and its sources

i. 1	Ancestry	B., c. 3; A(delard), Lect. i; O(sbern), c. 3
	Candle miracle	(A., Lect. i); O., c. 4
i. 2	Birth	B., c. 3; O., c. 5
	Dunstan's dream	B., c. 3; O., c. 5
i. 3	Illness	B., c. 4; A., Lect. ii; O., c. 7
	Vision of barking dogs	B., c. 4; A., Lect. ii; O., c. 7
	Ascent of scaffolding	B., c. 4; A., Lect. ii; O., c. 7
i. 4	Educated by Irishmen	B., c. 5; O., cc. 7, 8
i. 5	Fom Athelm to Æthelstan	(A., Lect. iii); O., c. 9
i. 6	Harp plays of itself	B., c. 12; O., c. 10
	Expulsion from court	B., c. 6; O., c. 11
i. 7	D. becomes a monk	B., c. 7; O., c. 12
	Satan casts stone	B., c. 8
i. 8	Ælfheah's prophecy	
i. 9	D. at Glastonbury	O., c. 13
	Devil grasped with tongs	O., c. 14
i. 10	The dead Wulfred's prophecy and its fulfilment	B., c. 9; (O., c. 17)
i. 11	Æthelflæd at Glastonbury	B., c. 10; O., c. 15
i. 12	Unfailing supply of wine	B., c. 10; O., c. 15
i. 13	Death of Æthelflæd presaged	B., c. 11; O., c. 16
i. 14	D. slandered to K. Edmund	B., c. 23; (O., c. 18)
i. 15	Edmund repents at Cheddar	B., c. 14; O., c. 18
i. 16	D.'s building at Glastonbury	(B., c. 15); O., c. 19
i. 17	D.'s illustrious pupils Æthelwold and D.'s dream of him	B., c. 15; (O., c. 19) See below, p. 206 n. 4
i. 18	Devil as wild beasts	B., c. 16; (O., c. 19)
i. 19	Devil as bear	B., c. 17; (A., Lect. vi; O., c. 26)
i. 20	Devil throws another stone	B., c. 18
i. 21	D.'s vision of nobles' immorality Edmund's murder	B., cc. 31–3; (O., c. 21)
i. 22	D. and K. Eadred	B., c. 19; O., c. 22
i. 23	D. tempted with bishoprics	B., c. 19; A., Lect. iv; O., c. 22
i. 24	D.'s vision of three saints	(B., c. 20; A., Lect. iv); O., c. 22

i. 25	D. presages Eadred's death	(B., c. 20; A., Lect. v); O., c. 24
i. 26	Building-miracle at Glastonbury	(A., Lect. vi); O., c. 26
i. 27	D. corrects Eadwig at his coronation	B., c. 21; (O., c. 27)
i. 28	D. exiled to Flanders	(B., c. 22); A., Lect. vi; O., c. 27
i. 29	D. protected by Count Arnulf	(B., c. 23); A., Lect. vi; O., c. 27
i. 30	Dream about Glastonbury monks	B., c. 23
i. 31	D. presages Eadwig's death	O., c. 30
ii. 1	Prophecy of Edgar's peaceful reign	A., Lect. iii; (O., c. 19)
ii. 2	E. vows to restore ruined monastery	See below, p. 238 n. 2
ii. 3	Rebellion against K. Eadwig	(B., c. 24); O., cc. 25, 28
ii. 4	D. made bp. of Worcester	B., c. 25; A., Lect. vii; O., c. 29
	Archbp. Ælfheah's inspired error	A., Lect. vii; O., c. 29
ii. 5	D. made bp. of London	(B., c. 25; A., Lect. vii); O., c. 31
ii. 6	Bp. Ælfsige's temerity punished	(B., c. 26); O., c. 32
	D. made archbp. of Canterbury	(B., c. 26; A., Lect. vii); O., c. 32
ii. 7	D. goes to Rome	B., c. 27; (O., c. 32)
	Miraculous provision of food	B., c. 27
	Privilege of Pope John XII	See below, p. 249 n. 3
ii. 8	Appearance of dove at Canterbury	(A., Lect. viii); O., c. 33
ii. 9	D.'s ecclesiastical reforms	(A., Lect. viii, xii); O., cc. 34–5; and see below, p. 254 n. 2
ii. 10	D. restores Glastonbury and Malmesbury	O., c. 16, and see below, pp. 258–9
ii. 11	D.'s eloquence and energy	
ii. 12	Æthelwold's reforms	See below, p. 262 and n. 1
ii. 13	Reforms of Oswald and Wulfsige	See below, p. 262 and n. 4
ii. 14	Edgar's achievements	
ii. 15	Water from a rock	O., c. 34
ii. 16	Vision of young Glastonbury monk's death	B., c. 34; (O., c. 20)
ii. 17	Prophecy of death of Glastonbury monk	B., c. 35
ii. 18	Edgar's death and ensuing decline	O., c. 37
ii. 19	Miracles at Councils of Winchester and Calne	O., c. 36
ii. 20	Death of St Edward	

ii. 21	Prophecies of the bad reign of Æthelred	O., c. 37 (one prophecy only)
ii. 22	Prophecy about bp. of Rochester	O., c. 39
ii. 23	Prophecy of Eadgyth's death	See below, p. 275 n. 6
ii. 24	Prophecy of Æthelwold's death	O., c. 38
	Vision of his successor	A., Lect. viii; O., c. 38
ii. 25	Vengeance on Ælfwold	
ii. 26	D.'s inner life	B., cc. 29, 37; O., c. 34
ii. 27	Antiphon learned in a vision	B., c. 29; (O., c. 40)
ii. 28	Vision of the B. V. M.	B., c. 36; (O., c. 40)
ii. 29	Introduction to D.'s passing	
ii. 30	Vision of angels	A., Lect. ix; O., c. 41
ii. 31	D.'s last sermons	(B., c. 38); O., c. 42
ii. 32	Secret levitation	B., c. 38 [p. 52 n.]; O., c. 43
ii. 33	Death	A., Lect. xi; O., c. 44
ii. 34	Coming of the Danes	O., c. 46
	D. appears to Archbp. Ælfheah	
ii. 35	Criticisms of Osbern	O., c. 4
ii. 36	Envoi	

TABLE II. *VD*'s use of B.

Uncertain cases are distinguished by brackets.

B.	*VD*	B.	*VD*
1 (prol.)		20	(i. 24–5)
2		21	i. 27
3	i. 1–2	22	(i. 28)
4	i. 3	23	(i. 28–9), 30
5	i. 4–5	24	(ii. 3–4)
6	i. 6	25	ii. 4–(5)
7	i. 7	26	ii. (6)
8	i. 7	27	ii. 7
9	i. 10–11	28	ii. 7 and 26
10	i. 12	29	ii. 27
11	i. 13	30	
12	i. 6	31	i. 21
13	i. 14–15	32	i. 21
14	i. 15	33	i. 21
15	i. (16)-17	34	ii. 16
16	i. 18	35	ii. 17
17	i. 19	36	ii. 28
18	i. 20	37	ii. 26
19	i. 22–3	38	ii. (31)-3

TEXT AND TRANSLATION

Incipit prologus de uita sancti Dunstani archiepiscopi

Dominis suis uenerabilibus et fratribus patribusque in sancta Glastoniensi aecclesia Deo famulari gratulantibus, Willelmus uester deuotione seruus, commilitio frater, dilectione filius.

In beatissimi patris uestri Dunstani amore et honore celebrando nostra, sanctissimi patres, cum omni Anglia deuotio emulo decertat exemplo; et nescio an maior sit nostra in hoc certamine gloria, cum nos eum diligamus ut alumnum[1] quem illi suspitiunt ut sanctum et archiepiscopum. Iungimus ergo amorem reuerentiae, in neutro Cantuaritis cedentes, qui se olim eum gloriantur primatem habuisse. 2. Vnde factum est ut, scripta de uita eius diligentius rimantes, expectationi uestrae*a* non respondere doleamus. Antiquis enim sermonum gratiam, recentibus integritatem fidei deesse deprehendimus.[2] Quare non immerito indulsimus eatenus mestitiae, quia et agrestia parum delectant, et pudet recitare quae solida ueritate non constant. Ille profecto abutitur litteris et otio qui de operibus sanctorum falsa scribendo, dum negligit famam, consciscit infamiam. Quod nouo scriptori[3] uitae beati Dunstani accidisse utinam nescirem! Plerumque enim aut opinione decipitur aut fauore inflectitur. 3. Sed hoc si pace animae ipsius dici potest, delictorum singula exempla, licet plura suppetant, subitiam.

Primo, cum de miraculo luminis in templo exhibiti sermonem adoriretur, 'maternis' inquit 'sinibus sacro puerperio intumescentibus'.[4] Egregie et pulchre dictum si esset catholicum! Non enim recte dicitur sacrum puerperium[5] quod, iniquitati originali obnoxium, nondum est sacro baptismo dilutum. Cuius dicti mei rationem in fine uitae Sancti Deo iuuante persoluere meditor.

4. Secundo, cum de indole studiorum puerilium loqueretur, sensum secundi prologi de arithmetica pene totum induxit, loquens de philosophorum scientia de rebus quae sunt et quae aliter esse non

---

a *Perhaps read* nostrae

[1] This could be a reference either to William's status as a *confrater* of the Glastonbury community (see below, p. 234 n. 1), to his Somersetshire birth, or—perhaps most plausibly—to his early education at the abbey (otherwise unattested). Cf. *AG* prol. (pp. 40–1), where Glastonbury 'Dunstanum materno gremio in uirum confouit': he is her *alumnus*, she is his *nutricula*. Glastonbury is called his *nutricula* in *VD* ii.17.1 (cf. *AG*, c. 24 (pp. 72–5), probably interpolated).

[2] The Life by B. and perhaps a now-lost OE Life of similar date on the one hand, that by Osbern (and perhaps that by Eadmer) on the other. See above, pp. xviii–xx.

Prologue

To his revered lords, brothers and fathers who rejoice to serve God in the holy church of Glastonbury, William, your servant in devotion, your brother in fellow service, your son in affection.

Most holy fathers, in the celebration of the love and honour of your most blessed father Dunstan our pious zeal strives to compete with the whole of England. And it may be that ours is the greater glory in this contest, seeing that we love as a former pupil[1] one whom they look up to as a saint and an archbishop. So it is that we can join love to our reverence, yielding in neither to those of Canterbury, who boast that they once had him as their primate. 2. Hence it has come about that, for all our diligence in looking out writings concerning his life, we are sad that they do not come up to your expectation. For we have found that the old Lives lack polish, and the new reliability.[2] So we have reasonably enough been to that extent saddened: for rustic writings give no pleasure, and it is shaming to repeat things that lack a firm basis in truth. It is a misuse of learning and leisure to retail falsehoods about the doings of saints: it shows contempt for reputation, and condemns one to infamy. I should be glad to be unaware that this fate has befallen a recent author[3] of a Life of the blessed Dunstan; he is often either mistaken in his views or biased in his judgement. 3. But—if such a remark can be made with all respect to his soul—I shall subjoin some particular instances of his faults, though more are available.

First: in introducing the miracle of the light shown in the church, he says: 'when the mother's womb was swollen with her holy unborn child.'[4] That would be a very fine saying, if it were not heretical. For it is not proper to describe as holy an unborn child[5] that, not having been washed clean in holy baptism, is still subject to original sin. If God comes to my aid, I mean at the end of my Life of the saint to justify this remark of mine.

4. Second: when speaking of the character of Dunstan's pursuits as a boy, this writer brought in almost the whole contents of the second prologue on arithmetic; he talked of the philosophical doctrine

[3] Osbern of Canterbury, for whom see *GR*, c. 342. 1 n. William was more complimentary to him in *GR*, c. 149. 3. See above, p. xx.

[4] Osbern, c. 4 (p. 72). William's refutation is at ii. 35.

[5] William here uses 'puerperium' to mean the foetus or unborn child (as Augustine invariably does). His objection to Osbern's expression is that an unbaptized infant cannot be called 'sacer'. But at ii. 35. 2 below he seems to use it in the more usual classical sense of 'childbirth'.

possunt, ut sunt magnitudines et aliae earum sibi adhaerentes, aliae separatae, multitudinesque aliae per se, aliae in relatione positae.[1] Videtis, domini, quantos fumos excitauit, cum potuisset simpliciter dicere puerum arithmeticae et cognatis artibus inuigilasse.

Tertio quod, Glastoniam regali fisco addictam et Dunstanum ibi fuisse primum abbatem dicendo, non mediocriter in historiae ueritate delinquit.[2] 5. Quod quantum a uero exulet testantur abbatum uestrorum nomina, qui annis quadringentis quinquaginta tribus, sicut ex consequentibus liquebit, ante natiuitatem Dunstani fuere in Glastonia. Ipsa quippe multo ante beatum Patritium, qui anno incarnationis Dominicae quadringentesimo septuagesimo secundo decessit,[3] in ius aecclesiasticum transiuit, et ipse nongentesimo uicesimo quinto anno eiusdem incarnationis, qui fuit Ethelstani regis primus, cum esset Glastoniae abbas Aldhunus, in lucem uenit. Nec minus quod Edgarum regem, unicum scilicet totius religionis tutorem, cum sanctimoniali uolutatum asseuerat.[4] 6. Illud cum omni historiarum testimonio careat, etiam si probari posset, magis pie dissimulari quam improbe propalari et in uulgus efferri deceret.

Quarto, quia dixit eundem Edgarum Sceftoniae monasterium fundasse, ut feminei animi tanto gloriarentur fundatore, cum multo ante tempore sub Elfredo rege constet ibi monachas habitasse.[5]

His igitur falsitatibus offensi, fraternitate qua uobis obnoxius sum obedientiam meam pulsastis, ut gesta beati uiri renouarem, et quasi quodam laboris mei prelo falsitatis fecem depellens, rerum puritatem eliquarem. 7. Quod ut fidentius facerem, scripta michi tam Latina quam Anglica in antiquissimo armario uestro reperta exhibuistis,[6] e quibus sicut e speculo rerum michi resultaret ueritas. Quae falsa nullo modo crediderim, quia calente adhuc gestorum memoria, ad Elfricum, qui tertio anno post decessum patris Dunstani successit in archiepiscopatu,[7] sunt edita. Nam ut mendatia demerem et studio meo

---

[1] Osbern, c. 8 (p. 78). The 'second prologue' refers (inaccurately) to Boethius, *De institutione arithmetica*, ed. G. Friedlein (Leipzig, 1867), pp. 7–8, part of the proem to the *first* book. William tries to show off by identifying Osbern's source, but gets the reference wrong.

[2] See also i. 15. 5 and ii. 10. 2. Osbern, cc. 6, 19 (pp. 74, 92). William reproaches Osbern on the second topic (without naming him) in *AG*, c. 55 (pp. 114–15).

[3] The same date for Patrick's death is in *AG*, c. 10 (pp. 61–2); and see below, p. 340 and n. 1.

[4] Osbern, c. 35 (p. 111).

[5] Osbern, c. 35 (p. 112). William's own accounts of the foundation of Shaftesbury are in *GR*, c. 122. 3 (with note), and *GP*, c. 86 (pp. 186–7).

[6] Osbern also mentions writings in OE (epist., c. 1; p. 70). For William the Latin writings certainly included the Life by B., in more than one version, and he probably knew

on things that are and cannot be otherwise, like magnitudes (some of them joined together, some separate) and multitudes (some in their own right, some in relation to others).[1] My lords, you see what a lot of smoke he has stirred up, when he could simply have said that the boy spent time on arithmetic and cognate arts.

Third: when he says that Glastonbury was subject to the royal fisc, and that Dunstan was first abbot there, he makes a not inconsiderable historical slip.[2] 5. His distance from the truth is witnessed to by the list of the names of your abbots, who ruled over Glastonbury for 453 years, as will appear from what follows, before Dunstan was born. In fact, Glastonbury passed under the sway of the church long before St Patrick, who died in AD 472;[3] while Dunstan saw the light of day in AD 925, the first year of King Æthelstan, when Ealdhun was abbot of Glastonbury. It is just as bad that he asserts that King Edgar, who was actually a supreme guardian of religion in all its aspects, took his pleasure with a nun.[4] 6. There is absolutely no evidence for that; and even it could be shown to be true, it would be better for it to be passed over piously than circulated and publicised with malice.

Fourth: he said the same King Edgar founded the monastery at Shaftesbury, so that the women there could boast of so eminent a founder; but it is established that nuns lived there long before, under King Alfred.[5]

It was because you had taken offence at such mistakes that you appealed to me to display the obedience our confraternity demands, and to give a new description of the saint's doings, using (as it were) the press of my labours to remove the lees of untruth and strain out a purified version of the facts. 7. So that I could do this with the more assurance, you showed me writings, both in Latin and in English, that you had found in an ancient chest of yours;[6] from these I would find the truth reflected as though from a mirror. I am not disposed to regard such writings as false, because they were dedicated to Ælfric while memory of the events was still fresh; for he succeeded to the archbishopric two years after the death of father Dunstan.[7] It has not been my plan to

---

a now-lost OE Life (see above, pp. xviii–xx). In 1247 Glastonbury still possessed many books in OE, among them a 'passionale sanctorum anglice scriptum': *English Benedictine Libraries*, p. 194. For another OE source which William undoubtedly used and which does survive, see below, ii. 2. 2 and n.

[7] William does not mean that Ælfric was Dunstan's *direct* successor. In *GP*, c. 20 (p. 32), he (rightly) has Æthelgar (988–90) as Dunstan's immediate successor, but then wrongly transposes Ælfric (995–1005) and Sigeric (990–4). His version of *ASC* should have put him right.

interruptam seriem resarcirem, non fuit consilium; quin esset laciniosum et uanum.[1] Liber enim ita dilaniatus nec alterius esset nec meus.

Preceptis ergo uestris festinus parui, et ut Sancti et uestrum
mercarer fauorem, maledicorum me dentibus fortasse exhibui.
8. Non enim defuturos opinor qui me ista ob aliorum scriptorum
reprehensionem scripsisse pronuntient. Sed ab his Dominus Iesus
bonam michi ueniam impetret, qui me in his dumtaxat scriptis nichil
uel odio uel liuori deferre uidet.[2] Ego enim michi conscius sum
numquam me laboribus insidiatum alienis, sed ut uobis morem
gererem stilum his apposuisse gestis. Adde quod is de quo memoraui
scriptor, iam dudum uita defunctus et inuidia, diuinaeque subditus
censurae, humana paruipendit iuditia. 9. Facile autem excusabitur
quod minus continue fidem rerum attexuit, quia per incendium quod,
sicut ipse in prologo dixit, Cantuariensis aecclesia passa est, antiqua
scripta non habuit.[3] Quae cum ita sint, obedientiae meae pignus
iniunctum suscipite, et si maliuoli contra me iacula maledictorum
intorserint, umbone uestrae auctoritatis elidite, domini uenerabiles et
merito amabiles patres.

⟨*Incipit Vita sancti Dunstani archiepiscopi*⟩

1. Annus igitur regis Ethelstani primus[4] produxit in mundum
puerum Dunstanum, totius Angliae patronum futurum. Pater eius
Herstanus, mater Kinedrida nominati, ambo pietate in Deum et
nobilitate generis insignes,[5] pari uirtutum studio et concordi
morum elegantia aeuum exegere. Quam uero grata Deo eorum
fuerit uita, Deus ipse non dubitauit monstrare post funera. Siquidem
hic idem eorum filius de quo sermonem adorsi sumus, postea iam
archiepiscopus, utrumque parentem inter caelestium choros gauden-
tem, matrem etiam Dominicae genitricis familiari obsequio assisten-
tem, defecatae mentis conspexit intuitu.[6] 2. Dignum nimirum diuina

---

[1] William seems to be saying that he is not proposing merely to remove Osbern's
mistakes and patch up the resulting mess, but to produce a wholly new work on the basis of
the material just described. The word *laciniosum*, misread by Stubbs as 'lacrymosum', was
rarely used except by Jerome; William may be recalling Jerome's *Comm. in Ecclesiasten* 12:
1 (CCSL lxxii, p. 349) '[uerba] quae . . . laciniosa sunt et prolixa', or, less probably,
Tertullian, *De uirg. uel.* 4. 6 'sermo laciniosus et onerosus et uanus'.

[2] If not ironic, this remark may reflect the unease with some aspects of the *GR* and *GP*
that led William to revise parts of them so thoroughly not long after their first appearance.

[3] Osbern, c. 1 (p. 70).

[4] B., c. 3 (p. 6), only says 'huius . . . imperii temporibus'; Osbern, c. 3 (p. 71), specifies
'anno . . . imperio eius primo, aduentus . . . Anglorum in Britanniam quadringentesimo

remove the falsehoods and then patch up the broken sequence of events: indeed the result would be something redundant and empty.[1] A book so mangled would belong neither to another nor to myself.

And so I have made haste to obey your command, and in my anxiety to win your favour and that of the saint, I have perhaps laid myself open to the teeth of backbiters. 8. Indeed I am sure that there will be those who will judge that I have written merely to find fault with other writers. But I pray Lord Jesus to win me forgiveness from such critics, for He sees that, at least in this work, I have had no truck with dislike or envy.[2] I know well that I have never laid traps to catch out the productions of other men, and that I have applied my pen to this topic simply to do you a favour. Further, the author whom I have mentioned, now long dead and past envy, can have no care for what humans think, seeing that he is subject to the judgement of God. 9. But it will be easy to excuse him for gaps in his narrative, because he had to do without old documents as a result of the fire which, as he said in his prologue, ravaged the church of Canterbury.[3] All this being so, please accept, my revered lords and rightly loved fathers, the pledge asked of my obedience; if ill-wishers cast against me the spears of malicious words, ward them off, I beg you, with the shield of your authority.

BOOK ONE

1. So the first year of King Æthelstan[4] brought into the world the child Dunstan, who was destined to be patron saint of all England. His father Heorstan and his mother Cynethryth were both of them distinguished for their piety[5] towards God and their nobility of birth; and it was in equal zeal for virtue and in all concord of refined manners that they lived out their lives. How pleasing their life was in God's eyes He did not hesitate to show after their deaths: this same son of theirs, whose story I am now setting out to narrate, when archbishop later on, saw, thanks to the clear gaze of his unsullied mind, both his parents rejoicing amid the heavenly choirs, and his mother, too, helping in the service of the Lord's Mother.[6] 2. It was of

---

nonagesimo septimo'. William presumably took the AD date given in prol. 5 from *ASC* (F), though he usually followed a copy of (E), which gives the correct date of 924. For the difficulties posed by this date for Dunstan's later career, as opposed to one *c*.910, see N. Brooks, 'The career of St Dunstan', in *St Dunstan*, pp. 3–5.

[5] Cf. Virgil, *Aen.* i. 10: 'insignem pietate uirum'. Brooks, 'The career of St Dunstan', discusses the meagre information about Dunstan's parentage.

[6] The vision is an expansion of Adelard, lect. i (p. 54).

prouidentia opus, ut bonus futurus filius boni lineam non peregrinis
disceret exemplis, sed intra domesticos parietes[1] a bonis mutuaretur
parentibus. Hi ergo legitimo nuptiarum federe maturis amoribus in
iuuenta conuenere. Iamque post aliquantum copulae tempus Kinedrida in spem prolis grandescebat utero, cum eam luminosa Pur-
ificationis festiuitas Glastoniam inuitauit. Quo die sollemnibus iam
inchoatis offitiis in uetustam aecclesiam frequens matronarum ordo
cum Kinedrida conuenerat. Micabant per totum atrium[2] lumina, ipsa
constipatione turbae acrius oculos perstringentia. 3. Tum uero
cessante intra aecclesiam omni uentorum inquietudine, diuino
credo nutu, omnium lumina uno confusa et extincta sunt ictu.[3]
Perculit ingens pauor omnem populum, ambigentem de facto quid
diceret, utrumne casui an miraculo deputaret. Extorsit metus silentium, attonitisque*a* tantum oculis et uultibus mutam inter se agitabant
mestitiam. Sed non mora, propitia Diuinitas factum correxit, et
stuporem pauentum in suae laudis materiam transduxit.[4] Continuo
enim serenum lumen caelo emissum cereo Kinedridae infulsit,
communionemque lucis cunctis accurrentibus exhibuit. 4. Venera-
bile miraculum quod et antiquis respondit et futuris prelusit!*b* Ipsa
enim quondam die beata Dei genitrix et perpetua uirgo Maria tulit ad
templum Dei Dei Verbum, filium suum: quem senilis deuotio
benignis astringens complexibus ipsum predicauit esse qui lumen
aeternitatis, quondam per Adam amissum, declararet oculis omnium
populorum.[5] Nunc autem beata mulier, iubar Angliae per Dei gratiam
futurum aluo continens, collatione cerei sui dampna perditae lucis toti
reparauit agmini, hoc profecto significante Spiritu sancto, quod in
illius lateret uentre qui splendorem predicationis omni diffunderet
prouintiae.[6]

---

a *Perhaps read* attonitique   *b* *ed.*; preludit *Q*

---

[1] Sulpicius Severus, *Vita S. Martini*, ep. i. 1: 'intra domesticos parietes'.
[2] 'Atrium' here clearly means (some part of) the inside of the church (cf. ii. 27. 1, a
presumably indoor scene in heaven). That is apparently where the Devil laughs in i. 28. 2;
B., c. 22 (p. 34), seems to have written 'in parte occidentali templi'. Elsewhere, William
uses the word of churchyards: i. 10. 2 (with graves); and two strolls outside: i. 20. 2 (with a
reference back, apparently to i. 10. 2), and ii. 17. 1. In *GP*, c. 110 (p. 245), the scene is
certainly the *cimiterium*, a word used just before, and Osbern, c. 5 (p. 73), has 'per plana
atrii', the open space near the church at Glastonbury, where the old man points out the
buildings Dunstan is to build. *Mir.*, p. 106 line 1189 ('per atrium ecclesiae Romanae
transirent'), is ambiguous. *ODML* s.v. records the main ecclesiastical meaning as

course a suitable arrangement of divine providence that a son destined to be good should not learn the outline of the good from models abroad; instead he obtained it from good parents within the four walls of his home.[1] Well, these two, joined in lawful matrimony, came together in their youth to enjoy mature affection. After they had been married for some time, Cynethryth came to have hopes of a child; and when she was already growing big, she was attracted to Glastonbury by the brilliance of the feast of the Purification. On the great day the solemn rites had already begun, and a crowd of married women had come with her to the Old Church. Lights glittered down the nave,[2] the more dazzling because the worshippers were so tightly packed. 3. But then, though no wind stirred inside the church, the lights of them all flickered out (I suppose it was God's doing), at a single stroke.[3] A great fear took hold of the whole congregation, as they wondered whether to attribute the event to chance or miracle. Their fear enforced silence. They said nothing, but signified their grief to one another by startled looks and glances only. But they did not have long to wait. God looked favourably on them, and put things right, instead giving the frightened and amazed multitude cause for praise of Him.[4] For on an instant a clear light shone from the sky and blazed on Cynethryth's candle; everyone ran to her, and she shared her light with them. 4. A miracle indeed! It fitted in with what was past, and made a prelude to what was to come. For it was on that same day long ago that the blessed Mother of God, the ever virgin Mary, carried to the temple of God her son, God's Word. The old man [Simeon], clutching him in loving arms, proclaimed that it was He who would make bright to the eyes of all peoples the light of eternity that had once been lost through Adam.[5] And on this present occasion the happy woman, who held in her womb one who was by God's grace to be a light for England, was able by sharing her candle to restore to the whole company the light they had lost. The Holy Spirit signified by this that in her womb was hid one who would spread over the whole province the splendour of his preaching.[6]

'churchyard, precinct, or forecourt', and two late and ambiguous meanings as porch or galilee. It does not cite William.

[3] A briefer version in *GP*, c. 19 (p. 28). A similar miracle is recounted in the anon. *Miracula S. Wulfstani*, c. 6 (Darlington, p. 119).

[4] Cf. *VW* i. 2. 3: 'transiret in materiam laudis'.

[5] Luke 2: 25–32.

[6] Rather similarly *GP*, c. 101 (p. 230), on Wilfrid: 'non passa est premi lumen Britanniae, quod fax celica signauit cum adhuc genitrix alui pondus absolueret.'

2. Emensis ergo post conceptionem mensibus, absoluit partum femina, effuditque in uitam masculum, quem continuo per ministerium sacerdotis Deo renatum et in adoptionem filiorum eius translatum gauisa est. Dunstanus infanti nomen inditum, quod et montem et petram sonat:[1] conuenienti rerum presagio, quia, in utroque Saluatoris nostri pedisequus, et montem se per uirtutum sullimitatem et petram per fidei soliditatem exhibuit. Gratia enim eum diuina excepit, et in omnibus dono liberalitatis suae preuenit et prouexit. Et iam iunioribus annis decursis pueritiae infantia cesserat, uenitque ad soluenda uota Glastoniam illustris uir Herstanus cum religiosa coniuge et prosperrimae indolis sobole. 2. Illis igitur in prefata aecclesia excubias agentibus, puer irrepente somno indulsit quieti. Visus illi senior stellanti uultu, niueo habitu, assistere manuque prensum per circumiecta loca ducere, simul dulci affatu iocundari puero, et habili gestu dextrae mensuram edifitiorum inibi per eum construendorum deliniare. Ille solutus somno[a] et tunc parentibus assignauit uisionem et cum aetas tulit effectui mancipauit. Eadem enim forma posteriori tempore abbas erexit tecta qua recolebat sibi puero per angelicum inditium[b] presignata.[2] At uero parentes ad indaginem uisionis non hebetes felixque presagium libenter amplexi filium ibidem litteris imbuendum reliquerunt.

3. Nec uero illorum spei defuit pusio, sed raptim elementa litterarum addiscens ad reliqua etiam alacri tendebat animo. Meditantem occupat febris, tenerasque paulatim depasta medullas[3] desperabilem medicis facit. Sternitur ergo lecto et per horarum momenta morti accedere uidetur. Certe animo absentissimus nec quid ageret norat discernere nec quid ab aliis ageretur poterat aduertere. Adeo pestis cerebro insederat ut aliena iactaret uerba[4] et freneticus haud dubie putaretur. Spes itaque parentum quam sibi de filio proposuerant iam dabat terga,[5] cognatorum frigebat gaudium, languebat pollicitatio

---

[a] ed. (cf. *VW iii. 23. 2*); sonino *Q* (*as it seems*); somnio *Stubbs*   [b] *Stubbs*; iudicium *Q* (*as it seems*)

[1] From Adelard, lect. xii (p. 67). OE *dun* + *stan* = 'mountain' + 'stone'. The etymology of (the second element of) Dunstan's name is also referred to below, at i. 27. 5, and in *GR*, c. 147. 2.
[2] See below, i. 16. For Glastonbury in Anglo-Saxon times, see P. Rahtz, *The English Heritage Book of Glastonbury* (London, 1993), pp. 70–82, 91–4; L. Abrams, *Anglo-Saxon Glastonbury: Church and Endowment* (Woodbridge, 1996); R. J. Cramp, 'Monastic sites', in

2. The months after she had conceived passed, and the woman gave birth to a boy; at once she had the joy of his rebirth in God by the ministry of a priest, and of his enrolment among God's adopted sons. He was given the name Dunstan, which means both Mountain and Rock:[1] a fitting omen of what was to come, because in both respects he followed in the footsteps of our Saviour, showing himself a mountain by the grandeur of his virtues and a rock by the firmness of his faith. For the grace of God received him, and went before him and advanced him in every way, by the gift He gave him in His liberality. Now his early years were over; infancy had given place to childhood, and the distinguished Heorstan came to Glastonbury to pay his vows, together with his pious wife and promising son. 2. When they kept vigil in the church, sleep overcame the child, and he slumbered peacefully. He dreamed that an old man, with shining countenance and snow-white clothes, stood by him, took his hand, and led him through the neighbourhood, making pleasant conversation to the child (?) and sketching with practised gestures the dimensions of the buildings he was to construct there. When he woke up, Dunstan confided what he had seen to his parents; and when he grew up he put it into effect, for as abbot in aftertime he erected buildings on the plan which he remembered the angel had marked out for him as a boy.[2] His father and mother were not slow to interpret the vision, and gladly welcoming the happy omen they left their son at Glastonbury to be educated.

3. The child lived up to their hopes, quickly learning the elements of letters before eagerly going on to other subjects. But a fever attacked the scholarly boy. Gradually it fed on his delicate organs[3] until the doctors despaired of him. He lay prostrate in bed, and every second seemed to bring him closer to death. He was distracted in the extreme; he could not tell what he was doing, or make out what others were doing. The sickness had settled on his brain to such a degree that he ejected unintelligible words,[4] and was thought to be beyond question mad. The hopes that his parents had conceived of their son now turned tail,[5] his relatives' joy grew cold, the doctors'

The Archaeology of Anglo-Saxon England, ed. D. M. Wilson (London, 1976), pp. 201–52, at 241–6.   [3] See VW i. 15. 2 n.
    [4] Cf. GP, c. 101 (p. 231) 'aliena facere, insana dicere', and MW's emendation at VW i. 15. 4.
    [5] Cf. Mir., p. 54 line 195 'dedit terga timor'; GR, c. 384. 2 'terga iam dabat metus'.

medicorum. 2. Veruntamen accurrit necessitati nec diutius passa
puerum torqueri pietas Christi medicabili uisitationis suae presentia
cuncta propulsauit incommoda. Nec tamen modum remedii nouit
ipse qui sensit, sed nocte intempesta, quasi extasi raptaretur, domum
cursim exiuit. Exeuntem secuta est mulier quae ceteris tedio languoris
stertentibus*a* sola super alumnum sollicitas pretendebat uigilias.
Nactus ergo baculum quo uel uiam regeret uel obstantes repelleret,
nocturnam carpebat semitam, et ecce magnum latrantium*b* agmen
rabidis*c* in properantem inhians rictibus obuiam ueniebat. 3. Quorum
unus infestior dum etiam terga premeret, ille, aliud esse interpretatus
quam canem, baculum totis uiribus contortum, inuocato Christi
nomine, in os beluae seuientis intentat. Qua pueri constantia hostis
elusus furuis inferni unde emerserat se indidit umbris. Ita Dunstanus
Iesu Domini auxilio tutus ceptum ad aecclesiam callem persequitur.
Sed eam firmis intus repagulis offendens obseratam, machinas quibus
insistebant architecti conscendit.*d* Forte enim fastigium templi dir-
utum manus artificum prestolabatur. 4. Ita quem non sine cautela
talium rerum consueti molirentur ascensum, ille intrepidus inuasit.
Iam uero, quia in interiori parte superiora inferioribus nulli con-
tinuabant gradus, mirum quomodo descenderit. Descendit tamen,
inuentusque est mane a querentibus in una porticu[1] inter duos
aedituos tertius, leui*e* sopore membra confotus. Rogatus ut salutis
et descensus modum exponeret, respondit se neutrum scire, et non
minus quam ipsos de talibus miraculum habere. Mulier sane quae
preeuntis lento pede terebat uestigia, rerum usque ad ascensum index
fuit. Cetera ad hanc diem incognita.

---

a ed.; sternentibus *Q*   *b* Perhaps add canum   *c* ed. (*cf. GP p. 29* rabidorum);
rapidis *Q*   *d* Stubbs; consendit *Q*   *e* Perhaps read leni (*cf. GP p. 417*)

---

[1] In Anglo-Saxon ecclesiastical architecture *porticus* were side chambers, flanking the
apse or east end of the nave, serving as sacristies; further *porticus* might continue along the
nave to provide for burials and other purposes: E. Fernie, *The Architecture of the Anglo-
Saxons* (London, 1983), pp. 42–6; R. Gem, 'Architecture, ecclesiastical', in *Blackwell
Encyclopaedia*, p. 44. William uses the word quite frequently, and seems to have
understood both of these meanings. In this passage Dunstan is found 'in una porticu'
inside the church (Eadmer, c. 2 (p. 167), says 'coram altari'); cf. *GP*, c. 112 (p. 246) (of a
place of burial at York). In other passages the position is specified: (1) *orientalis VD* i. 23. 3
from Wulfstan of Winchester, *Vita S. Æthelwoldi*, c. 10 (p. 19 and n. 4); *GP*, c. 65 (p. 121),
describing the burial-place of Anselm. (2) *occidentalis VW* i. 3. 4, with an altar to All Saints.
(3) *australis GP*, c. 155 (p. 293), concerning burial-places found at Gloucester. (4) 'Both'
porticus at Coventry, with burials, *GP*, c. 175 (p. 311); *anfractus porticuum: GR*, c. 47. 3
(Bangor), *GP*, c. 100 (p. 217) (Ripon). So 'in una porticu' above might mean 'one of the

reassurances waned. 2. Yet Christ in His pity came to meet the crisis and would not let the boy be tormented any longer; He visited him with His healing presence, and drove off all the symptoms. Dunstan felt the cure without knowing how it had come about; but at dead of night, as though rapt in a trance, he left the house at a run. As he left, he was followed by the woman who single-handed was keeping an anxious watch over her charge while all the others, exhausted by his illness, slumbered. Dunstan found a staff to support his progress or drive off anyone in his path, and set off on a sleep-walk. Suddenly a great pack of barking dogs, their teeth bared in rabid jaws, met the hurrying boy. 3. One more hostile than the rest was already at his heels when, judging that this was something more than a hound, he flung his stick with all his strength into the muzzle of the ravening beast, calling on the name of Christ as he did so. The Enemy, baffled by the boy's pluck, betook himself to the murky shades of Hell from which he had emerged, and Dunstan, saved by the Lord Jesus' aid, continued his journey to the church. Finding the door firmly barred from inside, he climbed up the scaffolding employed by builders to support them (for, as it happened, the church roof had caved in and awaited the attention of workmen). 4. So Dunstan, without a qualm, essayed a climb which not even those accustomed to such heights would lightly attempt. But there were no steps leading down inside the building from roof to floor, and how he came down again is a mystery. But down he did come, to be found in the morning by those seeking him in a *porticus*,[1] making a third between two church-wardens, peacefully sleeping. When he was asked to explain the manner of his recovery and his descent, he said both were equally inexplicable to him, and as miraculous to himself as to the inquirers. Of course, the woman who had slowly dogged his footsteps could tell what happened up to the point when he started to climb; the rest of the story is unknown to this day.

two'. (5) Most self-conscious is *VD* i. 16. 1 'alas uel porticus quas uocant adiecit', to make the building more square; here *porticus* along each side of the nave are clearly meant. For the *porticus* at Glastonbury, prior to the extensions made by Dunstan as abbot (see below, i. 16), see Taylor and Taylor, *Anglo-Saxon Architecture*, i. 252–3; C. A. Ralegh Radford, 'Glastonbury abbey before 1184: interim report on the excavations, 1908–64', in *Medieval Art and Architecture at Wells and Glastonbury*, ed. N. Coldstream and P. Draper (British Archaeological Association, Conference Transactions iv, 1981 for 1978), pp. 110–34, at 116–18, and Fernie, *The Architecture of the Anglo-Saxons*, p. 95. They flanked the chancel.

4. Vbi ergo Dunstano salutis refusus uigor, intermissum litterarum studium acrius aggressus, nichil quod cura sua dignum estimaret inexpertum reliquit.[1] Conueniebat honestis studiis diuinae serenitatis assensus, conciliando ei magistros, cum*a* indigenas tum et Hibernenses. Huiusce quippe nationis homines cum magna frequentia locum incolebant illum, uiri usquequaque peritissimi, et qui liberales artes ad plenum subdidissent ingeniis, quique ut perfectius philosophiae inseruirent, relicto natali solo cunctarumque necessitudinum affectibus abiuratis,*b* Glastoniam contenderant, Patritii primi predicatoris sui amore adducti, cuius corporales exuuiae ibi ab antiquo habentur repositae.[2] 2. Horum ergo discipulatui Dunstanus deditus sacram scripturam medullitus ad extremam satietatem hausit. Secularium litterarum quiddam ⟨non⟩*c* negligendum, nonnichil etiam appetendum putauit. Poetarum siquidem scripta, dumtaxat quae fabulis strepunt,[3] et artes quae citra utilitatem animae armant eloquium transeunter audiuit. Arithmeticam porro, cum geometria et astronomia et musica[4] quae appendent, gratanter addidicit et diligenter excoluit. 3. Est quippe in illis et magna exercitatio scientiae et ueritatis integra castitas, et mirabilium Dei non uana consideratio. Harum artium scientiam hodieque Hibernenses pro magno pollicentur; ceterum ad formanda Latine uerba et ad integre loquendum minus idonei.[5] Quapropter[6] cum ceterarum tum maxime musicae dulcedine captus, instrumenta eius cum ipse libenter exercere, tum ab aliis exerceri dulce habere. 4. Ipse citharam si quando ⟨a⟩*d* litteris uacaret sumere, ipse dulci strepitu resonantia fila quatere.[7] Iam uero illud instrumentum quod antiqui barbiton, nos organa dicimus,[8] tota diffudit Anglia, ubi ut fistula sonum componat per multiforatiles tractus 'pulsibus exceptas follis uomit anxius auras'.[9] Hoc porro

---

a ed. (*see VW i ep. 2*); tum *Q*   *b* ed.; obiuratis *Q*   *c* Supplied by ed.
d Supplied by ed. from Leland, *Comm.*, p. 162

[1] Cf. Virgil, *Aen.* iv. 415.

[2] William mentions Patrick's presence at Glastonbury, and visits of subsequent Irish there, in *GR*, cc. 22–4, *AG*, cc. 8, 10, 12, and 13 (pp. 54–5, 60–3); also B., c. 5 (pp. 10–11). Commentary by H. P. R. Finberg, 'St Patrick at Glastonbury', in his *West-Country Historical Studies* (Newton Abbot, 1969), pp. 70–88, and Lapidge, 'The cult of St Indract at Glastonbury' (above, p. xxvi n. 87), pp. 419–23 and nn. See also below, pp. 368–71 and notes.

[3] Cf. *GP*, c. 139 (p. 281) 'preter fabulas poetarum'. Similar views were expressed by Aldhelm, cited in *GP*, c. 214 (p. 359).

[4] Cf. below, p. 188 and n. 2, and *GR*, c. 167. 3, where the context is Gerbert's education and unwise striving towards what is forbidden.

4. So when Dunstan had regained health and strength, he returned the more enthusiastically to his interrupted literary studies, leaving nothing untouched[1] that he thought worthy of his trouble. The wholesomeness of his labours received divine approval, as was only fitting, for God won for him teachers both English and Irish. Irishmen frequented the place in great numbers: men with a wide range of expertise, who had mastered the liberal arts fully. Wishing to give themselves over to philosophy more completely, they had abandoned their native soil, rejected all family ties, and made their way to Glastonbury, led on by love for their first preacher, Patrick, whose mortal remains are held to have lain buried there from time immemorial.[2] 2. So it was to their teaching that Dunstan devoted himself. He drank down the Holy Scriptures to his very depths, even to surfeit. As for lay writings, he thought some should not be neglected and some even sought out. To poetry, at least the sort that rings with fable,[3] and the arts that arm the speaker without benefiting his soul, he gave only cursory attention. Arithmetic, with its appendages geometry, astronomy and music,[4] he learned with pleasure and worked at hard. 3. They provide sound training in knowledge, and their truth is pure and uncontaminated; indeed, they turn the mind to God's miracles with profit. Even today the Irish ask a great price for teaching these arts; but they are less good at training in composition and correct speech in Latin.[5] Hence[6] Dunstan was captivated by music in particular; he took delight in playing musical instruments, and thought it agreeable when they were played by others. 4. Whenever he had time left over from reading, he took up the harp, and in person 'struck the resounding strings with pleasant noise'.[7] He spread through England knowledge of what the ancients call *barbiton* and we 'organs',[8] in which, to cause the pipe to resound through a channel with many holes, 'the anxious bellows vomit out the air they receive from blows'.[9] Dunstan practised on this

---

[5] An interesting observation, doubtless correct; see F. J. Byrne, *A Thousand Years of Irish Script: An Exhibition of Irish Manuscripts in Oxford Libraries* (Oxford, The Bodleian Library, 1979), pp. 14–15, commenting on Bodl. Libr., MS Auct. F. 3. 15 (Chalcidius, John the Scot).

[6] i.e. rather than studying Latin with them.

[7] Cf. Statius, *Achill.* ii. 157–8, also apparently echoed in *GR*, c. 131. 4.

[8] *Barbiton* derives from 'barbitos', the ancient word for a lyre, but see *ODML* s. v., for its medieval uses to denote an organ or other wind instrument. William himself uses the word to describe an organ's wind-chest in *GR*, c. 168. 2 (and see n. ad loc.). *Organa* was commonly in the plural, sometimes specified as 'a pair'. See below, p. 258 and n. 7.

[9] *GP*, c. 255 (p. 407), also gives the (untraced) verse, somewhat differently.

exercebatur non ad lenocinium uoluptatum sed ad diuini amoris incitamentum, ut etiam ad litteram impleretur illud Dauiticum 'Laudate Dominum in psalterio et cithara; laudate eum in chordis et organo.'[1]

5. Interea aetas progressior et adolescentiae foribus insistens spem parentum olim de puero conceptam in maius animabat. Quam[a] illi religiosis alentes affectibus ut sacros ordines reciperet inuitauerunt filium, diuinum circa eum fauorem non negligendum arbitrati. Ille, ne precipientibus durus uideretur, supposuit collum, minoribus gradibus titulatus ad Dei genitricis aecclesiam prouectus, sui maternique miraculi consciam. Ita sacris initiatus ad patruum suum (ex monacho[b] Glastoniensi primus Wellensis episcopus)[2] Cantuariensem archiepiscopum, Athelmum,[3] contendit, ex cognati pectoris auctoritate religionis exemplum sumpturus. 2. Excepit nepotem archiepiscopus qua decebat dignatione, patrio affectu quaecumque commoda liberaliter et affluenter indulgens. Deinde spectata eius alacritate ingenii, cui etiam mores non dissiderent, regi Ethelstano, quem sacra unctione in regem ipse sullimauerat, commendare curauit. Accessit curae pontificis industria adolescentis, qua breui effectum ut per se commendabilior esset tam regi quam aulicis. Familiarium ergo partium habebatur, nec erat quisquam in curia id aetatis iuuenis qui posset cum rege aut esse secretius aut loqui iocundius. 3. Denique frequenter ante illum uel uocali melo citharaeue[c] uel timpani sono psallebat, nunc ut curas depelleret, nunc ut soporem induceret, plerumque etiam ut torporem somni discuteret. Felix euentus excitauit cognatorum inuidiam, qui adolescentis successum reputarent suae felicitatis detrimentum. Quocirca opinionem eius apud regem lacerare aggressi, dicebant eum maleficis artibus niti, proindeque[d] gratiam regalem mercari. Repulit ille primo susurronum calumnias, liuori attribuens delationis amaritudinem. Hoc illi acrius instare et occasiones rimari donec rem diuinae dignationis in argumentum concinnarent furoris.

---

[a] *Stubbs*; quem *Q*   [b] *Stubbs*; m̊ (*sc.* modo) *Q. The clause can hardly be sound (one expects* qui ex . . . episcopus fuerat *or the like: cf. JG, c. 61); it may be interpolated from AG p. 137 or GR 184. 2.*   [c] cithare ue *Q. One expects rather* uel citharae timpaniue sono (*cf. Osbern p. 80* psallebat in tympano siue in cithara)   [d] *Perhaps read* perindeque (*cf. GP p. 169*)

[1] Ps. 150: 3–4.
[2] The Latin is ungrammatical; a gloss has been incorporated into the text.

instrument not because of its enticing pleasures, but to arouse his love for God, so that to the very letter might be fulfilled the injunction of David: 'Praise the Lord with the psaltery and harp. Praise him with stringed instruments and organs.'[1]

5. Meanwhile Dunstan grew older, till he stood on the threshold of adolescence, making yet more lively the hopes his parents had long conceived of the boy. They nurtured that hope religiously, and encouraged their son to take holy orders, for they reckoned that God's favour towards him should not be ignored. Rather than seem obstinate in the face of their instructions, he submitted, and set out, qualified with the minor orders, to the church of the Mother of God, which knew so well the miracle that had marked out himself and his mother. Thus initiated, he went off to join his uncle Athelm,[3] archbishop of Canterbury (he had been first bishop of Wells, after being a monk of Glastonbury),[2] intending to find a model for religious practice in the person of his prestigious relative. 2. The archbishop welcomed his nephew with all due attention, and showed a father's affection in liberally and bounteously furnishing all his needs. Then, observing his quickness of mind and his corresponding qualities of character, he made it his concern to recommend him to King Æthelstan, whom he had himself consecrated. The archbishop's favour was backed by the young man's diligence, which soon made him personally acceptable to king and court alike. He was taken into the inner circle, and there was no one of his age at court who could move more familiarly in the king's presence, or converse more agreeably with him. 3. For instance, he would often sing or play the harp or drum before the king, now to drive care away, now to bring on slumber, often too to dispel drowsiness. His success aroused the envy of his relatives, for they thought his advancement threatened their own fortunes. They therefore set themselves to tear his reputation to shreds in the king's eyes, alleging that he relied on black arts to win the king's regard. At first he refuted the calumnies of these back-biters, putting the bitterness of their accusations down to envy. But that made them the more urgent in their attacks and the more keen to find openings; and finally they contrived to make a mark of divine favour into a proof of madness.

---

[3] Bp. of Wells c.909–923/5, after which he became archbp. of Canterbury, dying 8 Jan. 926. See *GR*, cc. 129. 3, 184. 2.

6. Rogatus est Dunstanus a quadam matrona Ethelwinna[a] nomine domum suam uenire, quatinus in casula sacerdotali faceret picturam, unde puellae suae insuendi auri traherent formam. Opus plumarium uocant Latini.[1] Erat enim Dunstanus etiam pingendi artifex: emulari arte naturam, et quicquid uidisset uspiam spetiosum a uiuo animali in mutum transferre simulacrum.[2] Venit ergo et assedit operi. Interim cithara eius paxillo appensa canoros edere sonos, et sine ullo digitorum pulsu huius antiphonae melodiam modulari audita est: 'Gaudent in caelis animae sanctorum' et cetera.[3] **2.** Mirum id, ut erat, uideri ceteris et maxime mulierculis, laeto plausu gannientibus.[4] Dunstano autem, cuius et sensus perspicatior et oculus interius mundior, non tam uideri presentis rei miraculum quam futurae misterium. Intellexit enim cantu hoc se ammonitum ad tribulationum tolerantiam, quo fidentius Christi operiretur gloriam. Respondit rerum ueritas ueraci presagio. Namque sutores calumniarum rem quasi Dunstani malefitium curiae auribus intulerunt. Serpsit rumor ab unis in alteros, omnesque liuidis obtutibus adolescentem aspitiebant. Quod quanuis ille animaduerteret, omnes tamen susurros malignantium sicut Scilleos latratus placido et potius obturato transibat auditu.[5] **3.** Nec minus, secundum preceptum Saluatoris bona pro malis reddens,[6] persecutores suos blande alloqui, ipsis etiam benigne et oportune obsequi. Quo illi nichil infractiores calumnias serere in uulgus non cessabant, nec prius abstiterunt quam res et regis aures obsedit et animos a Dunstano auertit. Ita turbatis rebus adolescens curia ultro cedendum putauit. Excedentem machinatores flagris adorsi parum abfuit quin exanimarent. Nam equo deiectum fedeque cesum, calcibus quo tardius exsurgeret pressum, egerunt in caenum. Tum quasi furori probe satisfecissent abierunt. Ille uero uix egreque luto emergens in uillam cuiusdam affinis sui e uicino commanentis concessit. **4.** Iam uero domui propinquantem[b] canes domestici, oblitum caeno et horrendum uisu conspicati, pene fuit ut inuaderent. Sed mox blandientis uoce cognita frenarunt impetum et adulantibus caudis domum introduxerunt. Hanc canum mutationem primo Dunstani excepit suspirium, mox etiam huiusmodi dictum:

---

[a] *ed.*; Alwinna *Q*   [b] *ed.*; propinquante *Q*

[1] Bede uses the expression five times in *De tabernaculo* ii.

[2] On Anglo-Saxon vestments, see C. R. Dodwell, *Anglo-Saxon Art: a New Perspective* (Manchester, 1982), pp. 180–7, and the references to this passage at pp. 39, 70.

[3] R.-J. Hesbert, *Corpus Antiphonalium Officii* (6 vols.: Rome, 1963–79), no. 2927. Similarly B., c. 12 (p. 21), Osbern, c. 10 (p. 80), Eadmer, c. 5 (p. 170). According to

6. Dunstan was requested by a married lady called Æthelwynn to come
to her house to draw a picture for a priest's stole, so that her girls could
use it as a pattern in sewing the gold design. The Latins call it 'feather-
work'.[1] Dunstan, you see, was also a skilled painter, able to ape nature in
art: anything beautiful he saw anywhere he could transfer from living
reality to dumb representation.[2] So along he went, and took his seat for
the task. As he worked, his harp, which hung on a peg, gave out
harmonious sounds; without touch from any finger, it was heard to play
the melody of the antiphon 'In heaven the souls of the holy rejoice . . .'.[3]
2. That seemed, as indeed it was, wonderful to the others, especially
the women, who chattered[4] a cheerful response. But Dunstan was more
perceptive, and had a clearer vision: he thought it not a miracle lasting
for a moment but a veiled prophecy of the future. He realized that this
anthem was warning him to bear with tribulations so that he could await
Christ's glory with the more confidence. The event corresponded with
this truthful presage. The sowers of calumny brought the story to the
ears of the courtiers, representing it as an instance of Dunstan's evil
arts. Rumour spread, and everyone looked askance at the young man.
He was aware of this, but listened quietly, or rather barred his ears, to all
the malign whispers as though they were the baying of Scylla's hounds.[5]
3. As our Saviour commanded,[6] he returned good for evil, addressing
his tormentors pleasantly and even doing them good turns. But
undeterred they went on sowing libels abroad, and did not let up
until the king was hemmed in and withdrew his favour from Dunstan.
All was up, and the young man thought it best to leave the court
voluntarily. As he went, the plotters attacked him with whips and all
but killed him: they threw him from his horse, beat him up, and
plunged him in a filthy bog, stamping him down to delay his emergence.
Then, feeling that they had made a good job of their folly, they left the
scene. Dunstan struggled out of the mud with difficulty, and betook
himself to the vill of a relative who lived nearby. **4.** As he approached,
the house dogs nearly attacked him, seeing him covered in mud and
horrid to behold. But they soon recognized his coaxing voice, stayed
their assault, and escorted him into the house, tails wagging. This
change of heart on the part of the dogs drew from Dunstan first a sigh,

Byrhtferth, *Vita S. Oswaldi*, p. 458, Dunstan heard this antiphon in the vision recounted at
ii. 28. 1–3 below. Eadmer has both versions, the second at c. 31 (p. 208).

[4] For this verb, see p. 33 n. 4.

[5] Cf. Jerome, *Vit. Hil.* 1: 'uerum destinato operi imponam manum, et Scylleos canes
obturata aure transibo.' There the hounds are possible critics of the work, like the *maliuoli*
of *VD* i. prol. 9.   [6] Luke 6: 27.

'Alternat, ut uideo, natura rerum, dum cognati bestiali feritate seui et canes in me humana lenitate sint blandi. Sed patienter ferendum est quod Deus iubet, quia pulchrum sua gratia dedit commertium, quoniam assentantur canes etsi aduersantur homines.'[1]

7. Huius tempestatis iactatione discussa, Dunstanus Wintoniam ire perrexit. Erat tum ibi*ª* Deo acceptissimus sacerdos Elfegus cognomento Caluus, cuius consanguinitatis lineam proximo gradu Dunstanus attingebat.[2] Hunc fuisse monachum Glastoniensem certum †et abbatem†*ᵇ* constans apud Wintonienses opinio est.[3] Vnde perspicuum est quod is, quisquis est, fallitur qui beatum Dunstanum monachos in Glastonia posuisse et primum ibi abbatem fuisse allegare conatur.[4] Nam, ut in epistola dixi,[5] et tempore natiuitatis eius Aldhunus abbas ibidem fuisse cognoscitur et hic Elfegus ante monachus quam abbas Dunstanus. 2. Ad hunc ergo ueniens sepeque ab eo salubribus monitis pulsatus ut monachus fieret, distulit facetis responsis episcopum uel eludens uel suspendens, nonnumquam etiam monachorum uitam non magis placere Deo quam laicorum cauillatus. Irrepserat enim iam adolescenti uoluptatum fomes,[6] ut nichil minus quam monachum cogitaret. Quapropter Deo dilectus episcopus, qui preuideret in spiritu quantum deperiret religioni dilatione*ᶜ* habitus mutandi, totius deuotionis in orationem diffudit uiscera, quatinus adolescens flagello ammoneretur corporeo ne animae obstaret commodo. 3. Auditum est continuo in caelis quod ille summurmurauerat in terris, et scintilla caritatis ex corde procedens episcopi reluxit in Dunstano ad flammam egrotationis. Ita enim uesicis turgentibus per totum corpus intumuit ut morbo intercutis uel regia[7] ualitudine laborare uideretur. Hoc periculo territus nuntiis missis rogauit eius aduentum. Maturauit iter episcopus, et ueniens audit quod diu optauerat, Dunstanum anxie expetere quod ante rogatus supersederat facere. Datur ergo effectus desiderio: alteratur Dunstanus et fit monachus.

ª Perhaps add episcopus   *ᵇ Apparently corrupt*   *ᶜ ed.*; dilacio *Q*

[1] Note the untranslatable word-play. Cf. Avitus, *Poem.* iii. 243–5: 'cumque canes miti perlambant uulnera lingua/blandior et fesso feritas medicabilis adsit,/sola hominum nescit mens semper dura moueri.'

[2] Similar wording is used to express relationship in *GR*, c. 209. 1.

[3] Ælfheah I, bp. of Winchester 934–51, *not* Ælfheah II, bp. of Winchester 984–1006, archbp. of Canterbury 1006–12. In *GR*, c. 184. 2, and *AG*, c. 67 (pp. 136–7), William says that the *second* had been prior. Either he or Winchester tradition may have confused the earlier careers of both men.

then words on these lines: 'I can see that the world is turned upside down; my relations are treating me like wild animals, and dogs like the gentlest of humans. But one must put up patiently with what God commands, for He has in His grace produced an excellent exchange: dogs fawn, even if men turn against me.'[1]

7. When the storm was over, Dunstan proceeded to Winchester. At that time the bishop there was Ælfheah the Bald, a priest most acceptable to God, and a close relation of Dunstan's.[2] It is certain he was a monk of Glastonbury, and there is a firm belief at Winchester that he was actually abbot.[3] Hence it is quite clear that he is mistaken (whoever he is) who tries to affirm that the blessed Dunstan settled monks at Glastonbury and was first abbot there.[4] For, as I said in my introductory letter,[5] Ealdhun is known to have been abbot there at the time of Dunstan's birth, and this Ælfheah was a monk there before the abbacy of Dunstan. 2. Anyway, he came to Ælfheah, who bombarded him with good advice—to become a monk. Dunstan put the bishop off with witty retorts, evading him or keeping him in suspense, and sometimes even sophistically arguing that the life of monks is no more pleasing to God than that of laymen. For the young man had by now been infected by the germ of pleasure,[6] and the last idea in his head was to become a monk. So the bishop, beloved of God as he was, seeing in the spirit how much would be lost to the religious life if Dunstan delayed conversion, poured out all his devotion of soul in prayers that the youth should be warned by bodily affliction not to stand in the way of the good of his own soul. 3. What Ælfheah had murmured on earth was on an instant heard in heaven, and a spark of charity from the bishop's heart blazed up in Dunstan into a flame of illness. His whole body so swelled with blisters that he looked to be suffering from dropsy or the King's Evil.[7] Terrified at the danger he was in, he sent off messengers to beg Ælfheah to come to him. The bishop hurried over, and on his arrival heard what he had long wished: Dunstan was anxiously seeking what he had previously refused. His desire was granted; Dunstan changed his way of life, and became a monk.

<hr />

[4] William continues his criticism of Osbern.
[5] See above, i. prol. 5. But William did not there name Ælfheah.
[6] B., c. 7 (p. 13), says that he was tempted to marry.
[7] For the range of diseases covered by the term 'King's Evil', see *GR*, c. 222 n. and the literature cited there, with the addition cited above, p. 74 n. 2.

4. Inaequalitate[1] igitur corporis fugata, mansionem circa Elfegum protelauit, ut in eius uita legeret quid regulare*a* tenere deberet. Interea oblitterandum non est quanta sub illo tempore prouidentiae diuinae pietas ambobus consuluerit. Rogatu ciuium suorum dedicauerat pontifex aecclesiam extra occidentalem ciuitatis portam. Sollemniis expletis, petitus ut domum unius conuiuio dignaretur suo, caritati non defuit inuitatoris. Iam uero luce occidua cum uespertinum crepusculum uideret accedere, data benedictione conuiuis Dunstano comitante ualefecit. 5. Tum forte uiantibus obtulit[2] se beati papae Gregorii aecclesia[3] uiae contermina. Illam ex uoluntate presulis ingressi completorium dicturiebant. Iamque pro more iunctis et inclinatis capitibus confitebantur, et ecce ingens lapis, ambiguum quo casu, tecto elapsus, ita illorum periculo proximus fuit ut amborum libaret cesariem sed non turbaret salutem. Crediderim insidias antiqui hostis fuisse, qui totis machinis saxum contorserit, cum saluti[4] utrorumque inuidens tum etiam alterius celsitudinem futuram suspectam habens. Sed e uicino repulit eius calliditatem diuina dignatio, uolens ut illi de hoste opimam*b* raperent predam, non ille de ipsis usurparet uictoriam.

8. Eisdem diebus[5] Dunstanus, eodem antistite iubente, ad gratiam presbiteratus accessit, habens ad eundem gradum collaterales collegas Athelwoldum et Ethelstanum. Hi uiri, sicut par in bono habuere principium, ita diuersum habuerunt exitum. Quod, spiritu medullis influente, Elfegus presentiens, ipsa eadem die ordinationis cum mensae assideret, tali secretum mentis sermone resoluit: 'Hodie sub ope Dei tribus uiris manum imposui, quorum primus erit apud Cantiam archiepiscopus, secundus michi quandoque in hac sede successurus, tertius abiecto religionis quo nunc uelatur simulacro uitam terminabit in uoluptatum uolutabro.' Nichil hac prophetia mirabilius aut diuinius, nichil eius effectu uerius aut sincerius. Dunstanus siquidem postea culmen archiepiscopatus, Athelwoldus

---

a Perhaps read regulae   *b* ed. (cf. GP pp. 332, 419); optimam Q

[1] Cf. *VW* iii. 26. 2, and *ODML* s. v. 'inaequalitas' 7 for this use of the word.
[2] Cf. *Mir.*, p. 118 line 201.
[3] Probably the chapel of St Gregory in the precinct of New Minster: *Winchester in the Early Middle Ages*, ed. M. Biddle (Winchester Studies i: Oxford, 1976), p. 316. No other dedication to St Gregory at Winchester is known.
[4] William seems to be playing on two meanings of the word: bodily safety and spiritual salvation (as forwarded by confession). In this incident, the Devil does not succeed in harming either.

4. In this manner he drove his illness[1] away; and he extended his stay with Ælfheah, intending to read in his life the rule he should cleave to. Meanwhile, I should not omit an instance of the way in which God in His merciful foresight took thought for them both at that period. The bishop had, at his people's request, dedicated a church outside the west gate of the city. After the ceremony, he was asked to honour the house of an individual by dining there; and he did not spurn the well-meant invitation. But when he saw the light failing and evening coming on, he blessed the gathering and made his farewell, along with Dunstan. 5. As they went along, they happened to pass[2] a wayside church dedicated to Pope Gregory [I],[3] and going inside at the bishop's wish they felt the urge to say Compline. They were making confession with their bowed heads close together, as is customary, when all of a sudden a great stone somehow became dislodged from the roof and came so near to hitting them that it shaved both their heads, without doing them harm. I should conjecture that this was a trap laid by the Old Enemy, projecting the stone with all his artillery, out of envy of the salvation[4] of both men, and resenting the future eminence of one of them. But God deigned to be at hand to repel his wiles; His wish was that *they* should win a rich booty from the Enemy, not that *he* should be victorious over them.

8. Around this time[5] Dunstan, at Ælfheah's insistence, attained the grace of the priesthood. His colleagues in this promotion were Æthelwold and Æthelstan, who, though making a similar start in good, came to very different ends. This Ælfheah was inspired by the Holy Spirit to foresee. Seated at table on the very day of the ordination, he revealed his secret thus: 'Today I have, with God's aid, laid my hands on three men. The first will be archbishop of Canterbury, the second will one day succeed me here. But the third will cast aside the pretence of religion in which he is now masquerading, and end his life wallowing in pleasure.' Nothing could be more wonderful or more heaven-sent than this prophecy, nothing more true or precise than its fulfilment. For Dunstan later ascended to the height of an archbishopric and Æthelwold to the rank of bishop,

---

[5] The prophecy is also recounted in *GP*, c. 75 (pp. 164–5), from Wulfstan of Winchester, *Vita S. Æthelwoldi*, c. 8. A similar story is recounted of Gundulf bp. of Rochester in *GP*, c. 72 (p. 137).

ordinem episcopatus conscendit; Ethelstanus ut canis reuersus ad uomitum[1] miserabile apostasiae fuit exemplum.

9. Nec multo post Dunstanus Glastoniam a pontifice missus est, ut qui habunde mores ad unius composuerat speculum, nunc ad multorum coaptaret exemplum. Ibi preter cotidianam cantandi sollertiam, ne mens inerti marceret otio, manuum se dedit exercitio. Sed, ut operanti suppeteret diuersorium, quoddam prope Dei genitricis aecclesiam tecto appendice continuauit spatium. Iam uero par est animaduertere quanta cura colebat animum, ut eo loci sedem poneret quo etiam licentiores cogitatus interpellaret et argueret. Mentem ergo frenabat loci reuerentia, simulque corpus arctabant ieiunia. 2. Ibi manus applicabat operi, labia psalmis, animos caelis. Ibi currebat per tabulam stilus, per paginam calamus, ibi sumebat pincillum ut pingeret, scalpellum ut sculperet, et, ut fatiam compendium, ibi exercebat*[a]* quicquid est licitarum et utilium artium.[2] Denique et fabrile studium quondam aggressum uicinia frequens ad emendandas recellas suas precibus fatigabat. Ille, in commune bonus omnibus,[3] nichil alicui negare, aequum affectum cunctis prestare. Inde diabolus occasionem aucupatus, quadam die sole iam occasum meditante, ad fenestram astitit quidlibet operis molienti. 3. Intuitus Dunstanus eum, qui et oris hilaritatem et hominis pretenderet effigiem, dolos non attendit. Quocirca rogantem ut, opere quod ceperat intermisso, suis seruiret usibus, non aspernatus manum eius suggestioni applicuit. Inter haec inimicus sermone collato uerba delicata iactabat in medium, mollitiem inferebat feminarum. Veruntamen ne aperta fronte proderentur argutiae, simulationis uelabatur pallio, eludens iuuenem religionis fuco. Nec mora, relictis bonis redibat ad noxia, talia commemorans quae possent cuiuslibet religiosi robur eneruare, uigorem inflectere.[4] 4. Audiebat haec Sanctus, et multa uolutabat animo. Tandemque, instinctu credo Dei, artificem doli comperiens ad ultionem armatur. Forcipes itaque ferrarias celeriter expedit, easque foco immittens uiuatiori flatu fornaculam

---

[a] ed.; exercebatur *Q*

[1] Prov. 26: 11.
[2] Similarly *Mir.*, p. 119 lines 225–6: 'licitas artes . . . illicitas'. Cf. above, p. 178 and n. 4, and Augustine, *De civ. Dei* x. 9, x. 28. William is concerned that no one should think that Dunstan was involved in black arts (see 5. 3).
[3] Cf. Lucan ii. 390: 'in commune bonus' (Dunstan is therefore being tacitly compared to Cato the Younger).

while Æthelstan returned like a dog to his vomit[1] and provided a pitiable instance of apostasy.

9. Not long afterwards the bishop sent Dunstan off to Glastonbury. He had formed his character sufficiently on the model of an individual; now he was to school it to follow the example of many. Once at Glastonbury, he daily showed his skill in singing; but so that his mind should not grow dull with inactivity, he devoted himself to working with his hands. Now to supply himself with a private retreat, he covered over a space adjoining the church of the Mother of God with a lean-to roof. We should notice how carefully he cultivated his mind, for he positioned himself where he could also interrupt and rebuke licentious thoughts. So the holiness of the place put a curb on his mind, while his body was trammelled by fasting. 2. In this shed he applied his hands to his job, his lips to psalms, his mind to heaven. There his stylus ran across the tablet, his pen across the page. There he wielded a brush to paint and a knife to carve. And (to sum up) there he practised all permitted and useful arts.[2] For example, he once took up carpentry, and was bombarded by the requests of the whole neighbourhood to mend their trumpery belongings. He was good to all alike,[3] denied no one anything, and gave everyone his equal affection. That gave the Devil his opportunity. One day, as the sun was going down, he stood at the window while Dunstan was busy with some job. 3. Dunstan saw him; he looked cheerful and entirely human, and Dunstan was unaware of his guiles. He asked Dunstan to lay aside his work and do something for him; Dunstan agreed, and set his hands to what the Devil proposed. As time went on, they fell into conversation, and the Devil introduced risqué topics, like the attractions of women. But to ensure that his cunning should not become obvious, he veiled himself in a cloak of pretence, misleading the young man with a gloss of piety. Soon he went back from healthy topics to harmful ones, retailing things capable of sapping the strength of the most religious man and weakening his energy.[4] 4. The saint listened, and pondered deeply. Finally, thanks I imagine to God's prompting, he recognised the trickster and armed himself for revenge. He quickly deployed his smith's tongs, thrust them into the fire, and roused the furnace to a greater draught. The fire roared,

---

[4] With this very graphic representation of the power of sexual temptation, cf. below i. 23. 3.

exsuscitat. Stridebat ergo incendium, feruebant tenacula. Quae candentia corripiens in fatiem portenti, iam se deprehensum intelligentis iamque fugam parantis, uibrat. Ille longe reducta fatie ictum cauet. Sed insistit pronis nisibus presbiter, iamque impudentes fauces ignito ferro precluserat. Nec uero ullo modo effugisset pestifer nisi, ad notas recurrens artes, inter manus tenentis in nocturnas elaberetur auras. 5. Fugiens tanto hiatu insonuit ut, procul repercusso aere, huiusmodi uox pene toti audiretur prouintiae: 'O quid fecit caluus iste? o quid fecit caluus iste?', iocatus uel potius grassatus in hominem cui, refugis a fronte capillis,[1] dampnosa cesaries erat. Diluculo uicinis a Dunstano auctorem ululatus percunctantibus, respondit diabolum fuisse: ipsum inquam[a] nunc sibi struere insidias qui quondam in palatio conflasset calumnias, ipsum nunc blandientem ad uitia, sed post exacturum suplitia:[2] cuius commoti clamor intolerabilis monet ut caueatur consortium in penis. Dixit plura fortassis ad hanc sententiam, quae magis conitienda sunt animo quam committenda scripto.[3]

10. Eodem tempore Glastoniensis aecclesiae monachus, felicem uitae sortitus terminum, feliciter supremum incurrit arbitrium. Is erat Wlfredus nomine, diaconus ordine, adolescens aetate, Dunstano iam inde a pueritia sancta deuinctus amicitia. Quae inter eos parili uirtutum et morum coaluerat studio, nec eam ulla umquam amara dumtaxat interpellauerat offensio. Hic post paucum decessus sui tempus amico apparuit nocte, familiari qua cognosceretur spetie. Tum uisus futurae uitae seriem ad unguem exponere, aduersa et prospera iuxta et incunctanter predicere. 2. Nec tamen ad audita Dunstanus credulo statim exiliuit gaudio, doctus in omnibus apponere cautelam, adhibere diligentiam. Quapropter, ut etiam in somniantis animo contempleris sapientiam, uisus est talia referre: 'Pulchra sunt' inquit 'quae promittis, sed quo inditio habeam fidem promissis?' Tum ille manu ut uidebatur comprehensum duxit ad australem partem atrii aecclesiae sepe nominatae. Scatebat ibi tota humus defunctorum memoriis, ita ut, sicut hodieque apparet, uix alicubi pedem poneres si non ad aliquod sepulchrum offenderes. 3. Paruulum modo erat spatium huius immune iniuriae, ubi uidebatur intactus cespes et herbosa uirens planitie. 'Hic' ait (et digito locum

---

[a] *Apparently corrupt; but William seems to be confused as to whether he intends direct or indirect speech.*

[1] Cf. Lucan x. 132; also in *GR*, c. 439. 2, *VW* iii. 17. 2.
[2] In the form of Dunstan's subsequent exile.

the tongs glowed. When they were white hot, Dunstan snatched them
out and brandished them in the monster's face. Realizing he was
caught out and already looking to flee, the Devil drew his face well
back and avoided the blow. But the priest persevered in his assault,
and soon had the shameless jaws gripped in the burning iron. The
Evildoer would indeed never have escaped had he not had recourse to
his well-known tricks and, slipping between his captor's hands,
disappeared into the night air. 5. As he fled his gaping jaws gave
out such a noise that the echo went far and wide, and half the
province heard the words: 'O what has this bald one done? O what has
this bald one done?'—a joke or rather a slander directed against one
whose locks had receded from his forehead,[1] leaving his hair thin. In
the morning the neighbours inquired of Dunstan who had been
responsible for the screams. He said: 'It was the Devil. Previously he
spread slanders in the palace; now he is plotting against me here. Now
he is trying to lure me into vice, but later he will exact a penalty.[2] The
appalling racket he made when he was upset shows how careful one
has to be to avoid sharing his punishment.' He perhaps said more
along these lines: things better imagined than set down in writing.[3]

10. Around the same time a monk of Glastonbury came to a happy
end of his life, and happily faced the Last Judgement. This was
Wulfred, a young deacon who had been attached to Dunstan in a holy
friendship ever since they were boys. The attachment had grown firm
thanks to their shared enthusiasm for virtuous behaviour, and no
serious disagreement had ever interrupted it. Not long after his death
Wulfred appeared to his friend one night, looking as he always had
looked, and easy to recognize. In the dream he went over Dunstan's
future life in detail, fluently predicting good as well as ill. 2. Dunstan
had learned to be cautious and careful in everything, and so he did not
leap up at once in joyful belief. Even in his dreaming state, you could
get an idea of his good sense. 'What you promise is very fine,' he
answered, 'but what sign is there to make me trust your promises?'
Then, in the dream, Wulfred took him by the hand and led him to the
southern part of the churchyard. The whole surface of the ground
there was so thickly covered with memorials of the dead that, as is
true today, you could scarcely put your foot down without running
into some tomb or other. 3. There was just one tiny spot free of such
obstruction, where the turf was unsullied and the grass grew green on

---

[3] Apparently related to the criticism of Osbern in ii. prol. 1.

ostendit) 'ad uerae uisionis inditium sepelietur presbiter infra triduum, qui nullum adhuc patitur incommodum, corpus autem eius ab occidentali parte huc deferetur tumulandum.' Dixit et euanuit; alter etiam sopore solutus surrexit. Nec uero diu ingrato indulsit silentio, quin continuo mane amicis uisionem communicaret. Simulque ad fidem dictorum iaculatus calculum in locum predictum, subiecit: 'Si uera est uisio, illic infra hoc triduum tumulabitur presbiteri corpus qui adhuc est alacer et sanus.' 4. Vix illi discesserant, et ecce capellanus matronae nobilis Ethelfledae ad eundem se locum matutinus agebat.[1] Is cum totum cimiterium circuisset oculis tantillumque spatii mortuorum uidisset carere reliquiis, ait his qui in tempore aduenerant aedituis: 'Paciscar queso uobiscum hanc gratiam, ut cum anima exuerit corpus hic sit requietionis meae locus.' Assentientibus illis abiit, statimque tactus incommodo naturaeque cedens, ubi rogauerat ante triduum sepulchrum promeruit. Nichil erat ultra quod de uisione[a] Dunstanus ambigeret. 5. Quapropter ad uirtutum incrementa exsurgere, ludicris mundanis, si quae animo eius restiterant, ualefacere; conari prorsus ut labor suus accederet Dei gratiae, quatinus quae sibi promittebantur gratuito non conferrentur immerito. Nec uero eius industria in uacuum cessit, quin potius cum multiplici Dei gratia fauor potentum hominum bene uiuenti non defuit. Quod uno exemplo fatiam in propatulo, si prius quaedam ad id pertinentia, quasi extrinsecus a materia, posuero. Breui ergo diuerticulo[2] utar, si forte relationis necessitatem fatiat breuitas lectionis excusabilem.

11. Neptis Ethelstani regis Ethelfleda,[b 3] summae potentiae femina, de cuius presbitero paulo ante dixi, uiro de compari nobilitate nupsit primo uere adolescentiae. Is cum diem clausisset, castitatem suam Deo consecrauit, ut numquam post primi dampna tori secundos experiretur ignes. Quod ut expeditius teneret, Glastoniam sese in otium contulit, edificatis propter[c] aecclesiam domibus, siue ut Dei genitricis familiarius inhereret obsequio, siue ut Dunstani liberius frueretur colloquio. 2. Erat enim eius proxima cognata,[4] et, ad bonum audiendum salutaribus animata monitis, cotidianis etiam ne

---

[a] de uisione (*corrected from* diuisione) *Q*; de missione *Stubbs*   [b] *ed.*; Ethelfreda *Q* (*so too at i. 12. 4*)   [c] prope *Q*[p.c.]

[1] Virgil, *Aen.* viii. 465; also at *VW* iii. 13.
[2] William marks its end at i. 13. 1.
[3] Called Æthelflæd by B., c. 9 (p. 16), variants of Æthelgifu or Ælfgifu in the copies of

the sward. 'Here,' he said, pointing out the place, 'to confirm the truth of the vision, a priest will be buried within three days. He is still in perfect health; yet his corpse will be brought from the west end for burial here.' Thereupon he vanished. Dunstan awoke and got up. But he did not keep sullen silence for long, and straightaway in the morning let his friends know of his dream. To guarantee his words he tossed a pebble down on the appointed spot, remarking: 'If my dream is true, within three days there will be buried in that place the body of a priest who is today active and well.' 4. They had scarcely parted when lo and behold! the chaplain of the noble lady Æthelflæd betook himself there of a morning.[1] He surveyed the whole cemetery, and noticed that a tiny spot was still without memorials of the dead. 'May I ask a favour of you?' he said to the church-wardens who had opportunely arrived on the scene. 'When my soul is freed from my body, may this be the place of my resting.' They agreed, and he went away. At once he succumbed to illness, yielded to nature, and before three days were out received burial where he had asked it. No need for Dunstan to have any further doubts about his vision! 5. He strove to increase in virtue, and bade farewell to any remaining worldly frivolities. All his efforts went into ensuring that his work forwarded the grace of God, so that what was promised him for no return should not be awarded without his deserving. Nor was his diligence in vain: rather, along with the manifold grace of God went the favour of powerful men towards one so righteous. I will make this clear by a single example, first mentioning certain matters relevant to it but tangential to my story. So I shall introduce a short digression,[2] hoping that my brevity will excuse the necessity of its telling.

11. King Æthelstan's niece Æthelflæd,[3] the influential lady of whose chaplain I spoke a little while back, married in the first flower of her youth a man of equal rank. When he died, she vowed her chastity to God: never after the loss of her first husband would she undergo the flames of a second love. To help her hold to this resolution the more easily, she took herself off to the calm of Glastonbury, building quarters near the church, so as either to serve the Mother of God more intimately or to have freer converse with Dunstan, (2) for she was closely related to him.[4] Dunstan spurred her on with salutary advice to listen to what was good, and strengthened her every day by

Osbern, c. 15 (p. 85 and n. 5), Ælfgifu by Eadmer, c. 8 (p. 175). Nothing further is known of her.   [4] Perhaps embroidering B., c. 10 (p. 17): 'causa . . . propinquitatis'.

deficeret roborabatur exemplis. Vtrumque ergo agebat sedulo, tantumque corporis curae deerat quantum illis operam impendebat.
Proinde uicario dilectionis munere tantum illi Domina nostra imper-
tiebatur gratiae ut nec in minimis eam contristari sustineret.[1] Quod
dictum ut euadat ambiguitatis offensam argumentum subnectam.

12.[2] Rex Ethelstanus, quo nullus umquam regum uel in pace iustior
uel in bello uictoriosior fuit, Glastoniam ueniebat. Quo Ethelfleda
cognito matrona, quae cum in omnes tum pronius in regiam sobolem
semper fuisset dapsilis, mandat ei ut non aspernanter ad se pransurus
introeat. Expositis mandatis onerauit frontem regiam pudor. Si enim
obaudiens dicto non esset, reuerebatur ne ancillam Dei commoueret;
si ueniret, timebat ne minus suffitientem paratum ostenderet.
2. Librato ergo consilio, ut nec neptis precibus resisteret nec ipse
uerecundiam suam urgeret, misit ministros qui suffitientiam uictus
explorarent. Illi concito equorum cursu arua morantia rapientes[3]
iussum exsequuntur, renuntiantque inuitatrici de ceteris quidem
plurimum, de hidromelle[a] uero minimum esse. Huius si possit
emendari detrimentum, nichil obstare quin rex ad eius concordet
uotum. Quod ubi accepit mulier immodicae in Deo spei respondit:
'Nolit umquam sancta Christi mater ut propter minus suffitientem
huiusmodi potum dominus rex declinet meam domum.' 3. Et cum
dicto templum ingressa compellat Virginem ut quod deerat de
industria[4] suppleret ipsa ex misericordia; ipsa dolium emendaret,
ipsa pateras spumantes coronaret.[5] Has preces cassas non fuisse
ostendit miraculum e uestigio subsecutum. Assedit rex mensae
totas secum in prandium trahens cateruas. Accelerant pincernae
inter et post dapes frequentioribus poculis inuitare conuiuarum
hilaritatem. Apportant ultro citroque potionem Anglis gratam et
pene naturalem.[6] Contendebat liquor cum haustoribus, et quasi de
fonte scaturiens dampnis increscebat suis. 4. Crederes hidriam
farinae et lecithum olei quibus Sareptenam uiduam[7] ipse pascebat

---

[a] *One expects* hidromello (*cf. VW iii. 15. 2, where the genitive is given as* hidromelli)

[1] Cf. *Mir.*, p. 67 lines 136–7: 'illos nec in modico contristari sustineo'; *GP*, c. 44 (p. 71)
'nullum umquam tristem permitteret'; also *VW* iii. 8. 1, 19. 3, 25. 1.
[2] For similar stories, told of Wulfstan and Æthelwold, cf. *VW* iii. 15, and Wulfstan of
Winchester, *Vita S. Æthelwoldi*, c. 12 (see above, p. 129 n. 3). Another version in *Mir.*,
pp. 161–2, is attributed to 'auctor uitae beati Dunstani' (presumably Osbern, c. 15 (pp. 85–
7); but see above, p. xx).   [3] Cf. *VW* iii. 23. 2.
[4] i.e. the pious lady does not approve of such carousals.
[5] Cf. Virgil, *Aen.* i. 724 'uina coronant', *Georg.* ii. 528 'cratera coronant', *Aen.* i. 793
'spumantem pateram'. A similar echo in *GP*, c. 139 (p. 281).

his example to ensure that she did not falter. She pursued both ends assiduously, and neglected the care of her body in proportion as she devoted herself to them. Rewarding her affection, Our Lady granted her such grace that she would not have her saddened even in small matters.[1] To remove any doubt about this, I will add an instance.

12.[2] King Æthelstan, just in peace and victorious in war as no king has ever been, was proposing to come to Glastonbury. Æthelflæd got to know of this; she had always been generous, especially to the royal family, and she asked the king to deign to come to lunch with her. On learning of this request, the king felt great embarrassment. If he disobeyed her, he feared he would upset the pious lady; if he accepted, he was worried that her hospitality would be shown up as insufficient. 2. So, devising a plan to avoid refusing his niece's prayers and adding to his own embarrassment, he sent messengers to spy out the adequacy of the supplies available. They spurred their horses to eat up the miles that delayed their journey,[3] carried out their orders, and reported back that the hostess was well stocked in other respects, but very short on mead. If this deficiency could be remedied, there was nothing to stop the king complying with her wish. Learning of this, the lady—whose hopes of God knew no bounds—replied: 'May the holy Mother of Christ never wish that my lord the king avoid my house for lack of a drink like that.' 3. Straight on her word, she went into the church and asked the Virgin of her mercy to supply what she had purposely[4] omitted: *she* must fill up the barrel, *she* must crown the foaming glasses.[5] The miracle that immediately followed showed that her prayers had not been in vain. The king sat down to table, accompanied by his whole retinue. The servants bustled about, during and after the meal, to encourage the good cheer of the company with repeated rounds of drinks. Back and forth they brought the drink that is agreeable and even natural to an Englishman.[6] The liquor kept pace with those who gulped it down; it bubbled up as though from a spring, and grew with its own loss. 4. You might have supposed it 'the barrel of meal' and 'the cruse of oil' with which he [Elijah] who had come to be fed himself fed the widow of Zarephath.[7] But perhaps here was the greater miracle, a

---

[6] Eadmer, c. 8 (p. 176) ('medo'). English drinking habits are alluded to in *GR*, c. 245. 4 (more in *GR* Index s. v. England), and *GP*, cc. 139–40 (pp. 281–2).

[7] 3 Sam. (1 Kgs.) 17: 16. The parallel had already been drawn by Osbern, c. 15 (p. 87). Cf. *VW* iii. 15. 3.

qui pasci uenerat. Veruntamen nescias an hic maiore miraculo et excellentiore gratia, quia ibi unius sustentata est natura, istic multorum oppleta est gula. Sed profecto imitata est mater Domini filii miraculum in deserto, quando sub dentibus creuit panis, et maius augmentum inuenit in mensa quam in unda piscis.[1] Applausit rex miraculo per ministros cognito, nimietatem suam ultro inculpans, qua potuisset Ethelfleda premi si noluisset ei Maria opitulari.

13. Expedita re quae aliquantum deuiabat a proposito,[2] nunc eam aggrediar quae partem Dunstani spectat e proximo. Haec eadem matrona, decursa religiosissime presentis uitae meta, letalem ualitudinem iniit. Iamque morbus quatiebat uitalia, et illa, Dunstano quadam die accito, ad ingressum alterius seculi oratione et confessione animam composuit. Haec occupatio Sanctum auocauerat ne illa die uesperis monachorum interesset. Curis explicitis, cum dampnum sarcire uellet, ad aecclesiam cum scolasticis contendit. 2. Stabat ergo pro foribus clauigerum opperiens, et ecce porrectis in sullime oculis uidit alitem pernici uolatu aera secare. Diligentius intuitus animaduertit esse columbam scintillanti alarum plausu flammeam, intellexitque esse Spiritum sanctum, qui quondam eiusdem auis mutuatus simulacrum apud Iordanem descendit in Dominum Christum.[3] Laetis igitur luminibus tam gloriosam uisionem hauriens, acuto uolantem prosequebatur intuitu, donec tecto decumbentis uidit illapsum. Reflexo proinde pede, eo unde uenerat impigre reuertitur. 3. Pulsanti ostium patuit, sed murmur intra cortinam auditur,[a] gradum festinantis continuit. Interrogat ancillas forinsecus excubantes quisnam cum domina interius consereret sermones. Nichil illae certum referunt nisi quod nuperrime iubar splendidissimum domo infulgens omnem tenebrarum crassitudinem dispulerit. 'Et ex tunc' inquiunt 'usque modo, pretento ante nos uelo, loquitur cum aliquo.' Persistit pius explorator, aure apposita, donec cessaret sermocinatio alterna. Tum immissus cortinae domestica personam collocutoris percunctatur audatia. 4. At felix matrona uultu placido renitens 'Quasi uero tu' inquit 'non illum uideris de quo percunctaris! Ipse tibi pro foribus aecclesiae uisus est; ipse a me omnem huius

---

[a] *Perhaps read* auditum

---

[1] The reference is to the 'Feeding of the five thousand': Matt. 14: 15–21; Mark 6: 35–44; Luke 9: 12–17; John 6: 5–13.

[2] See i. 10. 5 n.

[3] At the baptism of Jesus: Matt. 3: 16; Mark 1: 10; Luke 3: 22.

more abounding grace; *there* the bodily needs of a single man were met, *here* the greed of a multitude was satisfied. But assuredly the Lord's Mother used as a model her Son's miracle in the desert, when bread grew beneath the teeth, and the fish increased more on the table than in the water.[1] The king applauded the miracle when his servants told him of it, and found fault with his own excessive demands, which would have been a burden to Æthelflæd if Mary had been unwilling to help her.

13. Now that I have finished with a matter that was a little aside from my plan,[2] I shall enter upon one that is directly concerned with Dunstan. This same lady, after running the race of this life in all devotion, fell desperately ill. The illness was shaking her to the core when she summoned Dunstan to her side one day and composed her soul with prayer and confession for entry into the other world. This had had the effect of diverting the saint from attending the monastery Vespers that day. But when he had done what he had to do, he formed the resolution of remedying his lapse, and hurried to the church with his pupils. 2. So it was that he found himself standing at the door, waiting for someone to bring the key, when lo and behold! as he looked up into the sky he saw a bird cutting its swift way through the air. On closer examination he saw that it was a dove of flame, its wings flickering with sparks; and he knew it to be the Holy Spirit, which once borrowed the form of that same bird to light on the Lord Christ by the Jordan.[3] He drank in this glorious sight with joyful eyes, and keenly followed the bird's flight until he saw it settle on the house where his friend lay ill. Then he retraced his steps, and hurried back the way he had come. 3. The door was opened at his knock, but he heard a murmur behind a curtain, and checked his step, for all his hurry. He asked the maids keeping watch by the door who it could be who was talking with their mistress inside. All they could say for sure was that just now a ray of brilliant light had blazed on the house and dispelled every trace of shadow. 'From then till now,' they said, 'she has been talking with someone, with a curtain separating us from her.' He persisted in his kindly enquiries, keeping an ear open till the conversation was over. Then he passed through the curtain, and with the freedom allowable to a close friend asked her who she had been speaking to. 4. The fortunate lady was unperturbed, her face glowing: 'As if you did not yourself see Him about whom you ask! It was He you saw at the door of the church; and it is He who has

mortis sollicitudinem demolitus est. Quapropter de hoc excessu nec
tibi nec ceteris amicis meis lamentandum censeo, quia non est haec
uitae amissio sed de captiuitate in libertatem migratio.[1] Tibi autem
spetiales gratias et ago et habeo, quoniam hanc beatitudinem meam
tuis monitis, tuis exemplis debeo. 5. Nec uero fructu laborum
tuorum excides, quoniam quod cum aliquanto labore in me seuisti
cum gaudio metes.[2] Hanc porro unam et supremam petitionem
dilectricis tuae, dilecte dilector, ne respuas, ut, cum aurora in
primos ortus eruperit, ad ingrediendum longum iter sacra unctione
et uiuifica communione me communias.' Dixit, et conualescente
morbo exercebatur. Nichil fuit ex his quod segniter impleret Dunstanus, omnium obsequiorum offitiis abeuntem animam prosecutus,
pulchro et mirabili prorsus ordine, ut, cum ille mane missam cantans
eam communicasset, ipsa supremum efflaret.

14. Defuncto interea Ethelstano rege, frater eius Edmundus successit
solio, annorum decem et octo adolescens. Qui, ut teneritudinem
aetatis maturiori firmaret consilio, beatissimum Dunstanum inter
primos optimates primum prefecit palatio. Non enim exciderat
animo amicitia tempore fratris cum eodem uiro federata. Herebant
menti prudentia in consilio, facundia in uerbo, constantia in facto.
Quocirca cum iam omnia nutum eius spectarent, citra rationem
putauit nisi cum eo participaret potestatem nouam cui ueterem
communicauerat amicitiam. Assensus est precibus rogantis Dunstanus, remansitque in curia, quae sunt Cesaris Cesari reddens et quae
sunt Dei Deo.[3] 2. Regem ergo et principes primo de iustitia
conuenire, nec ut flecterentur omnino sinere, post etiam inferiores
in eandem instruere formam, in delinquentes acrem exercere disciplinam. Nam et hoc non leui momento animos eius impulerat ut
regiis se commodaret precibus, quatinus Anglorum regno consuleret
et iam dudum laborante iustitia labefactatum in statum priscum
erigeret. Rigor igitur uiri, mentes procerum turbans, ignes irarum
quondam sopitos exsuscitauit, donec in immensum flamma excanduit. Ad nocumentum ergo eius nec temperabant palam conuitio nec
clam maledicto. 3. Furor arma ministrat:[4] inuenit ira quod confingat,
exculpit liuor quod arrodat. Et quia malignitas numquam complicibus
caret, cum per se tum per satellites regem temptantes in eandem

---

[1] Cf. *GP*, c. 148 (p. 287), spoken by the dying Wulfstan; also *GR*, c. 347. 12–15.
[2] Cf. Ps. 125(126): 5.   [3] See *VW* i. 1. 1 n.
[4] Virgil, *Aen.* i. 150. Cf. also *GP*, c. 66 (p. 124).

removed from me all anxiety about the death that faces me. So it is my judgement that neither you nor my other friends need lament this passing, for this is not to lose a life, but to journey from captivity into liberty.[1] But I must give you particular thanks, for I owe this my blessedness to your advice, to your example. 5. And you will not fail to receive the reward of your labours: what you have sown in me with some toil you will reap with joy.[2] But, beloved lover, do not spurn this one last request of one who loves you. At the first break of day, fortify me for my long journey with the holy unction and the communion that gives life.' She spoke, and was overcome by her increasing illness. None of this could Dunstan fail to carry out with a will. He did all he could for the departing soul; and it was a beautiful and even miraculous sequence of events that she breathed her last only after he had sung morning mass and given her communion.

14. Meanwhile King Æthelstan died. He was succeeded on the throne by his brother Edmund, a youth of eighteen. To give his own tender years the support of maturer judgement, he at first granted Dunstan a place among the highest nobles in charge of the palace. For he had not forgotten the friendship he had formed with him in his brother's time, and he well remembered his good sense in counsel, his eloquence, and his firmness in action. So now that everything was at his beck and call, he thought it senseless not to share his new power with one whom he had admitted to his intimacy of old. Dunstan yielded to his entreaties and stayed on in court, rendering to Caesar the things which are Caesar's and to God the things that are God's.[3] 2. At first he lectured king and nobles on justice, not allowing them to diverge at all from it. Later he instructed those of lower rank on the same lines, and exercised sharp discipline over delinquents. Indeed, one crucial factor in his decision to comply with the king's request was just the desire to look after the interests of the kingdom of the English, and, at a time when justice had long been under threat, to bring the tottering land back to its former state. So it came about that Dunstan's austere approach upset the nobility; he aroused fires of anger that had for some time been damped down, until the flame blazed out to terrible effect. They did not hesitate to abuse him in public or slander him privately, if it had the effect of hurting him. 3. Madness provided weapons:[4] anger found what it could invent, envy dug up what it could gnaw on. Malice never lacks an accomplice; and sometimes alone, sometimes using hirelings, they

traducunt sententiam. Postposito enim iure amicitiae, oblitus saltem humanae uerecundiae, iubet eum omnibus necessariis ablatis curia eliminari: stulte prorsus et proterue, quia nichil turpius est quam si cum eo bellum geras quocum familiariter uixeras. Hac tempestate Sanctus perculsus fluctuabat animo et sententiae ambiguo. Ita quippe hostes omnes aditus precluserant, omnes calles obsederant, ut ei ad Glastoniam commeatus non esset, quanuis nec ibi posset*a* commorari tuto, auerso a se regis animo.[1] 4. Res apud Ceddrum gerebatur. Erant ibi exterarum gentium legati,[2] quos Dunstanus conueniens eis hostiles exponit calumnias, implorans ut fortunas tutentur suas. Illi dignitate uiri et indignitate rei permoti, ciuilem induerunt animum, bona terrae suae maxima polliciti, si uellet comitari secum. Et profecto nisi Deus illius tempestatis soluisset nebulam, amisisset tunc Anglia lucem clarissimam. Sed enim statim in crastinum*b* serenior aura regis afflauit animum per Dei omnipotentis miraculum. Quod quatinus factum sit breuiter expediam.

15. Mons est in Ceddro arboribus opacus, decliui crescens super-cilio,[3] faucibus immane quantum patentibus. Ibi cerui et ceterae ferae uenatibus aptae[4] in preruptis posuere cubilia[5] saxis. Ad eas perse-quendas rex mane surrexerat, ingenita diuitum consuetudine[6] ut nichil putent uoluptuosius quam indulgere uenatibus. Canes ergo emissi copulis exciuerant feras lustris, inter quas ingenti corpore ceruum cursu insuperabilem, cornibus ramosis minacem.[7] Hunc alipede cursu per plana, per auia fugientem animosius rex perseque-batur. Iam fera decliuia percurrerat, iam in summum montis iugum euaserat. 2. Ibi quoque canibus terga eius uellicantibus, negata omni fugiendi copia, precipiti ad ima saltu compleuit fata. Nec uero rapacitas canum molliori mortis genere absumpta. Horum casu rex perterritus et equi rapiditatem frenare conatus, lusit operam,[8] uires consumpsit anhelas.[9] Nam nisui hominis repugnante bestia, habenae

---

a ibi posset *ed.*; ubi possit *Q*   *b* crastino *JG, c. 62 (without* in), *preferably*

[1] This detail is not in any of the earlier Lives, and may only be William's embroidery.
[2] They were apparently envoys from Otto I: see Stubbs in *Memorials*, p. xvii; Lapidge, 'B. and the *Vita S. Dunstani*', (above, p. xviii n. 32) p. 282; K. Leyser, 'The Ottonians and Wessex', in his *Communications and Power in Medieval Europe: The Carolingian and Ottonian Centuries*, ed. T. Reuter (London and Rio Grande, 1994), pp. 73–104, at 92–3.
[3] For *decliuis* cf. *GR*, c. 377. 5 n., for *supercilium* Virgil, *Georg.* i. 108, with the commentary by R. A. B. Mynors (Oxford, 1990), p. 24.
[4] Cf. Ovid, *Met.* iv. 302.   [5] Statius, *Theb.* ii. 37.

laid siege to the king and brought him over to their way of thinking. Edmund turned his back on what was owing to a friend, and forgot, even, the shame any man should feel; and he told Dunstan to pack his bags and leave the court. A stupid and wanton act, for nothing is worse than to wage war with a one-time intimate. Rocked by this storm, the saint was thrown into great perplexity; for his enemies had closed all approaches and blocked all routes in such a way that he could not gain passage to Glastonbury—though even there he had no chance of living in safety, now that the king had turned against him.[1]
4. The crisis came at Cheddar, where ambassadors from abroad were present.[2] Dunstan interviewed them, told them the slanders his enemies were hurling at him, and begged them to grant him their protection. They found the man worthy, his treatment unworthy, and were moved to kindness, promising him wealth in their land if he was ready to go with them. Indeed, if God had not dispersed the mists of that tempest, England would at that point have been deprived of its brightest light. But all at once, next day, a more favourable breeze blew on the king's heart, thanks to a miracle sent by God. I will tell you briefly how it came about.

15. There is a hill at Cheddar, dark with trees, and rising steeply to an overhang[3] where the gorge opens up alarmingly. There deer and other beasts fit for the chase[4] have made their lairs[5] among the sheer rocks. The king had risen early to hunt them, it being the inborn habit[6] of the rich to think nothing more exquisitely pleasurable than to indulge in the chase. So the hounds were slipped from their leashes, and started the animals from their lairs, among them a stag of great size, an unsurpassed runner and branched with threatening antlers.[7] It fled in its winged career over deserted plains, and hot in pursuit went the king. Now it had mounted the slope, and come to the highest ridge of the hill. 2. The dogs were still snapping at its back, and it had no hope of escape; with a headlong leap to the bottom of the gorge, it met its end. And the greedy hounds could not avoid an equally harsh fate. The king was terrified by their fall. He tried to rein back his swift steed. But to no avail: his efforts were wasted,[8] and he ran out of breath and strength.[9] For as the beast fought back against

---

[6] Cf. *GR*, c. 45. 1: 'familiari . . . et pene ingenita illi nationi consuetudine'.
[7] Cf. Virgil, *Ecl.* vii. 30.
[8] With 'lusit operam' cf. *GP*, p. 336 n. 6; *Mir.*, p. 123 line 339.
[9] Cf. Statius, *Theb.* xii. 600.

diruptae et procul disiectae. Ita conatu irrito equus furens regem sub ipsum hiatum fautium peruexit. Non tamen ille in tanto periculo sui oblitus, sensatas cogitationes uoluebat animo, et fortassis expromebat dicto:[1] se in proximis diebus nullum aliqua temerasse iniuria, nisi quod Dunstanum summa lesisset arrogantia, quod expulisset amicum curia, prius addictum quam conuictum, ante dampnatum quam auditum; (3) id se plane correcturum ex placito, si eum Deus ipsius meritis a presenti eximeret periculo. Tua Deus misericors gratia, tua Christe omnipotens clementia! Vix haec uel cogitauerat uel dixerat, et equus, iam positis in uoragine pedibus anterioribus, qui ante seuierat tirannico cursu superbius,[a] constitit oue placidius.

Haec res tantum apud Edmundum ualuit ut ex illa die in reliquum nullus in animo eius fuerit Dunstano gratiosior, nullus in regno gloriosior. Denique statim accitum benigno quidem respexit oculo, sed dissimulato paulisper animo iussit ut ascenso equo secum Glastoniam contenderet. 4. Quo ubi peruentum est, rex inclinatus ad preces de sua liberatione Deo recitauit grates. Comitabantur orationem[b] lacrimae ueris singultibus expromptae.[2] Quas ubi et ratione resorbuit et digito compescuit, auide beatam beati uiri dextram apprehendens grato eam demulsit osculo. Tum deinde, ut ueteris scriptoris uerba subitiam,[3] ducens eum ad sacerdotalem cathedram et eum imponens dixit: 'Esto istius sedis princeps potensque insessor,[c] et presentis aecclesiae fidelissimus abbas.'[4] Siquidem proxime episcopus factus fuerat abbas Elfricus successor Aldhuni.[5] Adiecit deinde rex quod quicquid necessariorum habitatoribus deesset ipse regia liberalitate suppleret. 5. Quibus uerbis nouus scriptor[6] indiscretionis, ut molliter dicam, arguitur, qui, ut alias dixi, dicit et repetit sanctum Dunstanum primum abbatem Glastoniae concedente rege monachos posuisse. Quid enim per cathedram sacerdotalem nisi sedes abbatis intelligitur, cui Dunstanus a rege

---

[a] ed.; superbus Q   [b] ed. (orationes is also possible); omnes Q   [c] Stubbs (cf. B. p. 25); incessor Q

[1] Cf. 3 below 'Vix haec uel cogitauerat uel dixerat'. More doubts about exact words (cf. ii. prol. 1); Osbern, c. 18 (p. 91), is doubtless the principal target, though even B., c. 14 (p. 24), has the king's alleged words.

[2] Cf. VW iii. 24. 1.

[3] B., c. 14 (p. 25). For the formula, see Stubbs in Memorials, p. lxxxiv.

[4] For the appointment, see AG, c. 55 (p. 114), with reference back to this passage ('ut ante dictum est'). The significance of this is discussed above, p. xv. King Edmund alludes to the appointment in a charter cited in GR, c. 143. 1.

the struggles of its rider, the reins broke and fell at a distance. Maddened by the king's fruitless efforts, the horse carried him to the very brink of the precipice. But he kept his nerve in the crisis, and thought rationally—perhaps even expressed his thoughts in words:[1] 'I have not these past days done injury to anyone, except that I harmed Dunstan with the utmost arrogance, expelling my friend from court, sentence preceding conviction, condemned before he was heard. 3. I will make full amends, if only God, for Dunstan's merits, saves me from this present peril.' Yours, God, the pity and grace, yours, Christ, the almighty power to save! He had scarcely thought or uttered these words when the horse, its front feet already over the edge, stopped still more peaceably than any sheep, where before it had been madder than a tyrant in full career.

This event made such an impression on Edmund that from that day on no one was closer to his heart, no one more honoured in his kingdom, than Dunstan. For instance, he sent for him at once and looked favourably on him; but he kept his intentions secret for a while. For the moment he told him to get on his horse and accompany him to Glastonbury. 4. Once there, the king bowed in prayer, giving thanks to God for his escape. Tears and sincere sighs accompanied his prayers.[2] The king controlled himself and brushed the tears away. Eagerly taking the saint's saintly right hand, he gave it a kiss of gratitude. Then—to quote the words of the old biographer[3]—he led him to the priestly chair, sat him in it, and said: 'Sit in this seat in supreme power, as the faithful abbot of this church.'[4] For very lately Ælfric, who was Ealdhun's successor,[5] had been made a bishop. The king then added that he would of his royal largesse make up any deficiencies in the necessaries of life that the monks might feel. 5. These words find a new biographer[6] guilty of (to put it mildly) carelessness; for, as I have remarked elsewhere, he says, and says again, that the holy Dunstan was the first abbot of Glastonbury, and settled monks there with the permission of the king. For what is to be understood by 'the priestly chair' if not the seat of the abbot, in which Dunstan is said to have been placed by the king? And how it came to

---

[5] Dunstan was made abbot in 940 (*Heads*, p. 50). The order of Glastonbury abbots prior to this date is difficult to establish. See J. A. Robinson, 'The Saxon abbots of Glastonbury', in his *Somerset Historical Essays* (London, 1921), pp. 26–53, and S. Foot, 'Glastonbury's early abbots', in *The Archaeology and History of Glastonbury Abbey*, ed. Abrams and Carley, pp. 163–89. For Ælfric's bishopric see below, p. 260 n. 3.

[6] Osbern (see above, i. prol. 4–5). William refers to the statements in Osbern, cc. 6 (p. 74), and 19 (p. 92).

impositus dicitur? Quae quomodo ibi sine monachis et abbate fuerit, dicat qui intelligit.

Ceterum quanti penderit Edmundus Glastoniam ab eo tempore notius est quam ut nostro indigeat illustrari relatu.[1] 6. Ob hunc in Deo fauorem arridebat ei omnis prosperitas et omnium bellorum inuicta felicitas. Denique et Northanimbros, magnum et gentile tumentes,[2] ita contudit ut omnem laborem successoribus suis abstulerit. Illud fuit tempus quo sanctus Odo Cantuariensis archiepiscopus ossa beati Wilfridi ab ea regione ablata[3] apud sedem suam aurea recondidit theca.[4] Quomodo autem et quo auctore reliquiae sanctorum ex Transhumbranis Glastoniam sint aduectae, in libro de antiquitate eiusdem aecclesiae occasione accepta inserere non pigebit, si Deus mentem meam ad quod intendo direxerit.[5]

16. At Dunstanus, regiae liberalitatis et amicitiae compos, monasterium Dei dignatione sibi concessum in summum prouehere contendit. Est ibi aecclesiae ligneae, ut ante dixi,[6] lapidea contermina, cuius auctorem Inam regem non falsa confirmat antiquitas.[7] Hanc ille adiecta turri ad multum spatium prorogauit, et ut latitudo longitudini conquadraret alas uel porticus quas uocant adiecit.[8] Ita uir industrius impendit operam ut, quantum antiquae structurae patiebatur scema, utrobique fieret ingens basilica. 2. Vbi etsi aliquid desideratur uenustae[a] pulchritudinis, nichil deest necessariae capacitatis. Cimiterium monachorum ab australi aecclesiae pariete maceria in multos pedes protenta inclusit. Ipsum spatium quadratis lapidibus excitauit in tumulum,[9] uideturque quasi pratum amenissimum ab omni

---

[a] Perhaps read uetustae (*there is play on the two words in Mir. p. 167, line 1655); and cf. Wulfstan's regrets at the destruction of Oswald's church in VW iii. 10. 3*

---

[1] Cf. *GR*, cc. 142–3, and c. 34. 3: 'notius est quam ut nostro indigeat illustrari relatu'.

[2] Statius, *Theb.* viii. 429; cf. *VW* i. 16. 1 n.

[3] *GP*, cc. 15, 109 (pp. 22, 244). The bones had been at Ripon.

[4] Eadmer, *Vita S. Wilfridi*, c. 63 (ed. B. J. Muir and A. J. Turner (Exeter, 1998), pp. 146–7), gives a detailed account of the translation, but says that the relics were located by Oda in the high altar, not in a 'golden shrine'. He continues by observing that the relics were re-translated by Lanfranc into a shrine (*scrinium*), then 'after a number of years . . . a tomb (*sepulcrum*) was constructed for them on the northern side of the altar'. William must be describing the second or third state of Wilfrid's remains.

[5] Referring to *AG*, cc. 21, 55 (pp. 68–9, 116–17, and 194 n. 55). The significance of this is discussed above, p. xv.

[6] The only previous reference is to the 'old church' at i. 1. 2, without further details. The account in *AG*, cc. 6, 40 (pp. 52–3, 94–5) is somewhat more complex.

[7] *AG*, c. 40 (pp. 94–5).

[8] These details are not in the earlier Lives, but may have come to William as part of

be there in the absence of monks or abbot is up to whoever understands it to explain.

But how great the store Edmund set by Glastonbury from that day on is too well-known to require my narration to publish it abroad.[1] 6. Because of this favour under God, every good fortune shone on him, and he enjoyed unmarred success in every war. For instance, he so crushed even the Northumbrians, 'for all the boastfulness of their race',[2] as to leave his successors no problems with them. That was the time when the holy Oda, archbishop of Canterbury, translated the bones of the blessed Wilfrid from that area,[3] and gave them a new home in a golden shrine in his see.[4] But how, and on whose authority, the relics of saints came to Glastonbury from beyond the Humber, I shall be happy to relate when the right moment arises in my book on the antiquity of the church, so long as God directs my mind to what I purpose.[5]

16. Dunstan was now assured of the king's generosity and friendship, and he proceeded to raise to new heights the monastery that God had seen fit to entrust to him. At Glastonbury, as I mentioned before,[6] there is, next to the wooden church, a stone one, whose founder is said by an old and reliable tradition to be King Ine.[7] Dunstan extended it greatly, adding a tower, and also, so that length and breadth should be in proportion, wings or what they call *porticus*.[8] The energetic Dunstan's aim was that, so far as the plan of the old structure allowed, the church should be vast on both sides. 2. And even if there is some deficiency in attractiveness, the space that was needed is not lacking. The monks' cemetery he enclosed with walling that extended many feet from the south wall of the church, raising its whole area into a mound revetted with the squared stone.[9] The

Glastonbury tradition. For Dunstan's church, see Taylor and Taylor, *Anglo-Saxon Architecture*, i. 251–5; Fernie, *Architecture of the Anglo-Saxons*, pp. 95–6; C. A. Ralegh Radford, 'Glastonbury abbey before 1184', pp. 117–22; Rahtz, *Glastonbury*, pp. 76–7. The excavated evidence corroborates William's account. For William's noticeable interest in church architecture, see *GR*, c. 228. 6 n., and R. A. Brown, 'William of Malmesbury as an architectural historian', in his *Castles, Conquests and Charters: Collected Papers* (Woodbridge, 1989), pp. 227–34.

[9] Again, these details are not in the earlier Lives. For the sanctity of the churchyard, see *AG*, c. 18 (pp. 66–7) = *GR*, c. 20. 3. William's wording is obscure. It seems that the 'quadratae lapides' were what the 'maceria' was made of, and that Dunstan raised the ground level of the cemetery within, presumably because it was full (cf. i. 10. 2). So Taylor and Taylor, *Anglo-Saxon Architecture*, i. 251, Ralegh Radford, 'Glastonbury abbey before 1184', p. 123, and J. P. Carley, *Glastonbury Abbey* (London, 1988), pp. 11, 149, 152, 178.

ambulantium strepitu alienum, ut merito de sanctis ibi pausantibus dici queat: 'Corpora eorum in pace sepulta sunt.'[1]

17. Itaque ob preconium religionis eius, quae dulci compatriotarum fines impleuerat aura, undatim ad eius disciplinam confluebant homines. Suscipiebat ille omnes et offerebat Deo, promouens eos tam uerbo quam exemplo. Dedit felix emolumentum diuinitas magistri doctrinae et auditorum obedientiae, dum ex eodem grege abbatibus electis multae per Angliam et emendatae et fundatae sunt abbatiae. Quid dico de abbatibus? Episcopi et archiepiscopi, de conuentu illo procedentes, dederunt orbi Britannico[2] inditium quale de Dunstano mundus deberet habere iuditium.

2. Vnum pro exemplo Athelwoldum aduoco, quia de pluribus dicere in immensum esset pergere. Is nec iners nec imprudens nec preterea tenuis patrimonii clericus, cum multa monasteria uoluntati eius occurrerent quae illum obuiis manibus exciperent, solum omnium mortalium Dunstanum suae uitae consiliarium elegit, illius commilitium, illius contubernium desiderans, ei conuiuere, ei commori exestuans. Venit ergo Glastoniam, et ibi grammaticam artemque metricam edoctus, postremo etiam monachus factus monachi uigilauit in actus.[3] Cuius religio quantum conferret mundo Deus ipse ostendit Dunstano ueraci et perspicuo somnio.
3. Visus[4] est sibi uidere infra septa monasterii arborem patulis ramis omnem Angliam obumbrantem, ramos omnes monachilibus tunicis onustos, in summo culmine unam latitudine sui ceteras obuelantem. Dunstanus, uisionis subtilitatem discernere impotens, ducem uenerandae ut uidebatur canitiei presbiterum consulendum putauit. Ille remotis ambagibus dilucide omnia prosecutus est. 'Arbor' ait 'est haec insula. Maior cuculla est Athelwoldi monachi tui religiosa gratia. Ceterae sunt multorum monachorum animae, quas ille contra diabolum religionis suae uelo et quodam iustitiae defendet umbraculo.'[5] Hanc uisionem abbas tunc quidem silentio dedit, sed cum uidisset spem suam, quam de Athelwoldo taciturnus alebat, in effectum procedere, non dubitauit quae uiderat multis coram ingerere. 4. Secutus est rerum effectus caeleste oraculum, tantaque ac tot per illum uirum, postea Wintoniensem episcopum, constructa

---

[1] Ecclus. 44: 14.

[2] For the phrase 'orbi Britannico' and similar expressions, see *GR*, c. 54. 1 n.

[3] 'monachus . . . actus' is almost a complete hexameter.

[4] The dream is from Wulfstan of Winchester, *Vita S. Æthelwoldi*, c. 38 (pp. 56–7). It is also told in *GP*, c. 75 (pp. 165–6).

impression given is of a delightful meadow, free of the noise of any footstep. Truly can it be said of those who rest here in their holiness: 'Their bodies are buried in peace.'[1]

17. So as a result of the fame of his way of life, which had filled the country as with a sweet breath, men flocked to be taught by him. He welcomed them all, and dedicated them to God, advancing them by word and example. God granted a happy reward to the master's teaching and the obedience of his pupils, for from this flock abbots were chosen, and as a result abbeys founded and restored throughout England. Why do I say merely abbots? Bishops and archbishops from that house gave to Britain[2] an indication of what sort of judgement the world should pass on Dunstan.

2. I cite one example, that of Æthelwold, for it would be an enormous task to try to cover more. He was a cleric neither lazy nor foolish, and possessed too of no small fortune. Though many monasteries were available to his choice and ready to receive him with open arms, he chose from among all men Dunstan as counsellor for his life, desiring to serve and dwell with him, thirsting to live and die with him. So he came to Glastonbury, learned grammar and metre there, and finally became a monk and took up a monk's duties.[3] God himself showed Dunstan, in a clear and true dream, how much Æthelwold's vocation would contribute to the world. 3. He dreamed[4] that he saw, within the monastery precinct, a tree that shaded all England with its spreading branches. All the branches were laden with monks' tunics; but one of them, at the very top, shrouded the rest, so wide was it. Dunstan was unable to solve the riddle of this vision, and thought it best to consult his guide, a priest with (as it seemed in the dream) venerable grey hair. His clear exposition went through every detail, leaving no uncertainty. 'The tree,' he said, 'is this island. The largest cowl is the religious grace of your monk Æthelwold. The rest are the souls of many monks which he will defend against the Devil with the veil of his religious belief and a kind of umbrella of justice.'[5] The abbot for the time being suppressed his dream; but when he saw the hopes he silently nurtured for Æthelwold coming to fruition, he did not hesitate to press what he had seen upon many ears. 4. The prophecy from heaven was fulfilled, and so many great monasteries were built thanks to this man, who was afterwards

[5] Not from Wulfstan of Winchester. See *Mir.*, p. 172 line 1793, for another instance of *umbraculum*.

sunt monasteria quanta ut aggrediatur nullius regis modo spirare ausit industria. Sed de his contraham stilum, ne uideatur uagari extra propositum, quanuis a meta dicendi haec relatio non exorbitauerit, cum deceat abbatem subiectorum bona prouehere et prosperitates animo presagire.[1] Quocirca hoc de uita eiusdem Athelwoldi sumptum quo minus apponerem non abstinui, quia, ut scriptum est, 'Gloria patris est filius sapiens'.[2] Omnia ergo Athelwoldi benefacta in Dunstanum redundant, quorum fructum eo gratiosius tulit quo cumulatius semen in alterum transfudit.

18. Horum ergo et similium bonorum fundamenta Dunstanus probe iatiebat in Glastonia.[3] Sed enim antiquus hostis sepenumero aperta monstrabat impudentia quantus eum de presentibus liuor angeret, quantus de futuris timor torqueret. Armatus enim feralibus et malitiae suae congruis simulacris, beluinosque indutus uultus, crebris eum fatigabat impulsibus. Denique nocte quadam orantem ter appetiit, trium ferarum figuram ementitus.[4] 2. Primo uisus ursus hians et horrendis hispidus setis, secundo canis premisso latratu toruos in eum rictus irritans, tertio ganniens uulpecula dolosaque alludens cauda. Quibus omnibus Christi signo in fugam actis, non solum non motus sed etiam materiam laetitiae nactus est. Seueritatem quippe frontis risu soluens, ultro iniecit hosti obprobrium quod spetiem mutuaretur ferarum: ille qui quondam par Deo appetisset fastigium nunc se ostenderet in urso seuum et sanguinarium, improbum et ingratum in cane, uersipellem et mendacem in uulpe.

19. Confusus diabolus de Sancti uictoria, consilia, ut credi fas est, uoluebat uersuta. Et quoniam uigilanti non preualuerat, arbitratus fortassis, si solutis in somnum sensibus eum adoriretur, leui negotio cessurum, has non neglexit insidias. Sedebat ille quadam nocte ante beati Georgii martiris altare[5] et exercitio psalmodiae nocturnas protelabat excubias. Peccauit in psallentem lassitudo, quae paulisper eum dormitare coegit. Iamque somno in oculos serpente et summissis palpebris nutabat mento, cum affuit ille cui nulla festinatior est

---

[1] Cf. *VW* ii. 16. 1.

[2] Jerome, *Epist.* lii. 7, also quoted in *GR*, c. 54. 6.

[3] For the sources of the miracles in 18 and 19, see below, pp. 235 n. 10, 236 n. 1, 237 n. 2.

[4] Another multiple attack is recounted in *Mir.*, p. 97.

[5] A shrine of St George was given by Brihtwold, bp. of Ramsbury (1005–45), a former monk of Glastonbury: *AG*, c. 68 (pp. 138–9).

bishop of Winchester, that no king nowadays would be bold enough
to undertake such a task. But I will forbear to write further on this
subject in case I should seem to be digressing, though in fact this
story has meant no swerving aside from the goal of my book, for an
abbot should always try to advance the good of his subjects and have a
presentiment of their successes.[1] That is why I have not hesitated to
add here a detail from the Life of Æthelwold, for, as it is written, 'the
glory of the father is a wise son'.[2] Thus all Æthelwold's good deeds
reflect on Dunstan, who welcomed their fruit the more warmly
because he had sown the seed so lavishly in another.

18. Thus Dunstan laid the foundation for these and similar good
things in his fine work at Glastonbury.[3] But the Old Enemy
frequently showed with open shamelessness how much he was
pained by envy at present happenings and tortured by fear for the
future. Armed with the likeness of wild animals very appropriate to
his evil character, and putting on beast-faces, he often tried to wear
him out with his assaults. For instance, one night as he was praying,
the Devil attacked him three times, pretending to the appearance of
three animals.[4] 2. First he looked like a bear, jaws wide open, shaggy
with bristles; second, he was a dog, sending his barks before him and
savagely snarling at Dunstan; third, he was a yelping fox, wagging his
tricky tail. All three apparitions Dunstan put to flight with the sign of
the Cross. He was not merely unmoved: he won from his victory
cause for happiness. For he relaxed his severe brow in a smile, took
the offensive, and taunted the enemy for borrowing animal shapes: he
who had once coveted a height equal to God was now reduced to
showing himself as a bear, savage and bloody, as a dog, wicked and
disagreeable, and as a fox, crafty and lying.

19. The Devil was confounded by the saint's victory, and (as we may
suppose) started to turn cunning plots over in his mind. And because
he had failed with Dunstan when awake, and thinking that he might
yield easily enough if he were to attack him while asleep, he tried that
approach. Dunstan was sitting one night before the altar of the
blessed martyr George,[5] keeping the night watch by going through
the psalms. Tiredness sinned against him as he sang, and he could not
help dropping off for a while. As sleep crept over his eyes, his eyelids
drooped, and his chin was ready to fall on to his breast. Then the Evil
One arrived—he whose favourite occupation is to plot against a good

uoluptas quam ut bono uiro machinetur insidias. 2. Villosam enim ursi spetiem assumens et pedibus super ambos humeros insistens, pestifero hiatu minari et unguibus arpagare uisus est. Timor quietem depulit, statimque arrepto quem pro more gerebat baculo, dum informe portentum percutere conatur inanes uentilauit auras. Ictus uero non cassis uiribus in lapidem proximum delatus terribilis stridore soni aecclesiam impleuit. Ita interruptum psalmodiae ordinem continuans, ubi dimiserat incepit: 'Exsurgat Deus et dissipentur inimici eius, et fugiant qui oderunt eum a fatie eius.'[1] Quibus uerbis se notatum intelligens hostis, exuit formam alienam et recepit suam. Namque nebulosa obtectus fuligine, uisus est paulatim ante oculos uiri in subtilem aerem euanescere.

20. Nocturno aggressui diurnae successere insidiae. Habuerat hic Sanctus fratrem, Wlfricum nomine, bonae religionis laicum. Huic exteriorum curam delegauerat,[2] ut ipse ab omni strepitu causarum feriatus auidius caelestia gaudia prelibaret.[3] Wlfricus fideliter et grate offitium exsecutus uitae dies expleuit. At Dunstanus germanae necessitudinis pietate deuinctus funus honorifice curari iussit. Monachi omnes, ut patri morem gererent, communem dolorem priuato luctui accommodarunt. 2. Itaque quidam ut corpus adueherent longe profecti, quidam ut acciperent extra septa progressi, cenobium uacuefecerant. Solus pater remansit, cum puero qui aeuo accedente factus episcopus huiusce relationis index fuit. Lento ergo gradu intra atrium quod supra dixi[4] spatiabantur, aduentum, ut credo, monachorum prestolantes, et ecce, dubium quo euentu, uelut funda emissus ingens lapis stridulas euerberans auras in Dunstani caput uenit. Nec uero ille preuidit ictum uel precauit, sed Deus ab eo auertit. Nam citra ullam lesionem capitis pilleo excusso lapis longe ruit. Bone Deus! quid hoc monstri fuit? Mortales cuncti aberant, de puero porro nulla suspitio. 3. Nam quomodo ei fuisset saxum iaculabile, quod cum sibi Dunstanus afferri iussisset uix potuit humo tollere? Preterea forma, Sumersetensi*[a]* pago incognita, omnem de hominibus suspitionem purgabat. Quapropter demonis fuisse missile telum[5] Sanctus et intellexit et dixit, qui suae inuideret

---

[a] *ed.*; Summertensi *Q*

[1] Ps. 67(68): 2.

[2] Cf. *GR*, c. 271. 1: 'prefeceratque rebus forensibus' (= *GP*, c. 132 (p. 271)), and M. Lapidge, 'Abbot Germanus, Winchcombe, Ramsey and the Cambridge Psalter', in *Anglo-Latin Literature 900–1066*, pp. 387–417, at 406 n. 81.

man. 2. He took on the appearance of a shaggy bear, stood with his paws on both Dunstan's shoulders, and seemed to be threatening him with his terrible jaws and tearing at him with his claws. Fright drove sleep away. Dunstan snatched up his usual staff, and swished it through the empty air in an attempt to hit the hideous monster. The blow was not unrewarded; it struck a stone nearby, and echoed terribly through the church. Dunstan continued his psalm-singing at the point where he had been interrupted: 'Let God arise, let His enemies be scattered: let them also that hate Him flee before Him.'[1] The Enemy realized that these words were aimed at him, and giving up his borrowed form he resumed his own. Surrounded by a cloud of sooty smoke, he gradually disappeared into thin air before Dunstan's eyes.

20. Upon this night attack followed ambush by day. The saint had had a brother, called Wulfric, a layman of sound principle. To him he had delegated responsibility for affairs outside the monastery,[2] so that he himself could stay free from all the babble of business and have a more lavish foretaste of the joys of heaven.[3] Wulfric did his job loyally and agreeably, and then died. Dunstan felt bound by the ties of brotherly affection, and ordered a ceremonious funeral. To please their father, the monks to a man added their shared grief to his private laments. 2. As a result they had emptied the monastery: some had gone far afield to fetch the body, others had ventured outside the precinct to welcome it on its arrival. Only the abbot stayed behind, along with a boy who grew up to be a bishop and to witness to this story. Well, they paced slowly about the yard I mentioned before,[4] awaiting, I imagine, the arrival of the monks. Suddenly, who knows by what chance, a great stone screeched through the air as though a sling had sent it on its way, and came for Dunstan's head. He did not see it coming, and could not take steps to avoid it; but God diverted it away from him. Indeed, though it knocked off his hat, it caused no damage to his head, and fell some way away. Good God! What kind of portent was this? Everyone was away, and no one could suspect a child. 3. For how could he have flung a stone which he could hardly lift off the ground when Dunstan asked it to be brought to him? What is more, the type of stone, unknown in Somerset, cleared *men* of suspicion. Dunstan knew, and affirmed, that this was from the armoury[5] of the Devil, who resented a

---

[3] Similar wording in *GP*, c. 19 (p. 28).   [4] Presumably i. 10. 2.
[5] Cf. Virgil, *Aen.* x. 773. 'missile', already in B., c. 18 (p. 28), served to remind William of the quotation.

saluti, quam seruire uideret multorum profectui. Assignauit tamen cautelae lapidem perditum iri non debere, ut hostiles insidias monachi tanto cauerent promptius quanto earum formam conspicarentur presentius.

21.[1] Interea suprema dies regis Edmundi mortis pulsabat ianuam, accitusque nescio qua de causa Dunstanus uenit ad curiam. Pergebant[2] ex more de uilla in uillam, quod unus locus diu tantam non sustineret frequentiam. Adequitabat Sancto dux Elfstanus,[3] et serebatur inter eos sermo uarius, cum Dunstanus, porrectis ad agmen tubicinum[4] oculis, uidit demonem histrionicos motus agere, gesticulari et saltare, quasi plane ipsum deceret inter eiusmodi artifices esse. Diu hesit obtutu intento petulantiam hostis ammiratus. 2. Mox ducem percunctatus an idem ille uideret, ubi eum nichil preter solitum uidere intellexit, 'Signa,' inquit, 'uir illustrissime, signa oculos tuos crucis signaculo, si forte possis uidere quod uideo.' Paruit is et non distulit; nec mora, lux adeo clara bruta prius exacuit lumina ut non minus quam ipse Sanctus conspicaretur impudentis monstri saltus. Inde abbas malum regi ominatus mortem eius non quidem aperto sed suspenso prodidit uaticinio. Tum pretenta cruce et disparente fantasmate, protulit dux in medium proximae noctis somnium: (3) uisum sibi regem inter medios conuiuii strepitus obdormiscere, proceres omnes in hircos et capras mutatos esse. Corripuit uerbum Dunstanus ab ore loquentis,[5] et subiecit: 'Dormitio ergo regis mors est. Mutatio procerum in petulcas pecudes est eorum uita putida et lasciua perfidia.'[6] Mirum id dictu et uerum! Nam partem prophetiae in tempora regis Edwii fortuna distulit, partem continuo in effectum rapuit. Quod nimirum palam fecit eodem die repetita demonis uisio et inter cenantes discursatio. Haec adeo Sanctus preclare uidebat et ostendebat ut a quibusdam putaretur uel male credere uel parum prospere mente ualere.

4. Iam[7] lux fatalis illuxerat, et rex auditis offitiis ad curam corporis ab aecclesia in aulam festinabat. Ibi obuius quidam Dunstano rotulam

---

[1] The story is also told in *GR*, c. 144, 'Communi . . . benefitii' verbatim as the **CB** version. See note ad loc.

[2] i.e. the royal court. The subsequent anecdote occurs while Dunstan is at the itinerant court, not on his way to it.

[3] A man of this name was 'dux' in Wiltshire in 931 and 934: he witnessed S416, 425.

[4] The trumpeters are called 'regios' by B., c. 31 (p. 44), that is, they were part of the king's entourage, not Dunstan's.

[5] See above, p. 100 n. 2.　　　　　　　　　　　　　　[6] Cf. B., c. 32 (p. 45).

life that he saw giving so much to others. But as a precaution he laid down that the stone should not be disposed of, so that the monks should be the more careful of the Enemy's tricks because they had an instance of them constantly before their eyes.

21.[1] Meanwhile the last day of King Edmund was at hand, and he was knocking at death's door. For some reason Dunstan had been summoned to court. They[2] travelled as usual from vill to vill, because a single place could not endure the burden of so great a company for very long. With the saint rode Ealdorman Ælfstan,[3] and they were carrying on a conversation on various topics when Dunstan happened to glance at the column of trumpeters.[4] There he descried the Devil making such movements as an actor might, gesturing and dancing about, as though he was quite qualified to join such a troupe of players. Dunstan stared long in wonder at the impudence of the Enemy. 2. Then he asked the ealdorman if he could see the same as he could. But realizing *he* saw nothing out of the ordinary, he said: 'My lord, sign your eyes with the mark of the Cross, and perhaps then you will see what I see.' Ælfstan obeyed without a pause, and at once so clear a light sharpened eyes previously dim that he no less than the saint could make out the capers of the shameless monster. The abbot knew that this boded sure ill for the king, and foresaw his death, though he did not at once reveal his thoughts. Then, after the apparition had disappeared at the sign of the Cross, the nobleman revealed a dream he had had the night before: (3) the king had gone to sleep amid the racket of a feast, and all the nobles had changed into goats, male and female. Dunstan took up his words[5] and answered: 'The king going to sleep is his dying. The changing of the great men into randy beasts is their disgusting life and wanton lack of faith.'[6] A remarkable and true saying! Part of the prophecy was put off by fate till the times of King Eadwig, but part was fulfilled at once. And this was made public when the Devil reappeared the same day, prancing among the dinner guests. The saint saw and pointed all this out so lucidly that some thought he was either heretical or not right in the head.

4. Now[7] dawned the fatal day, and the king, having heard mass, hurried away from the church to his court to attend to the needs of his body. There someone came up to Dunstan, carrying a roll written

[7] *GR* (c. 144) also gives dark hints about the story of the king's death at Pucklechurch.

undique perscriptam manu gestitabat. Consultus quis esset, respondit Anglice, iuxta polite ut indigena, ex orientali regno se uenisse, quaedam se regi secreto communicanda deferre. Ei nuntiatus iussusque introduci, reperiri non potuit. Hac de causa questione inter aulicos orta, dum res diligentius disquiritur positis mensis rex discubuit. Adduxerat eo funesta sors quendam sicarium, quem quondam uiolatarum legum reum patria expulerat. 5. Hunc intuitus Edmundus, ira preferuidus et animum continere impotens, nemini quicquam dicens, in capillos inuolat. Latrunculus, qui ad tale infortunium se parauerat, sica uelociter extracta regem antequam a satellitibus accurri posset confodit. Exiuit in orbem fabula, magno dedecore Angliae, quod nulla possit emendare memoria. Communi ergo decretum consilio et funus Glastoniam delatum, ibique in aquilonali parte turris magnifice humatum. Id eum uoluisse pro familiari abbatis amicitia per nonnulla claruerat inditia. Data in inferias uilla in qua occubuerat, ut quae semel conscia fuerat homicidii, semper in posterum pro anima eius esset adiutrix benefitii.

22. Quia[1] uero filii Edmundi pro aetate puerili ad regnandum non uidebantur idonei, substituerunt proceres Edredum, ut regnaret loco fratrum suorum, uirum paci et iustitiae accommodum, hominibus morigerum et iocundum, Deo deuotum non minus pene quam monachum. Temptabat eum frequenter improspera ualitudo, et uehementer ad patientiam exercebat. Nam preter alia quibus cotidianis horis anhelabat ad exitum, interraneorum maxime cruciatu uexabatur, cibum omnem stomacho nausiante reitiens. 2. Annis ergo nouem in regno non tam uixit quam uitam traxit, totius corporis tormentis infractus et debilis. Quapropter Dunstanum, qui eum primus in regem acclamauerat,[2] et aliis et sibi[3] prefecit, ut pro scientia imperitaret regno, pro religione mederetur incommodo. Preterea quicquid pretiosissimum mortales opinantur eius delegauit tutelae, thesauros ab antecessoribus elaboratos et sibi hereditario iure transfusos. Suscepit ille et suo reposuit monasterio, non auri spetie captus sed depositoris amore deuinctus. 3. Tunc iustitiae normam per totum regnum extendere, et quae ultra uagarentur seuere simul et

---

[1] On Eadred's illness and death, see *GR*, c. 146. 2 and nn.
[2] Apparently based upon B., c. 19 (p. 29).
[3] Cf. Adelard, lect. iv (p. 56): 'tam se quam omne commisit imperium'.

all over. Asked who he was, he replied in English as urbanely as any Englishman, that he had come from a kingdom to the east and brought information that the king must hear in private. He was announced to the king and instructions were given for him to be brought in; but then he failed to appear. The courtiers were puzzled, and they were making careful enquiries on the matter when the king sat down to dine. Ill luck had brought that way a murderer, once banished the kingdom for breaking the law. 5. Edmund caught sight of him. Livid with rage, and unable to control himself, he said nothing to anyone, but went straight for the man's hair. The desperado had prepared himself for such an eventuality. He drew his dagger in a flash, and stabbed the king before any of his train could intervene. The story got out, to the great disgrace of England: a stain that no passage of time (?) can expunge. A decree was issued in common council, and the body taken to Glastonbury, where it was buried with every honour in the north part of the tower. Edmund had desired this, as was clear from various indications, because of his close friendship with the abbot. The vill where he had been killed was made an offering for the dead, so that having once witnessed his murder it might be for ever a source of spiritual benefit to his soul.

22. Because[1] Edmund's sons were too young to be thought suitable to reign, the nobles put up Eadred to be king in succession to his own brothers: a man of peace and justice, affable and compliant to men, and towards God almost as devout as any monk. He was often plagued by ill health, which stretched his endurance to the limits. For apart from other complaints that made him long for death every hour of the day, he was particularly tormented by internal pains, and brought up all his food from his nauseous stomach. 2. So for nine years on the throne he did not live so much as cling to life, broken and weakened by pain throughout his body. So it was that he put Dunstan, who had been the first to hail him king,[2] in charge both of others and of himself,[3] hoping that he would of his wisdom rule the kingdom and of his devotion cure his ill-health. Further, he handed over to his guardianship all that men think of most value, the treasures so laboriously acquired by his predecessors and passed down to him as heir. Dunstan took them and stored them in his monastery; it was not that he was allured by the sight of all that gold, rather that he was bound by love for him who entrusted it to his care. 3. Then he made justice hold sway through the whole kingdom, pruning severely and in good time everything that

oportune recidere. Pati nullum peccatis insolescere, cunctis primum*a*
Dei iuditium, secundo legum uigorem proponere: cuncta regis gratiae,
regis fidei attribuens, magnis suis laboribus commoda eius sepe
nundinatus; Dei timorem semper pre oculis habens, nichil quod eum
offenderet in se regnare permittens. Sciebat enim scriptum 'Deum
timete, regem honorificate'.[1] Nec minus Edredus grato benefatienti
concurrebat animo, nec umquam eum aliquis ullo potuit concutere
maledicto, ut existimaret*b* praue de Dunstano. 4. Aderat ille pene
semper et mansitabat in palatio, quanuis eius curam cuncta in Anglia
expectarent negotia; adeo eum amor regis sibi deuinxerat ut ne puncto
quidem temporis abesse pateretur. Frequenter etiam captatis occasio-
nibus cum in eum tum in sibi subiectos perliberalis et munificus fuit.
Denique Athelwoldum, de quo supra dixi,[2] Glastonia extractum in
abbatem Abbendoniensem prouexit, multa de suo uiro largitus;
tantumque amori eius detulit ut raro stipatus satellite ipse per se ad
monasterium uenire officinasque monachorum metiri non erubesceret.

23. Iam uero relatu arduum est quotiens Dunstano ut episcopatum
dignaretur suaserit nec persuaserit.[3] De duobus narrare suffitiet.
Ethelgari Cridiensis episcopi senis anima, uetustate corporis deposita,
in iuuentam aquilae transierat.[4] Eius locum Edredus per Dunstanum
supplere conatus plurimas in irritum fudit preces. Excusationis eius
ratio fuit in causa quod dominum regem, et debilem et presertim sui
amantem, occasione tam longinqui episcopatus deserere uideretur
barbari et minime mitis animi; preterea rem esse magni oneris et se
minimae religionis, nec expedire ut episcopatum accipiat nondum
patientibus meritis. 2. Ne tamen nichil pro rege, qui tam prona
deuotione amori suo deditus erat, facere uideretur, de consilio suo
electus est Alfwoldus,*c* qui maturis moribus iuuenis sedi succederet
boni senis. Hoc consilio rex deiectus molimen alterum aggreditur.
Nam Elphego Wintoniensi episcopo, de quo supra diximus,[5] ad
felicem quietem composito, res suggerere uidebatur ne Dunstanus
ulterius petenti regi negaret assensum. Nam et ipse Sanctus rudimenta
religionis in eadem urbe conceperat, et Edredus episcopali aecclesiae

---

a *One expects* primo   *b* *Stubbs*; exintimaret *Q*   *c* *ed.*; Alwoldus *Q*

[1] I Pet. 2: 17.
[2] i. 17. 2–4. Cf. Wulfstan of Winchester, *Vita S. Æthelwoldi*, cc. 11 and (for the building) 12; *GP*, c. 88 (p. 191).
[3] *GP*, c. 25 (p. 40): 'suasit et persuasit'.
[4] Ps. 102(103): 5. Æthelgar was bp. 934–952/3.   [5] i. 7.

strayed out of line. He allowed no one to grow accustomed to sinning, and placed before the eyes of all first the judgement of God and second the rigour of the law. All this he ascribed to the king's good will, and the king's piety; and he often bought Eadred's advantage at the price of his own labours. He always kept in view his fear of God, allowing to reign over himself nothing that would offend Him. For he knew that it is written: 'Fear God, honour the king.'[1] Equally Eadred, in gratitude for his services, was glad to fall in with his wishes, and no one's slander could cause him to think ill of Dunstan. 4. The abbot was almost always at his side, and lived in the palace, though all the business of England clamoured for his attention. For the king in his love for him had so attached him to himself that he would not let him be away for a second. Often, too, he seized every opportunity to be generous and munificent towards Dunstan and his flock. For instance, Æthelwold, of whom I have spoken before,[2] he removed from Glastonbury and promoted to be abbot of Abingdon, giving him much from his own store; and so greatly did he love him that with but a small retinue he did not blush to come of his own volition to the monastery and help measure out the monastic buildings.

23. It is hard work to tell how often Dunstan was asked by the king to become a bishop, but would not be persuaded.[3] Two instances will suffice. The soul of the old bishop of Crediton, Æthelgar, had laid aside its ancient body and passed into an eagle's youth.[4] Eadred wanted to replace him with Dunstan, but very many were the prayers he wasted. His reason for declining was that it looked like an act of cruelty, even barbarity, to desert, in favour of so distant a see, his lord king, in all his weakness, and especially when he loved him so much. Further, the job was burdensome, and he himself (he said) was a man of little religious standing: it was improper for him to accept a bishopric before his merits could support it. 2. But so as not to seem to be altogether failing the king, who was so devotedly affectionate towards him, his was the counsel by which Ælfwold was elected, a young man of mature character succeeding a good old man. The king, thwarted in this plan, tried another. Ælfheah bishop of Winchester, of whom I have spoken earlier,[5] came to a peaceful and happy end, and everything seemed to suggest that Dunstan would not refuse the king a second time. For the saint had himself taken his first steps towards religion at that city, and Eadred had put his mind to distinguishing the cathedral there. For, to employ the words of the

honorificandae mentem addixerat. Quippe, ut uerba illius qui uitam
sancti Athelwoldi composuit,[1] apponam, erat rex 'ueteris in Wintonia
cenobii spetialis amator et defensor, ut plura testantur' quae ibi larga
manu contulit; (3) 'qui etiam, si uita comes esset, orientalem porticum
eiusdem aecclesiae auratis imbricibus adornare disposuerat.' Ad hunc
ergo episcopatum Dunstanum sullimare intendens, sed pudori suo
consulens ne iterum repulsam pateretur, simulque sciens quantum
femina ualeat uiriles animos tentare uiresque inflectere, Elfgiuae[a] [2]
matri suae opus iniungit. Monentis fuit sermo ut Dunstanum communem amicum, tutorem unicum, precibus ad suscipiendum episcopatum
impelleret: id conuescens faceret, quo facilius hilaritas conuiuii et
astantium frequentia eum a sententia negandi deduceret. 4. Illa,
quae non minore dignatione Sanctum suspiceret, nescio etiam an ei
maiori dilectione obnoxia esset, adornat probe conuiuium, adornato
amicum introducit, affectat blanditias, sermones componit, precibus
pulsat, promissis onerat, postremo quantum femina, quantum amans,
quantum regina potest aggreditur. Sed parum procedit, parum aut
nichil ille omnibus his motus urget propositum, rationes quas predixi
allegans. Nec uero adhuc illa desineret nisi Sanctus nonnichil stoma-
chatus diceret: 'Certissimum tibi, domina, constet quod numquam in
diebus filii tui ero episcopus.' Quo dicto et reginae silentium et sibi
otium indulsit.

24. Et quidem tanta placidi uiri ex intentione boni procedebat
obstinatio, sed eam minus Deo placere sequentis noctis ostendit
uisio. Qua etiam luce clarius constitit quanta illum semper gratia
miseratio diuina preuenerit. Adhuc puero senex in somnis apparens
Glastoniam per eum reparandam promiserat. Iuueni aeque iuuenis
uisus ad summos eum gradus prouehendum predixerat.[3] Nunc uero,
ut omne uisionum suarum eluctaretur inuolucrum, soluit ipse Deus
per apostolos suos omne ambiguum, quarum aecclesiarum pontifex
esset futurus palam preconatus. Visus sibi erat Romam isse et apud
apostolos deposita oratione pedem ad reditum reflectere. 2. Tum ad
locum citra Sutrium uenisse cui Mons Gaudii nomen a peregrinis
datum.[4] Ibi enim ab itinerantibus Romana cernuntur menia, ibi

---

[a] Rightly Edgiuae (*cf. Memorials pp. 57,* [*95,*] *185*); *cf. p. 238 note c.*

[1] Wulfstan of Winchester, *Vita S. Æthelwoldi*, c. 10 (pp. 18–19).
[2] In fact Eadgifu.   [3] The early visions at i. 2. 2, i. 10. 1.
[4] Not in B.; first named by Osbern, c. 22 (p. 96), then by Eadmer, c. 13 (p. 185), who
both place Mons Gaudii near Rome, without mentioning Sutri (which was on the Via

writer of the Life of St Æthelwold,[1] the king was 'a special lover and
guardian of the Old Minster at Winchester, as is witnessed to by many
generous gifts he made to it': (3) 'if he had lived, the king had also
intended to decorate the east *porticus* of the church with golden tiles.'
This was the see to which Eadred thought of advancing Dunstan. But
he was shy of being repulsed a second time, and so, knowing how good
a woman is at testing a man and sapping his resistance, he gave his
mother Ælfgifu[2] the task. His suggestion was that she should appeal to
Dunstan, as their common friend and only protector, to take up the
bishopric. She should do it at a meal, when the good cheer of the
banquet and the surrounding company might dispel his resolve to say
no. 4. The queen regarded the saint with no less respect, and loved
him perhaps even more dearly. So she made the arrangements for a
good party and brought her friend into it; she tried coaxing, made
speeches, battered him with entreaties, loaded him with promises, and
generally did all a woman, a loving friend and a queen could do. To no
avail: he was hardly, if at all, moved by any of this, and pressed his
point, giving the reasons I have mentioned. But she would be going on
to this day, if the saint had not said in some pique: 'My lady, you may
rest assured that I shall never be bishop while your son lives.' That
silenced the queen and gave him some peace.

24. Of course, such obstinacy on the part of a man who was never
ruffled proceeded from the best of motives. But that God was
displeased by it was shown by a vision on the following night, one
that made it quite obvious how great was the grace with which God's
mercy ever attended Dunstan. While he was still a boy, an old man
had come to him in a dream and promised him the task of repairing
Glastonbury. Similarly, as a young man, a man no less young had
appeared to him and prophesied his promotion to the highest ranks.[3]
Now, so that he could completely penetrate the veil of his visions,
God Himself, through His own apostles, removed any doubt, by
giving a clear indication of which churches Dunstan was to rule over
as bishop. He dreamed that he had gone to Rome, prayed duly at the
shrines of the apostles, and turning his steps homeward (2) had come
to the place this side of Sutri which the pilgrims call *Mons Gaudii* (the
Hill of Joy);[4] for it is there that travellers first glimpse the walls of

Cassia, the route normally taken by pilgrims: e.g. Archbishop Sigeric's itinerary of 990 in
Memorials, p. 392). The place is now the Monte Mario, a small hill (455 feet/157 m. high),
a little north of St Peter's on the right bank of the Tiber. It was near the end of the Via

magnae uiae laboribus emensis peregrini felicis spei presumunt gaudia.[1] Eo loci Petrus et Paulus et Andreas apostoli ei occurrere uisi, singulos gladios tenentes singuli. In duorum autem gladiis eorum nomina legeres; porro in beati Petri ense aureis litteris scriptum cerneres: 'In principio erat Verbum et Verbum erat apud Deum.'[2] 3. Omnes ergo parili liberalitate gladios Dunstano prebuere, Andreas autem hilariori uultus laetitia uisus amicum perstringere; quantum enim mortales possunt supernorum herere contubernio, familiari ab aeuo ineunte famulatus ei fuerat obsequio, multa eius benefitia frequenter expertus. Ille igitur quasi ethimologiae cognominis sui alludens, qua mitissimus sanctorum et sentitur et dicitur,[3] simulque legationem allegans suam, suaui melo insonuit: 'Tollite iugum meum super uos, quia mitis sum et humilis corde.'[4] 4. Deinde Dunstanus dulci beati Petri conuentus imperio manum porrigere, blandientisque uirgulae crepitum persentiens, audire[5] promeruit hanc esse pridie refutati presulatus uindictam et ulterius non refutandi suadelam. Hoc excitus sono finem dedit somno. Pro magno sane miraculo quasi alienatus animo interrogauit prope accumbentem monachum quisnam eum perculerit. Illo percussorem negante, sobria tandem ad se reuersus mente dixit: 'Nunc scio, fili, nunc scio, inquam, quis me perculerit.' 5. Nec mora, noctis reliquias in Dei egressus laudibus, prorumpente diluculo, ad regem ingressus totius uisionis non falsus index fuit. Tunc gloriosus rex concepto uaticinii spiritu futura incunctanter exsoluit: gladios apostolorum aecclesiasticum significare pontificatum; futurum ergo eum episcopum aecclesiarum quae predictorum apostolorum operiuntur nutum. Porro scripturam quae de beati Petri micabat gladio significare futurum eum in Cantia primatem; ibi est enim Saluatoris Iesu Christi aecclesia,[6] de quo ea[a] protulit uerba beatus et uerus simmista.[7] 6. Dixit haec ille, non coniectantis

---

[a] de quo ea *ed.*; depostea (q̊ *was mistaken for* p̊) Q

Cassia, and provided an excellent view of the Leonine wall and the city beyond: G. Tomassetti, *La campagna romana antica, medioevale e moderna*, ed. L. Chiumenti and F. Bilancia (7 vols., Florence, 1979–80), iii. 22–9, omitting the English references; R. Krautheimer, *Rome: Profile of a City, 312–1308* (Princeton, 1980), p. 264 and fig. 202. By mentioning Sutri, William seems to imply—perhaps unintentionally—that the Mons was further from the city than this. Cf. the Mons Gaudii (Monte del Gozo), now Monte San Marcos, 5 km east of Compostela: *The Pilgrim's Guide to Santiago de Compostela: A Gazetteer*, ed. A. Shaver-Crandell and P. Gerson (London, 1995), pp. 87, 243, 420.

[1] The pilgrims, on seeing Rome, are given some idea of the joys of heaven, their hope of reaching which is being forwarded by their earthly journey. [2] John 1: 1.

[3] Jerome, *Liber interpretationis Hebraicorum nominum* (CCSL lxxii, pp. 134, 142),

Rome, there that pilgrims have a foretaste of the joys of their good hope after the travails of their long journey.[1] It was here that Dunstan dreamed that the apostles Peter, Paul and Andrew met him, each carrying a sword. On two of the swords you could read the names of the saints who held them; but on the sword belonging to the blessed Peter you could see in letters of gold the words: 'In the beginning was the Word, and the Word was with God.'[2] 3. All three held out their swords to Dunstan with equal generosity, but Andrew seemed to dazzle his friend with a particularly joyful look. For, so far as mortals can find a place in the company of heavenly ones, Dunstan had throughout his life served Andrew closely and loyally, and received many benefits from him. So now Andrew, as if playing on the etymology of his own name, by which he is said, as he is felt, to be the gentlest of saints,[3] and alluding at the same time to his calling, sang in a sweet voice: 'Take my yoke upon you, for I am meek and lowly in heart.'[4] 4. Then Dunstan was told by Peter with sweet insistence to hold out his hand. He felt the crack of the caressing cane, and was found worthy to hear[5] the words: 'This is your punishment for refusing the bishopric yesterday, and a warning to you not to refuse in future.' He woke up at the sound, and felt stupified by such a wonder. He asked the monk lying nearby who had struck him. He replied that no one had. Dunstan finally recovered himself, and said: 'Now I know, my son, now I know, I say, who hit me.' 5. He wasted no time; after seeing the night out in praises of God, he went to the king as dawn broke and reported the vision without holding anything back. The great king assumed a spirit of prophecy, and without hesitation foretold what was to be. The swords of the apostles signified the position of bishop, so he would become bishop of the churches subject to those apostles. The writing that gleamed on St Peter's sword meant that he would be archbishop of Canterbury, where is to be found a church of the Saviour Jesus Christ,[6] concerning whom Peter's comrade,[7] true and blessed, spoke those

interprets *Andreas* as *decorus, respondens pabulo, decus in statione*, or *uirilis*; similarly Isidore, *Etym.* vii. 9. 11. All of these seem somewhat remote from William's inference.

[4] Matt. 11: 29. The 'legatio' is presumably Christ's calling of the apostles.

[5] From Andrew, according to B., c. 20 (p. 30).

[6] For the church of the Saviour at Canterbury, see below, ii. 5. 4, *GP*, cc. 16, 20 (pp. 23, 32), and *Mir.*, p. 79 line 475.

[7] Meaning St John, writer of the words quoted at 24. 2. William is recalling Rufinus' translation of Origen, *In Levit. hom.* 7. 2 (PG xii. 478B), where John was described as *symmista*: 'Iohannes symmista eius [scil. Christi]'. (This is apparently the only occurrence of the word in Latin patristic literature.)

animo sed ueraci presagio, sicut et rerum effectus ostendit et lectionis continuatio manifestabit. Quid in his mirabilius dicam non diffinio, Dei gratiam occurrentem uiro, an uiri meritum concurrens Deo, an regis mentem accurrentem uaticinio. Sed tua, Christe Deus, sunt omnia: tua fluxit in Dunstanum gratia, Dunstani excreuit per te gloria, tuo munere fuit uera regis prophetia.

25.[1] Non post multum tempus Edredus uiolentia morbi pressus lento in mortem agebatur spiritu. Mandatum ergo curauit Dunstanum uitae arbitrum, mortis tutorem. Ille tristi perculsus rumore celer equum insilit. Tantum morae in medio ut iumenta thesauris oneraret quos rex supremae uoluntatis arbitrio dispensaret. Conficit iter nocte dieque stimulis amoris negotium accelerans. Nulla uiro pausa, nulla requies calcaribus; labor ingens subinde mutatis animalibus. Sed Deus, et amici pectoris sollicitudinem et afflicti corporis laborem miseratus, utrumque demissa superne uoce compescuit. 2. 'Modo' inquit 'Edredus rex obdormiuit in Domino.' Tum iumentum cui sedebat caelestis tonitrus impatiens animam amisit, sed ipse itineris continuationi securior indulsit. Turbauit sodales uocis crepitus et animalis interitus, qui sonum quidem audierant sed sensum non discreuerant. Absoluit Dunstanus timorem, rem ut erat ordine pandens,[2] et pro regis anima preces Deo medullitus fundens. Modicum inde cum progressus esset, uenientibus nuntiis post nuntios alteris post alteros, caelestis oraculi fidem approbauit. Iam uero, ubi ad locum peruentum, fuit uidere miseriam:[3] exanime regis corpus pene sine custode iacere, familiam omnem diffugisse. 3. Momentum fortunae[4] sequebatur procerum fides, et qui olim adulantes astiterant uiuo nunc subsannantes abibant a mortuo. Fit enim fere in rebus hominum ut in diuitibus magis quidam sectentur pecuniam quam gratiam, magis auaritiae famem quam amicitiae fidem. Indoluit uisu[5] uir beatissimus, cum^a defuncti modestiam recordatus, tum in desertores uehementer indignatus. Regales ergo exuuias suo diuersorio intulit, eisque cum presbiteris et monachis suis

---

^a *ed.*; tum *Q*

---

[1] The story of Dunstan's premonition of the king's death is also told, more succinctly, in *GR*, c. 146. 2.

[2] Cf. Virgil, *Aen.* iii. 179: 'remque ordine pando'. Echoed again below, ii. 32. 3.

[3] Cf. *GR*, c. 283. 1: 'tunc fuit uidere miseriam'.

[4] Cf. *GR*, c. 230. 1 and n.

[5] Statius, *Theb.* xii. 297.

words. 6. The king said all this not by guesswork but in true
prophecy; events bore him out, as will be made clear later in my
book. I hesitate to determine what is more marvellous in all this,
God's grace coming to meet a man, or the man's deserts concurring
with God, or the king's mind taking on the role of prophet. But,
Christ God, yours are all things. It was your grace that flowed into
Dunstan, it was through you that Dunstan's glory grew, and it was by
your gift that the king's prophecy came true.

25.[1] A little later, Eadred fell prey to a severe illness, and slowly
drifted towards death. He therefore asked them to send for Dunstan,
guide of his life, guardian of his death. Spurred by the sad tidings,
he leapt to horse, leaving only enough delay to pile on the beasts'
backs the treasure he wanted the king to dispose of by his last
testament. Pricked on by love, he travelled night and day to speed
his business. The man had no rest, the spurs were never spared;
great was the labour, and the horses were frequently changed. But
God had pity on his friend's heartache and bodily labours, and
brought relief to both by sending down a message from on high: (2)
'Now King Eadred has fallen asleep in the Lord.' The horse on
which he sat could not withstand the thunder from heaven, and
dropped dead, while Dunstan himself went on with his journey, his
anxiety less urgent. His friends were perturbed by the thunderous
voice and the death of the animal; they had heard the sound, but did
not understand its purport. Dunstan calmed their fears, telling them
all the details,[2] and pouring out heartfelt prayers for the king's soul.
When he had gone on a little, relays of messages arrived, and
Dunstan saw that the heavenly oracle had told the truth. But when
they at last came to the spot, it was a sad sight to behold:[3] the king's
lifeless body lay there with scarcely a guard, for his whole retinue
had fled. 3. The change of fortune[4] took with it the loyalty of the
nobility: those who had previously stood fawning by the man in life
now deserted his corpse with sneers and mockery. For such is the
way of the world: where the rich are concerned, some are more
interested in cash than in friendship, and feel the hunger of avarice
more than the tug of loyalty. The saint grieved at what he saw,[5]
recalling the dead man's lack of pretension and angry beyond
measure at those who had abandoned him. So he brought the
king's remains to his own lodgings, and with his priests and
monks carried out the proper rites over them. In the morning

iusta persoluit. Mane autem succollantibus ministris Wintoniam in episcopatum peruectas, quieti aeternae sedis imposuit.[1]

26. Quo sepulto curiales tumultus perosus monasterii sui sinibus exceptus est. Ibi dulci pace componens animum religionem de integro nouat, diuinae contemplationis sedulus explorator. Sed quanuis Mariae partem elegerit, Martham tamen non usquequaque aspernatus[2] semper aliquid utilis fabricae comminiscebatur. Vnde factum est ut turri quae proxime facta erat tectum iuberet imponi. Feruebat igitur labor artificum, stridebat funalis machina[3] immensas rapiens ad fastigium trabes. Et ceterae quidem ordines agnouerant, una uero ruptis, ut credo, funibus deorsum uergere cepit. 2. Tum fragore cadentis trabis et strepentis uulgi clamore concitatus abbas impiger accurrit. Rogantibus ceteris ipse immanitate periculi constantior et fidei arma concutiens[4] ore Christi auxilium asciscit, et manu signum crucis emittit in auras. Vis signaculi trabem ruentem retro depulit et in altum actam suo loco restituit. Hoc miraculum sicut et cetera quibusdam in eodem monasterio fratribus bonis erant ad augmentum in patrem gratiae, malis ad cumulum inuidiae. Nec enim uir ille, cuius purissimam uitam nullius umquam contagionis neuus infecit, liuorem suorum effugere potuit, quo minus in eum occultis dumtaxat seuirent calumniis.

27. Sed haec postmodum etiam diuino claruere inditio. Tunc[5] autem causa extitit ut omnibus principibus patriae conuocatis ad curiam deesse non deberet. Nam e duobus filiis Edmundi superioris regis maior electus est qui patruo succederet, Edwius nomine: iuuenculus aeuo, immaturus consilio; pernitiosus omnibus, pestifer sibi; preceps ad omne uitium, maxime crudelitatem petulantiamque, altera in omnium et in bonorum potissimum fortunas et uitas seuiens, altera pudicitiam suam omni pene momento ledens. 2. Captus enim

---

[1] Not in the earlier Lives. William's source could have been e.g. *ASC* (D) s.a. 955.

[2] Luke 10: 38–42. So *GR*, c. 149. 1.

[3] Also mentioned in *GP*, c. 216 (p. 362), in the context of another building miracle. 'Funalis machina' could in principle mean any contrivance involving rope; we translate it as 'pulley' because 'stridebat' seems inappropriate for something *made* of rope (such as a sling).

[4] Cf. *Mir.*, p. 108 line 1223.

[5] The story, including the exile, is told more succinctly in *GR*, c. 147. 1–2. See 147. 1 n., and B. A. Yorke, 'Æthelwold and the politics of the tenth century', in *Bishop Æthelwold: his Career and Influence*, ed. B. A. Yorke (Woodbridge, 1988), pp. 65–88, at 80–1, 87; N. Brooks, 'The career of St Dunstan', in *St Dunstan*, pp. 1–23, at 14–16.

they were shouldered by servants and borne to Winchester Cathedral, where they were laid to rest for ever.[1]

26. After the burial of Eadred, Dunstan grew tired of the stormy life at court, and returned to the welcoming embrace of his own monastery. There he relaxed in the sweet calm of the place, renewing his religious life from the foundations, and assiduously seeking to contemplate God. But though his choice was the role of Mary, he did not altogether spurn Martha,[2] and was always organizing some useful piece of construction work. So it came about that he ordered the roofing of a tower that had been built hard by. The workmen buzzed with activity, accompanied by the rattle of the pulley[3] taking the great beams up to the roof. The other beams had all found their proper places, but one—no doubt because the ropes broke—began to tip downwards. 2. His attention caught by the crash of the fall and the shouts of the crowd, the indefatigable abbot came at a run. While others begged for mercy, the terrible danger only made him the more determined. Brandishing the arms of faith,[4] he used his mouth to call on Christ's aid and his hand to make the sign of the Cross above his head. The power of the sign sent the headlong plank back in its tracks; up it went, and returned to its rightful position. This miracle, like others, caused in the monastery an increase of favour towards their father in the good brothers, while bringing to a head the envy of the wicked. For this man, whose purity of life was stained by not the slightest blot, could not escape the jealousy of his own people, or stop them taking out their resentment against him at least with covert slanders.

27. This came to light later by a sign from heaven. But for the moment[5] there was compelling reason for Dunstan to be present at court, at a meeting of all the princes of the realm. For of the two sons of Edmund, the previous king, the elder was chosen to succeed his uncle. His name was Eadwig, young and immature in counsel; a source of damage to all and of disaster to himself; headlong in the pursuit of every vice, but in particular cruelty and incontinence, led by the one to mad assaults on the fortunes and lives of all (and especially of the good), by the other to violate his own chastity almost every hour of the day. 2. For he had fallen captive to the wondrous

miraculo pulchritudinis[1] cuiusdam Elfgiuae,[2] quae sullimitatem
generis prauitate morum premeret, nichil non arbitrio eius fatiebat.
Herebat mulierculae filia plenis iam nubilis annis[3] quae genitrici haud
absimilis uitricum delinimentis etiam suis deuinxerat. Ferebaturque
Edwius lasciuire tam in matrem quam in filiam et in ambabus satiare
uoluptatem uicariam. Sed huius dicti credulitas penes antiquos
auctores sit. Vtinam in hoc dumtaxat sim uanus, nullusque ad
imitandum[a] michi fidem accommodet, quod umquam Christianus
se tali probro subiecerit.

3. Enimuero tunc, sicut est ignara futuri mens hominum,[4] qui
plerumque magno fauore aliquid fatiendum commendant, quod
postea magno dolore factum deplorant, consensu principum aulam
uacantem occupauit Edwius. Conuenerunt ad eum coronandum, ut
mos est, omnes patriae magnates, episcopi et abbates, uocibus in
gaudium profusis futurum sui dispendium urgentes. Dictis missis
cum cibo curassent corpora, ille quasi uentris desiderio pulsatus
primo in secretum, mox in triclinium feminarum[5] concessit. Cum
moram faceret, res interrogantes latere non potuit. Tum Odo
Cantuariensis archiepiscopus, omnium aeuo et gradu maximus,
paterno cunctos frementes leniuit hortatu: (4) iret aliquis et regem,
dedecoris quod fatiebat ammonitum, ad consessum reduceret optimatum, renuentem excommunicationis minis percelleret. Cunctis pro
inertia conscientiae fugientibus, duo se uoluntati archiepiscopi obtu-
lere, qui periculo suo rem tractarent iustitiae, Kinesius episcopus[6] et
Dunstanus abbas, par insigne constantiae nec minus affines sanguine.
Abeuntes comitatus est sedentium plausus, more hominum qui
nonnumquam in aliis laudare sciunt quod ipsi[b] facere non presumunt.
Egerunt illi primo legationem placide, constanti animo, non titubanti
uerbo. Veruntamen parum promouentes terruerunt eum excommunicationis suspendio. Volutabatur ille inter meretriculas, diademate
procul excusso et humi iacente. 5. Quapropter adhuc cunctantem
Dunstanus apprehendit dextra, impositaque corona uiolenter eduxit
triclinio. Is nichil contra, siue auctoritate uiri motus siue conscientia
sua territus. At Elfgiua muliebris impatientiae signifera,[7] toruos in
eum uibrans oculos, 'Quia' inquit 'tam audax es ut educas regem,

---

[a] ad imitandum *is dubious (not translated)*   [b] *Stubbs*; ipse *Q*

[1] Cf. *VW* iii. 28. 2 'spetiei miraculo' and n.
[2] *GR*, c. 147. 1 n.   [3] Virgil, *Aen.* vii. 53.
[4] Cf. Virgil, *Aen.* iv. 65, x. 501, Lucan ii. 14–15, Statius, *Theb.* v. 718–19.
[5] Cf. Esther 2: 13.
[6] Bp. of Lichfield 946/9–963/4: Stubbs in *Memorials*, p. lxxxviii n. 8; *HBC*, p. 218.

beauty[1] of one Ælfgifu,[2] whose depraved character brought disgrace to her high family, and he followed her whim in everything. The wretched woman had in constant attendance on her a daughter, old enough for matrimony,[3] who was a match for her mother and had also bewitched her stepfather with her blandishments. And the story went that Eadwig played around with both mother and daughter, having his way with them alternately. But belief in this must rest on the authority of old writers. I only wish that I am wrong, at least in this respect, and that no one credits my story that a Christian ever laid himself open to such insinuations.

3. Men can have no knowledge of the future,[4] and often warmly advocate an action they later deplore. Accordingly it was with the general consent of the great that Eadwig took over the vacant throne. There flocked to his coronation, as is usual, all the magnates of the realm, bishops too and abbots, pouring out their joy and speeding on an event they would later rue. Masses were said, and a banquet was held. Then the king, alleging the necessities of nature, went off first to a privy, then to the room where the women were.[5] When he seemed to be staying away a long while, there was no avoiding questions. Oda archbishop of Canterbury, senior to all in age and rank, calmed the hubbub with fatherly advice: (4) 'Let someone go and remind the king of the shame he is incurring. Bring him back to where the noblemen are seated, and if he refuses threaten him with excommunication.' Everybody hung back out of faintheartedness; only two took up the archbishop's notion, ready to do the right thing to their own cost, Bishop Cynesige[6] and Abbot Dunstan, a notable pair of stout souls, and related too by blood. As they went off, the nobles shouted applause from their seats, as men do who at times are capable of praising others for doing what they are not prepared to do themselves. The two of them at first carried out their mission in a calm tone, though in a firm spirit and with firm language. But when they found they were making no headway, they frightened the king with talk of excommunication. There he sprawled between his girls, his crown flung off, some way away on the floor. 5. When he went on havering, Dunstan took him by the hand, replaced the crown, and dragged him forcibly from the room. Eadwig made no resistance, either out of respect for Dunstan or for conscience's sake. But Ælfgifu gave vent to a woman's impatience.[7] Flashing her eyes grimly at Dunstan, she said: 'If you are so bold as to drag the king

[7] Cf. *Mir.*, p. 157 line 1433: 'uirginitatis signifera'.

uelit nolit, triclinio, fatiam ego ut huius diei meique semper
memineris cum potero'. Sed licet illa sacrilega in ipsum caelum
uerba iactaret, Dunstanus iuxta firmitatem nominis sui,[1] uelut
pelagi rupes immota resistens,[2] ut ceperat regem educens prostibulo,
collocauit et sedere fecit in solio.

28.[a] Tum uero mulier, ad omnem se proteruiam armans, suasionum
suarum classico uirum in bellum contra Deum accendit. Excogitato
enim quid Dunstano maxime posset esse dolori, feralia per totam
Angliam mittuntur edicta. Tunc res monachorum preceps agi, tunc
monachi proscribi, tunc monasteria fisco regio addici.[3] Putabat enim
adultera minus regiae maiestati conuenire, si omnem in unum
hominem uim furoris effunderet, nisi, ut de quodam dicitur, incendium suum ruina extingueret.[4] Iamque proscriptores Glastoniam
uenerant, et arrosis omnibus eum loco excedere iubebant. 2. Conuenerat frequens uicinia, uelut ad patris exequias; omnes preter paucos
de quibus diximus et dicemus[5] susurrones lamentabantur in caelum,
onerabant aethera suspiriis.[6] Interim non potuit dissimulare laetitiam
suam diabolus, fedos et petulantes cachinnos in atrio aecclesiae
ingeminare auditus. Dunstanum auctor risus non latuit, qui etiam,
quanuis maiora urgerent, dicere hosti non abstinuit: 'Nichil est,
diabole, quod de abscessu meo gaudeas si uaticinari possis quam
multiplitius in reditu[b] doleas.'[7] 3. Cedendum ergo tempori ratus, ne
presentia sua furentes exstimularet, transito mari Flandriam intrauit.[8]
Quo audito, altera Iezabel[9] nichilo modestior ministros direxit e
uestigio, scrutarique iussit eos quicumque sanctum Dei caritatis
suscepissent hospitio. Omnes itaque accusati, proscripti uel absumpti.
Quid enim non auderet[10] furiarum maxima,[11] quae illius oculos, oculos
columbinos, oculos semper superius intentos, si forte inuentus esset,
intentauerat cauis orbibus euellere. Sed preuenit audatiam femineam

---

[1] See above, p. 174 n. 1.
[2] Cf. Virgil, *Aen.* vii. 586, also echoed in *GR*, c. 175. 3, *HN*, c. 69.
[3] Cf. *GP*, c. 251 (p. 403).
[4] Sallust, *Cat.* xxxi. 9.
[5] i. 5. 3, 6. 2, 14. 2–3, ii. 9. 4, 19. 1.
[6] Cf. *VW* i. 3. 4 and n.
[7] A similar story (of Wilfrid) in *GP*, c. 100 (p. 220).
[8] So Adelard, lectio vi (p. 59); B. says only that Dunstan was exiled in 'ignotam
regionem iam dictae Galliae' (c. 23; p. 34).

willy-nilly from the room, I shall make sure you always remember
this day, and me—when I have the chance.' But though the impious
wretch let her words fly up to heaven itself, Dunstan—firm as his
name suggested[1]—remained as unmoved as a rock in the sea;[2] he
completed the removal of the king from his brothel, and replaced him
in his seat.

28 (27 Stubbs). Then indeed did the woman gird herself to every
form of impudence. She used the trumpet of her persuasions to
inflame the king to war against God. Thought was given to what
might most hurt Dunstan, and brutal proclamations went out over all
England. The property of monks fell victim; the monks themselves
were proscribed, and their monasteries handed over to the royal fisc.[3]
For the adulteress thought it unbefitting the king's majesty if he spent
all the force of his fury on a single man, without, as is said of
someone, extinguishing his own fire in the general ruin.[4] By now the
bailiffs had arrived in Glastonbury; they gnawed away at everything,
and began to insist on the departure of Dunstan. 2. The neighbourhood was there in force, as though at their father's funeral; apart from
a few cavillers, of whom I have spoken before and will speak again,[5]
everyone raised their laments to the skies and loaded the air with
sighs.[6] Meanwhile the Devil, unable to conceal his joy, was heard in
the church to utter repeated cackles of a disgusting and insolent
nature. Dunstan was well aware who was responsible for the laughter,
and, though he had more pressing business to attend to, could not
resist saying to the Devil: 'You would have no reason to rejoice at my
departure if you could know how much more sorely you will rue my
return.'[7] 3. He now thought it best to yield to circumstance, so as not
to spur on these madmen by his presence; and he crossed over to
Flanders.[8] At this news, the second Jezebel[9] was not appeased, but
straightway sent underlings with orders to investigate everyone who
took in the holy man of God with charitable hospitality. All of them
were accused, proscribed or eliminated. For what would not have
been dared[10] by this greatest of the furies,[11] seeing that she had had it
in mind, if she got hold of him, to tear from their hollows Dunstan's
eyes, the eyes of a dove, eyes always directed upwards. But a woman's
audacity was foiled by the holy foresight of the holy man, or, to be

[9] So Adelard, lectio vi (p. 59).
[10] So *Mir.*, p. 129 line 530: 'Quod (*leg.* quid) enim non auderet qui . . .'.
[11] Virgil, *Aen.* iii. 252, vi. 605.

sancta sancti uiri prouidentia, immo, ut uerius fatear, Dei omnipotentis qui Angliae consultum uolebat clementia.

29 (28 Stubbs). Erat eo tempore Arnulfus comes Flandriae, Elfredi
superiorum regum aui ex filia Ethelswitha[1] pronepos: princeps
magnificus et Dei amori deditus, qui monasterium apud Gandauium,[a]
olim a beato Amando episcopo constructum, nobiliter eo tempore
ampliabat. Cui etiam ad tutelam sui et patriae corpora sanctorum
intulit, Wandregisili, Ansberti, Wlmari.[2] Quorum primus Fontanellae
abbas, secundus et tertius primum ibidem abbates, mox alter apud
Rotomagum,[b] alter apud Senones archiepiscopi fuerant. Hoc ergo
audito et expulsionis suae causis expositis, conuenientem religioni
suae benignitatem eius expertus est. 2. Siquidem eo iubente in
predicto exceptus monasterio, non mansitabat ibi ut exul et incola,[3]
sed colebatur ut domesticus et abba. Frustra enim certabatur totis
Angliae tumultibus aduersus eum cui Deus aderat, frustra gloria-
bantur quidam expulsum patria, cui familiaris sui Andreae apostoli
non deerant suffragia. Ipse uigilanti quaecumque placita suppedita-
bat, ipse dormienti consolationes diuinitus exhibebat. In eodem
quippe monasterio multa ei caelitus ostensa, quibus uel dolorem de
suorum perfidia extenuaret uel exitium hostile cognosceret. Verbi
causa utrorumque sequantur exempla.

30 (29 Stubbs). Visus est sibi quadam nocte in Glastoniae choro esse,
ibique a monachis hanc antiphonam cantari audire: 'Quare detraxistis
sermonibus ueritatis? Ad increpandum uerba componitis et subuer-
tere nitimini amicum uestrum.'[4] Ibi antiphonam interruptam silentio
monachosque scientia sequentium uerborum frustratos, quanuis
multiplici temptarent repetitione, numquam potuisse titubantem
memoriam emendare. 2. Tum se uehementi eos inuectione arguere,
quod ita sequentia nescirent, 'Veruntamen quae cogitastis explete'.
Sed mox diuinum oraculum auditum a templi latere: 'Ideo fraudantur

---

   [a] *Stubbs*; Grandauium *Q* (*similarly in i. 31. 1*)   [b] *ed.*; Retomagum *Q*

   [1] *recte* Æthelthryth; see *GR*, c. 121. 13 and n. Adelard (lectio vi; p. 59), alone of
William's predecessors, names Count Arnulf, but his relationship to King Alfred is
William's own addition (*GR*, c. 123. 5 and n.).
   [2] Of William's sources only Adelard, a monk of Blandinium (St Peter's, Ghent),
mentions the monastery, its founder, and its renovation by Count Arnulf. Adelard (pp. 59–
60) says that he transferred there the relics of S. Wandrille (Wandragesil) 'cum sociis
archipraesulibus'. William adds their names (Ansbert and Wulmar), and the details of their
careers. Wandragesil and Wulmar both appear in the calendar of the Eadwine Psalter,

more accurate, by the mercy of God Almighty, who had the good of England at heart.

29 (28 Stubbs). The count of Flanders at this time was Arnulf, great-grandson by his daughter Æthelswith[1] of Alfred, grandfather of the previous kings, a magnificent prince devoted to the love of God, who at this time was splendidly enlarging the monastery at Ghent, the foundation of St Amand of old. To protect himself and the county he introduced the bodies of saints—Wandregesil, Ansbert and Wulmar.[2] The first of these had been abbot of Fontanelle, the second and third abbots there, and then archbishops, Ansbert at Rouen and Wulmar at Sens. Dunstan heard of all this, told him why he had been expelled from England, and was received with a kindness that matched his religious distinction. 2. At Arnulf's insistence, he was welcomed at Ghent, and dwelt there not like an exile and mere visitor,[3] but rather as a revered abbot and member of the family. Vain were all the tumultuous attempts in England to thwart one by whom God stood; vain too the boasts of some that they had removed him from his country, for he did not lack the help of his close friend, the apostle Andrew. Andrew gave him all manner of advice while he was awake, and when he slept supplied consolations from God. For many were the portents vouchsafed him in that monastery, which enabled him to grieve less at the treachery of his friends and to learn of the downfall of his enemies. I will give examples of both types.

30 (29 Stubbs). He dreamt one night that he was in the choir at Glastonbury, and heard the monks singing the antiphon: 'Why have you detracted from the words of truth? You put words together in order to rebuke, and strive to overturn your friend.'[4] Here the antiphon was interrupted and silence fell, for the monks could not recollect what came next. Though they made repeated attempts to start again, they were unable to put themselves right. 2. Then (in his dream) Dunstan sharply rebuked them for not knowing the next words, 'but complete what you have planned'. But soon the word of God was heard from the side of the church: 'They are robbed of

made at Christ Church Canterbury c.1155–60; Ansbert was rarely commemorated in England: R. W. Pfaff in *The Eadwine Psalter*, ed. M. Gibson, T. A. Heslop and R. W. Pfaff (London and University Park, PA, 1992), p. 70 and n. 32.

[3] Difficult to translate. *GP*, c. 278 (p. 442), makes it clear that *incola* distinguishes the new arrival from the *indigena*, or native. Cf. the way in which Dunstan feels at home at Glastonbury in ii. 17. 1.   [4] Job 6: 25–8. Hesbert, *Corpus antiphonalium*, no. 4448.

horum uerborum notitia quo minus ea dicere sciant, quia numquam explebunt opere quod cogitant, ut te a possessione huius monasterii funditus extrudant.' Quibus auditis somno excedens rediit ad uigilias, misericordi et omnipotenti Deo de tam manifesta consolatione quales decebat referens gratias.

31 (30 Stubbs). Nec minus mors Edwii regis, quae quomodo acciderit sequens libellus declarabit,[1] mors inquam Edwii Dunstano in Gandauio preclaro monstrata est inditio. In ipsa nocte obitus eius ante altare pro more orans stabat (eiusmodi quippe consuetudinem pene in naturam traxerat),[2] et ecce (mirabile dictu!) uidet comminus transeuntes piceae fuliginis formam indutos demones. Nec uero ipse more nostro inerti pauore refugit, sed diligentius in ipsas tenebras exacuens oculos uidit ab eis trahi regis animam continuo Gehennae mancipandam.[3] 2. Id illi et tripudio laetitiae suae et imperioso Sancti iussu coacti prodidere. Stetit confestim ante oculos Dunstani huma-nae conditionis miseratio, et si quid residuum erat rancoris fugit ex animo. Haec consideratio scaturiuit in corde beati hominis, et profudit uberem fontem lacrimarum ab oculis, gratum Deo sacrifi-tium et suaue holocaustum:[4] quod ille prostratus in humum thur-ificauit in caelum pro eo qui se patria expulerat,[a] qui denique, suum sanguinem sitiens, cupiditate si non mucrone illum libauerat. Quo facto Dunstanus palam fecit mundo quam bonus esset in amicos qui tam gratus erat in hostes. Oderat ergo in Edwio non naturam sed culpam; amauerat quidem hominem, etsi execrabatur libidinem.

32 (31 Stubbs). Hactenus librum primum protraxisse et de hoc miraculo dixisse suffecerit. Ceterum uerba Sancti ad demones uel demonum ad ipsum, preterea precibus eius animam a demonibus extortam, narrare refugio,[5] quia in ueteri exemplari nec haec nec alia perplura inuenio. Talia enim nouus scriptor,[6] ut esset sermo politior et uoluminis moles grandior, ex suo aditienda putauit. Sed nos ea inserere fastidiuimus, intelligentes quod nostrae laudis, presertim falsae, non est indigus Dunstanus.

Explicit liber primus

---

[a] *Another short* qui *clause may have fallen out*

[1] Below, ii. 4. 1, though it hardly explains 'quomodo acciderit'.
[2] Cf. *VW* i. 4. 1 n.
[3] William refers briefly to the story in *GR*, c. 147. 4. Cf. the similar ones (of Ælfheah) in *GP*, c. 76 (pp. 169–70), and (of Wilfrid) in Eadmer, *Vita Wilfridi*, c. 47 (p. 106).
[4] Cf. Num. 29: 36.

knowledge of these words and of the ability to sing them because never *will* they complete what they plan by expelling you once and for all from possession of this monastery.' At these words he awoke and returned to his vigil, giving proper thanks to almighty and merciful God for so clear a consolation.

31 (30 Stubbs). The following Book will tell how Eadwig died.[1] His death too was announced by a brilliant sign to Dunstan in Ghent. The very night of his decease Dunstan as usual stood praying before the altar, for this had become second nature to him.[2] And behold a wonder! He saw passing before his very eyes devils clothed in soot-black shapes. *He* did not, as *we* might have done, flinch in cowardly fear, but trained his eyes the more intently on the darkness; he was granted the sight of the king's soul being dragged away by the demons for immediate consignment to Hell.[3] 2. For this their transports of joy and the authoritative order of the saint forced them to declare. At once Dunstan was confronted by the pitiful nature of man's lot, and all remaining resentment fled from his mind. This thought welled up in the blessed man's heart, and he poured forth a rich fountain of tears, a pleasing sacrifice to God and a sweet offering,[4] which, prostrate on the ground, he sent like incense up to heaven on behalf of the man who had driven him from his native land, and who in his thirst for Dunstan's blood had shed it in his desires, if not with his sword. By so doing Dunstan made clear to the world how good must he be to his friends who showed such kindness towards his enemies. He had hated in Eadwig not his nature but his fault; he had loved the man, though he deplored his lust.

32 (31 Stubbs). So much will suffice for Book One, and on the subject of this miracle. As for the saint's words to the demons, and theirs to him, and the story of how the king's soul was saved from them by his prayers, I forebear to tell,[5] for like many other details I do not find these in the old Life. This is the sort of thing that the new biographer[6] thought fit to add on his own account to make his style more elegant and his book more massive. *I* have shrunk from putting them in, well aware that Dunstan has no need of our praise, particularly when it has no foundation.

[5] William again objects to the words attributed by Osbern to his characters (see ii. prol. 1–2). In fact B. ('in ueteri exemplari') does not tell the story at all.

[6] Osbern, c. 30 (pp. 104–5).

Incipit prologus secundi

Antiquitatem istius sanctissimi cenobii Glastoniensis, in quo caelestem profitemur militiam,[1] alio opere quantum diuinus fauor affuit
absoluimus;[2] quam si cui uoluptati erit legere, poterit alias[3] apud nos
inuenire. Negotium sane illud nos frustra suscepisse non causabitur
posteritas, quoniam subinde legens intellexerit quam immaniter
Cantuariensis cantor[4] in describenda patris nostri uita peccauerit.
Nam, preter paucissima in quibus rectam semitam tenuit, multa sunt
uel pene omnia ubi uel turbauit miraculorum ordinem uel minuendo
et augendo neglexit ueritatem, rethorum morem[5] in primis emulatus
multorum representans uerba quae dici quidem potuerunt in
tempore, sed quis (queso) ea nostro seculo intulit integra ueritate?
2. Vix enim, uix, inquam, tenuis ad nos gestorum manauit fama,
nedum ego crediderim potuisse teneri uerba cum ipso dicto uolatica.[6]
Nichil tale scriptores antiqui, secundum quorum tenorem ego,
uestris obsecundans iussis, miracula ordini suo reddidi et rerum
integritatem restitui. Adieci quae deerant, abscidi quae superflue-
bant.[7] Sed huic dicto timeo ne difficulter ab improbis detur uenia,
quanuis, secundum sententiam oratoris egregii,[8] in re uera crimen
arrogantiae non debeam uereri. 3. Inter quae notandum quod
utriusque linguae scriptores,[9] quos michi ad exemplum dedistis,
dicunt quidem plerumque unus plus altero, sicut se habebat
scribentium memoria uel intentio, ceterum in his quae utrique
dicenda putauerunt in unanimem concurrunt assensum, ut nichil
uideatur diuersum. Solum excipiatis licebit quod diaboli fantasma[10]

---

[1] For William's confraternity at Glastonbury, see Stubbs in *GR* I, pp. xxix–xxx.

[2] *AG.* For its date, see above, p. xv.

[3] i.e. (it seems) in *GR* (**CB**) cc. 19. 3–29. 1, as well as in *AG.*

[4] Once again William targets Osbern.

[5] This could refer either to the preceding remarks about diminishing and exaggerating, or to what follows about imaginary speeches.

[6] Compare the objection to 'declamatiunculae' (i.e. 'invented speeches') in *VW* i. 16. 5. Similar expressions in i. 9. 5, i. 32, ii. 21. 2; *VW* i. Ep. 4; *Mir.*, p. 67 lines 148–9: 'nam ipsa uerba prae fastidio lectorum praetereo'.

[7] Cf. *GR*, c. 29. 3, on the desirability of using more than one ancient source to construct a more complete account.

[8] Cicero, *Orator* 132; probably via Augustine, *Tract. in Ioann.* 58. 3 (CCSL xxxvi, p. 473).

[9] Cf. i. prol. 2, 7. For the possible identity of the OE writings referred to see above, pp. xviii–xx.

BOOK TWO

Prologue

I have dealt in another work,[2] as well as God allowed me, with the antiquity of this most holy monastery of Glastonbury in which I profess my heavenly service.[1] If anyone is desirous of reading about it, he will be able to find it elsewhere in my output.[3] Posterity will surely not say that my trouble was taken in vain, for any reader will frequently notice how heinously the Chanter of Canterbury[4] went astray in relating the life of our father. For apart from a very few details in which he kept on the right track, there are very many others—almost all, in fact—where he confused the order of the miracles, or strayed from the truth by diminishing or exaggerating events. In particular, following the practice of the rhetoricians,[5] he often attributes to speakers words which they might indeed have spoken in those circumstances—but who, I ask you, could have passed them on to our day with all accuracy? 2. Scarcely, scarcely I repeat, has a slender report of *events* trickled through to us; far less could I believe that *words*, which flew away the moment they were spoken, could have been held on to.[6] There is nothing of the sort in the old writers following whose account I have on your instructions brought back the miracles to their proper order and corrected the details of events. I have added what was lacking, and cut out what was superfluous.[7] But I am afraid it will be difficult to gain pardon for this remark from the ill-disposed, even though—to quote the opinion of a great orator[8]—I should not be afraid to be called arrogant when I am speaking the truth. 3. Amidst all this it should be observed that the writers of both languages[9] whom you have given me as models may often differ in the amount of information they impart, according to what the individual remembered or intended; but when they have both thought fit to narrate something, they agree strictly between themselves. The only exception is that one says the appearance of the Devil[10] in the shape of bear, dog,

---

[10] O. A. Erich, *Die Darstellung des Teufels in der christlichen Kunst* (Berlin, 1931), p. 60: 'wie denn England überhaupt schon früh eine Tendenz zur Vertierung des Teufels zeigt'. This assault seems to come under Edmund in B. (c. 16 (pp. 26–7); Edmund's death follows at c. 19 (p. 29)), and the lost OE Life (Eng.) therefore presumably specified Eadwig. But B.'s dating is followed by Osbern, c. 19 (p. 93) (hence Eadmer, c. 11 (pp. 182–3); not in Adelard, but see below), as well as by William (above, i. 18). Thus this passage cannot be used to support our hypothesis (pp. xviii–xix above) about Osbern's use of Eng.; in this instance he seems, for whatever reason, to have preferred to follow B. against Eng. It may be important that Adelard (lect. vi; p. 59), telling the separate story of Dunstan driving

in urso, cane et uulpe[1] alter tempore regis Edmundi, alter Edwii[a]
Dunstano intentatum asserit.[2] Sed quid hoc sugillare attinet, in quo
etsi discrepant de tempore, nichil dissident de facti ueritate? 4. Nec
illud generabit litem quod alter Ethelgari Cridiensis, alter Elphegi
Wintoniensis episcopatum ab Edredo rege Dunstano dicit oblatum;[3]
credibile enim est ut quod unus dixerit alter tacuerit, et rex utrumque
obtulerit, sed de neutro impetrauerit. Haec dixi fortassis quam lex
prologi sinit[b] loquatius; sed quia dicenda erant non dici potuerunt
breuius. Quapropter, quia omnia quae in scrupulum uenire poterant
uera fide absolui, nunc secundum librum de uita Dunstani ab ortu
regis Edgari incipiam. Et quoniam primo minores eius annos et
gradus percurri, nunc eum per auxiliatricem Dei gratiam ad brauium
supernae coronae per summos honores deducam.

Explicit prologus

1. Edmundus rex, de quo superius diximus,[4] duorum fratrum regum
medius, in spem heredum pruriens, accepit uxorem Elfgiuam summo
loco natam, pudicitia et sanctitate prestantem. Ea fecunda utero
contulit marito liberos, Edwium, quem superior sermo infamauit,[5]
et Edgarum, de quo nunc dicere pergam. Cuius futuram magnitudi-
nem et felitia tempora ipse auctor felicitatis Deus Dunstano suo
prenuntiare dignatus est.[6] 2. Sub ipso enim momento quo eum mater
effundebat in lucem, audiuit Dunstanus tum abbas uocem de caelo
dicentem: 'Pax Anglorum aecclesiae, exorti nunc pueri et nostri
Dunstani tempore.' Audiuit haec ille fatienda, nos audiuimus et
uidimus facta; nam quanta fuit eis uiuentibus pax in Anglorum
aecclesia non est in promptu dicere. Ceterum Edgaro defuncto per
aliquanta monasteriorum membra pax elanguit, sed Dunstano exce-
dente hic fax bellorum aeterna, illic febris interna malorum per omne
Angliae corpus excanduit.

---

    [a] *Stubbs*; Edwio *Q*   [b] *ed.*; sit *Q*

---

away an unaccompanied bear with his staff (recounted, with probably significant
differences of detail, by B., c. 17 (pp. 27–8), Osbern, c. 26 (p. 100), Eadmer, c. 15
(p. 189), and William, i. 19), has the Devil disappear 'per subdola bestiarum transforma-
tum fantasmata' (more than one beast, then, as well as the original bear), and that he places
the event just before mention of Eadwig. One might think then of Eng. (followed by
Adelard) telling a single story that combined elements of the two stories told in B.,
especially as *GP*, c. 19 (p. 29), knows a single story of Dunstan using his staff to drive away
the Devil in the form 'either of a fox or a bear'.

   [1] Only wolf and fox in Osbern (and Eadmer), perhaps to avoid two stories involving a
bear (see the previous n.).

and fox[1] was inflicted on Dunstan in the time of King Edmund, the other in that of Eadwig.[2] But why cavil about this, when, whatever the discrepancy on the date, they are agreed on the truth of the story? 4. Nor will we go to law over the fact that one says Eadred offered Dunstan the bishopric of Æthelgar of Crediton, the other that of Ælfheah of Winchester;[3] for it is conceivable that what one said the other omitted, and that Eadred offered both sees to Dunstan without getting his agreement on either occasion. I have perhaps gone to greater length in saying this than the rules of the prologue allow, but it had to be said, and I could not have said it more briefly. So, having dealt in good faith with everything that could have raised a question, I shall now begin the second book of the Life of Dunstan from the birth of King Edgar. And since I have in the first book described his youthful years and lower offices, I shall now escort him, with the aid of God's grace, through the highest honours to the trophy of the crown on high.

1. King Edmund, of whom I spoke above,[4] and who came between two brothers who were also kings, lusted for heirs, and took to wife the noble lady Ælfgifu, who excelled in chastity and holiness. She proved fertile and provided her husband with children, Eadwig, whose reputation is destroyed in my earlier narrative,[5] and Edgar, of whom I now proceed to speak. His future greatness and prosperity God, author of that prosperity, deigned to announce in advance to his servant Dunstan.[6] 2. For at the precise moment when his mother was bringing him into the light of day, Dunstan, then an abbot, heard a voice from heaven saying: 'Peace to the church of the English, in the time of the child that is now born and of our Dunstan.' Dunstan heard that this was to happen, we have heard and seen the results; for the peace that prevailed in the English Church while they lived cannot be described. But when Edgar was dead peace began to languish in certain monasteries, limbs of England, while at Dunstan's passing the constant firebrand of war or the fever of internal evils blazed out through the whole body of the land.

---

[2] See above, i. 18–19.

[3] Crediton: B., c. 19 (p. 29); Winchester: Adelard, lectio iv (p. 57), Osbern, c. 22 (p. 95), Eadmer, c. 12 (p. 185), following (so we argue above, p. xviii) the OE Life (Eng.). In i. 23 William presents the compromise he suggests here.

[4] i. 14. 1. The two brothers were Æthelstan and Eadred.   [5] Esp. i. 27.

[6] The prophecy of Edgar's birth and its fulfilment were also described by William in GR, c. 148. 1–2.

2. Edgarus, per incrementa temporum in pueritiam prouectus, crebro adhuc priuatus monstrabat inditio cui se in regno applicaturus esset studio.[1] Spirabat enim tenera aetas illustris et prudentis pueri quod robustiores anni mirifico dedere effectui.[a] Denique, ut in cuiusdam prologo legi[2] qui regulam Benedicti Anglico enucleabat stilo, dum quadam die ludibundus sagittis exerceret animum, animaduertit procul edifitia magna, sed situ et ruinis deformia. 2. Consuluit ergo sotios quid esset, indaginem ueri sollicita mente rimatus. Dictum est ab eis fuisse ibi monasterium olim magnificum, nunc, uel bellica hostium clade uel tirannica regum[3] ⟨superbia⟩[b] destructum, raro incoli habitatore. Tum ille leuatis in altum oculis huic se uoto fecit obnoxium, ut si umquam regnaret et istud et alia in statum pristinum excitaret. Per haec Deo, qui scrutatur interna, et hominibus, qui presentem indolem futuri boni uiderent interpretem, carus, statim ut anni tulere ascitus est in regnum magna hominum felicitate.

3. Grauabat adhuc superas auras[4] uiuendo Edwius, cuius quanto extendebatur uita, tanto augebatur malitia. Nam preter insaniam, quam retuli superius, in aecclesiam et Dunstanum, etiam in auiam suam Edgitham[c 5] crudelitatem anhelauit et euomuit, feminam[d] cuius nulla umquam littera digne mores effigiabit, nobilitate et religione[e] iuxta prestantem. Contempsit in ea Edwius dignitatem quod regina, quod duorum fuisset mater regum; paruipendit generis affinitatem, quod tulisset utero patrem suum; despexit annorum maturitatem, quod iam uergebat in senium; nichili duxit dapsilitatem, quod esset omnium gentium quasi fidum aerarium. 2. Conscidit igitur omnia, interdicens ei curia et patrimonio. Non potuerunt ultra ferre Angli proteruiam insani iuuenis qui etiam in proprios seuiret affectus. Vno ergo consensu plusquam ciuile bellum[6] consciscunt. Quicumque[7]

---

[a] ed. (*cf. i. 2. 2 and the n. at ii. 4. 4*); affectui *Q*   [b] *Supplied by ed. exempli gratia*
[c] *Rightly* Edgiuam (*cf. i. 23. 3 n.*)   [d] *Stubbs*; femina *Q*   [e] relligione et nobilitate *Q*[a.c.]

[1] For his building of monasteries, see *GP*, c. 73 (p. 143).
[2] Prol. to Æthelwold, OE version of the *Benedictine Rule*: ed. *Councils* i(1), no. 33 (pp. 142–54). See Robinson, *Times*, pp. 159–68; D. Whitelock, 'The authorship of the account of King Edgar's establishment of monasteries', in her *History, Law and Literature in 10th–11th Century England* (Variorum Collected Studies Ser., cxxviii: London, 1980), VII, pp. 125–36, esp. 127–8. The unique copy in BL, MS Cotton Faustina A. x, fos. 102–51, probably written during William's lifetime, has a tenuous connection with Worcester: Gameson, *Manuscripts of Early Norman England*, no. 384.
[3] Cf. *GP*, c. 75 (p. 159): 'eiusdem regis tirannide'. Eadwig is called 'tirannus' at ii. 3. 4. The reference is to Abingdon.

2. Edgar, advancing by degrees to boyhood, frequently showed while still a private citizen what would be his concerns when he came to the throne.[1] This brilliant and sensible boy even in his tenderest years gave a flavour of what maturity was to bring to marvellous fruition. For instance, as I have read in the prologue[2] of someone who translated the Rule of St Benedict into English, Edgar was on one occasion practising his skills at archery when he noticed some way off buildings of some size, but defaced by neglect and collapse. 2. He asked his companions about them, eager to search out the truth. They told him that there had once been a splendid monastery there, but that it had been destroyed by enemy action or the arrogance of tyrannical kings,[3] and now had only a few inhabitants. Edgar lifted his eyes, and bound himself by a vow: if he should ever be king, he would restore this place and others like it to their original state. In such ways he grew dear to God, who sees our inmost thoughts, and to men, who judged his present disposition an omen of good to come. And as soon as he was old enough he was summoned to the throne with general enthusiasm.

3. Eadwig was still alive to pollute the upper air;[4] the longer his life went on, the worse his evil character became. Apart from his mad attacks (already described) on Dunstan and on the Church, he breathed out—even vomited out—cruelty against his own grandmother Eadgyth,[5] a woman whose character will never be worthily portrayed by any description, so outstanding was she in nobility and piety alike. Eadwig despised her eminence, for she had been queen and the mother of two kings; he belittled his relationship with her, for she had borne his own father in her womb; he looked down on her mature years, for she was already growing old; and he rated her generosity low, for she was, as it were, the steadfast treasury of all peoples. 2. He tore all this up, banning her from court and inheritance alike. The English could not brook longer the insolence of a crazy youth who was prepared to turn his rage even on his own relatives. With one consent they undertook a 'more than civil' war.[6] All the peoples[7] this side the

---

[4] Virgilian (e.g. *Aen.* vi. 128), and cf. Statius, *Theb.* xii. 566–7: 'campum . . . caelum uentosque grauantem'.

[5] Eadgifu, wife of Edward the Elder. William knew the name perfectly well (e.g. *GR*, c. 126. 3), and it is odd that he gets it wrong twice (see *app. crit.* on i. 23. 3).

[6] Cf. Lucan i. 1, much used by William (see *GR*, c. 113. 1 n.).

[7] The account which follows considerably supplements that in *GR*, c. 147. 4, which says of Eadwig only that 'He paid the price, even in this life, for his rash daring [in oppressing monasteries], when, stripped of the most part of his kingdom, . . . he died'. The remarks in 3 on the submissiveness of the people to the kings of Wessex are striking.

citra Humbram, quicumque citra Tamensem fluuium populi erant in Edwium pari armantur sententia. Ita multis conspirantibus, nullis uel paucis auxiliantibus, facili negotio pulsum ultra Tamensem reliquere, has interim ei partes ad tutandam quam ei polliciti fidem concedentes.[1] 3. Fuerunt enim semper tenaces fidei, nec umquam in dominos quantumlibet asperos rebelles. Denique per ducentos et quinquaginta annos audiuimus, cum eos Westsaxonum reges multis sepe irritassent iniuriis, semper tamen illorum ditioni succiduis subdebantur seculis. Quocirca cum istum, ut dixi, iustis et necessariis causis parte tantum regni mutilassent,[2] Edgarum fratrem prefecerunt alteri, uoluntati nimirum Dei consentanei. 4. Ille statim, ut aetatis infirmitatem (non enim maior quam sedecim annorum erat)[3] maturiori fulciret consilio,[a] partis suae optimates indicto conuocauit concilio. Ibi cum aliis illud precipue decretum, ut priuilegia aecclesiarum, quae seculo suo tirannus inuiderat, prona libertate restituerentur. Quod ut enucleatius fieret, Dunstanum ab exilio reuocandum, qui et ea omnia nosset et quo minus renouarentur nulli potestati pro conscientia religionis cederet.

4. Edwius interim fatali sorte uitam exiuit, festinatae mortis benefitio multis exemptus iniuriis,[4] siue dolor repulsae obitum celerauerat, siue sustulerat Deus hominem de medio parum aecclesiae profuturum, non dico multum nociturum. At Dunstano ab exilio reuerso ab omnibus optimatibus libenter occursum, a rege fauor effusus. Parum intercessit temporis et, coacto apud Bradford concilio,[5] censitum est ab episcopis ut Dunstanus episcopatus gradum sumeret, quo maiori auctoritate regis tirocinia posset regere. Tunc enim Kenwaldus[b] Wigornensium antistes moriens ei locum uacuefecerat. 2. Properabat quippe impleri quod uiderat somnium, quod uerius quilibet uocet diuinum uaticinium. Tunc enim beatus Petrus suum

---

[a] *ed.* (*cf. Osbern p. 103*); concilio *Q; so too in ii. 4. 1*   [b] *ed.*; Kenenwaldus *Q*; Cynewaldus *B. p. 37*

[1] William's use of 'citra' and 'ultra' in relation to the rivers Humber and Thames is noteworthy. In relation to the Humber, 'citra' excludes the Northumbrians, though according to JW s.a. 957 they as well as the Mercians were in revolt against Eadwig. However, McGurk ad loc., n. 6, suggests that JW only included the Northumbrians among the rebels by inference. In relation to the Thames, 'citra' makes sense only if it means the northern side, thus denoting the Mercians, as against the West Saxons, who continued to support Eadwig. This is easier to imagine if William was thinking from a Malmesbury rather than a Glastonbury perspective.

[2] Cf. *GR*, c. 147. 4: 'maxima parte regni mutilatus'.   [3] *GR*, c. 148. 1.

Humber and Thames took up arms in unison against Eadwig. Many were the conspirators, few or none those who came to his aid; he was easily driven out and left beyond the Thames;[1] for they were ready to concede him this region for the moment so as to keep the oath they had sworn him. 3. For they were ever loyal to their promises, and never rebellious against masters however harsh. Indeed we have heard that for 250 years, for all the constant injuries with which the West Saxon kings provoked them, they always submitted to their control, century after century. So after, as I have said, for honourable and compelling reasons depriving Eadwig of only part of his kingdom,[2] they put his brother Edgar in control of the other part, surely conforming thereby to God's will. 4. Edgar at once summoned the noblemen of his half to a council, wishing to bring maturer advice to underpin his infirmity of years (for he was no more than sixteen).[3] At the council it was in particular decreed that the privileges of the churches, which the tyrant had in his day resented, should be restored with all liberty. To make sure this was carried out with the more precision, Dunstan was to be restored from exile, for he knew all their provisions and was too pious to yield to any authority the power to prevent their renewal.

4. Eadwig meanwhile died by a stroke of fate, and escaped many injuries thanks to this swift demise;[4] perhaps the grief he felt at his downfall had hurried it on, or God had removed from our midst a man who would not have much benefited the Church and indeed would have much harmed it. When Dunstan returned from exile, he was welcomed warmly by all the nobility; the king's favour was signal, and it was not long before a council was held at Bradford,[5] where the bishops gave their view that Dunstan should become a bishop to give him greater authority to guide the pupillage of the king. For Cenwald, bishop of Worcester, had just died, leaving a place open for him. 2. Indeed the dream Dunstan had had—rather to be called a prophecy from heaven—was hastening to its fulfilment. In it, St Peter

---

[4] A variation on the topos 'felix opportunitate mortis' (Tacitus, *Agricola* xlv. 3), normally applied to good men: see J. D. H. Scourfield, *Consoling Heliodorus* (Oxford, 1993), p. 196.

[5] 957 × 958: *Councils*, i(1), no. 24 (pp. 86–8), from B., c. 25 (pp. 36–7). Cenwald bp. of Worcester d. 28 June in one of these years. Eadwig did not die until 1 Oct. 959, after which Edgar became king of all England. The place ('Bradanford' in MSS AC, 'Brandanford' in MS D of B.'s Life) is not identified; it cannot have been Bradford-on-Avon, which is not in Edgar's part of the kingdom, but in Wessex.

tradidit ensem, quum*a* ei in Wigornia suam non inuidit sedem. Nam thronus pontificalis in Wigornia nondum transierat in nomen beatae Dei genitricis.[1] Quomodo autem et quando transierit sequens sermo elucidabit.[2] Quo deinceps ambiguo*b* Osbernus multa casso labore uerba consumpsit,[3] dum aliquid ueri simile conaretur procudere quare Dunstanus in Wigornia episcopus fuerit, cum eam sedem a Domini matre sibi datam non uiderit. 3. Vnde comperio parum eum inuestigasse historias, qui suae patriae nescierit aecclesias. In hanc ergo sedem consecrandus, pro more Cantuariam contendit. Durabat adhuc in rebus humanis beatus Odo archiepiscopus, infractus aetate sed integer mente. Is super electum egit consecrationis sollemnia, non ut Wigorniae pontificem sed ut Cantuariae primatem.[4] Nec, quanuis multo circumstantium interpolatus murmure, abstitit, quin immo susurros eorum leui*c* sermone compescuit: non se oris uel mentis titubantia peccasse, sed esse factum suum non inane, ore suo loqui Spiritum sanctum, qui presignaret beatum illum post se fore archiepiscopum. 4. Huius denuntiationis presagio Dunstanus insignis omnia constanti reuerentia et reuerenti constantia agere; uitae suae potissimum intendere, postea subiectorum mores non negligere, postremo tota niti solertia ut minae quibus obstrinxerat diabolum prodirent in effectum.*d* Credo nequam spiritum sepe momentaneam deplorasse laetitiam, cum tantam uideret a se dissotiari turbam. Hoc quippe cotidianum pontificis erat exercitium, comminisci unde faceret gaudium bonis, tristitiam spiritibus proteruis.

5. Impleta erat iam uisionis portio,[5] pars implenda restabat. Petrus fidem pollicitam soluerat; ut Paulus idem faceret supererat. Nec uero distulit, sed, ut credi fas est, exorato Deo Lundoniensem episcopum in quietas sedes transduxit.[6] Tum uero rex, qui nullam occasionem pretermitteret quo minus Dunstanum sullimaret, eum ad Pauli aecclesiam gubernandam crebro inuitauit; prudens*e* primi episcopatus amministratio regis animum exstimulauerat, spem auxerat. 2. Nichil

---

a *Probably read* quoniam   *b* quo deinceps ambiguo] *Hardly sound; perhaps read* de quo anceps (*cf. GR 48. 3*) ambiguo   *c* *Perhaps read* leni (*cf. GR 113. 1* leni oratione)   *d* affectum *Q*^*a.c.*   *e* *Perhaps add* enim

[1] See *VW* i. 3. 4 n.   [2] Below, c. 13.
[3] Osbern, c. 31 (p. 106).
[4] The senile consecration is also in *GP*, c. 17 (p. 25).
[5] See i. 24. 2–5, with Eadred's interpretation at 5. 'Verbum Dei' suggests that the church of Christ the Saviour, Canterbury, is meant (cf. above, p. 221 n. 6). The saints

handed his sword to Dunstan because he did not grudge him his see at Worcester. For the bishop's throne at Worcester had not yet come to be called after the blessed Mother of God.[1] How and when the name changed will appear later.[2] Osbern spent many words and wasted much labour on this problem,[3] trying to manufacture some plausible reason why Dunstan should have been made bishop at Worcester, though Dunstan in his dream did not see the bishopric being given to him by the Mother of God. 3. My conclusion is that Osbern did not go deep enough into history, seeing that he was ignorant of his own land's churches. Anyway, Worcester was the chosen see, and Dunstan set off for Canterbury to be consecrated in the usual way. The blessed Archbishop Oda was still alive, broken by age but sound of mind. And it was he who carried out the consecration ceremony for the elect, blessing him not as bishop of Worcester but as primate of Canterbury.[4] Despite the murmurs of those around trying to interrupt him, he carried on regardless, and even gently stilled their whispers, saying that he had not made a slip of the tongue or of memory; this was no meaningless occurrence, but the Holy Spirit was speaking through him, in order to signal the blessed Dunstan as eventual archbishop. 4. Marked out by this omen, Dunstan did everything with constant reverence and reverent constancy; he laid especial stress on regulating his own life, but after that did not neglect the morals of his subjects; and lastly he strove with all his skill to bring to effect the threats he had made to bind the Devil. I can well believe that the evil spirit often had cause to regret its moment of joy when it saw so great a multitude being removed from his power. This indeed was the daily concern of the bishop, to plan how to bring joy to good men and grief to impudent spirits.

5. Part of the vision had now been fulfilled,[5] part remained for fulfilment. Peter had duly paid what he had promised; it remained for Paul to do the same. He did not delay, but, as we may surmise, secured from God the removal of the bishop of London to the abode of the dead.[6] The king, not one to lose an opportunity to advance Dunstan, pressed him repeatedly to rule the church of Paul; for the good sense he had brought to the administration of his first bishopric had excited the king and increased his hopes of Dunstan. 2. Indeed,

---

designate the cathedral churches of which they were patrons: Peter = Worcester, Paul = London, and Andrew = Rochester; cf. ii. 6. 6.

[6] Cf. Virgil, *Aen.* i. 205. The bp. was Brihthelm, 951/3–957/9.

quippe nimium uidebatur committi ei in cuius animo ad multa gubernanda concordabat sapientia cum religione, ingenium cum uirtute. Renuit ille diu, frustraque triuisset Edgarus preces nisi communis episcoporum assensus renitentem superasset, quanuis et mentem eius sollicitare potuit*ᵃ* supradicta uisio, ne obstinate putaret negandum quod per apostolum iam nouerat presignatum. Quapropter subiecit ⟨se⟩*ᵇ* iugo quod imponebat caritas ex fratèrno episcoporum animo. 3. Nec fuit hoc transgredi canones,¹ quia cedunt leges humanae ubi promulgantur diuinae. Quocirca nulla sanctum uirum transgressionis pulset inuidia, ubi non fuit ambitus honoris, non appetitus potestatis. Nam quid horum in eius pectore potuit esse qui fuit per apostolos designatus, per collegium sacerdotum ascitus? Sed de his cuique liberum erit iuditium, dum modo non auertatur in prauum sed declinet in bonum. 4. Ego ceptam narrationem prosequar, quomodo secundum prophetiam*ᶜ* regis Edredi pro 'In principio erat Verbum', quod erat scriptum in gladio Petri, fuerit Dunstanus constitutus princeps et primas Angliae in aecclesia Saluatoris Cantuariae, nec minus quomodo Andreae gladium acceperit,*ᵈ* quia Rofensis aecclesia, eidem apostolo dedicata, sequitur Cantuariensem sicut matrem filia, sicut dominam pedisequa. Qui enim Cantuariensis archiepiscopus est in Rofensi aecclesia proprius uel dominus si seuus uel patronus si bonus. Haec igitur dicturus quaedam ad rem pertinentia premittam.²

6. Maturus erat iam caelo sanctus archiepiscopus Odo, poscebaturque a superis ciuibus, ut eius aduentu eorum augeretur numerus.³ Nec ille, ui morbi tactus, ulla tristitia excusauit aduentum, sed 'exultauit ut uideret diem Domini, uidit et gauisus est'.⁴ Tum uero Edgarus rex, oblatum sibi tempus existimans quo Dunstano facere bene tantum posset pene quantum uellet, ut archiepiscopatum susciperet preces ingessit et regessit; sed nichil profecit. 2. Quapropter⁵ Elfsius Wintoniensis episcopus sedem summam inuolauit

---

ᵃ One expects a subjunctive   *ᵇ Supplied by ed.*   *ᶜ ed.;* prophesiam *Q*   *ᵈ ed.;* acceperat *Q*

¹ i.e. by holding two sees at once. William excuses Dunstan's pluralism, as does Osbern, c. 31 (pp. 105–6).
² William refers forward to Dunstan's promotion to the see of Canterbury. His account of this begins at ii. 6. 5.
³ Cf. *GP*, c. 223 (p. 375): 'gratissimus fuit hic obitus caelestibus, quod pro sanctitate preteritae uitae numerum eorum ampliaret'.

nothing seemed to him too great to be entrusted to one in whom wisdom went hand in hand with piety, talent with virtue, in the governance of many offices. Long did Dunstan refuse, and Edgar's prayers would have been quite wasted had not the unanimous agreement of the bishops overcome his protests: though he might also have been influenced by the vision to think he should not be obstinate in rejecting something he knew the apostle had marked out for him. So he subjected himself to the yoke which the brotherly charity of the bishops laid upon him. 3. Nor was it a question of going against canon law,[1] because the laws of men have to retreat when those of God are proclaimed. Accordingly the holy man should not be imputed with any transgression in a case where there was no canvassing for a post and no lust for power. How could there have been any room for such sentiments in the heart of one who had been chosen by apostles and called to office by the college of priests? But everyone may take his own view on these matters, so long as it tends towards good rather than ill. 4. As for me, I shall go on with the story I have begun, how, to fulfil the prophecy of King Eadred, in accordance with the words 'In the beginning was the Word' written on the sword of Peter, Dunstan was made first bishop and primate of England in the church of the Saviour at Canterbury, and equally how he took the sword of Andrew. For the church of Rochester, which is dedicated to that apostle, follows the church of Canterbury as a daughter follows her mother, or a maid her mistress. Whoever is archbishop of Canterbury is for Rochester her own master if he is tyrannical and her own patron if he is good. But before I proceed to this, I shall first mention certain relevant matters.[2]

6. That holy man Archbishop Oda was by now ripe for heaven; those who live on high were clamouring for him, anxious that his arrival should increase their number.[3] When he fell ill, he was in no way sad, and he did not try to make excuses, but 'rejoiced to see the day of the Lord; he saw it, and was glad'.[4] King Edgar now recognized the opportunity to do for Dunstan almost as much as he wished in the way of good, and he urged and urged him again to take up the archbishopric. But to no avail. 2. Accordingly,[5] Ælfsige bishop of

---

[4] John 8: 56.
[5] The story is also told in *GP*, c. 17 (pp. 25–6). See also Byrhtferth, *Vita S. Oswaldi*, pp. 408–9, and Stubbs in *Memorials*, p. xciii. Ælfsige was bp. of Winchester 951–8, archbp. of Canterbury 958–9.

continuo, surreptis per aduocatos suos regis edictis: homo intract-
abilis auaritiae, ambitionis nimiae, qui multum diuque Cantuariae
inhiauerat. Quod ipso die processionis suae dissimulare non potuit.
Magna enim cum fuisset pompa exceptus, sacrilegum spirans accessit
ad tumbam beati Odonis. Putabant fortasse comites quod sanctae
animae uellet offitium deferre. At ille (o dolendum nefas!) et tumbam
pede depulit et in defunctum conuitia effudit. 'Tandem' inquit
'uiuacem animam effudisti, pessime senex! Tandem tua mala gratia
potior sede cupita.' 3. Facinus miserandum et seuum, fuisse pontificem qui in memoriam defuncti pontificis tam execrandas ructaret
iniurias! Sequenti sane nocte, apparente sibi Sancto, temeritatis
ammonitus et in futurum minis territus, nichilo setius Romam pro
pallio ire perseuerauit. Iam uero prope Alpes uentum cum esset,
miserabile frigus medullae concipiens, nulla copia uestium, nullo
ignis admotu calefieri potuit. Itaque exinteratis equorum uentribus
pedes immittens, cum nec*a* in teporem eos animare posset, anima
fugiente diriguit.

4. Hoc*b* Angliam nuntio delato, iterum ad Dunstanum de archiepiscopatu preces relatae, iterumque cassatae. Tum fuere qui dicebant
Brihtelmum[1] Dorsatensem episcopum pro animi modestia et uitae
munditia debere Cantuariam migrare. Facilis fuit regis concessio, qui
ad hoc animum induxerat suum, ut amplitudine fortunae non abutens
bonorum precibus refragari non uideretur. Veruntamen post paucos
dies cognitum est quia illud quod putabatur in Brihtelmo mentis
modestia erat potius inertia. Quapropter remissioris animi iudicatus
minusque magno regimini accommodus, ex uoluntate regis ualefecit
alienis honoribus, in suos regressus. 5. Ita rex, adiuncto sibi omnium
episcoporum et procerum suffragio, Dunstanum precibus temptauit,
nec destitit quoad ille importunitati succumbens omnium uoluntati
manus daret. *'*Omnes enim illi, non tam humani casus quam diuini
nutus, seruierant somno Dunstani et uaticinio regis Edredi;*c* non
enim otiosum esse uel in uanum cedere poterat quod gloriosus rex per
Spiritum dixerat. Suscepit ergo Dunstanus nostrarum aecclesiarum
principem, aecclesiam olim sibi precellentis metalli litteris in gladio
principis apostolorum designatam.[2] 6. Suscepit Domini Saluatoris

---

a Perhaps add sic (cf. GP p. 26)   *b* Q m.2 adds in   *c–c* The sentence seems corrupt

[1] Bp. of Wells 956–73, archbp. of Canterbury during 959.
[2] See i. 24. 2. For the obscure circumstances of Dunstan's succession as archbishop, see
D. Whitelock, 'The appointment of Dunstan as archbishop of Canterbury', in her *History,
Law and Literature in 10th–11th Century England* (London, 1981), no. IV.

Winchester at once pounced on the highest see, using his supporters to extract decrees from the king; for he was a man of uncompromising greed and excessive ambition, who had long cast greedy eyes on Canterbury. He could not hide this lust even on the day of his installation. After being received with great ceremony, he went to the tomb of the blessed Oda breathing sacrilege. It may be that the company thought he wanted to pay his respects to the holy man's soul; but shockingly he kicked the tomb and poured out abuse of the dead man: 'At last you have breathed your life out, you wicked old man! At last I have the see I wanted—no thanks to you!' 3. It is an appalling crime that there should have been a bishop ready to stain the memory of a dead bishop by emitting such deplorable insults. The following night he was visited by Oda in a vision, admonished for his rash deed, and threatened fearsomely as to his future behaviour. But none the less he persisted in his plan to go to Rome to fetch the pallium. As he approached the Alps, he caught a wretched and deep-seated chill, and could not get warm, however many clothes he put on or however near the fire he sat. He was reduced to having horses disembowelled and sitting with his feet in their guts; but he could not even take the chill off them, and eventually froze to death.

4. When the news reached England, the entreaties to Dunstan to take up the primacy were renewed, and again disappointed. There were those who said that Byrhthelm,[1] bishop of Dorset [sc. Wells], should move to Canterbury, for he was a modest and clean-living man. The king readily agreed, for he had resolved not to abuse his high fortune by seeming to resist the requests of good men. But a few days later it became clear that what had in Byrhthelm been thought modesty was in fact sloth. He was judged too slack to rule a great see, and at the instance of the king he bade farewell to an office to which he was unsuited and returned to his own. 5. The king then summoned to his aid all the bishops and noblemen, and did not stop badgering Dunstan with his request until he gave way to his importunity and surrendered to the universal will. For all had paid the closest heed to Dunstan's dream and the prophecy of King Eadred, as being the will of God and not a matter of chance. What a glorious king had foretold, under the inspiration of the Holy Spirit, could not be idle or without effect. And so it came about that Dunstan took over the first of our churches, a church long ago marked out for him by the letters in precious metal on the sword of the first of the apostles.[2] 6. He took up the yoke of the Lord Saviour in the church

in eiusdem basilica iugum, qui ipse principium, et ipse in principio Verbum, caro factus est in fine seculorum. Non minus, ut ante dixi,[1] cum Cantuariensi primatu suscepit beati Andreae in urbe Rofensi sedem, quae numquam potest diuelli ab eius caritate, sicut nec membrum a capite. Nichil ergo restabat*a* de debito, solutum est quicquid debebatur ex promisso. Itaque probatur non fuisse friuolum somnium quod tam nobili ordine constat esse impletum.

7. Pro more igitur antecessorum, pro insigni primatus sui suscipiendo ad Romam iter composuit. Currente per regiones uiae conterminas fama, turmatim ad eum ruebant populi, hi uictum, hi uultum, omnes benedictionem eius optantes. Impertiebat ipse omnibus necessaria, et dabantur eo iubente cibi, effundebaturque pecunia. Suggerentibus*b* crebro ministris iam exhaustum esse marsupium, iam in angusto esse uictum, semper pretendebat Christum: darent illi libenter, redderet Christus liberaliter. 2. Preterea conuenire archiepiscopo ut omni die omnem hominem suo illustret benefitio. Non erat ministris obniti *c*constanti auctoritate uiri deuictis.*c* Ita quanuis darentur omnia quae uel extulerant patria uel largitas contulerat aliena, numquam tamen eis defuit Christus. Denique cum quadam die, consumptis sumptibus, ne diurnus quidem suppeteret uictus, secessit pontifex iam illatus hospitio, ut uesperas hora monente conficeret. 3. Cauillante interea ministro cui dispensandi prouintia fuit delegata, quod frustra sibi de Christo applauserat,[2] ex insperato abbas e uicino commanens multa intulit xenia, tanta congessit*d* obsonia ut eo et sequentibus diebus non solum tolleret famem sed etiam cumulauit*e* satietatem. Sic ministro ne grunniret cohibito, presul *f*liberalitatis in pauperes propensior*f* Romam peruenit. Ibi ab apostolico Iohanne dignanter exceptus, pallium cum gratia, cum gloria reditum inpetrauit. Priuilegium etiam intulit patriae quod hic pro antiquitatis inditio uolo apponere:

4. *g*'Iohannes[3] episcopus, seruus seruorum,*h* confratri Dunstano Dorobernensis aecclesiae archiepiscopo uitae*i* permanendam in Christo salutem.

---

a *ed.*; restat *Q*   *b* *N adds* autem   *c–c* constanti (*or* -tia et) . . . deuictis *ed.*; constantia . . . deuinctis *Q*   *d* *Stubbs*; congesset *Q*   *e* *The mood is out of line* *f–f* *The phrase seems corrupt*   *g* *This letter is edited in Councils, i(1), pp. 90–2. We normally follow Q, but give some variants from other witnesses (Ead. = Eadmer, Historia Novorum (ed. M. Rule) pp. 274–6; GP pp. 61–2 (only in part); and P = Paris, Bibl. Nat. lat. 943).*   *h* *GP, Ead. add* Dei (*P adds* Domini), *rightly*   *i* *GP, Ead. add* perpetuae

of the Lord Saviour, who is the beginning, and in the beginning was the Word, and became flesh world without end. Equally, as I have said,[1] he took over with the primacy the see of St Andrew at Rochester, which can never be sundered from its dear sister any more than limb from head. So nothing was left of the debt, everything promised was now paid. Here is the proof that a dream so splendidly fulfilled in all its detail was not empty of meaning.

7. Like his predecessors, Dunstan arranged to travel to Rome to receive the insignia of his primacy. The news spread through the country bordering on his route; and people flocked to him, some wanting food, others a glimpse of him, but all his blessing. He gave to them all the necessities of life: at his orders food was supplied and money lavished. Often did the servants represent to him that the purse was exhausted and their very livelihood straitened, but he always used Christ as his answer: *they* should give willingly, *He* would give back bountifully. 2. Moreover, it was proper for an archbishop to bring the light of his good works to every man every day. The servants could not object; they were overawed by the man's firm authority. So although everything they had brought from home or received from the largesse of others was being given away, Christ never failed them. For instance, one day everything was finished and they had not food even for a day. The archbishop had already been taken to his lodgings, and he retired to say vespers as the hour demanded. 3. The servant who had the task of doling out supplies was grumbling that Dunstan had been wrong to pride himself on Christ's help,[2] when suddenly an abbot living nearby brought in a host of presents, and produced such a pile of provisions that on that and the succeeding days he not only averted hunger but heaped up a surfeit. That stopped the servant's grumbles, and the archbishop arrived in Rome even more inclined to be liberal to the poor. He was welcomed as befitted him by Pope John, and won from him the grace of the pallium and a return in glory. He also brought home a privilege, which I wish to put in here as a witness to times past.

4. 'John,[3] bishop, servant of servants, to his brother Dunstan, archbishop of Canterbury, lasting health and life, in Christ.

---

[1] ii. 5. 4.

[2] Cf. the grumbles of the steward in B., c. 27 (p. 39). For the phrase, see *Mir.*, p. 134 lines 681–2.

[3] *Regesta Pontificum Romanorum . . . ad annum 1198*, ed. P. Jaffé, 2nd edn. by S. Loewenfeld *et al.* (2 vols.: Leipzig, 1885–8), no. 3687, in a version edited at Canterbury

'Si pastores ouium solem geluque pro gregis sui custodia nocte ac die*ᵃ* ferre contenti sunt, et oculis circumspectant*ᵇ* uigilantibus ne aliqua ex ouibus aut errando pereat aut ferinis laniata*ᶜ* morsibus rapiatur: quanto sudore quantaque cura debemus esse peruigiles ob salutem animarum qui dicimur pastores earum! 5. Attendamus igitur nos offitium exhibere erga custodiam Dominicarum ouium, et ne quasi lupo ueniente territi fugiamus, *ᵈ*ne in die diuini examinis pro desidia nostra ante summum pastorem ex*ᵉ* negligentia nostra excruciemur.*ᵈ* Vnde modo honoris reuerentia in sullimiore arce ceteris diiudicamur. Primatum itaque tuum, in quo tibi ex more antecessorum tuorum uices apostolicae sedis exercere conuenit, ita tibi ad plenum confirmamus, sicut beatum Augustinum eiusque successores prefatae aecclesiae pontifices plenius habuisse dinoscitur. 6. Pallium uero fraternitati tuae ex more ad missarum sollemnia celebranda commendamus, quo tibi non aliter aecclesiae tuae priuilegiis in suo statu manentibus uti concedimus, nisi quem usum antecessores nostri*ᶠ¹* prodiderunt.

'Neque tua prudentia hoc incognitum habet,*ᵍ* quoniam indumenti honor moderatione actuum tenendus*ʰ* erit. Honestati morum tuorum haec ornamenta conueniant,*ⁱ* quatinus auctore Deo possis esse conspicuus, ita ut uita tua filiis tuis sit regula, et in ipsa si qua tortitudo illis inest dirigatur, dum in ea quod imitentur aspitiunt,*ʲ* in ipsa semper considerando profitiant, ut tecum Deum per hoc quod bene uixerint uidere mereantur. 7. Cor ergo tuum neque prosperis quae temporaliter blandiuntur extollatur neque aduersis deiciatur. Quicquid illud fuerit aduersi uirtute in Christo patientiae deiciatur.*ᵏ* Nullum apud te locum fauor indiscretus inueniat, in omnibus discretionem alii in te cognoscant. Insontem apud te culpabilem suggestio mala non fatiat, nocentem gratia non excuset. Remissum te delinquentibus non ostendas, nec quod illis non profuerit hos perpetrare permittas. 8. Sit in te*ˡ* boni pastoris dulcedo, sit et iudicis seuera districtio,*ᵐ* unum scilicet quo*ⁿ* innocentes foueas, aliud quo*ᵒ*

ᵃ die ac nocte *GP, Ead., P*   *ᵇ* conspectant *GP, Ead., P*   *ᶜ Perhaps read* lanianda   *ᵈ⁻ᵈ The text is uncertain*   *ᵉ* et *GP, Ead.*; pro *P*   *ᶠ GP, Ead., P*; uestri *Q*   *ᵍ Ead., P add* uel cuiusque (uel cuiuscumque *GP*)   *ʰ* tremendus *GP, Ead., P*   *ⁱ* conueniunt *GP, Ead., P*   *ʲ* aspician *GP, Ead., P*   *ᵏ* a te deuincatur *Ead., P* (deuincatur *is translated*)   *ˡ Ead., P add* et   *ᵐ Ead., P*; districtio *Q*   *ⁿ* quod *Ead., P*   *ᵒ* quod *Ead., P*

---

not earlier than Lanfranc's time: *Councils*, i(1), no. 25 (pp. 88–92), dated 21 Sept. 960. Part in *GP*, c. 39 (pp. 61–2); complete in Eadmer, *Historia novorum*, ed. M. Rule (RS, 1884), pp. 274–6. The genuine version is in the Sherborne Pontifical, Paris, Bibl. nat., MS lat.

'If shepherds are happy to put up night and day with sun and frost to look after their flock, and look about with watchful eyes to make sure none of their sheep strays and perishes or is snatched away, torn by the jaws of wild beasts: how much sweat, how much care *we* should expend in our watch over the salvation of souls, we who are called shepherds of those souls! 5. Let us therefore make sure that we do our duty in our guardianship of the sheep of the Lord, and let us not flee in terror when (as it were) a wolf approaches, so that on Judgement Day we are not tortured in the presence of the supreme Shepherd for our sloth and our negligence. It is because of this responsibility that in this world we are judged worthy of honour and reverence in a citadel that is higher than that of others. And so your primacy, in which it is for you, like your predecessors, to act for the apostolic see, we fully confirm to you, as fully as it is recognized that St Augustine and his successors as bishops of the same church held it. 6. As to the pallium, we commend it to you in the traditional manner, brother, for the solemn celebration of Mass, and we allow it for your use, so long as the privileges of your church remain in their present form, in no other way than that which our[1] predecessors set forth.

'You are of course well aware that the honour of wearing this needs to be preserved by moderation in action. Let these ornaments correspond to the uprightness of your character, so that with God to back you you may stand out, making your life a rule for your sons which they can use to correct any crookedness in their lives, looking upon it as something to follow and profiting by continual contemplation of it, so that like you they may deserve to see God because of their good lives. 7. Let your heart therefore not be puffed up by the blandishments of temporal prosperity, or cast down by adversity. Let anything that goes wrong be overcome by the virtue of patience in Christ. Let indiscriminate favour find no place in you; let others recognize discretion in you in all respects. Let evil insinuations make no innocent man guilty in your eyes. Let influence not find excuses for a guilty man. Do not show yourself slack to those who break the rules, or permit one person to do something that disadvantages another. 8. Show the sweetness of the good shepherd and the severity of a judge, that with the one you may foster the innocent, with the

943, fos. 7–8v (s. x²). See T. Symons, 'Notes on the life and work of St Dunstan—II', *The Downside Review*, lxxx (1962), 355–66, at pp. 357–8.

[1] We have for once accepted the reading of other witnesses against the text of our manuscript, which makes no sense.

inquietos feriendo a prauitate compescas. Sed quoniam nonnumquam prepositorum zelus, dum districtius malorum uindex est, transit in crudelitatem, correptionem in iuditio refrena, et censuram disciplinae discute, ut et culpas ferias et a dilectione peruersorum quos corripis non recedas. Misericordiam, prout uirtus patitur, pauperibus exhibe. Oppressis defensio tua subueniat, opprimentibus modesta ratione contradicas. 9. Nullius fatiem contra iustitiam accipias, nullum querentem iusta despitias. In custodia aequitatis excellas, ut nec diuitem pro^a potentia sua apud uos aliquid querentem^b extra uiam^c de accusatione audias, nec pauperem fatiat humilitas sua^d desperare: quatinus Deo miserante talis possis existere qualem sacra lectio precipit dicens: "Oportet episcopum irreprehensibilem esse."[1] Sed his omnibus uti salubriter poteris si magistram caritatem habueris: quam qui secutus fuerit a recto^e tramite non recedit. 10. Ecce, frater carissime, inter multa alia ista sunt sacerdotum, ista sunt pallii iura; quae si studiose seruaueris quod foris accepisse ostendis^f intus habebis.^{g} Sancta Trinitas fraternitatem uestram gratiae suae protectione circumdet, atque ita in timoris sui uiam te dirigat ut post uitae huius amaritudinem ad aeternam simul peruenire dulcedinem mereamur.

'Et hoc scriptum est per manum Leonis scrinialis sedis apostolicae, in mense Octobri, indictione quarta, data^h die i. kalendas Octobres, anno duodecimo summi pontificis Iohannis.'[2]

8. Beatum ergo pontificem feliciter totum iter emensum desideriis patriae sospes carina restituit.[3] Cuius reditum tam sibi prosperum quam suis uotiuum, primo exceptionis suae die[4] in Cantia, miraculum diuinitus ostensum commendauit. Assistebat candidatus[5] altari, archiepiscopatus sui redimitus insigni, cum interim templum lucida oppleuit nubes, et columba,[6] incertum unde ueniens, sacrificantem diu multumque plausibili uolatu circuiuit. 2. Ad postremum eius uertici, familiari scilicet sancti Spiritus subsellio, insidens ante

---

^{a} om. *Ead.*, P ^{b} om. *Ead.*, P ^{c} *Ead.*, P add suam ^{d} tua *Ead.*, P
^{e} *Ead.* (*after corr.*), P add aliquando ^{f} ostenderis *Ead.*, P ^{g} habes *Ead.*, P
^{h} sic Q; datarum *Ead.*, P (om. GP)

---

[1] 1 Tim. 3: 2.
[2] John XII reigned 955–63, so the regnal year is wrong: *Councils* i(1), p. 92 n. 4.
[3] Cf. to some extent *GR*, c. 3. 2, and, more closely, *HN*, c. 76.
[4] A phrase also used in *GP*, c. 17 (p. 25), apparently of Ælfsige's installation (*before* he goes off to Rome).
[5] The archbishop wears white robes; cf. also *Mir.*, p. 145 line 1036. This sense lacks in *ODML* s. v. 'candidare'.

other you may strike trouble-makers and restrain them from wickedness. But since at times the zeal of those in authority too rigorously
punishes evil men and passes over into cruelty, rein back in your
judgements the urge to correct, and consider carefully how far to
enforce discipline, so that while striking at fault you do not forget to
love the wrongdoers you are punishing. Show pity to the poor, so far
as virtue permits; let your protection come to the aid of the down-
trodden, and stand up without arrogance to those who oppress them.
9. Be not a respecter of persons against justice, despise no one who
seeks justice. Be prominent in guarding fairness: do not give ear to a
rich man who uses his power to obtain in an accusation before you
anything that goes beyond the limit, and do not let his humble
position make a poor man despair. In this way you may, by God's
mercy, be the kind of man prescribed in the Bible: "A bishop must be
blameless."[1] Now you will be able to win salvation in all these
respects if your master is Charity; anyone who follows Charity does
not diverge from the straight path. 10. These, then, dearest brother,
among many other things are the rules governing priests and the
pallium: if you keep them conscientiously, you will possess inwardly
what you show you have received externally. May the Holy Trinity
surround you, brother, with the protection of its Grace, and so direct
you to the way of fear of it that after the bitterness of this life we may
deserve to come together to the sweetness of the eternal.

'This was written by the hand of Leo, scribe of the apostolic see, in
the month of October, the fourth indiction, and sent on the day
before the kalends of October, in the twelfth year of the supreme
bishop John.'[2]

8. The blessed bishop successfully completed his journey, and his
ship brought him safely back to the land that had so much missed
him.[3] His return, so fortunate to himself and so much prayed for by
his flock, was on the first day of his welcome back[4] to Canterbury
marked by a miracle from heaven. He was at the altar, in his white
robes,[5] and wearing the token of his archbishop's rank, when a bright
cloud filled the church, and a dove,[6] coming from who knows where,
for a long time circled round Dunstan as he sacrificed, wings flapping.
2. Finally, it alighted on his head, the familiar resting place of the
Holy Spirit, and did not fly away until the office was over. Then it

[6] *GP*, c. 19 (p. 30).

peractum offitium non abscessit. Inde super sepulcrum beati Odonis pausam habuit, quod modo piramidis in australi edis parte fabrefactum fuit. Quod pontifex intuitus tantum reuerentiae in sepultum concepit ut non facile locum transiret nisi et genua flecteret et caput summitteret. Nec dubitabat cum*ᵃ* omni occasione Sanctum uocare et patrio sermone utens concinna urbanitate 'Ode se gode'*ᵇ* dicere.[1]

9. Sedit ergo in Cantia Dunstanus, ut uerbis illius qui uitam beati Athelwoldi composuit utar,[2] 'uultu angelicus, quasi columna immobilis, elemosinis, doctrina et actione precipuus, prophetia*ᶜ* prepollens'. Paucis profecto scriptor ille comprehendit beati pontificis uitam: cuius ego particulatim enodabo sententiam.

Nam quod in Dunstano nitori animi responderit claritas fatiei testantur multae quas sepe legi epistolae ad eum missae, quae niui capitis[3] candorem morum dicunt conuenisse: (2) quanuis quantulum hoc ad eius attingit laudem, in quo maiora fuerunt omnia quam ut ea quaelibet possit adornare facundia, nisi maior uideatur Dei gratia in homine quando hilaritas frontispitii concordat pectoris puritati!

Fuit porro uir ille columna immobilis quoniam nullius umquam potestatis terrore concussus est a ueritatis soliditate. Namque, ut a sanctuario Dei exordiar, eo tempore omnium aecclesiarum in Anglia clerici omnino a canonum regula desciuerant: nundinis negotiorum dediti,[4] (3) aleae lusores studiosi; fluxu uestium, uoluptatum luxu laicis uel pares uel preminentes; cibo intenti ad gulam, potui ad uomicam;[5] litterarum perinde nescii quasi dedecus esset si clerici essent litterati; usitata offitia citra intellectum uerborum uix egreque balbutientes. Huic uerecundae miseriae et miserae uerecundiae antistes medendum arbitratus, ita consilium expediuit ut nullum ad aecclesiasticos honores, episcopatus dico, aspirare pateretur nisi religiosae uitae abbatem aut monachum: id ideo ut subiectis clericis

---

ᵃ Probably to be deleted (cf. HN 74) *ᵇ ed. (cf. GP p. 30);* the goode *Q* *ᶜ ed. (cf. Wulfstan, Vit. Æth. 14);* prophesia *Q (cf. ii. 5. 4 above, and so too below ii. 17. 2, 24. 1, 35. 4 and 5, where the correction has not been signalled)*

[1] The phrase is also given in English in Eadmer, c. 27 (p. 203), and in his *Vita S. Odonis* (*Anglia Sacra* ii. 86); William repeats it in *GP*, c. 19 (p. 30).
[2] Wulfstan of Winchester, *Vita S. Æthelwoldi*, c. 14 (pp. 26–7), re-ordered, doubtless to suit the needs of William's subsequent discussion, which uses the words as a framework: *uultus* (9. 1–2), *columna* (9. 2–7), *eleemosinae* (10), *doctrina et actio* (11, with appendix on pupils and effect on the king 12–14), *prophetia* (from 14. 2).
[3] Cf. Horace, *Carm.* iv. 13. 12, Prudentius, *Cathem.* praef. 27.

came to rest on the tomb of the blessed Oda, which was built in the form of a pyramid on the south side of the building. Dunstan saw this, and conceived such a feeling of reverence towards the man buried there that he did not find it easy to pass the place without genuflecting and lowering his head. And he had no hesitation in calling him 'saint' at every opportunity, and in doing him the graceful compliment of calling him, in his native English, 'Oda the good'.[1]

9. So Dunstan ruled over Canterbury. He was, to use the words of the author of the Life of the blessed Æthelwold,[2] 'in countenance like an angel, like a pillar that cannot be moved, outstanding in alms, learning, and action, strong in prophecy'. Of course that writer is summing up the blessed bishop's life in short compass; but *I* will interpret his opinion point by point.

That in Dunstan his shining mind was matched by the brilliance of his features is testified to by many letters addressed to him, which I have often read; they say that his candour of character suited the snow-white of his hair.[3] 2. But how little relevant this is to the praises of one in whom everything was too great for any eloquence to decorate it!—unless perhaps the grace of God seems greater in the case of a man whose good-humoured face matches the purity of his character.

Then the man was like a pillar that cannot be moved because he could not be dislodged from the solidity of the truth by fear of any power. For, to start with the sanctuary of God, the clerks of every church in England had at that time fallen completely away from canon law: they involved themselves in business;[4] (3) they were ardent gamblers; they equalled or surpassed laymen in laxity of dress and excess of pleasures; they carried their enthusiasm for food to the point of gluttony, for drink to the point of vomiting;[5] they were as ignorant of letters as though it were a matter of shame for clerks to be literate; and they had great difficulty, thanks to their lack of understanding of the words, in mumbling out the customary services. The bishop thought measures were needed to remedy this deplorable and shameful state of affairs; his policy was to allow no one except an abbot or monk of devout behaviour to aspire to the

[4] Presumably simony: cf. *GP*, c. 23 (p. 35): 'prorsus publicas nundinas ex episcopatibus et abbatiis fatiens'.

[5] Cf. *GR*, c. 245. 5: 'in cibis urgentes crapulam, in potibus irritantes uomicam'; *Mir.*, p. 148 lines 1114–15: 'gulae dedita, ingluuie ciborum urgens crapulam, in potu irritans uomicam'.

tales presules uerbo et exemplo fatienda formarent.*ᵃ* 4. Paruerunt
sedulo pontifices summo primati ad emendationem clericorum,
parum*ᵇ* propemodum hac profecerunt industria.¹ Tum ille, seuerior-
ibus remediis inueteratos rescindens morbos, clericos omnes hoc
conuenit edicto: 'Aut canonice uiuite aut aecclesiis exite.' Illi calci-
trantes contra stimulum² mollioremque uitam eligentes aecclesias
monachis uacuarunt. Cumque miserabiliter per patriam uagabundi a
fortunis suis exularent, et regem et principes fautores apud archiepiscopum habuerunt ut sententiam temperaret. 5. Veruntamen
numquam ille ullis precibus adduci potuit ut canonicos sumptus³
haberent qui canonice uiuere nollent. Quapropter rex, rei aequitate
et archiepiscopi uoluntate permotus, cessauit ultra illis suum exhibere
fauorem qui turpiter uiuentes antistitis non mererentur absolutionem,
quia uulnerarent mentem. Nichil enim putabat expetendum quod uel
saltem eius turbaret uultum, in omnibus ei deferens, obnoxius ut
gratissimo parenti filius. 6. Nam ubi antistitis in delinquentes minus
operabatur sermo, ipse iuditium exercens*ᶜ* legali utebatur gladio,
omnes legum rebelles earundem seueritate cohercens. Itaque omnes
uel clam fures uel palam predones exitio dati uel exilio deportati.
Monetarii qui dampno prouintialium suum infartiebant marsupium, si
corrigi nollent, pedibus et pugnis expoliati. Veneficae, et quae caritatem conubii oblitae uiros necassent, incendio datae. Alieni matrimonii expugnatores⁴ ab aecclesiae liminibus coherciti. 7. Qui coniugia
incesta contraxerant diducti; quod si qui eorum opibus freti subrepti-
tiis a rege uel apostolico papa epistolis niti cepissent,⁵ nichil quod suis
artibus conduceret*ᵈ* in Dunstani pectore inuenientes, uigorem*ᵉ* apos-
tolicum inflexibilem in eo mirabantur. Haec erat columnae immobilis
constantia, hoc robur, hic status, quibus factum est ut omnes peccata
committere timerent, dum illa impunita non fore scirent.

10. Iam uero quam liberalis illa quae uulgo dicitur elemosina in
pauperes fuerit, alio scripto non constat. Veruntamen huius fides non

---

　　ᵃ *Text uncertain*　　　　ᵇ *Perhaps read* sed parum　　　ᶜ *ed.* (*cf. HN 47* iuditium . . .
exercuit; *note the variants at HN 30*); exserens *Q*　　　ᵈ *ed.* (*cf. GR 90, Mir. p. 73, line
303*); conducerent *Q*　　　ᵉ *Perhaps read* rigorem (*cf. VW i. 10. 2* rigorem apostolicae
sedis; *but note also e.g. GP p. 102* apostolicae sedis uigorem; *Mir. p. 120, line 270* 'de uigore
canonum flectendum ratus')

---

　　¹ Cf. below, ii. 12, *GP*, c. 18 (p. 27).　　　　　　　　　　² Acts 26: 14.
　　³ For this use of *sumptus* (= 'incomes'), see *GP*, c. 100 (p. 220), *Mir.*, p. 129 lines 532–3,
VW i. 6. 2.
　　⁴ Cf. *GR*, c. 314. 5 and n. To the references given there add Cyprian, *Epist.* lv. 26:
'matrimonii expugnator alieni'.

ecclesiastical honours (that is of bishoprics), so that prelates of this kind might lay down by word and example how clerks subordinate to them should act. 4. The bishops carefully followed the instructions of the primate to bring about the improvement of the clerks, but to little effect, for all their pains.[1] He then used harsher remedies to cut away maladies that had become ingrained: he confronted the clerks with a stern choice—'Either live according to the canons or get out of your churches.' They kicked against the pricks,[2] opted for a softer existence, and emptied the churches in favour of monks. When they found themselves wretched vagrants in the countryside, in exile from their fortunes, they used king and nobles to back them in their appeals to the archbishop to temper his strictness. 5. But he could never be prevailed on by any entreaties to allow those who would not live canonically to possess canonical incomes.[3] Whereupon the king, moved by the rights and wrongs of the matter and by the archbishop's wishes, withdrew his favour from clerks who offended the primate by their shameful life and so could not win his forgiveness. For the king thought it wrong to request anything that might even bring a frown to Dunstan's forehead; he deferred to him in everything, and obeyed him as a son obeys a beloved father. 6. Indeed, when the words of the archbishop had no effect on offenders, the king drew the sword of judgement, bringing all rebels against the laws to heel by the laws' severity. All thieves, whether furtive or flagrant in their crimes, were executed or deported. Moneyers who filled their own pockets at the expense of the people were deprived of feet and hands if they could not be reformed. Female poisoners, and women who forgot marriage ties so far as to murder their husbands, were burned. Adulterers[4] were banned from entering churches. 7. Those who contracted incestuous marriages were forcibly divorced; or if they had money to support them and started to rely on letters extracted from king or pope,[5] they could find nothing in Dunstan's heart that gave countenance to their wiles, and marvelled at the rigorous apostolic energy he displayed. Such was the firmness of the immovable pillar, such the toughness, such the stature(?); and as a result everyone was afraid to sin when they knew that sin would not go unpunished.

10. No other writing records how liberal his almsgiving (in the common sense) was to the poor, but there is no doubt of it. Yet if

---

[5] Alluding to a particular case, of a *comes* who obtained a papal letter supporting his unlawful marriage: Adelard, lect. xii (p. 67); Eadmer, c. 26 (p. 201).

uacillat. Quod si gratum Deo est perituras hominum carnes cibo ne
defitiant sustentare, quam eo gratius monasteria in aeternum uictura a
fundamentis erigere. Haec sunt illius opera in Domino stabilita,[1] has
eius elemosinas enarrabit omnis aecclesia sanctorum. Nam si Osberno
credimus,[2] quinque monasteria de suo patrimonio fecit, Glastoniense
uero monachis, prediis, edifitiis ampliauit, (2) antiquum id quidem,
ut dixi,[3] et multum eius anticipans tempora, sed quod, ut prioribus
ueterem fundationem, ita Dunstano nouam sullimitatem debeat.
Certe, quod procul ambiguo et exacta fide dico, cenobium Mal-
mesberiense, clericis eiectis quos Edwius intruserat illuc, ad pristinum statum, id est ad monachorum habitationem, reparauit,[4] multa
ibi largitus insignia, quorum quaedam ad hunc diem obliuionis
senium potuerunt eluctari:[5] (3) mirae magnitudinis signa, non
quidem, ut nostra fert aetas, dulci sed incondito sono strepentia;[6]
organa[7] quae concentu suo in festiuitatibus laetitiam populo excitar-
ent (in quorum circuitu hoc distichon litteris aeneis affixit:

Organa do sancto presul Dunstanus Aldhelmo;
perdat hic aeternum qui uult hinc tollere regnum);[8]

de fuluo aere uas aquatile fusili opere, in quo scriptum erat cernere:

Idriolam hanc fundi Dunstan mandauerat archi-
presul, ut in templo sancto seruiret Aldhelmo.[9]

4. Erant tunc eiusdem sancti Aldhelmi ossa composita in scrinio,[10]
pretiosi metalli mole operosa.*a* Haec ille scrinio exempta reposuit
tumulo, dictante Spiritu, non ignarus quantus post dies suos Danorum
turbo prouintiam esset inquietaturus, maturum commentus*b* consilium

---

a Perhaps read operoso　　　　*b* Stubbs; cometus Q

---

[1] Ecclus. 31: 11.　　　　　　　　　　　　　　　　　　[2] Osbern, c. 16 (p. 89).
[3] William is still concerned to refute Osbern's view (see i. prol. 4 n.) that Dunstan was
Glastonbury's first abbot.
[4] See GP, cc. 251, 255 (pp. 403, 407); there, however, the return of the monks is
credited to the initiative of Edgar, who appointed Ælfric as abbot in 974 (GP, c. 252;
pp. 404–5).
[5] The gifts and　verses were already recorded in the *Vita S. Aldhelmi* by Faricius of
Abingdon (d. 1117), which William drew on in GP: PL lxxxix. 76.
[6] GP, c. 255 (p. 407): 'sono et mole prestantia'. AG, c. 67 (pp. 136–7), gives one line of
verses on the refectory bell (there distinguished from the *signa*). See M. Lapidge, 'St
Dunstan's Latin poetry', in *Anglo-Latin Literature 900–1066*, pp. 151–6, at 153–5.
[7] For Dunstan playing the instrument, see above, pp. xxxvi–xxxvii, and i. 4. 4. There is
detailed commentary in P. Williams, *The Organ in Western Culture 750–1250* (Cambridge,
1993), chs. 6, 12, esp. pp. 199–200, 202–3, 229–30, 354.
[8] The verses are given again in GP, c. 255 (p. 407).
[9] The couplet is also given in GP, c. 255 (p. 407), with a note telling us that here and in
the other distich the author intended the spelling 'Adelmo'. AG, c. 67 (pp. 136–7), has the

it is pleasing to God to feed the perishable flesh of men so that it does not fade away, how much more pleasing is it to build from the first stone monasteries that will last for ever! These are the works of Dunstan that are established in the Lord,[1] these the alms which the whole Church of the saints will tell over. For if we are to believe Osbern,[2] Dunstan built five monasteries from his own resources, while adding to that at Glastonbury in number of monks, estates, and buildings. 2. It was an ancient place, as I have said,[3] going back well beyond his time; but though it owes its first foundation to earlier benefactors, it is indebted to Dunstan for its new pre-eminence. There is, in any case, no doubt whatever about Malmesbury, which Dunstan restored to its old state[4]—that is, to be a house of monks— after expelling the clerks intruded there by Eadwig. He bestowed on the place many ornaments, some of which have managed to fight off age and oblivion to this day.[5] 3. First, bells of amazing size (though they rang raggedly,[6] lacking the sweet sound of modern bells). Then, an organ[7] to rouse the people to joy on festive days by its harmony. Around it Dunstan inscribed a distich in letters of bronze:

> I Bishop Dunstan give St Aldhelm this organ;
> May he who wishes to remove it lose his share of the eternal
>   kingdom.[8]

Finally, a stoup cast from yellow brass, on which one could see the words:

> This water pot Archbishop Dunstan caused to be cast,
> So as to serve St Aldhelm in the church.[9]

4. At that time the bones of St Aldhelm were kept in a shrine,[10] elaborately worked with a mass of precious metal. Dunstan removed them, and put them in a tomb, well aware—for the Spirit moved him—of the great whirlwind of Danes that was after his time destined

---

(faulty) lines 'In urceolo altaris: "Idriolam hanc fundi Dunstan mandauerat archi/presul, Cunctipotens quem saluet in euum".' The Malmesbury inscription has apparently been adapted for a Glastonbury ewer. The words 'urceus/urceolus' and 'uas' were those regularly used in Anglo-Norman England for the ewer (later called *aquamanile*) from which the priest ritually cleansed his hands with water at Mass: C. R. Dodwell, *Anglo-Saxon Art: A New Perspective* (Manchester, 1982), pp. 159 and n. 220, 205 and n. 160, 217 and n. 2. (For *hydriola*, ODML cites only William and Higden after him.) No example survives from Anglo-Saxon England, but this one might have looked like a larger version of the gilt-bronze spouted jug (9. 5 cm. high), dated s. x, illustrated in *The Golden Age of Anglo-Saxon Art 966–1066*, ed. J. Backhouse *et al.* (London, 1984), no. 72 (p. 89 and pl. XXII), and D. M. Wilson, *Anglo-Saxon Art* (London, 1984), p. 160 and pl. 210.

[10] Also mentioned in *GP*, c. 236 (pp. 389–90), as commissioned by King Æthelwulf: 'with solid silver figures chased on the front part, while at the back he represented in raised metal-work the miracles I have already listed'.

ne quis barbarus auri spetie captus scrinium occuparet, ossa quoque pariter exportata et sanctissimos cineres caelo alicubi exponeret.[1] Et certe paulo minus contigit quod spectabilis uiri prouidentia cauit, quanuis ultioni suae Aldelmus non defuerit.[2] Dum enim Dani post multos annos per monasterium grassarentur, unus eorum cui mens preruptior, extracto cultello, aurum excrustare conatus, sine mente in terram ruit retroactus et illisus.[a] 5. Sed haec postmodum; tum uero Dunstanus ibidem Elfricum, cui multum religionis, plurimum litterarum inesse cognouerat, abbatem constituit, nec multo post in episcopatum Cridiensem,[3] qui nunc Exoniensis, promouit, uirum singularis utrobique industriae, hic in construendis edifitiis, ibi in refrenandis clericis. Talia archiepiscopus elemosinae opera per totam serebat Angliam, commilitonibus suis, fortissimis et magnanimis uiris, singulas prouintias delegans, et rempublicam Dei multorum collato umbone et communicato labore uelut strenuissimus imperatorum amministrans.

11. Doctrinam multam, sicut ante dictum est,[4] per Dei gratiam hauserat, quia in eius animo cum strenuitate studii precedebat[b] uiuacitas ingenii. Doctrinae porro res duae amminiculabantur, eloquentia elimata sed illaborata, dictorumque exsecutio prompta et impigra. Neque enim tantam procerum ceruicositatem suo umquam subdidisset eloquio, si ei defuisset bona operatio, quorum alterum in predicatore pendet ex altero, quia neutrum ualet, uel si bona dicta male uiuendo destruxeris, uel bonum exemplum sermone non firmaueris. Vtrumque autem in Dunstano uigebat, qui esset et facundus uerbo et fecundus exemplo. Sed quod dico proprio nititur argumento, si quam efficax eius in auditoribus fuerit doctrina paucorum discipulorum exemplo monstrauero.

12.[5] Athelwoldus, ut supra dixi,[6] ex monacho Glastoniensi abbas Abbendoniensis, idemque post haec episcopus Wintoniensis, tot et tanta monasteria fecit quod uix modo uideatur credibile ut talia fecerit

---

[a] (in pauimentum) elisus *GP p. 409* (in terram elisus *GP p. 284; cf. also VD ii. 19. 3* ad terram elisis) 　　[b] precellebat *Leland, Comm., p. 162, rightly?*

---

[1] Cf. *GP*, cc. 251 (p. 403), 255–6 (pp. 407–9), for Dunstan's precautions and the outcome. Note also *GP*, c. 91 (p. 196), 'turbo bellorum', of Danes.
[2] Cf. *GR*, c. 309. 2: 'non defuit patrocinio suo.'
[3] Ælfric became bp. of Crediton in or very soon after 977 (JW s.a. 977).
[4] i. 4.

to shatter the peace of the country. His advance plan was to counter the possibility that some barbarian, attracted by the gleam of gold, might grab the shrine, take it away, and somewhere expose to the sky the bones and holy ashes that went with it.[1] Indeed what the prudent Dunstan had tried to guard against all but happened, though Aldhelm came to his own defence.[2] For when the Danes many years later were rampaging through the monastery, one of the more headstrong of them took out a knife and tried to scrape off the gold; but he was flung back and dashed unconscious to the ground. 5. But this came later. Meanwhile Dunstan appointed as abbot one Ælfric, whom he knew to be both pious and learned; and not much later he advanced him to the bishopric of Crediton[3] (now Exeter). He worked peculiarly hard in both places, at Malmesbury in building, at Crediton in curbing the excesses of the clerks. Such were the works of almsgiving that the archbishop sowed through all England, delegating particular departments to his fellow-workers, brave and high-minded persons, and administering the republic of God like the most energetic of generals. And many were those who stood alongside him and shared in the work.

11. By the grace of God, Dunstan had, as we have seen,[4] imbibed much learning, for his mind combined quickness of wit with ability to work hard. Two further factors gave assistance to his learning: a polished but spontaneous eloquence, and a ready swiftness in carrying out what he had said. He could never have brought such stiff-necked nobles under the sway of his words if he had not excelled at putting them into action: and indeed in a preacher one thing depends on the other, for it is equally disastrous if you spoil the force of good words by living badly, or fail to reinforce your example by appropriate words. Dunstan, however, scored on both counts: he was eloquent in word and fertile in example. But what I am asserting will find its proof if by pointing to a few of his pupils I show what an effect his teaching had on those who heard him.

12.[5] Æthelwold, as I said before,[6] was a monk of Glastonbury before becoming abbot of Abingdon and then bishop of Winchester. So many great monasteries did he found that now it seems scarcely credible that the bishop of a single city should be able to accomplish

---

[5] The material in 12–13. 1 is similarly treated by William in GR, c. 149. 4–6.
[6] i. 17. 2–4, 22. 4.

unius urbis episcopus qualia uix posset rex Angliae totius. Mentior si
non palam sit quod loquor. Qualia sunt cenobia de Heli, Burh,
Thornig, quae ille a fundamentis suscitauit et sua industria perfecit!¹
Quae cum semper exactorum uellicet*ᵃ* nequitia, sunt nichilominus
habitatoribus suis suffitientia. Taceo quod monasteria quae sunt apud
Wintoniam monachis uel*ᵇ* monachabus repleuerit, quod clericos de
episcopatu proiecerit, qui cum, data optione ut aut regulariter
uiuerent aut loco cederent, magis delicatam uitam elegissent, pulsi
nec umquam redire permissi sunt.

13. Oswaldus Odonis archiepiscopi nepos, per Dunstanum Wigornensis episcopus et Eboracensis archiepiscopus, titulos non inferiores
Athelwoldo promeruit. Nam easdem terens orbitas, monachorum
regulam iure suo ampliauit, monasteria plura, inter quae precipuum
Ramesiense, construens. Sedem episcopalem Wigorniae, clericis non
ui expulsis sed sancto ingenio circumuentis,² regularibus impleuit
monachis. Siquidem aecclesiam beati Petri, cui sedes illa seruiebat
antiquitus, artifici negligentia destituens presentia sua, in aecclesia
beatae Dei genitricis, quam in cimiterio construxerat, cum monachis
suis pontificale offitium agebat. 2. Ita populis ad episcopum et
monachos confluentibus clerici destituti aut effugere aut monachatui
collum subdere.³

Sanctissimae memoriae Wlsius,*ᶜ*⁴ ex abbate Westmonasterii Dunstano agente Scireburnensis episcopus, monachos ibidem posuit,
posteris factum uel gaudendo emulantibus uel inuidendo patientibus.

Ita per beatum archiepiscopum, multiformi sanctorum lampade
Angliam serenante, crassae tenebrae uitiorum euanuere. Sic uigebat
religio, sic florebat iustitia, sic omnia bona,*ᵈ* ut crederes de caelo
renidere sidera.⁵

ᵃ ed. (*cf. GR 149. 4*); uellice Q (uellitae *Stubbs*)　　　*ᵇ* non *Qᵃ·ᶜ·* (*corr. m.2*)
ᶜ *Called* Wlfsinus *at GP p. 178*　　　*ᵈ* *A verb seems to lack*

¹ Wulfstan of Winchester, *Vita S. Æthelwoldi*, cc. 23–4 (pp. 38–43), in the same order.
² See above, p. xxi and n. 64.
³ For an attempt to describe the reality, probably less dramatic than William and his
contemporaries thought, see J. Barrow, 'The community of Worcester, 961–*c.*1100', in *St
Oswald of Worcester*, pp. 84–99.
⁴ Cf. *GP*, c. 81 (pp. 178–9). Wulfsige III, abbot of Westminster 958–993/7, bp. of
Sherborne *c.*993–1002 (*HBC*, p. 222; *Heads*, p. 76), established monks in his cathedral in

what would scarcely be practicable for the king of all England. What I assert is clear to all. Look at the houses of Ely, Peterborough, and Thorney, all raised from their foundations and completed by the labours of Æthelwold![1] They are always being picked away at by wicked tax-collectors, but they still can support those who live in them. I need not mention that he filled with monks and nuns the monasteries at Winchester, and that he ejected the clerks from the cathedral. Given the choice between life according to the Rule and departure from the place, they chose the easier existence, were turned out, and were never allowed to come back.

13. Oswald, nephew of Archbishop Oda, became by Dunstan's influence bishop of Worcester and archbishop of York, thereby winning positions not inferior to Æthelwold's. He trod the same path, for he used his power to widen the scope of the Rule by constructing a number of monasteries, chief among them Ramsey. He filled Worcester with regular monks, having got rid of the clerks not by force but by a clever though pious ploy.[2] Purposely neglecting the church of St Peter, the old seat of that bishopric, by depriving it of his presence, he conducted the episcopal office with his monks in the church of the blessed Mother of God which he had constructed in the churchyard. 2. The people flocked to bishop and monks, while the clerks, left out on a limb, either fled the scene or submitted to the life of a monk.[3]

Wulfsige,[4] of most holy memory, who thanks to Dunstan became bishop of Sherborne after being abbot of Westminster, introduced monks at Sherborne, something that later generations gladly imitated or tolerated with envy.

And so, through the works of the blessed archbishop, the fair light of many a saint flooded England, and the gross darkness of vice was dissipated. Religion was vigorous, justice flourished, and there was such an abundance of every good thing that one might have thought the stars were smiling down from heaven.[5]

---

998 (S895). William may have read Goscelin's *Vita* (*BHL* 8753): ed. C. H. Talbot, 'The Life of Saint Wulsin of Sherborne by Goscelin', *RB* lxix (1959), 68–85, esp. cc. 3–4 (pp. 75–6), although Goscelin attributes Wulfsige's abbacy rather than his bishopric to Dunstan's influence.

[5] Cf. *GR*, c. 149. 1: 'ut crederes e caelo arridere sidera'.

14. Postremo in Edgari regis pectore quantam Dunstani doctrina frugem tulerit, graue cogitatu, nedum non facile dictu. Nam preter seueritatem in improbos quam superius explanaui,[1] bonis dulcis, religiosis acclinis,[a] monachis affabilis erat. Nec ullus fere annus eius in Cronicis[2] preteritus est quo non magnum aliquod et patriae necessarium fecerit, quo non monasterium nouum fundauerit. Nemo eius tempore priuatus latro, nemo popularis predo, nisi qui mallet in fortunas grassari alienas propriae uitae dispendio. 2. Per haec Dei fauore tuto quantum pacis arriserit,[b] quantum fauoris suorum, quantum timoris hostium accesserit, libenter dicerem, si non a proposito uagabundus[3] indulgere uiderer eloquio.[4] Ceterum cui curae sit de talibus legere, Gesta Regum Anglorum, quae ante aliquot annos edidi,[5] dignetur inuenire; hic quod ad rem attinet diximus, sententiamque antiqui scriptoris[6] de Dunstano intellectu latiori diffudimus. Quapropter quaedam miracula quae ad nos fama sua manarunt, necnon et uaticinia de quibus dicere restat,[7] apponemus, quae ita conspicue uidebat et enuntiabat ut nulli prophetarum uideatur esse secundus.

15.[8] Eo tempore quo primum post susceptum pallium archiepiscopatum reditu suo nobilitauit, a quodam magnate ad aecclesiam quam in uilla sui iuris fecerat consecrandam inuitatus, non recusauit offitium. Processum est ad[c] aecclesiam. Antistes ad consecrationem stabat accinctus. Veruntamen fefellit offitiales incuriositas, quo minus omnia procurassent. Nam ministraturo aqua defuit, cuius copiam in tali offitio esse debere nemo fere est qui nesciat. 2. Cursitabant ministri, stabat attonitus dominus magno pudore frontem oneratus; pallebat illorum culpa, huius tumebat uerecundia. Erat pontificis pro amico confusio. Erat ingens uulgi expectatio, presertim quia non erat aqua de proximo. Omnibus his humanitas Sancti consuluit, et oratione fusa de rupe proxima aquam affluentem elicuit.[9] Crediderim

---

[a] *ed.* (*cf. VW i. 3. 4*); accliuis *Q*　　　[b] *ed.*; arriserat *Q*　　　[c] *N* (*cf. VW iii. 23. 1*); *om. Q*

[1] ii. 9. 6–7. There is overlap with the wording of *GR*, c. 155. See also *GP*, c. 18 (pp. 26–7).
[2] *ASC* (E) s.aa. 959, 964, 969, 975.
[3] Cf. *Mir.*, p. 74 line 336: 'uacabit [*leg.* uagabitur?] a proposito'.
[4] William does not mention here the penance imposed on Edgar by Dunstan (*GR*, cc. 158, 159. 2), though it appears in Osbern, c. 35 (pp. 111–12), and Eadmer, c. 33 (pp. 209–11).
[5] The latest date in *GR* is 10 Febr. 1126 (*GR* II, p. xviii n. 2). The reference here is to cc. 148–56, 160.

14. Finally, it is difficult to imagine, let alone express, what fruit the teaching of Dunstan bore in the heart of King Edgar. Besides the severe treatment of offenders, of which I have spoken,[1] he was agreeable to the good, favourable towards the pious, approachable to monks. Hardly a year passed in the Chronicles[2] when he did not do something great and politically important, or found a new monastery. In his time no one stole in private or plundered in public, unless he was prepared to harass the fortunes of others at the cost of his own life. 2. This made him safe in God's favour; and I should gladly tell how peace smiled upon him, and how he enjoyed the favour of his own and the fear of his enemies, if I might not thereby seem to be indulging myself in a digression[3] merely to show off my style.[4] But anyone who cares to read of such matters may wish to look out the *History of the English Kings*, which I published some years back.[5] But on the present occasion I have said what mattered, as well as giving wider publicity to the old biographer's[6] judgement on Dunstan. So I shall now proceed to record certain miracles which their fame has brought down to us, as well as prophecies still to be spoken of,[7] which he so notably witnessed and publicised that he seems inferior to none of the prophets.

15.[8] When he for the first time since taking the pallium honoured the archbishopric by his return, he was invited by a nobleman to consecrate a church he had built in a vill under his jurisdiction. He agreed to officiate, and they went in procession to the church. The archbishop stood there, all ready for the consecration. But the staff had failed to take sufficient care to get everything ready. For the ministrant had no water to hand—and almost everybody knows that a lot is needed on such an occasion. 2. The servants bustled about, the lord stood there thunder-struck, frowning in embarrassment: they pale with guilt, he swelling with shame. The archbishop was upset for his friend. The big crowd was all agog, especially as there was no water anywhere nearby. To all these the saint gave his kindly attention: he poured out a prayer, and brought water gushing from a nearby rock-face.[9] I can well believe the ealdorman at that moment

---

[6] Presumably meaning B., who is remarkably reticent on the reigns of Edgar and Æthelred.

[7] e.g. that on Æthelred at ii. 21. 3.

[8] Cf. *GP*, c. 19 (p. 29), and a similar story at c. 84 (p. 185), again 'there to this day'.

[9] The prototype for this miracle is Moses striking the rock to bring forth water in Exod. 17: 6; see *GR*, c. 377. 5.

ducem tunc amasse negligentiam suam, per quam sanctus sacerdos tanti miraculi rapuisset causam; facit certe in presenti hominibus eius prouintiae gaudium, qui uident per rupis anfractus leni*ᵃ* susurro dulcis aquae serpere riuum.[1]

16. Beatus igitur pontifex, ut nichil quod sui offitii interesset negligeret, sepe obibat cenobia, ut quae bene fiebant auctoritate sua muniret, quae perperam corrigeret. Hac consuetudine Bathoniam uenit, ubi calidae aquae uis emergens bullatis*ᵇ* scatebris balneas quibusdam egritudinibus salubres euaporat.[2] Susceptus dapsili fratrum caritate. Iam cibo curatus inter eos pro more assedit, et ecce animo caelum transuectus uidet cuiusdam Glastoniensis scolastici[3] animam supernis sacrariis magno angelorum plausu importari. Laetatus de felicis pueri gloria, gaudium considentibus participauit. 2. Postero die prepositus Glastoniensis eo uenit, antistitem de quibusdam necessariis consulturus; quem*ᶜ* statim post impertitam benedictionem interrogauit rectene an secus circa fratres constaret. Ille, cuius menti mors innocentis exciderat, recte omnia Dei gratia et eius orationibus agi respondit. Non se putare retulit Dunstanus eos sine proximo funere fuisse. Tunc demum prepositus, memoriae redditus, omnia dixit bene procedere, preter quod quidam puer pomeridianis horis excessit pridie. 'Hoc est' ait pontifex 'quod dixi! Anima ergo eius requiescat in pace. Amen.'

17. Ita[4] cum cenobia cetera tum frequentius uisitabat Glastoniam, felicitatis et religionis suae nutriculam. Ibi non ut in peregrino diuersorio sed ut in domestico contubernio, seposita episcopalis comitatus pompa, commanebat. Exierat quadam uice in atrium aecclesiae spatiatum uno tantum fratre obambulante (Elfsius ei nomen). Venerat ad occidentalem ueteris aecclesiae partem cum uox caelestis aethere pulso sonuit: 'Veni, ueni, Elfsi, ueni.' Continuoque Dunstanus concepto uaticinio, respitiens comitem, 'Praepara ergo' inquit 'te, frater, et uiaticum compara quo possis ingredi tantum iter. Instat enim uocationis tuae dies.' 2. Paruit patri monachus, post paucos dies prophetiae ueritatem expertus.

ᵃ N (*cf. Jerome cited in n. 1*); leui *Q*   ᵇ *For this word cf. VW* i. 1. 7   ᶜ *ed.*; cum *Q*

[1] Cf. Jerome, *Vita S. Pauli*, c. 3: 'cum leni iuxta murmure aquarum serperet riuus'.
[2] There is more on the springs of Bath in *GP*, c. 90 (p. 194).
[3] One of his own, according to Osbern, c. 20 (p. 94) (who dates the miracle to the period of Dunstan's abbacy). B., c. 34 (p. 46), dates the prophecy as William does.

blessed his own negligence, seeing that it had given the holy priest the chance to perform such a miracle. It certainly provides pleasure to men of those parts to this day, when they see a flow of sweet water gliding with a faint murmur[1] through the rocky gorge.

16. To ensure that he neglected nothing pertaining to his office, the blessed archbishop often visited monasteries, using his authority to consolidate what was going well and to correct what was going ill. In conformity with this custom, he once came to Bath, where a gush of hot water bubbling forth warms baths that are efficacious in the treatment of certain illnesses.[2] He was received by the brothers with a generous meal, and afterwards was sitting in their midst as usual when lo! he was carried to heaven in his mind, and saw the soul of a certain pupil[3] from Glastonbury being borne into the sacred places of heaven amid loud applause from the angels. He was overjoyed to see the boy so fortunate in his glory, and shared his happiness with those who sat with him. 2. Next day the prior of Glastonbury came to Bath to consult the archbishop on certain important matters, and Dunstan, immediately after giving him his blessing, asked whether or not all was well with the monks. The prior had forgotten about the innocent child's death, and said that thanks to the grace of God and Dunstan's prayers all was well. Dunstan retorted that he thought that they had had a death there recently. That brought the matter back to the prior's mind, and he said that all was going well except that the day before a boy had died during the afternoon. 'That is what I meant,' said the archbishop. 'So may his soul rest in peace. Amen.'

17. He[4] used to visit all his monasteries, but none more often than Glastonbury, the nurturer of his good fortune and religious vocation. He would stay there not as in some foreign lodging but as if at home, and laid aside there all episcopal pomp. On one occasion he had gone out into the churchyard to walk, with a single brother to accompany him; his name was Ælfsige. He had come to the west end of the old church when a voice thundered out from heaven: 'Come, come, Ælfsige, come!' Dunstan immediately took on a spirit of prophecy. He looked at his companion, and said: 'So you must prepare yourself, brother, and take the sacrament that will enable you to enter on so great a journey; for the day of your calling is upon you.' 2. The monk obeyed his father, and after a few days found the prophecy come true.

[4] Also in B., c. 35 (pp. 47–8), and Eadmer, c. 15 (p. 189).

Quid hoc diuinius, quid hoc mirabilius homine? Curauerunt alii
paucorum ualitudines corporum, hic depulit innumerabilium morbos
animarum; fuerunt alii prudentes in seculo, ille et hoc non omittebat
et totus inherebat Deo; fecerunt alii duo uel ut multum tria
monasteria,[1] hic a fundamentis multa extruxit noua, et quae iam
ruinam minitabantur reparauit uetera.

18. Interea Edgarus renuntiauit uitae, uir omni aeuo predicandus.
Namque non infirma inter Anglos fama est nullum nec eius ⟨nec⟩[a]
superioris aetatis regem in Anglia aequilibri iuditio comparandum
Edgaro. Ita nichil uita eius sanctius, nichil iustitia probabilius fuit, qui
patriam suam preclara fortitudine illustrauit et rerum gestarum
claritate et Deo seruientium multiplicitate,[2] in paucorum annorum
angustia rem seculorum includens. Sepultus est Glastoniae. Corpus
tunc quidem terra opertum, sed post scrinio argenteo[b] et inaurato
locatum pro merito personae honoratur.[3]

2. Successit[4] ei Eduardus filius, annitente Dunstano quanuis
obnitentibus proceribus,[5] et maxime nouerca, quae uixdum septem
annorum puerulum Egelredum filium prouehere conabatur, ut ipsa
potius sub nomine eius imperitaret. Ex tunc malitia hominum pull-
ulante felicitas regni immutata; iam enim Edgarus in supernum
regnum abierat,[c] cuius tempore futuram pacem caelestis uox Dunstano nuntiauerat.[6] Tunc ergo [d]uisus cometes[7] qui[d] uel pestem
hominum uel mutationem regni portendere pro uero asseueratur.
Nec mora, secuta sterilitas anni,[e] fames hominum, mors iumentorum,
apud uicum regium qui[f] uocatur Calna casus insolitus, quem
equidem scriptores uitae Dunstani preterisse miror,[8] cum in Cronicis
ad eius precipuam gloriam annotatus sit.[9]

---

[a] *GR 160. 3; om. Q*   [b] *GR 160. 2 (TA)*; in argenteo *Q*   [c] *ed. (cf. GP p. 124* in
alterum seculum abiit); obierat *Q*   [d ... d] uisa . . . quae *GR 161. 1*   [e] arui *GR
161. 1*   [f] *GR 161. 2*; que *Q*

[1] Three for Æthelwold (ii. 12), *plura* for Oswald (ii. 13. 1); Dunstan himself is credited
by modern authorities with the founding or repair of between four and eleven monastic
communities: *Regularis Concordia*, ed. and trans. T. Symons (NMT, 1953), pp. xx–xxi;
D. Knowles, *The Monastic Order in England*, (2nd edn., Cambridge, 1963), pp. 49–50.
[2] 'non infirma . . . multiplicitate' = *GR*, c. 160. 3, almost verbatim.
[3] 'Corpus . . . honoratur' = *GR*, c. 160. 2 (TtA). Cf. also *AG*, c. 62 (pp. 130–1). There
is more on the translation in *AG*, c. 66 (pp. 134–5).
[4] For the sequence of events in 18. 2–19, see also *GR*, c. 161, similarly worded.
[5] Cf. Osbern, c. 37 (p. 114).   [6] See ii. 1. 2.
[7] *ASC* (DE) s.a. 975.
[8] William's reference to the silence of the 'scriptores uitae Dunstani' is puzzling. The

Who could be more inspired or more marvellous than Dunstan? Others have cured the illnesses of a few bodies; he drove away the diseases of souls beyond counting. Others have been wise in this world; he, without neglecting that, cleaved wholly to God. Others built two or at most three monasteries;[1] he constructed many new ones from the foundations, and repaired others whose age threatened their collapse.

18. Meanwhile Edgar gave up this life, a man to be praised in every age; indeed there is a strong tradition among the English that no king of theirs, of that or any earlier time, could justly be compared with him. His life was incomparably holy, his justice incomparably pure; he brought lustre to his country by his brilliant bravery, his splendid feats, and the increased number of those serving God;[2] and he brought within the narrow compass of a few years the achievements of centuries. He was buried at Glastonbury. For the moment he was put below ground, but later the body was placed in a silver-gilt shrine, in which it is honoured as it deserves.[3]

2. His son Edward was his successor,[4] thanks to the efforts of Dunstan, though there was opposition from the nobility[5] and especially from his stepmother, who endeavoured to advance the claims of her little son Æthelred, a child of barely seven, in order to reign herself in his name. From then wickedness blossomed, and the happiness of the kingdom underwent a change. For now Edgar had gone to heaven, and it was in his time that the voice from above had told Dunstan that there would be peace.[6] It was accordingly then that a comet was seen,[7] something rightly claimed to portend either plague or constitutional change. Hard on its heels came crop failure, famine, cattle pest, and, at the royal vill called Calne, an unusual event which I am surprised the biographers of Dunstan have missed,[8] though the Chronicle records it to his especial glory.[9]

story is not in B. or Adelard, but it is told by both Osbern (c. 36, pp. 113–14) and Eadmer (c. 34, p. 213); and it would seem from the last sentence of this chapter (see n. ad loc.) that William was using Eadmer at least at that point. One wonders whether an adjective has dropped out: 'ueteres' (cf. esp. ii. 29) or 'antiquos' (cf. i. 27. 2, ii prol. 2 with n. and ii. 14. 2). If William did thus limit his remark to the old writers, one would like to know whether he meant by them B. plus Adelard, B. plus the lost Old English Life (Eng.; see pp. xviii–xx), or B. plus both. In other words, was Osbern here reproducing Eng.'s account, or adding new material of his own?

[9] *ASC* s.a. 978. William makes use of this entry, in which, as above and in the parallel account at *GR*, c. 161 (where *ASC* is not mentioned), Dunstan is stranded on a single joist, whereas both Osbern and Eadmer have him left sitting calmly with his people. As to the

19. Nam Edgaro rebus exempto, clerici quondam ab aecclesiis expulsi rediuiua prelia suscitarunt: ingens esse et miserabile dedecus ut nouus aduena ueteres colonos expelleret;[1] hoc nec Deo[a] gratum uideri, qui ueterem eis a longinquis seculis habitationem concessisset, nec alicui probo homini, qui sibi idem timere posset quod aliis preiuditio accidisse cerneret. Ea de re in clamores et iras surrectum et ad Dunstanum perrectum, proceribus precipue, ut laicorum mos est, succlamantibus preiuditium quod[b] passi fuerant leniori consilio succidi debere. 2. Itaque frequenti sinodo coacta primo Wintoniam uentum. Quis ibi fuerit finis certaminis aliae docent litterae.[2] Cum enim omnes aduersariorum obiectiones rationalibus responsis confutasset archiepiscopus, illi contentione irrita uersi ad preces fauore optimatum fulciebantur. Is[c] responsum non retulit, ne uel in tempore optimatibus aduersari uel nefandis precibus assentire uideretur. Quapropter Dominicae crucis imago, quae adhuc Wintoniae habetur, antistitem dubietatis absoluit periculo, repetens tertio 'Absit hoc ut fiat'. 3. Sed adhuc non sedatis animis Calnae concilium[d] indictum, ubi, cum in cenaculo, absente propter aetatem rege, considentibus[e] totius Angliae senatoribus magno conflictu res ageretur, et ualidissimum illum aecclesiae murum,[3] Dunstanum dico, multorum iacula impeterent conuitiorum,[f] nec quaterent, suas partes cuiusque ordinis uiris summo studio tuentibus, solarium totum repente cum axibus et trabibus dissiluit et concidit. Omnibus ad terram elisis, solus Dunstanus stans super unam trabem quae superstes erat probe euasit.[4] Reliqui uel exanimati uel perpetui languoris compede detenti. Hoc miraculum archiepiscopo exhibuit pacem de clericis, omnibus Anglis tunc et deinceps in eius sententiam concedentibus.[5]

20.[6] Interea Elfrida mater Egelredi, nouercali odio[7] uipereum dolum ruminans, insidias priuigno struere, quas hoc modo consummauit.

---

[a] *GR 161. 2;* dico *Q*   [b] *GR 161. 2 adds* clerici   [c] his *N*   [d] *N, GR 161. 3;* consilium *Q*   [e] *N, GR 161. 3;* insidentibus *Q*   [f] conu. iac. imp. *N, GR 161. 3*

dating of the incident: *ASC* does not mention Winchester, and places Calne before the death of Edward. Osbern describes Winchester under Edgar (presumably early in his reign), but seems to place Calne as much as a generation later (p. 113 'per successionem filiorum prior discordia renouata est'); similarly Eadmer (p. 213). William characteristically tries to find a compromise position. He places Winchester after the death of Edgar, presumably under Edward (in *GR* c. 161.2 the council reacts to the insolence of Ælfhere, dated by *ASC* to 975), and Calne (it would seem) not long afterwards, but implicitly under Æthelred (note 'absente propter aetatem rege').

[1] Cf. Virgil, *Ecl.* ix. 2–4, also echoed in *GP*, c. 272 (p. 434).

19. After Edgar's death, the clerks who had previously been driven from their churches renewed their struggle. It was, they said, a crying shame that a newcomer should turn out old tenants:[1] something pleasing neither to God, who had granted them homes there for ages back, nor to any respectable man who might fear the same fate for himself as he saw afflicting others. So they grew obstreperous and angry, and went off to Dunstan, the nobles in particular, as laymen will, shouting that what they [the clerks] had suffered should be cut short by the adoption of a more friendly policy. **2.** So a large synod was called. It met first at Winchester. The outcome of the contest there may be read elsewhere.[2] For when the archbishop had refuted all his adversaries' objections by his reasonable replies, they [the clerks], finding argument got them nowhere, turned to entreaty, relying on the support of the nobles. Dunstan made no reply, so as to avoid either opposing the nobility for the moment (?) or assenting to wicked requests. Whereupon the image of the Lord's Cross that is still preserved at Winchester rescued the archbishop from any danger of doubt by three times uttering the words 'Far be it that this should happen!' **3.** But passions still rode high, and a council was called at Calne. Here the king was absent because of his age, but the elders of all England took their seats in an upstairs room, to wrangle about the matter. Dunstan, that stalwart wall of the Church,[3] was the target for much abuse, though it did not shake him, and men of both orders defended their points of view with a good deal of heat. Amidst all this, the whole room suddenly gave way, beams, planks and all, and crashed to the ground. Everyone was dashed down; Dunstan alone made good his escape,[4] left standing on a single remaining joist. The rest were either killed or permanently disabled. This miracle led to peace for the archbishop from the clerks, and all the English then and thereafter came over to his way of thinking.[5]

20.[6] Meanwhile Ælfthryth, Æthelred's mother, was indulging her stepmotherly hatred[7] by scheming against her stepson like some

---

[2] Taken over from *GR*, c. 161. 3, where the reference can only be to Osbern/Eadmer. Here the reference might be to them, or to *GR*.

[3] Alluding to the etymology of his name; see above, i. 2. 1.

[4] For 'probe euasit', see also *GR*, c. 333. 5, *Mir.*, p. 140 line 864.

[5] Cf. Eadmer, c. 34 (p. 213): 'Hoc igitur modo calumnia clericorum est sopita, et usque hodie monachorum conuersatio in ipsa ecclesia stabilita.' The sentence has no counterpart in Osbern.

[6] The story in 1–2 is told, with similar wording, in *GR*, c. 162; see notes ad loc.

[7] Cf. Osbern, c. 37 (p. 114): 'nouercali fraude'.

Lassus uenatione reuertebatur propter laborem siti anhelus. Comites quo quemque casus tulerat canes consequebantur; auditoque quod illi in contigua uilla habitarent, equo concito illuc contendit iuuenculus solus, nichil propter innocentiam metuens, aliorum quippe animos ex suo ponderans. Tunc illa muliebri blanditia aduenientem allitiens sibi fecit intendere, et post libata oscula porrectum sibi auide poculum haurientem per satellitem sica transfodit.¹ 2. Quo uulnere sautius cum quantis potuit animae reliquiis sonipedem calcaribus monuisset*ᵃ* ad suos reuerti, uno pede lapsus alteroque per deuia tractus, undante cruore inditia interitus sui se querentibus dedit. Et tunc quidem sine honore apud Werham sepeliri iusserunt, inuidentes scilicet mortuo cespitem aecclesiasticum cui uiuo inuiderant decus regium.² Sed affuit diuinae serenitatis assensus qui innocenter cesum miraculorum sullimaret gloria. Quapropter Elferius dux, sacro corpore*ᵇ* de ignobili loco leuato, iustas et egregias inferias apud Sceftoniam soluit. 3. Creditumque et celebriter uulgatum quod propter Elfridae in Eduardum insolentiam multo post tempore tota patria seruitutem infremuisse barbaricam, quam fidem minae Dunstani firmarunt, sicut paulo post narrabitur.³ Nam et regis sanctitas antistitis proxime attingebat gloriam, quod eius suffragio imperium conscendisset, quod eius monitis paternae religionis uestigia triuisset,⁴ quod eius meritis commertium regni caelestis pro terreno fecisset.

21.⁵ Tunc obsedit regnum Egelredus frater eius de patre, cuius uitae cursus seuus in principio, miser in medio, turpis in exitu asseritur: ita parricidio⁶ cui coniuentiam adhibuerat immanis, ita fuga et mollitie infamis, ita morte miserabilis fuit. Ignauiam eius predixerat Dunstanus fedo exemplo ammonitus. Nam cum pusiolus in fontem baptismi mergeretur, circumstantibus episcopis, alui profluuio sacramenta interpolauit. 2. Qua re ille turbatus 'Per Deum' inquit 'et Matrem eius, ignauus homo erit.' Matris ergo suffragio proceribus

---

ᵃ *GR 162. 2*; mouisset *Q*   ᵇ corpori *GR 162. 4, rightly?*

---

¹ Not very clearly told. According to the *Passio S. Edwardi*, ed. C. E. Fell, *Edward King and Martyr* (Leeds Texts and Monographs, new ser. iii: Leeds, 1971), pp. 4–5, Ælfthryth had a house near the wood, in which Edward had been brought up. Edward approached this alone, his companions being scattered through the wood. It was there that his stepmother killed him.
² Similarly *GR*, c. 49. 8.   ³ ii. 22.   ⁴ *GR*, c. 162. 1.
⁵ The story is told, with similar wording, in *GR*, c. 164 (see notes ad loc.). For Dunstan and Æthelred, see *GP*, cc. 19, 20 (pp. 30, 33).
⁶ It is hard to see how so young a child could have been guilty, but William had already

treacherous viper. This is how she carried out her plan. Edward was coming back tired out from the chase, thirsty and breathless with his efforts. His companions were still following the hounds wherever chance took them. Hearing that they were lodged in a nearby vill, the young man spurred his horse in that direction, quite alone, too innocent to feel fear; for he measured the character of others by his own. When he arrived, Ælfthryth used her woman's wiles to catch his attention, kissed him and gave him a drink. As he was greedily draining the cup, she got a hireling to run him through with a dagger.[1] 2. Despite his injury he used what remained of his breath to spur his horse on to rejoin his friends. One foot slipped from the stirrup, and he was dragged by the other through the lonely countryside, his fast-ebbing blood giving signs of his death to those who looked for him. For the moment they had him buried unceremoniously at Wareham, obviously grudging church ground when he was dead to one to whom they had grudged the royal dignity while he lived.[2] But God granted that he who had been slain for no good cause should be exalted by glorious miracles. So it was that Ealdorman Ælfhere raised the sacred body from its humble grave, and gave it proper and dignified burial at Shaftesbury. 3. It was believed and published abroad that it was just because of Ælfthryth's wanton treatment of Edward that much later the whole country had to endure the tumult of enslavement to the barbarians: a belief that the threats of Dunstan strengthened, as will be told a little later.[3] For the king's holiness was closely associated with the archbishop's glory: it was by Dunstan's help that he had ascended the throne, on his advice that he had trodden the path of his fathers' religion,[4] by his merits that he made the exchange of reign on earth for the kingdom of heaven.

21.[5] Next, his half-brother Æthelred laid siege to the throne. His life story was cruel at the start, pitiable in the middle, and shameful in its end—or so they say. For the foul murder[6] at which he had connived made him a monster of savagery, his flight and effeminacy destroyed his reputation, and his death was wretched. Dunstan had foretold his worthlessness, with a sordid sign to prompt him. For when the baby was being plunged in the water for baptism, surrounded by bishops, he interrupted the ceremony by opening his bowels. 2. This upset Dunstan, who said: 'By God and His Mother, this will be a worthless

made the allegation in *GR*, c. 164. 1, 3, though at 2 he seems to throw the blame on the mother.

congregatis, dies dicta ut Dunstanus adueniret[a]. Ille licet infensus esset supersedit resistere, pontifex aeui maturioris et in secularibus emeritus; iam uero diadema componens non se continuit quin spiritum propheticum totis medullis haustum ore pleno effunderet. Verba ipsa quae alias legi dicturus sum, quanuis, ut in prologo huius libri dixi, eis consensum non obligem meum qui uerba nusquam audita uel lecta apponunt quia dici potuerunt.[1] 3. 'Quia' inquit 'per mortem fratris tui aspirasti ad regnum, propterea audi uerbum Domini. Haec dicit Dominus Deus: "Non delebitur peccatum ignominiosae matris tuae, et peccatum uirorum qui interfuerunt consilio illius nequam, sine multo sanguine miserorum prouintialium; et uenient super gentem Anglorum mala qualia non passa[b] ex quo Angliam uenit usque in tempus illud."'

Nec multo post simile uaticinium effudit, eius peruicatia hoc modo irritatus. 22. Surrexerat[2] inter regem et episcopum Rofensem simultas, incertum qua de causa. Quocirca contra ciuitatem exercitum duxit. Mandatum ei ab archiepiscopo ut furori[c] desisteret, nec sanctum Andream, in cuius tutela episcopatus est, irritaret, sicut ad indulgendum facilem, ita ad ulciscendum terribilem.[3] Verborum nuditate contempta adornat preceptum pecunia, et mittit centum libras ut obsidionem solueret, pretio emptus abiret. Quo ille accepto receptui cecinit, procinctum militum feriari permisit. Miratus Dunstanus hominis cupiditatem haec per nuntios retulit: 'Quoniam pretulisti argentum Deo, pecuniam apostolo, cupiditatem michi, uelociter uenient super te mala quae locutus est Dominus. Sed haec me uiuente non fient, quia et hoc locutus est Dominus.'[4]

23.[5] At non ita melior Edgari soboles Edgitha, non ita Dunstani animum offendebat, sed eius potius gratiam sedulo demerebatur. Vnde quiddam quod in eius Vita[6] legi apponere non fastidiam: quod quia alienum non est a Dunstano, non interim a materia uagabitur oratio. Ea abbatissa Wiltoniae, uideratque illam Dunstanus in

---

[a] GR 164. 2 adds regem iure archiepiscopi coronaturus   [b] GR 164. 3 adds est
[c] furore Q[p.c.] (cf. GR 165. 1 n.)

[1] See ii. prol. 1–2 and n. on 2. In the following direct speech, William adapts Osbern, c. 37 (pp. 114–15).

[2] Also in GR, c. 165. 1. The event took place in 986 (ASC s.a.), when the bishop of Rochester was Ælfstan (955/64–994/5).

[3] The same expression is in Mir., p. 67 lines 132–3.

[4] So Osbern, c. 39 (p. 117). GR says 'et haec locutus'; so William re-consulted Osbern rather than just copying out GR.

man.' At his mother's instance the nobles assembled and a day was set for the arrival of Dunstan [to crown Æthelred]. For all his hostility, Dunstan decided not to object, for he was an archbishop of ripe years, and great experience in secular matters. But as he put the crown on the king's head, he could not forebear to draw the spirit of prophecy from deep within him and pour it out at the top of his voice. I will record the actual words I have read elsewhere, though, as I said in the prologue to this book, I do not guarantee my agreement with those who put down words that no one has heard or read anywhere just because they *could* have been spoken.[1] 3. 'Because' he said 'you exploited your brother's death in striving for the throne, hear the word of the Lord. The Lord God says: "The sin of your shameful mother, and the sin of the men who took part in her wicked plan, will not be expunged without much bloodshed for this unfortunate land. And there will come on the race of the English ills such as it has not suffered ever since it came to England."'

Not much later, provoked by Æthelred's obstinacy, he poured out a similar prophecy. **22.** For some reason, a quarrel[2] had arisen between the king and the bishop of Rochester, and he accordingly led an army against the city. The archbishop instructed him to desist from his folly and avoid provoking St Andrew, patron saint of the see, who, though generous in showing kindness, could be terrible in revenge.[3] Mere words being ignored, he decked out his counsel with cash, sending a hundred pounds for the king to raise the siege and go away well paid. The king took the money, beat a retreat, and let his force of soldiers have a furlough. Dunstan, amazed at the man's avarice, sent this message: 'Since you have put silver before God, money before the apostle, and greed before myself, there will swiftly come upon you the evils of which the Lord has spoken; but not during my lifetime, because the Lord has said that too.'[4]

23.[5] But Eadgyth, a better scion of Edgar, did not offend Dunstan like this, but rather took care to win his regard. So I shall not avoid adding something I have read in her Life;[6] it is not irrelevant to Dunstan, and will not involve me in digression. She was abbess of Wilton, and, at the consecration of the church of St Denis, which she

---

[5] The story is also in *GR*, c. 218. 3–4; *GP*, cc. 19 (p. 30), 87 (pp. 189–90).

[6] Goscelin, *Vita S. Edithae*, ed. A. Wilmart, 'La légende de Ste Édith en prose et vers par le moine Goscelin', *Analecta Bollandiana*, lvi (1938), 5–101, 265–307, at pp. 88, 91, 265–9. See also *GR*, c. 342 n. (on Goscelin).

consecratione aecclesiae sancti Dionisii, quam illa in amorem martiris
edificauerat, pollicem dextrum frequenter protendere, et signum
crucis fronti e regione pingere. 2. Delectatusque admodum 'Numquam' inquit 'putrescat hic digitus', continuoque intra missarum
agenda prorupit in lacrimas[1] adeo profluas ut singultiente uoce[a]
discipulum[2] propter astantem concuteret. Reique causam quesitus,
'Cito' ait 'haec florida rosa marcescet, cito auis dilecta Deo auolabit,
post sex ab hoc die septimanas.' Consecuta est igitur rerum ueritas
pontificale uaticinium. Namque illa, nobilis propositi tenax, predicta
die citra iuuentae terminum efflauit, cum esset annorum uiginti
trium. Nec multo post idem beatus uidit somni uisione sanctum
Dionisium uirginem amicabiliter manu tenentem, et ex oraculo
diuino constanter iubentem ut a famulis honorificaretur in terris,
sicut a Sponso et Domino uenerabatur in caelis. 3. Ita crebrescenti-
bus ad tumbam miraculis, edictum ut corpus uirgineum leuaretur et
altius efferretur; inuentumque totum in cineres solutum, preter
digitum et aluum et aluo subiecta. Vnde disputantibus nonnullis,
uni ⟨ex his⟩[b] qui uiderant[3] dormienti ipsa uirgo astitit, dicens non
mirum[c] si partes illae corporis putruerint, quod usus habeat exani-
mata corpora in quosdam archanos recessus defluere, et ipsa, utpote
puella, membris illis peccauerat; ceterum iuste[d] uentrem nulla
putredine corrumpi, qui nulla sit umquam aculeatus libidine: immu-
nem se fuisse crapulae et carnalis copulae.

24.[4] Similem prophetiam in prenuntiando Athelwoldi Wintoniensis
episcopi excessu Dunstanus exhibuit. Is ueniens Cantiam benigno et
liberali aliquandiu confotus est hospitio. Suspitiebat enim in eo
archiepiscopus uerae uirtutis specimen et non fictae religionis
simulacrum, quod ab eo in se rapuerat et emulo exemplo pretendebat.
Post[e] dies abeuntem, cum Rofensi episcopo qui eo forte uenerat,
dignanter prosequebatur. Et iam aliquantum uiae confecerant, et
uesper occiduus tenebras[f] minabatur, quoniam in mouendo moras
nexuerant. 2. Tum Rofensis antistes sanctum summissis precibus

[a] uoce GR 218. 3, GP p. 189; uoce ut Q   [b] ex his GR 218. 4; om. Q   [c] non
mirum GR 218. 4, GP p. 190; nimirum Q   [d] Q adds dicit in the margin   [e] A word
like aliquot seems to have fallen out   [f] ed.; tenebris Q

[1] Osbern, c. 38 (p. 116), tells of another incident when Dunstan 'erupit in fletum,
fletum adeo magnum ut uix . . .'. In GR, c. 218. 3 (CB) 'prorupit in lacrimas, lacrimas adeo
profluas ut . . .', TA, like VD, omit one set of lacrimae: GP, c. 87 (p. 189), has both.

had built for love of the martyr, Dunstan had seen her frequently
stretch out her right thumb and make the sign of the Cross full on her
forehead. 2. Very pleased, he said: 'May this finger never decay!'
And straightway amid the ceremony of the Mass he burst into tears,[1]
so torrential that his choking voice caught the attention of a pupil[2]
standing nearby. Asked the reason, Dunstan said: 'Soon will this
blooming rose fade, soon will the bird beloved of God fly away, six
weeks from today.' The event bore out the archbishop's prediction.
Eadgyth, still cleaving to her noble resolve, breathed her last on the
assigned day, still a young woman, aged 23. Not much later, the
blessed man had in his sleep a vision of St Denis, holding the girl by
the hand in a friendly fashion and firmly proclaiming the will of God
that her servants should honour her on earth as she was revered in
heaven by her Bridegroom and Lord. 3. Miracles took place freely at
her tomb, and it was decreed that the virgin's body should be
translated and raised aloft. It was found to be entirely reduced to
dust, except for the finger, the belly and the parts below the belly.
There was some dispute; then the girl herself stood by one of the
witnesses[3] as he slept, saying: 'No wonder those parts of my body
rotted, because it is normal for dead bodies to flow away into certain
secret recesses, and being a girl I had sinned with those limbs. But it
was right that my belly did not rot, for it had never been stung by any
lust, and I was untouched by gluttony or carnal intercourse.'

24.[4] Dunstan showed no less power of prophecy in foretelling the
death of Æthelwold bishop of Winchester. Æthelwold had come to
Canterbury, and was received there for a while with kindness and
generosity. For the archbishop admired him as a model of true
goodness and an image of sincere devotion; indeed he had borrowed
these qualities eagerly for himself, and competed to equal him in
them. Dunstan did Æthelwold the honour of escorting him when he
left after some days, together with the bishop of Rochester, who had
come there by chance. They had gone some of the way when evening
began to come on, with the threat of darkness, because they had been
dilatory in starting out. 2. The bishop of Rochester then humbly

[2] A deacon in *GP*, c. 87 (p. 189).
[3] Dunstan, according to *GP*, c. 87 (p. 190).
[4] The story is alluded to in *GP*, c. 19 (p. 30). There is nothing of this in Wulfstan of
Winchester, *Vita S. Æthelwoldi*, c. 41 (pp. 62–3) (where he dies at Beddington). Æthelwold
died in 984, but this does not seem to fit any bishop of Rochester (*HBC*, p. 221).

ambit archiepiscopum ut non refutaret diuersorium quod sui iuris erat, uiae proximum. Qui cum in Athelwoldum suae uoluntatis refudisset arbitrium, Athelwoldo exorato Rofensis utrorumque obtinuit assensum. Fugata nocte, mane inclaruerat et illi uiam adoriebantur. Cumque collem ascenderent qui plurimus uillae imminet, postulant a summo pontifice benedictionem episcopi mox digressuri.*ª* 3. Ille porrecta dextra et benedictionis uerba concipiens suspirium dedit; liquitur doloris imber ex oculis, succutitur singultu pectus, uestes lacrimis infunduntur. Pauefacti ambo tam subiti et tam effusi fletus portento, inter se diu multumque mussitare; demum lacrimarum occasionem placide percunctati, audierunt doloris sui esse causam ⟨mortem⟩*ᵇ* illorum proximam. Contra illi orare ut asperum amoueret uaticinium: futurum Deo auctore sepe huiusmodi conuentum; si quid presagii uidisset alio intellectu diuinandum. 4. Nec minus Dunstanus sententiam astruere, sed spe blandienti lenire: morituros eos seculo, sed uicturos cum Deo; presentibus carituros, sed gaudiis perpetuis fruituros. Ita unusquisque diuersis affectibus uiam suam abiit, ille uaticinii sui conscius, hi curiosi de hora imminentis transitus. Et Rofensi quidem ingresso menia suae urbis statim occurrit exitus uitae. Athelwoldus porro, priusquam iter a Cantia emensus esset, decubuit incommodo quod eum intulit caelo.

5. Cuius¹ excessus magnas turbas consciuit in Wintonia, clericis olim amisso loco inhiantibus, monachis regis Edgari priuilegia obtendentibus. Ita dum quisque sui ordinis cupit habere episcopum partes fecere, creuissetque immanis tumultus nisi Dunstanus arbitrium litis refudisset in Deum, orans ut litigantibus bonae uoluntatis suae obiceret scutum.² Statim consecutus precum effectum, uidit Andream apostolum Dei manifeste dicentem sibi orationem suam caelum penetrasse, prouidisse Deum desolatae*ᶜ* pastorem aecclesiae; proinde securus abbati Bathoniensi Elphego episcopatum imponeret, cuius ad utramque religionem temperata tantam seditionem sedaret modestia. 6. Nec potuit beatus uates, quem nullum umquam fefellerat presagium, de uisione dubitare, quippe qui fatiem apostoli probe norat et sepe beniuolentiam comperisset. Itaque per nuntios regem Egelredum rei certum facit, uoluntatem simul allegans suam. Ille quamquam insulsus in ceteris, in hoc tamen resipuit, ne uoluntati Dei

---

ª Stubbs; digressum *Q*   *ᵇ Supplied by ed.*   *ᶜ Stubbs*; dissolatae *Q*

¹ For this incident, see *GP*, c. 76 (p. 170).   ² Cf. Ps. 5: 13.

prayed the archbishop not to reject lodgings which he had under his jurisdiction near the road. Dunstan left the decision to Æthelwold, who consented; and so the bishop won the agreement of them both. The night passed, bright morning came, and they set out again. As they climbed a high hill overlooking the vill, the bishops asked the archbishop's blessing, now that they were about to part. 3. He held out his right hand, and was formulating the blessing when he gave a sigh. Tears of grief cascaded from his eyes, his breast shook with sobs, his clothes grew drenched. Both men were terrified by what this sudden flood might mean, and they discussed the matter for some time in low voices. Finally they gently asked the reason for the tears— and learnt that it was their own imminent death which was the cause of his grief. They begged him to take back this painful prophecy. If God willed, they would often meet again like this; he should put some other interpretation on any omen he had seen. 4. Dunstan would not change his position, though he put a more optimistic gloss on it: they would die to this world, but live with God; they would lose what is present, but gain joys eternal. So each man went his separate way with different emotions: Dunstan well aware of his gift of prophecy, the two bishops worrying about the hour set for their impending deaths. Rochester died as soon as he entered the walls of his city, while Æthelwold took to bed of the illness which brought him to heaven even before he completed the journey from Canterbury.

5. His death[1] convulsed Winchester. The clerks were all agog to regain the place they had lost, the monks brandished privileges they had been given by King Edgar. Each man wanted to have a bishop from his own order. Factions formed, and there would have been a most unseemly dispute if Dunstan had not passed the decision to God, praying that He might hold before the litigants the shield of His good will.[2] He at once had his prayers answered: he had a clear vision of God's apostle Andrew, telling him that his prayers had reached heaven, and that God had looked out a shepherd for the bereaved church. He was to put care aside and give the bishopric to Ælfheah abbot of Bath, who, with a modesty that built a bridge between the two ways of life, would calm the crisis down. 6. Dunstan, who had never been found wanting by any presage, could not doubt the vision, for he knew the apostle's face well and had often experienced his good will. He therefore informed King Æthelred by messenger of the circumstances, and made his own wishes clear. Foolish the king may have been in other matters, but here he showed good sense enough

contrastare presumeret. Ita Elphegus episcopatui datus, quinque annis Dunstano uiuente, decem et octo post eius excessum Wintoniae prefuit. Tum archiepiscopatu septem annis potitus, postremo martirium iniit.[1]

25. Illud erat in Dunstano mirabile quod etiam uerba quae casu non studio effunderet effectu non carerent, nichil umquam pene dixerit quod inani pondere in leues auras efflueret, ut illud: Opulentus quidam Alwoldus nomine, pulsatus ualitudine agensque penitentem, monachi pannos apud Glastoniam petierat et impetrauerat. Accessio temporis, uel potius sanctorum uirorum conuersatio, incommodum depulit, uisusque est aliquanto tempore integerrimae sospitatis compos. Qua elatus iterum spirauit seculum, concepitque regulae et monasterii nauseam. Obstinata intentio*ᵃ* peruersam cogitationem aluit, donec reiecto habitu in mundum prosiluit.[2] 2. Ante, cum morbus insedisset precordiis, parui fatiens diuitias contulerat monasterio quasdam possessiunculas. Tunc uero abbatis et monachorum aures cum*ᵇ* per se tum per amicos fatigabat de restitutione. Cum nichil promoueret, regis Egelredi animum oblatione nummorum temptauit. Ille, sub cuius regimine magnus erat labor iustitiae, sub quo nullus tutus nisi pecuniosus, missis apparitoribus Alwoldo quicquid interrogabat in solidum restituit. Ita rusticus inuadens omnia, etiam multa preter haec monasterio inflixit incommoda, ut est agrestium*ᶜ* cum incipiunt seuire proteruia.[3] 3. Monachi, ad unicum recurrentes patronum, archiepiscopo de fugitiuo monacho querelam deponunt. Multa*ᵈ* respondit ille plangentibus, sed haec fuit summa: 'A Domini matre ultionem exigite; illum comedant uulpes.' Quod illum non crediderim dixisse maledicentis animo, sed uel pro casu lapsum uel uaticinio impulsum. Nec tamen secus euenit. Nam post aliquantum tempus preuaricator morbo corripitur, excruciatur, defungitur. Prius tamen, anima in egressum festinante, iusserat ut cadauer suum Glastoniam deferretur, quatinus locum, quem superbe contempserat uiuus, supliciter occuparet mortuus. 4. Effertur ergo corpus exanime. Aliquantum uiae processerant qui ferebant, et ecce undique uulpes, incertum quo spiritu agente, accurrunt. Acclamatur undique 'Vulpes,

---

ᵃ *ed.*; intensio *Q*   *ᵇ* *ed.*; tum *Q*   *ᶜ* *Stubbs*; agrestum *Q*   *ᵈ* *ed.*; multis *Q*

---

[1] *GR*, c. 165. 5–6. Ælfheah was bp. of Winchester 984–1006, abp. of Canterbury 1006–12.
[2] For another renegade monk, see *GP*, c. 83 (p. 183) ('ut fere fit in talibus').

not to try to stand out against God's will. So it was that Ælfheah was given the see, and he ruled Winchester for five years while Dunstan lived, and for eighteen after his death. Then he was archbishop for seven years, before his final martyrdom.[1]

25. A remarkable feature of Dunstan was that even words he uttered by chance and not of set purpose did not lack fulfilment, and that he said almost nothing that fell without weight on the light breezes. Thus: A rich man called Ælfwold, attacked by illness and playing the penitent, had sought to become a monk at Glastonbury. He was taken in, and the passage of time, or rather the company of holy men, drove off his disease; and he for some time seemed fully recovered. This encouraged him to hanker after the things of this world again, and he began to feel disgust for the Rule and the monastery. His obstinacy fostered this improper thought, until finally he threw off his habit and bounded back into the world.[2] 2. Previously, when the disease had settled on his vitals, he had made light of wealth, and had given the monastery some small estates. But now he plagued the abbot and monks, both in person and through friends, to give his property back. Making no headway, he tried out King Æthelred by offering money. Under this king's rule justice was in a poor way, and no one was safe if he was moneyless; and so he sent bailiffs and restored to Ælfwold every penny of what he asked. The boor reoccupied everything, and did other damage besides to the house, such is the impudence of country folk once they start to lose their tempers.[3] 3. The monks had recourse to their only protector, and laid a complaint with the archbishop concerning the runaway monk. He made a long reply to their complaints, but this was the upshot: 'Look for vengeance to the Mother of the Lord. As for him, let foxes eat him.' I do not believe that he said this with any intention of cursing, but rather that it slipped out by chance or in a moment of prophetic inspiration. But the outcome proved his words true. After some time the sinner fell ill and died in agony. Earlier, however, when his soul was hastening towards departure, he had ordered his body to be taken to Glastonbury, so that he could, as a suppliant, lay claim when dead to a place he had haughtily belittled while he lived. 4. The bearers had proceeded some way when suddenly foxes ran up from all directions, who knows what devil driving them on. There was a general cry of

---

[3] Cf. *VW* ii. 20. 2: 'quanuis semel incitatis agrestium animis nulla queat obsistere uis rationis'.

uulpes!', et exceptum clamorem aetheris conuexa multiplicant. Strepit uulgus ignobile,[1] ita ut uespillones[a] etiam deposito cadauere ad bestiolas insequendas incurrerent. Illae parumper fugientes mox compendiaria uia sunt reuersae; antequam accurri posset, cadauer inuadunt, corrodunt, disiciunt, nec scio si aliquid superfuit quod posset condi humo: tremendo Dei iuditio, ut parum aut nichil de illo in placiditatem sinus[2] sui terra susciperet qui Dei matris benignitatem irritasset.

26. Hactenus forensia eius lectoris notitiae intuli; nunc interiorem uitam eius paucis absoluam.[3] At primum ille uetus uitae scriptor[4] eum obseruasse potissimum commemorat, ut nichil citra[b] doctrinam suam ageret, nichil quod a subiectis digne reprehenderetur aut diceret[c] aut faceret. Et diebus quidem hoc fere modo uiuebat, si aliae curae non auocarent,[d] ut[e] himnodiae iugi indefessaeque orationi insudaret, aut litterarum studio et librorum emendationi totum diem insumeret, nec aliud preter curam corporis actitaret: hoc post peracta sollemnia, statim subeunte aurora, incipiens. 2. Sin uero infirmis[f] negotiis hominum seruire cogeretur, rectum semper pensabat iuditium ut nec diuitem pro persona susciperet[g] nec pauperem pro fortuna despiceret, precipuum studium habens legitima coniugia conciliare, illicita diducere, pronuntians frigidam esse uirtutem sobolis adulter-inae,[5] et parum ualentem ad defensionem patriae quae furtiuo conciperetur calore; pacifici salubritate sermonis iurgia sedare, et turbulentos animorum motus in serenam quietem reuocare, uiduis et orphanis non solum patrocinium exhibens, sed etiam dignanter eos iuxta preceptum Iacobi reuisens.[h][6] 3. Omnibus postremo pauperibus sepe et oportune adesse, his uictum, illis uestimentum largiri; aliquibus tectum, nonnullis nummum, cunctis auxilium. Edifitia labantia et uetera restituens, noua nec ignaue aggrediens nec auare absoluens, prouisioni monasteriorum curam suam in patria exponere, nec transmarina maximeque in Flandria negligere.[7] Predicationis ex

---

[a] uespilliones $Q^{p.c.}$ [b] *Perhaps read* contra   [c] *ed.*; doceret Q [d] *ed.*; euocarent Q [e] ut (*or* ut aut) *ed.*; aut Q [f] *Dubious* (*hardly* infimis)   [g] *Perhaps read* suspiceret (*cf. GP p. 293* suspicere . . . contempnere; *but contrast VD ii. 7. 9* accipias . . . despitias)   [h] *It is unclear why William uses the compound*

---

[1] Virg. *Aen.* i. 149: 'saeuitque animis ignobile uulgus'. What precedes ('exceptum clamorem aetheris conuexa multiplicant') also sounds poetic.

[2] There is an underplayed allusion to the idea of Mother Earth (alongside Mother Mary). Cf. ii. 33. 5: 'dulci naturae gremio'.

[3] See above, p. 106 n. 3.   [4] B., cc. 28 (p. 40), 37 (pp. 49–50).

'Foxes, foxes!'; the vaults of heaven received the shout, and echoed it back. The rabble[1] was in high excitement, and the bearers went so far as to put down their burden and race off in pursuit of the little beasts. They fled for a while, but soon returned by a short cut, and, before anyone could intervene, assaulted the corpse, nibbled, and dismembered it. I doubt if there was anything left to be buried: a terrifying judgement of God, that a man who had provoked the benign Mother of God should leave little or nothing for the earth to receive to its tranquil bosom.[2]

26. Up to this point I have brought to the reader's notice Dunstan's public behaviour. Now I shall deal briefly with his inner life.[3] First of all, the old biographer[4] records that it was his especial rule to do nothing that conflicted with his own teaching, to say or do nothing that could reasonably be found fault with by those subject to him. By day, it was his usual practice, if he was not called away by other cares, either to labour at constant hymn-singing and untiring prayer, or to spend a whole day in literary study and the emending of books, doing nothing else apart from seeing to his bodily needs, beginning immediately at dawn, after mass. 2. But if he was forced to attend to the unstable affairs of men, he always maintained the right balance—not to have regard to a rich man's person or to look down on a poor man's fortune. It was his particular care to promote legal marriages and to end illicit ones, for, as he remarked, cold is the virtue of one born of adultery,[5] of little effect in the defence of his country one conceived in a torrid affair. With calm and healing words he would take the heat out of quarrels, and quieten roused emotions. To widows and orphans he gave not merely his protection: he visited them, in proper accordance with James's precept.[6] 3. Finally, he was often available at moments of need to all poor men, giving them now food, now clothing, some a roof, some money, all help. He restored old and tottering buildings, while strenuously turning his hands to new ones and completing them without stinginess. He looked after the upkeep of monasteries at home and also abroad, especially in Flanders.[7] There fell continuously from his

---

[5] With this contrast William's praise of the bastard Robert earl of Gloucester in *GR*, Ep. 3, and cc. 446–9.   [6] James 1: 27.

[7] Not in the earlier Lives. William's source was probably the letter written to Dunstan 980 × 986 by Wido abbot of St Peter's, Ghent (*Memorials*, pp. 380–1), requesting aid because the monks' crops had failed. He may also have noticed the letter sent by Odbert abbot of Saint-Bertin to Archbp. Sigeric in 990, mentioning Dunstan's support for his

eius ore manabat imber continuus, bonis lenis et profluus, malis ut fulmen et tonitrus. Hoc agere ad presentes uerbis, ad absentes epistolis. 4. Iam uero in ipsis negotiorum tumultibus constitutus, reducta ex his cogitatione, sepe quidem oculum, semper autem animum librabat in caelum, nec umquam eum tantarum rerum moles inquietare poterant*ᵃ* quin animo tranquillo uultuque immoto decederet.*ᵇ* Quietem mentis fatiei commendabat alacritas, simulque quod statim imperturbato uocis sono psalmodiam incipiens in curam transibat animae. Quanta sane ipsi compunctionis inesset gratia, quae possit explicare lingua? Numquam dedicationes aecclesiarum, numquam ordinationes sacerdotum sine lacrimis peregit.¹ 5. Quicquid in aecclesiis maioribus fiebat sollemniis, suis nobilitabat*ᶜ* fletibus, tanto diluuio beatam irrorabant animam irriguum superius et irriguum inferius.² Haec diebus; noctibus porro numquam ad plenam satietatem indulsit somno, nec uero peruigiliam fabulis uel inerti consumebat otio, sed orationibus assiduis, genuflexionibus, crebris suspiriis ex imo petitis. Vnde factum est ut defecato carnis et mentis intuitu utriusque substantiae oculis hauriret diuina misteria, dum adhuc grauaretur mole terrena, multoties audiens agmina superna suaue Kirrieleison cantantia.³

27. Quadam deinde*ᵈ* nocte post multas uigilias delinito in soporem corpore, mente in caelum euasit; ibi festiuam*ᵉ* frequentiam supernorum ciuium uidit,*ᶠ* ibi concentum inestimabilis suauitatis audiuit. Sedebat mater eius, ut uidebatur, instar sponsae compta crinem stellanti*ᵍ* diademate, sedebat inquam sullimi solio nixa, cuidam prepotenti regi nuptura. Erat magna constipantium caterua, feruebat uigor laetitiae, resultabant atria uocum dulcedine; solus Dunstanus diuturnum premebat silentium, uel melo captus uel gaudio attonitus. Tum iuuenis de proximo stans, cuius prestabilis forma reuerberabat oculos, arguit tacentem, cum uel propter matris gloriam debuisset in

---

ᵃ Probably read poterat (*cf. GR 447* tantarum occupationum mole [*sing.*])
ᵇ Perhaps read secederet   *ᶜ ed.*; nobilita Q   *ᵈ om. N; perhaps* denique (*'for example'; used in second position at GP p. 421*)   *ᵉ N;* festinam Q   *ᶠ N; om. Q*
ᵍ N (cf. i. 2. 2; VW iii. 23. 1); stellante Q

---

house (*Memorials*, p. 389). Both letters are found in BL, MS Cotton Tiberius A. xv, a manuscript of Alcuin's letters known to William: Thomson, *William of Malmesbury*, pp. 158–63. See generally P. Grierson, 'The relations between England and Flanders before the Norman Conquest', in *Essays in Medieval History*, ed. R. W. Southern (London, 1968), pp. 61–92, at 74–5.

¹ For Dunstan's tears cf. i. 31. 2, ii. 23. 2, 24. 3, 27. 2.

lips the rain of preaching, flowing forth softly for the good, but for the evil accompanied by thunder and lightning. He did this orally when he addressed those present, and by letter to reach the absent. 4. Yet in the very midst of the calls of business he could withdraw his thoughts from it, directing his eyes often, his mind always, towards heaven; such mountains of work could never so disconcert him as to prevent him abstracting himself with quiet mind and unmoved countenance. The tranquillity of his mind was set off by the animation of his expression, and also by the fact that, while beginning a psalm with untroubled voice, he could pass straight over to care for his soul. What tongue could express how rich he was in the grace of compunction ? He never carried out the dedication of a church or the ordination of a priest without shedding tears.[1] 5. Every event in church at high feasts he distinguished by his weeping, with such floods did 'the upper springs and the nether springs'[2] bedew his blessed soul. All this by day. At night, he never slept as long as he might have done. Nor did he spend his vigils in gossip or slothful ease, but with constant prayer, genuflexions and frequent sighs brought up from the depth of his being. So it came about that his bodily and spiritual sight was cleansed, and he could see with eyes of both kinds the secrets of heaven even while he was still burdened with the weight of earth. And he many times heard the heavenly choirs sweetly singing *Kyrie Eleison.*[3]

27. One night, when his body was soothed into sleep after long periods of vigil, his mind escaped to heaven. There he saw the citizens on high at a crowded festival, and heard harmonies of ineffable sweetness. His mother, in his dream, sat like a bride, her hair done up in a starry diadem; sat, I repeat, on a high throne, ready to marry a high king. Great was the throng about her, the scene hummed with joy, and the halls resounded with pleasant voices. Only Dunstan maintained silence, and he did so for a long while, captivated by the music or overcome by joy. Then a youth standing nearby, whose distinguished beauty dazzled the beholder, rebuked him for his

---

[2] Judges 1: 15.
[3] Cf. Osbern, c. 40 (p. 117), as part of the vision-story recounted by William in ii. 27; Byrhtferth, *Vita S. Oswaldi*, p. 459; and, an elaboration of Byrhtferth's account, Eadmer, c. 30 (p. 207). In *GP*, c. 19 (p. 31), William says 'Et credo equidem, nec uana fides, quod etiam angelorum cantum audierit, kirrieleison psallentium, quod nunc libenter aecclesiae discunt et docent Anglorum', which is a summary of the Byrhtferth–Eadmer version. See Stubbs in *Memorials*, pp. cxiv–cxv, 357–8.

Christi erumpere laudem. 2. Cumque ille retulisset se nec ignauum nec ingratum, sed huius concentus esse ignarum, 'Vis' inquit 'ut doceam te?', simulque cum dicto ita modulatus est: 'O rex gentium, dominator omnium, propter sedem maiestatis tuae da nobis indulgentiam, rex Christe, peccatorum. Alleluia',[1] his uerbis frequenter ad subsidium memoriae repetitis. Pontifex somno amisso cunctis prope cubantibus monachis et clericis statim uerba et melum[a] insonuit, quibus in disciplinam propere surgentibus, ipse interim largo imbre humectabat fatiem,[2] subinde repetens: 'Discite, filii, quia fidelis et bonus est a quo ego haec didici.'

28.[3] Hac uigilandi consuetudine noctibus ad cenobium beati Augustini extra muros Cantuariae procedebat. In eo cenobio est beatae Dei genitricis aecclesia, a sancto Adriano abbate constructa. Illuc una noctium, post consummatos in maiori aecclesia psalmos, cum tenderet, eminus quoddam caeleste murmur auribus captauit. Vlterius felici audatia progressus, uidet totam aecclesiam crebris micare luminibus.[4] 2. Nec cunctatus cuncta rimari, rimis hostiatim patentibus oculo apposito, conspicatur in solio sedentem ipsam Dei genitricem, quam circumdabat chorus uirginum, et uultibus et uestium cultibus insigne Deitatis preferentium. Has omnes domina imperatrix blando sono ad Christi laudem hortabatur[b] his uersibus: 'Cantemus Domino, sotiae, cantemus honorem; dulcis amor Christi personet ore pio.'[5] Respondebantque beatae uirgines herae precinenti uersus sequentes hoc modo: 'Femina sola fuit patuit qua ianua leti; per quam uita redit, femina sola fuit.' 3. Magna sunt haec ad ostendendam hominibus beatae Mariae dulcedinem, quam exhibuit seruulo qui eam multo mulcebat obsequio; magna uiri preconia, ut, lutea nondum compage[6] solutus, uideret oculis, hauriret auribus quod in futura uita concedendum alii sancti magno et diuturno suspirant desiderio. Senserint alii quodlibet: ego unam beatissimae Dominae

---

[a] *A dubious form (W. usually writes* melos)   [b] *N, Mir. p. 80, line 494;* hortatur *Q*

[1] Not in Hesbert, *Corpus Antiphonalium*. The text as B. (MS A), c. 29 (p. 41), and Eadmer, c. 29 (p. 206). B. MSS C and D omit *alleluia*; Osbern, c. 40 (p. 118), has an entirely different version.

[2] Cf. Statius, *Theb.* iv. 591: 'largis umectant imbribus ora'.

[3] The vision is also recorded in Byrhtferth, *Vita S. Oswaldi*, p. 458, on the basis of [B.'s] 'liber uitae [Dunstani]' (p. 457). William repeats the story in *GP*, c. 19 (pp. 30–1), and *Mir.*, c. 7 (pp. 79–81).

[4] Virgil, *Aen.* i. 90: 'crebris micat ignibus aether'.

silence; he should have burst out (he said) into praises of Christ if only to mark the glory of his mother. 2. Dunstan rejoined that he was neither lazy nor ungrateful, but that he did not know the song. 'Shall I teach you?' the young man said, and he at once sang: 'O king of the peoples, ruler of all, at the seat of your majesty give us, King Christ, forgiveness for our sins. Alleluia.'[1] And he kept repeating the words to help him fix them in his memory. When he woke, the archbishop at once sang words and music to all the monks and clerks lying nearby, and when they hurriedly got up to learn them he himself wet his face with a flood of tears,[2] saying over and over again: 'Learn, my sons, for trustworthy and good is He from whom *I* learned these things.'

28.[3] In accordance with this habit of conducting vigils, he used at night to go off to the monastery of St Augustine outside the walls of Canterbury. In that house there is a church of the blessed Mother of God, built by the holy abbot Hadrian. When he was walking there one night after the end of psalms in the great church, he caught from some distance a sound of a heavenly nature. He went nearer with happy daring, and saw the whole church sparkling with many a light.[4] 2. He did not hesitate to investigate, but put his eyes to the cracks that opened like doors in the wall, and saw sitting on a throne the very Mother of God, surrounded by a company of virgins whose faces and dress betrayed their divine nature. All of these were being encouraged to praise Christ by the Lady Empress, who was in a kind voice reciting these verses: 'Companions, let us sing, let us sing in honour of the Lord; let the sweet love of Christ resound from our pious lips.'[5] The blessed virgins followed the lead of their mistress by saying the verses that follow: 'It was a woman alone who opened the door to death: and a woman alone by whom life returned.' 3. Great are these proofs to show to men the sweetness of the blessed Mary, which she displayed to a servant who gave her long and pleasant service. And great the praise redounding to the man, that, though not yet free of the muddy frame of the body,[6] he saw with his eyes and heard with his ears what other holy men can only long with a great and long-lasting desire should be conceded them in a future life. Let others

---

[5] Sedulius, *Hymn* i. 1–2, 7–8. The first couplet also in *GP*, c. 19 (p. 31), lines 1–8 in *Mir.*, p. 80; also in B., c. 36 (p. 49), Osbern, c. 40 (p. 118), and Eadmer, c. 31 (p. 208). B. gives only 1–2, Byrhtferth 1–4. Osbern and Eadmer have the virgins responding to 1–2 with 3–8 and 3–4 respectively. William's line 8 seems to be his own adaptation of Sedulius's text.

[6] Alcimus Avitus, *Poem.* v. 288; cf. also *GP*, cc. 19, 148 (pp. 31, 287).

uisionem toti preponerem mundo, et omnia miracula quae quisquam fecit facturusue sit*ᵃ* in eius libra minus pondero.

29. Multa sunt eiusmodi et quae numerum excedunt, nec erit ulla meta referenti, qui consideret quantum Anglia bonorum uirorum copia et pacis sereno floruerit per gratiam Dei agente Dunstano, uiro cuius, ut ita dicam, uita tota in uirtutes transierat. Pauca tantum eademque strictim libauimus, perpenso*ᵇ* ad utrumque consilio, ut ⟨. . .⟩*ᶜ* lectoris mederemur fastidio. Nunc quia suffitienter ostensum et pene digito notatum quam pure et gratiose hunc incolatum coluerit, restat paucis absoluere quam sancte et gloriose migrauerit*ᵈ* ad patriam. In quibus dicendis, sicut et in antedictis, hanc paciscor regulam, ut nichil uerborum apponam nisi quod ueterum scriptorum adornet sententiam.[1]

30. Annus erat incarnationis Domini nongentesimus octogesimus octauus, et in Ascensione Domini, quae tunc ad xvi. kalendas Iunias fuit, Dunstano in caelum struebatur ascensus.[2] Cuius rei gloriam presaga mente uidit Elfgarus, tunc beati antistitis curialis presbiter,[3] post episcopatui datus, qui tunc apud Helmaham,*ᵉ* nunc apud Norwic sedem tenet. Is igitur ipsa Dominicae Ascensionis nocte preclarum imaginatus est somnium, esse se in Saluatoris aecclesia, sedere Dunstanum in throno pontificali forma quam solebat augustiori.*ᶠ* 2. Tum undatim per omnes fores angelorum cateruas irruere, adeo ut confertae multitudinis constipatione uideretur hostiorum*ᵍ* laxari capacitas.[4] Compositis autem ordinibus ante pontificem, stationis offitium exhibentes gratissima illum salutatione impertire: 'Salue,' aiunt, 'Dunstane noster, quia iam tempus est ut consortio fruaris nostro. Esto compositus die sabbati ut nobiscum hinc abeas, et aeternas laudes ante summum pontificem[5] psallas aeternaliter.' His

---

ᵃ One expects est (but cf. Mir. p. 81, line 521)   *ᵇ* ed. (cf. GP p. 408); propenso Q
ᶜ Supply e.g. ut Dunstani satisfaceremus laudibus et   *ᵈ* ed.; migrauit Q   *ᵉ* ed.;
Helmam Q   *ᶠ* agustiori Q (corr. to ang- , as it seems)   *ᵍ* ed.; hostium Q

[1] See above, Ep. 7.
[2] The calculation is correct, the day being Thursday. All the other Lives agree with William that Dunstan died on the following Saturday (19 May). None supplies the year, which William presumably found in *ASC* (see below, p. 294 n. 7).
[3] Cf. *VW* i. 2. 1 n., for this use of *curialis*. Ælfgar's connection to Dunstan is not specified in the earlier Lives, though it may only be William's reasonable interpretation of Adelard, lect. x (p. 64): 'unus ex clero ecclesiae Christi'. He became bp. of Elmham in 1001, resigning between 1012 and 1016, and dying in 1020 (*HBC*, p. 216).
[4] William apparently means that the doors seemed narrow because of the numbers

think what they will; *I* should prefer to the whole world a single glimpse of the blessed Lady, and weighed in that balance I count as nothing all the miracles anyone has done or will do.

29. There is much to be told of that kind, beyond measure indeed; and the teller will find no end if he bears in mind how much England flourished in the number of good men and the tranquillity of peace, by God's grace through the agency of Dunstan, a man whose whole life had, so to say, passed over into virtue. I have only mentioned a few details, and those concisely, with the double intention of ⟨doing justice to Dunstan's virtues while⟩ avoiding satiety for the reader. But now, since I have sufficiently shown and indeed virtually pointed out with my finger the purity and grace he brought to life in this world, it remains to deal briefly with the holiness and glory of his departure to his heavenly home. Here as before my rule is to include nothing that does not build on the words of the old writers.[1]

30. The year was AD 988; and it was on Ascension Day—then 17 May—that Dunstan's ascent to heaven began to be brought about.[2] The prophetic soul of Ælfgar foresaw the glory of this event; he was at this time the chaplain of the blessed archbishop,[3] though later he was to become bishop of the see that was then at Elmham but is now at Norwich. On the very night of the Lord's Ascension he dreamed a remarkable dream, that he was in the church of Our Saviour, and that Dunstan was sitting on the episcopal throne looking more august than ever before. 2. Then wave on wave of angels came rushing through all the doors, and so crowded became the throng that the doors seemed too narrow to let them through.[4] But they ranked themselves before the bishop, standing in his honour, and gave him an agreeable salutation: 'Hail, Dunstan, our friend,' they said, 'for now is the time for you to enjoy our company. Be prepared on Saturday to go away from here with us, and sing for ever eternal praises before the supreme bishop.'[5] On these words the vision of the angels was

coming through them; cf. *GP*, c. 73 (p. 145): 'tanta criptae laxitas, tanta superioris aedis capacitas, ut quamlibet confertae multitudini uideatur posse sufficere.' Another crowded scene is in *VW* iii. 19. 1.

[5] Presumably meaning Christ, not the pope (as it does at ii. 7. 10); but cf. the mysterious passage in Adelard, lect. x (p. 65), where the cherubim and seraphim order Dunstan 'Paratus esto die Sabbati nobiscum hinc *Romam* transire, quia oportet te coram summo pontifice nobiscum Sanctus, Sanctus, Sanctus, aeternaliter canere'. At this point Adelard, Osbern, and Eadmer recorded a reply of Dunstan's, which William omits: Adelard, lect. x (pp. 64–5), Osbern, c. 41 (p. 121), Eadmer, c. 37 (p. 218).

dictis angelorum sullata est uisio, et presbiter excessit somno, tacitumque quod uiderat usque ad missam tulit, quid tam manifesta uisio portenderet quodam stupore mentis opperiens.

31. Interea procedit dominus archiepiscopus ad sollemnia sine ullius incommodi sensu, sed imminentis transitus, ut post palam fuit, haud dubie conscius. Ter ea die infudit populo uerba salutis, primo post euangelium, quem morem omnes terunt, secundo post benedictionem episcopalem,[1] tertio post perceptam eucharistiam, semper tanta sermonum gratia, tanta uultus elegantia, ut nichil supra. Procedebat ex ore tanta uerborum copia, ex fatie claritas quanta prius numquam; profecto aderat ei de cuius aduentu loquebatur Spiritus, ut claritate fatiei nichilo minus quam angelus, a^a predicationis ubertate nichil minus uideretur quam apostolus. 2. Inhiabat populus uerbis eius, suspirabat uultui,^{b} quasi et ipse presagiret quod eum ulterius uisurus non esset. Volebat antistes eis suam gloriam manifestare,[2] sed dicturientem retrahebat passio, superabat affectus. Magno ergo suo gaudio obstrepebat et aliquantum meroris nubilum pretendebat filiorum desolatio. Iam uero tertio, ut dixi, sermonem adorsus, erupit in uocem, uocem qua eis incomparabilem effudit dolorem: haberent caritatem et dilectionem fraternam qua sola cum Deo federatur mortalis hominis anima. 3. Hanc reliquisse Dominum Saluatorem in signum sui amoris discipulis; hanc se commendare illis, hoc munus extremum.[3] Haec suae dilectionis esse pignora, quae filiis suis continuo decessurus contraderet. Neque enim se cum illis ulterius commoraturum, sed celeriter ingressurum uiam patrum. His dictis surrexit in aecclesia ingens clamor omnium, 'eheu pater, eheu^c domine' clamantium. Itum est in planctum, itum in singultum, profluebantque lacrimae doloris interpretes, precordiorum arbitrae. 4. Quibus iterum sermonem eius rogantibus supliciter, uerba quidem sufficere respondit; ueruntamen ad multos amplexu mutuo, ad omnes osculi caritate decurrit. Nam et Elfgarus sacerdos uisionis suae iam compos,[4] cum quae uiderat tulisset in medium, haud incertum dedit inditium pontificem sabbato proximo migraturum. Ille igitur, omnibus, ut dixi, quoquomodo consolatis, dedit extremae benedictionis gratiam et auctoritate sibi tradita peccatorum absolutionem et remissam.

^{a} *Probably to be deleted* ^{b} *Perhaps read* uultum ^{c} *Stubbs*; heu *Q*

[1] *Before* the blessing, according to Osbern, c. 42 (p. 122).
[2] i.e. announce his approaching death (cf. ii. 33. 2).
[3] Virgil, *Ecl.* viii. 60.
[4] Cf. ii. 30.

removed. The priest woke from his sleep, and kept what he had seen hidden till mass, waiting in some confusion of mind to learn what so clear a vision might signify.

31. Meanwhile the lord archbishop proceeded to the solemnities with no feeling of discomfort, though, as became clear later, he was certainly aware of the imminence of his passing. Three times that day he poured into the people the words of salvation: first after the Gospel, as everyone does, second after the episcopal blessing,[1] and third after receiving the Eucharist, but always with unsurpassed grace of language and beauty of countenance. From his mouth came such abundance of words, from his face such resplendence, as never before. Surely he was attended by the Spirit of whose advent he was speaking, so that in brilliance of face he seemed no less than an angel, in richness of preaching no less than an apostle. 2. The people hung on his words and sighed to look on his face, as though themselves conscious they would not see him again. The archbishop wished to make his glory manifest to them,[2] but when he tried to speak of it he was held back by emotion and overcome by his feelings. The need to abandon his sons fought against his own great joy, and cast a certain pall of sorrow over it. But when he was, as I have said, essaying a sermon for the third time he burst forth into words that caused them grief as never before. They should (he said) practise the charity and brotherly love that is the only bond between a mortal soul and God. 3. The Lord Saviour had left this to His disciples as a sign of His love for them; and this (Dunstan said) he now commended to them, this was his final gift.[3] These were the guarantees of his affection, which he was handing on to his sons just before his death. He would not dwell longer with them, but would shortly go the way of his fathers. At these words there arose in the church a mighty clamour, as all cried: 'Alas, father, alas lord.' They wailed and sobbed, and shed tears that told their grief and witnessed to their inmost feelings. 4. They asked him on their knees to speak again, but he said these words were enough, though he embraced many and gave all the kiss of charity. The priest Ælfgar too, who had had the vision earlier,[4] told what he had seen, thus giving a sure indication that the bishop would depart on the following Saturday. And so Dunstan, having, as I have said, given such consolation as he could to all of them, granted the grace of his last blessing, and by the authority vested in him the absolution and remission of sins.

32. Ita pransurus cum zetam[1] intrasset, omnes participare uolentes hilariter excepit, liberaliter pauit; prandio sancte et sobrie ut solebat celebrato, editiorem locum ascendit. Ibi, ut, quia claudicante iam uere tempus in aestatem uergebat, calorem effugeret, uel ut meridianum somnum more solito inuitaret, assedit subsellio. Erat sedile uiminea crate contextum et ita fulciendis lateribus accommodum ut etiam dormitantem a casu defenderet.[2] 2. Ministri qua quisque poterat in circuitu indulsere quieti. Iamque ille et quidam eorum in soporem concesserant, cum ipse primum quodam leni motu percussus, mox cum ipso sedili ad tectum usque subuectus[a] est, inaudito seculis omnibus miraculo, ut cum grauis carnis pondere uacuum per inane[3] ferretur. Diriguere omnes metu,[4] stratisque excussi per angulos diffugiunt;[5] sed delinimentum fuit pauoris, ea modestia qua sub-uectus fuerat, demissio pontificis. 3. Demissum ergo atque exper-rectum ritu obsequentium circumstant, reliquias formidinis pallidis uultibus preferentes; eos antistes blando filiorum nomine compellans, interrogat quid uidissent quod ita buxeum colorem[6] et exanimem induissent. Illi[b] rem ordine pandunt,[7] et se miratos in tempore aiunt. Tum ille 'Si haec' inquit 'uidistis, filii, uidete ne dum supersum diuulgetur hoc factum cuiquam; si dixeritis, Deum et obedientiam meam offendetis.'[8]

33. Incubuit interim ualitudo, et tota illa die cum sequente usque ad sabbatum uires accepit in corpore, sed animam nesciuit grauare; liberum illa uolatum moliebatur in caelum, quantoque ergastulum erat dissolutius tanto illa emicabat plausibilius. Excubabant propter monachi et clerici de pastoris uocatione suspensi et solliciti. Quibus ille indefesse salubria uerba inculcans deliniabat in memoria quae-cumque uidebat necessaria. Multa tunc et singulis et patriae in posterum profutura uaticinatum crediderim, quoniam propior aeter-nae uitae capatior erat prophetiae. 2. Quae tamen illa fuerant, quia in ueteribus libris non inuenio, dicere non presumo. Nam, ut alias

---

[a] *ed.* (*cf. below*); subiectus *Q* (euectus *s.l.*, *m.*2)   [b] hi *Q[p.c]*

[1] = *dietam*, i.e. *refectorium*. The word was used in a non-monastic context by Aldhelm, *De Virg. pros.* 33 ('tunc ad palatinas ducitur zetas et imperialis ypodromi uestibulum'). William's use is found in Osbern, *Vita S. Ælfegi* (*Anglia Sacra* ii. 127): 'Zetam uero cum ueluti pransurus intraret'.

[2] This description of Dunstan's couch is not in the earlier Lives. It is unlike William's characteristic embroidery, and is the sort of homely detail that might have been in the lost OE Life that he seems to have used.

[3] Virgil, *Aen.* xii. 906.   [4] Ovid, *Met.* vii. 115. Also echoed in *GR*, c. 204. 6.

32. So when he had entered the refectory[1] to lunch, he gave a hearty welcome to all who wished to take part, and fed them liberally. After the meal had been celebrated with the usual holy sobriety, he went up to a higher room. Here, either to avoid the heat (for spring was drawing to an end and summer was coming on) or to induce his customary siesta, he sat on a seat woven from osiers that so supported the sides as to save even a sleeper from a fall.[2] 2. His servants, seated wherever they could in a circle around him, gave themselves over to rest. When he and some of them were asleep, he was first shaken by a gentle movement, and then carried right up to the ceiling, chair and all: a miracle without precedent, that one weighed down by the burdensome flesh should be borne through empty space.[3] They all froze in fear,[4] shot from their beds and fled to all corners of the room.[5] But it calmed their panic that the archbishop was let down as gently as he had gone up. 3. When he was back on the ground and wide awake, they stood round as though to do his bidding, showing the remnants of their fright in the pallor of their faces. The bishop spoke to them kindly, calling them his sons, and asked what they had seen to give them so yellow[6] and deathly a colour. They told him the story[7] and said that they had been astonished for a time. Then he said: 'If you have seen these things, my sons, make sure no one is told of this while I yet live; if you reveal it, you will offend God and your duty of obedience to me.'[8]

33. Meanwhile his illness struck him, and all that day and the next until Saturday, though he was ready to take sustenance for his body, he was unwilling to weight down his soul; it was trying to fly to heaven unimpeded, and the more its prison cell crumbled, the more anxious(?) it was to sally forth. Near him watched monks and clerks, on tenterhooks of anxiety about their shepherd's summons from life. He was untiring in dinning into them words that bring salvation, and he impressed upon their memories all he saw to be necessary. I can well believe that at this time he made prophecies of use to individuals and to the realm for the future, for the nearer he came to eternal life the more capable of prophecy he became. 2. But what he foretold I do not presume to say, for I find nothing in the old books. As I have

---

[5] Cf. *VW* iii. 23. 3.

[6] Cf. Aldhelm, *De uirg.* (*metr.*) 1013: 'buxeus o quantos obtexit pallor inertes.'

[7] Cf. above, p. 222 n. 2.

[8] Jesus instructed His disciples not to tell others of His miracles in Matt. 8: 4, 9: 30, etc. This detail is found only in the MS D version of B. (c. 38; p. 52 n).

dixi,[1] quicumque de gestis sanctorum plus quam ab antiquo scripta sibi arrogat, profecto mente non constat. Iam ergo pollicitae quietis sabbatum accesserat, cum beatissimus presul, horam gloriae suae aduentare sentiens, fratres omnes adesse imperat. Festinus fuit eorum sed mestus accursus, exhibitumque inunctionis offitium patri amantissimo non indeploratum. 3. Doloris immensitatem uerbis amplificare otiosi est hominis;[2] quis enim non possit conicere quod, si umquam fuerint, ibi non defuerunt lacrimae, ubi plangebatur casus patriae, religionis ruina,[3] quae nitebantur in eo solo homine? Corpus Domini porrectum qua decebat ueneratione suscepit, eoque usus mente sobria, sensu integro, uoce sonora, hunc psalmi uersum concinit: 'Memoriam fecit mirabilium suorum misericors et miserator Dominus, escam dedit timentibus se.'[4] Haec uerba beato uiro fuerunt ultima, haec extremi anhelitus uestigia, dum inter has Dei laudes ad eum quem laudabat pretiosa subuolabat anima. 4. Magnum perfectae felicitatis inditium, ut egressum omnibus mortalibus suspectum tam facili meatu euaderet, dum sensu uerbisque non titubantibus supremum efflaret. Igitur Dominici thesauri splendidum margaritum, sanctique Paracleti caeleste quondam organum, humeris sacerdotum in aecclesiam delatum, ibidemque post offitia sollemnia in loco ubi ipse uiuens dictauerat[5] uenerabiliter sepulturae datum. 5. Et corpus quidem dulci naturae gremio[6] confouendum humus excepit, spiritus autem, iam dudum caelesti regno exhibitus, a Domino Christo premia meritorum petiit et accepit.

Transiit autem ad patres suos gloriosus amicus Dei Dunstanus anno aetatis, ut ex Cronicis supputare potui, sexagesimo quarto, archiepiscopatus, ut multum, uicesimo septimo:[7] uir senectutis non multae, sed sanctitatis immensae, qui famam uirtutibus uicerit,[8] qui gloriam meritis suis in aeuum omne propagarit, qui patriae iam diu nutantis ruinam ad suum exitum distulerit.

---

[1] William keeps to his rule (ii. prol. 1–2) of not giving the exact words of speeches not found in his oldest sources (B. and either Adelard or the OE Life or both). The target is Osbern, who introduces a long exhortation in c. 43 (pp. 124–5).

[2] Cf. *VW* i. Ep. 4.　　　　　　　　[3] As with Wulfstan: *VW* iii. 24. 1.

[4] Ps. 110(111): 4–5.

[5] See Osbern, c. 46 (p. 126), Eadmer, c. 42 (p. 221). Osbern adds the detail that Dunstan designated his place of burial two days before his death.

[6] Cf. ii. 25. 4.

[7] How did William compute his age and the length of his pontificate? (*a*) Above, at i. 1. 1, he followed Osbern in dating his birth to the first year of King Æthelstan (924). He presumably took the date of his death (988) from *ASC* (so also JW). (*b*) A 27-year pontificate would mean a date of 961 for Dunstan's consecration; this date is indeed found elsewhere, but only in *ASC* (F), a version not normally used by William. He gives the same

said before,[1] whoever claims to tell of the feats of saints, but goes beyond what has been written in the past, is surely of unsound mind. So now the Saturday that promised peace had arrived, and the blessed bishop, feeling the hour of his glory to be approaching, ordered all the brothers to assemble. They ran up in sad haste, and not without tears gave their beloved father the due anointing. 3. It is the part of an idle man to use words to exaggerate extremes of grief.[2] Who is unable to imagine for himself that then, if ever, tears were forthcoming—when it was a matter of bewailing the downfall of the whole country and the ruin of religion,[3] both of which depended on this one man? The body of the Lord was held out to him, and he took it with all proper reverence, and having eaten it, sober of mind and in full control of his understanding, he sang in a strong voice this verse from the psalms: 'He hath made His wonderful works to be remembered, the Lord gracious and full of compassion. He hath given meat unto them that fear Him.'[4] These were the blessed man's last words, these the traces left by his last breath; and it was amid these praises of God that his precious soul flew up to Him whom he was praising. 4. It was a great mark of his complete felicity that he made so easily a departure on which all mortals look askance, breathing his last with faculties and speech unimpaired. So the splendid pearl of the Lord's treasure, once the heavenly organ of the Holy Comforter, was carried on the shoulders of priests into the church, and there after the solemn rites buried with all reverence in the place which he had prescribed while alive.[5] 5. His body the earth received, to cherish in the sweet bosom of nature,[6] while his soul, which had long since been displayed to the kingdom of heaven, asked for and received from Christ the Lord the reward for its services.

Dunstan, glorious friend of God, passed to his fathers in the 64th year of his age, so far as I could calculate from the Chronicles, and at most in the 27th of his archbishopric;[7] he was not particularly old, but of enormous holiness, one who surpassed his fame by his virtues,[8] made his glory extend to all ages by his merits, and put off until his own death the collapse of a land which had been tottering for so long.

---

figure for the length of Dunstan's pontificate in *GP*, c. 19 (p. 31), having altered it from 33. The date of Dunstan's consecration, not easy to determine, is discussed by Stubbs in *Memorials*, pp. xcii–xcvi, and Plummer in *Two Saxon Chronicles*, ii. 154. According to *HBC*, p. 214, Dunstan was translated from London in 959, and consecrated archbishop on 21 Oct., probably in 960, dying on 19 May 988. This would actually give him a pontificate of 28 years and seven months.

[8] Cf. *AG*, c. 62 (pp. 130–1) (of Edgar!).

34.[1] Nam ut sine fastidio legentium breuiter ostendam quantam Dunstani uaticinium[2] in Egelredum intortum habuit[a] efficatiam, statim post obitum eius, qui decimo anno regis[b] fuit,[3] Dani uenerunt in Angliam, quibus omnia littora infestantibus et leuitate piratica discurrentibus, decretum ut repellerentur argento qui non potuerunt ferro; ita decem milia librarum persoluta cupiditatem Danorum expleuere:[4] exemplum infame et uiris indignum, libertatem pecunia redimere, quam ab inuicto animo nulla uiolentia possit excutere. 2. Et tunc quidem paulisper ab excursibus cessatum. Mox, ubi otio uires resumpserunt, ad superiora redeunt. Tantus timor regem incesserat ut nichil de resistendo cogitaret. Itaque Northanimbria tota[c] populata, occidentali prouintia pessumdata, ad sedecim milia librarum soluenda coactus est.[5] Cantia depredationi data, urbs metropolis et patriarcharum sedes incendio data, ipse archiepiscopus Elphegus, de quo superius dixi,[6] abductus et uinculis[d] tentus, ad extremum apparente sibi Dunstano ad gloriam benigne inuitatus, lapidatusque et securi percussus, anima caelum glorificauit.[7] 3. Durat ad hoc tempus et recens eius sanguis et illibata integritas corporis, miraculoque ducitur posse cadauer exanimari et non posse tabefieri.[8] Rex interea strenuus et egregie ad dormiendum factus oscitabat,[9] qui, ut pernitiosus in posteros esset, commentatus est qualiter successio sua omnem Angliam amitteret, Emmam filiam Ricardi comitis Normanniae coniugio asciscens; (4) unde succedenti tempore factum ut Normanni Angliam iure suo clamitantes ditioni subicerent, sicut hodie melius uidetur oculo quam exaratur stilo.[10] Interea felix Dunstani spiritus non[e] feriabatur,[f] sua tantum in caelis gloria contentus, sed in terris miraculis plurimus affuit, miseriis expostulantium plurimus assistebat. Eorum copia uetustate obsoleta[g]

---

[a] *One expects* habuerit   [b] regni eius *GR 165. 2*   [c] *Stubbs (cf. GR 165. 3)*; toto *Q*
[d] in uinculis *GR 165. 5*   [e] *Deleted in Q*   [f] *ed.*; feriebatur *Q*   [g] *ed. (cf. GP p. 172)*; absoleta *Q*

[1] This chapter is largely summarized from *GR*, c. 165; see the notes in *GR* II ad loc.
[2] ii. 20. 3, 21. 3.
[3] *ASC* (CDE) s.aa. 978, 988.
[4] *ASC* (CDE) s.a. 991.
[5] *ASC* s.aa. 993, (CDE) 994.
[6] i. 8. 1 etc. For his vision of Dunstan, see *GP*, c. 20 (p. 33); Osbern, *Vita S. Ælfegi*, p. 135, and JW s.a. 1011 for the burning of Canterbury. Ælfheah's martyrdom is mentioned above, ii. 24. 6.
[7] 'Cantia . . . glorificauit' = *GR*, c. 165. 5, almost verbatim. At about this point William

34.[1] For—to show briefly and without boredom to the reader how great was the effect of the prophecy[2] directed by Dunstan at Æthelred—the Danes came to England immediately after his death in the tenth year of the reign.[3] They harried every shore and raced hither and thither as briskly as pirates. As a result it was decided that as the sword had failed they should be driven away by gold. Ten thousand pounds was paid out to sate the greed of the Danes[4]—a shameful precedent, not worthy of true men, to buy for money the liberty that no violence can tear away from a heart that does not know the meaning of defeat. 2. For the moment, there was a short cessation of the raids. But the Danes renewed their strength thanks to this rest and returned to their previous ways. Such fear had gripped the king that he had no thought of resistance, but was forced to pay sixteen thousand pounds after the devastation of the whole of Northumbria and the wasting of the west.[5] Kent was given over to plunder, the metropolitan city and seat of the archbishops was set on fire. The archbishop himself, the Ælfheah of whom I spoke above,[6] was hauled off to captivity. In the end Dunstan appeared to him and invited him with kind intent to meet a glorious end; he was stoned and beheaded, and brought glory to heaven with his soul.[7] 3. To this day his blood remains fresh and his body incorrupt, and it is thought a miracle that a body can be killed yet not rot.[8] Meanwhile our energetic king, well formed by nature for slumber, dreamed away his existence.[9] To prolong the harm he did so that it affected posterity, he contrived that his successors should lose all England, by marrying Emma, daughter of Richard duke of Normandy, (4) the result being that in after years the Normans were able to claim England as of right and bring it under their control, something better seen today than put down in writing.[10] Meanwhile Dunstan's spirit took no rest, and did not content itself merely with its own glory in heaven; he was frequently present on earth to work miracles, and frequently helped when the wretched appealed to him. Much of this material has been lost to

---

might (had he so wished) have referred to the story of the alleged translation of Dunstan's remains to Glastonbury; see above, pp. xxii–xxiii.

[8] 'Durat . . . tabefieri' = *GR*, c. 165. 6, almost verbatim.

[9] 'Rex interea . . . oscitabat' = *GR*, c. 165. 7.

[10] William is hard on Æthelred in *GR*, cc. 164–5, 176–80, but does not blame him in this way for his marriage. The assertion amounts to a very strong and surprising identification with Englishness by the Anglo-Norman William (see also above, p. xxxiv).

memoriae excidit; pauca quae per patrocinium litterarum supersunt
sequentis libelli pagina sibi uendicabit.*ᵃ* ¹

35. Nunc auxiliante Dei gratia hoc quod in epistola libro primo
premissa promisi conabor expedire.² Quidam enim michi uitio
uertunt quod scriptorem uitae Dunstani arguerim eo quod maternos
sinus sacro puerperio intumuisse dixerit. 'Potest' inquiunt 'dici
sacrum puerperium sicut dicitur*ᵇ* bonum coniugale³ et honorabiles
nuptiae.' Assentirer⁴ si idem esset coniugium quod puerperium.
Enimuero, ut Augustinus ait, coniugium non facit tantum commixtio
corporum quantum consensus animorum.⁵ 2. Nam et Ioseph et
beatissima Maria dicti sunt coniuges, inter quos nulla fuit uirginitatis
defloratio, sed placida et Deo grata uoluntatum consensio. Puerperium autem, ut nomen ipsum indicat, non tantum est prolis in uentre
gestatio quantum in lucem effusio;⁶ omnem autem hominem in
iniquitatibus concipi et pari psalmista testatur: 'Ecce enim' inquit
'in iniquitatibus conceptus sum, et in delictis peperit me mater mea'
(sic enim habet antiqua translatio).⁷ Siquidem quod in peccatis
concipitur in peccatis nascitur, et eorundem inuolucro uoluitur,

---

ᵃ *Stubbs*; uendicabunt *Q*   ᵇ *ed*.; dicit *Q*

---

¹ It seems that William at least projected a separate book on Dunstan's posthumous
miracles, on the analogy of Osbern and Eadmer. It is either lost now, or was never written
(see above, p. xxiii). It may only be coincidental that in the Rawlinson MS, William's *Vita*
is followed by Osbern's *Miracula*. See Stubbs in *Memorials*, pp. xxxiv–xxxv, li, liii, where
he (wrongly) says that the *Miracula* are Eadmer's.
² i. prol. 3. The reference is to Osbern, c. 4 (p. 72). What follows would seem to reflect a
genuine verbal debate between William and one or more monks from Canterbury. One is
tempted to think that Osbern's defender, or one of them, might have been Eadmer.
³ We have not located 'coniugale' elsewhere as a noun; the context ensures that it must
be equivalent to 'coniugium', which we translate. It would seem (unless the text is corrupt)
that William (or the reported objector) mistakenly thought that in the phrase 'bonum
coniugale', found in patristic texts, 'bonum' is adjective rather than noun. There could well
be a specific allusion to Augustine's treatise *De bono coniugali* (CSEL xli, pp. 187–231; note
that in c. 8 [p. 198] there is a citation of Hebr. 13: 4 in the form 'Honorabiles nuptiae in
omnibus et torus immaculatus'), countered by William's reference to Augustine below
(see n. 4).
⁴ The argument proceeds thus: William objects to Osbern's words 'sacrum puerperium'
because the unborn child's state of original sin has not yet been redeemed by baptism; his
opponents riposte that this adjective may be properly applied to an unborn child, in just
the same (modified) way as 'bonum' to 'coniugium' or 'honorabiles' to 'nuptiae'. For (we
may supply) though the marital state involves sin (i.e. sex), it is still 'good', and better than
fornication, though not as good as continence: Augustine, *De bono coniug.* c. 8 (p. 198) 'non
ergo duo mala sunt conubium et fornicatio, quorum alterum peius, sed duo bona sunt
conubium et continentia, quorum alterum est melius'. William counters that, according to
Augustine's own view, marriage does not have to involve sex at all, an example being the

memory in the course of time, but a few things that have been preserved in writing will claim a place in the following book.[1]

35. Now with the help of God's grace I shall try to clear up something I promised in the letter prefacing Book One.[2] For some people find fault with me for condemning the biographer of Dunstan because he said that the mother's womb swelled with her sacred unborn child. 'We can' they say 'talk of a sacred unborn child, just as we talk of a good marriage[3] or an honourable wedding.' I should agree,[4] if a marriage were the same thing as an unborn child. In fact, as Augustine says, marriage is made not so much by the coming together of bodies as by the consent of minds.[5] 2. For both Joseph and the blessed Mary are called married partners even though there was no deflowering of her maidenhead, but only a tranquil and God-pleasing agreement of wills. But *puerperium*, as the etymology shows, is not so much the carrying of offspring in the belly but rather its bringing out into the light of day.[6] But that every man is conceived and brought to birth in iniquity is attested by the psalmist: 'Behold, I was conceived in iniquity; and in sin did my mother bear me' (such being the wording of the Old Translation).[7] For what is conceived in sin is born in sin, and is wrapped up in a covering of that same sin

Holy Family; it can therefore be 'good' in a full sense. That is not the case with a child; in the womb, and especially when born, it is subject to sin (authorities are given). Osbern's defenders, to show the possibility of an unborn or newly born child being free from sin, then propose as examples John the Baptist and Jeremiah; but William replies that neither case is comparable, because the first was miraculous, the second metaphorical.

[5] Cf. *Serm.* li. 21 (PL xxxviii. 344): 'coniugium facit non commixtio carnalis sed caritas coniugalis'. Augustine, like William, uses the example of the Holy Family. Cf. also *De bono coniugali* c. 3 (pp. 190–1): 'in bono licet annoso coniugio, etsi emarcuit ardor aetatis inter masculum et feminam, uiget tamen ordo caritatis inter maritum et uxorem, qui quanto meliores sunt, tanto maturius a conmixtione carnis suae pari consensu se continere coeperunt. . . . etiamsi languescentibus et prope cadauerinis utrisque membris, animorum tamen rite coniugatorum . . . tanto securior quanto placidior castitas perseuerat'. In the same tradition is *VW* i. 1. 1 'coniugali affectu magis quam pruritu coniuncti'.

[6] See above, p. 167 n. 5. William moves from 'puerperium' in Osbern's sense of 'unborn child' to the ordinary sense of 'childbirth' (or strictly, in William's phrasing, from the carrying of the child in the womb to its extrusion at birth), because he is going on to use confirmatory texts that speak of birth. As he says, the word 'puerperium' (from 'puer' + 'parere') implies the bearing of a child; this looks forward to 'peperit' in the passage from the Psalms.

[7] Ps. 50(51): 7. 'Antiqua translatio' means the Vetus Latina, but William is probably quoting from an intermediate source; the Vetus Latina version of this passage was much used e.g. by Ambrose and Augustine, but the context would suggest Augustine, *Contra Iulianum* ii (PL xliv. 673–5, 684). In the Vulgate, the second clause reads 'et in peccatis concepit me mater mea.'

priusquam per regeneratricem Dei gratiam renascatur. 3. Fallor si non omnes catholici tractatores idem asseuerant. Quorum unius Fulgentii testimonium ponam ex habundanti.[1] 'Firmissime' inquit 'tene et nullatenus dubites omnem hominem, qui per concubitum uiri et mulieris concipitur, cum originali peccato nasci, impietati sub-ditum mortique subiectum; et ob hoc natura irae filium nasci.' Quomodo ergo dicitur sacrum quod cum peccato nascitur, quod impietati subditur? Ad[a] hoc sane quod dicunt, posse dici de Dunstano quod dictum est de Iohanne Baptista: 'Spiritu sancto replebitur adhuc ex utero matris suae,'[2] respondeo miracula Dei in exemplum non trahenda. 4. Quis enim ad illius sanctitatis aspiret gloriam quo inter natos mulierum non surrexit maior,[3] qui dictus est angelus, si non natura, offitio tamen et gratia; qui sicut singulare meruit donum prophetiae, ita singulari[b] preuentus est munere? Nam quod ad Ieremiam prophetam dictum est, 'Priusquam te formarem in utero noui te, et antequam progredereris sanctificaui te',[4] magis ad spem predestinationis quam ad effectum rei presentis accipi debere, uerba sequentia preconantur, cum subditur 'et prophetam in gentibus dedi te.' 5. Neque enim Ieremias uel quilibet alius potuit ante exercere prophetiae munus quam esset natus: quanuis de Domino Christo absolutius intelligatur, qui gentium desideratus[5] predicationis gratiam in eas effudit ad quas numquam Ieremias accessit. Ex eadem forma predestinationis dictum Rebeccae: 'Duae gentes in utero tuo sunt, et duo populi ex uentre tuo progredientur.'[6] Non enim cateruatim et agmine facto[7] duo populi ex uentre mulieris prosiluere, sed in singulis paruulis singulae gentes sunt signatae.

36. Iam uero quod dicunt propter redargutionem aliorum scriptorum me posse inire odium,[8] illud[c] comicum dictum michi occurrit solatio, 'ueritas odium parit';[9] quanuis michi conscius sim multa merito redarguenda suppressisse silentio, et cauta egisse diligentia, ut non periclitaretur ueritas ubi superbiret falsitas. Facessat igitur inuidia,[10] malignus interpres absistat. Nullius innocentiam sautiaui, sed bona

---

[a] *ed.*; ab *Q*   [b] *Stubbs*; singulare *Q*   [c] *ed.*; ad illud *Q*

[1] *De fide ad Petrum*, c. 69 (xxvi) (CCSL xciA, p. 753).
[2] Luke 1: 15.
[3] = John the Baptist: Matt. 11: 11. Cf. Augustine, *Enarr. in Ps.* 49. 11: 'de Iohanne baptista dicitur: ecce mitto angelum meum ante faciem tuam, qui praeparabit uiam tuam ante te' (Mark 1: 2).
[4] Jerem. 1: 5.   [5] Haggai 2: 8.   [6] Gen. 25: 23.

until it is re-born through the regenerating grace of God. 3. Unless I
am mistaken, all orthodox treatises make the same claim. I shall give
the testimony of but a single witness, Fulgentius,[1] though there is no
need for it. 'Cleave firmly' he says 'to this, and have no doubt of it,
that every man conceived by the intercourse of man and woman is
born with original sin, subject to impiety and to death; and because of
this he is by nature born the son of wrath.' How then can something
be called sacred that is born in sin and subject to impiety? To their
claim that what is said of John the Baptist. 'He shall be filled with the
Holy Ghost, even from his mother's womb',[2] can be said of Dunstan,
I reply that miracles sent by God are not to be used as parallels.
4. For who would aspire to the glorious sanctity of one than whom
no greater arose among those that are born of women,[3] who was called
an angel, if not in nature at least in office and grace, and who, just as
he merited the unique gift of prophecy, was also preceded by a unique
grant. As to what was said to the prophet Jeremiah, 'Before I formed
you in the belly I knew thee; and before thou camest forth I sanctified
thee',[4] that these words are to be understood rather of the hope of
predestination than with immediate effect is shown by what follows:
'and I ordained thee a prophet unto the nations.' 5. For neither
Jeremiah nor any one else could have exercised the gift of prophecy
before being born: though the idea may be understood more literally
of Christ the Lord, who as the 'desire of the nations'[5] poured the
grace of preaching into peoples never approached by Jeremiah. Under
the same type of predestination falls what was said to Rebecca: 'Two
nations are in thy womb, and two manner of people will proceed from
thy belly.'[6] For two peoples did not spring from the woman's belly, in
close military formation,[7] but in each of the little ones a single race
was foreshadowed.

36. But as to my critics saying that I may incur hatred because I find
fault with other writers,[8] I take solace in recalling the saying from
comedy, 'Truth breeds hate'.[9] Yet I am aware that I have passed over
in silence much that I could have censured, and acted with care and
diligence to make sure that the truth was not endangered where
falsehood was triumphant. Let envy cease then,[10] and the malevolent
critic desist. I have wounded no innocent person, but covered the

---

[7] *GP*, c. 163 (p. 300). The phrase is Virgilian (e.g. *Aen.* i. 82).   [8] Cf. i. prol. 8.
[9] Modelled on Terence, *Andr.* 68 (Otto, *Sprichwörter*, p. 368).
[10] An expression favoured by Jerome in his Letters, e.g. xv. 2. 1.

integre, uitia parce perstrinxi.[1] 2. Decet enim scriptorem integritatis reuerentiam non deserere, qui dictorum suorum se nouit habere quot lectores tot iudices.[2] Quocirca, domini fratres, haec non abstinui dicere, ut purgarem suspitiones hominum, nec sinistrum de me relinquerem iuditium; meliori siquidem aetatis parte consumpta, quanto fini accedo, tanto curare debeo ne mea laceretur opinio.

Finis Vitae sancti Dunstani archiepiscopi

good fully while sparing the evil.[1] 2. For a writer should not lose his deep concern for probity, when he knows that his writings have as many judges as they have readers.[2] Wherefore, lord brothers, I have not held back from saying these things, in order to clear myself from men's suspicions, and to leave no perverse judgement of me behind. For the best part of my life is over, and the nearer I come to my end, the more I must have a care that my reputation remains unsullied.

---

[1] Cf. William's remarks on William the Conqueror in *GR* iii. prol. 1–2.
[2] Cf. Terence, *Phorm.* 454: 'Quot homines, tot sententiae'.

THE FRAGMENTARY
LIVES

INTRODUCTION

William's Lives of Patrick, Benignus, and Indract are lost to us. But they were still extant at Glastonbury when John Leland visited the abbey in the sixteenth century. His note of books in the library reads in part:[1]

Gulielmus Malmesbiriensis de antiquitate Glesconiensi.

Vita Patricii,
Vita Indracti,   } Autore Gulielmo Malmesbiriensi
Vita Benigni,
Vita Dunstani duobus libellis.

William himself refers to the same lost Lives in the letter prefacing *AG* (p. 40): 'illos ergo libellos [sc. the two of *VD*] set et uitam beati Patricii, miracula uenerabilis Benigni, passionem martiris Indracti, que simili cura procuderam, iam pridem in eorum [the monks of Glastonbury] permisi uersari manibus, ut si quid citra racionem dictum esset corrigeretur pro tempore'; and the monks passed them. They were all therefore written before *AG*, though all were clearly part of his Glastonbury production.

In another place (see below) Leland gives extracts from the Life of Patrick. Further, all three can be in some degree retrieved from the *Cronica* of John of Glastonbury. We print the relevant part of John's text (with the kind permission of the latest editor, Professor J. P. Carley: some minor corrections have been made), giving cross-references to the mentions of the saints in William's preserved works, and noting the many parallels with those works, not hitherto observed, which put John's basic dependence on William's lost Lives beyond doubt.[2]

[1] Leland, *Coll.* iv. 155; *English Benedictine Libraries*, p. 237. Some slight changes have been made (here and later) in the light of a collation of Leland's manuscript; but tiny orthographical divergences have been ignored. In the list of William's works in *Comm.*, p. 196, the Life of St Patrick is said to have been in two books, and the Life of Indract is given as 'Vita Indracti, Hiberniae reguli'.

[2] For the most striking of these see below, pp. 345 nn. 4–6; 357 n. 5; 360 n. 1; 369 n. 4; 370 n. 6; 371 nn. 8–9; 373 n. 7; 379 n. 2.

VITA PATRICII

This Life is excerpted in Leland, *Coll.* iii. 273–6 (he knew MSS, since lost, at Glastonbury [two, indeed: see below, p. 336] and at 'Twinham . . . in prouincia Avoniae littoralis'; cf. *Comm.*, p. 38 'Medimnae, alias Christeschyrche, antiquiori uero nomine Saxonico Twinhamburne'; also *Comm.*, p. 150). Some details can be added from his account of Patrick's life in *Comm.*, pp. 36–40; where his story and his own excerpts from William overlap, it is clear that he is re-writing his source, but he nevertheless preserves here details of William's narrative not available in the *Collectanea*. We have adjusted the punctuation (and used i for j and u for v). We have only included the more interesting of Leland's own marginalia, and we have not translated them. In the second column we provide supplementary material from other works of William and from John of Glastonbury (JG).[1]

William got information from at least three Patrician sources:[2] T = *Vita Tertia* (version II, the English family), (W = lost source of) SQ = *Vita secunda* and *Vita quarta* (both cited by the page of Bieler's edition), and C = Patrick's own *Confessio* (cited by chapter, and more than once mentioned by William; note too Leland's marginalia, and *Comm.*, p. 39). We comment mainly on William's own additions and characteristic phrasing.

VITA BENIGNI

This Life is also referred to in *AG*, c. 77 (p. 156), in connection with Benignus's translation, 'quam uirtutibus non incelebram [*sic*] alias stilus noster expediuit'. Apparently separate from the manuscript known to Leland is that in the Glastonbury library catalogue of 1247 mentioned by Carley, p. xli. These manuscripts have not survived.

Similarities of wording to preserved works of William show that we may confidently use John of Glastonbury's account as the basis for reconstruction of the lost Life. JG's narrative is to be compared with that in the *NLA* i. 112–14. They are close to each other up to the flowering of the staff (though *NLA*, unlike John, names *Ferramere* at this point).[3] *NLA*, however, is much fuller on the miracle of the water

---

[1] Correa, 'William of Malmesbury's *Vita S. Patricii*' [see p. xxiv n. 72], pp. 267–71, prints only the extracts from Leland's *Collectanea*, without comment.

[2] Bieler, pp. 22–4, corrected by Scott in *AG*, p. 7. And see above, p. xxiv.

[3] But note JG, c. 2 (p. 12), cited below, p. 348 n. 1.

and the meeting with the Devil. It also supplies a date for the death ('tertio nonas Nouembris': 3 November),[1] and details of miracles at the tomb not given by JG. Some or all of the *NLA* version may well be derived from William's lost Life (which he calls 'miracula . . . Benigni': above, p. 307), though William's linguistic fingerprints do not appear so clearly here as in JG. We have printed the accounts of JG and *NLA* in parallel columns.

Less problematic, perhaps, is the fragment from a narrative of the life of Benignus in Anglo-Norman verse, published by Robin Flower, *Notes and Queries for Somerset and Dorset*, xvii (1923), 205–17. This tells the story from the encounter with Patrick to the death and translation of Benignus. It survives as part of a single leaf used as a wrapper for sheets containing the list of rate-payers of the parish of West Pennard, dating from 1555.[2] The leaf is dated by Flower 1250–1300, well before John of Glastonbury (and John of Tynemouth). The outline of the story is identical to that in JG. But the author knows more. He cites not only the epitaph (which could have come from *AG*) but a Latin sequence on the miracles of the staff and the river (see also p. 348 n. 1). He knows that Benignus had to go west (or at least north-west) to reach Meare from Glastonbury (though of course that could be local knowledge). Near the end he says that the reader could read a written Life if he wished to learn of Benignus's miracles; those, presumably, later related by JG as accompanying the translation, which he has just mentioned. The Life he speaks of can hardly be anything else but William's, though it perhaps does not follow that all his new information is from that source.

Something should be said (cf. below, pp. 312–13 on Indract) of a passage cited by Scott, p. 62, from *AG* MS L (fo. 8v). This differs from Scott's text of *AG* (apart from slight details of wording) in the following ways:

(*a*)   Benignus comes to Glastonbury 'ob amorem sancti Patricii' (cf. JG, c. 5 p. 18 on Indract); that he found Patrick there is suppressed (cf. JG, c. 29 p. 68 'Patricium . . . repperit'). This is perhaps not intended to imply that Patrick was by now dead, for L repeats *AG*'s information that Benignus came in the year 460 (well within Patrick's lifetime; JG's date is 462).

(*b*)   A date is given for Benignus's death, 443, which Scott misread

---

as 404 and emended to 464. We do not know where this date comes from (the abbacy of Benignus is not dated at *AG*, c. 71 p. 146), or why the MS reading is emended in this particular way. The earliest Irish sources date the death of Benen, called Patrick's heir and successor, to 468.[1]

(*c*) The date of the translation is correctly given as 1091 (not 901).

It should be noted that this passage refers to the 'gesta' of both Patrick and Benignus, in apparent allusion to their Lives by William: below, p. 313.

VITA INDRACTI

William refers to this Life in *AG*, c. 12 (p. 60), 'sicut alias stilus noster non tacuit'. For a copy at Glastonbury in 1247, no doubt that seen by Leland, see Carley in JG, p. xl.

We can form some idea of William's Life from the account of the saint in JG, cc. 50–1, reproduced below (translated by G. H. Doble in his fundamental article, 'Saint Indract and Saint Dominic', *Somerset Record Society*, lvii (1942), 1–24, at pp. 11–13). JG again can be shown, by parallels from William's other works, to preserve at least some of the author's original wording. Parallel to this account we have printed some parts of the so-called Digby Life, edited with exemplary care by M. Lapidge from Bodl. Libr., MS Digby 112, in his 'The cult of St Indract at Glastonbury', *Anglo-Latin Literature 900–1066*, pp. 419–52, at 439–44 (a mine of information on everything concerning this obscure saint), and translated by Doble, pp. 4–8. This second Life, once thought to be the work of William (a view dismissed by Doble, 'Indract', p. 9), proclaims its faithful reproduction of an 'exemplar Anglicum' (9. 6–7: here as elsewhere we cite by Lapidge's chapter and lines). It differs in a number of details from JG, especially in the number of Indract's companions (seven in JG, nine in Digby), and in the place of the martyrdom (Shapwick in JG, *Hywisc* in Digby).[2] The Life in *NLA* (ii. 56–8; translated by Doble,

---

[1] D. Dumville, 'St Patrick and fifth-century Irish chronology: the saints', in Dumville, *Saint Patrick* (above, p. xxiv n. 72), pp. 51–7, at 51 and 53.

[2] Lapidge on Digby 1. 17 argues for identification with Huish Episcopi, some nine miles south-west of Glastonbury. But someone travelling from Glastonbury towards the sea at (say) Bridgewater would have done well to follow the pronounced ridge trending westwards above the marshes (the alternative venue, Shapwick, is just to the north of it), and so be more likely to have come to another Huish, that recorded in Domesday Book near Burnham (Ekwall, p. 256). But there remains a problem: neither Huish is known to

'Indract', pp. 14–15) is essentially a summary of Digby, but it introduces material from elsewhere; some of it, Horstman thought, from JG. We return to this point below.

It is impossible to be sure how William's Life and the English exemplar of the Digby Life are related. Lapidge (p. 437) thought that William drew on that exemplar. If this is the case, William may have 'corrected' and modified it in the light of his own research (i.e. his investigations of the oral tradition at Glastonbury and thereabouts).[1] The relevant part of Digby 112 is commonly dated *c.*1100 (so Lapidge, p. 425 n. 36), and Carley (*ASE* xxiii [1994], 275; cf. Doble, 'Indract', p. 4) thinks it was probably written at Glastonbury. It is difficult, however, to believe that, if the Digby Life itself was available at Glastonbury when William was there, he would have failed to read it (Lapidge, p. 437 n. 93); Lapidge (p. 436 n. 91) seems correct in denying that there are any *significant*[2] parallels in wording between JG and Digby, and his view (p. 425) that the book comes from Winchester has much to recommend it.[3]

Carley (p. xl, n. 31) asserts that *NLA* is 'an abridgement of the Digby *Life* with additions from lost Cornish sources'. This follows the view of Lapidge (p. 437), following Doble, 'Indract', pp. 16–17, who thought John of Tynemouth might have visited St Germans. The foundation of this opinion is that the *NLA* version describes a stay of the saint (en route to Rome) at 'Tamerunta' in Cornwall. But it has not been observed that Leland, after the information given above (p. 307), notes: 'Tamerwrth portus Cornubiae in vita S. Indracti.' Though the item 'Epistole Albini' has intervened, the implication is surely that the *Vita Indracti* is William's, so that William knew the Cornish episode (perhaps from his local oral sources).[4] The name intended by both *NLA* and Leland will be

have belonged to Glastonbury, though the Digby Life 7. 5–6 says that the place of the martyrdom was given by Ine to the abbey (Doble, 'Indract', p. 10).

[1] Alternatively, 'William's source was probably the same lost Old English account, to which he was more faithful than the Digby author' (Carley in JG, p. xl). That is to discount the Digby author's assertion of his fidelity to his source.

[2] Doble, 'Indract', p. 12 n. 2, lists some parallels that may be just coincidental.

[3] See *Bodleian Library Quarto Catalogues IX: Digby Manuscripts*, ed. W. D. Macray, new edn. by R. W. Hunt and A. G. Watson (Oxford, 1999), cols. 125–7, and pp. 60–1. It contains the best copy of the epigrams of Godfrey of Cambrai, prior of Winchester (1082–1107), ascribed in the heading to 'domini G. prioris'.

[4] This remains an odd entry: not the name of a book at Glastonbury but a jotting of something Leland found of interest, placed near (but not next) to the title of the book in which he found it.

'Tamermuthe' (cf. 'Hegelmuthe', discussed below at p. 338 n. 1), i.e. the mouth of the river Tamar, near modern Plymouth on the borders of Devon and Cornwall.[1] The harbour is mentioned in *ASC* (E) s.a. 997 (the Danes go *in to Tamer muthan*); hence Henry of Huntingdon v. 30 'Tamremutham'. It may appear an eccentric landfall for one coming from Ireland (contrast Patrick's arrival, by altar, on the northern shore of Cornwall); but Indract was going on to Rome. In view of this, it may be conjectured that *NLA*'s supplements to the Digby Life were taken, at least in part, direct from William's Life, and not from JG or lost Cornish sources.

There seems no doubt that William's Life, though differing in detail from the Digby Life, agreed with it in a crucial respect: both placed the martyrdom of Indract and his companions in the time of Ine (reigned 688–726), long after Patrick's death (placed by William in 472). Yet in other contexts William preserves a quite different chronology. *GP*, c. 91 (p. 197), may (or may not) imply that Patrick was dead; but a date under Ine seems hardly in question. *GR*, c. 23 (cf. 35C. 3), too, is not explicit on the dating (Scott in *AG*, p. 183 n. 17), but both it and the closely related *AG*, c. 12 (p. 60), might seem to put Indract in the same general period as St Brigid, whose visit to Glastonbury *AG* dates to 488. The translation, on this version, comes under Ine: 'postmodum' (*GR*, c. 23) or 'postea' (*AG*).[2]

Now this version is witnessed to by two related texts. One is a passage of *AG* MS L,[3] recorded by Scott, pp. 60 and 62 (we have corrected some errors of transcription): 'Ibidem etiam requiescit sanctus Indractus martir cum vii sociis suis commartiribus. Hii uero sancti ex regali Hiberniensium progenie Romam causa pere-grinacionis euntes et per Glastoniam ad patriam suam redeuntes, beato Patricio tunc ibidem existente abbate, ut eiusdem salubriter fruerentur colloquio, in quadam uilla iuxta Glastoniam, Shapewik nominata, hospitati, noctis silentio in lectulis suis dormientes ab infelicibus satellitibus martirizati sunt. Qualiter uero eorum corpora postmodum sanctissimo Ine regi Westsaxonum Dei prouidentia fuerunt reuelata et per eundem Glastoniam translata, in libris de

---

[1] *Pace* O. J. Padel, 'Glastonbury's Cornish connections' in *The Archaeology and History of Glastonbury Abbey*, ed. Abrams and Carley, pp. 245–56, at 246, followed by N. Orme, *The Saints of Cornwall* (Oxford, 2000), p. 110. Padel's suggestion of (North) Tamerton was anticipated by Dr C. Singer: see Doble, 'Indract', p. 16 n. 2.

[2] In *AG*, c. 20 (p. 68; 'Aliquantis annis elapsis'), the time reference is uncertain, as the item is misplaced.

[3] fo. 8v, not 8r; for the immediately preceding words about Benignus, see above, p. 309.

gestis eorum apud Glastoniam plenius habetur.' Scott recorded these remarks 'as they may be taken from William's missing *Life*'. They are certainly close to JG, c. 5 (pp. 16, 18), where in a preview of his later account he tells us that 'Ibi quiescit sanctus martir Indractus cum septem sociis suis commartiribus. Hii, ex regali Hiberniensium genere, Romam causa peregrinacionis euntes et per Glastoniam ob amorem Sancti Patricii ad patriam suam redeuntes in quadam uilla Schapewik nominata, noctis silencio dormientes, ab iniquis satellitibus martirisati sunt: quorum corpora post non modicum gloriosus rex Ina, miraculorum datis indiciis, Glastoniam transtulit.' It seems likely that JG was drawing directly on L. But if so he suppresses two items:

(*a*)   Patrick was still abbot at the time of Indract's arrival. JG does leave that possibility open; later in c. 50 (like Digby or *NLA*) he puts the martyrdom as well as the translation under Ine. It looks as though JG either carelessly combined different sources, or consciously changed his mind when he came to write the full account of Indract. Equally, William himself must have changed his mind. A story he had in *GR* and *AG* apparently placed in the fifth century he transferred to the seventh or eighth when he came to write his separate Life of Indract.[1] One can only speculate why he did this. One obvious possibility is that his Glastonbury researches turned up the Digby Life, or its English source, and that he felt he should follow this evidence on a matter dear to Glastonbury hearts (cf. Lapidge, p. 433, on the possible reasons for the invention of the details of the story).

(*b*)   Equally, JG does not say, as L does, that the story of the translation by Ine was said to be 'preserved more fully at Glastonbury in books concerning their deeds'. What books? One might think of any or all of William's Life; the English original of the Digby Life; the Digby Life itself.

That, of course, leaves open the question of where the author of L got his pre-Ine dating of the martyrdom. We take it that the answer to that is: by deduction from *AG*, c. 12 (p. 60). Otherwise the details in which L agrees with William's Life against Digby (seven companions, Shapwick) will come from the Life itself. It may be observed that in its account of Benignus L seems to know William's Lives of both Patrick and Benignus: see pp. 310 and 346 n. 1).

---

[1] As we have seen, he mentions that Life in the preface to *AG*. But that preface will have been written (much?) later than the bulk of *AG*.

TEXT AND TRANSLATION

VITA PATRICII

Coll. iii. 273–6 Ex primo libro Gulielmi Meldunensis, quem de uita S. Patr⟨itii⟩ ad monachos Glessoburgenses scripsit.

Auus eius Potitus presbyter, pater Calpurnius[1] diaconus,[2] Romanorum morem, qui tunc temporis in Britannia potentes erant, in uocabulorum decore tenuere. Mater porro Conches, filia Ocmis,[3] et soror Liupida [*var.* Luipida; *mg.* alias Lupida][4] barbariem Britan⟨nicam⟩ sonant. Nec minus ipse [*gl.* Patrit⟨ius⟩], Succet cog⟨nomento⟩,[5] a patriae appellationis more degenerare potuit.[6] Natus haud procul a mari per quod in Hiberniam transmittitur.[7] Locus exortus Banauen uicus in Taberniae campo, ex metatione tabernaculorum Romanorum, ut constans nec a uero dissimilis fama est, tale nomen sortito.[8] Ostenditur lapis puerperii conscius, in quo connixa mater sobolem effudit in lucem.[9] Magna in diem

---

[1] T 122. [2] C 1. [3] T 122.

[4] SQ 51 (see also Bieler's remarks on p. 23 n. 4).

[5] T 122. This (rather than 'cognomine') is William's normal expression, and is confirmed here by Leland, *Comm.*, p. 36. JG, c. 23 (p. 58; cf. Scott in *AG*, pp. 189–90) tells a quite different story about Patrick's names, only partly from Irish sources.

[6] William (himself of twin stock) contrasts the Roman names of Patricius himself, his grandfather and father, with the strange-sounding names of his mother, grandmother and sister. Cf. *GR* i prol. 4 'exarata barbarice Romano sale condire', c. 165. 6 'quorum nomina propter barbariem linguae [so *GP*, c. 181 (p. 319)] scribere refugio', *VW* i. 16. 5 'uocabulorum barbaries': all of Old English.

LIFE OF PATRICK

(Leland)
From the first book of William of Malmesbury which he wrote on the life of St Patrick to the monks of Glastonbury.

His grandfather, Potitus, a priest, and his father Calpurnius,[1] a deacon,[2] retained in the dignified form of their names the manner of the Romans, who were at that time powerful in Britain. But his mother Conches, daughter of Ocmis,[3] and his sister Liupida[4] have the ring of the barbarian British. Patrick himself, who was also known[5] as Succet, did not fall short of his father's type of name.[6] He was born not far from the sea which one crosses to go over to Ireland.[7] The place of his birth was the *vicus* of *Banauen* in the *Campus Taberniae*, so named, according to a long-standing and plausible report, from the marking out of the tents of the Romans.[8] The stone associated with his birth, on which his mother lay when she bore her child,[9] is shown to

---

[7] T 122. Cf. *VW* ii. 19. 2 (of Bristol).

[8] SQ 51–2 (but C 1 for 'Banauen uicus'). William adds the learned words *exortus* (used in *GR*, c. 19. 3, of the rise of the church of Glastonbury), and *metatio*, perhaps from Frontinus, *Strat.* iv. 3. 13; William had his own copy of this work: Thomson, *William of Malmesbury*, p. 87.

[9] SQ 52. Cf. *GP*, c. 100 (p. 212) 'in lucem effunderet'. There is perhaps a reminiscence of Virgil, *Ecl.* i. 14–15 'gemellos, / spem gregis, a! silice in nuda conixa reliquit'. (This use

modernum accolarum circa lapidem frequentia.

Iam uero in sortem Christi regenerandus puerulus exhibitus est uiro sancto, cui Gornias nomen.[1]

De basilica loquens fabricata eo loco ubi baptizatus erat S. Patritius.

Aiunt qui uiderunt ad altaris partem dexteram fontem esse quadratum, in crucis modum, uitreis undis perlucidum, cuius haustu nihil iucundius, intuitu nihil purius.[2] [*mg.* Fons miraculo ortus, in quo Patritius baptizatus fuit.]

In Banauen igitur uico, qui et Nenchor [*v.l.* Nantchor], educatus sanctiss⟨ima⟩ ut par erat disciplina et in ephebum aeuo crescente prouectus, religioni parentum non defuit.[3] [*mg.* Banauen uicus, alias Nenchor dictus.]

Assistit ipse sermoni meo astipulator idoneus his uerbis in confessione sua.[4] [*mg.* Gul⟨ielmus⟩ Meld⟨unensis⟩ frequenter citat librum Patritii de confessione, in quo res a se gestas et uitam suam scripsit.]

Habebat sororem, ut ante dixi, Lupidam, uenerabilium post

Comm. p. 36 cum Lupida, paruula sorore sua, foemina magnae

of 'conixa' is unique in classical Latin.) The next sentence is apparently William's own information. It suggests that people in his day knew, or thought they knew, where 'Banauen uicus in Taberniae campo' was, and that it was not very far from Malmesbury. Modern scholarship has wavered between a south-west and north-west location. R. P. C. Hanson, *Saint Patrick: His Origins and Career* (Oxford, 1968), discussing the problem at pp. 113–16, concluded that 'the probability is strongly in favour of locating it in the Lowland Zone of Roman Britain, and in the south-western part of that zone, in Somerset

visitors, and crowds of locals
flock around it even today.

The infant was now shown to
a holy man called Gornias for
baptism.[1]

Speaking of the church built
on the place where St Patrick was
baptized:

Those who have seen it say
that to the right of the altar is a
square fountain, shaped like a
cross, with water as pellucid as
glass, incomparable for its sweet
taste and clarity.[2]

So it was in the *vicus* of
Banauen, also called Nenchor,
that he was given (as was only
right) a most religious education,
and as he grew up he did not fail
to associate himself with his parents' faith.[3]

My words have an excellent
witness, Patrick himself, in
these words from his *Confession*.[4]

He had a sister, as I said before, called Lupida, a woman	*Comm.* He lived happily with his young sister Lupida, a woman

or Dorset or Devon'; so also J. B. Bury, *The Life of St. Patrick* (London, 1905), p. 17;
E. MacNeill, *Saint Patrick* (Dublin and London, 1964), p. 44. But Hanson dismisses,
perhaps too hastily, the ingenious suggestion of T. F. O'Rahilly (*The Two Patricks*
(Dublin, 1942), pp. 32–4), that Patrick was born near Glastonbury. O'Rahilly conjectured
that 'Banauen Taberniae' was originally 'Bannauenta Bruuiae', named after the river Brue,
on which Glastonbury is situated. The river name is accepted by Ekwall, p. 70, as of
British origin, and this would square nicely with William's comment. On the other hand
C. Thomas, *Christianity in Roman Britain to AD 500* (London, 1981), pp. 310–14, argues
strongly for a location close to Hadrian's Wall.

[1] SQ 52.
[2] SQ 53. William's 'qui uiderunt' echoes his source's 'periti loci illius', but the
rhapsodic description of the spring is his own (cf. *GR*, c. 377. 3 'quasi congelato uitro
totus perlucidus' and esp. *GP*, c. 214 (p. 359) [from Aldhelm] 'uitreorum fontium limpidis
laticibus'). Still, 'ad altaris partem dexteram' and the mention of flocking crowds may be
from local information.   [3] SQ 53 (see Bieler, p. 23).
[4] 'sermoni meo' and 'his uerbis' seem to have been left by Leland with no reference.
For the phrasing, cf. *GP*, c. 117 (p. 255) 'utrarumque rerum astipulator est idoneus Beda'.

haec meritorum feminam, cuius nunc reliquiae pausant in Ardmacha, urbe Hiber⟨niae(?)⟩ praecipua.[1]

[*mg.* Patritius a Scottis Hiberniensibus, qui littus Britanniae a Circio infestabant, captus.] Cum enim Hiberniensium classis, praedae allecta facilitate, Britanniam more suo adnauigasset, inter ceteros captiuos et Patritium, iam sedecim annorum adolescentulum, abduxit.[2]

Ipse certe in confessione caussam captiuitatis adscribit peccatis populi et suis.[3]

Latrunculorum ergo praeda factus Patritius ueniit in seruum, trans aquilonares remotioris Hiberniae partes distractus. Comparauit regionis illius regulus Milcu [*mg.* alias Miluc], filius Boin, pro paucorum nummorum commercio ingenuo potitus, et superbus spolio. Denique, ut splendorem natalium eius obfuscaret, subulcum instituit.[4]

Vt inuento thezauro Patritius se a seruitute redemerit.[5]

postea continentiae et uirtutis, feliciter, parentibus omnia abunde ministrantibus, uixit.

JG 23 (cf. Scott, pp. 189–90) Tradunt namque historie Constantinum et Maximum ac alios quosdam in Britannia imperatores creatos, transito mari, omnem armatam et militarem manum abduxisse et inermes absque tutela Britones reliquisse. Hoc percipientes hostes circumhabitantes Hibernienses et Picti in Britannos omnis expertes milicie irruentes, non ignobiles predas crebro abduxerunt. Quocirca inter ceteros captiuos eciam Patricium, iam sexdecim annorum adolescentulum, Hibernienses rapuerunt.

JG 23 (cf. Scott, p. 190) Latrunculorum ergo preda factus uenditus est in seruum. Comparauit eum regionis illius quidam regulus nomine Milchu atque eum suo seruicio mancipauit. Denique durius quam herilis clemencie interesset agens cum adolescente suum eum subulcum instituit.

JG 23 (cf. Scott, p. 190) Transierunt in hac seruitute sex anni

---

[1] SQ 51. William adds the gloss to help English readers, and invents the sister's merits: we hear no more than that she too became a shepherd. Leland, *Comm.*, p. 36, may be inventing too when he adds that Patrick's parents helped out at this period.

[2] T 121 + SQ 61. With the passage from John, cf. *GR*, cc. 2–3.

who later showed remarkable qualities; her remains now rest at Armagh, an important city in Ireland.[1]

who later showed great continence and virtue, their parents supplying everything in abundance.

JG History relates that Constantine and Maximus and some others, having been made emperors in Britain, crossed the sea, taking all the armed forces with them and leaving the Britons with no one to look after them. Seeing this, the enemies around about, Irish and Pict, bore down on the British, who were quite without martial skills, and often carried off fine booty. Among their prisoners the Irish took away Patrick, now a youth of sixteen.

For when a fleet of Irishmen, drawn by the prospect of easy plunder, as so often sailed over to Britain, it took away among other captives Patrick, now a youth of sixteen.[2]

At least he in his *Confession* puts his captivity down to the sins of his people and to his own.[3]

Become the prey of robbers, Patrick was sold into slavery, and disposed of across the remoter northern parts of Ireland. His purchaser was a petty king of the district, Milcu, son of Boin, who won possession of a freeborn man at tiny cost, and prided himself on his spoil. Then, to obscure the brilliance of his birth, he made him a swineherd.[4]

JG So, become the prey of robbers, he was sold into slavery. He was bought by a petty king of that district called Milchu, who put him to work for him. For instance, treating the young man more harshly than a kind master should, he made him his swineherd.

How Patrick found a treasure and bought himself out of slavery.[5]

JG Six years passed in this period of slavery. Finally, an

---

[3] C 1 'secundum merita nostra, quia a Deo recessimus . . .' .

[4] T 122–3 (the motivation in 'ut . . . obfuscaret' is apparently William's own).

[5] A summary or heading, not an extract; see T 124. JG is also abbreviating. Leland, *Comm.*, is mistaken in saying that William gave no clear indication of the length of this

Ille [*gl.* Miluc], metalli fulgore[1] perstrictus oculos, simul et pondere captus, se exorabilem praebuit, et adolescentem manumissum seruituti emancipauit.[2]

continui. Demum angelico oraculo aurum sub cespite quodam inueniens domino tribuit ac seruitute liberatus patriam rediit atque parentes expeciit. Leland, *Comm.* p. 36 Sed quamdiu seruiuerit ex Gulielmo non satis liquet. Scribit tamen dato pretio manumissum fuisse, dominumque postea poenitudine ductum cogitauisse de repetendo seruo.

Felicibus ergo uentis in altum prouecti, post triduum continentem attingebant, etc.[3] De erroribus Patritii per deserta loca.

Leland, *Comm.* pp. 36–7 At Patricius, secundo uento usus, festinanter abierat: ita tamen, ut per mare per terras multa pericula [antea] sit passus, quam ad parentes peruenisset.

Octauo ergo et uicesimo postquam appulerat die post errores multiuagos, quos deuius [*leg.* deuia] secutus inciderat, Patritius terram habitalem [*leg.* habitabilem] uidit.[4] Sed nec longum uisu laetatus est,[5] paulo post iterum a praedonibus interceptus et abductus.[6]

Sexagesimus postea dies uidit Patritium ab omni captiuitatis iniuria exemptum.[7]

Ita mag⟨nis⟩ laboribus perfunctus tandem in patriam, tandem in domum paternam receptui cecinit.[8]

period of slavery, unless JG is using another source beside William. The lord's tardy regret at freeing Patrick also derives from T 124.

[1] Cf. *GR*, c. 440. 2 'fulgore pecuniarum' (see also below, p. 373 n. 7).

[2] Cf. *GP*, c. 261 (p. 417) 'a seruitute diaboli emancipatus'.

[3] T 125. Another heading follows (T 125 'per desertum'). The sufferings mentioned by Leland, *Comm.*, do not come in T or C: he is probably embroidering (or William did: cf. below, 'magnis laboribus perfunctus').

Miluc, his eyes dazzled by the glint of metal,[1] and attracted by its weight, showed himself open to persuasion, and freed the young man.[2]

angel's warning enabled him to find gold under a sod. He gave it to his master, and freed from slavery went back to his homeland and sought out his parents. *Comm.* But how long he was a slave is not clear from William. However, he writes that he was manumitted after paying the price, and that his master was later smitten with remorse and thought about looking for his slave again.

They went out to sea before favourable winds, and after three days came to the mainland, etc.[3] Of the wanderings of Patrick through desert places.

Comm. But Patrick, on a favourable wind, had made a swift departure, though he was to undergo many dangers on land and sea before he came safe to his parents.

So on the 28th day after his landing, after many wanderings in out of the way country, Patrick saw civilization again.[4] But he could not enjoy the sight for long,[5] for soon afterwards he was a second time seized by pirates and led off.[6]

The sixtieth day after that saw Patrick freed from all the disgrace of captivity.[7]

Having thus come through great labours, he finally beat a retreat to his homeland and his father's house.[8]

---

[4] T 125. The unusual word *multiuagus* is used e.g. twice in Statius's *Thebaid* (i. 499, vi. 1). 'per deuia' is used three times in *GR*, and is common in patristic Latin. The finding of habitable land seems to reflect the encounter with the pigs (T 126).

[5] Cf. *GR*, cc. 14. 1 'nec . . . longum gloriatus est', 42. 3 'non longum . . . gloriatus'.

[6] T 127.   [7] T 128 'post duos menses'.

[8] T 128. For William's phrasing cf. e.g. *GP*, c. 259 (p. 414) 'in patriam receptui cecinit'.

JG 24 (cf. Scott, p. 190) Circa hec tempora, occiso proditore rege Constante qui prius monachus in Wintoniensi fuerat ecclesia Vortigernoque diadema regni indebite surripiente, uenerunt Saxones in Angliam.[1] Illis diebus fides Britonum plurimum fuerat labefacta tum propter Saxonum paganorum societatem tum eciam propter Pelagianam heresim qua multis diebus infecti fuerant. Quapropter Sanctus Germanus Altisiodorensis et Sanctus Lupus Trecasinus episcopi Britanniam mittuntur et fidem catholicam expungnantes euangelicis atque apostolicis confutarunt auctoritatibus. Inde in patriam meditantes reditum Patricium Sanctus Germanus ad familiare asciuit contubernium. Cuius discipulatui duobus de uiginti annis non segniter insudans, Patricius scripturarum diuinarum leccione quicquid deerat plenitudini adiecit sciencie. Cf. Leland, *Comm.*, p. 37 Erat circiter haec tempora Germanus episcopus Altisiodorensis, uir magnae eruditionis simul ac uirtutis, in summo pretio non modo apud Gallos suos, uerum etiam apud Britannos; quos semel, atque iterum a Pelagiana haeresi, et Saxonum

[*mg.* Patritius Sancti Germani discipulus] Cuius disciplinatui[2] duobus de uiginti annis non segniter insud⟨ans, Patritius⟩ scripturarum diuinarum lectione quicquid deerat plenitudini ⟨adiecit⟩ scientiae.[3]

---

[1] The nonsense of this first sentence of John's comes from Geoffrey of Monmouth (vi. 5–9), not from William. For what follows (to 'contubernium') cf. the shorter account in *AG*, c. 8 (p. 54), itself close to *GR*, c. 22. 1. Leland, *Comm.*, gives us a version at this point that accords well with the story given by JG/*AG* /*GR*. For 'in summo pretio . . .' cf. T 130 'uirum sapientissimum et honoratum ab omnibus Gallis'.

[2] JG's *discipulatui* is no doubt correct. Cf. *GP*, c. 91 (p. 197) 'Patritius . . . Germani . . .

LIFE OF PATRICK 325

JG Around this time, after the
killing of the traitor king Constans, formerly a monk at
Winchester, and the illegitimate
seizure of the throne by Vortigern, the Saxons came to England.[1] At that time the faith of
the Britons had been under-
mined both by intercourse with
the pagan Saxons and also
because of the Pelagian heresy
which had infected them over a
long period. So St Germanus
bishop of Auxerre and St
Lupus bishop of Troyes were
sent to Britain, and used the
authority of the gospels and the
apostles to refute those who were
assailing the catholic faith. Then,
when they were thinking of
returning home, St Germanus
brought Patrick into his intimate
Patrick worked hard as his   circle. Patrick worked hard as his
pupil[2] for eighteen years, and   pupil for eighteen years, and by
by study of Holy Scripture   study of Holy Scripture made up
made up any deficiencies in his   any deficiencies in his wide
wide knowledge.[3]   knowledge. *Comm.* Around this
time lived Germanus bishop of
Auxerre, a man of education and
virtue, who was highly regarded
not only in his native Gaul but
also among the British, whom he
saved more than once from the
Pelagian heresy and the violent
tyranny of the Saxons. Now free

discipulus'; *VD* i. 4. 2 'horum ergo discipulatui ['disciplinatu' Leland, *Comm.*, p. 162] . . .
deditus'.
   [3] The years are given as forty in T 130, thirty in SQ 74. For the studies, see T 130
('legens et implens diuinas scripturas'). We have supplemented Leland's damaged text
from JG. With the phrasing cf. *GP*, cc. 115 (p. 249) 'plenitudini litterarum adiecit', 189
(p. 334) 'liberales artes plenitudini scientiae adiecit'.

uiolenta tyrannide liberos fecit. Hunc Patricius libertati restitutus tanquam praeceptorem et patronum obseruauit, dilexit, coluit: nec ante ab eius recessit latere, quam totos duodeuiginti annos exegisset. Quo longo spatio tantum per omnes cum eruditionis, tum uirtutis numeros profecit, quantum illi ad immortalem gloriam satis erat.

[*mg.* Patritius, Segetio comitatus, Romam petit.] Missus cum eo ab episcopo [*gl.* Germano] Segetius presbyter spetiosiorem fecit com . . . .[1]

Leland, *Comm.* (contd.) Senserat haec Germanus, cupiensque uirum iustis modis illustrare, commendatissimum per epistolas ad Coelestinum P. R. una cum Segetio presbytero misit.

JG 24 (cf. Scott, p. 190) Iamque quadragenariam[2] etatem egressus, magistro [i.e. Germano] ualefaciens suam presenciam Romane intulit curie inuenitque gratiam . . . apostolus.

Inuenit gratiam in conspectu domini Papae. Is erat Caelestinus, ⟨a beato Petro quadragesimus quintus, anno Dominicae⟩ incarnat⟨ionis⟩ CCCCXXII° papatum ingressus. Ab eo Patritius Hiberniam ⟨in o⟩pu⟨s euan⟩gelii missus, datus est illis gentibus doctor et apostolus.[3]

Leland, *Comm.* p. 37 a quo [sc. Coelestino] non multo post ad Hibernos apostolus missus est, ut fidem et Christi euangelium praediceret.

---

[1] T 131. T's 'ut testem haberet idoneum' might suggest supplementing to 'spetiosiorem fecit com⟨item⟩', but the phrase would be strange.

[2] If Patrick was born, as JG believed, in 361, 'quadragenariam' is quite wrong. JG himself says (c. 26; p. 64) that Patrick was 64 when he was sent to Ireland; did William write, or mean to write, 'sexagenariam'? We might, for instance, imagine 'quadragenariam' as the error of a later copyist, using an exemplar with roman numerals, as was William's wont.

[3] T 132. JG, c. 24 (p. 60) (which we have again used to supplement Leland where he marks gaps) gives the date of Celestine's accession as 424 (not 422), and that of the mission

again, Patrick cultivated and loved him as a teacher and patron, and did not leave his side before full eighteen years had passed. For this long period he went through all the stages of learning and virtue, enough to qualify him for immortal fame.

The priest Segetius, who was sent with him by the bishop [i.e. Germanus], made a more beautiful . . .[1]

Comm. Germanus was well aware of this, and desiring to promote Patrick's reputation in every proper way, he sent him, with the priest Segetius, and a laudatory reference, to Pope Celestine.

JG Now beyond his fortieth[2] year, he bade farewell to his master and presented himself at the *curia* in Rome; he found favour . . .

He found favour in the sight of the lord pope. This was Celestine, forty-fifth after St Peter, who entered office in AD 422. Patrick was sent by him to evangelize in Ireland, where he became teacher and apostle for those peoples.[3]

Comm. Not much later Celestine sent him to the Irish as a missionary, to preach the faith and the gospel of Christ.

to Ireland as 425 (so also JG prol.; p. 6). The same date for the mission is found in *GR*, c. 22. 1, citing an unknown chronicle: 'Patritius ordinatur a Celestino papa in Hiberniam.' Leland, *Comm.*, p. 37, gives no dates, but adds, concerning Patrick's stay in Rome, the following information: 'Illud interim non praetereundum silentio, Piranum Hibernum, Domuelis filium, cuius fanum in Corinia ad Sabrinum litus eminet, Patricio Romae fuisse familiarem.' The reference is to St Ciaran of Saighir, who was wrongly identified with the Cornish Piran: see G. H. Doble, 'Saint Perran or Piran', in his *The Saints of Cornwall*, ed. D. Attwater, part 4 (Oxford, 1965), pp. 3–30; N. Orme, *The Saints of Cornwall*, pp. 220–3. Piran gave his name to Perranporth in N. Cornwall; the 'fanum' is presumably the church

Idem sane Caelestinus paulo ante Palladium quendam Hiberniam ad praedicandum miserat; ut uero autor est Beda anno Domini CCCCXXX°, etc.[1] Vt Palladius, pertaesus barbariei, reuersus sit in Britanniam, ubi mortuus est.[2]

Vnde colligitur Patritium eodem anno quo Palladium uel certe sequenti Hiberniam missum, quia non ultra nouem annos Caelestinus protendit pontificatum.[3]

Leland, *Comm.* (contd.) Nam Palladius, qui paulo ante eo se contulerat, non ferens ignotae gentis barbariem, Britanniam petiit; ubi et diem obiit.

[*mg*. Et haec Gul⟨ielmus⟩ Meld-⟨unensis⟩ ex libro Confessionis Patritii decerpsit.]

Nec non et praemia dabam regibus [*gl.* sup.(*sic*) Hiberniae][4] et filiis eorum qui propter securitatem meam mecum ambulabant. Sed tamen ipsi me auidissime uolebant interficere, et quicquid inuenerunt nobiscum rapuerunt, et me ferro uinxerunt. [*mg*. Patritius in uinculis.] Quartodecimo

at St Piran or Perranzabuloe, a mile from Perranporth: see N. Orme, *English Church Dedications: With a Survey of Cornwall and Devon* (Exeter, 1996), p. 221. It seems probable that Leland drew his information from the Life of the saint found in the *Nova Legenda Anglie* (*NLA* ii. 320–7), which tells of the meeting with Patrick and calls Piran's father Domuel (contrast the name Lugneus in another Life, printed by C. Plummer in *Vitae Sanctorum Hiberniae* (2 vols.: Oxford, 1910), i. 217–33). The *NLA* Life ends: 'Quiescit autem in Cornubia supra mare Sabrinum a Petrokstowe [Padstow, N. Cornwall] miliaribus quindecim et a Mousehole [nr. Penzance] uigintiquinque [Perranzabuloe is in fact 23 miles from Mousehole and nearly 15 from Padstow].' For the Cornish connection cf. below, p. 338 n. 1 on Patrick's alleged landing at *Hailemout*. But it remains possible that the information was available in William's Life. Leland does not here make a non-William source explicit, as he does when he cites Marianus earlier; and what John of Tynemouth knew William could have known too. The same problem arises with St Cairnech (p. 334 n. 3 below).

This same Celestine had shortly before sent one Palladius to Ireland to preach, but according to Bede in AD 430, etc.[1] How Palladius, tired of the lack of civilization, returned to Britain, where he died.[2]

The deduction is that Patrick was sent to Ireland in the same year as Palladius, or at least the following one, for Celestine's pontificate did not last more than nine years.[3]

Comm. For Palladius, who had gone there shortly before, could not tolerate the barbarous ways of a race he knew nothing of, and repaired to Britain, where he also died.

I also gave rewards to the kings[4] and their sons who walked with me to protect me. But they urgently desired to kill me, and whatever they found with us they took away, and bound me in chains. But on the

---

[1] According to Bede (*HE* i.13, v. 24), Palladius was sent to Ireland (cf. T 133) in the eighth year of Theodosius or 430; so also the 'Carta Patricii' in *AG*, c. 9 (p. 54), but probably corrected from 425, the date given in the version in JG, c. 24 (p. 60), and in *GR*, c. 22. 1 (see p. 326 n. 3 above). Patrick therefore went shortly after 430 (if Bede is believed), or in or soon after 425.

[2] A summary of William's narrative; cf. T 133. But 'pertaesus barbariei' (cf. Leland, *Comm.*, 'ignotae gentis barbariem') sounds like William's wording: cf. *VW* ii. 1. 7 'Normannis inaccessa et propter barbariem inpacata', of the see of Chester.

[3] Taken by RMT (*GR* II, p. 403) as Leland's own remark (though it is not marked as such, unlike the last paragraph of the series). This must be right, since the argument only works on Bede's (not William's) dating: if Palladius was sent by Celestine in 430, Patrick must have gone in 430 or 431, because Celestine did not reign for more than nine years (reckoning from 422). Leland's deduction is paralleled by a late thirteenth-century note in MS T of *AG* (see Scott, p. 54 note k): 'et eodem anno [430?—but almost certainly corrected from 425] uel precedente misit idem papa ad predicandum ibidem uirum nomine Palladium, Britannicum genere. Sed idem cito repatriauit sine ullo effectu.'

[4] Presumably = 'scil. Hiberniae'.

autem die absoluit me Dominus
de potestate eorum.[1]

Ex 2° libro de uita Patritii.

De puero Hunna nomine, in
Temoria, regione Hiberniae in qua
regnum erat Loegarii, qui nullo
modo a Patritio abesse uoluit.[2]
[*mg.* Hic est Benignus, qui sepultus est Glessoburgi.] Eum et
dignatus est lecto et insigniuit
Benigni uocabulo. Iussit ergo
baptizatum in currum suum
leuari, pronuntians illum futurum heredem regni sui.

JG 29 (see below, pp. 344, 346)
. . . eum dignatus est lecto et
insigniuit Benigni uocabulo. . . .
Iussit ergo baptisatum in currum
suum leuari, pronuncians eum
futurum heredem regiminis et
pontificii sui.

Vnus erat id temporis[3] ex Britannorum regibus, dubium an
adhuc paganus, certe ferocitate
deterrimus, nomine Cereticus.
Is animum sancti multis con-
ficiebat angoribus hac quae
sequitur caussa. Crebris enim,
ut supra dixi,[4] conflictibus Brit-
anni et Scotti summa ui utrinque
decertabant, et ut sunt incerta
bellorum modo illis modo his
uincentibus praedae insignes
agebantur. Hinc fiebat ut Hib-
ern⟨ienses⟩ captiui, qui ceci-
dissent in sortem Ceretici,
miseris excruciati modis, antici-
parent mortem suppliciis.[5] Hanc
cum in omnes exerceret carnifi-
cinam, tum maxime in eos quos

---

[1] As Leland remarks, this is quoted direct from the *Confessio* (52, in a text differing considerably from ours).

[2] A heading. See T 141. JG (for whose account see below, pp. 344–7) probably had the story available to him, in similar or identical versions, in both the *Vita Benigni* and the *Vita Patricii*. Leland's 'Hunna' should be 'Beonna'.

fourteenth day the Lord freed me from their clutches.[1]

From the second book of the Life of Patrick.

Concerning the boy called Hunna, in Temoria, the district of Ireland in which was the kingdom of Leoghaire, who refused to be parted from Patrick.[2]

He let him sleep in his bed, and marked him out with the name Benignus. He therefore gave the order for him to be baptized and lifted into his wagon, saying solemnly that he would be heir to his rule.

JG . . . he let him sleep in his bed, and marked him out with the name Benignus. . . . He therefore gave the order for him to be baptized and lifted into his wagon, saying solemnly that he would be heir to his rule and his bishopric.

One of the kings of the British at that time,[3] perhaps still a pagan, certainly far gone in savagery, was called Cereticus. He caused the saint much anguish for the following reason. As I have said above,[4] both the British and the Scots employed extreme violence in their constant quarrels, and such being the vagaries of war, now one side, now the other was victorious, and notable booty was taken. The result was that Irish captives who fell to Cereticus's lot were subjected to pitiful torture, so that they suffered the torments of death while still alive.[5] He practised butchery like this on everyone; but in

---

[3] Perhaps the only instance in William of this phrase without a preposition (*ad, per*).

[4] The passage referred to does not survive.

[5] The phrase is elucidated by reference to a remark in *GP*, c. 268 (p. 425), attributed there to Augustine: 'mens mali conscia ipsa sibi tormentum est, anticipatque uiuens mortuorum suplitia.' We have not succeeded in identifying it.

Patritius baptizasset totam fatigabat saeuitiam, saepius infrendens quod homo Britannus
Britannorum inimicis praedicaret
uerba salutis etc.[1] Vt Patritius
Cereticum tantae crudelitatis
admonuerit.[2]

De Maguilio quodam potenti
homine Hiberniae, ad fidem con-
uerso praedicatione et miraculis
Patritii.[3]

Maguilius autem, inuolucris
mundi expeditus,[4] ad mare contendit. Ibi, ut iussum erat, naui
conscensa, regente obedientia cui
parebat, felicibus auris in Meua-
niam insulam[5] euectus, duos
episcopos, assidentes littori, miraculo sui perculit.

Qui [*gl.* episcopi] mirati simul
et miserati hominem, marinis
iactatum periculis simul et com-
peditum, de profundo leuatum
asciscunt mensae, participant
hospitio; ubi et eorum charitate
confotus et dei gratia adiutus, ita
in bonum breui conualuit ut non
solum diuinitus expeditus [*gl.* a
compedibus] sed et episcopus
factus religiosam sui memoriam
usque hodie insulanis reliquerit.

Rex   Britonum   Munessam

---

[1] T 169, alluding to a protreptic letter (not the preserved one, most recently ed. A. B. E.
Hood, *St. Patrick* (Chichester, 1978), pp. 35–8) which Patrick sent to Corotic. The
preserved letter should be added to the list of works read by William, who doubtless
derived from it the information that Corotic slaughtered the *baptized* (c. 3). For copies at
Worcester and Salisbury containing both the *Confessio* and the Letter, see above, p. xxiv.
William could have known any of the surviving copies; even so, he seems to be spicing up
his sources.

[2] Another heading, referring to the preserved Letter.

[3] Yet another heading. For the story, see T 169–72.

particular he exhausted all his
savagery on those whom Patrick
had baptized, often grinding his
teeth in fury that a British man
should preach the word of salvation to the enemies of the British,
etc.[1] How Patrick warned Cereticus about such cruelty.[2]

About Maguilius, a potentate
of Ireland, who was converted to
the faith by the preaching and
miracles of Patrick.[3]

Now Maguilius, freed of the
toils of the world,[4] proceeded to
the sea. There, in accordance
with his orders, he boarded ship
as obedience demanded, and
came on favourable winds to
the Mevanian Isle,[5] where his
sudden appearance astonished
two bishops who were sitting on
the beach.

The bishops felt pity as well as
wonder at the sight of one who
had been tossed on the dangerous
sea and was also in chains; they
took him up from the deep, and
fed and lodged him. Refreshed
by their charity and assisted by
God's grace, he soon so recovered that he was not only freed
by God [from his shackles], but
was made a bishop and left a
pious memory that survives to
this day among the islanders.

A king of the Britons called

---

[4] Cf. *GP*, cc. 73 (p. 146) 'depositis . . . inuolucris mundi', 227 (p. 382) [from a poem
doubtless by William] 'inuolucris mundi . . . resolutus'.

[5] Manan T 171. William may mean either Man or Anglesey: see *GR*, c. 48. 3 n.

nomine, filiam unicam, cui
aetatis maturitas et spetiositas
formae suffragabatur, nuptum
dare uolebat, etc. Vt illa nullis
minis adduci potuerit ad nuptias,
quamuis adhuc pagana, utque
parentes Patricium de hac re
consuluerint, qui statim puellam
baptizauit. Quo facto, paulo post
obiit uirgo.[1]

De talibus quippe [signis et
miraculis] sexaginta sex libros
compegit antiquitas, sicut ea
exercebat per singulas regiones.[2]

JG 24 Ille opus iniunctum gnauiter executus, Hibernicos multis
miraculorum signis atque por-
tentis ad uiam ueritatis conuertit
atque in fide catholica solidauit.[3]
Cf. *AG* p. 54 Ille munus iniunctum gnauiter executus . . . (= *GR*
22. 2).

Finis 2[i]. libri

Nunc ad eius in patriam
gratiosum reditum et ad coelum
gloriosum transitum dirigam
mentem et stilum.[4]

Lelandus.

Comm. pp. 37–8 Nunc ad eius in
patriam gratiosum reditum, et ad
coelos gloriosum transitum, dirigam mentem simul et stylum.

---

[1] T 174–5. William dwells on the eligibility of the girl, as above on the sufferings and
reception of Maguil.   [2] T 182.

[3] After 'Ille . . . executus' based on the beginning of the 'Carta Patricii' (JG, c. 25; pp. 60,
62 = *AG*, c. 9; p. 54), and therefore not from William (Scott, p. 191 n. 35), though the 'Carta'
could have used material already in William's *Vita*. Further, see Leland, *Comm.*, p. 37 (placed
after the mention of the meeting with St Ciaran), 'Feruebat iam Patricius cura prouinciae sibi
delegatae: itaque Hiberniam recta profectus est, ubi, tonitru et fulmine uerbi euangelici,
multos ab idolorum cultura deterruit. Longum hic esset singula enarrare, quae ille ibidem
magna cum totius gentis gloria tum utilitate fecit. Quare ego in praesentia tantum unum, sed
quod reliqua omnia tanquam circulo complectatur, apponam; nempe illum tam diu, tamque
strenue in promouendo euangelii negotio laborasse, ut ab illo tempore Hiberni, gens antea
effera et pertinacissime pagana, Christianam religionem acceptam in hanc nostram usque
aetatem seruauerint.' This could be Leland's own gloss, or his report of similar sentiments of
William's (for the conversion, see also below, p. 340 n. 1; *GP*, c. 91 (p. 197)). He goes on:
'Ferunt Carantocum Britannum, filium Ceretici reguli, Hiberniam petiisse in Patricii

Munessan wished to give away in marriage his only daughter, who was grown up and pretty, etc. How no menaces could lead her to agree to wed, although she was still a pagan, and how her parents asked Patrick for advice on the problem; he at once baptized the girl, and she soon afterwards died.[1]

Antiquity saw the composition of 66 books on signs and miracles like this, as he brought them about in different regions.[2]

JG He executed his mission with vigour, and by many miracles and portents converted the Irish to the way of truth and confirmed them in the catholic faith.[3]

End of the second book.

Now I shall direct mind and pen to his welcome return to his homeland and his glorious passing to heaven.[4]

Leland.

Comm. similarly.

gratiam, et, accepto Cernachii nomine, causam una promouisse euangelicam. Vnde et postea in eius memoriam quaedam ciuitas Cirnachum dicta.' For St Carantoc/Cairnech, see Doble, 'Saint Carantoc', in *The Saints of Cornwall*, part 4, pp. 31–52; Orme, *The Saints of Cornwall*, pp. 83–5. Again (see p. 326 n. 3), Leland may well have been using the *NLA* (i. 177–9), which makes the saint son of Ceredig, tells how he 'perrexit tandem ad Hiberniam amore Sancti Patricii allectus', and goes on to mention his change of name ('et mutauit nomen eius in lingua eorum Cernath'), as well as his burial 'in ciuitate sua que a nomine suo uocata est Chernac'. But again, it does not follow that William did not have the information too. John of Tynemouth's source seems to have been the twelfth-century Life in BL, MS Cotton Vespasian A. xiv part I, *c.*1200 (ed. Wade-Evans, *Vitae Sanctorum Britanniae et Genealogiae*, pp. 142–9), but that does not mention the name-change. The saint's connections with Somerset (J. A. Robinson, 'St Carantoc in Somerset', *Downside Review*, xlvi (1928), 234–43; Doble, pp. 39–40) might have aroused William's interest.

[4] This is presumably the last sentence of the second book, despite the 'Finis' that Leland has placed just above.

Pollicetur hîc Gulielmus scrip-
turum se de reditu Patritii in
Britanniam. Sed hactenus in
nullo exemplari de reditu scriptum aliquid uidi, nescio an quod
ille opus forsan imperfectum reliquerit, an quod codices, in quos
incidi, mutili fuerint, quorum
duos Glessoburgi inueni, ubi
Patritium praedicant monachi
sepultum esse, reclamante hoc
disticho, ex Bedae (nisi fallor)
epigrammatibus desumpto:

Calpurnus genuit istum, alma
     Britannia misit,
Gallia nutriuit, tenet artus
     Scottia felix.[1]

Leland could find no third book of the Life (see also *Comm.* pp. 36,
38), but William no doubt wrote one (perhaps later than the first two,
just as *VD* i and ii were separated by some years). In *Comm.*, pp. 38–
40, Leland uses the (interpolated) *AG* to fill up the gap; but it is safer
to use *GR* 22. 2–3 as a framework.

Ille igitur munus iniunctum gnauiter exsecutus, et extremis diebus[2] in patriam reuertens, super altare suum Cornubiam appulit, quod hodieque apud incolas magnae uenerationi est propter sanctitudinem et utilita-tem propter infirmorum salutem. Ita Glastoniam ueniens ibique monachus et abbas factus,	*AG* p. 54 Ille munus iniunctum gnauiter executus, extremis diebus Britanniam remeans, priorem celsitudinem salutacion-esque in foro respuens, super altare suum Cornubiam appulit; quod usque hodie apud incolas magne ueneracioni est, tum prop-ter sanctitudinem et utilitatem, tum propter infirmorum salutem.

---

[1] For this epigram, in fact by an Irishman, see M. Lapidge, 'Some remnants of Bede's
lost *Liber Epigrammatum*', in his *Anglo-Latin Literature*, *600–899* (London and Rio
Grande, OH 1996), pp. 363–4, with bibliography of later work on p. 510. The whole
epigram is twice cited by Leland, *Coll.* iii. 114 and *Comm.*, p. 39), each time with *ossaque*
for *artus*, as in the manuscript that Leland was using, a fragment of which survives at

William here promises to write
of the return of Patrick to Britain. But so far I have seen nothing about his return in any copy,
either because he perhaps left
the work incomplete, or because
the manuscripts which I have
happened upon were mutilated.
I found two at Glastonbury,
where the monks say Patrick
is buried, though this distich,
taken, unless I am mistaken,
from the Epigrams of Bede,
tells a different story:

Calpurnius begot him, Britain
  sent him,
Gaul fed him, blessed *Scottia*
  holds his limbs.[1]

After executing his mission with
vigour, at the end of his life[2] he
came back home, and landed in
Cornwall, voyaging on his altar,
which is still held in great
veneration by the Cornish for
its holiness, and its value in
the treatment of the sick. So he
came to Glastonbury, and having
become a monk and abbot there,

AG After executing his mission
with vigour, he returned to Britain at the end of his life, rejecting
his previous lofty position and
public recognition. He landed in
Cornwall after voyaging on his
altar, which is to this day held in
great veneration by the Cornish
for its holiness and its usefulness,
and because of the health it
brings to the sick. So he came

Urbana, Illinois. This contained a collection of epigrams put together by Milred bp. of
Worcester 745–75 (Thomson, *William of Malmesbury*, pp. 126–30).
    [2] Aet. 72 (though he was to live much longer!). So *GP*, c. 91 (p. 197), with the comment
'uicino senio ammonitus'.

Inde Glastoniam ueniens, XII fratres anachoritice uiuentes ibidem repperiens, congregauit abbatisque suscipiens officium eosdem agere uitam docuit cenobialem . . . Cf. JG 24 (= Scott, p. 190).[1]

AG p. 58 Hic itaque . . . postquam predictos fratres regularibus disciplinis conuenienter informauerat et eundem locum terris et possessionibus de dono regum ac aliorum principum competenter ditauerat, post ali-

post aliquot annos naturae cessit.   quot annos decursos nature cessit . . . Cf. JG 26.

Cuius assertionis omnem absoluit scrupulum uisio cuiusdam fratris, qui post obitum beati uiri, iam nutante memoria utrum ibi monachus et abbas fuerit, cum de hoc frequens uerteretur questio, tali confirmatus est oraculo. (3) Resolutus enim in soporem, uisus est audire quendam legentem post multa eius miracula haec uerba: 'Hic igitur metropolitani pallii sanctitate decoratus est; postmodum uero hic monachus et abbas factus.' Adiecit etiam ut non integre credenti litteris aureis quod dixerat scriptum ostenderet.[2]

AG p. 60 (corrected from JG 27) Cum autem longe post obitum beati Patricii frequens questio ⟨uerteretur⟩ utrum ibi monachus et abbas fuerit, omnem scrupulum absoluit uisio cuiusdam fratris, qui post obitum beati uiri, nutante memoria utrum ibi monachus et abbas fuerit, cum de hoc frequens uerteretur questio, tali confirmatus est oraculo. Resolutus enim in soporem, uisus ⟨est⟩ audire quendam legentem post multa eius miracula, hec uerba: 'Hic igitur metropolitani pallii decoratus est sanctitate; postmodum uero hic monachus et abbas

---

[1] JG gives the same story as *AG* in similar words, but adds (*a*) that he landed at 'Hailemout' (a name known to William: see *GP*, c. 95 (p. 204) 'Hegelmuthe'), the Camel estuary in Cornwall (*GR* II, p. 76); see below, p. 368; and (*b*) that the date of his arrival in Glastonbury was 433/4 (*AG*, p. 190, an interpolation made s. xiv, gives 449). Both then back up their assertion that Patrick founded Glastonbury on the basis of twelve hermits whom he found there (cf. *AG*, c. 33 (p. 86), partly interpolated) by appeal to the 'Carta Patricii'. One wonders where Patrick's altar was venerated by the Cornish in William's time. But the whole story about the altar may rest on a confusion with the Cornish saint

to Glastonbury, and finding
twelve brothers there living as
hermits, he brought them together and taking on the position
of abbot taught them to live a
communal life.[1]

AG After fittingly training the
brothers in the discipline of a
rule and suitably enriching the
place with lands and property
given by kings and other great
after some years yielded to   men, he after some years had
nature.   passed yielded to nature.

Any hesitation about this state-   *AG* But when, a long time after
ment is dispelled by the vision of   St Patrick's death, there was
one of the monks, who after the   much dispute whether he had
saint's death, when the tradition   been a monk and abbot there,
was already uncertain whether he   all doubts were removed by the
had been monk and abbot there,   vision of a brother, who after the
and the question was much dis-   saint's death, when the tradition
cussed, had his faith established   was already uncertain whether he
by the following oracle. In his   had been monk and abbot there,
sleep, he seemed to hear someone   and the question was much dis-
reading, at the end of an account   cussed, had his faith established
of St Patrick's many miracles,   by the following oracle: . . . let-
the following words: 'So he was   ters of gold.
honoured with the sacred pal-
lium of an archbishop; but afterwards became a monk and abbot
here.' The reader added that, if
he did not fully believe, he would
show what he had said, written in
letters of gold.[2]

Petroc: H. P. R. Finberg, *West-Country Historical Studies* (Newton Abbot, 1969), p. 79;
Orme, *The Saints of Cornwall*, pp. 211, 214. For the evidence connecting Patrick with
Glastonbury, see L. Abrams, 'St Patrick and Glastonbury abbey: *nihil ex nihilo fit?*', in
Dumville, *Saint Patrick*, pp. 233–42.   [2] Cf. also JG prol. (p. 8).

factus est.' Adiecit eciam ut non integre credenti litteris aureis quod dixerat scriptum ostenderet.

Excessit ergo Patritius anno aetatis centesimo undecimo, incarnationis Domini quadringentesimo septuagesimo secundo, qui fuit annus ex quo Hiberniam missus est quadragesimus septimus.[1]

AG p. 60 (close to JG 26) Excessit ergo Patricius anno etatis sue CXI, incarnacionis uero Domini CCCCLXXII, qui fuit annus ex quo in Yberniam missus est XLVII. Si quidem anno Domini CCCLXI in lucem uenit et anno Domini CCCCXXV a Celestino papa in Hyberniam missus fuit (hic fuit annus etatis sue LXIIII), et anno Domini CCCCXXXIII Ybernicos ad fidem Christi conuertit. Demum Britanniam reuersus in optima conuersacione XXXIX annos in insula Auallonie permansit.

Requiescit in dextro latere altaris Vetustae Aecclesiae in piramide saxea, quam argento uestiuit posterorum diligentia.

AG p. 60, contd. [close to JG 26] Requieuit autem in uetusta ecclesia a dextro latere altaris per multorum annorum curricula, uidelicet DCC et decem annos, usque ad combustionem eiusdem ecclesie.[2] Corpus uero suum in piramide saxea[3] fuit collocatum iuxta altare uersus austrum quam, pro ueneracione eiusdem sancti, auro et argento postea nobiliter uestiuit domesticorum diligencia. *AG* p. 58 = JG 26

---

[1] The witnesses agree on a consistent framework. In *GP*, c. 91 (p. 197), William speaks of Patrick evangelizing 'multis annis' in Ireland; his chronological precisions may have come later, in his Glastonbury period. The assumption is made that Patrick's conversion of Ireland was instantly followed by his departure to England. The date of Patrick's death is also given as 472 at *VD* i pr. 5. It will be convenient to assemble the whole picture here:
361 Birth of Patrick
425 Mission to Ireland: aet. 64

So Patrick died in the one hundred and eleventh year of his age and the year of our Lord 472, which was the forty-seventh after his sending into Ireland.[1]

AG So Patrick died in the one hundred and eleventh year of his age, in the year of our Lord 472, which was the forty-seventh after his sending into Ireland. For he came into this world in AD 361, was sent to Ireland by Pope Celestine in 425, when he was 64, and in 433 converted the Irish to Christianity. Finally he returned to Britain, and lived an excellent life on the island of Avalon for 39 years.

He rests on the right side of the altar of the old Church, in a stone pyramid, which the devotion of later times overlaid with silver.

AG He rested in the Old Church on the right side of the altar for many years, 710 in fact, right up to the time when the church was burned down.[2] His body lay in a stone pyramid[3] near the altar towards the south, which, out of respect for the saint, the devoted monks of the house later overlaid splendidly with gold and silver.

---

433 Conversion of Irish and arrival in England
472 Death of Patrick, 39 years after arrival in England, 47 years after mission to Ireland: aet. III

[2] This part of the story is of course interpolated. The fire is here dated to 1182, though it should be 1184 (Carley, p. 282 n. 93).

[3] For the pyramid, and the position of Patrick to the right of the altar, see below, p. 380 n. 1.

(cf. 5 [p. 20]) sepulturam, angelo demonstrante flammaque ingenti de eodem loco cunctis uidentibus qui aderant erumpente, in uetusta ecclesia a dextra [dextris JG] altaris promeruit.

Hinc Hiberniensibus mos inolitus ad exosculandas patroni reliquias locum frequentare.

= *AG* p. 60

AG He was found fit to be buried in the Old Church to the right of the altar when an angel pointed out the place and a great flame burst from it that was seen by all those present.

Hence it is an established custom amongst the Irish to visit Glastonbury to kiss the relics of their patron saint.

VITA BENIGNI

JG 29. Venerabilis[1] pontifex
Sanctus Patricius, de quo superius est sermo, dum predicando
circuiret regiones Hibernicas,
peruenit in campum qui dicitur
Brei, spacio famosum et specie,
cuius pulcritudo animum pontificis illexerat ut ibi percelebraret
Pascha quod tunc instabat. Prima
illi in ea prouincia hospitalitatis
necessitudo cum quodam uiro
fuit qui continuo diuine predica-
cioni credulam aurem apponens[2]
baptismi sacramento alteratus est
in nouum hominem. Cuius filius,
Beonna nomine, etatis admodum delicate, alludens episcopo
blando amplexu pedem eius suo
astringebat pectori nonnunquam
osculabundus.[3] Euntem quoque
ad corporis pausam lacrimis prosecutus non nisi cum eo se uelle
dormire clamitabat. Quapropter
Patricius, perspicaci prophecie
intendens oculo[4] quanta uirtutum indoles[5] per Dei graciam
puero esset accessura, eum
dignatus est lecto et insigniuit
Benigni uocabulo.[6] Postero die
cum profeccionem adoriretur
antistes, mestis uagitibus puer

---

[1] The source for the Irish part of this story is the *Vita Tertia* of Patrick (T, version II),
c. 36, pp. 141–2 Bieler; but William's hand is very apparent. Leland, *Coll.* iii. 275 (see
above, p. 330), cites from William's Life of Patrick words close to part of the account here.
For the confusion of the Irish Benen/Benignus and the Anglo-Saxon Beonna, see e.g.

LIFE OF BENIGNUS

JG 29. This same revered bishop St Patrick[1] came, as he journeyed round Ireland preaching, to a plain called Bray, well known for its size and beauty. He was so charmed by it that he celebrated the coming Easter there. His first host in that district was a man who had immediately believed[2] the word of God, and had been baptized. His son Beonna, still very young, while playing near the bishop, grasped his foot affectionately and pulled it to his breast to kiss it[3] now and then. When Patrick went away to rest, the boy escorted him in tears, shouting that he would sleep only with him. Patrick saw with the keen eye of a prophet[4] what virtues[5] God in His grace would grant to the boy; he let him sleep in his bed, and marked him out with the name Benignus.[6] Next day, when he was setting forth, the child began to wail pitifully, asking him not to leave him, for he did not wish to live without him. He therefore

Finberg, *West-Country Historical Studies*, pp. 82–3. The cult at Glastonbury probably did not originate earlier than the eleventh century: Carley in JG, pp. xxxviii–xxxix.

[2]   This is a JG phrase (cf. c. 62 (p. 118) 'nimis credulam applicans aurem').

[3]   The word is used by William at *VW* i. 12. 2.

[4]   Cf. *GR*, c. 155 'porrecto prophetiae oculo'.

[5]   Cf. *VW* i. 1. 2 'futurarum uirtutum indolem crebris parturiebat inditiis'.

[6]   Cf. *GR*, c. 354. 3 'eam . . . uocabulo quoque insignies tuo'.

concrepare cepit; ne se desereret poposcit; sine illo se uiuere nolle dixit. Iussit ergo baptisatum in currum suum leuari, pronuncians eum futurum heredem regiminis et pontificii sui. Quod et factum est. Nam tercio loco[1] ei successit quemadmodum eorum gesta testantur. Hic igitur Sanctus Benignus post septem annos in regimine pontificali peractos, angelo monente, patriam pontificiique dignitatem ex uoto deserens, uoluntaria peregrinacione suscepta, anno Domini quadringentesimo sexagesimo secundo Glastoniam, Deo duce, peruenit ubi et Sanctum Patricium diuinis inuigilantem repperit[2] et ei peregrinacionis sue causas summopere aperuit. Quo exortante ut ceptis feliciter insisteret, 'proficiscere,' inquit, 'mi desideratissime, baculo contentus, cumque ad locum tibi a Domino predestinatum perueneris quocumque solo fixo baculo eum uirescere, frondes [*leg.* frondescere] et florescere uideris, ibi tibi habitaculum preparandum noueris.' Et sic collocucionibus alterius utrisque in Domino corroboratis, Sanctus Benignus, comitante secum quodam puero nomine Pincio, profectus per nemorosa et palustria loca. At ubi uenit ad

NLA Sanctus enim Benignus, in regimine pontificali transactis feliciter in Hibernia annis multis, quadam nocte soporatus, per angelum admonetur patriam suam relinquere et uoluntaria peregrinatione suscepta deserti secreta petere.

Mari igitur prospere transito Glastoniam ueniens sanctum Patricium inuenit;

qui ei dixit: 'Proficiscere, mi frater, baculo tuo contentus, et cum ad locum a Domino tibi predestinatum ipso ducente perueneris, quocumque solo fixo baculo tuo ipsum uirescere, florescere et frondescere uideris, ibi tibi habitandum et habitaculum preparatum noueris.'

Qui comitante quodam puero nomine Pincio profectus; per nemorosa et paludosa loca gradientes, ad quandam insulam

---

[1] *AG*, c. 13 (p. 62) 'successor in episcopatu eius tertius in Ybernia fuit, quemadmodum eorum gesta testantur'. The last clause apparently alludes to William's Lives of Patrick and Benignus; see above, p. 310. The source of 'successor . . . tertius' was doubtless an episcopal list. The list printed by H. J. Lawlor and R. I. Best, 'The ancient list of the

gave the order for him to be baptized and lifted into his wagon, saying solemnly that he would be heir to his rule and his bishopric. This came about. For as their *History* tells us, he was his third successor.[1] Now this Benignus, after seven years as bishop, was prompted by an angel to make a vow, abandon homeland and office, and go into voluntary exile. In AD 462, with God's guidance, he came to Glastonbury, where he found St Patrick[2] much concerned with religious observances.

NLA For St Benignus, after passing many successful years as bishop in Ireland, while asleep one night was prompted by an angel to leave his homeland, go into voluntary exile, and look for solitude in a deserted place.

Accordingly, after a favourable crossing, he came to Glastonbury, where he found St Patrick.

He gave him a full explanation of the reasons for his journey. Patrick urged him to continue in his excellent plans, saying: 'Go, my beloved, taking only your staff. When you come to the place the Lord means for you, wherever you plant the staff in the ground and see it bring forth green leaves and flowers, you will know that that is where you must make your dwelling place.'
Their conversation gave each other strength in the Lord, and St Benignus, accompanied by a boy called Pincius, set off through woods and swamps.

NLA Patrick said to him: 'Go, brother, taking only your staff, and when you come under His guidance to the place the Lord means for you, wherever you plant the staff in the ground and see it bring forth green leaves and flowers, you will know that that is where you must dwell and where a dwelling place is made ready for you.'

NLA Benignus set out, accompanied by a boy called Pincius; they proceeded through woods

coarbs of Patrick', *Proceedings of the Royal Irish Academy*, 3rd ser., xxxv. C (1919), 316–62, at p. 318, gives the order Patraic, Sechnall, Sen-Patraic, Benen.
    [2] *AG*, c. 13 (p. 62), 'hic igitur, angelo monente, patriam pontificiique dignitatem ex uoto deserens, uoluntaria peregrinacione suscepta, Glastoniam, Deo duce, peruenit, ubi et sanctum Patricium inuenit', with the date AD 460, not 462.

quandam insulam[1] ubi locum solitarium habitacioni congruum uidit mox, solo fixo baculo, mirum dictu! baculus uirescere, frondescere et florescere cepit. Ibi · Sanctus Benignus habitaculum preparauit, ibi Deo famulandum, ibi finetenus conuersandum censuit. Nam usque ad nostra tempora sanctitatis eius signifera ipsa arbor, sparsis late frondibus, iuxta beati uiri oratorium stare uidetur. Ibi austerius solito uigiliis, ieiuniis, oracionibus diuersisque spiritualium sollicitudinum laboribus carnem domabat. Et quamquam locus ille solitarius a populari frequencia remotus Dei famulatui esset opportunus, aque tamen longinqua remocione erat importunus.[2] Quapropter beati uiri puer Pincius cotidie ad aquam deferendam per tria fere miliaria egrediens, tum lassitudine fatigatus tum malignorum spirituum infestacionibus pregrauatus, a beato Benigno sepius est uerbis consolatoriis confortatus.

nomine Ferramere peruenerunt, et fixo ibi baculo uirescere frondes et flores producere cepit.

Illis enim temporibus fluuius quem nunc ibidem defluere cernimus non tunc defluebat, sed diebus singulis penuriam aque nimiam uir Dei cum puero paciebatur. Et cum die quadam puer aquam ei humeris de longe baiulans in itinere dormiret, hostis malignus uasculum auferens abcessit. Euigilans puer et merens protinus cum lachrymis in hanc uocem prorupit, dicens: 'Heus,' inquit, 'tibi loquor quicumque meum furatus es uasculum: en te per Deum celi adiuro quem meus magister beatus Benignus adorat, in quem credit ac fideliter seruit, ut illud michi festinanter restituas.' Nec mora, uas eius ulterius secum demon

---

[1] Identified by JG, c. 2 (p. 12), as *Ferramere* (Meare, about four miles NW of Glastonbury). *AG*, c. 13 (p. 62), renders the name as *Fernigemere*, mentioning 'ex eius baculo arido ingens arbor uirens et frondifera'. The sequence in the West Pennard

When he came to an island[1] and saw an isolated place fit to live in, he planted his staff, and lo and behold! it straightway began to sprout green leaves and flowers. St Benignus made his dwelling here, thinking that this was where he should serve God and live out his life. Indeed up to our own times the very tree that signifies his sanctity can be seen standing by the saint's chapel, its leaves spreading wide. Here he tamed his flesh with unusual rigour, practising vigils, fasts, prayers, and various spiritual exercises. Though this hermitage was far from the crowds and well suited for the service of God, it caused problems[2] by being so far from water. The saint's servant Pincius had to go out every day for about three miles to fetch water. He found this tiring, and troublesome too because of the evil spirits that plagued him; and Benignus often had to console and comfort him.

and swamps, and came to an island called *Ferramere*. Here he planted his staff, and it began to sprout green leaves and flowers.

NLA In those days the river we see flowing there now did not exist, and every day the man of God and the boy suffered sorely from lack of water. One day the boy was carrying water for Benignus on his shoulders from a long way off, when he went to sleep on the way; and the Devil carried away his water pot. The boy awoke and in his distress burst out with these words: 'Ho there, I am talking to whoever you are who stole my pot. I adjure you by the God in heaven whom my master the blessed Benignus worships, in whom he believes and whom he faithfully serves, to restore it to me at once.' With no delay, the

fragment (which has the form *Ferlingemere*), perhaps coincidentally, speaks of the 'arbor frondifera'.

[2] The contrast may go back to 2 Tim. 4: 2, used in *VW* ii. 16. 1.

Eius namque laboribus compassus, solo prostratus, ad Dominum ex corde conuersus, ut pietate sua fontis uenam aperiret et aquam sufficientem largiretur deuocius exorauit.

retinere nequiuit, sed dicto citius restituit, et cachinnando aufugit. Quod audiens sanctus Benignus, prostrato in terram toto corpore, cum preces ad Deum deuotas fudisset, angelus Domini, pennis fulgentibus alas habens flammeoque aspectu irradians,[1] apparuit ei dicens: 'Constans esto, serue Dei, exaudite sunt orationes tue; mitte puerum tuum Pincium ad orientalem celle tue plagam, ubi terram baculo tuo percutiens fontem perhennem abunde manare uidebit.'

At beatus uir celesti certificatus uisione et angelica roboratus uisitacione, tradito baculo puero suo Pincio, iussit ut ad quoddam iuncetum iret et aquam diu desideratam baculi ictu de terra producendam non dubitaret. Paruit puer, locum adiit, baculo patris terram terebrando ter in summe Trinitatis nomine percussit. Et mox fons affluens[2] erupit ex quo usque in hodiernum diem late manans flumen uidetur, quod et ad piscandum habile et ad diuersa salubre et utile habetur.

Perrexit ergo puer ad locum a uiro Dei designatum, et cum terram baculo percussisset, fons ingens statim erupit, a quo usque nunc magnum et latum fluuium creuisse uidemus.

30. Factum est autem ut, defuncto Sancto Patricio, ei in fratrum regimen succederet Sanctus Benignus[3] qui nonnunquam

Vir Dei Benignus solus in obscuro noctis silentio ad ecclesiam sancte Marie in Glastonia orandi gratia ire solebat. Cumque

---

[1] Perhaps cf. *VD* i. 13. 2 'columbam scintillanti alarum plausu flammeam'.

[2] *AG*, c. 13 (p. 62) 'data eius precibus aqua largissima'. The river was presumably the Brue, which flows through Meare. The staff appears in the s. xiv 'Titus relic list' from Glastonbury (Carley, pp. xxxviii–xxxix, xlvi).

Sympathizing with his difficulties, he prostrated himself and turned to the Lord in his heart, begging Him humbly in His pity to open up a spring and provide sufficiency of water.

Devil found he could not keep hold of the pot any longer, but quicker than I can tell it he gave it back, and retreated cackling. St Benignus, learning of this, prostrated himself full length on the ground, and poured out humble prayers to God. An angel of the Lord, winged with gleaming feathers and glowing like fire,[1] appeared to him, saying: 'Be of good resolve, servant of God, your prayers have been heard. Send your boy Pincius to the east side of your cell. There, after striking the ground with your staff, he will see a permanent spring well up with abundance of water.'

A vision from heaven and the visit of an angel gave the saint confidence and strength, and handing his staff to the boy he told him to go to a particular reed bed and be sure that a stroke of the staff would bring the longed-for water from the ground. Pincius obeyed, went to the spot, dug the father's staff into the ground, and struck it three times in the name of the Trinity most high. At once a fountain burst forth,[2] the source even today of a wide river, good for fishing and safe to use for various purposes.

So the boy went to the place the man of God had pointed out to him, and struck the ground with the staff; a great spring burst forth at once, the source of the big wide river we see even today.

30. It came about that on the death of St Patrick he was succeeded in his rule of the brethren by St Benignus,[3] who sometimes

NLA Benignus, man of God, used to go alone in the quiet of night to pray in the church of St Mary at Glastonbury. One night

---

[3] *GR*, c. 24 'successit Patritio in abbatis regimine Benignus, sed quot annis incertum'; *AG*, c. 33 (p. 86). Patrick and Benignus are listed as the first two abbots of Glastonbury in *AG*, c. 71 (p. 146).

diebus ac noctibus Glastoniam uenit tam orandi gracia quam fratres alloquendi causa. Vnde quadam nocte ut habuit in consuetudine Glastoniam oratum tendens communem obuiat aduersarium. Interrogatus a uiro quid uellet aud quid machinaretur mali, respondit quia 'te michi prorsus contrarium peruertere, te a recto diuertere festino.' 'Nequaquam,' ait uir Dei, 'quin Dominus in me et ego in Domino preualebo.' Admotaque leua baculo quem forte gerebat non segniter cesum in profundissimum puteum eidem loco contiguum impulit sicque monstrum preceps euanuit. Ex illo loco lutum fetidissimum frequenter ebulliri ac nullum fundum constat inueniri.

Glastoniam inde perueniens pro tanto triumpho gracias omnipotenti reddidit Deo, consummatisque oracionibus note solitudinis habitaculum repeciit. Nec multo post supramemorato flumine calmecum[3] illud per quod Glastoniam eundo et redeundo iter habere consueuerat meatu suo

nocte quadam per pontem quem fecerat transiret, uidit quendam demonem turpissimum, aspectu terribilem, obuiam sibi uenientem. Ad quem sanctus propius accedens, hiis uerbis eum alloquitur, dicens: 'Quid' inquit 'hic stas, cruenta bestia? cui insidiaris? cui hic expectando dampnum gestis inferre?' Cui demon ait: 'Te hic expecto, edentule[1] senex, te decipere cupio.' Ad quem sanctus 'Dominus' inquit 'michi est adiutor: non timebo quid faciat michi uel dicat malignus.'[2] Et hec dicens leua eum apprehendit manu, et baculo quem dextera gestabat diutissime uerberauit, et in quendam profundissimum puteum precipitauit; qui ultra non comparuit. Ex illo enim tempore usque in hodiernum diem nullus ad puteum illum ausus est accedere, quoniam fertur ibi fundum penitus non inueniri. Et ad Glastoniam pergens sanctus, facta ibi oratione solita, ad cellam rediit.

---

[1] Cf. Fulgentius Myth., *Serm. ant.* 23 (p. 118 Helm): 'Flaccus Tibullus[!] in Melene comedia ait: "Tunc amare audes, edentule et capularis senex?"; edentulum enim quasi iam sine dentibus dici uoluit.' Similarly the Harley gloss cited by *ODML* s.v. 'edentulus': 'i. senex sine dentibus'. William seems to have known Fulgentius' commoner *Mythologiae* (Thomson, *William of Malmesbury*, p. 61, where '*Met.*' should be '*Mit.*'). The adjective is mainly found in Plautus (whom William did not know).

came, by day or night, to Glastonbury to pray or to talk to the
monks. One night, when he came
as was his wont to Glastonbury
to pray, he met the Enemy of us
all. Asked what he wanted and
what mischief he was up to, the
Devil replied: 'I am in a hurry to
overthrow you and divert you
from the right path, for you are
my sworn enemy.' 'No, you will
not,' said the man of God. 'The
Lord will prevail in me, and I in
Him.' He put his left hand on the
staff he happened to have with
him, gave the Devil a hearty
blow, and projected him into a
deep well that was to hand; and
so the monster fell from sight. It
is a fact that from that spot the
most foul mud often bubbles,
and no bottom is to be found.

Benignus went on to Glastonbury and gave thanks to almighty
God for this great feat; then after
saying all his prayers he went
back to his familiar hermitage.

he was crossing over the bridge
he had made when he saw a foul
fiend of appalling aspect coming
to meet him. The saint came
nearer and addressed him: 'Why
are you standing here, you
bloody beast? Who are you
trying to ambush? Who are you
waiting here to harm?' The Devil
said: 'It is you I am waiting for,
you toothless[1] old man, you I
want to deceive.' The saint
replied: 'God is my helper, and
I shall not fear anything the evil
one does or says to me.'[2] So
saying he gripped him in his
left hand, gave him a prolonged
thrashing with the staff in his
right hand, and flung him into a
deep well, from which he did not
reappear. From that time on no
one has to this day dared to go
near that well, for there is said to
be no bottom to it. The saint
went on his way to Glastonbury,
offered his usual prayers, and
returned to his cell.

Soon after this, the river flooded
over the reed-bed[3] he used to
cross on his journeys to and
from Glastonbury, and he there-

---

[2] Cf. Ps. 117(118): 6, Hebr. 13: 6.
[3] See *ODML* s.v. 'calametum'. (One wonders if the mysterious 'carrecti' in the Digby
Life of Indract 6. 20 might be a corruption of the same word.) *NLA* mentions a bridge
(there the scene of the meeting with the Devil).

cooperiente, uir beatus, cellule tantum sue inhabitacione contentus,[1] de reliquo nec Glastoniam reuisere nec extra ipsius cellule terminos uspiam uoluit exire. Et post inmensos agones in dicta insula beato fine quieuit.[2]

Ieiuniis et orationibus assiduis uacans, supremam uite sue horam cotidie suspectam habuit. Cum igitur finem suum diuinitus imminere cognouisset, uocatis discipulis suis, horam qua ab hoc seculo migraturus erat innotuit. Eleuatis tandem in celum oculis, inter manus illorum felicem animam ad supernorum ciuium[3] beatitudinem tertio nonas Nouembris emisit.

Terrestresque exuuie[4] in ecclesia eiusdem loci ad austrum secus altare sunt sepulte cum tali epitaphio:[5]

Hoc patris in lapide Beonne
  sunt ossa locata,
Qui pater extiterat mona-
  chorum hic tempore prisco.
Hunc fore Patricii quondam
  fortasse ministrum
Fantur Hybernigene et Beon-
  nam de nomine dicunt.

Set nec defuere miracula[6] quibus Deus ostenderet sancti merita. Ibi enim requieuit usque ad tem-

Anno autem Domini millesimo nonagesimo primo eleuatum est

---

[1] GP, c. 91 (p. 198) 'Benignus confessor, qui non longe hinc anachorita fuerit'. 'Hinc', meaning 'from Glastonbury', is an addition to the autograph, and may date from William's period at the monastery. Cf. JG, c. 2 (p. 12), referring to the island of 'Ferramere, ubi Sanctus Benignus heremiticam quondam duxit uitam'. AG, c. 13 (p. 62), too, mentions his 'immensos agones' there. Cf. also Leland, Comm., p. 39: 'Benignum, Hibernorum episcopum, qui Aualloniam uenit, ut Patricium, a quo baptizatus et educatus fuerat, inuiseret; forsan et uitam ibidem solitariam duceret.'

[2] For the date, see above, pp. 309–10. [3] Cf. VD ii. 27. 1.

after contented himself with life in his tiny cell,[1] never wanting to go back to Glastonbury or anywhere beyond the bounds of his home. After immeasurable sufferings, he died a happy death on the island.[2]

NLA Constant in fasting and prayer, he every day expected his last hour. When he learned from God that his end was at hand, he called his pupils to him and told them the time at which he was to leave this world. He raised his eyes to heaven, and supported in their arms released his fortunate soul to join the blessed company of the citizens on high,[3] on 3 November.

His earthly remains[4] are buried in the church there, to the south by the altar, with the epitaph:[5]

Within this tomb his bones
    Beonna lays,
Was father here of monks in
    ancient days.
Patrick of old to serve he had
    the honour
(So Erin's sons aver, and name
    Beonna).

There was no shortage of miracles[6] sent by God to make the saint's merits obvious. In fact he   *NLA* His body was raised from

---

[4] Cf. e.g. *GR*, c. 20. 2 'corporales . . . exuuiae'.

[5] Also at *GR*, c. 24, with no variant: said to be at Meare (*Ferramere*). The lines are also given by *AG*, c. 33 (p. 86) (with *dudum* for *quondam*) and the West Pennard fragment (said to omit 'hic'). Leland, *Comm.*, p. 39, seems to have seen the tomb: 'nam eius tumulus adhuc ostenditur propter lacum Feranium, qui tribus aut quatuor passuum milibus distat a Glessoburgo.'

[6] Cf. *GR*, c. 24 (during life and after translation); *GP*, c. 91 (p. 198) (caused the translation).

pora regis Willelmi Rufi et tunc
Glastoniam translatus est.[1] . . .

86. Ad gloriam quoque temporis Turstini pertinet beatissimi Benigni translacio.[2] Huius
namque diebus translatus est a
loco Ferramere dicto ubi obierat,
ut supratactum est, et sepultus
fuerat usque Glastoniam. Nullus
itaque Glastoniencium abbatum
antea apposuerat mentem ut
ecclesiam principalem illo in-
signirent corpore. Hiis tandem
diebus predicti loci fratres
omnes in unam conuenientes sen-
tenciam Turstino abbati iustas de
hoc intulerunt querelas ne
lucerna[3] lateret sub modio que
totam illustrabat Angliam miraculorum corusco. Flexus hiis
abbas cessit bone uoluntati iusta
poscencium et die indicta religio-
sum propositum mancipauerunt
effectui.[4] Ossa enim effossa lota
et reuerenter sindone inuoluta ac
in locello ad hoc parato inclusa,
odorem spirabant suauiter fra-
grantem et balsamiticum.[5] Scrinio abbas sigillum impressit
ne quis clamdestina surrepcione
reliquias temeraret. Et consilio
habito nullatenus tunc decreuit
sacras transferri reliquias donec

corpus eius sanctum de terra,
et ad Glastoniensem ecclesiam
delatum.

---

[1] *GR*, c. 24 'nouae in maiorem aecclesiam translationis'. JG (below, p. 364) and *NLA*
date the move to 1091. For *AG*, c. 13 (p. 62), see above, pp. 309–10. For the *scrinium* 'in
quo nunc beati Benigni corpus requiescit', given by King Harthacnut, see *AG*, c. 66
(p. 134) = JG, c. 80 (p. 152).

[2] *AG*, c. 77 (p. 156), 'ad gloriam sane temporum Turstini pertinet beatissimi Benigni
translacio'.

rested here until the time of King William Rufus, when he was translated to Glastonbury. . . .[1]

86. To the glory of Thurstan's time also belongs the translation of the blessed Benignus.[2] For it was in his days that he was moved to Glastonbury from the place called *Ferramere* where he died (as was mentioned above) and was buried. None of the previous abbots of Glastonbury had applied their minds to distinguishing their main church with this body. It was only now that all the brethren of the place arrived at a unanimous view and quite reasonably complained to Abbot Thurstan about the way in which a light[3] was being hidden under a bushel that was illuminating all England with its brilliant miracles. The abbot was swayed by this and yielded to the good intentions of those who made this proper request; and on the appointed day they put the devout plan into effect.[4] The bones were dug up, washed, reverently wrapped in linen, and placed in a specially made shrine, exhaling a pleasant scent as of balsam.[5] The abbot sealed up the shrine to make sure no one sacrilegiously purloined the relics. After discussion he decreed that the holy remains

the ground in AD 1091, and taken to the church of Glastonbury.

---

[3] Cf. *GR*, c. 440. 2, where the familiar quotation is similarly used.
[4] An expression of William's: e.g. *GP*, c. 19 (p. 29).
[5] Cf. *GR*, c. 216 = *GP*, c. 171 (p. 306) 'balsamiti odoris'.

episcopus diocesanus edictum
proponeret, quo tanto patrono
transferendo populus undique
accurreret. Propositum namque
habuerant ut sequenti transferre-
tur dominica, set per uisionem
sanctus cuidam monacho factam
ad octo abinde ebdomadas fecit
deferri. Monachi interim septem
illuc missi circa sanctum corpus
sollicitas obseruabant excubias, in
Dei laudibus die ac nocte iugiter
meditantes. Elapsis deinde octo
septimanis illuxit dies quem pre-
signauerat sanctus. Ossa iterum
de locello eruta et lota in scrinio
aurato ad id misso sunt locata.
Aqua eciam dictarum reliquiarum
ablucione sanctificata diligenter
custodita, multis postea informi-
tatum [*sic*] generibus fuit medi-
cina. Nocte uero dominicam
translacionis diem precedente,
duo uiri per flumen contiguum
remigantes columpnam lucis in
celum usque porrectam[1] super
oratorium sancti uiderunt ac
eciam multis aliis ostenderunt.
Nec minus mane cum sancte reli-
quie nauigio uersus Glastoniam
deferentur [*sic*] duo in eadem
nauicula existentes, monachus
unus et alter laicus, eminus conspicati sunt ex aere quasi arcua-
tum tectum diuersorum colorum

---

[1] Cf. below, p. 376 n. 2.

should not be translated until the
diocesan bishop could put out a
proclamation to ensure a throng
of people from all quarters to
attend the transfer of such an
important benefactor. The original plan had been that he should
be removed on the following
Sunday, but the saint appeared
in a vision to one of the monks
and had it put off till eight weeks
hence. Seven monks were posted
there meanwhile, and kept a careful watch over the holy body,
singing God's praises without
cease day and night. After the
eight weeks had gone by, the day
marked out by the saint dawned.
The bones were brought out again
from the reliquary, washed and
placed in the gold shrine that had
arrived for the purpose. The
water made holy by being used
to wash the relics was carefully
preserved, and later proved healing for many people's infirmities.
On the night before the Sunday of
the translation, two men rowing
on the nearby river saw a column
of light going right up to heaven[1]
above the saint's chapel and
pointed it out to many others
besides. Again in the morning,
when the holy relics were being
brought down by water to Glastonbury, two men in the same
boat, one a monk, the other a
layman, saw from far off in the
air a sort of arched roof of different colours shading the whole

totum monasterium obumbrare
ut nullatenus dubitarent celestem
graciam illabi et adgaudere habi-
taculo cui tantus aduehebatur
habitator. Omnes itaque turbe
gaudentes et monachi ac clerici
sacris induti cum crucibus, turri-
bulis, luminaribus ac ceteris que
mos est in processionibus efferri,
obuiam procedunt cantibus et
laudibus sonoris concrepantes.
Sanctis reliquiis litori appulsis
atque ad locum congruum citra
flumen delatis, media fere uia
inter flumen et monasterium, ex
eminencioris stacionis edito de
sancti uiri uita et translacionis
causa ad circumstantem plebem
factus est sermo. Et in fine sermonis prolato uno ex ossibus sanctis
ac supra astantes signo crucis ex
eo facto, tanta diuine liberalitatis
in populum effluxit gracia ut
uexati langoribus uariis et diuersa
infirmitatum pericula sustinentes,
ceci, surdi, muti sanarentur, multi
eciam quos uiscerum cruciabat
torcio[1] mortem intus latentem
euomerent et multi coram omnibus colubros et multipedas effun-
derent.

Illo uero die abbas unum de ossibus sanctis arripiens, et signum
crucis super populum cum eo
faciens, nonnullos diuersis lan-
guorum cruciatibus uexatos sanitate recepta letari fecit, et ceci
quidam atque contracti optatam
salutem consecuti sunt, et plurimi
cerei in manibus populi a uento
et turbine prius extincti, per
merita beati Benigni ipsa hora
diuinitus sunt accensi. Plurimi
etiam colubros et diuersa dolo-
rum genera uisceribus habentes,
palam uidente populo, euomuer-
unt. Tanta etenim curationis
gratia in illo loco erat ostensa ut
uix debilis quisquam aut egrotus
ad tumbam sancti ueniens absque

---

[1] *GR*, c. 365. 4.

monastery, so that they were certain that the grace of heaven was coming down and rejoicing in the dwelling that so important a dweller was approaching. So all the delighted crowd went to meet him, monks and clerks in their vestments and carrying crosses, thuribles, lights, and all that is usually carried out in procession, loudly singing and praising God. When the relics came to the shore and had been carried to an appropriate place on land, perhaps half way between river and monastery, a sermon was preached from a raised place to the people standing around, concerning the saint's life and the reason for his translation. At the end of the sermon, one of the holy bones was brought forth and used to make the sign of the Cross over the bystanders; and such was the grace of God's generosity that flowed into the people, that people troubled with various illnesses and grave infirmities, the blind, the deaf and the dumb, found healing. Many too who had agonizing internal complaints[1] vomited up the deadly venom that lurked within them, and many brought up snakes and insects in public.

NLA On that day the abbot took one of the holy bones and made the sign of the Cross with it over the people, thus causing not a few to rejoice at recovering their health, though they had been troubled by various agonizing diseases. Certain blind and crippled persons got well again, as they had longed to do, and many candles held in the hands of the people, that had been extinguished by gusts of wind, were by the merits of St Benignus miraculously rekindled at that same hour. Many with snakes and various pains in their bowels vomited them up in full view of the people. Indeed so great a grace of curing was shown in that place

sanitate recepta discederet.[1]
Frater quidam longa infirmitate
decoctus[2] a fratribus rogatur ut
sanctum Benignum pro salute
sua exoraret; qui ita respondit:
'Re enim uera, sicut michi pro-
desse non ualet, ita nec michi
nocere potest.' Cumque sopori
membra dedisset, apparuit ei
sanctus Benignus, candidis uestibus ornatus, qui quasi indig-
nans sic eum affatur: 'Quid
nunc tibi' ait 'de Benigno seruo
Dei uidetur, frater? Quid tibi de
duobus credi potissimum sit, an
cum sanctis in regno gaudet, uel
cum impiis in penis torquetur?'
Et cum ille respondere non
auderet, comminando hoc intulit
sanctus: 'Cum secreta Dei iudicia
humane fragilitatis ingenio
comprehendi nequeant, cur
michi derogasti? Quare me
blasphemare uoluisti? Ecce enim
grauiorem quam hactenus passus
es infirmitatem et molestiam
inuitus sustinebis, eo quod
uerbis inanibus michi irridendo
detraxisti. Ceteri quoque quos
me in derisum habuisse cog-
nosco, illum maxime qui
dentem meum furto abstulit,
nisi penitentiam agendo resi-
puerint, penis cum impiis
amaris se torqueri cognoscant.'
Hiis dictis alapam ingentem in
faciem eius dedit, et mox exper-

---

[1] Cf. *GP*, c. 171 (p. 306), of the tomb of St Mildburh: 'ut nullus exinde nisi extincta uel mitigata ualitudine discederet'.

[2] Cf. *GP*, c. 272 (p. 434) 'hoc morbo decocta'.

that scarce did any weak or ill man come to the saint's tomb and go away without being made well.[1] A brother who had long been ill[2] was asked by his brethren to beg the saint to heal him. He replied: 'Well, he can do me no harm, just as he can do me no good.' When he had gone to sleep, St Benignus appeared to him, dressed in white, and spoke to him as though in anger: 'Brother, what do you think of Benignus, servant of God, now? What had you best believe, that he rejoices with the saints in the kingdom, or is tortured with the impious in hell?' He dared not make any reply, and the saint added in a threatening tone: 'The secret judgements of God can not be understood by the weakness of human understanding. Why then did you find fault with me? Why did you think of blaspheming against me? You will have to put up with an illness worse than hitherto, whether you like it or not, because you have mocked and slighted me with empty words. I know of others who have made fun of me, in particular the brother who stole my tooth; unless they repent and come to their senses, they must realize that they will be sorely tormented with the impious.' With these words he gave him a great slap in the face. Waking up in a short while, he began to fear

gefactus a sompno, quem ante despexerat, tunc timere et uenerari cepit, diris tamen correptus febribus per totum annum liberari nequiuit. Quod cum per ordinem abbas et fratres audissent, dens a fratre receptus in locum suum restituitur, et laudes et gratie ab omnibus Deo et sancto eius referuntur.

In loco autem illo quo tunc requieuit sanctum corpus ipsius sancti nomine fabricata est ecclesia continuo quam dedicauit Iohannes primus episcopus[1] qui Bathonie cathedram suam statuit, que usque in hodiernum diem perseuerat. Ita festiua laude in maiorem ecclesiam Sanctus Benignus deductus et ante magnum altare locatus cotidianis miraculis sue sanctitatis ostendebat preconium. Tanta quippe fuit hominum diuersorum utriusque sexus frequencia ut continuis quadraginta diebus uix quisquam ad altare pre pressura posset accedere. Hinc confluentes ex diuersis prouinciis uariis morborum ac infirmitatum molestiis grauati, ceci, muti, paralitici, leprosi, mente capti, idropici, contracti, mulieres eciam fetum mortuum in utero gestantes, per Sancti Benigni merita sospitate adepta, alacres redierunt ad propria. Facta est autem hec translacio anno Domini millesimo nonagesimo primo. Abbas uero

Cf. above, pp. 354, 356.

and respect one whom he had previously scorned; but for a whole year he was plagued by serious fevers that he could not throw off. When the abbot and monks heard the whole story, the tooth was got back from the monk and restored to its place; and everyone gave thanks and praise to God and His saint.

At the place where the holy body then rested was built forthwith a church in the saint's name, which was dedicated by John, the first bishop[1] to make his seat at Bath, where it is to this day. With festive praise St Benignus was brought to the larger church and placed before the high altar, where he began to demonstrate his sanctity by daily miracles. So great was the crowd of both men and women that for forty consecutive days scarcely anyone could get through the press to the altar. From many a province flocked in people afflicted with all kinds of illness, the blind, the dumb, the paralytic, the leprous, the mad, the dropsical, the crippled, women too who carried dead foetuses in their wombs; all were healed by St Benignus's merits, and went back home with a light step. This translation took place in AD 1091.

---

[1] For the move (in 1090) of John de Villula (bishop 1088–1122) from Wells to Bath, see *GP*, c. 90 (p. 194).

Turstinus,[1] aliquot annis monasterii regimen occupans et per
eiusdem possessiones peruagatus,
longe ab ipso ut dignus erat
misere uitam finiuit.

---

[1] His miserable end was earned by a career that culminated in the disgraceful scene described in JG, c. 85 (pp. 156, 158; cf. *GP*, c. 91 (p. 197); *GR*, c. 270; *AG*, c. 78 (pp. 156, 158), as a result of which he was packed off back to Caen, though he later regained office. The sentence does not make it clear that it is concerned with the last period of Thurstan's life, as we learn from JG's source, represented for us by *AG*, c. 78 (p. 158): [after

Abbot Thurstan,[1] who for some
years ruled the monastery or
wandered from one of its estates
to another, finished his life
wretchedly, as was only right,
far away from the house.

Thurstan's banishment to France] 'Rege tamen mortuo idem Turstinus auxilio parentum
suorum abbaciam Glastonie a filio suo Willelmo, dicto Rupho, quingentis libris argenti
dicitur redemisse, et monasterium aliquot annis occupans et per eiusdem possessiones
peruagatus, ⟨longe ab ipso, ut dignus erat,⟩ [supplemented in the margin of MS T (from
JG)] misere uitam finiuit.'

VITA INDRACTI

Digby 1 In cuius [sc. King Ine] tempore

JG 50 Hiis diebus [i.e. in the days of King Ine] Sanctus Indractus cum sociis suis uenit Glastoniam, cuius causa aduentus hec fuit. Cum Sanctus Patricius a Celestino papa missus Hibernicos[1] ad fidem Christi conuertisset atque eos in fide solidasset,[2] ut superius declaratum est, Britanniam rediit et in portum qui Hailemout nuncupatur appulit.[3] Ob cuius reuerenciam sanctitatisque excellenciam ibidem statuitur ecclesia, Sancti Patricii nomine, propter eius merita et frequencia miracula insignita. Tunc ex omni copia locorum Glastoniam potissimum elegit[4] ubi ei triumphorum de diabolo materia suppeteret et celestium premiorum gaudia promereri posset. Nam tunc locus ille, paludibus pene inuius, pro solitudine hominum celestibus excubiis[5]

---

[1] So in the same context at *AG*, c. 12 (p. 60), Patrick 'a Celestino papa in Hyberniam missus fuit . . . Ybernicos ad fidem Christi conuertit'. *Hibernicus* is apparently not found elsewhere in William.

[2] JG and *NLA* (but not Digby) have the same sequence of events: Patrick's conversion of Ireland, his coming to Glastonbury, the story of Indract. This was probably William's own order. Note the similarity of wording in *AG*, c. 12 (p. 60) (cited in the previous note), JG, and *NLA*: 'postquam . . . Patricius populum Hiberniensem ad fidem Christi . . . conuertisset'. The phrasing 'conuertisset . . . solidasset' is reminiscent of the interpolated 'Carta Patricii' (see above, p. 334 n. 3: 'conuerti. Et cum eos in fide catholica solidassem' (JG, c. 25; pp. 60, 62 = *AG*, c. 9 (p. 54), and JG himself, c. 24 (p. 60) 'conuertit atque in fide catholica solidauit', the passage to which 'ut superius declaratum est' here looks back).

[3] William may or may not have written that Patrick's Cornish landfall was at

LIFE OF INDRACT

Digby 1. In Ine's time

JG 50. At this time St Indract came with his companions to Glastonbury, for the following reason. When (as described above) St Patrick had been sent to Ireland by Pope Celestine, had converted the people[1] to Christianity, and had confirmed them in the faith,[2] he came back to Britain and put in at a port called *Hailemout*.[3] Because of the reverence felt for him and his outstanding holiness, a church is established there in his name, distinguished by his merits and frequent miracles. Then, from the whole wealth of sites available, he chose Glastonbury in particular[4] as a place where there would be wide scope for triumphs over the Devil and where he could earn the joys of reward in heaven. At this time the place was almost inaccessible amid its marshes, and its lonely position made it appropriate for serving God.[5]

'Hailemout' (*GR*, c. 22. 1, *AG*, c. 8; p. 54; see also JG, c. 24; p. 60, and above, p. 338 n. 1), or have mentioned the church built there. But we now come to material demonstrably from William's Life.

[4] Cf. *GP*, c. 24 (p. 38) 'ex omni abbatiarum copia Beccum apud Normanniam potissimum elegit [*sc*. Lanfrancus]' (also *VD* i. 17. 2 'cum multa monasteria uoluntati eius occurrerent . . ., solum omnium mortalium Dunstanum . . . elegit').

[5] Cf. *GP*, cc. 66 (p. 124), 213 (p. 357); also *GP*, c. 160 (pp. 296–7) 'dum solitudine inuitante frequentaret excubias', and *Vita Benigni* above, p. 348: 'locus ille solitarius . . . Dei famulatui . . . opportunus'.

cuiusdam regis Hybernensium filius, Indractus nomine, Romam de Hybernia uenit (quod ea tempestate magne uirtutis estimabatur), nouem sibi solummodo asseclis associatis, suppliciterque adoratis apostolorum reliquiis, circuiuit quas ualuit Romane urbis ecclesias atque in singulis pro nanciscendis superne uite gaudiis Domino preces fudit. Quo facto mox inde ouanti animo cum domni Apostolici benedictione ad propriam curauit patriam repedare. Qui cum exinde rediens ad Angliam peruenisset et ad Hybernensium mare ire decreuisset, suum iter diuertit ad Glastoniam quo Sancti Patricii sciebat esse reli-

erat oportunus. Ibi sanctissimam excurrens uitam die uocacionis sue reposcentibus astris[1] exhibuit animam. At uero gens Hibernica, non in fide barbara, quin pocius sui doctoris cupiens emulari uestigia, quia Rome ordinatum illum acceperat,[2] illuc indefessa excurrere et solennes ac annuos meatus cepit instituere atque redeundo ob uenerandas sui patroni reliquias Glastoniam frequentare.[3] Vnde Sanctus Indractus, gloriosus Christi martir futurus, cuiusdam Hiberniencium regis filius,[4] cum aliis septem[5] iteneris comitibus Romam est ingressus. Ibi triumphalibus apostolorum luminibus affusi,[6] deuotis precibus uota sua suppliciter compleuerunt et omnes Rome ecclesias circueuntes[7] preces cumulabant uberius ut exaudirentur efficacius. Votis peractis regressum adorsi sunt celebrius [leg. celerius]. Ingressos pelagus felici nauigio suscepit Britannicus sinus. Inde Glastoniam contendunt preter religionem[8] estimantes insalutatum patrem Patricium preterire.[9] Quo in loco

---

[1] Cf. GP, c. 6 (p. 12) 'hi ambo . . . reposcebantur celo'.

[2] For the 'ordination', see e.g. GP, c. 91 (p. 197).

[3] Cf. AG, c. 12 (p. 60) 'hinc Yberniensibus mos inolitus ad exosculandas patroni reliquias locum frequentare' = GR, c. 22. 3; cf. VD i. 4. 1, and NLA ii. 56 'Hibernienses . . . urbem Glastoniam orationis ac deuotionis gratia peregrini crebro uisitare solebant.'

[4] So GP, c. 91 (p. 197). Cf. GR, c. 23 (he and Brigid 'Hiberniae non obscuros incolas') = AG, c. 12 (p. 60).

[5] So GP, c. 91 (p. 197), GR, c. 23; JG, c. 5 (cited above, p. 313) extends royal birth to the others. Contrast the nine in Digby 1. 8 (note also 6. 16–18) and thence NLA.

[6] Cf. GP, c. 100 (p. 213) 'beato Andrea suffragante, cuius triumphalibus luminibus affusus opem . . . orauerat'.

There he ran the course of his holy life, and on the day of his calling gave up his soul to the stars that asked for his return.[1] Now the Irish were not primitive in the faith; rather, they were eager to follow in the footsteps of their teacher. They had heard he had been ordained in Rome,[2] and they began to travel there with tireless speed and to institute regular yearly visits; and on their return journey they would throng to Glastonbury because of the reverence they felt for the relics of their patron.[3] This is how St Indract, son[4] of an Irish king and destined to be a glorious martyr for Christ, came to travel to Rome with seven[5] companions. There they fell before the triumphant countenances of the apostles,[6] and humbly fulfilled their vows with devout prayers; going round all the churches[7] of Rome, they piled up their prayers the higher that they might be heard the more effectively. After completing their vows they returned swiftly. After a prosperous voyage they came to land in Britain. Then they proceeded to Glastonbury, judging it improper[8] to pass by father Patrick without greeting him,[9] and stayed there for some

the son of a king of the Irish, by the name of Indract, came to Rome from Ireland (a journey that at that date was counted very virtuous), taking but nine companions. He worshipped the relics of the apostles as a suppliant, and went round all the churches of Rome that he could, pouring out prayers in each to try to win the joys of the life above. Armed with the pope's blessing and triumphant at heart, he then put his mind to returning home. Arrived in England and aiming for the Irish Sea, he turned off to Glastonbury, where he knew the relics of St Patrick were to be found, to pray and to visit them. Leaving there at nightfall, he came one

---

[7] Cf. *GP*, c. 268 (p. 425) 'sanctorum aecclesias circuiret', but also Digby's 'circuiuit . . . ecclesias'.

[8] Cf. *GP*, c. 75 (p. 159) = *GR*, c. 29. 3.

[9] *VW* i. 15. 1 with n.

quias, orandi simulque uisendi gratia. Cumque inde, iam die ad occasum uergente, recessisset, facta oratione peruenit quadam die[1] forte ad quendam locum qui lingua Anglorum Hywisc dicitur, in prouincia Occidentalium Saxonum situm. Iuxta quem haud procul tunc temporis Inus rex Anglorum . . . in uilla quadam que ab incolis Pedred nominatur perendinando commorabatur.

Verum in eo loco ad quem uir Domini cum suis sociis uenerat, quidam ex principibus regis, Huna nomine, quod locus ille herbosus esset ad equos pascendos per campum late fixerat tentoria. Cuius satellites, cernentes seruos Dei ferentes pergrandes peras sub ascellis baculosque manu gestantes, ut Hybernensibus moris est, auricalco comptos,

aliquamdiu commorantes fessa membra recreare et tantorum laborum sudorem extergere quieuerunt.

Hiis diebus rex Ina in uilla que Pedred[2] dicitur commanebat. Vulgus satellitum contiguas curie uillas hospicio incubabat. Post more interuallum Sanctus Indractus cum sociis Hiberniam tendere proponebant, clementem flatum qui eos ad mare urgeret prestolantes. Sed aderat diuina miseracio[3] que eos ad melius regnum transueheret, cumque a Glastonia discessissent, peruenerunt ad quoddam oppidum quod Schapwik dicitur, non longe a Glastonia distans,[4] et ibidem pernoctare disposuerunt. Tunc quidam regiorum satellitum[5] maliciosi, rapinis inhiantes, in peregrinos auida defixerunt lumina, ingemuerunt inuidia, auiditatem traxerunt,[6] uidentes suffarcinatas peras quasi auro grauidas. Baculorum enim splendor alludebat oculis quasi fuluum[7]

---

[1] The passage 'Cumque . . . quadam die' is problematic: (1) Why did Indract apparently leave Glastonbury at day's end? (2) Had he already prayed, or did he do so during the journey? (3) Why did he reach nearby Huish 'quadam die'? One might wish to emend 'quadam' to 'eadem', if the saint had not begun his journey in the evening. Alternatively, one might emend 'quadam' to 'sequenti'.

[2] See Lapidge on Digby 1. 20. He points to a royal vill on the river Parret (formerly

day(?)[1] after praying to a place called in English Huish, in the province of the West Saxons. Not far from there Ine king of the English was at that time staying in a vill called *Pedred* by the locals.

Now in the place reached by the man of God and his companions one of the king's nobles, Huna, had pitched his tents far across the plain so as to feed his horses, the place being grassy. His minions saw the servants of God carrying big bags under their arms, and staffs in their hands decorated with brass in the Irish manner, and, being

time quietly to rest their tired limbs and wipe off the sweat of all their labours.

At this time King Ine was residing in a vill called *Pedred*,[2] while his troop of followers were lodged in vills near the court. After a while St Indract and his friends decided to go on towards Ireland, though they had to wait for a favourable breeze to take them out to sea. But God in His mercy was at hand[3] to carry them over to a better kingdom. After leaving Glastonbury they came to a town called Shapwick, not far away,[4] and determined to spend the night there. Then some villains in the king's retinue,[5] with a mind to plunder, cast avaricious eyes on the pilgrims, and groaned in their envy, looking greedily[6] at their well-filled bags, as they thought, heavy with gold. For the gleam of their staffs deceived them into thinking that tawny gold[7] lay hidden in the bags, though the

Pedred) near Muchelney and south of Huish Episcopi (perhaps Digby's *Hywisc*; but see above, p. 310 n. 2). These places are well to the south-west of Glastonbury, and a vill lower down the river seems more likely.   [3] A similar expression in *VD* i. 24. 1.

[4] See also JG, c. 5 (cited above, p. 313). *GR*, c. 23 has merely 'iuxta Glastoniam' (it is nearly five miles to the west. *AG*, c. 12 (p. 60) 'ibidem' is a little ambiguous, but the same word clearly refers to Glastonbury at *GP*, c. 91 (p. 198). *NLA*'s 'apud Shapwike' is an interpolation from JG, not present in John of Tynemouth.

[5] Cf. L at *AG*, p. 62 n. 'ab infelicibus satellitibus', as well as Digby 1. 24 and 5. 1.

[6] An odd phrase, perhaps meaning that they 'absorbed' greed into their systems.

[7] *GR*, c. 277. 3 'tantam auri copiam prodidere ut nostri seculi estimationem superaret fului congeries metalli' (also 135. 3 'fuluum . . . aurum': Virgilian). For the conjectured *fulgor*, cf. *GR*, c. 188. 6; Life of Patrick above, p. 322.

cum essent cupidi et auari animo, estimantes eos habere multam pecuniam simulque aurum esse compturam baculorum ipsorum, quasi sub pietatis studio hospitio indolo susceperunt. Sed famuli Domini non aurum neque pecuniam ullam, quemadmodum illi arbitrabantur, portabant, sed suas impleuerant peras de seminibus apii aliarumque herbarum, quod suam ad patriam secum deferre cupiebant, unde locus ille usque in hodiernum diem refertus est.

auri metallum iaceret in peris, cuius fuluor [*leg.* fulgor] tantum renitebat in baculis. Illi autem non auri laminis set semine apii peras impleuerant, gratum munus prouincialibus fore estimantes, si herbas afferrent que et suauem odorem preberent naribus et mederentur corporibus. At uero barbari quomodo effectu potirentur seduli rimabantur et susceptos hospicio

2. Susceptus est igitur uir Domini Indrachtus . . . a barbaris hospitio indolo. . . . Barbari autem intempeste noctis silentio surgentes ad sanctos Dei legentes et orantes quemadmodum premeditati fuerant interfecerunt, et in speluncam que in uicino aderat ramis arborum superpositis occuluerunt . . .

beatissimum Indractum cum suis commilitonibus, postquam se in plenam composuerant quietem, intempesta nocte[1] inpudentissimi latrones et celesti [*leg.* scelesti] carnifices, ausi facinus uix apud gentiles auditum, interfecerunt ad unum.[2] Et sic peregrinorum soporem mutauerunt in mortem, fefellerunt hospites ut facerent martires. Quamuis enim non faciat martirem pena sed causa,[3] credendum est tamen eos ad martirii peruenisse gloriam, qui uiuendo martirum seruauerunt innocenciam. Nec ad hoc credendum suam diuinus fauor

---

[1] A favourite phrase of William's (five times in *GR* alone). Digby has 'intempeste noctis silentio' (2. 5), and 'nocte quadam intempesta' (3. 3), neither, apparently, found in William.

[2] Cf. e.g. *GR*, c. 125. 2 'ad unum . . . interfecti'.

greedy and grasping by nature, they thought the travellers had a lot of money with them, and that what decorated their staffs was gold. So with a show of kindness they gave them treacherous lodging. But the servants of the Lord were carrying not gold or any money, as they thought, but had filled their bags with the seeds of celery and other plants, in which the district is rich to this day, meaning to take them home with them.

glint came in fact only from the staffs. The pilgrims had filled the bags not with gold leaf but with celery seed, thinking it would make a welcome present for their people if they brought home plants that had a pleasant smell and healing properties beside. The barbarians, however, cast round carefully to see how they could have their way.

2. So the man of the Lord Indract was received by the savages in a treacherous lodging. . . . But the barbarians got up at dead of night, and attacking the saints of God as they read and prayed they killed them as they had plotted, and hid them in a nearby cave by piling branches on them.

They gave the blessed Indract and his comrades lodging, and they fell into a deep sleep. At dead of night[1] the shameless robbers and wicked murderers, daring to undertake a deed scarcely heard of among the heathen, killed them to a man,[2] so turning the pilgrims' sleep into their deaths, and playing guests false to make martyrs of them. It is not the suffering but the motive that makes a martyr;[3] still, one must believe that they came to the glory of martyrdom, seeing that in life they had preserved the innocence of martyrs. And God's favour provided authority for this belief.

[3] Variants of this statement are found sixteen times in Augustine. The only occurrence with 'faciat' is Aug., *Ep.* cciv. 4.

Apparuit enim columna lucis radiis solis splendidior super sanctos, a terra ad celum usque porrecta, cuius splendore tota illa regio splendescere uidebatur. Que tam diu singulis noctibus uisa est donec longe lateque quod factum fuerat a multis dinosceretur. 3. Rex autem prefatus in uicinio aderat . . . nec tante rei facinus quod eius serui patrauerant adhuc ad eius notitiam peruenerat. Qui nocte quadam intempesta a stratu suo surgens, diuino ut autumo ammonitus instinctu, sala regia egressus est. Mox oculis ad celum eleuatis uidit predictam lucis columnam a terra ad celum usque extensam. Diriguit, stupuit, quid portenderet ammiratus. Nec multum inde locutus ad lectum reuersus est. Rursus nocte sequenti hora eadem foras exiit et ita lucis fulgorem ut prius prospexit. Similiter uero et tertia nocte progressus, ac columnam radiantem cum aspexisset, nil ultra moratus, statim sub nocturno tempore equum ascendit paucisque secum assumptis ministris recto itinere ad locum luminis usque peruenit. Et uidens corpora sanctorum in terra iacentia . . . de equo protinus exiliuit flensque humiliter adorauit.

subtraxit autoritatem. 51. Rex namque Ina qui apud uillam predictam aliquantam continuauerat moram, nocte eadem, nescio quid facturus egressus domo, per regionem oculos obliquans[1] uidit a loco in quo sancti iacebant limpidissimi iubaris columpnam in celum usque porrectam.[2] Visu tamen turbatus quidnam esset quidue portenderet animo fluctuabat.

Noctibus duabus sequentibus uigiliis operandans [*leg.* operam dans] conuenientem principiis inuenit exitum.[3] Non enim ociosum[4] fore estimabat quod tercia manifestacione animaduertebat.

Locum adiit, corpora sanctorum sine ordine, sine lege sepulture uili loco proiecta, inuenit. At ipse equo desiliens sanctorum

---

[1] Ovid, *Met.* vii. 412. Cf. *GR*, c. 188. 6 'Goduinum quoque obliquis oculis intuitus'.

[2] Besides Digby 3, cf. also Digby 6. 24–5 'lucis columna . . . a terra usque ad celum porrecta'; add JG, c. 86 (p. 160; above, p. 358) 'columpnam lucis in celum usque porrectam'.

A column of light brighter than the sun's rays appeared over the saints, stretching from earth to heaven, and making the whole district seem to glow with its brilliance. It was seen night after night until far and wide many knew what had happened. 3. King Ine was in the neighbourhood, . . . but the outrage perpetrated by his servants had not yet come to his notice. One dark night he rose from his bed, I think on some divine impulse, and left the royal apartments. Looking up, he saw the column of light spanning the sky. He stiffened in astonishment: what could it mean? Without saying much about it, he went back to bed. On the following night he went outside at the same hour and saw the brilliant light as before. So too on the third night; going out and seeing the column spreading its light, he put it off no longer, but at once, night though it was, mounted his horse, and taking a few servants with him went straight to the source of the light. Seeing the bodies of the saints lying on the ground, . . . he forthwith leapt off his horse, and weeping worshipped them in all humility.

51. King Ine had spent some time at *Pedred*. On the night in question he went out for some reason and was looking about him,[1] when he saw a column of very bright light stretching right up to heaven[2] from the place where the martyrs lay. He was perturbed at the sight, wondering what it was and what it meant.

On the two following nights he stayed awake and found the phenomenon unchanged.[3] He did not believe that something he had seen three times could be without meaning.[4]

He went to the place, only to find the saints' bodies strewn on the unsanctified ground without order or ceremony. Leaping from his horse he gave the remains the reverence due to them.

[3] Cf. *VD* i. 8 'par . . . principium, . . . diuersum . . . exitum'.
[4] Cf. *VW* i. 2. 1, *VD* ii. 6. 5.

[4. Sub eadem tempestate in eadem regione quedam degebat uidua, infidelitate gentilitatis adhuc irretita. Que cum forte nocte quadam de domo sua egressa esset et uidisset predictam lucis columnam, herebat stupens . . . quantocius uicinam ecclesiam petiit, quo baptizari promeruisset.]

Deinde per ordinem inquisiuit qui fuerant, uel unde uenere, uel quare siue a quibus occisi fuere. . . .

5. Satellites autem impietatis qui sanctos Dei propter auaritiam pecunie interfecerant, . . . fugere ceperunt. . . . Sed fuga nil ualuit: cura secuta fuit. Inuenti nanque rapiuntur operarii iniquitatis, et ad regem usque deducti ligatis manibus post tergum de restibus. Quos statim ira regis puniri iusta pena parabat. Sed ultio diuina non illos ab homine interfici sinebat. Nam hora eadem coram cunctis ab immundis spiritibus uexari ceperunt, adeo crudeliter ut sese inuicem more canum dentibus discerperent ac dilaniarent. . . .

6. Igitur his ita gestis rex cum suis proceribus consilium iniit quo in loco tante [*sic*] pretii margarite conderentur. Cui, ut fertur, mox ita responsa dedere: 'Non repperietur' inquiunt 'in Anglorum regno pro condendis horum martyrum reliquiis locus habilior

reliquias cultu ueneratus est quo decuit. Facta est autem eadem uisio columpne cuidam uidue nondum set postea ob hoc in Christo regenerate.[1]

Patratores autem sceleris et quicumque fuerant criminis complices seuissimo afflati demone torquebantur[2] coram rege et alterutros appetebant dentibus ac ferales cibos commedebant de sociorum carnibus.

Illustris autem regis inhesit animo ut quam honorifice posset sanctorum corpora magna cum solempnitate reconderet.

---

[1] The story is given more fully in Digby 4 ('renata').

[4. At the same time, in the same region, there was living a widow, still caught in the toils of heathendom. One night she chanced to come out of her house and see the column of light. She was struck dumb . . . she went quickly to the neighbouring church, and was found fit for baptism.] Then [the king] made strict enquiries who they were, where they had come from, and why and by whom they had been killed.

Now the same vision of the column of light had been seen by a widow who only afterwards, and as a result of this happening, was reborn in Christ.[1]

5. The conscienceless minions who had killed saints of God out of greed for money . . . started to flee. . . . But it availed them nothing: trouble was soon on their tracks. The workers of iniquity were discovered, arrested, and brought before the king, their hands roped behind their backs. The angry king at once set about making them pay a proper penalty. But God's vengeance would not allow them to be killed by man. At that very hour, with all watching, they began to be troubled by unclean spirits, so cruelly that they tore each other to pieces with their teeth like dogs. . . . 6. After this, the king in conclave with his nobles discussed where pearls of such price should be stored. We are told that the immediate reply was: 'No more suitable place will be found

The criminals and their accomplices fell in the king's presence under the influence of a savage and tormenting devil:[2] they snapped at each other with their teeth, and made a horrid meal off their companions' flesh.

The great king was determined to give the saints' bodies the most honourable burial rites possible with all ceremony.

---

[2] Cf. *GP*, c. 261 (p. 416) 'pessimo afflatus demone torquebatur'. There is no literal torture in either passage.

Glastonia, ubi gloriosa genitricis Dei habetur ecclesia. In qua in parte altaris dextra [*so MS*] Sanctus Patricius Hybernorum apostolus est ab antiquis temporibus humatus. Ad hanc ergo iubeat celsitudo uestra Sancti Indracti martyris una cum sociorum transferri reliquias . . .'. Cumque hoc regi consilium placuisset, statim libitinas fieri imperauit, quibus pretiosa martyrum corpora superimposita ad supradictum Glestoniense cenobium allata sunt . . . . Cuius corpus sanctissimum in sinistra parte altaris . . . sepelierunt. Verum octo socios eius simili modo conditos ante altare in pauimento tumulauerunt. Nonus uero ex sociis eorum non cum eis est repertus. . . .

7–8 *Miracles.*

Deferri namque fecit eos Glastoniam, Sanctum Indractum in uetusta ecclesia ad partem collocauit sinistram, occupante Sancto Patricio dextram.[1] Ceteri per solum pauimenti positi[2] totum basilice ambitum reddiderunt uenerabilem. Nisi enim sanctos istos gloriosos fuisse et esse martires temporis illius patres credidissent precipueque pater Dunstanus Sancto Spiritu influente repletus, nequaquam credulitate sua posteris confirmatum reliquissent. Quapropter non modo tantum credere set et uenerari nos decet quod illi uel assensu tradiderunt tacito uel diu librato perceperunt iudicio.[3] Nec defuere celestia miracula[4] quibus in celo Christus ostenderet sanctorum merita.

---

[1] For the spot add *GR*, c. 35C. 3 'in lapidea piramide ad sinistrum altaris' = *AG*, c. 20 (p. 68); Digby 6. 15 'in sinistra parte altaris', 8. 13 'de piramide sinistre partis altaris'; JG, c. 97 (p. 178). For Patrick (for a long time) on the right, see *GR*, c. 22. 3; *AG*, cc. 9 and 10 (pp. 58, 60); JG, cc. 5 (p. 16), 26 (p. 64; 'uersus austrum'), 97 (p. 178); Digby 6. 5 ('in parte altaris dextra'). For the two, and their pyramids, Digby 7. 27–8. For the churches of Glastonbury, see Lapidge on Digby 6. 5 and 7. 3; and for pyramids Lapidge on 7. 27.

[2] *GR*, c. 35C. 3 'ceterorum in pauimento, prout uel casus tulit uel industria locauit' = *AG*, c. 20 (p. 68). JG, c. 97 (p. 178), puts Indract and his companions on the left, Gildas under the pavement.

in the realm of the English for the burial of the relics of these martyrs than Glastonbury, where there is a noble church of the Mother of God. There, on the right of the altar, St Patrick apostle of the Irish was buried of old. That is where Your Majesty should order the remains of St Indract the martyr and those of his comrades to be taken. . . .' The king took this advice, and ordered the immediate construction of biers, on which the precious bodies of the martyrs were taken to the monastery of Glastonbury. . . . They buried [Indract's] holy body on the left of the altar, and eight companions similarly beneath the floor in front of the altar. . . . But the ninth of the company was not found with them.

He accordingly had them carried to Glastonbury, placing St Indract in the Old Church on the left hand side, St Patrick being in possession of the right,[1] while the rest were given graves under the floor of the church,[2] making its whole area worthy of reverence. Indeed if the fathers of that time, and in particular Father Dunstan (receptacle of the Holy Spirit), had not believed that these saints were and are glorious martyrs, they would never have left that belief to posterity with the seal of their approval. So it is fitting that *we* should not merely believe, but also feel reverence for what *they* handed down with tacit assent or judged to be the case after long deliberations.[3] Nor were there lacking miracles[4] by which Christ showed from heaven the qualities of His saints.

Miracles.

---

[3] *GR*, c. 332. 1. Cf. also the contrast in *GR*, c. 11. 1 'propensiore consilio . . . tacito iuditio'.

[4] It is by no means impossible that these were related by William; they survive for us in Digby 7–8, *NLA.* ii. 57–8.

INDEX OF SOURCES

ADELARD:
  Vita S. Dunstani 161–3, 171, 174, 214,
      228–30, 235–7, 257, 269, 288–9,
      294
ÆLFRIC:
  Homilies 32, 66
ÆTHELWOLD, *Prol. to OE Reg. Ben.* 238
ALDHELM:
  De virg. (metr.) 1013 293
  De virg. (prosa) c. 33 292
      c. 45 32
      c. 47 39
Anglo-Saxon Chronicle 40, 82, 131, 169,
      171, 224, 264, 268–70, 274, 288,
      294, 296
AUGUSTINE:
  De bono coniug., c. 3 299
      c. 8 298
  De civ. Dei x. 9 188
      x. 28 188
  Contra Iulianum ii 299
  De doctr. christiana iv. 96 12
  Enarr. in Ps. 49. 11 300
  Ep. cciv. 4 375
  Serm. li. 21 299
  De serm. Dom. in monte ii. 41 106
  Tract. in Ioann. 58. 3 234
  unidentified 331
AVITUS:
  Poem. iii. 243–5 184
      v. 288 287

B., *Vita S. Dunstani* 129, 161–3, 166, 168,
      170, 172, 178, 182, 185, 192–3,
      202, 211–12, 214, 218, 221, 228,
      233, 235–7, 241, 249, 266–7, 269,
      282, 286–7, 293–4
BEDE:
  Hist. eccles. 328–9
  De tabernaculo ii 182
  Vita Cuthberti, c. 1 18
BIBLE:
  Gen. 25: 23 300
      39: 6–12 33
  Exod. 17: 6 265
  Num. 29: 36 232

Judges 1: 15 284
3 Sam. (1 Kgs.) 17: 16 130, 195
Esther 2: 13 226
Ps. 5: 13 278
  15 (16): 1 116
  17 (18): 2 116
  24 (25): 1 80
  25 (26): 8 113
  50 (51): 7 298
  67 (68): 2 210
  85 (86): 1 119
  102 (103): 5 216
  110 (111): 4–5 294
  116 (117) 124
  117 (118): 6 28, 353
  118 (119): 24
  125 (126): 5 198
  129 (130) 124
  150 124
  150: 3–4 180
Prov. 18: 17 55
  19: 25 16
  21: 1 64
  26: 11 188
Ecclus. 15: 9 8
  31: 11 258
  44: 14 206
Jerem. 1: 5 300
Lam. 3: 41 55
Ezech. 18: 32 100
  33: 11 100
Job 6: 25–8 231
Haggai 2: 8 300
Matt. 3: 16 196
  5: 9 92
  5: 34–7 66
  8: 4 293
  9: 30 293
  10: 18–19 63
  11: 11 300
  11: 12 51
  11: 29 221
  14: 15–21 196
  16: 8 77
  21: 18–22 95
  22: 21 15

BIBLE (*cont.*)
  23: 11 126
  25: 36 55
  25: 40 118
Mark 1: 2 300
  1: 10 196
  5: 9–13 71
  5: 26 68
  6: 35–44 196
  12: 17 15
  13: 9 63
  13: 11 63
Luke 1: 15 300
  2: 14 90
  2: 25–32 172
  3: 8 46
  3: 22 196
  6: 27 183
  7: 42 138
  8: 26–39 71
  9: 12–17 196
  10: 38–42 224
  11: 3 44
  20: 25 15
  24: 36 90
John 1: 1 220
  1: 47 48
  4: 21 66
  6: 5–13 196
  8: 44 92
  8: 56 245
  13: 1 136
  13: 14 44
  14: 27 90
  19: 34 80
  20: 19 97
  20: 24–9 104
Acts 26: 14 256
Col. 3: 9–10 24
1 Tim. 3: 2 252
2 Tim. 4: 2 93, 349
Hebr. 13: 4 298
  13: 6 353
James 1: 27 283
1 Pet. 2: 17 216
BOETHIUS:
  De inst. arithmetica, i prol. 168
BYRHTFERTH:
  Vita Oswaldi 183, 245, 285–7

CAESARIUS:
  Serm. xl. 1 72

CASSIODORUS:
  Expos. S. Pauli: Rom., c. 9 72
CICERO:
  Orator 101 12
    132 234
(Ps.)-CICERO:
  Ad Herenn. i. 4. 6 13
CLAUDIAN:
  In Rufin. ii. 527 13
COUNCILS:
  Lisieux 1064 124
  Winchester 1070 43, 125, 128
  ?N. or S. Petherton 1071 64
  Rouen 1072 125
  Winchester and Windsor 1072 62, 65
  Winchester 1076 124
  Westminster 1125 34
CYPRIAN:
  Epist. lv. 26 256

EADMER:
  Historia nouorum 250
  Vita S. Dunstani 166, 182–3, 193, 195,
      218, 235–7, 254, 257, 264, 267,
      269–71, 285–7, 289, 294, 298
  Vita S. Odonis xx–xxii, 254
  Vita S. Wilfridi 204, 232
  Epigrammata 336

FARICIUS:
  Vita S. Aldhelmi 258
FRONTINUS:
  Strat. iv. 3. 13 317
FULGENTIUS:
  De fide ad Petrum, c. 69 300
FULGENTIUS MYTHOGRAPHUS:
  Serm. ant. 23 352

GILDAS 39
GOSCELIN:
  Vita S. Edithae 275
  Vita S. Wulfhildae 129
  Vita S. Wulfsini 263
GREGORY:
  Dial. i. 4 36

HORACE:
  Carm. i. 4. 13 120
    iv. 13. 12 254
  Epist. ii. 1. 251 84

ISIDORE:
  Etym. vii. 9. 11 221

xii. 1. 32 87
Sent. i. 16. 16 92

JEROME:
Comm. in Eccles. 12: 1 170
Comm. in Hos. 1. 2. 16–17 59
Dial. contra Pelag. iii. 5 59
Epist. xv. 2. 1 301
xxii. 30 38
lii. 7 208
De interpr. Hebr. nom. 220
Vita Hilar. 1 183
Vita Pauli, c. 3 266
JUVENAL:
vi. 273–4 54

LANFRANC:
Scriptum de primatu 61
LEONTIUS:
Vita S. Ioannis Eleemosynarii 66–7
Letters 283–4
LITURGY:
Antiphons 182, 230, 285
LUCAN:
i. 1 239
i. 492–3 136
i. 566 88
ii. 14–15 226
ii. 390 188
v. 483–4 52
vi. 543 58
x. 132 190

Memoriale qualiter 66

ORIGEN:
In Levit. hom. 7. 2 221
OSBERN:
Vita S. Ælfegi 292, 296
Vita S. Dunstani 161, 166–8, 170, 172,
182, 193–5, 202–3, 218, 233–7, 242,
244, 258, 264, 266, 268–71, 274,
276, 285–7, 289–90, 294, 298–9
OVID:
Heroid. xii. 61 49
Met. iv. 302 200
vii. 115 292
vii. 412 376

Passio S. Agnetis 32
Passio S. Edwardi 272
PATRICIUS:
Confessio 308, 316, 320–1, 330
Ep. ad Coroticum 332

PAUL THE DEACON:
Vita Gregorii i. 2 31
PAULINUS OF PÉRIGORD:
De uita S. Martini 54
PERSIUS, iii. 80 143
PRUDENTIUS:
Cath. praef. 27 254
iii. 148 94

(Ps.-) QUINTILIAN:
Decl. maiores xiii. 2 36

SALLUST:
Cat. xxxi. 9 228
Jug. iii. 3 68
SEDULIUS:
Hymn 1 286
SENECA:
Epist. xi. 8–10 16
STATIUS:
Achill. ii. 157–8 179
Theb. i. 499 323
ii. 37 200
iv. 591 286
v. 718–19 226
vi. 1 323
vi. 807 56
viii. 429 56, 204
xii. 297 222
xii. 566–7 239
xii. 600 201
SUETONIUS:
Aug. lxi. 1 106
Tib. xxi. 2 75
SULPICIUS SEVERUS:
Vita S. Martini 172

TERENCE:
Andr. 68 301
Phorm. 454 303
TERTULLIAN:
De uirg. uel. 170

VIRGIL:
Aen. i. 10 171
i. 82 301
i. 90 286
i. 149 282
i. 150 198
i. 205 243
i. 282 60
i. 387–8 8
i. 502 88

VIRGIL (*cont.*)
i. 723 110
i. 724 194
i. 793 194
ii. 268 84
ii. 274 145
ii. 428 94
iii. 179 222
iii. 252 229
iii. 457 81
iv. 2 31
iv. 65 226
iv. 415 178
v. 103 109
v. 318–19 18
v. 320 12
vi. 128 239
vi. 129–30 12
vi. 605 229
vii. 53 226
vii. 118–19 100
vii. 586 228
viii. 465 126, 192
ix. 24 25
x. 324 108
x. 501 226
x. 733 31

x. 773 211
x. 859–60 65
xii. 906 292
Ecl. i. 14–15 317
iii. 102 143
iv. 63 32
vii. 30 201
viii. 60 290
ix. 2–4 270
Georg. i. 108 200
ii. 528 194
Vita Ædwardi regis 42
Vitae S. Patricii 308, 316–26, 329–30,
332–4, 344

WULFSTAN OF WINCHESTER:
Vita S. Æthelwoldi
c. 8 187
c. 10 176, 218
cc. 11–12 216
c. 12 129, 194
c. 14 254
cc. 23–4 262
c. 34 38
c. 38 206
c. 41 277

GENERAL INDEX

Abbo of Fleury xix
Abingdon (Berks.) 217, 238; abt. of, see
Æthelwold
Adam 173
Adel (Yorks.) 39
Adelard of Ghent xvii–xx, xxvi, xxix,
230, 269
Ælfgar, Earl 45
Ælfgar, curial priest of Archbp. Dunstan,
bp. of Elmham 288–9, 291
Ælfgifu, w. of K. Edmund xiii, xxii, 237
Ælfgifu, mistress of K. Eadwig 227, 229
Ælfgifu, see Æthelflæd, Eadgifu
Ælfheah I ('the Bald'), monk of
Glastonbury, bp. of Winchester 161,
184–5, 187, 217, 237
Ælfheah II, monk of Glastonbury, abt. of
Bath, bp. of Winchester, archbp. of
Canterbury xiii, xix, xxiii, 162–3, 184,
232, 279, 281, 296–7
Ælfhere, Ealdorman 270, 273
Ælfric, archbp. of Canterbury xix, 34,
169
Ælfric, abt. of Glastonbury 203, 258
Ælfric, abt. of Eynsham 39
Ælfric, abt. of Malmesbury, bp. of
Crediton 260–1
Ælfsige, bp. of Winchester, archbp. of
Canterbury 162, 245, 247, 252
Ælfsige, thegn of K. Edward 95
Ælfsige, monk of Glastonbury 267
Ælfstan, Ealdorman 213
Ælfstan, bp. of Rochester 274
Ælfstan, prior of Worcester 30
Ælfthryth, w. of K. Edgar 271–3, 275
Ælfwold, bp. of Crediton 217
Ælfwold, rich man 163, 281
Æthelburh, St xiii
Æthelflæd (Æthelgifu, Ælfgifu), niece of
K. Æthelstan xxii, 161, 192–3, 195,
197, 199
Æthelgar, archbp. of Canterbury 169
Æthelgar, bp. of Crediton 216–17, 237
Æthelmær, a priest 74–5, 77
Æthelred II, k. of England xxxiv, 163,
265, 269–73, 275, 279, 281, 297

Æthelric, monk of Evesham 57, 69
Æthelric, archdeacon of Worcester 128–9
Æthelstan, k. of England xxxv, 80, 136,
161, 169, 171, 181, 183, 195, 199, 237,
294
Æthelstan, wastrel 187, 189
Æthelstan, f. of Wulfstan 15, 21
Æthelswith (recte Æthelthryth), d. of
K. Alfred 230–1
Æthelthryth, St xiii
Æthelwig, abt. of Evesham xxviii, 46–7,
50
Æthelwine, prior of Worcester xvii, 30
Æthelwold, monk of Glastonbury, abt. of
Abingdon, bp. of Winchester xiii, xviii,
xxix, 161–3, 187, 194, 207, 209, 217,
261, 263, 268, 277, 279
Æthelwulf, k. of W. Saxons 259
Æthelwynn 183
Agnes, St 32
Alcuin xvi, 284
Aldhelm, St, bp. of Sherborne, abt. of
Malmesbury xiii, xxxviii, 154, 178,
259, 261, 319; shrine of 259, 261
Alexander II, Pope 43, 62–3
Alfred, k. of West Saxons xxxv–xxxvi,
169, 230–1
Alps 247
altars 128–9
Amand, St 231
Ambrose, St 299
Andrew, St 221, 231, 243, 245, 275, 279
Anglesey, see Mevanian Isle
Anglo-Saxon Chronicle xxiii, 169, 265,
269, 295, 312
Ansbert, St, abt. of Fontanelle, archbp. of
Rouen 230–1
Anselm, archbp. of Canterbury xiii, xxi,
xxxiv, 63, 176
Armagh 321
Arnulf, count of Flanders 162, 230–1
Arthur (?the Frenchman), Wulfstan's
steward 74–5
Athelm, monk of Glastonbury, bp. of
Wells, archbp. of Canterbury 161, 181
Audoenus, St xiii

Augustine, St, of Hippo 167, 299, 331, 375
Augustine, St, archbp. of Canterbury xiii, 251
Avalon 341

B., *Vita S. Dunstani* xvii–xx, xxix, xxxv, 161–3, 265, 269
Bangor (Gwynedd) 176
Bannaven Taberniae (*also called* Nenchor) 317–19
Bari, an archbp. of 139
Barking (Essex) xxxi
Bath (Som.) 266–7; abt. of, *see* Ælfheah; bp. of, *see* John
Beaconsfield (Berks.) 77
Beddington (Surrey) 277
Bede xxxiii, xxxv–xxxvi, 152, 329, 337; church dedicated to xxxiii, 51
Benedict, St, Rule of xviii, 31, 53, 66, 147, 239, 263, 281
Benignus (Benen, Beonna), St xiii, xxiv, xxvi–xxvii, xxx, 307–10, 312–13, 331, 344–67; his staff sprouts 347, 349; makes a spring 349, 351; abt. of Glastonbury 351; death 355; translation 357, 359–65; miracles 355, 357, 361, 363, 365
Berengar of Poitiers xxiii
Bernard, bp. of St David's 122
Birinus, St xiii
Blockley (Glos.) 96–7
Boethius, on arithmetic 166
Bradenham (Bucks.) 78
Bradford 241
Bray (Ireland) 345
Breamore (Hants) 24
Bridgewater (Som.) 310
Brigid, St 312, 370
Brihtheah, bp. of Worcester 21, 23, 25, 35, 109
Brihthelm, bp. of London 243
Brihtwold, bp. of Ramsbury 208
Bristol (Som.) 98–9, 101, 317
Britain 207, 317–18, 321, 325, 329, 337, 341, 369
British 317, 319, 321, 325, 331, 333
Brue, R. (Som.) 319, 350
Bruton (Som.) xvi, 153
Buckinghamshire 78
Burnham (Som.) 310
Bury St Edmunds (Suff.) xviii, xxxi
Byrhthelm, bp. of Wells, archbp. of Canterbury 246–7

Byrnstan, bp. of Winchester xiii, 134
Byzantium 79

Caen 366
Cairnech (Carantoc), St 328, 335
Calne (Wilts.) 162, 269–71
Calpurnius, f. of St Patrick 317, 337
Camel, R. (Cornw.) 338, 369
Canterbury xxi–xxiii, xxxi–xxxii, 22, 133, 162, 187, 244, 247, 249, 253, 277, 279, 298; Christ Church ('church of Our Saviour') xix, xxi–xxiv, xxvi, xxx, 15, 221, 231, 242–3, 245, 247, 249, 255, 289; St Augustine's church xviii, xxx, 287; St Mary's church 287; and Dunstan 167, 243, 253, 255; primacy of 61, 65; fire at 171, 296; sacked by Danes 297; and Rochester 245, 249; Æthelwold visits 277, 279; archbps. of, *see* Ælfric, Ælfheah II, Ælfsige, Æthelgar, Anselm, Athelm, Augustine, Byrhthelm, Dunstan, Lanfranc, Oda, Sigeric, Stigand; abt. of, *see* Hadrian
Cato the Younger 188
Celestine (I), Pope 326–7, 329, 341, 369
Celts xiv
Cenwald, bp. of Worcester 241
Cereticus (Ceredig, Corotic), British k. 331–3, 335
Chalcidius 179
Charlemagne 80
Cheddar (Som.) 161, 201
Cheshire 65
Chester xxxi, 64–5, 67, 329
Christchurch (Hants) 308
churches, building of xxxvi–xxxvii; *atrium* 172–3, 210, 266; bells 38–9, 258; organs xxxvi–xxxvii, 179, 181, 258–9; *porticus* xxxvi, 24, 176–7, 205, 219; 'pyramids' 341, 380
Ciaran, St 327, 334
Cleeve, Bishop's (Glos.) 70–1
Cluny 30
Cnut, k. of England 15, 17, 36, 41
Coleman, monk of Worcester xv–xvi, xxxii–xxxiii, 93, 95, 98, 121, 123, 133; his Life of Wulfstan xv–xvii, xxvii, xxxii, xxxvi, 5, 50, 61, 64, 78, 100; style of xvi, xxxviii, 11, 59, 132; use of fictional speeches xvi, 59, 234; cited or alluded to 11, 21, 29, 31, 58–9, 65, 69, 79, 81, 85, 93, 95, 97, 99, 105, 133, 135; pupil and chaplain of Wulfstan 11;

unsuccessful preacher 93, 95; and
Westbury 123
Cologne 41–2
Columba, St 100
Compostela 220
Conches, mother of St Patrick 317
Constans 325
Constantine 321
Constantinople 79, 81
Cornwall, Cornish 311–12, 327–8, 337–8, 368
Cotton, Sir Robert 3–4, 160
councils 34, 36, 43, 61–5, 101, 107, 124–5, 128, 131, 162, 241, 270–1
Coventry 176
Cranbourne (Hants) 140
Crediton (Devon) xviii, 237, 261; bps. of, see Ælfric, Ælfwold, Æthelgar
Cricklade (Wilts.) 144–5
Cuthbert, St xiii
Cutsdean (Glos.) 129
Cynesige, archbp. of York 41–2
Cynesige, bp. of Lichfield 227
Cyneswith, St xiii
Cynethryth, St xiii
Cynethryth, m. of Dunstan 171, 173, 175, 285

Danes xxii–xxiii, xxxii, 60–1, 131, 163, 259–61, 297, 312
Denis, St 277; church of at Wilton 275
Devon 312, 319
Dominic, prior of Evesham xxxi
Domuel, f. of Piran 328
Dorset 319
Downpatrick (Ireland) xxiv
Droitwich (Worcs.) 84–5
Dunstan, archbp. of Canterbury xiv, xvii–xx, xxii–xxiii, xxvi–xxvii, xxix, xxxiv, xxxvii, 92, 109, 129, 160–3, 381; earlier Lives of 63, 166–7, 233, 235, 293, 295; birth 171, 173, 175; name 175; education 175, 179, 189; and music xxxvi–xxxvii, 179, 183, 258; and painting 183; works with his hands 189; with Athelm 181; at court of K. Æthelstan 181–5; with Ælfheah 185, 187; becomes a monk 185; becomes a priest 187; at Glastonbury xxi, xxiii, xxxvi, 169, 175, 189–99, 201, 203, 205, 207, 225, 258–9, 267; buildings at Glastonbury xxxvi, 172, 177, 205, 225; elsewhere 259, 268–9,

283; refuses bishoprics 217, 219, 237; becomes bp. of Worcester 241, 243; and of London 243, 295; and of Rochester 245, 249; as archbp. of Canterbury 246–7, 255, 257, 259, 263; travels to Rome 249, 251, 253; privilege from Pope John XII 249, 251, 253; and Malmesbury xxxvi–xxxvii, 259, 261; and K. Edmund 199, 201, 203, 205, 213, 215; and K. Eadred 215, 217, 219, 223; and K. Eadwig 225, 227, 233, 239; and Flanders 231, 233, 283; recalled to England 241; and K. Edgar 239, 265; and K. Edward 269; and K. Æthelred 273, 275, 279, 281; and Æthelwold 207, 261, 263, 277, 279; and Oswald 263; qualities 267; his inner life 283; tears 233, 277, 279, 285, 287; relatives of, see Athelm, Æthelflæd, Cynesige, Wulfric; and England xxii, 179, 201, 261, 263, 271, 275, 289, 295; miracles involving xx, xxxviii, 265, 267, 269, 293, 297; dealings with the Devil 177, 187, 189, 191, 209, 211, 213; visions and dreams of xx, xxii, 219, 221, 223, 231, 233, 235, 237, 267, 279, 285, 287, 289; heavenly voice speaks to 237, 267; prophecies of xx, xxxviii, 207, 209, 223, 267, 273, 275, 277, 281, 293; death 146, 288–9, 291, 293, 295; appears to Archbp. Ælfheah 297; events after his death 297; his body xxii–xxiii; cult xxvi
Dunstan, priest of Bruton xvi, 155
Durham xxv, xxxi, 3

Eadburh, St xiii
Eadgifu, w. of K. Edward the Elder, grandmother of K. Edgar 218–19, 239
Eadgyth, d. of K. Edgar, abbess of Wilton xiii, xx, 20, 163, 275, 277
Eadmer of Canterbury xx–xxii, xxx–xxxii, 22, 63, 78, 124, 159, 298; his Life of Dunstan xvii–xxiii, xxvi, xxix, 161
Eadred, k. of England xix, 161–2, 214–15, 217, 219, 223, 225, 237, 242, 245, 247
Eadric, monk of Worcester xiv, xvi, xxvii, 112–13
Eadwig, k. of England xx, 162, 213, 225, 227, 229, 233, 235–41, 259

Eadwine Psalter 230–1
Ealdhun, abt. of Glastonbury 169, 185, 203
Ealdred, as bp. of Worcester xvii, 30, 35,
    40–1, 43; as archbp. of York 41–3,
    45–7, 49–51, 60–1, 65; journey to
    Rome 41, 43
Ealdwine, prior of Great Malvern 65, 67
Ealdwulf, bp. of Worcester 123
Earnmær, plasterer of Worcester 95
Earnwig, teacher of Wulfstan, ?abt. of
    Peterborough 16–17
Ecgwine, St xiii, 54–5
Edgar, k. of England xxix, 162, 169, 237,
    239, 241, 243, 245, 247, 257–8, 264–5,
    269–71, 275, 279, 295
Edmund, k. and martyr xiii
Edmund, k. of England 146, 161, 199,
    201–3, 205, 213, 215, 225, 235, 237
Edmund Ironside, k. of England 40
Edward the Confessor, k. of England xiii,
    xxxiii, 41, 43, 45, 47, 57, 67, 95
Edward, son of Edmund Ironside 40
Edward the Elder, k. of England 239
Edward the Martyr, k. of England xiii,
    162, 269–70, 272–3
Einhard 138
Elias, archbp. of Bari 138
Elijah 131, 195
Elmham (Norfolk) 289; bp. of, see Ælfgar
Ely (Cambs.) xxxi, 263
Emma, d. of Richard II, duke of
    Normandy, w. of K. Cnut xxxiv, 17, 297
England xxxvii, 57, 59, 63, 101, 117, 145,
    147, 153, 167, 173, 207, 229, 231, 247,
    263, 271, 275, 340–1, 357, 371; coming
    of the Saxons 325; flourishes under
    Dunstan 289; coming of the Danes
    131, 297; disgraced by death of
    K. Edmund 215; problems at death of
    K. Edward 57; Normans arrive 59;
    Wulfstan famous throughout 15, 35;
    noblemen of 139; travelled over by
    Ealdred and cardinals 43; wooden altars
    in 128–9; kings of, see Æthelred,
    Æthelstan, Cnut, Eadred, Eadwig,
    Edgar, Edmund, Edward, William I,
    William II; see also Dunstan
English 381; like mead 111, 195;
    deplorable morals of 59; lavishness of
    45; time of (opposed to time of
    Normans) 59; rebel against K. Eadwig
    239, 241; approve of Edgar 269;
    tolerant of West Saxon kings 241; Bede

prince of English letters xxxiii, 51;
    Church xxviii, xxxii, 30, 42, 237, 255
English, Old xv, xviii–xix, xxv–xxvii,
    xxxii–xxxiii, xxxv–xxxvi, 11, 66, 90,
    168–9, 215, 234, 239, 254–5, 310–11,
    313, 316; translation into xviii–xix,
    xxxvi; Life of St Dunstan xviii–xx,
    xxix–xxx, xxxvi, 166, 169, 235, 237,
    269, 292, 294
Eorcenwald, St xiii
Ermenfrid, bp. of Sion xvii, 43
Escomb (Co. Dur.) 39
Eugenius III, Pope 122
Euthymius, patriarch of Jerusalem 138
Evesham (Worcs.) xxxi, 15, 47, 54–6;
    prior of 69, see also Dominic; abt. of,
    see Æthelwig, Ecgwine; monk of, see
    Æthelric
Exeter 261

Faricius, abt. of Abingdon xxxviii
Flanders 162, 229, 231, 283; count of, see
    Arnulf
Florence of Worcester xvii
Folcard of Saint-Bertin xxx
Fontanelle 231
France, French xxxiii, 83, 367; an
    unnamed Frenchman 83; the French
    know of Wulfstan 83
Frederick, archbp. of Mainz xiii
Freowine, deacon and monk of Worcester
    85, 103, 113, 115
Frideswide, St xiii
Fulgentius 301

Gaul 325, 337
Geoffrey, bp. of Coutances xxxiii, 107,
    109
Geoffrey of Monmouth 324
George, St 208–9
Gerald, abt. of Tewkesbury 140–1
Gerard, count of Galeria 43
Gerbert of Aurillac 178
Germanus, bp. of Auxerre 325, 327
Ghent 231, 233; St Peter's abbey xix,
    230–1; abt. of, see Wido
Gildas 380
Glastonbury (Som.) xv, xvii, xxi–xxiv,
    xxvi–xxvii, xxix–xxx, xxxii,
    xxxvi–xxxvii, 12, 159, 161–2, 166, 169,
    172–5, 193, 195, 201, 207, 217, 219,
    229, 231, 240, 259, 261, 267, 269, 281,
    297, 307–12, 319, 337–8, 340, 345, 348,

373; *see also* Ælfheah, Ælfsige, Ælfwold, Æthelwold, Athelm, Brihtwold, Dunstan, John, Wulfred; monks of xiv–xv, xxiii, xxvi, 167, 169, 317; history of 235, 259, 317; Irish at 178–9, 339, 343, 347, 368–9, 371; Patrick there 337–9, 341, 347, 371; Benignus there 347, 351, 353, 355, 357, 359, 361; Indract there 369, 371–3; favour of K. Edmund 203, 205; relics of saints at 205, 357, 359, 380–1; K. Edmund buried there 215; K. Edgar buried there 269; Dunstan not buried there xxii–xxiii, 297; Old Church (St Mary's) at 173, 177, 341, 343, 351, 357, 365, 381; cemetery xxxvi, 172, 191, 205; abts. of 169; *see also* Ælfric, Benignus, Dunstan, Ealdhun, Henry, Thurstan; prior of 184, 267; pupil of 267; steward of, *see* Wulfric

Gloucester 87, 89, 91, 176; abt. of, *see* Serlo

Gloucestershire 71

Godfrey of Cambrai, prior of Winchester 311

Godric, monk of Worcester 29

Gornias 319

Goscelin of Saint-Bertin xx, xxiii, xxx–xxxi, 275

Gregory, St xiii, 135, 187; Life of 31

Gregory of Tours xiii

Gundulf, bp. of Rochester 187

Gunnhild, d. of K. Harold 83

Hadrian, abt. of Canterbury xiii, 287

Hadrian's Wall 319

'Hailemouth', *see* Camel, R.

Harding 78

Harold III, k. of the Norwegians 56–7

Harold son of Godwine xxxiii–xxxiv, 35, 42, 45, 56–7, 59, 61, 83

Harthacnut, k. of England 356

Hastings, Battle of 60

Hawkesbury (Glos.) 108–9

Hearne, Thomas 159

Hemming, subprior of Worcester xxxiii, 20–1, 50

Hemming's Cartulary xxviii, xxxii, 20, 27, 30, 42, 46, 50, 60, 121, 124, 142

Henry III, emperor 40–1

Henry I, k. of England xv, xxxiv

Henry of Avranches xxv

Henry of Blois, abt. of Glastonbury, bp. of Winchester xv

Henry of Huntingdon 312

Heorstan, f. of Dunstan 171, 173, 175

Hereford, bp. of 41; *see* Robert

Hermann xxxi

Holm Cultram xxv, 3

Holy Lance 80–1

Hugh, bp. of Lincoln 4

Hugh, archdeacon of Worcester 129

Hugh the Chanter 50, 64

Hugh, count of Paris 80

Huish (Som.) 310, 372–3

Huish Episcopi (Som.) 310, 373

Humber, R. 205, 240–1

Huna 373

Hungary 40

Indract, St xiii, xxiv, xxvi–xxvii, xxx, 309–13, 368–81; at Glastonbury 371, 373; robbed and killed 373, 375, 377; burial 380–1; miracles 377, 379

Ine, k. of W. Saxons xxxvi, 154, 205, 311–13, 369, 373, 377, 379, 381

Innocent III, Pope xxvii, xxxiii

Iohannes Newynam 160

Ireland xxiv, 98–9, 101, 139, 312, 317, 321, 326–7, 329, 331, 333, 340–1, 345, 347, 368–9, 371, 373

Irish 98, 179, 316, 321, 327, 331, 335, 341, 343, 371; teachers at Glastonbury 178–9; Sea 371

Islip (Northants) 77

Italy 159

Itchington, Bishop's (Warw.) 14

Itchington, Long (Warw.) 14

Ivo, St xiii

James, St 283

Jeremiah 299, 301

Jerome, St 36, 38–9, 170

Jerusalem 67; a patriarch of 139

Jezebel 229

John, St 221

John XII, Pope 162, 249, 252–3; privilege of 249, 251, 253

John, K. xxxiii

John the Baptist 299–301

John, bp. of Bath 365

John of Glastonbury *or* Seen xxiii, xxvii, 160, 307–9, 312–13, 320–7, 330–1, 334–5, 338–40, 342, 344–61, 364–81

John Leland xxvii, 159–60, 307–8,
310–11, 317–43, 354–5
John the Scot 179
John of Tynemouth xxvii, 309, 311, 328,
335, 373
John of Worcester xiv, xvii, xxxiii, 14, 21,
24–6, 30, 40, 43–4, 46–50, 64, 74,
123–4, 142–5, 240, 294, 296
Jordan, R. 197
Joseph, husband of Mary 299
Joseph, Wulfstan a second 33

Kempsey (Worcs.) 74–5
Kenelm, St xiii
Kent 297; pauper from 75; earl of, see
Odo
'King's Evil' 74–6, 135, 185

Lanfranc, archbp. of Canterbury xxi,
xxviii, xxxiv, 15, 22, 63, 65, 131, 133,
204, 250, 369
Latins 183
Leeds (Yorks.) 39
Leo I, Pope 36
Leo IX, Pope 21
Leo, scribe of apostolic see 253
Leoghaire, Kingdom of 331
Leominster (Salop.) xxv, 3
leprosy, see 'King's Evil'
Letard, St xiii
Lichfield 64; bp. of, see Peter
Lincoln 78; bps. of, see Hugh, Remigius
Lisieux, council of 124
Liupida, sister of St Patrick 317, 319
London 76–7, 243; bps. of, see Brihthelm,
Dunstan
Longney (Glos.) 95
Lugneus, f. of Piran 328
Lupus, bp. of Troyes 325

Maguilius, Irish noble 333–4
Malcolm III, k. of Scotland 138–9
Malmesbury (Wilts.) xiii, xviii, xxix,
xxxvi–xxxvii, 154, 162, 240, 259, 261,
318; Dunstan's gifts to xxxvi–xxxvii,
259; abt. of, see Ælfric; see also Aldhelm
Malvern (Great, Worcs.) 65, 67, see also
Ealdwine
Man, Isle of, see Mevanian Isle

MANUSCRIPTS:
Aberystwyth, Nat. Libr. of Wales,
Peniarth 386 xxv

Arras, Bibl. municipale 812 xviii
Cambridge, Corpus Christi Coll. 9 159
163 40
265 125
391 110
Cambridge, Trinity Coll. R. 7. 5 48
CUL Kk. 3. 18 xxxiii
Ll. 1. 14 66
Durham Cath. B. IV. 39b 3
Gloucester Cath. 1 xxv, 3
BL Cotton Claudius A. v 3
Cleopatra B. xiii xviii
Faustina A. x 238
Nero E. i xxiv, 159
Tiberius A. xv xxiv, 284
Vespasian A. xiv 335
Vespasian E. ix 4
Vitellius E. xii 40
Harley 322 4
Lansdowne 436 4
Bodl. Libr. Auct. F. 3. 15 179
Digby 112 xxv, 310–11
Hatton 113 74–5, 92–3, 112, 142
Hatton 114 93
Hatton 116 66
Junius 121 93, 128
Rawlinson D. 263 159, 298
Paris, Bibl. nat. lat. 943 250–1
Salisbury Cath. 221 xxiv
223 xxiv
St Gall, Kantonbibl. (Vadiana) 337
xviii
Worcester Cath. F. 48 20
Dean & Chapter Muniments C. 370
106

Marcus, patriarch of Jerusalem 138
Margaret, w. of K. Malcolm 138–9
Marianus (Scotus) 328
Marlow (Bucks.) 113
Martha, St 225
Mary, St 197, 225, 243, 282–3, 287, 289,
299; dedications to: Canterbury 287,
Glastonbury 351, Shrewsbury 67, see
also Worcester; Hours of 111, 153
Maximus 321
Meare (Som.) 308–9, 348–50, 355
Mercia 15, 240
Mevanian Isle 333
Milcu, son of Boin 321, 323
Mildburh, St xiii, 362
Mildred, St xiii
Milred, bp. of Worcester 337

Mons Gaudii (Monte Mario, nr. Rome) 218–20
Monte San Marcos (nr. Compostela) 220
Moreton-in-Marsh (Glos.) 77
Moses 265
Mousehole (Cornw.) 328
Muchelney (Som.) 373
Muirchu xxiv
Munessan, a British k. 335

Nicholas, St 100
Nicholas II, Pope 42–3
Nicholas, prior of Worcester xiv, xvi, xxvii, 15, 119, 121, 123, 127, 131–3
Normandy, dukes of, see Richard II, William
Normans xxxi–xxxiii; coming of xxxiv, 59, 61, 297; time of 59; and Chester 65
Northumbria, Northumbrians 56–7, 205, 240, 297; see Tostig
Norwich xxv, 289
Nottingham 103–4

Ocmis, grandfather of St Patrick 317
Oda, archbp. of Canterbury xiii, xxii, 36, 204–5, 227, 243, 245, 247, 255, 263
Odbert, abt. of Saint-Bertin 283
Odelirius 67
Odo, earl of Kent and bp. of Bayeux 63
Orderic Vitalis 67
Osbern of Canterbury xvii–xix, xxvi–xxvii, xxix–xxxi, xxxv–xxxvii, 4, 161–3, 298; criticized by William xx–xxiii, xxxv–xxxvi, xxxviii, 163, 167, 169, 170–1, 185, 191, 202–3, 233–5, 243, 259, 275, 294–5, 298–9, 301
Osbert of Clare xxxiv
Oswald, k. of Northumbria xiii
Oswald, bp. of Worcester, archbp. of York xiii, xxi, xxix, 15, 23, 25, 27, 63, 123–4, 162, 263, 268
Otto I, emperor 200
Ouen, see Audoenus

Padstow (Cornw.) 328
Palladius 329
Parret, R. (Som.) 64–5, 372
Paternus, St xiii
Patrick, St xiii, xxiv, xxvi–xxvii, xxx, 168–9, 178–9, 307–10, 312–13, 347, 368, 371; also called Succet 317; parentage and birth 317; his

upbringing 319; enslaved 321, 323; missionary in Ireland 327, 329, 331, 333, 335, 345, 368–9; at Glastonbury 178, 338–9, 347, 351, 368; death and burial xxiv, 337, 339, 341, 343, 381; relics of 179, 371, 380–1; his writings xxiv, 308, 319, 321; Lives of xxiv
Paul, St 243, 245
Peace of God 91
Pedred, Pedridan 64, 373, 377
Pelagian heresy 325
Pennard, West (Som.) 309, 348
Penzance (Cornw.) 328
Perranporth (Cornw.) 327–8
Perranzabuloe (or St Piran) (Cornw.) 328
Pershore (Worcs.) 77
Peter, St 241, 243, 245, 247, 327; dedications to: Shrewsbury 67; see also Worcester
Peter, bp. of Lichfield 65
Peter Damian 43
'Peter's Pence' 43
Peterborough (Northants) 15, 19, 263
Petherton, North (Som.) 64
Petherton, South (Som.) 64
Petroc, St 339
Picts 321
Pincius 347, 349, 351
Piran, St 327–8
Plautus 352
Plymouth (Devon) 312
Potiphar, wife of 33
Potitus, grandfather of St Patrick 317
Powick (Worcs.) 74
Pucklechurch (Glos.) 213

Ramsey (Hunts.) xxxi, 263
Ranulf Higden 259
Ratcliffe (on Soar, Leics.) 104–5
Reading (Berks.) xxv, 3
Rebecca 301
Remigius, bp. of Lincoln 79
Rhetorica ad Herennium xxxv
Richard II, duke of Normandy xxxiv, 297
Richard, archdeacon of Worcester 129
Ripon (Yorks.) 124, 176, 204
Robert, earl of Gloucester 283
Robert, bp. of Hereford 107, 123, 140–1, 144–5, 147
Rochester 243, 249; and Canterbury 245, 249; and K. Æthelred 275; a bp. of 163, 275, 277, 279; see also Ælfstan, Dunstan, Gundulf

Roger de Montgomery 67, 96
'Romano-German Pontifical' 40
Romans 316–17
Rome 63, 218–19, 289; St Peter's 219; visited by Bp. Ealdred 41, 43; visited by Archbp. Ælfsige 247, 252; visited by Archbp. Dunstan 249, 251, 253; visited by Archbps. Thomas and Lanfranc 63; visited by St Patrick 327, 371; visited by St Indract 311–12, 371; and Peter's Pence 43; cardinals of 43, 45, see also Ermenfrid; customs of church of 43; pope of 47, 139; Leonine wall 220; popes of, see Alexander, Celestine, Innocent, John, Leo, Nicholas, Urban; see also Mons Gaudii
Romsey (Hants) xxv, 4
Rouen, council of 125; archbp. of, see Ansbert

Sæwig (Sewy) of Ratcliffe 104–5
St Germans (Cornw.) 311
Salisbury xxiv, 332
Samson, bp. of Worcester xxxii, 121
Saxons 325
Scots 331
Scottia 337
Scylla 183
Séez 67
Sechnall 347
Segetius, a priest 327
Segild, woman of Droitwich 85
Sen-Patraic 347
Sens, see Wulmar
Senatus, prior of Worcester xxv, xxvii, 3
Serlo, abt. of Gloucester 87, 89, 141
Severn, R. 95
Shaftesbury (Dorset) 168–9, 273
Shapwick (Som.) 310, 313, 373
Sherborne (Dorset) 263; bps. of, see Aldhelm, Wulfsige; Pontifical 250–1
Shrewsbury (Salop.) 67
Shropshire 65
Sigeric, archbp. of Canterbury 169, 219, 283
Simeon 173
Simeon of Durham xxxi
Siward, son of Æthelgar 67
slave-trade 100–1, 103, 321, 323, 329
Somerset 153, 166, 211, 318, 335
Staffordshire 65
Stamford Bridge, Battle of 57

Stigand, archbp. of Canterbury 42–3, 45, 47
Sutri (Lazio) 43, 218–20
Swertlin (Suarting, Swerting) of Wycombe 78–9
Swithhun, St xiii

Tamar, R. 312
Tamerton, North (Cornw.) 312
Temoria (Ireland) 331
Tewkesbury (Glos.) 140; abt. of, see Gerald
Thames, R. 240–1
Theodosius, emperor 329
Theulf, bp. of Worcester 133
Thomas, St 105
Thomas of Bayeux, archbp. of York xxviii, 47, 60–1, 63–4, 103
Thomas, prior of Worcester 141, 149
Thorney (Cambs.) xxx, 263
Thurstan, abt. of Glastonbury 357, 366–7
Tiber, R. 219
Tostig, earl of Northumbria 43, 57
Trent, R. 103–4

Urban II, Pope 138–9
Ursus, archbp. of Bari 138
Uxbridge (Berks.) 77

Via Cassia 218–20
Vikings, see Danes
Virgil xxxv, 373
Vortigern, k. of the Britons 325

Wærburh, St xiii
Wales, Welsh 145
Walkelin, bp. of Winchester 65
Wandragesil (Wandrille), St 230–1
Wareham (Dorset) 273
Warin, prior of Worcester xiv–xv, 9
Warwick 14
Warwickshire 15
Wells (Som.), bp. of 41; see also Athelm, Byrhthelm, John
Wessex 239, 241
West Saxons 240–1, 373; kings of, see Alfred, Ine
West, James 159
Westbury (on-Trym, Glos.) 120–1
Westminster xxxiii, 67, 74; abt. of, see Wulfsige; councils at xxxiv, 34, 101, 107
Westwood (Worcs.) 4

Wido, abt. of St Peter's Ghent 283
Wigstan, St xiii
Wihtburh, St xiii
Wilfrid, St xiii, 124, 173, 204–5, 228, 232
William, duke of Normandy 57, 61; as k.
   of England xxxiii, 61, 65, 83, 101, 103,
   131, 303
William II, k. of England xxxii, xxxiv,
   141–2, 145, 357
William the Bald of Gloucester 91
William of Malmesbury, as hagiographer
   xiii–xv; on origin of the *VW* 9, 11; on
   its purpose and style xvi–xvii, 13, 59,
   61; took six weeks to write 155; on its
   organization xvi, 11; knew Eadric xiv,
   112; knew Prior Nicholas xiv, 119;
   knew Prior Warin xiv; recalls Dunstan
   of Bruton 153, 155; reluctance to tell
   of Wulfstan's death 139; alludes to
   Gesta regum 131; connections with
   Glastonbury xiv, 12, 167–8, 234–5;
   with Worcester 12; on earlier Lives of
   Dunstan xviii, 169, 233, 235, 289, 293;
   cites B. xx, 265; his aims in *VD* 167,
   169, 171; on Osbern of Canterbury, *see*
   Osbern; his critics 171, 301; a
   'following book' on miracles of
   Dunstan 299
Wilstan, monk of Worcester, abt. of
   Gloucester 30
Wilton (Wilts.) xxxi, 81, 275; abbess of,
   see Eadgyth
Wiltshire 153, 212
Winchcombe (Glos.) xxxi
Winchester xviii, 83, 85, 145, 185, 219,
   225, 237, 263, 279, 281, 311, 325; St
   Gregory's chapel 186–7; bps. of, *see*
   Ælfheah, Ælfheah II, Ælfsige,
   Æthelwold, Byrnstan, Walkelin; prior
   of, *see* Godfrey of Cambrai; councils at
   43, 64, 124–5, 128, 162, 270–1; *see also*
   Wulfstan
Windsor (Surrey) 64
Winrich, monk of Worcester 36–9
Wissant 144
Witheric, monk of Worcester 30
Worcester xxi, xxxiii–xxxiv, xxxvi, 15,
   31, 43, 46, 76, 81, 85, 91, 125, 127,
   145, 151, 243, 332; Cathedral Priory
   xiv, xxiv–xxvi, xxviii, xxx, xxxii, 3–4,
   9, 12, 21, 40, 50, 74, 111, 120–1, 123,
   159–60, 238, 263; church of St Martin
   in 23; church of St Peter in 23, 263;

cathedral church of St Mary xxxvi,
   25–7, 38, 135 ('the greater church'),
   263; cathedral church of St Peter
   xxxvi, 24–5, 27; Wulfstan's father
   becomes a monk of 21; his mother
   becomes nun at 21; Wulfstan becomes
   monk of 25; plundered by Danes and
   Archbp. Ealdred 49–51, 60–1, 64;
   claimed by York 61, 63; confirmed as
   belonging to Canterbury 65; diocese of
   42–3, 47, 53, 85, 121, 128; rich lady of,
   misbehaves 31, 33; fire at 122–3; bps.
   of, *see* Brihtheah, Cenwald, Dunstan,
   Ealdred, Ealdwulf, Ecgwine, Milred,
   Oswald, Samson, Theulf, Wulfstan I,
   Wulfstan II; archdeacons of, *see*
   Æthelric, Hugh, Richard; priors of, *see*
   Ælfstan, Æthelmær, Æthelwine,
   Nicholas, Senatus, Thomas; subprior
   of, *see* Hemming; monks of xiv, 4, 9,
   46, 50, 99, 107, 144–5, 147, 153, 155;
   see also Coleman, Eadric, Florence,
   Freowine, Godric, John, Wilstan,
   Winrich, Witheric
Worcestershire 51
Wulfgifu, m. of Wulfstan 15, 21
Wulfred, monk of Glastonbury 191
Wulfric, br. of Dunstan 109, 211
Wulfsige, a recluse xvii, 49
Wulfsige, abt. of Westminster, bp. of
   Sherborne 162, 262–3
Wulfstan I, bp. of Worcester, archbp. of
   York 15, 46
Wulfstan II, bp. of Worcester xiii–xvii,
   xxvii–xxix, xxxii, 194, 198, 294; his
   forebears and parents 15; reason for
   name 15; education of xxxiii, 15, 17;
   and Earnwig's books 17, 41; chastity
   16–17, 19–21, 31, 33, 125, 127;
   becomes priest 23; becomes monk of
   Worcester 25; his offices there 25, 27,
   30; wrestles with Devil 27, 29; as
   provost (prior) of Worcester 31; and
   Harold 35, 57, 59; and kings and
   magnates 35, 45, 61, 139; election and
   consecration as bishop 45, 47, 49; in
   Northumbria 57; trouble with Ealdred
   over estates 51, 60–1, 65; dispute with
   Thomas of Bayeux 61, 63; receives
   visitation of Chester 65, 67; building
   works, esp. at cathedral xxxiii, xxxvi,
   25, 39, 41, 53, 121, 123; dedicates
   churches xxxvii, 51, 79, 89, 95, 105,

Wulfstan II, bp. of Worcester (*cont.*)
129; baptising and confirming xxxvii,
33, 35, 53, 79, 87, 89, 127; preaching of
35, 37, 39, 51, 79, 87, 89, 91, 93, 103,
105, 125; books of 110–13, 125, 128; on
dress 106–7, 109; and hair 58–9; on
oaths 66–7, 111; on peace 89, 91–3,
105, 107; on prayer 111, 115, 117, 119,
121, 125; and slave trade 100–3;
miracles by xxxvii, 39, 41, 55, 57, 59,
69–107, 129, 131, 133; appearance 107;
inner life and character 45, 51, 53, 55,
107–29, 135, 137, 139; last illness, death
and burial 139–47; events following
death of 122–3, 149–55; cult xxv

Wulfstan Cantor (of Winchester),
biographer of Æthelwold xvi, xxiii, 255
Wulmar, St, abt. of Fontanelle, archbp. of
Sens 230–1
Wycombe, High (Bucks.) 76–7, 81
Wycombe, West (Bucks.) 78–9

York 43, 45, 47, 60, 64–5, 103, 176;
Wulfstan consecrated at 47, 49;
archbps. of, *see* Cynesige, Ealdred,
Oswald, Thomas of Bayeux

Zarephath, widow of 131, 195

DATE DUE

DEMCO 13829810